Slovenia

Steve Fallon

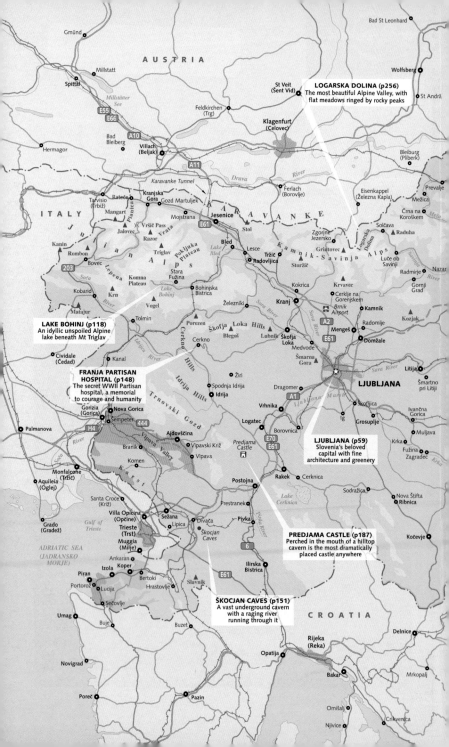

AUSTRIA

LOGARSKA DOLINA (p256)
The most beautiful Alpine Valley, with
flat meadows ringed by rocky peaks

ITALY

LAKE BOHINJ (p118)
An idyllic unspoiled Alpine
lake beneath Mt Triglav

**FRANJA PARTISAN
HOSPITAL (p148)**
The secret WWII Partisan
hospital, a memorial
to courage and humanity

LJUBLJANA (p59)
Slovenia's beloved
capital with fine
architecture and greenery

PREDJAMA CASTLE (p187)
Perched in the mouth of a hilltop
cavern is the most dramatically
placed castle anywhere

ŠKOCJAN CAVES (p151)
A vast underground cavern
with a raging river
running through it

ADRIATIC SEA
(JADRANSKO
MORJE)

CROATIA

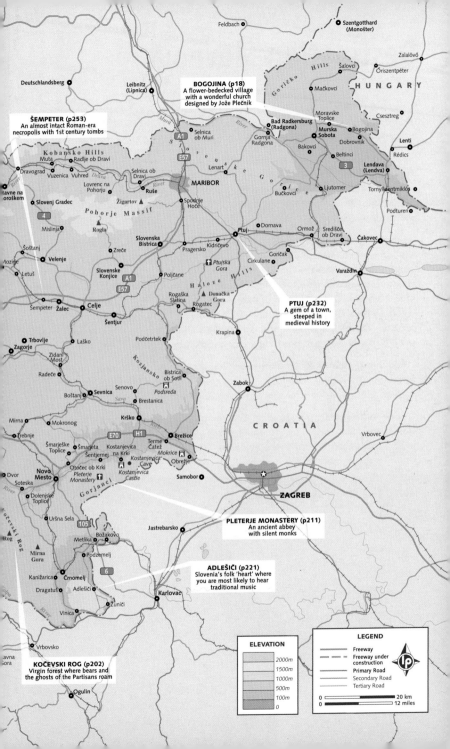

BOGOJINA (p18)
A flower-bedecked village with a wonderful church designed by Jože Plečnik

ŠEMPETER (p253)
An almost intact Roman-era necropolis with 1st century tombs

PTUJ (p232)
A gem of a town, steeped in medieval history

PLETERJE MONASTERY (p211)
An ancient abbey with silent monks

ADLEŠIČI (p221)
Slovenia's folk 'heart' where you are most likely to hear traditional music

KOČEVSKI ROG (p202)
Virgin forest where bears and the ghosts of the Partisans roam

HUNGARY

CROATIA

ZAGREB

ELEVATION

2000m
1500m
1000m
500m
100m
0

LEGEND

Freeway
Freeway under construction
Primary Road
Secondary Road
Tertiary Road

0   20 km
0   12 miles

Destination Slovenia

Every town in Slovenia has a general store where, locals like to say, you can buy anything *od šivanke do lokomoti* (literally 'from a needle to a train engine'). Similarly, Slovenija (Slovenia) itself, though undeniably small, has a wealth of attractions to rival a country many times its size.

Resting between the Alps and the Adriatic and poised above – but not a part of – the Balkan peninsula, Slovenia has been blessed with incredible natural beauty and has welded a great number of outside influences - from Roman and Venetian to Germanic and Hungarian - onto its Slavic core. The result is a physical and cultural alloy that is wholly distinctive and distinctly precious.

Slovenia has been dubbed many things – 'Europe in Miniature', 'The Sunny Side of the Alps', 'The Green Piece of Europe' – and they're all true. The place abounds in top-notch things to see – stunning mountains, lakes, rivers and a coast of jaw-dropping beauty as well as historic towns and cities with unforgettable architecture, museums and a unique energy all of their own. And in the land of the great outdoors the list of activities on offer here is almost endless. Throughout the year you'll encounter locals engaged in decidedly active pursuits – canoeing and kayaking in spring, swimming and water-skiing in summer, hiking and climbing in autumn, and skiing and snowboarding in winter.

And then there's what I consider to be Slovenia's greatest single attribute: the Slovenes themselves. The typical personality is quietly conservative but deeply self-confident, broad-minded, tolerant and very friendly and hospitable.

Don't misunderstand me, Slovenia ain't paradise. Like everywhere, it has its own share of difficulties. But when I die, and whoever is in charge decides I'm heading north and not south, I'll take along a copy of the *Avtoatlas Slovenija* (Road Atlas of Slovenia). You never know – it might prove useful.

GRANT DI

Castles & Grand Architecture

MARTIN MOOS

Marvel at the dizzying frescoes of the Chapel of St George (p71), Ljubljana Castle

CRAIG PERSHOUSE

The 16th-century City Tower (p234) pierces the skyline above Ptuj's town centre

The magnificent Predjama Castle (p187) has a history of court intrigue

NEIL WILSON

The Great Outdoors

B. KLADNIK / WWW.SLOVENIJA-TOURISM.SI

Rinka Waterfall (p256) has scenic trails for those whose boots were made for walking

OTHER HIGHLIGHTS

- Explore the underground world of the Škocjan Caves (p151)
- Once a dietary staple, the humble dormouse relives its popularity on Dormouse Night (p191)
- Lose your head on the wines of the Metlika district (p218)

MARTIN MOOS

Be humbled by the mountain panorama of Triglav National Park and Lake Bohinj (p118)

Chair lifts at Krvavec (p105) offer views over Slovenia's most popular ski grounds

A. FEVŽER / WWW.SLOVENIJA-TOURISM.SI

Raft, canoe, or kayak on the Soča River (p134)

B. KLADNIK / WWW.SLOVENIJA-TOURISM.SI

MARTIN MOOS

A. FEVŽER / WWW.SLOVENIJA-TOURISM.SI

Cure what ails you in the thermal waters
of Terme Olimia (p226), Podčetrtek

Get a rush from the swirling rapids and waterfalls
of Radovna River, Vintgar Gorge (p118)

Lake Bled (p113) is known for its quiet waters and charming walks

RICHARD I'ANSON

The Culture

MARTIN MOOS

A costumed local gets carried away at the Kurentovanje (p235) festival of spring

DAMIEN SIMO

Lipizzaners (p161) are the horses of kings

GRANT DIX

The Slovenian hayrack (p254) appears on as many postcards as it does hillsides

Traditional dress and colourful flowers welcome the herds' return at the Cows' Ball festival (p122), Bohinj

MARTIN MC

Contents

Regional Map Contents

The Author

STEVE FALLON

Steve has been travelling to Slovenia since the early 1990s, when a well-known publishing company at first refused his proposal to write a guidebook to the country because of 'the war going on' (it had ended two years before) and an influential American daily newspaper told him that their readers weren't interested in 'Slovakia'. Never mind, it was his own little private Idaho for a good 10 years. Though he hasn't reached the top of Triglav yet and *še govori slovensko kot jamski človek* (he still speaks Slovene like a caveman), Steve considers at least a piece of his soul to be Slovenian and returns to the country as often as he can, for a glimpse of the Julian Alps in the sun, a dribble of *bučno olje* and a dose of the dual.

My Favourite Places

How one goes about choosing the very best of paradise is anyone's guess, but if I really and truly had to choose my favourite spots in Slovenia they would run the gamut from mountains and rivers to towns and churches. Starting at the top, the **Vršič Pass** (p131) stands head and soldiers above the rest, and leads me directly down to sunny Primorska and the bluer-than-blue **Soča River** (p134). **Ljubljana** (p59), **Ptuj** (p232) and **Piran** (p171) top the list in the history league tables, but there's something special about 'second' towns like **Škofja Loka** (p97), **Radovljica** (p105), **Idrija** (p144) and **Kobarid** (p138) that let the imagination soar. In a country of magnificent houses of worship, I count my favourite churches in **Bohinj** (p119), **Hrastovlje** (p162) and **Ptujska Gora** (p237).

Getting Started

Slovenia is a dream destination for many reasons, but among the most obvious is that it requires so little advance planning. Tourist literature abounds, maps are excellent and readily available, and the staff at tourist offices, travel agencies, hotels, train stations and so on are almost universally helpful and efficient. And most speak English very well. Yes, Slovenia is so well developed and organised that you don't have to plan much of anything before your trip; almost everything can be arranged on the spot.

But this is fine only if your budget is unlimited, you don't have an interest in any particular activity, period of architecture or type of music, and you'll eat or drink anything put down in front of you. Those who have a limit as to the amount they can spend while travelling, or want better value for their money will benefit immensely from a bit of prior knowledge and careful planning. And if you have specific interests – from white-water rafting and mountaineering to bird-watching and folk music – you'll certainly want to make sure that the things you expect to see and do will be possible at the particular time of year when you intend to travel.

WHEN TO GO

For more specific information about Slovenia's climate, see p274.

Every season has its attractions in Slovenia. Snow can linger in the mountains until late June and even July, but spring is a great time to be in the lowlands and flower-carpeted valleys (though it can be pretty wet in May and June). At the same time the days are getting longer, the theatres and other cultural venues are in full swing, off-season rates still generally apply and local people are not yet jaded by waves of summertime visitors.

Summer (mid-June to sometime in September) is the ideal time for hiking and camping, but it's also the peak season for visitors, making accommodation (and a restaurant table) in Ljubljana and on the coast hard to come by without advance booking. September can be an excellent month, with plentiful local fruit and vegetables, shoulder-season tariffs in effect again and the tourist

---

DON'T LEAVE HOME WITHOUT...

Unless you plan to do some serious hiking or engage in sport, you don't have to remember any particular items of clothing for Slovenia – a warm sweater (even in summer) for the mountains at night, perhaps, and an umbrella, especially in spring or autumn. In general, Slovenian society dresses casually (though a bit smarter in Ljubljana than the provinces) when it goes out on the town. Besides taking the obvious (for visa information see p285) other items you may wish to include are:

- a swimsuit and thongs (flip-flops)
- a compass to help orient yourself in the mountains
- a torch (flashlight) if you intend to visit any caves
- an adapter plug for electrical appliances
- tea bags (since Slovenes drink buckets of the herbal variety but not the black stuff)
- sunglasses and sun block, even in the cooler months (those rays in the mountains can be fierce)
- a penknife, with such essentials as a bottle opener and strong corkscrew
- binoculars for when trekking or viewing detail on churches and other buildings

masses home and back at work. You can still swim comfortably in the Adriatic in September, but by mid-October most of the camping grounds have closed down and the days are growing shorter. Autumn is beautiful, particularly in the mountains of Gorenjska and Štajerska, and it's the best time for hiking and climbing (though October and November can be rainy).

Winter (December to March) in Slovenia is for skiers. It can be very cold and, away from the mountains, often quite bleak. At the same time, winter sees museums and other tourist sights closed or their hours sharply curtailed. Skiers should bear in mind that Slovenian school kids have winter holidays for about 10 days between Christmas and just into the New Year and again for a week in the second half of February.

COSTS & MONEY

Although prices are increasing, with imported items costing as much as they do in the rest of Europe, Slovenia is cheaper by as much as a third than neighbouring Italy and Austria. At the same time, everything costs at least 33% more than in nearby Hungary. Croatia has always been more expensive than Slovenia.

If you stay in private rooms or guesthouses, eat at medium-priced restaurants and travel 2nd class on the train or by bus, you should get by on under €50 a day. Travelling in greater style and comfort – restaurant splurges with bottles of wine, a fairly active nightlife, small hotels/guesthouses with 'character' – will cost about twice as much in the capital but an average of €75 to €80 in the provinces. Those putting up at hostels or college dormitories, eating *burek* (meat- or cheese-filled pastries) for lunch and at self-service restaurants for dinner could squeeze by on €30 a day.

READING UP

There's no shortage of books on Slovenia, but travellers writing diary accounts of southeast Europe have usually treated Slovenia rather cursorily or not at all, as they made tracks for 'more exotic' destinations like Croatia, Bosnia or even Serbia. In *Black Lamb and Grey Falcon*, her classic (and, at over 1000 pages, rather longwinded) look at Yugoslavia between the wars, Rebecca West allows Slovenia and the Slovenes fewer than a dozen brief references.

We know that a few other great writers did make it here, and there's documentation to prove at least one did. In Ljubljana's train station, for example, a brass plaque to the left of the staircase leading down from platform No 1 tells us that no less than James Joyce, together with his new paramour Nora Barnacle, spent the night of 19 October 1904 in Ljubljana. What the inscription fails to mention is that the couple, who had met just four months earlier and were on their way to teach English at Berlitz in Pula, had caught the wrong train.

Recommended reading:

The Making of Slovenia (Marko Štepec, ed) This succinct history of Slovenia in the 20th century, published by the Museum of Contemporary History in Ljubljana, is illustrated with many rarely seen photographs.

Questions about Slovenia (Matjaž Chvatal) This rather naff, 95-page book in oversized vest-pocket format will tell you the differences among Slovenia, Slovakia and Slavonia, what *koline* (pig-slaughters) are and just what makes Slovenes tick.

Slovenia 1945: Memories of Death and Survival after World War II (John Corsellis & Marcus Ferrar) This is the harrowing story of the forced return to Slovenia and execution of thousands of members of the anti-Communist Domobranci (Home Guards) after WWII.

Slovenia from the Air (Matjaž Kmecl et al) This trilingual coffee-table book has the standard wow-factor photographs of Slovenia's lakes, coast, towns and, of course, mountains from on high, and may even have you considering the ascent of Triglav.

HOW MUCH?

100km by train/bus
€5.50/9

Bicycle rental (per day)
€4.20-5.45

Bottle of ordinary/quality Slovenian wine
€4.20/8.35

Cup of coffee in a café
€0.75-1

Ski pass (per day)
€15.85-24.60

TOP FIVES

Festivals & Events

Slovenia marks red-letter days with festivals and special events throughout the year. The following are among the best:

- Kurentovanje (p235) in Ptuj in February
- Lent Festival (p242) in Maribor in June
- Ljubljana Summer Festival (p78) in July
- Rock Otočec (p277) near Novo Mesto in July
- Cows' Ball (p122) in Bohinj in September

Natural Wonders

In a land of hundreds of natural wonders – from ice caves and disappearing lakes to virgin forests and cobalt-blue rivers – it's difficult to narrow the list down to five. It's certain, however, that most travellers won't soon forget any of the following:

- Vršič Pass (p131)
- Škocjan Caves (p151)
- Logarska Dolina (p256)
- Soča River (p134)
- Vintgar Gorge (p118)

Outdoor Activities

Perhaps more than any other country in Europe outside Scandinavia, Slovenes are attached to the great outdoors (p43). We recommend:

- skiing in the Maribor Pohorje (p245)
- hiking in Triglav National Park (p128)
- kayaking on the Krka River (p199)
- horse riding at Lipica (p162)
- taking the waters at Dolenjska Toplice (p201)

Slovene Architecture of the Twentieth Century (Dr Stane Bernik) The quintessential guide and pictorial companion to modern and contemporary architecture across Slovenia, with everyone from Maks Fabian to Nande Kropnik represented.

Slovenia: My Country (Joco Žnidaršič) With Slovenia so diverse and physically attractive, there's no shortage of picture and art books on the country and this is the best: a heartfelt but never cloying paean to the photographer's homeland.

INTERNET RESOURCES

E-uprava (http://e-uprava.gov.si/e-uprava/en/portal.euprava) The 'State Portal of the Republic of Slovenia' has information about and links to just about anything you could want to know about the country – from today's pollution indices to how to trace your Slovenian roots.

Government Public Relations and Media Office (www.uvi.si/eng) Full of facts and figures about Slovenia's politics, economy, culture and environment.

Mat'Kurja (www.matkurja.com/eng) The 'Mother Hen' site is a vast directory of Slovenian web resources.

Najdi (www.najdi.si) The most popular search engine in Slovenia (mostly in Slovene).

Slovenia Times (www.sloveniatimes.com) Website of the independent free newspaper that comes out every two weeks.

TRAVEL WIDELY, TREAD LIGHTLY, GIVE SUSTAINABLY – THE LONELY PLANET FOUNDATION

The Lonely Planet Foundation proudly supports nimble nonprofit institutions working for change in the world. Each year the foundation donates 5% of Lonely Planet company profits to projects selected by staff and authors. Our partners range from Kabissa, which provides small nonprofits across Africa with access to technology, to the Foundation for Developing Cambodian Orphans, which supports girls at risk of falling victim to sex traffickers.

Our nonprofit partners are linked by a grass-roots approach to the areas of health, education or sustainable tourism. Many – such as Louis Sarno who works with BaAka (Pygmy) children in the forested areas of Central African Republic – choose to focus on women and children as one of the most effective ways to support the whole community. Louis is determined to give options to children who are discriminated against by the majority Bantu population.

Sometimes foundation assistance is as simple as restoring a local ruin like the Minaret of Jam in Afghanistan; this incredible monument now draws intrepid tourists to the area and its restoration has greatly improved options for local people.

Just as travel is often about learning to see with new eyes, so many of the groups we work with aim to change the way people see themselves and the future for their children and communities.

Slovenian Association of Historic Towns (www.zdruzenje-zg-mest.si) Great help in guiding you through the numerous town sites.

Slovenian Landmarks (www.burger.si) General and detailed information along with some 360-degree tours of Slovenia's towns and cities, museums and galleries, castles and manors, caves and waterfalls.

Slovenian Tourist Board (www.slovenia-tourism.si/) The Slovenian Tourist Board's ambitious but user-unfriendly site has information on every conceivable sight and activity in the republic.

STA (www.sta.si) News and views from the Slovenska Tiskovna Agencija (Slovene Press Agency).

Telephone Directory of Slovenia (http://tis.telekom.si) Nationwide telephone directory.

ITINERARIES
CLASSIC ROUTES

MOUNTAINS MAJESTY
One to Seven Days/Gorenjska Round Trip

What Slovenia has in spades is mountains, and they are 'just up the road' from Ljubljana.

From **Ljubljana** (p59) head north on route No 211. Before Medvode, detour through colourful **Škofja Loka** (p97). Head north along route No 210 to the historic town of **Kranj** (p101) and follow the road to Bled, passing through 'bee town' **Radovljica** (p105). Spend the night in picturesque **Bled** (p110) or carry on to the quieter and more atmospheric **Lake Bohinj** (p118).

From either place rejoin the main road and make tracks for the ski centre **Kranjska Gora** (p125) and the **Vršič Pass** (p131) in **Triglav National Park**. The road down will deposit you in Primorska's **Soča Valley** (p134). Following the Soča River will bring you to the activities centre of **Bovec** (p134) and the WWI battlegrounds around **Kobarid** (p138). From here follow route No 102 through Tolmin to **Idrija** (p144). Ljubljana, via Logatec and Vrhnika (route No 409), is only 55km to the northeast.

This unbelievably scenic, 329km circuit takes in some of the most attractive scenery in Slovenia: lakes, historic towns, mountain villages and the very mountains themselves. Although very safe except in the most inclement of weather (when it shuts), the Vršič Pass is *not* for the faint-hearted.

KARST & COAST   Two to Seven Days/Ljubljana to Primorska

This itinerary combines the best of two worlds: the evocative and sunbaked region of the Karst and the historic (although sometimes a little brash) Slovenian coast.

From **Ljubljana** (p59), follow motorway A1 to **Postojna** (p183). If you're not too caved-out after a visit, continue on to Divača and the awesome **Škocjan Caves** (p151). By then you'll need to take some R&R at the bucolic oasis that is **Lipica** (p161).

The fastest way to get to the Slovenian coast from Lipica is through Italy, just south of Trieste. If you'd rather stay on Slovenian soil, return to Divača and head south along the motorway (or follow alternative route No 10) to **Koper** (p164), a cheaper place to stay on the coast than the other Venetian towns. Follow the coastal road to **Izola** (p168), with a minor detour to **Strunjan** (p171) and its country park, **Piran** (p171), and eventually **Portorož** (p163), with all types of accommodation for different budgets. To the south along the coast is **Sečovlje** (p180) and its famous salt pans, a relaxing antidote to Portorož. A spur road just before the Croatian border follows the Drnica River and links up with route No 11 heading back for Ljubljana. At the Rižana exit head south for the Karst village of **Hrastovlje** (p162) and its wonderful church. Motorway A1, some 8km north of Hrastovlje, will take you back to the capital.

This 310km tour takes you through the Karst region – stopping at Slovenia's two most famous caves – and carries on to the coast before looping back up through the Karst.

ROADS LESS TRAVELLED

GOING POTTY   One Day/Prekmurje round trip

Prekmurje, lacking both mountains and coast, is a Slovenian 'neither fish nor fowl' but its great expanses of plain are unusual, and reminiscent of neighbouring Hungary.

From **Murska Sobota** (p265), head north along route No 232 and from **Martjanci**, with its important Gothic church, go east along route No 442 to the thermal spa of **Moravske Toplice** (p269). **Tešanovci**, a couple of kilometres east, is noted for its *lončarstvo* (pottery).

About 2.5km further east is the village of **Bogojina** and its **Parish Church of the Ascension,** which was redesigned by Jože Plečnik around 1926. To the original Romanesque and baroque structure, Plečnik added two asymmetrical aisles and a round tower. The interior is an odd mixture of black marble, brass, wood and brick; the oak-beamed ceiling is fitted with Prekmurje ceramic plates and jugs, as is the altar.

Filovci, another 2km beyond Bogojina, is famed for its *črna keramika* (black pottery). The **Bojnec Workshop**, 200m southwest of the main road, invites visitors to watch them work and sells wares.

Carry on southeast to **Dobrovnik** (p270), which has a couple of decent road-side *gostilna* (innlike restaurants). From here route No 439 leads southwest to **Beltinci**, known to philatelists as the place where one of the 1918 provisional stamps was overprinted on Hungarian stamps by the Serbian occupation forces during WWI. Today there is also a significant Roma minority living here. Murska Sobota and its well-renovated 16th-century castle are just 8km to the northwest.

This 40km trip, which can be done either by car or bicycle, follows a stretch of the so-called potters' road, running southeast from Moravske Toplice. To the north are the low-lying Goričko Hills covered in vineyards – while not Prekmurje's most important wine-growing region the hills are lovely nonetheless.

TAILORED TRIPS

WINE & WATER

If you're like us, you know that a sauna and/or a soak is the perfect treatment for a little too much of the good life. So why not combine the two – wine and water (thermal, that is) – and detox as you indulge?

The wine regions of **Posavje** and **Podravje** (p50), running almost the full length of eastern Slovenia, are delightful areas to visit from both scenic and wine-tasting points of view. They also happen to be as awash with thermal water as they are with wine.

A mere 18km beyond the charming **Bizeljsko-Sremič wine region** (p215), which effectively ends at Bizeljsko and is noted for its medium-dry whites and reds and for *repnice* (caves for storing wine), is the thermal spa of **Terme Olimia** (p226). Its healing waters are full of magnesium and calcium, and its attractions lie in both its curative powers and its recreational appeal. However, if you prefer something a little less of-this-century, go the extra distance to **Rogaška Slatina** (p228). Located some 15km further north, it overflows with magical 'olde worlde' charm, not to mention its very own 'drinking cure' (water this time).

The **Haloze wine region** (p238), celebrated for its pinot blanc, sauvignon and riesling, begins a mere 18km southwest of **Ptuj** (p232), where you'll find **Terme Ptuj** (p235).

The **Jeruzalem-Ljutomer wine district** (p238) begins at Ormož, due east of Ptuj. Were you to travel some 25km northeast along routes Nos 230 and 439, you'd come to **Terme Banovci** (p267), a spa with Slovenia's only naturist camping ground. But the shy and/or chilly may want to move on to the more reserved spa town of **Radenci** (p268), a modest 15km up the road.

Snapshot

On 1 May 2004 Slovenia joined the European Union but about the only difference you could tell at the time was that the electronic 'count-down' board in Miklošičeva trg had got stuck on '0 Days to Go'. Now you'll see the change every time you reach for your wallet. Welcome to Euroland.

Since then a new government has also been installed, this one a coalition led by Prime Minister Janez Janša of the Slovenian Democratic Party (SDS), who was a gadfly to the Communist honchos in the 1980s.

At the same time, former Prime Minister Janez Drnovšek, elevated to the presidency in 2002, has undergone a radical change. Once a dry, conservative political technocrat, the president has experienced some sort of epiphany, mutating into a fervent peace-and-love figure. Along his 'road to Damascus', Drnovšek detoured at Darfour to present a peace plan for the region, then moved on to Bangalore in India to meet with Ravi Shankar and to Lake Titicaca in Bolivia to chant along with shamans.

As a result, Drnovšek blew his annual travel budget within six months, so the Finance Ministry cut him off, refusing him any more funding for further trips. Complaining that the government was trying to control him, he left to form his very own Movement for Justice and Development, prompting an outpouring of speculation in the press.

More worrisome for many is the increasing role – both political and economic – of the Roman Catholic Church in Slovenia, epitomised by the elevation of Ljubljana's archbishop, the conservative Dr France Rode, to the role of cardinal in March 2006. Several political parties have proposed that Christian religious instruction be made compulsory in schools, and the Church continues to press for restitution of property seized after the war that's worth more than €233 million – a politically unpopular issue here despite the Church's significant influence within Slovenia. Indeed, in 2005 plans to build a mosque in the capital were stalled when it turned out that part of the land the city had proposed for sale to the Muslim community was subject to an ownership claim by the Church. The Church agreed to forgo its demand – if the city compensated it.

The first new member state to hold the presidency of the EU in 2008, it remains to be seen whether Slovenia will lose its unique role as conduit between Western Europe and the Balkans in the process of all this EU-ising. Will Slovenia find a new role for itself in the New Europe or content itself with becoming an economic satellite of Austria and Italy, just another nice, well-to-do social democratic republic?

History

EARLY INHABITANTS
The area of present-day Slovenia has been settled since the Palaeolithic Age. Tools made of bone that date back to between 100,000 and 60,000 BC have been found in a cave at Mt Olševa, north of Solčava in Štajerska's Upper Savinja Valley.

During the Bronze Age (around 2000 to 900 BC), marsh dwellers farmed and raised cattle in the area south of present-day Ljubljana – the Ljubljansko Barje – and at Lake Cerknica. They lived in round huts set on stilts and traded with other peoples along the so-called Amber Route linking the Balkans with Italy and northern Europe.

Around 700 BC the Ljubljana Marsh people were overwhelmed by the Illyrian tribes from the south who brought iron tools and weapons. They settled largely in Dolenjska, built hill-top forts and reached their peak between 650 and 550 BC, during what is called the Hallstatt period. Iron helmets, gold jewellery and *situlae* (embossed pails) with distinctive Hallstatt geometric motifs have been found in tombs near Stična and at Vače near Litija; you'll see some excellent examples of these findings at both the National Museum of Slovenia (p72) in Ljubljana and the Dolenjska Museum (p203) in Novo Mesto.

In about 400 BC, Celtic tribes from what are now France, Germany and the Czech lands began pushing southward towards the Balkans. They mixed with the local population and established the Noric kingdom, the first 'state' on Slovenian soil.

An easy-to-read but useful introduction to Slovenian history is Janko Prunk's revised *Brief History of Slovenia*, which starts with the territory of present-day Slovenia in pre-Roman times and ends at the dawn of the new millennium.

THE ROMANS
In 181 BC the Romans established the colony of Aquileia (Oglej in Slovene) on the Gulf of Trieste in order to protect the empire from tribal incursions, and Julius Caesar, after whom the Julian Alps in the northwest are named, actually visited in the 1st century AD. In the next century, the Romans annexed the Celtic Noric kingdom and moved into the rest of Slovenia and Istria.

The Romans divided the area into the provinces of Noricum (today's southern Austria, Koroška and western Štajerska), Upper and Lower Pannonia (eastern Štajerska, Dolenjska and much of Gorenjska) and Histria (Primorska and Croatian Istria), later called Illyrium, and built roads connecting their new military settlements. From these bases developed the important towns of Emona (Ljubljana), Celeia (Celje) and Poetovio (Ptuj), where reminders of the Roman presence can still be seen. Some fine examples are the Citizen of Emona statue (p72) in Ljubljana, the Roman necropolis at Šempeter (p253) and the Mithraic shrines (p234) near Ptuj.

THE GREAT MIGRATIONS
In the middle of the 5th century AD, the Huns, led by Attila, invaded Italy via Slovenia, attacking Poetovio, Celeia and Emona along the way. Aquileia fell to the Huns in 452. However, Attila's empire was short-lived and was soon eclipsed first by the Germanic Ostrogoths and then the Langobards, who occupied much of the Slovenian territory. In 568 the Langobards struck out for Italy, taking Aquileia and eventually conquering the Venetian mainland.

For as much information as you'll ever need on the ancient city of Aquileia, listed as a Unesco World Heritage Site since 1998, go to www.aquileia.it.

TIMELINE	400 BC	2nd decade AD
	Celtic tribes establish the Noric kingdom on Slovenian soil	Romans move into Slovenia from Italy and annex the Noric kingdom

THE EARLY SLAVS

The ancestors of today's Slovenes arrived from the Carpathian Basin in the 6th century and settled in the Sava, Drava and Mura river valleys and the eastern Alps. Under pressure from the Avars, a powerful Mongol people with whom they had formed a tribal alliance, the early Slavs migrated further west to the Friulian plain and the Adriatic Sea, north to the sources of the Drava and Mura Rivers and east as far as Lake Balaton in Hungary. Early Slavic burial grounds can be found at Kranj (p103) and Slovenj Gradec (p262).

In their original homelands the early Slavs were a peaceful people, living in forests or along rivers and lakes, breeding cattle and farming by slash-and-burn methods. They were a superstitious people who saw *vile* (both good and bad fairies or sprites) everywhere and paid homage to a pantheon of gods and goddesses. As a social group they made no class distinctions, but chose a leader – a *župan* (now the word for 'mayor') or *vojvoda* (duke) – in times of great danger. During the migratory periods, however, their docile nature changed and they became more warlike and aggressive.

Lake Balaton in Hungary, which the early Slavs reached in their roamings, takes its name from the Slovenian word *blato* (mud).

THE DUCHY OF CARANTANIA

When the Avars failed to take Byzantium in 626, the alpine Slavs united under their leader, the duke Valuk, and joined forces with the Frankish king Samo to fight them. The Slavic tribal union became the Duchy of Carantania (Karantanija), the first Slavic state, with its seat at Krn Castle (now Karnburg) near Klagenfurt (Celovec in Slovene) in Austria.

By the early 8th century, a new class of ennobled commoners called *kosezi* had emerged, and it was they who publicly elected and crowned the new *knez* (grand duke) on the *knežni kamen* ('duke's rock') in the courtyard of Krn Castle. Such a democratic process was unique in the feudal Europe of the early Middle Ages. The model was noted by the 16th-century French political theorist Jean Bodin, whose work is said to have been a key reference for Thomas Jefferson when he wrote the American Declaration of Independence in 1775–76.

EXPANSION OF THE FRANKS

In 748 the Frankish empire of the Carolingians incorporated Carantania as a vassal state called Carinthia and attempted to convert the population to Christianity. The new religion was resisted at first, but Irish monks under the auspices of the Diocese of Salzburg began to preach in the vernacular and were more successful.

By the early 9th century, religious authority on Slovenian territory was shared between Salzburg and the Patriarchate (or Bishopric) of Aquileia (opposite). The weakening Frankish authorities began replacing Slovenian nobles with German counts, reducing the local peasantry to serfdom. The German nobility was thus at the top of the feudal hierarchy for the first time in Slovenian lands. This would later become one of the key obstacles to Slovenian national and cultural development.

THE CARINTHIAN KINGDOM

With the total collapse of the Frankish state in the second half of the 9th century, a Carinthian prince named Kocelj established a short-lived (869–74)

6th century	7th century
Early Slavic tribes settle in the Sava, Drava and Mura River valleys and the eastern Alps	A union of Slavic tribes establishes the Duchy of Carantania, the first Slavic state

---

THE PATRIARCHATE OF AQUILEIA

You'd never guess from its present size (population 3350), but the Friulian town of Aquileia north of Grado on the Gulf of Trieste played a pivotal role in Slovenian history, and for many centuries its bishops (or 'patriarchs') ruled much of Carniola (Kranjska).

Founded as a Roman colony in the late 2nd century BC, Aquileia fell to a succession of tribes during the Great Migrations and had lost its political and economic importance by the end of the 6th century. But Aquileia had been made the metropolitan see for Venice, Istria and Carniola, and when the Church declared some of Aquileia's teachings heretical, it broke from Rome. The schism lasted only a century and when it was resolved Aquileia was recognised as a separate patriarchate.

Aquileia's ecclesiastical importance grew during the mission of Paulinus II to the Avars and Slovenes in the late 8th century, and it acquired feudal estates and extensive political privileges (including the right to mint coins) from the Frankish and later the German kings. It remained a feudal principality until 1420 when the Venetian Republic conquered Friuli, and Venetians were appointed patriarchs for the first time. Aquileia retained some of its holdings in Slovenia and elsewhere for the next 300 years. But the final blow came in 1751 when Pope Benedict XIV created the archbishoprics of Udine and Gorizia. The once powerful Patriarchate of Aquileia had outlasted its usefulness and was dissolved.

---

independent Slovenian 'kingdom' in Lower Pannonia, the area stretching southeast from Styria (Štajerska) to the Mura, Drava and Danube Rivers. It was to Lower Pannonia that the Macedonian brothers Cyril and Methodius, the 'apostles of the southern Slavs', had first brought the translations of the Scriptures to the Slovenes six years before. And it was here that calls for a Slavic archdiocese were first heard.

THE MAGYARS & GERMAN ASCENDANCY

In about 900, the fearsome Magyars, expert horsemen and archers, subjugated Lower Pannonia and the Slovenian regions along the Sava, cutting them off from Carinthia. It wasn't until 955 that they were stopped by forces under King Otto I at Augsburg.

The Germans decided to re-establish Carinthia, dividing the area into a half-dozen border counties (or marches). These developed into the Slovenian provinces that would remain basically unchanged until 1918: Carniola (Kranjska), Carinthia (Koroška), Styria (Štajerska), Gorica (Goriška) and the so-called White March (Bela Krajina).

A drive for complete Germanisation of the Slovenian lands began in the 10th century. Land was divided between the nobility and various church dioceses (Brixen, Salzburg, Freising), and German gentry were settled on it. The population remained essentially Slovenian, however, and it was largely due to intensive educational and pastoral work by the clergy that the Slovenian identity was preserved. The *Freising Manuscripts* (p33), the oldest example of written Slovene, date from this period.

Most of Slovenia's important castles were built and many important Christian monasteries – for example, Stična (p197) and Kostanjevica (p209) – established between the 10th and 13th centuries. Towns also developed as administrative, trade and social centres.

See www.uvi.si/eng /slovenia/background -information/freising -manuscripts for more information about and links on the Freising manuscripts, the oldest known writings in the Slovenian language.

748

Frankish empire incorporates Carantania as a vassal state called Carinthia

869–74

Carinthian Prince Kocelj rules a Slovenian 'kingdom' in Lower Pannonia

EARLY HABSBURG RULE

In the early Middle Ages, the Habsburgs were just one of many German aristocratic families struggling for hegemony on Slovenian soil. Others, such as the Andechs, Spanheims and Žoneks (later the Counts of Celje), were equally powerful at various times. But as dynasties intermarried or died out, the Habsburgs consolidated their power.

Between the late 13th century and the early 16th century, almost all the lands inhabited by Slovenes passed into Habsburg hands except for Istria and the Littoral, which were controlled by Venice until 1797, and parts of Prekmurje, which belonged to the Hungarian crown. Until the 17th century, rule was not direct but administered by diets (parliaments) of 'resident princes', prelates, feudal lords and representatives from the towns, who dealt with matters like taxation.

By this time Slovenian territory totalled about 24,000 sq km, about 15% larger than its present size. Not only did more towns and boroughs receive charters and rights, but the country began to develop economically with the opening of ironworks (eg at Kropa, p109) and mines (eg Idrija, p144). This economic progress reduced the differences among the repressed peasants, and they united against their feudal lords.

Ivan Cankar's *Hlapec Jernej in Njegova Pravica* (The Bailiff Yerney and His Rights), a tale of the unequal relationship between servant and master, is read as a metaphor for Slovenia under Habsburg rule.

PEASANT UPRISINGS & THE REFORMATION

More than a hundred peasant uprisings and revolts occurred on Slovenian territory between the 14th and 19th centuries, but they reached their peak between 1478 and 1573. Together with the Protestant Reformation at the end of the 16th century, they are considered a watershed of the Slovenian national awakening.

Attacks by the Ottoman Turks on southeastern Europe began in 1408 and continued for more than two-and-a-half centuries, almost reaching Vienna on several occasions. By the start of the 16th century, thousands of Slovenes had been killed or taken prisoner. The assaults helped to radicalise landless peasants and labourers, who were required to raise their own defences *and* continue to pay tribute and work for their feudal lords.

In most of the uprisings, peasant 'unions' demanded a reduction in feudal payments and the democratic election of parish priests. The three most violent uprisings took place in 1478 in Koroška, in 1515, encompassing almost the entire Slovenian territory, and in 1573, when Ambrož 'Matija' Gubec led 12,000 Slovenian and Croatian peasants in revolt. Castles were occupied and pulled down and lords executed, but none of the revolts succeeded as such.

The Protestant Reformation in Slovenia was closely associated with the nobility from 1540 onward and was generally ignored by the rural population except for those who lived or worked on Church-owned lands. But it raised the overall educational level of Slovenes and gave them their first books in their own language, thereby lifting the status of the vernacular and affirming Slovenian culture.

COUNTER-REFORMATION & PROGRESS

The wealthy middle class had lost interest in the Reformation by the time it peaked in the 1580s because of the widening economic gap between it and the nobility. They turned to the Catholic resident princes, who quashed

Late 13th–early 16th centuries	1478–1573
All Slovenian lands fall under Habsburg rule	Peasant riots in Slovenia at their peak

Protestantism among the peasants and banished noble families who persisted in the new belief.

In the early 18th century Habsburg economic decline brought on by a series of wars was reversed, and Empress Maria Theresa (1740–80) introduced a series of reforms. These included the establishment of a new state administration with a type of provincial government; the abolition of customs duties between provinces of the empire; the building of new roads; and the introduction of obligatory elementary school in German and state-controlled secondary schools. Her son, Joseph II (1780–90), went several steps further. He abolished serfdom in 1782, paving the way for the formation of a Slovenian bourgeoisie, and allowed complete religious freedom for Calvinists, Lutherans and Jews. He also dissolved the all-powerful (and often corrupt) Catholic religious orders.

As a result of these reforms, agricultural output improved, manufacturing intensified and shipping from Austria's main seaport at Trieste increased. The reforms also produced a flowering of the arts and letters in Slovenia, with the playwright and historian Anton Tomaž Linhart (p38) and the poet and journalist Valentin Vodnik producing their finest and most influential works at this time.

NAPOLEON & THE ILLYRIAN PROVINCES

The French Revolution of 1789 convinced the Austrians that reforms should be nipped in the bud, and a period of reaction began that continued until the Revolution of 1848. In the meantime there was a brief interlude that would have a profound effect on Slovenia and its future.

After defeating the Austrians at Wagram in 1809, Napoleon decided to cut the entire Habsburg Empire off from the Adriatic. To do this he created six 'Illyrian Provinces' from Slovenian and Croatian regions, including Koroška, Kranjska, Gorica, Istria and Trieste, and made Ljubljana the capital.

Although the Illyrian Provinces lasted only from 1809 to 1813, France instituted a number of reforms, including equality before the law and the use of Slovene in primary and lower secondary schools and in public offices. Most importantly, the progressive influence of the French Revolution brought the issue of national awakening to the Slovenian political arena for the first time.

Slovenia and the Slovenes: A Small State and the New Europe by James Gow and Cathie Carmichael offers excellent analyses not just of history and politics but of culture and the arts as well.

ROMANTIC NATIONALISM & THE 1848 REVOLUTION

Austrian rule, restored in 1814, was now guided by the iron fist of Prince Clemens von Metternich. He immediately reinstituted the Austrian feudal system and attempted to suppress every national movement from the time of the Congress of Vienna (1815) to the Revolution of 1848. But the process of change had already started in Slovenia.

The period of so-called Romantic Nationalism (1814–48) was one of intensive literary and cultural activity and led to the promulgation of the first Slovenian political program. Although many influential writers published at this time, no one so dominated the period as the poet France Prešeren (p34).

In 1848 Slovenian intellectuals drew up their first national political program under the banner Zedinjena Slovenija (United Slovenia). In essence it called for the unification of all historic Slovenian regions within an

The seventh stanza of France Prešeren's popular poem *Zdravljica* (A Toast) forms the lyrics of Slovenia's national anthem.

1540–80	1782
Protestant Reformation; first books in Slovene published	Habsburg Emperor Joseph II abolishes serfdom

> **SLOVENIA'S NATIONAL ANTHEM**
>
> God's blessing on all nations,
> Who long and work for that bright day,
> When o'er earth's habitations
> No war, no strife shall hold its sway;
> Who long to see
> That all men free
> No more shall foes, but neighbours be.
>
> *France Prešeren (1800–49), A Toast*

autonomous unit under the Austrian monarchy, the use of Slovene in all schools and public offices and the establishment of a local university. The demands were rejected, as they would have required the reorganisation of the empire along ethnic lines.

CONSTITUTIONAL PERIOD

The only tangible results for Slovenes in the 1848 Austrian Constitution were that laws would henceforth be published in Slovene and that the Carniolan (and thus Slovenian) flag should be three horizontal stripes of white, blue and red. But the United Slovenia programme would remain the basis of all Slovenian political demands up to 1918, and political-cultural clubs and circles began to appear all over the territory.

The rest of the 19th and early 20th centuries were marked by economic development: the railway from Vienna to Ljubljana opened in 1849, industrial companies were formed at Kranj and Trbovlje, and a mill began operating at Ajdovščina. Despite this, material conditions declined for the peasantry, and between 1850 and 1910 more than 300,000 Slovenes – 56% of the population – emigrated.

Some advances were made on the political side. Out of the influential *čitalnice* (reading clubs) and *tabori,* camps in which Slovenes of many different beliefs rallied, grew political movements. Parties first appeared toward the end of the 19th century, and a new idea – a union with the other Slavs to the south – was propounded from the 1860s onward by the distinguished Croatian bishop Josip Strossmayer. The writer and socialist Ivan Cankar even called for an independent Yugoslav ('south Slav') state in the form of a federal republic.

WWI & THE KINGDOM OF SERBS, CROATS & SLOVENES

Slovenian political parties generally tended to remain faithful to Austria-Hungary (as the empire was known from 1867). With the heavy loss of life and destruction during WWI, however, especially along the Soča (or Isonzo) Front (p139), support grew for an autonomous democratic state within the Habsburg monarchy. With the defeat of Austria-Hungary and the dissolution of the Habsburg dynasty in 1918, Slovenes, Croats and Serbs banded together and declared the independent Kingdom of Serbs, Croats and Slovenes, under Serbian King Peter I. The Serbian statesman Stojan Protić became prime minister, and the conservative Slovene leader of the Clerical Party, Fr Anton Korošec, was named vice-premier.

1809–13	1848
Ljubljana capital of the French-ruled Illyrian Provinces	Slovenian intellectuals issue a national political program called United Slovenia

The peace treaties after the war had given large amounts of Slovenian and Croatian territory to Italy (Primorska and Istria), Austria (Koroška) and Hungary (part of Prekmurje), and almost half a million Slovenes now lived outside the borders (some, like the Slovenes in Koroška, had voted to do so, however). The loss of more than a quarter of its population and a third of its land would remain the single most important issue facing Slovenia between the wars.

The kingdom was dominated by Serbian control, imperialistic pressure from Italy and the notion of Yugoslav unity. Slovenia was reduced to little more than a province in this centralist kingdom, although it did enjoy cultural and linguistic autonomy, and economic progress was rapid.

In 1929 Peter I's son King Alexander seized absolute power, abolished the constitution and proclaimed the Kingdom of Yugoslavia. But the king was assassinated five years later by a Macedonian terrorist in Marseilles during an official visit to France, and his cousin, Prince Paul, was named regent.

The political climate changed in Slovenia when the conservative Clerical Party joined the new centralist government of Milan Stojadinović in 1935, proving how hollow that party's calls for Slovenian autonomy had been. As a result, splinter groups began to seek closer contacts with the workers' movements. In 1937 the Communist Party of Slovenia (KPS) was formed under the tutelage of Josip Broz Tito (1892–1980) and the Communist Party of Yugoslavia (KPJ).

WWII & THE PARTISAN STRUGGLE

Yugoslavia managed to avoid getting involved in the war until March 1941 when Prince Paul, under pressure from Berlin and Rome, signed a treaty with the Axis powers. He was overthrown in a coup backed by the British, who installed King Paul II. Paul at first attempted neutrality, but German armies invaded and occupied Yugoslavia in April.

Slovenia was split up among Germany (Štajerska, Gorenjska and Koroška), Italy (Ljubljana, Primorska, Notranjska, Dolenjska and Bela Krajina) and Hungary (Prekmurje). To counter this, the Slovenian Communists and other left-wing groups formed a Liberation Front (Osvobodilne Fronte, or OF), and the people took up arms for the first time since the peasant uprisings. The OF, dedicated to the principles of a united Slovenia in a Yugoslav republic, joined the all-Yugoslav Partisan army of the KPJ and its secretary-general, Josip Tito. The Partisans received assistance from the Allies and were the most organised – and successful – of any resistance movement during WWII.

After Italy capitulated in 1943, the anti-OF Slovenian Domobranci (Home Guards) were active in Primorska and, in a bid to prevent the communists from gaining political control in liberated areas, began supporting the Germans.

Despite this assistance and the support of the fascist Ustaša nationalists in Croatia and later the Četniks in Serbia, the Germans were forced to evacuate Belgrade in 1944. Slovenia was not totally liberated until May 1945.

The following month, as many as 12,000 Domobranci and anti-communist civilians were sent back to Slovenia from refugee camps in Austria by the British. Most of them were executed by the communists over the next two months, their bodies thrown into the caves at Kočevski Rog (p202) in Dolenjska.

Josip Broz Tito was born in 1892 in Kumrovec, just over the Štajerska border in Croatia, to a Slovenian mother and a Croatian father.

France Štiglic's 1955 film *Dolina Miru* (Valley of Peace) is the bittersweet story of two children, an ethnic German boy and a Slovenian girl, trying to find a haven during the tumult of WWII.

The Axis History Factbook website (www.axishistory.com/index.php?id=95) details the strength and leadership of the controversial Domobranci (Home Guards) during WWII.

1918
Austria-Hungary dissolved and Kingdom of Serbs, Croats and Slovenes declared

1945
Occupied Slovenia liberated (May); Slovenia included in the Federal People's Republic of Yugoslavia (Nov)

POSTWAR DIVISION

Of immediate concern to Slovenia after the war was the status of the liberated areas along the Adriatic, especially Trieste. A peace treaty signed in Paris in 1947 put Trieste and its surrounds under Anglo-American administration (the so-called Zone A) and the Koper and Buje (Istria) areas under Yugoslav control in Zone B. In 1954 Zone A (with both its Italian and ethnic Slovenian populations) became the Italian province of Trieste. Koper and a 47km stretch of coast later went to Slovenia while the bulk of Istria went to Croatia. The Belvedere Treaty (1955) guaranteed Austria its 1938 borders, including most of Koroška.

TITO & SOCIALIST YUGOSLAVIA

Tito had been elected head of the assembly, providing for a federal republic in November 1943. He moved quickly after the war to consolidate his power under the strength of the communist banner. However, it soon became obvious that Slovenia's rights to self-determination and autonomy within the framework of a federal Yugoslavia would be limited beyond educational and cultural matters. Serbian domination from Belgrade would continue as before.

Tito distanced himself from the Soviet Union as early as 1948, but his efforts to create a communist state, with all the usual arrests, show trials, purges and gulags, continued into the mid-1950s. Industry was nationalised, private ownership of agricultural land limited to 20 hectares, and a planned central economy put in place.

For more information about the life and times of the founding father of the Federal Republic of Yugoslavia, go to http://josip-broz-tito .biography.ms.

But isolation from the markets of the Soviet bloc soon forced Tito to look to the West. Yugoslavia introduced features of a market economy, including workers' self-management. Greater economic reforms in the mid-1960s as well as relaxed police control and border controls brought greater prosperity and freedom of movement, but the Communist Party saw such democratisation as a threat to its power. A purge of the reformists in government was carried out in 1971–72, and many politicians and directors were pensioned off for their 'liberalism' and 'entrepreneurial thinking'. A new constitution in 1974 gave the Yugoslav republics more independence (and autonomy to the ethnic Albanian province of Kosovo in Serbia), but what were to become known as the 'leaden years' in Yugoslavia lasted throughout the 1970s until Tito's death in 1980. By that time, though, Slovenia was the most advanced republic economically in Yugoslavia.

CRISIS, RENEWAL & CHANGE

The economic decline in Yugoslavia in the early 1980s led to inter-ethnic conflict, especially between Serbs and ethnic Albanians in autonomous Kosovo. Serbia proposed scrapping elements of the 1974 constitution in favour of more state uniformity in economic and cultural areas. This, of course, was anathema to Slovenes.

Neil Barnett's relatively slim (175 pages) new biography Tito, an entertaining and timely read, offers a new assessment of the limits of holding a state like Yugoslavia together by sheer force of personality.

In 1987 the Ljubljana-based magazine Nova Revija published an article outlining a new Slovenian national program, which included political pluralism, democracy, a market economy and independence, possibly within a Yugoslav confederation. The new liberal leader of the Slovenian communists, Milan Kučan, did not oppose the demands, and opposition parties began to emerge. The de facto head of the central government in

1980	23 December 1990
Josip Broz (Tito) dies	Slovenian electorate overwhelmingly supports an independent republic

Belgrade, Serbian communist leader Slobodan Milošević, resolved to put pressure on Slovenia.

In June 1988 three Slovenian journalists, including the current prime minister, Janez Janša, working for the weekly *Mladina* (Youth) and a junior army officer who had given away 'military secrets' were tried by a military court and sentenced to prison. Mass demonstrations were held throughout the country in protest.

In the autumn, Serbia unilaterally scrapped the autonomy of Kosovo (where 80% of the population is ethnically Albanian). Slovenes were shocked by the move, fearing the same could happen to them. A rally organised jointly by the Slovenian government and the opposition in Ljubljana early in the new year condemned the move.

In the spring of 1989 the new opposition parties published the May Declaration, demanding a sovereign state for Slovenes based on democracy and respect for human rights. In September the Slovenian parliament amended the constitution to legalise management of its own resources and peacetime command of the armed forces. Serbia then announced plans to hold a 'meeting of truth' in Ljubljana on its intentions. When Slovenia banned it, Serbia and all the other republics except Croatia announced an economic boycott of Slovenia, cutting off 25% of its exports. In January 1990, Slovenian delegates walked out on an extraordinary congress of the Communist Party, thereby sounding the death knell of the party.

Among the four dissidents arrested, tried by a military court and sentenced to prison in June 1988 was the current prime minister Janez Janša.

INDEPENDENCE

In April 1990, Slovenia became the first Yugoslav republic to hold free elections. Demos, a coalition of seven opposition parties, won 55% of the vote, and Kučan, head of what was now called the Party of Democratic Renewal, was elected 'president of the presidency'. The leader of the Christian Democrats, Lojze Peterle, became prime minister.

In the summer, after Serbia had rejected the Slovenian and Croatian proposals for a confederation and threatened to declare a state of emergency, the Slovenian parliament adopted a 'declaration on the sovereignty of the state of Slovenia'. Henceforth Slovenia's own constitution would direct its political, economic and judicial systems; federal laws would apply only if they were not in contradiction to it.

On 23 December 1990, 88.5% of the Slovenian electorate voted in a referendum for an independent republic – effective within six months. The presidency of the Yugoslav Federation in Belgrade labelled the move secessionist and anticonstitutional. Serbia then proceeded to raid the Yugoslav monetary system and misappropriated almost the entire monetary issue planned for Yugoslavia in 1991 – US$2 billion. Seeing the writing on the wall, the Slovenian government began stockpiling weapons, and on 25 June 1991 Slovenia pulled out of the Yugoslav Federation for good. 'This evening dreams are allowed', President Kučan told a jubilant crowd in Ljubljana's Kongresni trg the following evening. 'Tomorrow is a new day.'

Indeed it was. On 27 June the Yugoslav army began marching on Slovenia but met resistance from the Territorial Defence Forces, the police and the general population. Within several days, units of the federal army began disintegrating; Belgrade threatened aerial bombardment and Slovenia faced the prospect of total war.

27 June–6 July 1991	May 1992
Slovenia fights a 10-day war with Yugoslavia	Slovenia admitted into the UN

The military action had not come totally unprovoked. To dramatise their bid for independence and to generate support from a less than sympathetic West, which wanted to see Yugoslavia continue to exist in some form or another, Slovenian leaders had baited Belgrade by attempting to take control of the border crossings first. Belgrade apparently never expected Slovenia to resist, believing that a show of force would be sufficient for it to back down.

As no territorial claims or minority issues were involved, the Yugoslav government agreed on 7 July to a truce brokered by leaders of what was then the European Community (EC). Under the so-called Brioni Declaration, Slovenia would put further moves to assert its independence on hold for three months provided it was granted recognition by the EC after that time. The war had lasted just 10 days and taken the lives of 66 people.

THE ROAD TO EUROPE

To everyone's surprise, Belgrade announced that it would withdraw the federal army from Slovenian soil within three months, and did so on 25 October 1991, less than a month after Slovenia introduced scrip of its own new currency – the tolar. In late December, Slovenia got a new constitution that provided for a parliamentary system of government. The National Assembly (Državni Zbor), the highest legislative authority, today consists of 90 deputies elected for four years by proportional representation; two of the deputies represent the Italian and Hungarian ethnic communities. The 40 members of the Council of State (Državni Svet), which performs an advisory role, are elected for five-year terms by social, economic, professional and special-interest groups. The head of state, the president, is elected directly for a maximum of two five-year terms. Milan Kučan, arguably the nation's most popular and respected politician to date, held that role from independence until 2002, when Prime Minister Janez Drnovšek was elected. Executive power is vested in the prime minister, currently Janez Janša of the Slovenian Democratic Party (SDS), who heads a four-party centre-right coalition, and a cabinet of 17 ministers (two without portfolio). The judicial system consists of a supreme court, four high courts that serve as appeals courts, 11 circuit courts and 44 district courts.

The EC formally recognised Slovenia on 15 January 1992, and it was admitted to the UN four months later as the 176th member-state.

Slovenia began negotiations for entry into the European Union (EU) in 1998 and, along with nine other countries, was invited to join the union four years later. In a referendum held in March 2003, an overwhelming 89.6% of the electorate voted in favour of Slovenia joining the EU, and 66% approved its membership in NATO. In March 2004, Slovenia became the first transition country to graduate from borrower status to donor partner at the World Bank and in May of that year entered the EU as a full member. In January 2007, Slovenia became the first of the 10 new EU states to adopt the euro, replacing the tolar as the national currency.

For a portrait of how Slovenia looks to an outsider at the moment, see p20.

May 2004

Slovenia joins the European Union

January 2007

Slovenia replaces the tolar with the euro as its national currency

The Culture

THE NATIONAL PSYCHE

Slovenes are a sophisticated and well-educated people. They have a reputation for being sober-minded, hard-working, dependable and honest – a Germanic bent that is the result of 600-plus years in the orbit of the Habsburgs. But they retain something of their Slavic character, even if their spontaneity is a little more planned and their expressions of passion a little more muted than that of their Slavic neighbours to the south. Think quietly conservative, deeply self-confident, broadminded and tolerant.

If you really want to understand Slovenes and *Sloventsvo* ('Slovene-ness'), there are two Slovenian words that you should know. The first is the adjective *priden,* variously defined as 'diligent', 'industrious', 'hard-working' and – tellingly – 'well-behaved'. Erica Johnson Debeljak , in her seminal (though as yet unpublished in English) memoir *And the Distance Smells of Apples: A Story of Migration* claims that *priden* 'comes close to defining the essence of the Slovenian soul'. Doing a spot of DIY, neighbour? How *priden* of you! Expecting that second child? Aren't we *priden*!

The second word is the noun *hrepenenje,* which expresses a more complicated concept. The dictionary says it means 'longing' or 'yearning' but that's only half the story. In truth it's the desire for something seemingly unattainable and the sorrow that accompanies it. '*Hrepenenje* is the exclusive property of the dispossessed,' writes Johnson Debeljak, citing 'the country's agonising history of border changes, emigration, alienation and powerlessness within a larger unit.' The medieval tale *Lepa Vida* could be seen as the very embodiment of this 'melancholy yearning'.

Luckily, Slovenes are gifted polyglots, and almost everyone speaks some English, German and/or Italian. The fact that you will rarely have difficulty in making yourself understood and will probably never 'need' Slovene – aside from those two words! – shouldn't stop you from learning a few phrases of this rich and wonderful language (which counts a full 34 dialects). Any effort on your part to speak the local tongue (p299) will be rewarded 100-fold.

LIFESTYLE

The population of Slovenia is divided almost exactly in half, between those who live in towns and cities and those who dwell in the country. But in Slovenia, where most urban folk still have some connection with the country – whether it's a village house or a *zidanica*, a cottage in one of the wine-growing regions, the division is not all that great. And with the arrival of large malls on the outskirts of the biggest cities and a Mercator supermarket in virtually every village in the land, the city has come to the country in Slovenia.

Most Slovenes believe that the essence of their national character lies in nature's plentiful bounty. For them a life that is not in some way connected to the countryside is inconceivable. At weekends many seek the great outdoors for some walking in the hills or cross-country skiing. Or at least a spot of gardening, a favourite pastime.

With farmhouse stays a popular form of accommodation in Slovenia, it's relatively easy to take a peek inside a local home. What you'll see generally won't differ too much from what you'd see elsewhere in Central and Western Europe, though you may be surprised at the dearth of children. Slovenes don't have many kids – the nation has one of Europe's lowest rates of natural population increase (8.98 per 1000 population, with a population

An excellent source book for all things cultural in Slovenia is the weighty, 520-page *Slovenia Cultural Profile,* published by the UK-based Visiting Arts in association with the British Council and the Slovenian Ministry of Culture.

The French novelist Charles Nodier (1780–1844), who lived and worked in Ljubljana for a couple of years in the early 19th century, called Slovenia 'an Academy of Arts and Sciences' because of the people's flair for speaking foreign languages.

growth of -0.05%) – and women usually give birth on the late side. Most families tend to have just one child and if they have a second it's usually a decade later.

ECONOMY

A largely heterogeneous and highly adaptable economy, and a very hard-working people have always been central to Slovenia's prosperity. The country's accession with nine other nations to the EU in 2004 also opened up a vast market for the country's goods. Slovenia was the first of these 10 nations to be allowed to adopt the euro as its national currency, when its average annual inflation rate had reached 2.5%. Overall unemployment remains a relatively high 10.4%.

The picture is not altogether rosy. Much of the economy remains in state hands and foreign direct investment in Slovenia is one of the lowest in the EU on a per-capita basis. Ljubljana is responsible for as much as 25% of the country's GDP, primarily thanks to industry (pharmaceuticals, petro-chemicals and food-processing), retailing, transport, communications, and financial and other business services. Agriculture accounts for only 6% of all economic activity.

POPULATION & MULTICULTURALISM

According to the most recent census figures, about 82% of the population claims to be ethnic Slovene, descendants of the South Slavs who settled in what is now Slovenia from the 6th century AD.

There are 6243 ethnic Hungarians and 3246 Roma (Gypsies), largely in Prekmurje, as well as 2258 Italians in Primorska. 'Others' and 'unknown ethnic origin', accounting for about 16% of the population, include ethnic Albanians, Bosnians, Croats, Serbs, those who identify themselves simply as 'Muslims' and many citizens of former Yugoslav republics who 'lost' their nationality after independence for fear that Slovenia would not grant them citizenship.

Cleveland, Ohio, in the USA is the largest 'Slovenian' city outside Slovenia.

The Italians and Hungarians are considered indigenous minorities with rights protected under the constitution, and they have special deputies looking after their interests in parliament. Although some members of the other groups have lived and worked in Slovenia for many years, most are relatively recent arrivals – refugees and economic immigrants from the fighting in the former Yugoslav republics. Their status as noncitizens in Slovenia is extremely controversial, and many Slovenes have very racist feelings about them.

Ethnic Slovenes living outside the national borders number as many as 400,000, with the vast majority (almost 75%) in the USA and Canada. In addition, 50,000 or more Slovenes live in the Italian regions of Gorizia (Gorica), Udine (Videm) and Trieste (Trst), another 15,000 in Austrian Carinthia (Kärnten in German, Koroška in Slovene) and 5000 in southwest Hungary.

SPORT

See www.eurobasket.com/slo/slo.asp for more about Union Olimpija and Slovenian basketball.

Slovenia – a land where *smučanje* (skiing) is king – has produced many world-class ski champions, including Roman Perko in cross-country racing, Mitja Dragšič in men's slalom and Špela Pretnar in women's slalom. But the national heroes in recent years have been Primož Peterka, the ski-jumping World Cup winner in 1996–97 and 1997–98, extreme skier Davo Karničar, who made the first uninterrupted descent of Mt Everest on skis in 2000, and new kid on the block Rok Benkovič, who took gold at the Nordic Ski World Championship at Oberstdorf in Germany in 2005.

Until recently Slovenia was one of the few countries in Europe where *nogomet* (football) was not a national passion, but interest in the sport increased following the national team's plucky performance in the 2000 European Championship, and again in 2004 when they finished second in their group, behind mighty France. In the 2006 FIFA World Cup qualifiers, Slovenia beat Moldova 3-0 at the new Športni Park stadium in Celje, and a shock 1-0 success against favourites Italy propelled them to the top spot in their group. But they failed to qualify as they had in 2002. There are 10 teams in the First Division, with HiT Gorica of Nova Gorica the champions for the past three years.

In general *kosarka* (basketball) is the most popular team sport here, and the Union Olimpija team reigns supreme. Other popular spectator sports are ice *hokej* (hockey) and *odjojka* (volleyball).

Slovenia punches well above its weight when it comes to winning Olympic medals, regularly claiming more gold medals per head of population than Russia or the USA. At the 2004 Olympic Games in Athens, Slovenia won a silver in men's double sculls and three bronzes in the women's 800m, judo and laser sailing. More impressively they walked away from the 2000 Sydney Olympics with two golds: in the men's double sculls and the 50m rifle shooting. The Slovenian ski-jumping team, which includes Damjan Fras, Primož Peterka, Robert Kranjec and Peter Zonta, took a bronze medal at the 2002 Winter Olympics in Salt Lake City, but no medals came back to Slovenia from the winter games in Turin in 2006.

Some 3500 sport societies and clubs count a total membership of 400,000 – 20% of the population – across the nation.

RELIGION

Although Protestantism gained a very strong foothold in Slovenia in the 16th century, the majority of Slovenes – just under 58% – identified themselves as Roman Catholic in the most recent (2002) census. The primate of Slovenia is Cardinal France Rode, based in Ljubljana. There are bishoprics at Maribor and Koper and, from 2006, at Celje, Novo Mesto and Murska Sobota.

Other religious communities in Slovenia include Muslims (2.4%), Eastern Orthodox Christians (2.3%) and Protestants (1%). Most Protestants belong to the Evangelical (Lutheran) church based in Murska Sobota in Prekmurje.

Jews have played a very minor role in Slovenia since they were first banished from the territory in the 15th century. In 2003 the Jewish community of Slovenia (www.jewishcommunity.si; population about 100) received a Torah at a newly equipped temporary synagogue in Ljubljana, the first since before WWII.

Maja Weiss's *Varuh Meje* (Guardian of the Frontier, 2002), the first Slovenian feature film directed by a woman, follows the journey of three young women on break from college. They take a perilous journey down the Kolpa River, crossing national, political and sexual boundaries.

WOMEN IN SLOVENIA

Women enjoy equal status with men under Slovenian law but, despite all the work done to eliminate discrimination against women, bias remains. The share of women in government positions of power is low: at present 12 members of parliament – just over 13% – are women. It's a little better in business, with about 20% of directorial posts filled by females.

ARTS
Literature

Slovenia is a highly educated society with a literacy rate of virtually 100% among those older than 15 years of age. Indeed, being able to read and write is ingrained in the culture. 'What is your surname?' in Slovene is '*Kako se pišete?*' or 'How do you write yourself?'

The oldest example of written Slovene (or any Slavic language for that matter) can be found in the three so-called *Freising Manuscripts* (Brižinski Spomeniki) from around 970. They contain a sermon on sin and penance

Slovenia is the third-smallest literature market in Europe and a fiction 'bestseller' in this country means 500 to 800 copies sold.

Valvasor's explanation of how the water system in Lake Cerknica worked earned him membership in 1697 in the Royal Society in London, the world's foremost scientific institution at the time.

and instructions for general confession. Oral poetry, such as the seminal *Lepa Vida* (Fair Vida), a tale of longing, homesickness and nostalgia, flourished throughout the Middle Ages, but it was the Reformation that saw the first book in Slovene, a catechism published by Primož Trubar in 1550. A complete translation of the Bible by Jurij Dalmatin followed in 1584, and in the same year Adam Bohorič published a grammar of Slovene in Latin, with the evocative title *Spare Winter Hours*. Almost everything else published until the late 18th century was in Latin or German, including Janez Vajkard Valvasor's ambitious account of Slovenia, *The Glory of the Duchy of Carniola* (1689), from which most of our knowledge of Slovenian history, geography, culture and folklore before the 17th century comes. Not only did Valvasor (1641–93) map huge areas of Carniola and its towns for the first time, he also explained the mystery of disappearing karst lakes and rivers, 'discovered' the unusual amphibian *Proteus anguinus*, introduced the world to Erazem Lueger, the 15th-century Robin Hood of Slovenia, and catalogued early Slovenian folk tales and dress. *Die Ehre des Herzogthums Crain* (as it was called in German) ran into four volumes, containing 3500 pages with 535 maps and copper engravings.

The Enlightenment and the reforms carried out under Habsburg rulers Maria Theresa and Joseph II raised the educational and general cultural level of the Slovenian nation. In large part due to the support and philanthropy of Baron Žiga Zois (1747–1819), Slovenia gained its first dramatist (Anton Tomaž Linhart), poet (Valentin Vodnik) and modern grammarian (Jernej Kopitar) at this time. But it was during the so-called National Romantic Period that Slovenian literature truly came of age and gained its greatest poet of all times: France Prešeren (below). Although many influential writers published at this time, including his friends and associates Matija Čop and Andrej Smole, no one so dominated the period as Prešeren. His bittersweet verse, progressive ideas, demands for political freedom and longings for the unity of all Slovenes caught the imagination of the nation and simply has never let it go.

Visit www.preseren.net /ang for English translations of the works of national poet France Prešeren.

FRANCE PREŠEREN: A POET FOR THE NATION

Slovenia's most beloved poet was born in Vrba near Bled in 1800 and educated in Ribnica, Ljubljana and Vienna, where he received a law degree in 1828. Most of his working life was spent as an articled clerk in the office of a Ljubljana lawyer. By the time he had opened his own practice in Kranj in 1846 he was already a sick and dispirited man. He died three years later.

Although Prešeren published only one volume of poetry during his lifetime (*Poezije*, 1848), which sold a mere 30 copies, he left behind a legacy of work printed in the literary magazines *Kranjska Čbelica* (Carniolan Bee) and the German-language *Illyrisches Blatt* (Illyrian Sheet). His verse set new standards for Slovenian literature at a time when German was the literary language, and his lyric poems, such as the masterpiece 'Sonetni Venec' (A Garland of Sonnets, 1834), are among the most sensitive, original and eloquent works in Slovene. In later poems, such as his epic 'Krst pri Savici' (Baptism by the Savica Waterfall, 1836), he expressed a national consciousness that he tried to instil in his compatriots.

Prešeren's life was one of sorrow and disappointment, which he met with stoicism and resignation. The sudden death of his close friend and mentor, the literary historian Matija Čop, in 1835 and an unrequited love affair with an heiress called Julija Primic brought him close to suicide. But this was when he produced his best poems.

In reality, Prešeren was a drunkard, a philanderer, a social outcast and maybe even a tad vain. He refused to have his portrait done and any likeness you see of him was done from memory after his death. But Prešeren was the first to demonstrate the full literary potential of the Slovenian language, and his body of verse – lyric poems, epics, satire, narrative verse – has inspired Slovenes at home and abroad for generations. And will do so for generations to come.

ANDREJ BLATNIK: FIRST PERSON SINGULAR

Andrej Blatnik (www.andrejblatnik.com), who started his artistic career in the early 1980s playing bass guitar in a punk rock band, has published two novels and four collections of short stories, including *Menjave Kož*, translated into English as *Skinswaps* and available from Amazon. Here are some of his views on:

Art in the previous regime 'Art was viewed as something high-class and intellectual. Punk rock brought art to street level in Slovenia.'

Censorship before independence 'By the 1980s things were very open here, even local communist cells were lenient. They'd call you in and say "It's OK if you think that, but do you have to write it?" The state was more interested then in what we were doing!'

Literature in Slovenia 'Literature has always had other duties in Slovenia beyond just art. Writers drew up early nationalist programs, the nation's constitution, they were the first to open up parts of our hidden history, putting the torture and the trials after WWII subtly in their novels. In a small country everything has a bigger effect, a greater echo. [Today] Literature has become more a personal task than one of team work. Once we used it to foster our identity and feed our pride. Now we have other successes and can rely on things like football. No one can rely on the previous experience of literature today.'

Themes in Slovenian writing '*Hrepenenje* [p31], the desire for something uncertain perhaps linked with the lack of independence over the centuries, is very prominent in the work of Prešeren and Cankar. Urban themes are few and far between as there is no real city life as such here. Most people in Ljubljana are only first or second generation. There are exceptions [for example, Andrej E Skubic's *Fužine Blues*], with some young writers focusing on what is an increasingly multi-ethnic society. But most urban novels have been traditionally written abroad and end with the protagonist coming back to Slovenia and the countryside – usually to their mother's burial in the mud and the rain.'

Being a writer in Slovenia 'Between 60 to 70 novels are published a year and 200 books of poetry. There is some funding from the state and also a certain amount of prestige. You can make a living as a writer in Slovenia. State grants help as do public readings but it is a very, very modest living.'

In the latter half of the 19th century, Fran Levstik (1831–87) brought the writing and interpretation of oral folk tales to new heights with his *Martin Krpan*: legends about the eponymous larger-than-life hero of the Bloke Plateau in Notranjska. But it was Josip Jurčič (1844–81) who published the first full-length novel in Slovene, *Deseti Brat* (The 10th Brother, 1866).

The period from the turn of the 20th century up to WWII is dominated by two men who single-handedly introduced modernism into Slovenian literature: the poet Oton Župančič (1878–1949) and the novelist and playwright Ivan Cankar (1876–1918). The latter has been called 'the outstanding master of Slovenian prose'. His works, notably *Hiša Marije Pomočnice* (The Ward of Our Lady of Mercy, 1904) and *Hlapec Jernej in Njegova Pravica* (The Bailiff Yerney and His Rights, 1907), influenced a generation of young writers.

Slovenian literature immediately before and after WWII was influenced by socialist realism and the Partisan struggle as exemplified by the novels of Lovro Kuhar-Prežihov Voranc (1893–1950). Since then, however, Slovenia has tended to follow Western European trends: late expressionism, symbolism (poetry by Edvard Kocbek, 1904–81) and existentialism (novels by Vitomil Zupan, 1914–87, and the drama of Gregor Strniša 1930–87).

The major figures of Slovenian post-modernism since 1980 are the novelist Drago Jančar (1948–) and the poet Tomaž Šalamun (1941–). Important writers born around 1960 include the poet Aleš Debeljak (1961–) and the writer Andrej Blatnik (1963–). Young talent to watch out for includes Andrej E Skubic (1967–), whose 2004 novel (and now play) *Fužinski Bluz* (Fužine Blues) is set in one of Ljubljana's less salubrious neighbourhoods on 13 June 2002, the day of the very first football match between independent Slovenia and Yugoslavia. A personal favourite is Boris Pahor (1913–), a member of the Slovenian minority in Trieste whose books – including *Nekropola*

(Pilgrim among the Shadows), a harrowing memoir of time spent in the Natzweiler–Struthof concentration camp at the end of WWII – are now being translated into English.

Architecture

Examples of Romanesque architecture can be found in many parts of Slovenia, including the churches at Stična Abbey in Dolenjska, at Muta and Dravograd in Koroška, and at Podsreda Castle in Štajerska.

Much Gothic architecture in Slovenia is of the late period; the earthquake of 1511 took care of many buildings erected before then (although both the Venetian Gothic Loggia and Praetorian Palace in Koper date back a century earlier). Renaissance architecture is mostly limited to civil buildings (eg the town houses in Škofja Loka and Kranj, and Brdo Castle in Gorenjska).

Italian-influenced baroque of the 17th and 18th centuries abounds in Slovenia, particularly in Ljubljana (eg the Ursuline Church of the Holy Trinity and the cathedral, p72). Classicism prevailed in architecture here in the first half of the 19th century; the Kazina building in Ljubljana's Kongresni trg and the Tempel pavilion in Rogaška Slatina in Štajerska are good examples.

The turn of the 20th century was when the Secessionist (or Art Nouveau) architects Maks Fabiani and Ivan Vurnik began changing the face of Ljubljana (Miklošičev Park, Prešeren monument, the Cooperative Bank on Miklošičeva cesta) after the devastating earthquake of 1895. But no architect has had a greater impact on his city or nation than Jože Plečnik (p76), a man who defies easy definition.

Postwar architecture is generally forgettable but among the most interesting contemporary architects working today are the team Rok Oman and Špela Videčnik, who designed the extraordinary new extension to the City Museum (p72) in Ljubljana.

Architectural Guide to Ljubljana by Janez Koželj and Andrej Hrausky is a richly illustrated guide to 100 buildings and other features in the capital, with much emphasis on architect extraordinaire Jože Plečnik.

Music

As elsewhere in Central and Eastern Europe, music – especially the classical variety – is very important in Slovenia and attendance at concerts and recitals is very high in cities and towns.

The conversion of the Slavs to Christianity from the 8th century brought the development of choral singing in churches and monasteries; the oldest Slovenian spiritual song dates from 1440. The most important composer in the late 16th century was Jakob Gallus (1550–91), who wrote madrigals and choral songs as well as 16 sung masses.

Baroque music had gone out of fashion by the time the Filharmonija was founded in Ljubljana in 1701, and classical forms had become all the rage. *Belin,* the first Slovenian opera, was written by Jakob Francisek Zupan in 1780, and Janez Novak composed classical music for a comedy written by Slovenia's first playwright, Anton Tomaž Linhart. The 19th-century Romantics, like Benjamin Ipavec, Fran Gerbič and Anton Foerster, incorporated traditional Slovenian elements into their music as a way of expressing their nationalism. Perhaps Slovenia's best-known composer at this time was Hugo Wolf (1860–1903), born in Slovenj Gradec.

Slovenian music between the wars is best represented by the expressionist Marij Kogoj and the modernist Slavko Osterc. Contemporary composers whose reputations go well beyond the borders of Slovenia include Primož Ramovš, Marjan Kozina, Lojze Lebič and the ultramodernist Vinko Globokar, who lives in Paris. Opera buffs won't want to miss out on the chance to hear Marjana Lipovšek, the country's foremost mezzo-soprano. There are a total of five professional orchestras and two operas in Slovenia.

Popular music runs the gamut from Slovenian *chanson* (eg Vita Mavrič) and folk to jazz and mainstream polka best exemplified by the Avsenik Brothers Ensemble (www.avsenik.com). However, it was punk music in the late 1970s and early 1980s that put Slovenia on the world stage. The most celebrated groups were Pankrti, Borghesia and Laibach, and they were imitated throughout Eastern Europe. The most popular rock band in Slovenia today remains Siddharta, still going strong after almost a decade. The most popular solo musician is Magnifico (aka Robert Pešut), who combines Balkan, funk, pop and electronic music, to reasonable degrees of success. New talent to watch out for is the versatile musician and singer Neisha.

The leader of celebrated punk band Laibach, Tomaž Hostnik, died tragically in 1983 when he hanged himself from a *kozolec*, the traditional Slovenian hayrack.

FOLK MUSIC

Ljudska glasba (folk music) in Slovenia has developed independently from other forms of music over the centuries, and the collection and classification of children's songs, wedding marches and fables set to music began only in the National Romantic Period of the 19th century. Traditional folk instruments include the *frajtonarica* (button accordion), *cymbalom* (a curious stringed instrument played with sticks), *bisernica* (lute), *zvegla* (wooden cross flute), *okarina* (clay flute), *šurle* (Istrian double flute), *trstenke* (reed pipes), Jew's harp, *lončeni bajs* (earthenware bass), *berdo* (contrabass) and *brač* (eight-string guitar).

Folk-music performances are usually local affairs and are very popular in Dolenjska, Bela Krajina and even Bled (especially during the August Okarina Etno Festival, p115). Črnomelj and especially Adlešiči in Bela Krajina are centres of Slovenian folk music, and as many as 50 bands are active in the area.

There's been a folk-music revival in recent years, and two groups to listen for include Katice and Katalena, who play traditional Slovene music with a modern twist. Terra Folk is the quintessential world-music band.

Visual Arts

There are 45 permanent art museums and galleries in Slovenia and another 800 temporary exhibition spaces, which will give you a rough idea of the role that visual arts play in the lives of many Slovenes.

Examples of Romanesque fine art are rare in Slovenia, surviving only in illuminated manuscripts. Gothic painting and sculpture is another matter, however, with excellent works at Ptujska Gora (the carved altar in the Church of the Virgin Mary; p237), Bohinj (frescoes in the Church of St John the Baptist; p101), and Hrastovlje (Dance of Death wall painting at the Church of the Holy Trinity; p163). Important painters of this time were Johannes de Laibaco (John of Ljubljana), who decorated the Church of the Assumption in Muljava (p196); Jernej of Loka, who worked mostly around Škofja Loka; and Johannes Aquila of Radgona, who did the frescoes in the magnificent church (p267) at Martjanci.

The colourful tome *Handicrafts of Slovenia* by leading ethnographer Janez Bogataj takes a close look at Slovenia's rich tradition of folk craft, with everything from ceramics and lace to woodcarving and painted beehive panels .

For baroque sculpture, look at Jožef Straub's plague pillar in Maribor, the golden altar in the Church of the Annunciation (p101) at Crngrob or the work of Francesco Robba in Ljubljana (Carniolan Rivers fountain in Mestni trg; see Robba Fountain p72). Fortunat Bergant, who painted the Stations of the Cross in the church at Stična Abbey (p197), was a master of baroque painting.

Classicism prevailed in Slovenian art in the first half of the 19th century in the works of the painter Franc Kavčič, and the Romantic portraits and landscapes of Josip Tominc and Matevž Langus. Realism arrived in the second half of the century in the work of such artists as Ivana Kobilca, Jurij Šubic and Anton Ažbe. The most important painters of that time, however, were the impressionists Rihard Jakopič, Matija Jama, Ivan Grohar and Matej Sternen, who exhibited together in Ljubljana in 1900.

In the 20th century, the expressionist school of Božidar Jakac and the brothers France and Tone Kralj gave way to the so-called Club of Independents (the painters Zoran Mušič, Maksim Sedej and France Mihelič) and later the sculptors Alojzij Gangl, Franc Berneker, Jakob Savinšek and Lojze Dolinar. The last two would later create 'masterpieces' of socialist realism under Tito without losing their credibility or (sometimes) their artistic sensibilities. Favourite artists to emerge after WWII include Janez Bernik, Rudi Španzel and, from Slovenj Gradec, Jože Tisnikar.

Since the 1980s postmodernist painting and sculpture has been more or less dominated by the artists' cooperative IRWIN, part of the wider multimedia group Neue Slowenische Kunst (NSK). Among notable names are that of the sculptor Marjetica Potrč and the video artist Marko Peljhan.

Check out www.ljudmila .org/nsk/1.html to learn more about what the Neue Slowenische Kunst and IRWIN are up to.

Theatre & Dance

Slovenian attendance of theatre productions is close to 900,000 a year, evidence that this art form is a vital and popular discipline.

The exact birth date of Slovenian theatre is considered to be 28 December 1789, as it was on that night that Anton Tomaž Linhart (1756–95), Slovenia's first playwright, staged the inaugural performance of his comedy *Županova Micka* (Micka, the Mayor's Daughter). In 1867 a Dramatics Society was founded in Ljubljana and a national theatre founded in 1892. Today Ljubljana and Maribor enjoy a vibrant theatre scene. Experimental theatre, best exemplified by Grejpfrut and director Dragan Živadinov, is particularly interesting. The Ana Desetnica International Festival of Street Theatre (p78) is organised by the Ana Monro Theatre in Ljubljana in early July.

Much of Slovenian dance finds its origins in folk culture, and *ljudski ples* (folk dance) has a long tradition in Slovenia, including polkas, circle dances and Hungarian-style czardas. The first ballet group was established in 1918 as part of the National Theatre, and a ballet school was set up. The Ljubljana Ballet now performs at the Opera House and there's another company in Maribor. Avant-garde dance is best exemplified by Betontanc, a dance company established by Matjaž Pogrejc, which mixes live music and theatrical elements – called 'physical theatre' – with some sharp political comment, Iztok Kovač's EbKnap troupe and Tomaš Pandur.

Cinema & TV

Slovenia was never on the cutting edge of film-making as were some of the former Yugoslav republics (eg Croatia). However, it still managed to produce about a dozen full-length features annually, some of which – like Jože Gale's *Kekec* (1951) and France Štiglic's *Dolina Miru* (Valley of Peace, 1955) – won international awards. Today that number has dropped to between four and six.

Only two films were produced in Slovenia between the wars. In the 1950s Slovenian film tended to focus on subjects like the Partisan struggle – eg Štiglic's *Na Svoji Zemlji* (On Their Own Land, 1948) and *Akcija* (Action, 1960) by Jane Kavčič – and life among the Slovenian bourgeoisie under the Austro-Hungarian empire (eg Bojan Stupica's *Jara Gospoda* or Parvenus, 1953). The 1960s brought a new wave of modernism, best exemplified by the work of the late Boštjan Hladnik (*Ples v Dežju* or Dance in the Rain, 1961) and Matjaž Klopčič (*Na Papirnatih Avionih* or On Wings of Paper, 1967).

What is now touted as the 'Spring of Slovenian Film' in the late 1990s was heralded by two films: *Ekspres, Ekspres* (Express, Express, 1997) by Igor Šterk, an award-winning 'railroad' film and farce, and *Autsajder* (Outsider,

The first film shot in Slovenia was a documentary called *V Kraljestvu Zlatoroga* (In the Realm of the Goldenhorn) in 1931.

1997) by Andrej Košak, about the love between a Slovenian girl and Bosnian 'outsider'. Subsequent successes were Sašo Podgoršek's *Sladke Sanje* (Sweet Dreams, 2001) and *Kruh in Mleko* (Bread & Milk, 2001) by Jan Cvitkovič. Damjan Kozole's *Rezervni Deli* (Spare Parts, 2003) won international acclaim for its almost brutal treatment of the trafficking of illegal immigrants through Slovenia, from Croatia to Italy, by a bunch of embittered misfits. Up for a Foreign Language Oscar in 2007 was Cvitkovič's *Odgrobadogroba* (Grave Hopping), a tragicomedy about a professional funeral speaker. The Slovenian Film Festival takes place in Celje in September.

The website of the Slovenian Film Fund (Filmski Sklad Slovenije; www .film-sklad.si) can tell you everything you need to know about films and filming in Slovenia.

Radiotelevizija Slovenija (RTV SLO) broadcasts on two channels: SLO 1, which has everything from children's programs to news and films, and SLO 2, which shows mostly sporting events. A subsidiary called TV Koper-Capodistria broadcasts in Italian on the coast, and there is a regional station in Maribor. The top two private commercial channels are the immensely popular Pop-TV and Kanal A, which often show films and other programmes in English with Slovene subtitles, and there are about 30 regional cable stations. Locally produced public TV is not very good in Slovenia – you may have noticed all those satellite dishes on the rooftops pulling in Sky, BBC World and CNN.

Environment

THE LAND

Slovenia is a Central European country with a surface area of only 20,273 sq km – about the size of Wales or Israel. It borders Austria for 318km to the north and Croatia for 670km to the south and southeast. Shorter frontiers are shared with Italy (280km) to the west and Hungary (102km) to the northeast.

The terrain is predominantly hilly or mountainous: about 90% of the surface lies more than 300m above sea level at an average elevation of 557m. Forest, some of it virgin, and woodland cover 57% of the country. Land under agricultural use is rapidly diminishing and now accounts for just under a quarter of the total.

Geographers divide the country into as many as a dozen different areas, but there are basically four topographical regions. The Alps, including the Julian Alps, the Kamnik-Savinja Alps, the Karavanke chain and the Pohorje Massif, are to the north and northeast. Spreading across their entire southern side are the pre-Alpine hills of Idrija, Cerkno, Škofja Loka and Posavje. The Dinaric karst lies below the hills and encompasses the 'true' or 'original' Karst plateau between Ljubljana and the Italian border. The Slovenian littoral follows its small 47km of coastline along the Adriatic Sea, and the essentially flat Pannonian plain spreads to the east and northeast of the country.

Much of the interior of Slovenia is drained by two rivers – the Sava (221km) and Drava (144km) – both of which flow southeastward and empty into the Danube. Other important rivers are the Soča to the west, which flows into the Adriatic, the Mura in the northeast, the Krka to the southeast and the Kolpa, which forms part of the southeastern border with Croatia. There are several 'intermittent' rivers (eg the Unica, Pivka and Reka), which disappear into karst caves and potholes, only to resurface elsewhere under different names. Slovenia's largest natural lakes are Cerknica in Notranjska, which is dry for part of the year (usually July to September or later), and Bohinj in Gorenjska.

Main Regions

Although Slovenia is divided up into 194 *občine* (municipalities or administrative communes), this doesn't help when travelling. Instead, Slovenia is best viewed as a country with a capital city (Ljubljana) and eight traditional *regije* (regions): Gorenjska, Primorska, Notranjska, Dolenjska, Bela Krajina, Štajerska, Prekmurje and Koroška.

Greater Ljubljana, by far the nation's largest city, is pinched between hills to the west and east and the nonarable Ljubljana Marsh to the south.

Gorenjska, to the north and northwest of the capital, is Slovenia's most mountainous province and contains the country's highest peaks, including Triglav (2864m) and Škrlatica (2740m). The landscape is Alpine and the provincial centre is Kranj. Primorska, a very diverse region of hills, valleys, karst and a short coastline on the northern end of the Istrian peninsula, forms the country's western border, and the countryside feels Mediterranean on the whole. It has two 'capitals', Nova Gorica and Koper, and Slovenia's Italian minority is concentrated here. Notranjska, to the south and southeast of Ljubljana, is an underdeveloped area of forests and karst – Slovenia's 'last frontier'. Its main towns are Cerknica and Postojna.

Dolenjska lies south of the Sava River and has several distinct areas, including the Krka Valley, the hilly Kočevje and also the remote Posavje

The National Atlas of Slovenia, produced by a team of geographers, historians and social scientists to commemorate the 10th anniversary of Slovenia's independence, looks at the country's geography, settlement, emigration and environment and has over 100 maps.

Because the Karst region, a limestone plateau in Primorska, was the first such area to be described, it is also called the 'classic', 'real', 'true' or 'original' Karst and always spelled with an upper-case 'K'.

Slovenia ranks 150th in size out of a total 190 nations on earth.

regions. Novo Mesto is the main city. Bela Krajina, a gentle land of rolling hills and birch groves south of Dolenjska, is washed by the Kolpa River. Its most important towns are Metlika and Črnomelj.

Štajerska, by far Slovenia's largest region, stretches to the east and northeast and is a land of mountains, rivers, valleys, vineyards and ancient towns. Maribor and Celje are the centres, and Slovenia's second- and third-largest cities respectively. Sitting north of Štajerska is little Koroška, with its cultural heart at Slovenj Gradec.

Prekmurje, which roughly translates as 'beyond the Mura River', is basically a flat plain in Slovenia's extreme northeast, although there are hills to the north. Most of Slovenia's Hungarian minority lives within its borders, and the capital and administrative centre is Murska Sobota.

There are more Parisians (2.14 million) in central Paris than Slovenes (2 million) in all of Slovenia.

WILDLIFE

Slovenia, a small republic in the heart of Central Europe, is not the obvious place to view wildlife. However, common European animals abound and its forests, marsh areas and short coast attract a tremendous amount of birdlife. There are upwards of six dozen types of plants that you'll find only in Slovenia.

Animals

While Slovenia counts some 15,000 animal species, most are common European varieties such as deer, boar, chamois, wolves and lynx, all of which live here in abundance, especially in the Alpine areas and the Kočevje region of Dolenjska. The latter is also home to Europe's largest population of brown bears *(Ursus arctos)*, which currently numbers between 500 and 700 and has to be culled annually. There are also much rarer species such as the moor tortoise, cave hedgehog, scarab beetle and various types of dormice. Two species unique to Slovenia are the marbled Soča trout *(Salmo trutta marmoratus)* and *Proteus anguinus,* a blind salamander that lives in karst cave pools (p185) and is the only exclusively cave-dwelling vertebrate in the world.

www.gov.si/zgs/medved has information about the conservation of large carnivores in Slovenia, including brown bears.

Plants

Slovenia is home to 3200 plant species, and about 70 of them – many in the Alps – are unique to Slovenia or were first classified here. Triglav National Park is especially rich in endemic flowering plants, including the Triglav 'rose' (actually a pink cinquefoil), the blue Clusi's gentian, yellow hawk's-beard, Julian poppy, Carniola lily and primrose, tufted rampion and the purple Zois bellflower.

NATIONAL PARKS

About 8% of the countryside is protected under law at present. Further statutes have already been approved by parliament, and eventually more than a quarter of the territory will be conservation land of some kind.

There is one national park – the 83,808-hectare Triglav National Park (p128), which encompasses almost all of the Julian Alps – although proposals have been made to set aside others in the Kamnik Alps, the Pohorje Massif, the Karst and the Kočevje-Kolpa regions. There are three regional parks – in the Kozjansko region (p228) of southeast Štajerska, the area around the Škocjan Caves in Primorska (p151) and in Notranjska (p188) – and 44 areas designated as country (literally 'landscape') parks. There are also about 50 protected nature reserves, including 200 hectares of primeval forest in Kočevski Rog region (p202) of Dolenjska, and some 623 natural heritage sites, such as tiny Divje Jezero (Wild Lake; p147) at Idrija in Primorska.

RESPONSIBLE TOURISM

The rules and regulations in most protected parks and nature reserves are fairly obvious: no litter-ing, no picking flowers, no setting fires except in designated areas and so on. But also remember that certain landscapes, Triglav National Park in particular, are very fragile, and there is no wild camping and mountain bikes are banned from trails.

Minimise the waste you must carry out by taking minimal packaging and bringing no more food than you will need. Don't use detergents or toothpaste in or near watercourses, even if they are biodegradable. Bear in mind that sensitive biospheres, for both flora and fauna, may be seriously damaged if you depart from designated paths in protected areas.

Traffic congestion on Slovenia's roads is a problem in peak season, and visitors will do them-selves and residents a favour if they forgo driving and use public transport. You can also do your bit by resisting the temptation to drive your own or a rental car in fragile areas, like the Logarska Dolina and Robanov Kot in Štajerska, and go instead by bicycle or on foot. Use the recycling banks on the streets of larger towns or the litter bins at the very least.

ENVIRONMENTAL ISSUES

Although Slovenia is a very green country, pollution is a problem here, and it is now being tackled by the National Environment Protection Program, a seven-year plan approved by parliament in 2005, and the Environmental Agency of Slovenia(Agencija za Okolje), a branch of the Ministry of the Environment and Spatial Planning.

Over the past two decades the biggest concern has been air pollution. Climatic change is particularly worrying in a country that calls itself 'the garden of Europe', and the reduction of greenhouse gas emissions is a primary objective.

To learn more about the Environmental Agency of Slovenia, visit www .arso.gov.si.

In particular, nitrous oxides emitted by cars on the highway connecting Gorenjska with the coast are hurting the pine forests of Notranjska and damaging buildings, outdoor sculptures and other artwork in many histori-cal cities. Sulphur dioxide levels are especially high in cities and towns like Šoštanj, Trbovlje and Ljubljana where coal was the main fuel. The nation's sole nuclear power plant (at Krško in Dolenjska) provides about 40% of electric power, but half of it is owned by Croatia, and Slovenia plans to stop using it altogether in 2023.

From 1990 to 2000, steps taken to clean up the mess – including the con-struction of water-purifying plants, the monitoring of companies discharg-ing waste, the installation of filters on power plants and the introduction of gas heating – saw sulphur dioxide emissions fall by almost two-thirds and nitrogen oxide levels reduced by just over 10%.

In the past several years Slovenia has also introduced a series of environ-mental taxes, including a waste-disposal and water-pollution tax, in a bid to hit the biggest abusers in the pocket. The Sava, Mura and lower Savinja Rivers are especially vulnerable, though the quality of water in most Slov-enian rivers is acceptable. Even so, rain has washed underground all sorts of filth dumped in the Karst region, and waste carried by the 'disappearing' Unica and Ljubljanica Rivers could threaten the Ljubljana Marsh. Slovenia produces almost 4.7 million tonnes of waste a year, 61% of which is now recovered and 27% disposed.

Slovenia Outdoors

Slovenes live very active, very outdoorsy lives, and it won't be long before you're invited to join in the fun. Indeed, these are the people who invented skiing almost four centuries ago, and hiking and climbing clubs across the country count some 55,000 paid-up members. And according to local tradition, Slovenes can't even describe themselves as such until they have reached the top of Mt Triglav (p128). It is a tradition in Slovenia to greet everyone you pass while hiking or climbing. Generally a simple '*Dober dan*' (Hello) and/or a smile will suffice.

As a result of all this enthusiasm, the choice of activities and range of facilities available are endless. From skiing and climbing to caving and cycling, it's all on offer and very affordable compared with other parts of Europe. The **Slovenian Tourist Board** (www.slovenia.info) publishes specialist brochures and maps on skiing, hiking, cycling, golfing and horse riding, as well as one on the nation's top spas and heath resorts.

You'll find these activities available throughout the country, and most described below are cross-referenced to the appropriate sections under individual towns. You can always go it alone, but if you really want to be in safe, experienced hands, engage the services of any of the travel agencies specialising in adventure sport. These are usually found in this book's Information section of each town or city.

HIKING & WALKING

Slovenia has an excellent system of trails – 7000km of them – almost all of which are marked by a red circle with a white centre. At crossings, there are signs indicating distances and walking times. The Julian Alps, the Kamnik-Savinja Alps and the Pohorje Massif are the most popular places for hiking, but there are some wonderful trails in the lower hills and valleys as well.

The 350km E6 European Hiking Trail running from the Baltic to the Adriatic Seas enters Slovenia at Radlje ob Dravi in Koroška and continues for 280km to a point south of Snežnik in Notranjska. The 600km E7 European Hiking Trail, which connects the Atlantic with the Black Sea, crosses into Slovenia at Robič in Primorska, runs along the Soča Valley and then continues through the southern part of the country eastward to Bistrica ob Sotli in Štajerska before exiting into Croatia. Both are marked by a red circle with a yellow centre.

The Slovenian Alpine Trail, which opened in 1953 and was the first such trail in Europe, runs for 500km from Maribor to Ankaran on the coast via the Pohorje Massif, the Kamnik-Savinja Alps, the Julian Alps and the Cerkno and Idrija hills. It too is marked with a red circle with a white centre.

Slovenia has joined Austria, Germany, Liechtenstein, Switzerland, Italy, France and Monaco to develop **Via Alpina** (www.via-alpina.com), a 161-stage long-distance trail of two parts (Red Trail: 220km, Purple Trail 120km) that follows the entire arc of the Alps from Trieste to Monaco. Some 22 stages pass through Slovenia.

The Ljubljana-based **Alpine Association of Slovenia** (Planinska Zveza Slovenije, PZS; Map pp62-3; ☎ 01-434 56 80 general info, 434 56 90 huts info; www.pzs.si; Dvoržakova ulica 9; ☼ 8am-5pm Mon, 8am-3pm Tue-Fri), the umbrella organisation of 248 local hiking and climbing clubs, which has 55,000 fully paid members, is the fount of all information and can also organise mountain guides. It publishes hiking maps and a very useful list of mountain huts, refuges and bivouacs throughout Slovenia. This association provides information about specific trails in Triglav National Park and elsewhere as well as huts.

According to a government survey, every third Slovene takes part in active leisure pursuits.

For more on the E6 and E7 European Hiking Trails, see www.wander theglobe.com/trekking /europe.shtml.

All but one of the Category I mountain huts in Slovenia are in the Alps.

SLEEPING IN THE MOUNTAINS

A *bivak* (bivouac) is the most basic hut in the mountains of Slovenia, providing shelter only, whereas a *zavetišče* (refuge) has refreshments, and sometimes accommodation, but usually no running water. A *koča* (hut) or *dom* (house) can be a simple cottage or a fairly grand establishment like some of those close to Triglav.

A bed for the night runs from €10 to €20 in a Category I hut, depending on the number of beds in the room, and from €7.50 to €13.35 in a Category II. Category III huts are allowed to set their own prices but usually cost less than Category I huts.

A hut is Category I if it is at a height of over 1000m and is more than one hour from motorised transport. A Category II hut is within one hour's walking distance from motorised transport. A Category III hut can be reached by car or cable car directly.

Ten of the highest huts, including most of those around Triglav, are Category I huts. Members of the PZS, along with visitors holding a UIAA-affiliated club membership card, get a 50% discount.

Food prices at PZS huts are regulated as well. A simple meal should cost between €3 and €5 in a Category I hut and €2.50 and €3.75 in a Category II hut. Tea is €0.85 to €1.25 and 1.5L of mineral water are €1.25 and €2.50.

There are some 56 mountain huts (42 of them Category I huts) in the Julian Alps, most of them open at least between June and September; some huts at lower altitudes are open all year. Huts are never more than five hours' walk apart. You'll never be turned away if the weather looks bad, but some huts on Triglav can be unbearably crowded at weekends – especially in August and September. Try to plan your hikes for midweek if possible, and phone or even email ahead – most huts now take bookings.

Of the 167 mountain huts and other accommodation maintained by the Alpine Association of Slovenia across the country, some are very basic indeed whereas others come close to hotel-style accommodation (above).

The Slovenian Tourist Board publishes the excellent (and free) *Hiking in Slovenia* pamphlet with suggested itineraries. More comprehensive sourcebooks and guides include *Walking in the Julian Alps* (Cicerone) by Justi Carey and Roy Clark, with 50 walking routes and short treks, as well as *A Guide to Walks and Scrambles in the Julian Alps* (Zlatorog Publications) by Mike Newbury. Several shorter treks are outlined in the *Sunflower Guide Slovenia* (Sunflower Books).

SKIING

Skiing is by far the most popular recreational pursuit in Slovenia, and why not? On the basis of written references that go back to the 17th century, many people believe that skiing was born on the slopes of the Bloke Plateau in Notranjska. Today around 300,000 people – 15% of the population – ski regularly. Just about everyone takes to the slopes or trails in season (mainly December to March), and you can too on some 40 ski grounds and resorts of varying sizes across the country. They're most crowded over the Christmas holidays and in early February.

Most of Slovenia's ski areas are small and unchallenging compared to the Alpine resorts of France, Switzerland and Italy, but they do have the attraction of lower prices and the scenery is lovely. The latest weather and snow reports are available on the website www.smucisca.7-s.si, or you could call the **Snow Hotline** (Snežni Telefon; ☎ 041-182 500, 031-182 500). Both are in Slovene only, however.

The biggest downhill skiing area in Slovenia is Maribor Pohorje (p245) at altitudes of 336m to 1346m in the hills immediately south of Maribor in Štajerska, with 80km of linked pistes suitable for skiers of all levels. It offers a ski and snowboard school, equipment rental and floodlit night skiing, as well as being a good starting point for ski touring through the forested hills of the Pohorje.

Kranjska Gora (p124), at 810m to 1570m in Gorenjska, has 20km of pistes, but the skiing here is fairly dull and suited mostly for beginners and intermediates. Nevertheless, for foreign visitors, it is probably Slovenia's best-known and most popular ski resort, being easily accessible from Austria and Italy.

Krvavec (p105), at between 1450m and 1970m in the hills northeast of Kranj in Gorenjska, is one of the best-equipped ski areas in the country, with ski (alpine and telemark) and snowboard schools, equipment rental, a good variety of piste and off-piste skiing, a freestyle mogul course, a speed-skiing track, a half-pipe and snowboard cross trail, a ski shop and some good restaurants and bars. However, as it's only an hour's drive from Ljubljana, it's best avoided at the weekends unless you like long queues.

Many Slovenian skiers think that the Cerkno Ski Centre (p149), at between 900m and 1290m north of Idrija in Primorska, offers some of the country's best downhill skiing. There are only 18km of marked pistes and 5km of cross-country trails served by six modern (and covered) chairlifts and two tows, but all are covered by snow cannon, which guarantee adequate snow cover throughout the season.

For spectacular scenery, you can't beat Kanin (p136), which perches above Bovec in Primorska and at 1600m to 2300m is by far Slovenia's highest ski resort, and Vogel (p121), some 570m to 1800m above shimmering Lake Bohinj in Gorenjska. Both resorts enjoy stunning views north to Triglav and the Julian Alps, and from the top station at Kanin you can even see the Adriatic. Vogel is more suited to experienced skiers and has great opportunities for off-piste and ski-touring.

Snowboarders can find fun parks at Krvavec (p105) and Stari Vrh (p100), at 580m to 1210m near Škofja Loka in Gorenjska, and there are also half-pipes at Vogel and Rogla (p247), at 1517m near Zreče, north of Celje in Štajerska.

There are marked cross-country ski trails at most Slovenian resorts, but the major ones are at Kranjska Gora (40km), Maribor Pohorje (36km), Rogla (18km), and Logarska Dolina (15km).

Website www.slo-skiing .net is the best single source for information on Slovenian skiing grounds and centres.

SPAS & HEALTH RESORTS

Taking the waters is one of the most enjoyable ways to relax in Slovenia, especially after a day on the slopes or mountain trails. Slovenia has 15 thermal spa resorts – two on the coast at Portorož and Strunjan and the rest in the eastern half of the country in Štajerska, Dolenjska and Prekmurje. They are excellent places not only for 'taking the cure' but also for relaxing and meeting people. Many resorts use the Italian *terme* for 'spa' instead of the proper Slovene word *toplice* (thermal spring) or *zdravilišče* (health resort).

Only three towns – Dolenjske Toplice (p200) in Dolenjska, Rogaška Slatina in Štajerska (p224) and Radenci (p268) in Prekmurje – are really spa towns as such, with that distinctive *fin-de-siècle* feel about them. Others, such as Terme Olimia in Štajerska and Terme Čatež in Dolenjska, are loud, brash places dedicated to all the hedonistic pursuits you care to imagine, complete with swimming pools, waterslides, tennis courts, saunas, beauty parlours and massage services. The Banovci spa (p267) near Veržej, about 13km south of Murska Sobota in Prekmurje, is reserved for naturists.

The Slovenian Tourist Board publishes a useful brochure entitled *Wellness – Tailor-made for You,* which describes the spas as well as wellness centres throughout the country.

The hottest thermal water in Slovenia is at Moravske Toplice, with an egg-boiling temperature of 72°C at source.

MOUNTAINEERING & ROCK CLIMBING

The foothills of the Alps cover almost a third of Slovenia.

The principal rock- and ice-climbing areas include Triglav's magnificent north face – where routes range from the classic Slovene Route (Slovenski Pot; Grade II/III; 750m) to the modern Sphinx Face (Obraz Sfinge; Grade IX+/X-; 140m), with a crux 6m roof – as well as the impressive northern buttresses of Prisank overlooking the Vršič Pass. The best mountaineering guidebook readily available is Tine Mihelič's *Mountaineering in Slovenia* (published by Sidarta), which describes more than 80 tours in the Julian Alps as well as the Kamnik-Savinja Alps and the Karavanke.

Slovenia set up its first mountain association back in 1893, one of the first in the world.

Športno plezanje (sport climbing) is very popular here too. *Slovenija Športnoplezalni Vodnik* (Sport Climbing Guide of Slovenia; Sidarta) by climber Janez Skok covers 70 sport-climbing crags in the country, with good topos and descriptions in English, German and Italian as well as Slovene. The closest sport-climbing crags to Bled are only a few kilometres away at Bohinjska Bela and Bodešče.

CYCLING & MOUNTAIN BIKING

Slovenia is a wonderful country for cycling and mountain biking; the Slovenian Tourist Board publishes a cycling map-brochure called *Biking in Slovenia* that introduces dozens of road- and mountain-bike trails. Places where you can rent bicycles and/or mountains bikes are listed in the Activities or Getting Around sections of each town.

The uncrowded roads around Bled and Bohinj are a joy to cycle on. Other excellent areas for cycling are the Upper Savinja Valley in Štajerska, the Soča Valley in Primorska, the Drava Valley in Koroška and especially the Krka Valley in Dolenjska, which has become something of a cycling centre.

Mountain-bike enthusiasts should make tracks for Notranjska Regional Park (p186), southwest Koroška (p262), the Maribor Pohorje (p245) and/or the Central Pohorje Region (p246) in Štajerska. Please note that mountain bikes are banned from the trails in Triglav National Park.

KAYAKING, CANOEING & RAFTING

River sports are hugely popular and practised anywhere there's running water in Slovenia, particularly on the Krka River in Dolenjska (for example at Žužemberk and Krka, p199), the Kolpa in Bela Krajina, especially at Vinica (p221), the Sava River in Gorenjska (Bohinj, p121), the Savinja River at Logarska Dolina (p256) in Štajerska, the Drava River near Dravograd (p258) in Koroška but especially the Soča River at Bovec (p136) in Primorska.

The Soča is famed as one of the best white-water rafting and kayaking rivers in Europe, and it is one of only half-a-dozen rivers in the European Alps whose upper waters are still unspoiled. Agencies offering rafting and canoeing trips are detailed in the relevant regional chapters, especially under the Bovec section of the Primorska chapter.

CAVING

It is hardly surprising that the country that gave the world the word 'karst' is riddled with caves – around 8100 have been recorded and described. There are about 20 'show caves' open to visitors, most of which – Škocjan (p151), Postojna (p183), Križna (p189), Planina (p185), Pivka (p185), Predjama (p187) – are in the karst areas of Primorska and Notranjska.

The deepest cave in Slovenia – Čehi II on Jelenk peak northwest of Bovec – goes down 1380m.

The main potholing regions in Slovenia are the Notranjska karst, centred on Postojna, and the Julian Alps of Gorenjska and Primorska. For more information, club contacts and expeditions, contact the **Speleological Association of Slovenia** (Jamarska Zveza Slovenije; ☎ 01-429 34 44; www.jamarska-zveza.si; Lepi pot 6) in Ljubljana.

SAILING & WINDSURFING

Sailing is big on the Adriatic, but most yachties prefer the delights of Croatia's island-studded Dalmatian coast to the strictly limited attractions of Slovenia's 47km littoral. The country's main marinas are at Izola and Portorož (p177), where you can charter yachts and powerboats.

FISHING

Slovenia's mountain streams are teeming with brown and rainbow trout and grayling, and its lakes and more sluggish rivers are home to pike, perch, carp and other coarse fish. The best rivers for angling are the Soča, the Krka, the Kolpa, the Sava Bohinjka near Bohinj and the Unica in Notranjska. As elsewhere, angling is not a cheap sport in Slovenia – a permit at the more popular rivers will cost from €55 to €95 a day and €275 to €470 a week. Catch-and-release permits are cheaper.

For information on licences and seasons, contact the **Slovenian Fishing Institute** (Zavod za Ribištvo Slovenije; ☎ 01-244 34 00; www.zzrs.si; Župančičeva ulica 9) in Ljubljana.

The cobalt-blue Soča River in Primorska is recognised as offering some of the finest trout fishing in all of Europe.

HORSE RIDING

Slovenia is a nation of horse riders. The world's most famous horse – the Lipizzaner of the Spanish Riding School in Vienna – was first bred at Lipica in Primorska. About a dozen riding centres registered with the Ljubljana-based **Equestrian Association of Slovenia** (Konjeniška Zveza Slovenije; ☎ 01-434 72 65; www .konj-zveza.si in Slovene; Celovška cesta 25) rent horses and offer lessons. There are just as many smaller stables and ranches renting privately.

Among the best and most professional places to ride in Slovenia are, of course, the Lipica Stud Farm (p162) in Primorska and the Novo Mesto Sport Equestrian Centre (p204) in Dolenjska

If you'd like to see yourself mounted on a proud Lipizzaner, see www.lipica.org.

PARAGLIDING, BALLOONING & FLYING

Paragliding has really taken off in Slovenia, especially in Gorenjska around Bohinj (p121) and at Bovec (p136), where you can take a tandem flight from the upper cable-car station on Kanin peak and descend 2000m into the Bovec Valley.

The tourist information centre in Ljubljana organises hot-air balloon (p76) flights around the year.

Every self-respecting town in Slovenia seems to have an airstrip or aerodrome, complete with an *aeroklub* whose enthusiastic members will take you 'flight-seeing'. The Ljubljana-based **Aeronautical Association of Slovenia** (Letalska Zveza Slovenije; ☎ 01-422 33 33; www.lzs-zveza.si in Slovene; Tržaška cesta 2) has a complete list.

GOLF

There are 18-hole golf courses at Bled and Volčji Potok (both Gorenjska), Mokrice Castle (Dolenjska), Ptuj (Štajerska) and Moravske Toplice (Prekmurje). Nine-hole courses can be found at Bled and Brdo near Kranj (both Gorenjska), Lipica (Primorska) and Podčetrtek and Slovenske Konjice, southeast of Zreče (both Štajerska). The newest course in the country is the nine-hole one at Otočec in Dolenjska.

The best links in Slovenia are the par 73 King's Course in Bled at Bled Golf & Country Club (p114), which opened in 1937, and the par 71 Golf Course Ptuj (p235).

For information, contact the **Slovenian Golf Association** (Golf Zveza Slovenije; ☎ 01-585 17 53; www.golfportal.info in Slovene; Šmartinska cesta 152) in Ljubljana. The Slovenian Tourist Board publishes the useful *Golf Courses in Slovenia* brochure.

BIRD-WATCHING

Although many Slovenes don't realise it, Slovenia has some of the best bird-watching in Central Europe. At least 375 species have been sighted here, 220 of which are breeders and 11 of which are under threat. The Ljubljana Marsh (Ljubljansko Barje), south of the capital, Lake Cerknica (p188) in Notranjska and the Sečovlje saltpans (p180) in Primorska are especially good for sighting water birds and waders, as is the Drava River and its reservoirs in northeast Slovenia. An especially wonderful (though messy) sight is the arrival of the white storks in Prekmurje (p270) in April. Other important habitats are the Julian and Savinja Alps, the Karst area and the Krakovski forest north of Kostanjevica na Krki in Dolenjska.

For more information, contact the Ljubljana-based **Bird Watching & Study Association of Slovenia** (Društvo za Opazovanje in Proučevanje Ptic Slovenije; ☎ 01-426 58 75; www.ptice.org in Slovene; Tržaška cesta 2), a member of Bird Life International.

There's no guidebook devoted specifically to the birds of Slovenia but Gerard Gorman's **Birding in Eastern Europe** (www.probirder.com) published by **Wildsounds** (www.wildsounds.com) contains a section on the country.

See www.fatbirder.com /links_geo/europe/slovenia.html for more information on bird-watching in Slovenia.

DIVING

You can dive in all Slovenian rivers, lakes and of course the sea, with the exceptions of the fish hatchery in Lake Bohinj and the shipping lanes and harbour areas. The sport is popular in Lake Bled, in the Kolpa River in Bela Krajina and at Ankaran, Portorož and Piran (p174) on the coast, and you can even take lessons and qualify at the last. For more information, contact the **Slovenian Diving Federation** (Slovenska Potapljaška Zveza; ☎ 01-433 93 08; www.spz.si in Slovene; 25 Celovška cesta) in Ljubljana.

Cave diving is a popular sport in Slovenia but is permitted only under the supervision of a professional guide. Cave diving has been done at Postojna, Škocjan and in the tunnel at Wild Lake (Divje Jezero) near Idrija.

HUNTING

We don't like it either, but hunting is big business in Slovenia, and many Europeans (especially Italians) will pay big – um – bucks to bag a deer, a brace of grouse, a boar or even a bear, which now number up to 700 in Slovenia (p41) and need to be culled. The **Slovenian Hunting Association** (Lovska Zveza Slovenije; ☎ 01-241 09 10; www.lovska-zveza.si in Slovene; Župančičeva ulica 9) in Ljubljana can provide more information.

Food & Drink

Little Slovenia can boast an incredibly varied cuisine, with many different regional styles of cooking. Unfortunately, except for a few national favourites such as *žlikrofi* (stuffed pasta) from Idrija and *brodet* (fish soup) from the coast in Primorska, the distinctive *bučno olje* (pumpkinseed oil) from Štajerska and an incredibly rich dessert called *gibanica* from Prekmurje, you're not likely to encounter many of these regional specialities on restaurant menus. This is home-cooking at its finest, and you should do everything within your charm-the-socks-off-them power to wangle an invitation to a Slovenian home, where food is paramount.

There are several truisms concerning Slovenian cuisine. In general, it is plain and simple, pretty heavy and fairly meaty. The most important thing to remember about it, however, is that it is heavily influenced by its neighbours' cuisines. From Austria, there's *klobasa* (sausage), *zavitek* (strudel) filled with fruit, nuts and/or *skuta* (curd cheese), and *dunajski zrezek* (Wiener schnitzel). The ravioli-like *žlikrofi*, *njoki* (potato dumplings) and *rižota* (risotto) obviously have Italian origins, and Hungary has contributed *golaž* (goulash), *paprikaš* (piquant chicken or beef 'stew') and *palačinke* (thin pancakes filled with jam or nuts and topped with chocolate). From Croatia and the rest of the Balkans have come such popular grills as *čevapčiči* (spicy meatballs of beef or pork) and *pljeskavica* (meat patties)

STAPLES & SPECIALITIES
Bread

Nothing is more Slovenian than *kruh* (bread), and it is generally excellent, especially *(kmečki temni kruh)* (whole wheat bread). Real treats are the braided loaves made around Christmas not dissimilar to Jewish *challah* and *pisan kruh* ('mottled bread') in which three types of dough (usually buckwheat, wheat and corn) are rolled up and baked.

Soup

Most Slovenian meals start with *juha* (soup) – of which there are said to be a hundred different varieties – year-round but especially in winter. As a starter, this is usually chicken or beef broth with little *kokošja* or *goveja juha z rezanci* (egg noodles). More substantial varieties include *jesprenj* (barley soup); *jota*, a very thick potage of beans, potatoes, sauerkraut and smoked pork or sausage; and *obara*, a stew, often made with chicken or veal.

Meat & Fish

For most Slovenes, a meal is incomplete without a *meso* (meat) dish. The pig is king in Slovenia; in these parts the favourite flesh is *svinjina* (pork), although *teletina* (veal), *govedina* (beef) and, in season, *divjačina* (game), such as *srna* (deer) and *fazan* (pheasant), are also eaten. Indeed, even *konj* (horse) finds its way to the Slovenian table.

Some excellent prepared meats are *pršut,* air-dried, thinly sliced ham from the Karst region that is related to Italian *prosciutto,* and *divjačinska salama* (salami made from game). For some reason, *piščanec* (chicken) is not as common on a Slovenian menu as *puran* (turkey), while *gos* (goose), *jagnjetina* (lamb) and *koza* (goat) are seen but rarely.

Slovenes are big eaters of *riba* (fish) and *morski sadež* (shellfish) even far away from the coast. *Postrv* (trout), particularly the variety from the Soča River, is superb.

The Cuisine of Slovenia: Four Seasons of Culinary Masterpieces by Janez Bogataj et al is a richly photographed tome that follows Slovenian cuisine through the year, introducing both traditional and new dishes.

You'll find up to 274 recipes from around Slovenia at www.kulinarika .net/english/cook.asp.

It's the fiercely cold northeast wind in the Karst region called the *burja* that gives *pršut* its distinctive taste.

TRAVEL YOUR TASTEBUDS

Slovenes don't eat a lot of offal and won't tempt you with an eye of newt or even a frog's leg. But they do eat something nobody else does: dormouse or *polh* (loir), a tree-dwelling nocturnal rodent not unlike a squirrel that grows to about 30cm long and sleeps through several months of the year. But unless you are in Notranjska, where it was once a staple, during the loir-hunting season (late September) and have friends there, it's unlikely you'll get to try the incredible edible varmint.

Like the French, Slovenes have a taste for horseflesh – literally – and are especially fond of *žrebe* (colt). They like the taste (it's sweeter than beef or mutton), the low fat and the deep, almost ruby-red colour. You can try it at one of two fast-food outlets called Hot Horse (p84) in Ljubljana.

Groats

Distinctively Slovenian dishes are often served with *žganci,* groats made from barley or corn but usually *ajda* (buckwheat). A real rib-sticker is *ajdovi žganci z ocvirki,* a kind of dense buckwheat porridge with the savoury addition of pork crackling or *ocvirki* (scratchings).

Dessert

Slovenian cuisine boasts two unique and very different desserts. *Potica,* a national institution, is a kind of nut roll (although it's often made with savoury fillings too) eaten after a meal or with coffee or tea during the day. *Prekmurska gibanica,* from Slovenia's easternmost province, is a caloric concoction of pastry filled with poppy seeds, walnuts, apples and/or sultanas and cheese and topped with cream.

DRINKS
Nonalcoholic Drinks

Most international brands of soft drinks are available in Slovenia, but *mineralna voda* (mineral water) is the most popular libation for teetotallers in pubs and bars. *Sok* (juice) is more often than not boxed fruit drink with lots of sugar.

Italian espresso is the type of *kava* (coffee) most commonly served, but thick, sweet Turkish-style coffee is also popular, especially at home. If you don't want it too sweet, say: '*Ne sladko, prosim*'.

Local people drink lots of *čaj* (tea) made from herbs, berries, blossoms or leaves but seldom what they call 'Russian' (ie black) tea. It is still difficult to find black tea in the shops, so bring your own supply of tea bags if you need that morning cuppa.

Alcoholic Drinks
WINE

Wine *(vino)* has been made in what is now Slovenia since Roman times, and many of the country's wines are of a very high quality indeed. Unfortunately, most foreigners know Slovenian wine – if at all – from the el cheapo bottles of dull and unmemorable white Laški Rizling served at college parties; a trip to Slovenia will convince travellers that the best wines stay at home. Be warned, though, that cheaper 'open wine' (*odprto vino*) sold by the decilitre (0.1L) in bars and restaurants are usually pure rot-gut. For more detailed information, contact the **Commercial Union for Viticulture & Wine of Slovenia** (Poslovna Skupnost za Vinogradništvo in Vinarstvo Slovenije; ☎ 01-24 4 18 04, 244 18 00; www.slovino.com/psvvs; Kongresni trg 14; 1000 Ljubljana).

Slovenia counts around 10 distinct wine-growing districts, though there are really just three major regions you should be concerned about. Podravje (literally 'on the Drava') extends from northeast Štajerska into Prekmurje and produces whites almost exclusively, including Laški Rizling (Welschriesling) and Renski Rizling (a true German Riesling), Beli Pinot (Pinot Blanc), Traminec (Gewürtztraminer) and Šipon (Furmint).

Posavje is the region running from eastern Štajerska across the Sava River into Dolenjska and Bela Krajina. This region produces both whites and reds, but its most famous wine is Cviček, a distinctly Slovenian dry light red – almost rosé – wine with a low (8.5% to 10%) alcohol content.

The Primorska wine region excels at reds, the most famous being Teran, a ruby-red, peppery wine with high acidity made from Slovenian Refošk (Refosco) grapes in the Karst region. Other wines from this region are Malvazija (Malvasia), a yellowish white from the coast that is light and dry, and red Merlot, especially the ones from the Vipava Valley (Vipavska Dolina) and the Brda Hills (Goriška Brda).

On a Slovenian wine label, the first word usually identifies where the wine is from and the second the grape varietal: Vipavski Merlot, Mariborski Traminec etc. But this is not always the case, and some wines bear names according to their place of origin, such as Jeruzalemčan, Bizeljčan or Haložan.

There is no *appellation contrôlée* as such in Slovenia; *zaščiteno geografsko poreklo* is a trademark protection that usually – although not in every instance – suggests a certain standard and guarantees provenance. When choosing wine, look for the words *vrhunsko vino* (premium wine) and a gold label and *kakovostno vino* (quality wine) and a silver one. *Namizno vino* means ordinary 'table wine'. They can be red, white or rosé and dry, semidry, semisweet or sweet. Very roughly, anything costing more than €4.50 in the shops is a serious bottle of wine; pay more than €8.50 and you'll be getting something very fine indeed.

One excellent Slovenian sparkling wine that employs the demanding *méthode classique* is Zlata Radgonska Penina from Gornja Radgona, which is based on Chardonnay and Beli Pinot. The award-winning No 1 Cuvée 1 Spéciale from Janez Istenič's winery in Bizeljsko is another. Kraška Penina, a sparkling Teran, is unique. Late-harvest dessert wines include Rumeni Muškat, a 'Yellow Muscat' from Kamnica near Maribor and from Haloze southeast of Ptuj.

Slovenes usually drink wine with meals or socially at home; it's rare to see people sit down to a bottle at a café or pub. As elsewhere in Central Europe, a bottle or glass of mineral water is ordered along with the wine when eating. It's a different story in summer, when *brizganec* or *špricar* (spritzers or wine coolers) of red or white wine mixed with mineral water are consumed in vast quantities. Wine comes in 0.75L bottles or is ordered by the *deci* (decilitre, 0.1L). A normal glass of wine is about *dva deci* (0.2L), but no-one is going to blink an eye if you order three or more.

Of those polled, some 92.5% of Slovenes said that Slovenian wine is the best in the world (though the industry is braced to lose a 20% share of the market to cheap EU imports over the next five years).

A total of 24,500 hectares is under vine cultivation, producing an annual 100 million litres of wine (of which the average Slovene drinks 40).

The oldest vine in the world, planted more than four centuries ago and still producing grapes and wine, is in Maribor.

A MATCH MADE IN HEAVEN

The pairing of food with wine is as great an obsession in Slovenia as it is in other wine-producing countries. Most people assume *pršut* with black olives and a glass of ruby-red Teran is a match made in heaven, and it is. But what is less appreciated is the wonderful synergy other wines from the Karst – red Rebula, even white Malvazija – enjoy with these two foodstuffs. With heavier and/or spicier meat dishes such as goulash and salami, try Cviček. Malvazija, a yellowish white from the coast, is also good with fish, as is Cabernet Sauvignon and even Laški Rizling. And with sweet food such as strudel and *potica*, it's got to be a glass of late-harvest Rumeni Muškat.

Most of the wine-producing districts have a *vinska cesta* (wine route) or two that you can follow in a car or on a bicycle. Many are outlined in the free *Next Exit: Byways are More Attractive than Highways* by the **Slovenian Tourist Board** (Slovenska Turistična Organizacija, STO; www.slovenia.info). Along the way, you can stop at the occasional *klet* (cellar) that offers wine tastings or at a *vinoteka* in wine towns or in such cities as Maribor, Metlika, Ptuj, Črnomelj and Dobrovo near Nova Gorica.

The Wines of Slovenia by Julij Nemanič and Janez Bogataj is currently the best single source book on viticulture and wine in Slovenia.

BEER

Pivo beer is very popular in Slovenia, especially outside the home and among younger people. Štajerska *hmelj* (hops) grown in the Savinja Valley are used locally, and are also widely sought by brewers from around the world. They have been described as having the flavour of lemon grass.

Slovenia has two major breweries: Union in Ljubljana, and Laško in the town of that name south of Celje. Union is lighter-tasting and sweeter than Zlatorog, the excellent and ubiquitous beer brewed by Laško, which also makes Laško Club. Union produces an alcohol-free beer called Uni, a decent stout called Črni Baron (Black Baron) and a low-alcohol (2.5%) shandy called Radler. Smile, also produced by Union, is consumed with a slice of lemon like Corona.

Laško's alcohol-free brew is called Gren, and its shandy is called Roler (Bandidos throws in tequila and lemon). It also makes a light beer called Lahko Laško and a dark lager called Laško Temno.

In a *pivnica* (pub), *točeno pivo* (draught beer) is drunk in *veliko pivo* (0.5L mugs) or *malo pivo* (0.3L glasses). Both locally brewed and imported beers are also available at pubs, shops and supermarkets in 0.5L bottles or 0.3L cans.

SPIRITS

You'll learn lots more about Slovenian viticulture, regions and wine labelling by visiting www.matkurja.com/projects/wine.

An alcoholic drink as Slovenian as wine is *žganje,* a strong brandy or *eau de vie* distilled from a variety of fruits. Common types are *slivovka* (made with plums), *češnjevec* (with cherries), *sadjevec* (with mixed fruit) and *brinjevec* (with juniper). Another type is *medeno žganje* (or *medica*), which is flavoured with honey. One of the most unusual (if not the best) is Pleterska Hruška, a pear brandy (also called *viljamovka*) made by the Carthusian monks at the Pleterje monastery near Kostanjevica na Krki (p211) in Dolenjska.

Many Slovenes enjoy a *špička* – slang for a little glass of schnapps – during the day as a pick-me-up. You'll probably receive the invitation '*Pridite na kupico*' ('Come and have a drop') more than once.

CELEBRATIONS

Like most people in this increasingly globalised world, Slovenes mark things like birthdays in the indistinguishably developed-world Hallmark kind of way. But at Easter there's always a ham cooked with herbs and decorated Easter eggs. And a Slovenian Christmas wouldn't be Christmas without a *potica*.

Although it's not a public holiday, St Martin's Day (11 November) is important, as on this day, the winemakers' *mošt* (must), which is essentially fermenting grape juice, officially becomes wine and can be sold as such. In the evening families traditionally dine on goose and drink new wine, and some restaurants offer a special *Martinovanje* dinner accompanied by folk music. According to the legend, St Martin hid himself in a flock of geese when the faithful were looking for him to tell him he'd just been made a bishop.

SLOVENIA'S TOP FIVE

Aska in Volk (p82) In the capital, 'The Lamb and Wolf' is a very stylish place for Bosnian and other South Slav specialities, including roast lamb.

Lovenjak (p267) This *gostilna* northwest of Murska Sobota serves Prekmurje specialities in upmarket but comfortable surrounds.

Oštarija Peglez'n (p116) Bled's new 'Iron Inn' has interesting retro décor and serves some of the best fish dishes in town.

Ribič (p236) The 'Angler' faces the Drava River in Ptuj and the speciality here is – not surprisingly – fish, especially trout.

Topli Val (p140) One of Slovenia's finest restaurants, the 'Warm Wave' in Kobarid serves superb fish and seafood fishes and boasts an enviable wine card.

WHERE TO EAT & DRINK

Restaurants go by many names in Slovenia, but the distinctions are not very clear. At the top of the heap, a *restavracija* is a restaurant where you sit down and are served by a waiter. A *gostilna* or *gostišče* has waiters too, but it's more like an inn, with rustic decor and usually (but not always) traditional Slovenian dishes. A *samopostrežna restavracija* is a self-service establishment where you order from a counter and sometimes eat standing up. An *okrepčevalnica* and a *bife* serve simple, fast food such as grilled meats and sausages. A *krčma* may have snacks, but the emphasis here is on drinking (usually alcohol). A *slaščičarna* sells sweets and ice cream whereas a *kavarna* provides coffee and pastries. A *mlečna restavracija* (milk bar) sells yogurt and other dairy products as well as *krofi* – tasty, jam-filled doughnuts.

Almost every sit-down restaurant in Slovenia has a menu with dishes translated into English, Italian, German and sometimes French and Russian. It's important to note the difference between *pripravljene jedi* or *gotova jedilna* (ready-made dishes) such as goulash or stew that are just heated up and *jedi po naročilu* (dishes made to order). Lists of *danes priporočamo* or *nudimo* (daily recommendations or suggestions) are frequently in Slovene only.

Many restaurants and inns have an inexpensive *dnevno kosilo* (set lunch menu). Three courses can cost less than €6.

It's important to remember that not many Slovenes eat in city-centre restaurants, unless they have to because of work or because they happen to be entertaining after work. At the weekend, most will head 5km or 10km out of town to a *gostilna* or *gostišče* that they know will serve them good, home-cooked food and local wine at affordable prices. See the Directory (p274) for opening hours.

Slovenian Cookery: Over 100 Classic Dishes (Založba Mladinska Knjiga) by Slavko Adamlje is a practical illustrated guide to Slovenian cuisine.

Quick Eats

The most popular street food in Slovenia is a Balkan import called *burek* – flaky pastry sometimes stuffed with meat but more often cheese or even apple – that is not unlike Turkish *börek*. It's sold at outdoor stalls or kiosks and is very cheap and filling. Other cheap *malice* (snacks) available on the hoof are *čevapčiči*, *pljeskavica* (spicy meat patties), *ražnjiči* (shish kebab) and pizza (which sometimes appears spelled in Slovene as *pica*).

VEGETARIANS & VEGANS

Slovenia is hardly a paradise for vegetarians, but there are a couple of meat-free eateries in Ljubljana and you're sure to find a few meatless dishes on any menu. *Štruklji* (dumplings made with cheese) often flavoured with chives or tarragon are widely available, as are dishes like *gobova rižota* (mushroom risotto) and *ocvrti sir* (deep-fried cheese). Another boon for vegies is that

Mushroom-picking is almost a national pastime in the hills and forests of Slovenia in autumn.

> **ORGANIC GROWTH**
>
> The number of organic farms in Slovenia has mushroomed over the past decade – from a mere 41 in 1998 to 1400 by the time Slovenia joined the EU in 2004. The farms raise and process everything from cereals, dairy products and meat to fruits and vegetables, oils, nuts and wine. Only products inspected and certified by the Ministry of Agriculture, Forestry and Food may bear the government's *ekološki* label or the organic farmers' union logo 'Biodar'.

Slovenes love fresh *solata* (salad) – a most un-Slavic partiality – and you can get one anywhere, even in a countryside *gostilna*. In season (late summer and autumn) the whole country indulges in *jurčki* (wild cep mushrooms) – in soup, grilled or in salads.

EATING WITH KIDS

Although Slovenia has one of the lowest birth rates in the world and the average Slovenian family numbers just three – well, actually 2.8 – people, Slovenes love children, and it is a very child-friendly country. The family goes everywhere together, and you'll see youngsters dining with their parents in even the most sophisticated restaurants here.

HABITS & CUSTOMS

Diners at the same table wish one another 'Dober tek!' (Bon appetit!) before starting a meal.

On the whole, Slovenians are not big eaters of breakfast *(zajtrk)*, preferring a cup of coffee at home or on the way to work. Instead, many people eat a light meal *(malica)* at around 10.30am. Lunch *(kosilo)* is traditionally the main meal in the countryside, and it's eaten at noon if *malica* has been skipped. Dinner *(večerja)* – a supper, really – is less substantial when eaten at home, often just sliced meats, cheese and salad at 7pm or 8pm.

EAT YOUR WORDS

For pronunciation guidelines see p299.

Useful Phrases

Do you have a menu in English
Ali imate jedilni list v angleščini?   a·lee ee·*ma*·te ye·*deel*·nee list v an·*glesh*·chee·nee
Is service included in the bill
Ali je postrežba všteta v ceno?   a·lee ye pos·*trezh*·ba *vshte*·ta v *tse*·no
I'm a vegetarian.
Vegetarijanec sem.   ve·ge·ta·ree·*ya*·nets sem
I don't eat (meat/chicken/fish).
Ne jem (meso, piščanca, ribo).   ne yem (me·*so*, pish·*chan*·tza, *ree*·bo)
Do you have some typical Slovenian dishes?
Ali imate kakšne pristne slovenske jedi?   a·lee ee·*ma*·te *kak*·shne *preest*·ne slo·*ven*·ske ye·*dee*
What is the house speciality
Kaj je domača specialiteta?   kay ye do·*ma*·cha spe·tsee·a·lee·*te*·ta
I'm hungry/thirsty.
Lačen/žejen sem.   *la*·chen *zhe*·yen sem
I'd like the set lunch, please.
Rad bi menu, prosim.   rad bee me·*nee* pro·seem
I'd like some ...
Rad bi nekaj ...   rad bee *ne*·kay ...
Another, please.
Še enkrat, prosim.   she *en*·krat *pro*·seem
The bill, please.
Račun, prosim.   ra·*choon* pro·seem

Food Glossary

JUHE (SOUPS)

čista juha	*chis*·ta *yoo*·ha	clear soup, bouillon
dnevna juha	*dnev*·na *yoo*·ha	soup of the day
gobova kremna juha	*go*·bo·va *krem*·na *yoo*·ha	creamed mushroom soup
goveja juha z rezanci	*go*·*ve*·ya *yoo*·ha s *re*·zan·tsee	beef broth with little egg noodles
grahova juha	*gra*·ho·va *yoo*·ha	pea soup
paradižnikova juha	pa·ra·*deezh*·nee·ko·va *yoo*·ha	tomato soup
prežganka	pr·*zhgan*·ka	toasted rye-flour soup thickened with cream
zelenjavna juha	ze·len·*yav*·na *yoo*·ha	vegetable soup

HLADNE ZAČETNE JEDI/HLADNE PREDJEDE (COLD STARTERS)

domača salama	do·*ma*·cha sa·*la*·ma	home-style salami
francoska solata	fran·*tzos*·ka so·*la*·ta	diced potatoes and vegetables with mayonnaise
šunka z hrenom	*shoon*·ka s *hre*·nom	smoked/boiled ham with horseradish
kraški pršut z olivami	*krash*·kee pr·*shoot* s o·*lee*·va·mee	air-dried Karst ham (prosciutto) with salted black olives
narezek	na·*re*·zek	smoked cold meats
prekajena gnjat	pre·ka·*ye*·na gnyat	smoked ham
riba v marinadi	*ree*·ba v ma·ree·*na*·dee	marinated fish

TOPLE ZAČETNE JEDI/TOPLE PREDJEDI (WARM STARTERS)

drobnjakovi štruklji	drob·*nya*·ko·vee *shtrook*·lee	dumplings of cottage cheese and chives
omlet z sirom/šunko	om·*let* s *see*·rom/*shoon*·ko	omelette with cheese/ham
ocvrti sir s tartarsko omako	ots·*vr*·tee sir s tar·*tar*·sko o·*ma*·ko	deep-fried cheese with tartar sauce
rižoto z gobami	ree·*zho*·to s *go*·ba·mee	risotto with mushrooms
špageti po bolonjsko	shpa·*ge*·tee po bo·*lon*·sko	spaghetti Bolognese
žlikrofi	*zhlee*·kro·fee	'ravioli' of cheese, bacon and chives

PRIPRAVLJENE JEDI/GOTOVA JEDILNA (READY-MADE DISHES)

bograč golaž	*bog*·rach *go*·lash	beef goulash served in a pot
jota	*yo*·ta	beans, sauerkraut and potatoes or barley cooked with pork in a pot
kuhana govedina z hrenom	*koo*·ha·na go·*ve*·dee·na s *hre*·nom	boiled beef with horseradish
kurja obara z ajdovimi žganci	*koor*·ya o·*ba*·ra s *ay*·do·vee·mee *zhgan*·tsee	chicken stew or 'gumbo' with buckwheat groats
pečen piščanec	pe·*chen* peesh·*cha*·nets	roast chicken
prekajena svinjska rebrca z kislim zeljem	pre·ka·*ye*·na *sveen*·ska *rebr*·tza s *kees*·leem ze·lyem	smoked pork ribs with sauerkraut
ričet	*ree*·chat	barley stew with smoked pork ribs
svinjska pečenka	*sveen*·ska pe·*chen*·ka	roast pork

JEDI PO NAROČILU (DISHES MADE TO ORDER)

čebulna bržola	che·*bool*·na br·*zho*·la	braised beef with onions
ciganska jetra	tsee·*gan*·ska *yet*·ra	liver Gypsy-style
dunajski zrezek	*doo*·nay·skee *zre*·zek	Wiener schnitzel (breaded cutlet of veal or pork)
kmečka pojedina	*kmech*·ka po·*ye*·dee·na	'farmer's feast' of smoked meats and sauerkraut

kranjska klobasa z gorčico	*kran*·ska klo·*ba*·sa s gor·*chee*·tso	Carniolan sausage with mustard
ljubljanski zrezek	lioob·*lian*·skee *zre*·zek	breaded cutlet with cheese
mešano meso na žaru	*me*·sha·no me·*so* na *zha*·roo	mixed grill
ocvrti piščanec	ots·*vr*·tee peesh·*cha*·nets	fried chicken
pariški zrezek	pa·*reesh*·kee *zre*·zek	veal cutlet fried in egg batter
puranov zrezek z šampinjoni	poo·*ra*·naw *zre*·zek sham·pee·*nyo*·nee	turkey cutlet with white mushrooms

RIBE (FISH)

brancin z maslom	bran·*tseen* s *mas*·lom	sea bass in butter
kuhana/pečena postrv	*koo*·ha·na/pe·*che*·na pos·*trv*	boiled/grilled trout
lignji/kalamari na žaru	*leeg*·nyee/ka·la·*ma*·ree na·*zha*·roo	grilled squid
ocvrti oslič	ots·*vr*·tee *os*·lich	fried cod
orada na žaru	o·*ra*·da na *zha*·roo	grilled sea bream
morski sadež	*mor*·skee *sa*·dezh	shellfish
morski list v belem vinu	*mor*·skee list v *be*·lem *vee*·noo	sole in white wine
pečene sardele	pe·*che*·ne sar·*de*·le	grilled sardines
ribja plošča	*reeb*·ya *plosh*·cha	seafood plate
škampi na žaru	*shkam*·pee na *zha*·roo	grilled scampi (prawns)
školjke	*shkol*·ke	clams

SOLATE (SALADS)

fižolova solata	fee·*zho*·lo·va so·*la*·ta	bean salad
kisla rdeča pesa	*kees*·la *rde*·cha *pe*·sa	pickled beetroot (beets)
kisle kumarice	*kees*·le *koo*·mar·tse	pickled gherkins
kumarična solata	*koo*·mar·chna so·*la*·ta	cucumber salad
paradižnikova solata	pa·ra·*deezh*·nee·ko·va so·*la*·ta	tomato salad
sezonska/mešana solata	se·*zon*·ska/*me*·sha·na so·*la*·ta	seasonal/mixed salad
srbska solata	*srb*·ska so·*la*·ta	'Serbian salad' of tomatoes and green peppers
zelena solata	ze·*le*·na so·*la*·ta	lettuce salad
zeljnata solata	*zel*·na·ta so·*la*·ta	coleslaw

SLADICE/SIRI (DESSERTS/CHEESES)

jabolčni zavitek	*ya*·bol·chnee *zvee*·tek	apple strudel
krofi	*kro*·fee	jam-filled doughnuts
orehova potica	o·*re*·ho·va po·*tee*·tsa	Slovenian nut roll
palačinke z marmelado/ orehi/čokolado	pa·la·*cheen*·ke z mar·me·*la*·do/ o·*re*·hee/cho·ko·*la*·do	thin pancakes with marmalade/ nuts/chocolate
prekmurska gibanica	*prek*·moor·ska *gee*·ba·nee·tsa	layered pastry with fruit, nut, cheese and poppy-seed filling and cream
sadna kupa	*sad*·na *koo*·pa	fruit salad with whipped cream
sirova plošča	*see*·ro·va *plosh*·cha	cheese plate
sladoled	sla·do·*led*	ice cream
torta	*tor*·ta	cake

MALICE (SNACKS)

burek	*boo*·rek	pastry filled with meat, cheese or apple
čevapčiči	che·*vap*·chee·chee	spicy meatballs of beef or pork
pica	*pee*·tsa	pizza
pljeskavica	*plyes*·ka·vee·tsa	spicy meat patties
pomfrit	*pom*·freet	chips (French fries)

| ražnjiči | *razh*·nyee·chee | shish kebab |
| vroča hrenovka | *vro*·cha *hre*·nov·ka | hot dog |

BASICS

hrana	*hra*·na	food
delikatesa	de·lee·ka·*te*·sa	delicatessen
jajca	*yay*·tsa	eggs
jedilni list	ye·*deel*·nee list	menu
kosilo	ko·*see*·lo	lunch
kozarec	ko·*za*·rets	glass
krožnik	*krozh*·neek	plate
kruh	krooh	bread
maslo	*mas*·lo	butter
menu	me·*nee*	set menu
natakar/natakarica	na·*ta*·kar/na·*ta*·ka·ree·tsa	waiter/waitress
nož	nozh	knife
poper	*po*·per	pepper
restavracija	res·tav·*ra*·tsee·ya	restaurant
samopostrežna trgovina	sa·mo·pos·*trezh*·na tr·go·*vee*·na	grocery store
sir	seer	cheese
sladkor	*slad*·kor	sugar
sol	saw	salt
steklenica	stek·le·*nee*·tsa	bottle
topel/hladen	*to*·pel/*hla*·den	hot/cold
tržnica	*trzh*·nee·tsa	market
večerja	ve·*cher*·ya	dinner, supper
vilica	*vil*·tsa	fork
vinska karta	*veen*·ska kar·ta	wine list
z/brez	z/brez	with/without
zajtrk	*zay*·trk	breakfast
žlica	*zhlee*·tsa	spoon

MEAT & FISH

govedina	go·*ve*·dee·na	beef
meso	me·*so*	meat
piščanec	*peesh*·cha·nets	chicken
puran	poo·*ran*	turkey
riba	*ree*·ba	fish
svinjina	sveen·*yee*·na	pork
teletina	te·*le*·tee·na	veal

VEGETABLES & SIDE DISHES

ajdovi/koruzni žganci	*ay*·do·vee/ko·*rooz*·nee *zhgan*·tsee	buckwheat/corn groats
bučke	*booch*·ke	squash or pumpkin
cvetača/karfijola	tsve·*ta*·cha/kar·fee·*yo*·la	cauliflower
grah	grah	peas
korenje	ko·*ren*·ye	carrots
kruhovi cmoki	*kroo*·ho·vee *tsmo*·kee	bread dumplings
mlinci	*mleen*·tsee	pancakes
pire krompir	pee·*re* krom·*peer*	mashed potatoes
pražen krompir	*pra*·zhen krom·*peer*	fried potatoes
riž	rizh	rice
špinača	shpee·*na*·cha	spinach

stročji fižol	*stroch·*yee fee·*zhaw*	string beans
testenine	tes·te·*nee·*ne	pasta
zelenjava	ze·len·*ya·*va	vegetables

FRUIT

ananas	*a·*na·nas	pineapple
breskev	*bres·*kav	peach
češnje	*chesh·*nye	cherries
češplja	*chesh·*plya	plum
grozdje	*groz·*dye	grapes
hruška	*hroosh·*ka	pear
jabolko	*ya·*bol·ko	apple
jagode	*ya·*go·de	strawberries
kompot	kom·*pot*	stewed fruit (many types)
lešniki	*lesh·*nee·kee	hazelnuts
maline	ma·*lee·*ne	raspberries
marelica	ma·*re·*lee·tsa	apricot
orehi	o·*re·*hee	walnuts
pomaranča	po·ma·*run·*cha	orange
višnje	*veesh·*nye	sour cherries (morellos)

NONALCHOLIC DRINKS

brezalkoholne pijače	*brez·*al·ko·hol·ne pee·*ya·*che	soft drink
čaj	chai	tea
kapučino	ka·poo·*chee·*no	cappuccino
kava	*ka·*va	coffee
kava z smetano	*ka·*va z *sme·*ta·no	coffee with whipped cream
limonada	lee·mo·*na·*da	lemonade
pomaranчni sok	po·ma·*ranch·*nee sok	orange juice
sok	sok	juice
tonik z ledom	*to·*neek z *le·*dom	tonic water with ice
zeliščni čaj	ze·*leesh·*chnee chai	herbal tea

WINE

belo vino	*be·*lo *vee·*no	white wine
brizganec (špricar)	*breez·*ga·nets (*shpree·*tsar)	wine cooler (spritzer)
črno vino	*chr·*no *vee·*no	red (literally black) wine
peneče vino	pe·*ne·*che *vee·*no	sparkling wine
rose	*ro·*ze	rosé wine
sladko (desertno) vino	*slad·*ko (de·*zert·*no) *vee·*no	sweet (dessert) wine
vino	*vee·*no	wine

BEER & SPIRITS

brinjevec	*breen·*ye·vets	juniper-flavoured brandy
češnjevec	*chesh·*nye·vets	cherry brandy (kirsch)
hruškovec	*hroosh·*ko·vets	pear brandy
jabolčnik	ya·*bolch·*nik	apple cider
medica	me·*dee·*tsa	honey-flavoured brandy
pivo	*pee·*vo	beer
slivovka	*slee·*vov·ka	plum brandy
sadjevec	*sad·*ye·vets	fruit brandy
svetlo pivo	*svet·*lo pee·vo	lager
temno pivo	*tem·*no *pee·*vo	dark beer/stout
viljamovka	*vil·*ya·mov·ka	pear brandy
žganje	*zhgan·*ye	fruit brandy

Ljubljana

With a dazzling hilltop castle as her crown and the emerald-green Ljubljanica River at her feet, Ljubljana is a princess in size (petite). But her pint size conceals a wealth of culture, sights, activities and good old-fashioned fun that would be the envy of a city twice her extent. And best of all, everything is within such easy reach – a mere stroll or cycle away.

The princess, whose name *almost* means 'beloved' *(ljubljena)* in Slovene, is also a working girl. As the country's political, economic and cultural capital, this is where virtually everything of national importance begins, ends or is taking place. Of course that might not be immediately apparent in spring and summer, when café tables spill into the narrow streets of the Old Town and street musicians and actors entertain passers-by in Prešernov trg and on the little bridges spanning the Ljubljanica River.

Ljubljana's buzzing student community – there are some 56,650 students attending Ljubljana University's 20 faculties, three art academies and three university colleges – and alternative-lifestyle centre at Metelkova are added bonuses. Admittedly, the city may lack the grandeur or big-ticket attractions of, say, Prague or Budapest, but the great museums and galleries, atmospheric bars and varied, accessible nightlife make it a wonderful, relaxed place to visit and stay awhile – perhaps longer than you had planned.

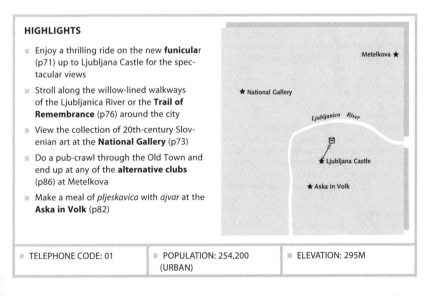

HIGHLIGHTS

- Enjoy a thrilling ride on the new **funicular** (p71) up to Ljubljana Castle for the spectacular views
- Stroll along the willow-lined walkways of the Ljubljanica River or the **Trail of Remembrance** (p76) around the city
- View the collection of 20th-century Slovenian art at the **National Gallery** (p73)
- Do a pub-crawl through the Old Town and end up at any of the **alternative clubs** (p86) at Metelkova
- Make a meal of *pljeskavica* with *ajvar* at the **Aska in Volk** (p82)

Metelkova ★

★ National Gallery

Ljubljanica River

★ Ljubljana Castle

★ Aska in Volk

| ▪ TELEPHONE CODE: 01 | ▪ POPULATION: 254,200 (URBAN) | ▪ ELEVATION: 295M |

HISTORY

The first written reference to Ljubljana as the town of Laibach appeared in 1144, but the area had been inhabited for at least three millennia before then. An infertile bog to the south of the present city was settled during the Bronze Age by marsh dwellers who lived in round huts built on stilts. These early people – mostly hunters and fisherfolk – were followed by the Illyrians and, sometime in the 4th century BC, by the Celts, who established themselves along the Ljubljanica River.

The first important settlement in the area, however, came with the arrival of the Romans who built a military camp here in around 50 BC. Within a hundred years, what had become known as Emona was a thriving town of 5000 inhabitants and a strategic crossroad on the routes linking Upper Pannonia in the south with the Roman colonies at Noricum and Aquileia to the north and east. Legacies of the Roman presence – remnants of walls, dwellings and early churches – can still be seen throughout Ljubljana.

Emona was sacked and destroyed by the Huns, Ostrogoths and Langobards (Lombards) from the mid-5th century, but the 'Ljubljana gate' remained an important crossing point between east and west. Tribes of early Slavs settled here at the end of the 6th century.

Ljubljana changed hands frequently in the Middle Ages. The last and most momentous change came in 1335, when the Habsburgs became the town's new rulers. Except for a brief interlude in the early 19th century, they would remain the city's (and the nation's) masters until the end of WWI in 1918.

The town and its hilltop castle were able to repel the Turks in the late 15th century, but a devastating earthquake in 1511 reduced much of the medieval Ljubljana to rubble. This led to a period of frantic construction in the 17th and 18th centuries that provided Ljubljana with many of its pale-coloured baroque churches and mansions – and the nickname 'Bela (White) Ljubljana'. The most important engineering feat was the building of a canal to the south and east of Castle Hill in the late 18th century that regulated the flow of the Ljubljanica and prevented flooding.

When Napoleon established his Illyrian Provinces in 1809 in a bid to cut Habsburg Austria's access to the Adriatic, he made Ljubljana the capital; Austrian rule was restored in 1813. In 1821 members of the Holy Alliance (Austria, Prussia, Russia and Naples) met at the Congress of Laibach to discuss measures to suppress the democratic revolutionary and national movements in Italy.

Railways linked Ljubljana with Vienna and Trieste in 1849 and 1857, stimulating economic development of the town. Not long after the Ljubljana Tobacco Factory was established in 1871 it was employing 2500 people. By then this city had become the centre of Slovenian nationalism under Austrian rule. But in 1895 another, more powerful earthquake struck, forcing the city to rebuild once again. To Ljubljana's great benefit, the Secessionist and Art Nouveau styles were all the rage in Central Europe at the time, and many of the wonderful buildings erected then still stand.

During WWII Ljubljana was occupied by the Italians and then the Germans, who en-

LJUBLJANA IN...

One Day

From Prešernov trg cross the Triple Bridge to Mestni trg in the Old Town. Ascend Ulica na Grad from Gornji trg to Ljubljana Castle (p70). Grajska Kavarna (p85) has outdoor seating and is a convenient spot for a snack or light lunch. In the afternoon visit the National Museum or the National Gallery (p73), then walk through Park Tivoli (p74) to cool off (or warm up – depending on the season) at the Ilirija swimming pool (p77) or Zlati Klub sauna (p77). End the day with a drink at Kavarna Pločnik (p85) and a meal at Taverna Tatjana (p83).

Two Days

The next day follow the walking tour on p77 for an introduction to what Ljubljana looks like off the beaten track. In the afternoon rent a bike from Ljubljana Bike (p91) and cycle through Park Tivoli (p74) to the Ljubljana Zoo (p74) or along the Ljubljanica River. In the evening take in a performance at the Križanke or Cankarjev Dom (p72) and then visit one of the clubs (p86.

circled the city with a barbed-wire fence creating, in effect, an urban concentration camp. Ljubljana became the capital of the Socialist Republic of Slovenia within Yugoslavia in 1945 and remained the capital after Slovenia's independence in 1991. Today, Ljubljana is the nation's largest and most vibrant city.

ORIENTATION

Ljubljana lies within the Ljubljana Basin (Ljubljanska Kotlina), which extends 25km to the north and northwest along the Sava River to Kranj. The basin has two distinct parts: the Ljubljana Marsh (Ljubljansko Barje) to the south and the fertile Ljubljana Plain (Ljubljansko Polje) to the north and east. The city is wedged between the Polhov Gradec hills to the west and Golovec hills (including Castle Hill) to the east and southeast.

Ljubljana is traditionally divided into two dozen districts, but only a handful are of any importance to travellers. Center is the commercial area on the left bank of the Ljubljanica River, to the west and north of Castle Hill and the Old Town. Tabor and Poljane are the easternmost parts of Center, and Bežigrad, where the bulk of the university buildings are, lies to the north of them. Krakovo and Trnovo, two old suburbs south of Center, retain a lot of traditional charm.

Certain streets and squares (eg Čopova ulica, Prešernov trg, most of Trubarjeva cesta) and much of the Old Town are pedestrianised. The Ljubljanica is crossed by more than a dozen vehicular bridges and footbridges, and three of them – Cobbler Bridge (Čevljarski Most), Triple Bridge (Tromostovje) and Dragon Bridge (Zmajski Most) – are most useful to travellers and historically important.

Brnik airport, 27km to the northwest, is easily accessible by bus and taxi (p91). The train and bus stations are opposite one another on Trg Osvobodilne Fronte (Trg OF) at the northern end of Center. You can reach the centre by walking south along Slovenska cesta, the capital's main thoroughfare some 300m to the west.

Maps

The tourist office hands out its own free 1:35,000-scale *Ljubljana City Map*; ask them for the more useful tear-out map of the central district with street index. For extended stays, you might want to pick up the 1:20,000-scale commercial *Mestni Načrt Ljubljana* (Ljubljana

City Map; €7) published by Kod & Kam (p61), which has an enlarged 1:7000 plan of the centre and a 1:75,000 map of the surrounding areas on the reverse. The 1:15,000 *Atlas Mesta Ljubljana in Okolica* (€13) is a street atlas of the capital and its suburbs. The town centre appears on a scale of 1: 6600.

INFORMATION
Bookshops

Geonavtik (Map pp66-7; ☎ 252 70 27; www.geo navtik.com, in Slovene; Kongresni trg 1; ⏰ 8.30am-8.30pm Mon-Fri, 8.30am-4pm Sat) Superb shop with travel and nautical guides, maps, books about Slovenia and a popular café/bar (p87).

Knjigarna Vale-Novak (Map pp66-7; ☎ 422 34 10; Wolfova ulica 8; ⏰ 10am-8pm Mon-Fri, 9am-2pm Sat, 10am-noon Sun) Inviting, well-run and very large, this bookshop is in the heart of town.

Kod & Kam (Map pp66-7; ☎ 200 27 32; www.kod -kam.si; Trg Francoske Revolucije 7; ⏰ 9am-8pm Mon-Fri, 8am-1pm Sat) 'Whence & Whither' stocks local city, regional and hiking maps as well as imported maps and guides (enter from Gosposka ulica).

Mladinska Knjiga (Map pp66-7 ☎ 241 06 51; 1st fl, Slovenska cesta 29; ⏰ 9am-7.30pm Mon-Fri, 9am-2pm Sat) Miklošičeva cesta (Map pp62-3; ☎ 234 27 81; Miklošičeva cesta 40; ⏰ 8.30am-7pm Mon-Fri, 9am-noon Sat) 'MK' is the biggest and best-stocked bookshop in Ljubljana, with lots of guidebooks, maps, pictorials, fiction and newspapers and periodicals in English.

Cultural Centres

British Council (Map pp62-3; ☎ 300 20 30; www .britishcouncil.si; Tivolska cesta 30; Center Tivoli; ⏰ 11am-8pm Mon-Fri)

SLOVENIAN HERITAGE

If you are searching for your Slovenian roots, check first with the *mestna občina* (municipal government) or *občina* (county office); they have birth and death certificates going back a century. Vital records beyond the 100-year limit are kept at the **Archives of the Republic of Slovenia** (Arhiv Republike Slovenije; Map p75; ☎ 241 42 00; www.arhiv.gov.si; Gruber Palace, Zvezdarska ulica 1; ⏰ 8am-3pm Mon, Tue & Thu, 8am-4.30pm Wed, 8am-2pm Fri). Ethnic Slovenes living abroad should contact the **Slovenian Emigrants Centre** (Slovenska Izseljenska Matica, SIM; Map pp66-7; ☎ 241 02 80; www .zdruzenje-sim.si; 2nd fl, Cankarjeva cesta 1; ⏰ by appointment).

LJUBLJANA

LJUBLJANA

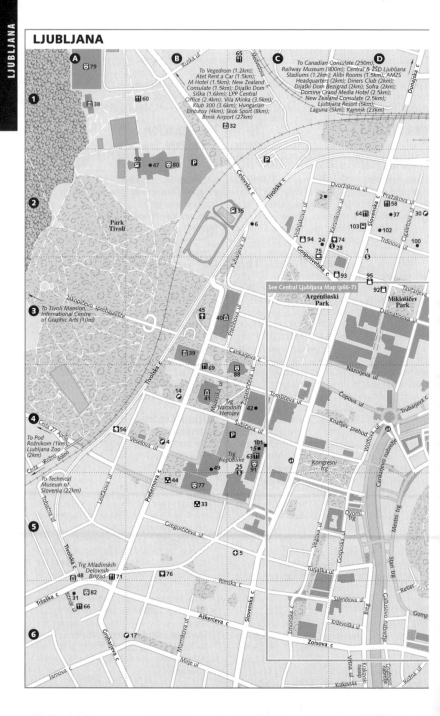

To Vegedrom (1.2km);
Atet Rent a Car (1.5km);
M Hotel (1.5km); New Zealand
Consulate (1.5km); Dijaški Dom
Šiška (1.6km); LPP Central
Office (2.4km); Vila Minka (3.5km);
Klub 300 (3.6km); Hungarian
Embassy (4km); Skok Sport (8km);
Brnik Airport (27km)

To Canadian Consulate (250m);
Railway Museum (800m); Central & ŽSD Ljubljana
Stadiums (1.2km); Alibi Rooms (1.5km); AMZS
Headquarters (2km); Diners Club (2km);
Dijaški Dom Bezigrad (2km); Sofra (2km);
Domina Grand Media Hotel (2.5km);
New Zealand Consulate (2.5km);
Ljubljana Resort (5km);
Laguna (5km); Kamnik (23km)

Park
Tivoli

To Tivoli Mansion,
International Centre
of Graphic Arts (10m)

See Central Ljubljana Map (p66-7)

Argentinski
Park

Miklošičev
Park

To Pod
Rožnikom (1km);
Ljubljana Zoo
(2km)

To Technical
Museum of
Slovenia (22km)

Trg
Narodnih
Herojev

Trg
Republike

Trg Mladinskih
Delovnih
Brigad

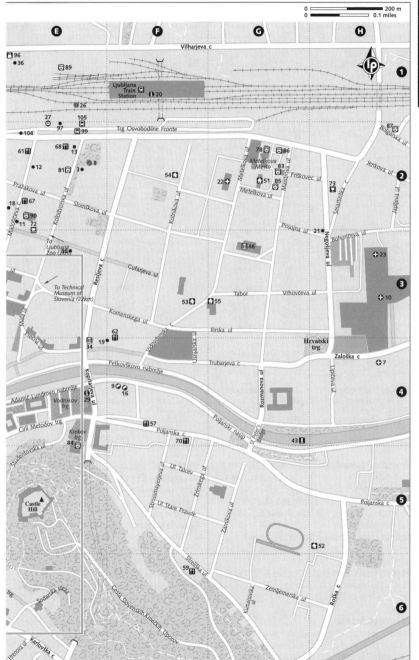

INFORMATION
Abanka 1 D2
Alpine Association of Slovenia 2 C2
Atlas Express 3 E2
Australian Consulate (see 49)
Austrian Embassy 4 B4
Barsos-MC 5 C5
British Council 6 C2
Dental Clinic 7 H4
Deutscher Lesesaal (see 49)
DrogArt 8 E2
Dutch Embassy 9 F4
Emergency Medical Assistance Clinic 10 H3
Erazem 11 E2
Foto Grad 12 E2
Foto Grad Branch 13 E2
German Embassy 14 B4
Globtour 15 C4
Irish Embassy 16 F4
Italian Embassy 17 B6
Kiber Pipa (see 74)
Kompas 18 E2
Label 19 F4
Ljibljana Tourist Information Centre Branch 20 F1
Ljubljana Pharmacy 21 H3
Medical Centre 22 G2
Medical Emergency Unit 23 H3
Miklošič Educational Centre (see 11)
Mint International House Ljubljana 24 C2
Nova Ljubljanska Banka 25 C4
Portal.si Internet Kotiček 26 E1
Post Office Branch 27 E2
ŠOU Information Centre 28 D2
Slovenian Tourist Information Centre 29 E4
South African Consulate 30 D2
Trek Trek 31 A6

SIGHTS & ACTIVITIES
Brewery Museum 32 B1
Ferant Garden (Roman Ruins) 33 B5
House of Experiments 34 E4
Ilirija Outdoor Swimming Pool 35 C2
Ljubljana Fairgrounds 36 E1
Ljubljana Stock Exchange 37 D2
Museum of Contemporary History of Slovenia 38 A1
Museum of Modern Art 39 B3
National Gallery 40 B3
National Museum of Slovenia 41 B4
Parliament Building 42 C4
Plečnik Monumental Lock 43 G4
Roman Wall Remains 44 B5
Serbian Orthodox Church 45 B3
Slovenian Ethnographic Museum 46 G3
Slovenian Museum of Natural History (see 41)
Tivoli Recreation Centre 47 B2
Tobacco Museum 48 A5
TR3 49 B4
Union Brewery (see 32)
Zlati Klub 50 B2

SLEEPING
Celica Hostel 51 G2
Dijaški Dom Ivana Cankarja 52 H5
Dijaški Dom Tabor 53 F3
Orka 54 F2
Park Hotel 55 G3
Vila Veselova 56 A4

EATING
Ali Baba 57 F4
Burek Stand 58 D2
Don Felipe 59 F6
Hot Horse 60 B1
JB 61 E2
Kebapči 62 F3
Maximarket 63 C4
Mercator 64 D2
Mexico 1867 65 C1
Mirje 66 A6
Nobel Burek 67 E2
Noč in Dan 68 E2
Pen Club 69 B4
Restavracija 2000 (see 63)
Shanghai 70 F4
Tramvaj Ekspress 71 A5

DRINKING
Ambiente 72 E3
Druga Pomoč 73 H2
Klub Metropol 74 D2
Slamič KavaČaj 75 C2
Žmavc 76 B5

ENTERTAINMENT
100% Mizart (see 78)
Čajnica pri Mariči (see 85)
Cankarjev Dom 77 B5
Channel Zero (see 78)
Gala Hala 78 G2
Hala Tivoli 79 A1
Katastrofa 80 D3
Kino Dvor 81 E2
Kinoklub Vič 82 A6
Klub Gromka 83 G2
Klub K4 (see 28)
Ljubljana Puppet Theatre 84 E4
Menza pri Koritu 85 G2
Monokel 86 G2
Orto Bar 87 H2
Slovenian National Opera and Ballet Theatre 88 C4
Slovenian Youth Theatre 89 E1
Slovenska Kinoteka 90 E2
Ticket Office (Cancarjev Dom) 91 C4
Tiffany (see 86)

SHOPPING
Almira Sadar 92 D3
Darila Rokus 93 D3
Lovec 94 C2
Torbice Grošelj 95 D3
Wine Cellars of Slovenia 96 E1

TRANSPORT
AutoRent 97 E2
Avis 98 E3
Bus Station 99 E2
Hertz 100 D2
Ljubljana Bike 101 C4
LPP Information Centre 102 D2
LPP Kiosk 103 D2
Private Airport Van Stop 104 E2
Public Airport Bus Stop 105 E2

Deutscher Lesesaal (Map pp62-3; ☎ 476 37 24; 1st fl, Trg Republike 3, TR3 Tower; 10am-3pm Mon, Wed & Thu, 1am-6pm Tue, 10am-1pm Fri)

European Union House (Map pp66-7 ☎ 252 88 00; http://europa.eu.int/slovenia in Slovene; Breg 14; 9am-5pm Mon-Fri)

Institut Français Charles Nodier (Map pp66-7 ☎ 200 05 00; 2nd fl, Breg 12; 10am-6pm Mon-Thu, 10am-2pm Fri)

Škuc Cultural Centre (ŠKUC; Map pp66-7; ☎ 432 73 68, 421 31 42; www.skuc.org; Stari trg 21; 4-8pm Sep-Jun, 5-9pm Jul & Aug)

Internet Access

Web connection is available at virtually all hostels and hotels. The Slovenian Tourist Information Centre (p68) offers access for €1 per 30 minutes, and the STA Ljubljana café (p68) has a rate of €1 per 20 minutes. It is open from 8am till late Monday to Friday, but closes at 3pm on Saturday.

Other options:

Cyber Café Xplorer (Map pp66-7; ☎ 430 19 91; Petkovškovo nabrežje 23; per half/1/5hr €2.45/4/11; 10am-10pm Mon-Fri, 2-10pm Sat & Sun) Ljubljana's best internet café, with 10 super-fast computers and wireless connection (per hr €3.25).

DrogArt (Map pp62-3; ☎ 438 72 70; Kolodvorska ulica 20; 15 min free, per hr €1.70; 10am-6pm Mon-Fri) Across from the train station.

Kiber Pipa (Cyber Tap; Map pp62-3; ☎ 438 03 05; www.kiberpipa.org; basement, Kersnikova ulica 6; free with drink; during the university term 10am-10pm Mon-Fri)

Portal.si Internet Kotiček (Map pp62-3; ☎ 090-42 30; Trg OF 4; per hr €3.75, then every 10 min €0.65; 7am-8.30pm) In the bus station.

Internet Resources

In addition to the websites of the Slovenian Tourist Information Centre and Ljubljana Tourist Information Centre (p67), the following sites might be useful:

City of Ljubljana (www.ljubljana.si) Informative official site direct from city hall.

Ljubljana Digital Media Lab (www.ljudmila.org) Excellent site with links to all forms of alternative culture, music, venues and publications.

Ljubljana Information (www.ljubljana.info)

Ljubljana Life (www.ljubljanalife.com) Website of the quarterly freebie (p86), with listings and articles.

University of Ljubljana (www.uni-lj.si) Useful info for students.

Laundry

A couple of the *dijaški dom* (student dormitories) have washing machines and dryers, but they may be closed outside the academic year. Washing machines are available, even to nonguests, at the Celica Hostel (p80) for €5 per load, including washing powder. Commercial laundries, including **Chemo Express** Center (Map pp66-7; ☎ 251 44 04; Wolfova ulica 12; 7am-6pm Mon-Fri); Tabor (Map pp62-3; ☎ 231 07 82; Vidovdanska cesta 2; 7am-7pm Mon-Fri), charge from €3.75 a kilo.

Left Luggage

Bus station (Map pp62-3; per day €1.80; 5am-9.30pm)

Train station (Map pp62-3; per day €2.10; 24hr) Coin lockers on platform 1.

Discount Cards

The excellent-value Ljubljana Card (€12), valid for three days and available from the tourist offices, offers free and discounted admission to many museums, unlimited city-bus travel and discounts on organised tours, accommodation, rental cars etc.

Medical Services

Barsos-MC (Map pp62-3; ☎ 242 07 00; info@barsos .net; Gregorčičeva ulica 11; 8am-3pm Mon, Wed & Fri; 8am-2pm Tue & Thu) Recommended (and tested!) private clinic charging €20 to €30 per consultation.

Dental Clinic (Stomotološka Klinika; Map pp62-3; ☎ 431 31 13; Zaloška cesta 2; 8am-noon Mon-Sat)

Central Pharmacy (Centralna Lekarna; Map pp66-7; ☎ 244 23 60; Prešernov trg 5; 7.30am-8pm Mon-Fri, 8am-1pm Sat)

Emergency Medical Assistance Clinic (Klinični Center Urgenca; Map pp62-3; ☎ 232 30 60; Bohoričeva ulica 4; 24hr) East of the Hotel Park in Tabor.

Ljubljana Pharmacy (Lekarna Ljubljana; Map pp62-3; ☎ 230 62 30; Prisojna ulica 7; 24hr) All-night pharmacy near the Klinični Center.

Medical Centre (Zdravstveni Dom Center; Map pp62-3; ☎ 472 37 00; Metelkova ulica 9; 7.30am-7pm) For nonemergencies.

Money

There are ATMs at every turn, including in the train and bus stations (Map pp62-3), where you'll also find a bureaux de change, open 6am to 10pm. They charge no commission but change cash only.

Some of the best exchange rates in Ljubljana are available at **Nova Ljubljanska Banka** (Map pp62-3; Trg Republike 2; 8am-6pm Mon-Fri), **Ljubljana City Savings Bank Building** Center (Mestna Hranilnica Ljubljanska; Map pp66-7; Čopova ulica 3; 9am-1pm & 3-5pm Mon-Fri) and the Old Town (Map pp66-7; Mestni trg 16; 8am-noon & 2.30-4.30pm Mon-Fri).

Ljubljana still has a few *menjalnice* (private exchange bureaus) taking no commission and offering good rates, including one in the Central Market called **Hida** (Map pp66-7; Pogačarjev trg 1; 7am-7pm Mon-Fri, 7am-2pm Sat).

CREDIT CARDS

Atlas Express (Map pp62-3; ☎ 430 77 20; Kolodvorska ulica 16; 8am-5pm Mon-Fri) This is the Slovenian representative for foreign American Express card-holders. It can make advances partly in cash and partly in travellers cheques; limits depend on the card you are carrying.

Abanka (Map pp62-3; ☎ 471 81 00; Slovenska cesta 50; 9am-5pm Mon-Fri, 9am-noon Sat) A local rep for Visa, Abanka can issue a euro cash advance on your card. If you have problems with your Visa card when Abanka is closed, call the **Visa Centre** (☎ 471 81 00; 24hr)

Diners Club (Map pp62-3; ☎ 589 61 11; Dunajska cesta 129) Headquarters is in Bežigrad.

Nova Ljubljanska Banka (☎ 477 20 00; 24hr) For Eurocard and MasterCard holders.

Post

Main post office (Map pp66-7; Slovenska cesta 32) *Poštno ležeče* (poste restante) is held here for 30 days.

Post office branch (Map pp62-3; Trg OF 5; 7am-9pm Mon-Fri, 7am-6pm Sat) West of the train station.

Toilets

Convenient public toilets (€0.20) are in the Plečnikov podhod (Map pp66-7), the underpass/subway below Slovenska cesta linking

LJUBLJANA

CENTRAL LJUBLJANA

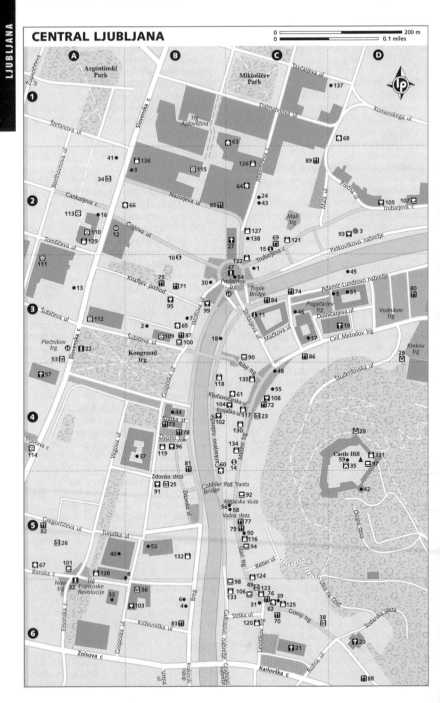

Kongresni trg with Plečnikov trg, and on Hribarjevo nabrežje (Map pp66-7) below Kavarna Pločnik (p85) on Prešernov trg.

Tourist Information

Alpine Association of Slovenia (Planinska Zveza Slovenije; Map pp62-3; general info ☎ 434 56 80, accommodation info ☎ 434 56 90; www.pzs.si; Dvoržakova ulica 9; ☺ 8am-5pm Mon, 8am-3pm Tue-Fri) Information about hiking and mountain huts throughout the country, with maps and guides for sale.

Ljubljana Tourist Information Centre Kresija Bldg (TIC; Map pp66-7; ☎ 306 12 15; www.ljubljana-tourism. si; Kresija Bldg, Stritarjeva ulica; ☺ 8am-9pm Jun-Sep,

INFORMATION
Central Pharmacy..................... **1** C3
Chemo Express........................... **2** B3
Cyber Café Xplorer **3** D2
European Union House.............. **4** B6
Geonavtik.............................(see 112)
Hida Exchange Bureau............... **5** D3
Institut Franřais Charles Nodier... **6** B6
Knjigarna Vale-Novak................ **7** B3
Kod & Kam................................ **8** B5
Kompas....................................**9** B2
Ljubljana City Savings Bank
  Building..............................**10** B3
Ljubljana Tourist Information
  Centre (TIC)........................**11** C3
Main Post Office.......................**12** A2
Mladinska Knjiga......................**13** A3
Nova Ljubljanska Banka............**14** C4
Škuc Cultural Centre..............(see 49)
ŠOU Information Centre...........**15** C2
Slovenian Emigrants Centre......**16** A2

SIGHTS & ACTIVITIES
Bishop's Palace........................**17** C3
Cankarjevo Nabrežje Pier
  (Boat Tours).......................**18** B3
Cathedral of St Nicholas..........**19** D3
Chapel of St George.............(see 59)
Church of St Florian..................**20** D6
Church of St James..................**21** C6
Citizen of Emona......................**22** A3
City Gallery...............................**23** C4
Cooperative Bank......................**24** C2
DESSA Architectural Gallery..... **25** B3
Equrna Gallery..........................**26** A5
Franciscan Church of the
  Annunciation.......................**27** C2
Funicular Lower Station............**28** D3
Funicular Upper Station...........**29** D4
Grand Hotel Union................(see 64)
Grand Hotel Union................(see 63)
Hauptman House (Ura
  Building)..............................**30** B3
Hercules Fountain.....................**31** C6
Ilirija Column............................**32** A6
Križanke.................................. **33** A6
Little Gallery.............................**34** A2
Ljubljana Castle........................**35** D4
Ljubljana City Museum.............**36** B6
Ljubljana University..................**37** B4
Luwigiana Gallery.....................**38** C6
Medieval Houses...................... **39** C6
National and University
  Library................................**40** A5
Nebotičnik..............................**41** A2
Pentagonal Tower....................**42** D5
People's Loan Bank...................**43** C2
Philharmonic Hall.....................**44** B4
Plecčvnik Colonnade................**45** D3
Plečnik Cone............................**46** C3

Prešeren Monument.................**47** C3
Robba Fountain........................**48** C4
Škuc Gallery.............................**49** C6
Schweiger House......................**50** C5
Seminary..................................**51** D3
Slovenian Academy of Arts and
  Sciences..............................**52** B5
Slovenian School Museum........**53** A3
Tourist Train.............................**54** C3
Town Hall..................................**55** C4
Tranča.....................................**56** C5
Urbanc...............................(see 122)
Ursuline Church of the Holy
  Trinity.................................**57** A4
Valvasor's Birthplace................**58** C5
Viewing Tower..........................**59** D4
Virtual Museum..................(see 59)

SLEEPING 🏠
Alibi Hostel...............................**60** B4
Alibi K5....................................**61** C4
Antiq Hotel..............................**62** C6
Grand Hotel Union Business......**63** C1
Grand Hotel Union
  Executive............................**64** C2
Hotel Emonec..........................**65** B3
Hotel Slon Best Western............**66** B2
Pri Mraku................................**67** A5
Tour As....................................**68** D1

EATING 🍴
Ajdovo Zrno.............................**69** C2
Aska in Volk.............................**70** C6
Cantina Mexicana....................**71** B3
Chez Eric..................................**72** C4
Covered Market..................(see 51)
Delikatesa Ljubljanski Dvor......**73** B4
Fish Market...............................**74** C3
Gostilna As...............................**75** B3
Gostilna Pri Pavli.....................**76** C6
Julija..**77** C5
Ljubljanski Dvor.......................**78** B4
Lunch Café...............................**79** C5
Open-air Markets.....................**80** D3
Paninoteka...............................**81** B4
Pizzerija Foculus......................**82** A5
Pri Vitezu.................................**83** B6
Ribka.......................................**84** C3
Smrekarjev Hram.....................**85** B2
Sokol.......................................**86** C3
Sushimama..............................**87** B3
Taverna Tatjana........................**88** D6
Triglav......................................**89** C2

DRINKING 🍷🍸
Abecedarium Cafe....................**90** C3
As Pub.................................(see 75)
BiKoFe.....................................**91** B5
Čajna Hiša...............................**92** C5
Čarli..**93** D2

Cafe Antico..............................**94** C5
Café Galerija........................(see 23)
Cutty Sark................................**95** B3
Dvorni Bar................................**96** B4
Grajska Kavarna.......................**97** D4
Kafeterija Lan..........................**98** C6
Kavarna Pločnik........................**99** B3
Kavarna Zvezda......................**100** B3
Le Petit Café...........................**101** A5
Maček....................................**102** B4
Pod Skalco..............................**103** B6
Pr'Skelet.................................**104** C4
Salon......................................**105** D2
Slaščičarna Pri Vodnjaku.........**106** C6
Trubadur.................................**107** D2
Vinoteka Movia.......................**108** C4

ENTERTAINMENT 📺
As Pub.................................(see 75)
Bacchus Centre Club...............**109** B3
Glej Theatre........................(see 26)
Global....................................**110** A2
Jazz Club Gajo.........................**111** A3
Kavarna Geonavtik..................**112** A3
Kino Komuna..........................**113** A2
Križanke..............................(see 33)
Philharmonic Hall................(see 44)
Slovenian National Drama
  Theatre..............................**114** A4
Tramontana............................**115** B2

SHOPPING 🛍
Akultura.................................**116** C5
Antika Ferjan.........................**117** C4
Antiques Flea Market..............**118** B4
ArtGlass Atelje.......................**119** B4
Butanoga................................**120** C6
Carniola Antiqua....................**121** C2
Centromerkur Department
  Store..................................**122** C3
Devetka..................................**123** C6
Galerija Fortuna.....................**124** C5
Katarina Silk...........................**125** C6
Ljubljanček............................**126** C2
MCD Shop..............................**127** C2
Musikalije...............................**128** A5
Nama Department Store..........**129** A2
Piranske Soline.......................**130** C4
Rustika....................................**131** D4
Skrina.....................................**132** B5
Spin Vinyl...............................**133** C6
Studio Irma Vončina...............**134** C4
Trubarjev Antikvariat..............**135** C4
Vino Boutique........................**136** B2

TRANSPORT
ABC Rent a Car.......................**137** D1
Budget.................................(see 63)
Europcar.............................(see 137)
Ljubljana Bike Stand..............**138** C2

8am-7pm Oct-May); Train station (Map pp62-3; ☎ 433 94 75; central hall, Ljubljana train station, Trg OF; ☺ 8am-10pm Jun-Sep, 10am-7pm Oct-May) Run by the innovative Ljubljana Tourist Board (Zavod za Turizem Ljubljana), these outlets are excellent sources of information on Ljubljana and the rest of Slovenia. Knowledgeable, enthusiastic staff dispense information and useful literature (*Ljubljana City Map*, *Where to?* in *Ljubljana tourist guide*, *Ljubljana from A to Z* booklet etc) and can check accommodation availability.

Slovenian Tourist Information Centre (STIC; Map pp62-3; ☎ 306 45 75; www.slovenia.info; Krekov trg 10; ☺ 8am-9pm Jun-Sep, 8am-7pm Oct-May) Good source of information for the rest of Slovenia. Internet and bicycle rental also available.

Student Organisation of the University of Ljubljana (Študentska Organizacija Univerze Ljubljani; ŠOU; Map pp66-7; ☎ 433 01 76, 438 02 00; www.sou-lj .si/english; Trubarjeva cesta 7; ☺ 10am-6pm Mon-Thu, 10am-3pm Fri) Information and student cards.

Travel Agencies

Erazem (Map pp62-3; ☎ 430 55 37; www.erazem.net; basement, Miklošičeva cesta 26; ☺ 10am-5pm Mon-Fri, 10am-1pm Sat Jun-Sep; noon-5pm Mon-Fri Oct-May) Popular with backpackers and students; staff make plane, train and ferry bookings and sell ISIC, ITIC and IYTC cards.

Globtour (Map pp62-3; ☎ 244 13 20; www.globtour .si; Maximarket passageway, Trg Republike 1; ☺ 9am-7pm Mon-Fri, 9am-noon Sat)

Kompas Slovenska cesta (Map pp66-7; ☎ 200 62 22; www .kompas.net; Slovenska cesta 36; ☺ 9am-7pm Mon-Fri, 9am-12.30pm Sat); Miklošičeva cesta (Map pp62-3; ☎ 200 63 40; Miklošičeva cesta 11; ☺ 9am-5pm Mon-Fri)

Label (Map pp62-3; ☎ 051-200 743; www.label.si; Trubarjeva cesta 47; ☺ 9.30am-7.30pm Mon-Fri, 9am-1pm Sat) Subtitled 'Board Culture Shop', this agency organises adventure-sport excursions around Slovenia.

STA Ljubljana (Map pp66-7; ☎ 439 16 90, 041-612 711; www.staljubljana.com, in Slovene; 1st fl, Trg Ajdovščina 1; ☺ 10am-1pm & 2-5pm Mon-Fri) Offers discount airfares for students and its café has internet access. Located in the Mobitel Centre.

Trek Trek (Map pp62-3; ☎ 425 13 92, 041-521 655; www.trektrek.si; Bičevje ulica 5; ☺ 10am-5pm Mon-Fri) Specialising in adventure travel, with emphasis on trekking and cycling holidays in southeast Slovenia.

SIGHTS

The easiest way to see the best that Ljubljana has to offer is on foot. The oldest part of town, with the most important historical buildings and sights (including Ljubljana Castle) lies on the right (east) bank of the Ljubljanica; on the left (west) side is Center and the lion's share of the city's museums.

Prešernov Trg

This central and very beautiful square (Map pp66-7) forms the link between Center and the Old Town. Taking pride of place is the **Prešeren monument** (1905) designed by Maks Fabiani and Ivan Zajc, and erected in honour of Slovenia's greatest poet, France Prešeren (1800–49). On the plinth are motifs from his poems. Just south of the monument is the **Triple Bridge** (Tromostovje), once called Špital Bridge (1842), which leads to the Old Town. The prolific architect Jože Plečnik added the two sides in 1931.

To the east of the monument at No 5 is the Italianate **Central Pharmacy** (Centralna Lekarna), an erstwhile café frequented by intellectuals in the 19th century. To the north, on the corner of Trubarjeva cesta and Miklošičeva cesta, is the delightful Secessionist **Urbanc** building (1903), now the Centromerkur department store. Diagonally across the square at No 1 is another Secessionist gem: the **Hauptman House** (or Ura building). Peer two doors down Wolfova ulica and at No 4 you'll see a terracotta figure peeking out from a 'window'. It's Julija Primic looking at the monument to her lifelong admirer Prešeren.

The 17th-century Italianate **Franciscan Church of the Annunciation** (Frančiškanska Cerkev Marijinega Oznanjanja; ☎ 242 93 00; Prešernov trg 4; ☺ 6.45am-noon & 3-8pm) stands on the northern side of the square. The interior is not so interesting with its six side altars and enormous choir stall, though the main altar was designed by the Italian sculptor Francesco Robba (1698–1757).

Miklošičeva Cesta

This 650m-long thoroughfare links Prešernov trg with Trg OF and the train and bus stations; the southern end boasts a splendid array of fine Secessionist buildings. The cream-coloured former **People's Loan Bank** (Map pp66-7; 1908) at No 4 is topped with blue tiles and the figures of two women holding symbols of industry (a beehive) and wealth (a purse). The one-time **Cooperative Bank** (Map pp66-7) at No 8 was designed by Ivan Vurnik, and the red, yellow and blue geometric patterns painted by his wife Helena in 1922. Just opposite is the **Grand Hotel Union** (Map pp66-7), the *grande dame* of Ljubljana hotels built in 1905. About 150m to the north is **Miklošičev Park** (Map pp62-3 & Map pp66-7), laid out by Fabiani in 1902.

All the buildings facing it are Art Nouveau masterpieces, with the exception of the unspeakable one housing offices, trade unions and a bank to the south.

Central Market

The Central Market (Centralna Tržnica; Map pp66-7) lies across Triple Bridge to the southeast of Prešernov trg. The elegant covered walkway along the river, the **Plečnik Colonnade** (Plečnikov Arkada), forms part of the market to the north.

Walk through **Pogačarjev trg** and on to **Vodnikov trg**, with their wonderful open-air market stalls selling everything from wild mushrooms and forest berries, to honey and homemade cheeses, such as soft white *sirček*.

The curious **cone** at the entrance to Pogačarjev trg was erected in honour of Plečnik in 1993. It represents the similarly shaped parliament building he designed, but never built, for the top of Castle Hill. The building on the southern side of the square is the Renaissance **Bishop's Palace** (Škofijski Dvorec), with a lovely arcaded central courtyard. The **Seminary** (Semenišče; 1708) to the east, its entrance framed by a pair of Atlas figures sculpted by Andrea Pozzo of Atlases, contains ornate baroque furnishings and a library with priceless incunabula, 16th-century manuscripts and frescoes. The interior can be visited by appointment only; contact the tourist office. There's a covered market with meat, fish and dairy products on the ground floor (p84).

Dominating Pogačarjev trg is the **Cathedral of St Nicholas** (Stolnica; Map pp66-7; ☎ 234 26 90; Dolničarjeva ulica 1; ☼ 10am-noon & 3-6pm). A church has stood here since the 13th century, but the existing twin-towered building dates from the start of the 18th century. Inside it's a palace of pink marble, white stucco and gilt, with frescoes by baroque master Giulio Quaglio

and 19th-century artist Matevž Langus. Have a look at the magnificent carved choir stalls, organ and the angels on the main altar – another Robba creation. Two stunning bronze doors were added in 1996 to commemorate the late Pope John Paul II's visit – the (main) west door facing the Bishop's Palace symbolises 1250 years of Christianity in Slovenia, and the six bishops on the south door fronting Ciril-Metodov trg depict the history of the Ljubljana diocese.

Old Town

Ljubljana's Old Town (Staro Mesto; Map pp66-7) is its oldest and most important historical quarter. A large portion of the buildings here are baroque, although some houses along Stari trg and Gornji trg have retained their medieval layout.

MESTNI TRG

The first of the Old Town's three 'squares' (the next two are more like narrow cobbled streets), Mestni trg (Town Square) is dominated by the **town hall** (rotovž; ☎ 306 30 00; ☼ 7.30am-4pm Mon-Fri), the seat of the city government and sometimes referred to as the Magistrat. It was erected in the late 15th century and rebuilt in 1718. The Gothic courtyard inside, arcaded on three levels, is where theatrical performances once took place and contains some lovely sgraffiti. If you look above the south portal leading to a second courtyard you'll see a relief map of Ljubljana in the second half of the 17th century.

In front of the town hall stands the **Robba Fountain** (1751); the three titans with their gushing urns represent the three rivers of Carniola: the Sava, Krka and Ljubljanica.

STARI TRG

'Old Square', the true heart of the Old Town, is lined with 19th-century wooden shop

---

WAGGIN' DRAGONS

Ljubljana's town hall is topped with a golden dragon, a symbol of Ljubljana but not an ancient one as many people assume. Just before the turn of the 20th century a wily mayor named Ivan Hribar apparently persuaded the authorities in Vienna that Ljubljana needed a new crossing over the Ljubljanica, and submitted plans for a 'Jubilee Bridge' to mark 50 years of the reign of Franz Joseph. The result, the much-loved Dragon Bridge (Zmajski Most) was built to the northeast, off Vodnikov trg, and renamed in 1919. City folk say the winged bronze dragons wag their tails whenever a virgin crosses the bridge. To his credit, Mayor Hribar even suggested that a lift be built to Ljubljana Castle, something has finally been realised in the form of a funicular (p71).

fronts, quiet courtyards and cobblestone passageways. From behind the medieval houses on the eastern side, paths once led to Castle Hill, which was a source of water. The buildings fronting the river had large passageways built to allow drainage in case of flooding. Where No 4 is today a prison called **Tranča** formerly stood until the 18th century, and those condemned to death were executed at a spot nearby. The great polymath Janez Vajkard Valvasor (p198) was born in the house next door in 1641.

A small street to the north called Pod Trančo (Below Tranča) leads to **Cobbler Bridge** (Čevljarski Most). During the Middle Ages this was a place of trade, and a tolled gateway led to the town. Craftsmen worked and lived on the bridges (in this case 16 shoemakers) to catch the traffic and avoid paying town taxes; it was a kind of medieval version of duty-free.

Between Stari trg 11a and No 15 – the house that *should* bear the number 13 – there's a lovely rococo building called **Schweiger House** with a large Atlas supporting the upper balcony. The figure has his finger raised to his lips as if asking passers-by to be quiet (the owner's name means 'Silent One' in German). In this part of the world, bordellos were traditionally located at house No 13 of a street, and he probably got quite a few unsolicited calls.

In Levstikov trg, the southern extension of Stari trg, the **Hercules Fountain** is a recent copy of the 17th-century statue now in the town hall. To the southeast is the **Church of St James** (Cerkev Sv Jakoba; Map p66-7; ☎ 252 17 27; Gornji trg 18; ⌚ 7am-8pm) built in 1615. Inside the church, far more interesting than Robba's main altar (1732) is the one in the church's **Chapel of St Francis Xavier** to the left, with statues of a 'White Queen' and a 'Black King'.

Across Karlovška cesta is **Gruber Palace** (Gruberjeva Palača; Map p75; Zvezdarska ulica 1). Gabriel Gruber, the Jesuit who built the Gruber Canal (Gruberjev Prekop) that regulates the Ljubljanica, lived here until 1784. The palace is in Zopf style, a transitional art style between late baroque and neoclassicism, and now contains the national archives (p61). If you look eastward on Karlovška cesta to No 1, you'll see what was once the **Balkan Gate** (Map p75), the southernmost point of the Old Town. From here the town walls ran up Castle Hill.

GORNJI TRG

'Upper Square' is the eastern extension of Stari trg. The five **medieval houses** at Nos 7 to 15 (Map pp66-7) have narrow side passages (some with doors) where rubbish was once deposited so that it could be washed down into the river. The most important building on this elongated square is the **Church of St Florian** (Cerkev Sv Florijana), built in 1672 it was dedicated to the patron saint of fires after a serious blaze destroyed much of the Old Town. It was renovated by Plečnik in 1934.

The footpath **Ulica na Grad**, leading up from the church, is an easy way to reach the castle.

Botanical Garden

About 800m southeast of the Old Town along Karlovška cesta and over the Ljubljanica River, this 2.5-hectare **botanical garden** (Botanični Vrt; Map p75; ☎ 427 12 80; Ižanska cesta 15; admission free; ⌚ 7am-7pm Apr-Oct, 7am-5pm Nov-Mar) was founded in 1810 as a sanctuary of native flora. It contains 4500 species of plants and trees, about a third of which are indigenous, and is overseen by the University of Ljubljana. You can also reach here on bus 3 from Slovenska cesta (stop: Strelišče).

Ljubljana Castle

Known as Ljubljana Castle (Ljubljanski Grad), there have been fortifications of one kind or another on Castle Hill (Grajska Planota) since at least Celtic times, but the existing **castle** (Map pp66-7; ☎ 232 99 94; www.festival-lj.si; admission free; ⌚ 9am-10pm May-Sep, 10am-9pm Oct-Apr) mostly dates from a 16th-century rebuilding following the 1511 earthquake. It was a royal residence in the 17th and 18th centuries and a prison and barracks in the 19th and first half of the 20th centuries. About 80% of the castle has been renovated in recent years, and it is now frequently used as a venue for concerts and other cultural activities, and as a wedding hall on Wednesday, Friday and Saturday.

The **Viewing Tower** (Razgledni Stolp; Map pp66-7; adult/senior & student/family €3.30/2/4.15; ☎ 9am-9pm May-Sep, 10am-6pm Oct-Apr), which is the tower on the western side of the castle courtyard, contains the **Virtual Museum** (Virtualni Muzej), a 20-minute 3D video tour of Ljubljana and its history in four languages. The climb up to the top of the tower, via a double wrought-iron staircase (95 steps from the museum level) of the 19th-century tower and a walk along

LJUBLJANA

the ramparts, is worth the effort for the views down into the Old Town and across the river to Center.

Attached to the Viewing Tower, the **Chapel of St George** (Kapela Sv Jurija; 1489) is covered in frescoes and the coats of arms of the Dukes of Carniola. In the castle's southern wing, the **Pentagonal Tower** (Peterokotni Stolp) hosts changing exhibitions, smaller concerts and theatrical performances.

Castle tours (Map pp66-7; adult/senior/student & under 18 €4/6/3.30; � 10am & 4pm Jun–mid-Sep) depart from the bridge at the castle's main entrance and include admission to the tower and museum.

You can reach the castle from the Old Town on foot in about 15 minutes via any of three routes: Študentovska ulica, which runs south from Ciril-Metodov trg; steep Reber ulica from Stari trg; and Ulica na Grad from Gornji trg. The fastest way to reach the castle is via the new **funicular**, which ascends from Krekov trg in just one minute. You can also take the hourly **tourist train** (Map pp66-7; adult/child €2.50/1.70; ☎ 11am-6pm Apr–mid-Jun; 9am-9pm mid-Jun–Sep, 9am-7pm Oct, 11am-3pm Nov-Mar) from Prešernov trg.

Tabor

North of Castle Hill across the Ljubljanica River, this district (Map pp62-3) is leafy, residential, and home to the pulsating Metelkova district of alternative culture (p86). Some say it also holds Ljubljana's best museum.

SLOVENIAN ETHNOGRAPHIC MUSEUM

This new **museum** (Slovenski Etnografski Muzej; Map pp62-3; ☎ 300 87 45; www.etno-muzej.si; Metelkova ulica 2; adult/student & senior €3.35/2.10, admission free last Sun of month; ☎ 10am-6pm Tue-Sun), housed in the 1886 Belgian Barracks on the southern edge of Metelkova, has a permanent collection on the 3rd floor. There's traditional Slovenian trades and handicrafts – everything from beekeeping and blacksmithing to glass-painting and pottery making – and some excellent exhibits directed at children. Temporary exhibits are on the 1st and 2nd floors. Allow extra time for this one; it's excellent.

Žale

This suburb about 2km northeast of Tabor contains Plečnik's largest masterpiece, the monumental **Žale Cemetery** (Pokopališče Žale; Map pp62-3; ☎ 420 17 00; med Hmeljniki 2; ☎ 6am-8pm Apr-

Sep, 7am-6pm Oct-Mar). It has a series of chapels dedicated to the patron saints of Ljubljana's churches, and the entrance is an enormous two-storey arcade. Ljubljana's own Père Lachaise or Highgate is a very peaceful, green place and 'home' to a number of Slovenian actors, writers, painters and a certain distinguished architect – Gospod Plečnik himself. There are also the graves of Austrian, Italian and German soldiers from both world wars and a Jewish section. You can reach Žale on bus 2, 7 or 22 (stop: Žale).

Center

This district on the left bank of the Ljubljanica is the nerve centre of modern Ljubljana. It is filled with shops, commercial offices, government departments and embassies. There are several areas of interest to travellers as well.

NOVI TRG

'New Square' (Map pp66-7), south of Cobbler Bridge, was a walled settlement of fisherfolk outside the town administration in the Middle Ages, but it became more aristocratic from the 16th century. It suffered extensive damage in the 1895 earthquake, but medieval remnants include the very narrow street to the north called **Židovska ulica** (Jewish Street) and its offshoot Židovska steza (Jewish Lane), once the site of a synagogue and the centre of Jewish life here in the Middle Ages. **Breg**, the city's port when the Ljubljanica River was still navigable this far inland, runs south from the square. At Novi trg's western end is the **Slovenian Academy of Arts and Sciences** (Slovenska Akademija Znanosti in Umetnosti; Map pp66-7; ☎ 470 61 00; Novi trg 3), housed in a 16th-century building that was the seat of the provincial diet under the Habsburgs. The **National and University Library** (Narodna in Univerzitetna Knjižnica; Map pp66-7; ☎ 200 11 00; Gosposka ulica 14; ☎ 8am-8pm Mon-Fri, 9am-2pm Sat), Plečnik's masterpiece completed in 1941, is just opposite. To appreciate more of this great man's philosophy, enter through the main door (note the horse-head doorknobs) on Turjaška ulica 1 – you'll find yourself in near darkness, entombed in black marble. But as you ascend the steps, you'll emerge into a colonnade suffused with light – the light of knowledge, according to the architect's plans. The Main Reading Room (Velika Čitalnica), now closed to nonstudents, has huge glass walls and some stunning lamps, also designed by Plečnik. Check out the Art Deco **Plečnik Café** in the basement.

TRG FRANCOSKE REVOLUCIJE

'French Revolution Square' was for centuries the headquarters of the Teutonic Knights of the Cross (*Križniki*). They built a commandery here in the early 13th century, which was transformed into the **Križanke** (Map pp66-7; ☎ 241 60 00; Trg Francoske Revolucije 1-2) monastery complex in 1714. Today it serves as the headquarters of the Ljubljana Summer Festival (p78), with an open-air theatre seating 1400 people. The **Ilirija Column** in the centre of the square is dedicated to Napoleon and his Illyrian Provinces (1809–13), when Slovene was taught in schools for the first time.

At the eastern end of Trg Francoske Revolucije is the excellent **Ljubljana City Museum** (Mestni Muzej Ljubljana; Map pp66-7; ☎ 241 25 00; www.mm-lj.si; Gosposka ulica 15; adult/child €2.10/1.25; ☎ 10am-6pm Tue-Sun), which has reopened after a four-year renovation and focuses on Ljubljana's history, culture and politics. The reconstructed Roman street that linked the eastern gates of Emona to the Ljubljanica, and the collection of well-preserved classical artefacts in the basement are worth a visit in themselves.

KONGRESNI TRG

This lovely square can be reached from Trg Francoske Revolucije by walking north along Vegova ulica, a pleasant street lined with trees and busts of Slovenian writers, scientists and musicians. Named in honour of the Congress of the Holy Alliance, convened by Austria, Prussia, Russia and Naples in 1821 and hosted by Ljubljana, 'Congress Square' contains several important buildings. To the south at No 12 is the central building of **Ljubljana University** (Univerza v Ljubljani; Map pp66-7; ☎ 241 85 00; Kongresni trg 12), erected as a ducal palace in 1902. The **Philharmonic Hall** (Filharmonija; Map pp66-7; ☎ 241 08 00; Kongresni trg 10) in the southeast corner is home to the Slovenian Philharmonic Orchestra, which was founded in 1701 and is one of the oldest in the world. Haydn, Beethoven and Brahms were honorary members, and Gustav Mahler was resident conductor for a season (1881–82).

The **Ursuline Church of the Holy Trinity** (Uršulinska Cerkev Sv Trojice; Map pp66-7; ☎ 252 48 64; Slovenska cesta 21; ☎ 5.30-7.30am, 9-11am & 4-7pm), which faces the square from across Slovenska cesta and dates from 1726, is the most beautiful baroque building in the city. It contains a multicoloured altar by Robba made of African marble. To reach the church use the Plečnik underpass (Plečnikov podhod) at the western end of Kongresni trg and, as you descend, look to the right for a small gilded statue on top of a column. It's a copy (the original is in the National Museum) of the Roman-era **Citizen of Emona**, dating from the 4th century and unearthed nearby in 1836. At the other end of the underpass is the entrance to the rather esoteric **Slovenian School Museum** (Slovenski Šolski Muzej; Map pp66-7; ☎ 251 30 24; www.ssolski-muzej .si; Plečnikov trg 1; admission free; ☎ 9am-1pm Mon-Fri), which explores how Slovenian kids learned the three Rs in the 19th century.

Some 300m north of the Ursuline church along Slovenska cesta is the impressive Art Deco **Nebotičnik** (Skyscraper; Map pp66-7; Štefanova ulica 1), designed by Vladimir Šubic (1933) and, at nine storeys, the city's tallest building for decades.

TRG REPUBLIKE

'Republic Square' is Center's main plaza. Unfortunately, it is basically a car park dominated by a pair of glowering, grey tower blocks – **TR3** (Map pp62-3; Trg Republike 3), housing offices and embassies, and the headquarters of **Nova Ljubljanska Banka** (Map pp62-3; Trg Republike 2) – and a couple of garish revolutionary monuments. The renovated **Parliament Building** (Map pp62-3; ☎ 478 97 87; Šubičeva ulica 4; admission free; ☎ 9am, 10am & 11am every 2nd Sat), built in 1959 at the northeast corner of the square, is no beauty pageant winner on the outside but the mammoth portal festooned with bronze sculptures is noteworthy. It's worth joining one of the infrequent guided tours at the weekend to see the inside, especially the period-piece mural in the vestibule of the Large Hall depicting the history of Slovenia. **Cankarjev Dom** (Map pp62-3; ☎ 241 71 00; 10), the city's premier cultural and conference centre (p87), squats behind the TR3 building to the southwest.

Behind Cankarjev Dom is **Ferant Garden** (Map pp62-3; Erjavčeva cesta 18; ☎ 10am-4pm Mon-Fri, 10am-1pm Sat Apr-Oct), with the remains of an early Christian church porch and baptistery with mosaics from the 4th century. To visit you must first contact the City Museum (p72). Opposite and to the west of the Cankarjev Dom are the remains of a **Roman wall** dating from 15AD.

Museum Area

Four of Ljubljana's most important museums are located in this area (Map pp62-3), which is only a short distance to the northwest of Trg Republike.

NATIONAL MUSEUM OF SLOVENIA

On the western side of parklike Trg Narodnih Herojev, this **museum** (Narodni Muzej Slovenije; Map pp62-3; ☎ 241 44 00; www.narmuz-lj.si; Muzejska ulica 1; adult/student & senior/family €3/2.10/5.85, incl Natural History Museum €4.60/3.35/9.20, admission free 1st Sun; ☺ 10am-6pm Fri-Wed, 10am-8pm Thu) occupies an elegant 1888 building. It has a large collection but at the time of writing only highlights from the rich archaeological and coin collections were on display. The Roman glass and the jewellery found in 6th-century Slavic graves is pretty standard fare, but the *chef d'oeuvre* here is the highly embossed Vače situla, a Celtic pail from the late 6th century BC unearthed in a town east of Ljubljana. Make sure you check out the ceiling fresco in the foyer, which features an allegorical Carniola surrounded by important Slovenes from the past and the statues of the Muses and Fates relaxing on the stairway banisters.

SLOVENIAN MUSEUM OF NATURAL HISTORY

Housed in 16 rooms and hallways of the same impressive building as the National Museum, the **Natural History Museum** (Prirodoslovni Muzej Slovenije; Map pp62-3; ☎ 241 09 40; www2.pms-lj.si; Muzejska ulica 1; adult/student & senior/family €3/2.10/5.85, incl National Museum €4.60/3.35/9.20, admission free 1st Sun; ☺ 10am-6pm Fri-Wed, 10am-8pm Thu) contains the usual reassembled mammoth and whale skeletons, stuffed birds, reptiles and mammals. However, the mineral collections amassed by the philanthropic Baron Žiga Zois in the early 19th century and the display on Slovenia's unique salamander *Proteus anguinus* (p185) are worth a visit.

NATIONAL GALLERY

Slovenia's foremost collection of fine art is at the **National Gallery** (Narodna Galerija; Map pp62-3; ☎ 241 54 34; www.ng-slo.si; Prešernova cesta 24; adult/student & senior €4.20/2.90, admission free 2-6pm Sat & 1st Sun; ☺ 10am-6pm Tue-Sun). It offers portraits and Slovenian landscapes from the 17th to 19th centuries (check out works by 'national Romantics' Pavel Künl, Marko Pernhart and Anton Karinger), copies of medieval frescoes and a wonderful Gothic statuary (1896) in its old south wing. Although the subjects of the earlier paintings are the usual foppish nobles and lemon-lipped clergymen, some of the later works are remarkable and provide a good introduction to Slovenian art. Take a close look at the works of the impressionists Jurij Šubic (*Before the Hunt*) and Rihard Jakopič (*Birches in Autumn*), the pointillist Ivan Grohar (*Škofja Loka in the Snow*) and Slovenia's most celebrated female painter Ivana Kobilca (*Summer*). The bronzes by Franc Berneker and Anton Gangl are truly exceptional. The

A GALLERY OF GALLERIES

Ljubljana is awash in galleries both public and commercial. The following are among the best.

- **City Gallery** Mestni trg (Mestna Galerija; Map p66-7; ☎ 241 17 70; www.mestna-galerija.si; Mestni trg 5; admission free; ☺ 10am-6pm Tue-Sat, 10am-1pm Sun); Cankarjevo nabrežje (☎ 241 17 90; Cankarjevo nabrežje 11; ☺ same hr) Rotating displays of contemporary painting, sculpture and graphic art.
- **DESSA Architectural Gallery** (Map p66-7; ☎ 251 40 74; www.dessa.si; Židovska steza 4; admission free; ☺ 10am-3pm Mon-Fri) Small gallery spotlighting contemporary architecture and architects.
- **Equrna Gallery** (Galerija Equrna; Map p66-7; ☎ 252 71 23; www.galerija-equrna.si; Gregorčičeva ulica 3; admission free; ☺ 10am-7pm Mon-Fri, 10am-1pm Sat) Among the most innovative modern galleries in town.
- **Little Gallery** (Mala Galerija; Map p66-7; ☎ 241 68 00; www.mg-lj.si; Slovenska cesta 35; admission free; ☺ 10am-6pm Tue-Sun) Rotating exhibits in the heart of Center.
- **Luwigiana Gallery** (Galerija Luwigiana; Map p66-7; ☎ 252 73 69; www.studiocerne-jc.si; Gornji trg 19; admission free; ☺ 11am-7pm Mon-Fri) Well-respected space in the Old Town.
- **Škuc Gallery** (Galerija Škuc; Map p66-7; ☎ 421 31 40, 432 73 68; www.galerija.skuc-drustvo.si; Stari trg 21; admission free; ☺ 10am-6pm Tue-Sun) Cutting-edge gallery in the Old Town.

gallery's modern north wing facing Puharjeva ulica has a permanent collection of European paintings from the Middle Ages to the 20th century on the 1st floor and is also used for temporary exhibits.

MUSEUM OF MODERN ART

Housed in an ugly modern building (Edvard Ravnikar; 1939–51), the inwardly vibrant and inspiring **Museum of Modern Art** (Moderna Galerija; Map pp62-3; ☎ 241 68 00; www.mg-lj.si; Cankarjeva cesta 15; adult/student & senior €4.20/2.10; ⌚ 10am-6pm Tue-Sun) exhibits a permanent collection of 20th-century Slovenian art on two floors that helps put some of the socialist-inspired work of sculptors such as Jakob Savinšek (*Protest*) into artistic perspective. Watch out for works by Tone Kralj (*Peasant Wedding*), the expressionist France Mihelič (*The Quintet*) and the surrealist Štefan Planinc (*Primeval World* series). Some people might consider the works by multimedia group Neue Slowenische Kunst (NSK; *Suitcase for Spiritual Use: Baptism under Triglav*) and the artists' cooperative IRWIN (*Kapital*) 'fun' rather than 'serious' art.

OTHER HISTORIC BUILDINGS

The graceful **Opera House** (Map pp62-3; ☎ 241 17 40; www.opera.si; Župančičeva ulica 1), northeast of the National Museum, opened in 1892 as the Provincial Theatre, and plays in German and Slovene were performed here. After WWI it was renamed the Opera House and is now home to the Slovenian National Opera and Ballet (p87) companies.

The interior of the **Serbian Orthodox Church** (Srbska Pravoslavna Cerkev; Map pp62-3; ☎ 252 40 02, 041-744 402; Prešernova cesta; ⌚ 2-6pm Tue-Sun), built in 1936 and dedicated to Sts Cyril and Methodius, is covered from floor to ceiling with colourful modern frescoes. There is a richly carved iconostasis separating the nave from the sanctuary.

Park Tivoli

You can reach Tivoli, the city's leafy playground laid out in 1813 and measuring 5 sq km, via an underpass from Cankarjeva cesta. Straight ahead, at the end of **Jakopičevo sprehajališče**, the monumental Jakopič Promenade designed by Plečnik in the 1920s and 30s, is the 17th-century **Tivoli Mansion** (Grad Tivoli), which now contains the **International Centre of Graphic Arts** (Mednarodni Grafični Likovni Center, MGLC; Map pp62-3; ☎ 241 38 00; www.mglc-lj.si; Pod turnom 3; adult/senior & student €3.35/1.70; ⌚ 11am-6pm Wed-Sun). The centre has new exhibitions every three months and hosts the International Biennial of Graphic Arts (p78) every odd-numbered year.

The **Museum of Contemporary History of Slovenia** (Muzej Novejše Zgodovine Slovenije; Map pp62-3; ☎ 300 96 10; www.muzej-nz.si; Celovška cesta 23; adult/student €2.10/1.25; ⌚ 10am-6pm Tue-Sat), housed in the 18th-century Cekin Mansion (Grad Cekinov) just northeast of the Tivoli Recreation Centre (p77), traces the history of Slovenia in the 20th century through multimedia and artefacts. Note the contrast between the sober earnestness of the communist-era Room G and the exuberant, logo-mad commercialism of the neighbouring industrial exhibit in Room H. A portrait of Stalin lies 'discarded' behind the door between the two. The glor-iously baroque Ceremonial Hall (Viteška Dvorana) on the 1st floor is how the whole mansion once looked.

The 20-hectare **Ljubljana Zoo** (Živalski Vrt Ljubljana; Map pp62-3; ☎ 244 21 88; www.zoo-ljubljana.si in Slovene; Večna pot 70; adult/senior & student/child 2-10 5.70/4.85/3.25; ⌚ 9am-7pm May-Aug, 9am-6pm Apr & Sep, 9am-5pm Mar & Oct, 9am-4pm Nov-Feb), on the southern slope of **Rožnik Hill** (394m), contains 580 animals representing more than 150 species. There's also a petting zoo for children. It's an upbeat and well-landscaped menagerie.

Krakovo & Trnovo

These two attractive districts south of Center are Ljubljana's oldest suburbs, and they have a number of interesting buildings and historic sites. The neighbourhood around Krakovska ulica, with all its two-storey cottages, was once called the 'Montmartre of Ljubljana' because of all the artists living there. There are many market gardeners here who sell their produce (notably lettuce) at Ljubljana's market.

The **Roman wall** running along Mirje from Barjanska cesta dates from about 15AD; the archway topped with a pyramid is a Plečnik addition. Within the **Jakopič Garden** (Mirje 4; Map p75; ⌚ 10am-1pm & 4-6pm) to the southeast, where the impressionist painter once worked in his summerhouse, there are more Roman ruins, including household artefacts, mosaics and the remains of sophisticated heating and sewage systems. Contact the City Museum (p72) if you want to visit.

KRAKOVO & TRNOVO
0 200 m
0 0.1 miles
Jakopic Garden
Zoisova c
Krakovska ul
Gradaščica Canal
Eipprova ul
Trnovska ul
Švabičeva ul
Zihertova ul
Karunova ul
Emonska c
Krakovski nasip
Ljubljanica River
Karlovška c
Cesta Slovenskih Kmečkih Uporov
Gruberjevo nabrežje
Gruber Canal
Dolenjska c
Velika Čolnarska ul
Opekarska c
Hladnikova c
C na Mesarico
Jeranova ul
Staretova ul
Jefovškova
Mencingerjeva ul
Mirje
Murnikova
Groharjeva c
Janežičeva c
Prule
Privoz
Ižanska c
INFORMATION
Archives of the Republic of Slovenia (see 6)
Croatian Embassy 1 D2
French Embassy 2 B1
SIGHTS & ACTIVITIES
Botanical Garden Entrance 3 D2
Church of St James 4 C1
Church of St John the Baptist 5 B1
Former Balkan Gate 6 C1
Gruber Palace 7 C1
Ljubljana Rowing Club 8 C3
Plečnik Collection 9 B2
Plečnik Pyramid 10 A1
Roman Walls 11 A1
Trovo Bridge 12 B1
EATING
Harambaša 13 B1
Kitajska Zvezda 14 C1
Manna 15 B1
Pri Škofju 16 B1
Trta 17 C1
Yildiz Han 18 D2
DRINKING
Breskvar 19 B3
Sax Pub 20 B1
Šank Pub 21 B1
ENTERTAINMENT
KUD France Prešeren 22 B2
SHOPPING
Annapurna Shop 23 B1

Spanning the picturesque canal called Gradaščica to the south is little **Trnovo Bridge**, designed in 1932 by Plečnik, who added five of his trademark pyramids. On the south side is the **Church of St John the Baptist** (Cerkev Sv Janeza Krstnika; Map p75; ☎ 283 50 60; Kolezijska ulica 1; 6-8pm Mon-Sat, 8am-noon Sun), which has a lovely carved altar and where the poet Prešeren met the love of his life, Julija Primic.

A short distance south is the house where Jože Plečnik lived and worked for almost 40 years. Today it houses the Ljubljana Architectural Museum's **Plečnik Collection** (Map p75; ☎ 280 16 00; Karunova ulica 4; adult/child €4.20/2.10; 10am-2pm & 4-6pm Tue-Thu, 9am-3pm Sat). There's an excellent introduction by guided tour to this almost ascetically religious man, his inspirations and his work.

Other Museums & Galleries

Ljubljana contains many more interesting museums, some of them a bit further out from the centre.

Ljubljana Architectural Museum (Arhitekturni Muzej Ljubljana; Map pp62-3; ☎ 540 97 98; www.aml.si; Fužine Castle, Pot na Fužine 2, Studenec; adult/senior, student & child 6-16 €2.10/1.05; 9am-3pm Mon-Fri, 11am-6pm Sat, 11am-2pm Sun) Much emphasis on Plečnik, focusing on his work at home and abroad, and some stunning unrealised projects (bus 20 to Fužine).

Brewery Museum (Pivovarski Muzej; Map pp62-3; ☎ 471 73 40; www.pivo-union.si; Union Brewery, Pivovarniška ulica 2; admission free; 8am-1pm every 1st Tue & by appointment) Beer-making displays, film and a tour of the brewery (bus 1, 3 or 5 to Pivovarna).

Railway Museum (Železniški Muzej; Map pp62-3; ☎ 291 26 41; www.slo-zeleznice.si/en/about_us/rail way_museum; Parmova ulica 35; adult/senior, student & child 6-16 €3.15/2.10; 10am-6pm Tue-Sun) Locomotives, carriages, uniforms and railway-related art north of Centre (bus 14).

Technical Museum of Slovenia (Tehniški Muzej Slovenije; Map pp62-3; ☎ 750 66 70; www.tms.si; Bistra Castle, Bistra pri Vrhniki; adult/student & child €3.75/3; 8am-4pm Tue-Fri, 8am-5pm Sat, 10am-6pm Sun Mar-Nov) Huge collection of antique motor vehicles and bicycles, water-driven and horse-powered mills, and implements used in agriculture, weaving, forestry, smithing, fishing and hunting. It's 22km southwest of Ljubljana; bus to Vrhnika or train to Verd.

Tobacco Museum (Tobačni Muzej; Map pp62-3; ☎ 477 73 44; www.mm-lj.si; Tobacco Factory, Tobačna

JOŽE PLEČNIK, ARCHITECT EXTRAORDINAIRE

Few architects anywhere in the world have had as great an impact on their birthplace as Jože Plečnik. His work is eclectic, inspired, unique – and found everywhere in Ljubljana and elsewhere in Slovenia.

Born in Ljubljana in 1872, Plečnik was educated at the College of Arts in Graz and studied under the architect Otto Wagner in Vienna. He lived for 10 years in Prague from 1911, where he taught and later helped renovate Prague Castle.

Plečnik's work in his hometown began in 1921. Almost single-handedly he transformed the city, adding elements of classical Greek and Roman architecture with Byzantine, Islamic, ancient Egyptian and folkloric motifs to its baroque and Secessionist faces. The list of his creations and renovations is endless – from the National and University Library and the colonnaded Central Market to the magnificent cemetery at Žale.

Plečnik was also a city planner and designer. Not only did he redesign the banks of the Ljubljanica River (including the Triple Bridge and the monumental lock downstream), entire streets (Zoisova ulica) and Park Tivoli, but he also set his sights elsewhere on monumental stairways (Kranj), public buildings (Kamnik) and outdoor shrines (Bled). An intensely religious man, Plečnik designed many furnishings and liturgical objects – chalices, candlesticks, lanterns – for churches throughout the land (eg Škofja Loka's Church of St James, p99). One of Plečnik's designs that was never realised was an extravagant parliament, complete with an enormous cone-shaped structure, to be built on Castle Hill after WWII.

Plečnik's eclecticism and individuality alienated him from the mainstream of modern architecture during his lifetime, and he was relatively unknown outside Eastern and Central Europe when he died in 1957. Today he is hailed as a prophet of postmodernism.

ulica 5; admission free; 🕙 10am-6pm 1st Wed & 3rd Thu of month) Ljubljana's first factory (bus 6 to Tobačna).

ACTIVITIES
Adventure Sports

Agencies like Label (p68) and Trek Trek (p68) and **Adrenaline-Check** (☎ 041-383 662, 040-150 600; www.adrenaline-check.com) at the Celica Hostel (p80) can organise a wide range of outdoor activities around Ljubljana and further afield across the rest of Slovenia, including trekking, mountaineering, rock climbing, ski touring, cross country skiing, mountain biking, rafting, kayaking, canyoning, caving and paragliding.

Ballooning

The Ljubljana Tourist Information Centre (p67) organises **balloon rides** (adult/child €87/45; 🕙 7am & 6pm Apr-Aug, 8am & 5pm Sep-Mar) year-round lasting three to four hours (one to 1½ hours actually in the air) departing from the Slovenian Tourist Information Centre (p68).

Boating & Rafting

The **Ljubljana Rowing Club** (Veslaški Klub Ljubljana; Map p75; ☎ 283 87 12; www.vesl-klub-ljubljanica.si in Slovene; Velika Čolnarska ulica; 20; per hr from €2.50; 🕙 10am-7pm mid-May–Sep) in Trnovo has dinghies and larger rowing boats for hire on the Ljubljanica River.

Skok Sport (Map pp62-3; ☎ 512 44 02, 040-218 000; www.skok-sport.si; Marinovševa cesta 8) in Šentvid, 8km northwest of Center, organises rafting trips on the Sava, from Medvode to Brod for €15 and from Boka to Trnovo for €30. They can also arrange kayak and canoe excursions (from €25) on the Ljubljanica and run a kayaking school (bus 8 to Brod).

Bowling & Billiards

Klub 300 (Map pp62-3; ☎ 510 39 40; www.bowling klub300.com; Regentova cesta 35; game €2.10-3.35, rental shoes €1.50; 🕙 2pm-midnight Mon, Tue, Thu & Fri, noon-midnight Wed, 10am-midnight Sat & Sun) is a super-modern 16-lane bowling centre with four billiard and pool tables. It's located northwest of Center (bus 7 to Plešičeva stop). For a drugless high, try **cosmic bowling** (per hr €22.50; 🕙 9pm-midnight Fri & Sat), with special lighting effects and music.

Hiking

The marked **Trail of Remembrance** (Pot Spominov) is popular with walkers and joggers. It runs for 34km around the city, where German barbed wire once completely enclosed

Ljubljana during WWII. The easiest places to reach the trail are from the **AMZS headquarters** (Map pp62–3; bus 6, 8 or 21 to AMZS stop) on Dunajska cesta (No 128), or from Trg Komandanta Staneta just northwest of the central office of the public transport authority LPP (Map pp62–3; bus 1 to Remiza stop), on Celovška cesta (No 160). You can also join it from the northwestern side of **Žale Cemetery** (Map pp62–3; bus 19 to Nove Žale stop) or south of **Trnovo** (Map p75; bus 19 to Veliki Štradon stop).

Another popular destination from Ljubljana is **Šmarna Gora**, a 669m-high hill above the Sava River, 12km northwest of Ljubljana. Take bus 15 from Slovenska cesta or Gosposvetska cesta to the Medno stop or bus 8 to Brod and begin walking. Another way to go is via the Smlednik bus from the main station and then follow the marked path from the 12th-century Smlednik Castle. There's swimming and boating in Zbilje Lake nearby.

Swimming & Sauna

Tivoli Recreation Centre (Map pp62–3; ☎ 431 51 55; Celovška cesta 25) in Park Tivoli has an indoor swimming pool (open mid-September to June), a fitness centre, clay tennis courts and a roller-skating rink (which becomes an ice rink from mid-August to February). It also has a popular sauna called **Zlati Klub** (Gold Club; morning €12, afternoon €14.60; ☼ 10am-10pm Mon, Wed, Thu & Sun, 10am-11pm Fri & Sat, women only 10am-10pm Tue) with saunas, steam room, splash pools and outside swimming pool surrounded by high walls so you can sunbathe *au naturel*. Towels are an extra €2.

Southeast of the Tivoli Centre is the **Ilirija outdoor swimming pool** (Map pp62–3; ☎ 231 02 33, 439 75 80; Celovška cesta 3; adult/child 6-10/child 11-14/student €4.20/2.50/3/3.35; ☼ 10am-7pm Jun-Aug). The most modern of its kind in Yugoslavia when built in 1929, it's now a bit rough around the edges.

Ljubljana boasts two enormous water parks. **Atlantis** (Map pp62–3; ☎ 585 21 00; www .atlantis-vodnomesto.si; BTC City, Šmartinska cesta 152; Adventure World day pass Mon-Fri adult/child €12.50/10.40, Sat & Sun €14.20/12.10; ☼ 9am-11pm) is the more swish, with separate theme areas: Adventure World for kids, with a half-dozen pools and water slides; Thermal Temple with indoor and outdoor thermal pools; and Land of Saunas with 11 different types of saunas. Get there on bus 2, 7 or 17. **Laguna** (Map pp62–3; ☎ 568 39 13; www.laguna.si; Dunjaska cesta 270; day pass adult/student & child over 10/child under 10 €10/8/5.85 Mon-Fri, €12/10/6.70 Sat & Sun; ☼ 9am-8pm Jun-Sep) at the Ljubljana Resort (p79) is more traditional, with several outdoor swimming pools and sunbathing areas, as well as fitness studio with sauna, badminton and volleyball courts. Take bus 8 to its terminus or the more frequent no 6 (stop Ježica).

WALKING TOUR

This is a short and straightforward walk that will give you a taste of the Old Town, the banks of the Ljubljanica River and Krakovo. Start the tour on **Prešernov trg** (p68) in the very heart of Ljubljana. Cross the celebrated **Triple Bridge** and head north (left) at the tourist office for a stroll though the **Central Market** (p69), with its colourful stalls and Plečnik's elegant colonnades. Turn west (right) onto Ciril-Metodov trg and walk towards Old Town, Ljubljana's historical centre. Make a brief visit to the **Cathedral of St Nicholas** (p69) before crossing into cobbled Mestni trg. Past the impressive **town hall** (p69) and renovated **Robba Fountain** (p69), explore the narrow lanes that lead down to the river from the square before continuing on to Stari trg, where you might take a relaxing tea break at **Čajna Hiša** (p84) and ruminate over some contemporary art at the **Škuc Gallery** (p73). Walk to the end of the Levstikov trg and head east (right) onto Karlovška cesta in front of the **Church of St James** (p70), crossing the Ljubljanica River via the foot and vehicular bridge. Walk south along the riverbank for a short while and then turn west (right) into Krakovska ulica. You're in the heart of Krakovo, an 'inner suburb' that often feels more like the country – just check out all those vegetable (mostly lettuce) patches. Peek through the gates of the atmospheric courtyards before finishing off with a scrumptious bite at **Pri Škofju** (p81) on Rečna ulica.

WALK FACTS

Start Prešernov trg
End Krakovo (Rečna ulica)
Distance 2km
Duration 1½ hours
Fuel Stop Čajna Hiša or Pri Škofju

COURSES

A free 1½-hour mini course in Slovene organised by the Centre for Slovene as a Second/Foreign Language (p275) is held at the Slovenian Tourist Information Centre (p68) at 5pm on Wednesday from June to mid-September. Those more serious about learning the language should see p275.

LJUBLJANA FOR CHILDREN

The free monthly *Where to? in Ljubljana* tourist guide available from tourist offices lists events and activities for children, as does the Ljubljana Tourist Board's website (www.ljubljana-tourism.si).

Park Tivoli (p74), with a couple of children's playgrounds, swimming pools and a zoo, is an excellent place to take children as are the two water parks **Laguna** (p77) and especially **Atlantis** (p77).

Kids love moving conveyances of any kind and they'll get a special kick out of both the **funicular** and the **tourist train** that transports the young, the old, the infirm and the lazy (ie just about all of us) to **Castle Hill** (p70).

In the warmer months the **Mini Summer for Children International Festival** (☎ 434 36 20; www.mini-teater.si; 🕙 11am & 6.30pm Sun Jul–mid-Sep) stages puppet shows from around the world for kids at Ljubljana Castle. At other times of the year, check out the programme at the **Ljubljana Puppet Theatre** (p88).

A super place for kids is the **House of Experiments** (Map pp62-3; ☎ 300 68 88; www.h-e.si; Trubarjeva cesta 39; admission €4; 🕙 11am-7pm Sat & Sun), a hands-on science centre with almost four dozen inventive and challenging exhibits that successfully mixes learning with humour. There's a science adventure show at 5pm.

TOURS

The Ljubljana Tourist Information Centre (p67) organises a number of guided tours of the city.

A two-hour guided **walking tour** (adult/student & senior €6.25/3; 🕙 10am Apr-Sep, 11am Fri-Sun Mar & Oct) in English departs from the town hall on Mestni trg year-round.

In the warmer months a glass-enclosed vessel called the *Ljubljana I* offers one-hour English-language **boat tours** (adult/child €6.25/3) on the Ljubljanica River, departing from the little Cankarjevo nabrežje pier (Map pp66-7) just down from Ribji trg on Cankarjevo nabrežje. In April, May and October, boats

depart at 5.30pm, with an additional sailing at 10.30am on Saturday and Sunday. From June to September they leave at 6.30pm daily, with another departure at 10.30am at the weekend.

For tours from Ljubljana to other parts of Slovenia, see p294.

FESTIVALS & EVENTS

The number one event on Ljubljana's social calendar is the **Ljubljana Summer Festival** (www.festival-lj.si), a celebration from early July to late August of music, opera, dance and street theatre held in venues throughout the city, but principally in the open-air theatre at the Križanke (p72).

Druga Godba (www.drugagodba.si), a festival of alternative and world music, takes place in the Križanke in late May and early June. The **Ljubljana Jazz Festival** (www.cd-cc.si) at both the Križanke and the Cankarjev Dom in late June has been taking place for almost half a century.

Vino Ljubljana is an international wine fair and competition held in early June at the **Ljubljana Fairgrounds** (Ljubljanski Sejem; Map pp62-3; www.ljubljanafair.com; Dunajska cesta 10) northwest of the train station.

Ljubljana is at its most vibrant in July and August during the so-called **Summer in the Old Town** season when there are four or five free cultural events a week in the city's historic squares, courtyards and bridges.

The **Ana Desetnica International Festival of Street Theatre** (ana.monro@kud-fp.si) organised by the Ana Monro Theatre in early July is not to be missed and **Trnfest** (www.kud-fp.si), an international festival of alternative arts and culture, takes place in Trnovo in August.

City of Women (www.cityofwomen.org), held in the first half of October in venues throughout Ljubljana, showcases all forms of artistic expression by women. The **Ljubljana Marathon** (http://maraton.slo-timing.com) takes off on the last Saturday in October.

The **International Biennial of Graphic Arts** (www.mglc-lj.si) at the International Centre of Graphic Arts in Park Tivoli, the Museum of Modern Art and several other venues, is held from mid-June to September every odd-numbered year. Another biennial event is **Lutke**, the International Puppet Festival (Mednarodni Lutkovni Festival) held at the Ljubljana Puppet Theatre (p88) in September every even-numbered year.

SLEEPING

Ljubljana is not overly endowed with accommodation choices, especially at the midrange level; in fact, the following selection includes the lion's share of central budget and midrange options available. The tourist office websites have comprehensive details of hotels further out in the suburbs and of the half-dozen other top-end hotels such as the **Domina Grand Media Hotel** (www.dominahotels.com) north of Center and the world-class **Hotel Mons** (www.hotel.mons.si) in a wooded track on the fringe of the city to the southwest.

Budget

Ljubljana Resort (Map pp62-3; ☎ 568 39 13; www.ljubljanaresort.si; Dunajska cesta 270; camp site per adult €7.10-12.10, per child €5.30-9.10; ☻ year-round; P 🖳 🏊) It's got a pretty grandiose name, but wait till you see the facilities at this attractive 7-hectare camping ground-cum-resort 5km north of the centre. Along with a 62-room midrange **hotel** (single/doubles from €54/75) and five **chalets** (rooms €75), there's the **Laguna water park** (p77) next door, which is free for guests. Take bus 8, 6 or 11 to the Ježica stop.

Dijaški Dom Ivana Cankarja (Map pp62-3; ☎ 474 86 00; www.dic-lj.com; Bldg B, Poljanska cesta 26; dm/s/d/tr €6/17/30/37; ☻ late Jun-late Aug; 🗶) About 1.2km east of Center in Poljane (bus 5 or 13 to Roška stop), this place has 480 beds (some of which may be available at weekends and holidays at other times of the year).

Dijaški Dom Bežigrad (Map pp62-3; ☎ 534 28 67; dd.lj-bezigrad@guest.arnes.si; Kardeljeva ploščad 28; s/d/tr €29/38/48, without bathroom dm/s/d €9/19/32; ☻ late Jun-late Aug; 🗶) This 278-bed dorm is in Bežigrad, 2km north of the train and bus stations (bus 6, 8 or 21 to Mercator stop).

Dijaški Dom Tabor (Map pp62-3; ☎ 234 88 40; www2.arnes.si/~ssljddta4; Vidovdanska cesta 7; dm €10-18, s/d €26/38; ☻ late Jun-late Aug; 🗶) In summer five colleges in Ljubljana open their *dijaški dom* to travellers but only this 300-bed one, a 10-minute walk southeast of the bus and train stations, is truly central. Enter from Kotnikova ulica.

Dijaški Dom Poljane (Map pp62-3; ☎ 300 31 37; dd-poljane@guest.arnes.si; Potočnikova ulica 3; per person €12-23; ☻ mid-Jun-Jul; 🗶) This 244-bed dorm is 300m northeast of the Ivana Cankarja dormitory; reach it on bus 5 or 13 (stop: Gornje Poljane).

Ljubljana Youth Hostel (Map pp62-3; ☎ 548 00 55; www.yh-ljubljana.com; Litijska cesta 57; dm HI member/nonmember €16.50/17.50; 🖳) This HI-affiliated hostel has six rooms with shared facilities at the BIT Center Hotel (p80). While not in the most central of locations, some 3km east of the centre, the hostel is easily reached on bus 5, 9 or 13 (stop: Emona). A boon is the attached sport centre (open 7am to 11pm), where guests get a 50% discount.

Dijaški Dom Šiška (Map pp62-3; ☎ 500 78 04; www.ddsiska.com; Aljaževa ulica 32; adult/student dm €14/11, s €28/22; ☻ Jun-late Aug; 🗶) Popular with Eastern European groups, this dormitory is northwest of Center in Šiška (bus 1, 8 or 15 to Stara Cerkev stop).

Orka (Map pp62-3; ☎ 041-444 063; www.accommodation-ljubljana.com; 3rd fl, Kotnikova ulica 25; s/d/tr/q €30/40/51/68; P 🗶 🖳) This new kid on the block is a spotlessly clean pension with three rooms of between two and four beds. It's in a new building just a hop, skip and a jump from Metelkova and the bus and train stations. There's a kitchen washing machine, free tea and coffee, and the manager can arrange any number of day trips.

Alibi Hostel (Map pp66-7; ☎ 251 12 44; www.alibi.si; Cankarjevo nabrežje 27; dm/d €20/60; 🗶 🗶 🖳) This unbelievably well-situated 110-bed hostel is changing the face of budget accommodation in Ljubljana. It's right on the Ljubljanica, in the former headquarters of the British Council, and has brightly painted, airy dorm rooms, with six to 12 wooden bunks and five doubles on four floors. The double room 13 and 14 have great views of the river. Alibi's sister hostel, the tiny **Alibi K5** (Map pp66-7; ☎ 252 49 60; Krojaška ulica 5) just around the corner takes the overspill. **Alibi Rooms** (Map pp62-3; ☎ 433 13 31; Kolarjeva ulica 30; dm €20, d €50; P 🗶 🖳), further afield in Bežigrad (bus 14), has nine rooms with between two and six beds in an old villa with a lovely garden. It's out of the way but a leafy and very chilled spot.

Most tourist offices (p67) have about 20 **private rooms** (s/d from €19/27) on its list, but only a couple are in Center and most require a bus trip north to Bežigrad or beyond. **Tour As** (Map pp66-7; ☎ 434 26 60; www.apartmaji.si; Mala ulica 8; reception ☻ 8.30am-6pm Mon-Fri, 8.30am-1pm Sat) has 35 very comfortable apartments and studios – six of which are very central – with one to three bedrooms for €58 to €118 a night.

Midrange

Vila Veselova (Map pp62-3; ☎ 059-926 721, 041-678 000; www.v-v.si; Veselova ulica 14; dm €20-25, d/tr/q €70/90/110; P 🗶 🗶 🖳) This very attractive freestanding

THE AUTHOR'S CHOICE

Celica Hostel (Map pp62-3; ☎ 230 97 00; www
.hostelcelica.com; Metelkova ulica 8; dm/s/d/tr
€17/44/48/57; P ☒ ☐ ⟨⟩) This revamped
former prison (1882) in Metelkova has 20
designer 'cells', complete with original bars,
rooms and apartments with three to seven
beds, and a popular 12-bed dorm. The all-
blue room 116 with the circular bed is like
sleeping in an eye. The ground floor is home
to three cafés (set lunch €3.15 to 5.25): a traditional Slovenian *gostilna*, a western-style
café (with two internet stations) and the
Oriental Café, with cushions, water pipes,
and shoes strictly outside. Celica has become such a landmark that there are guided
tours every day at 2pm.

villa in the centre of the museum district has
its own garden and 40 beds on three floors. It
offers mostly hostel accommodation in three
rooms with four to eight beds, but a double
and an apartment with en suite facilities make
it an attractive midrange option. Some rooms
face Park Tivoli across busy Tivolska cesta.
Reception is on first floor.

BIT Center Hotel (Map pp62-3; ☎ 548 00 55; www
.bit-center.net; Litijska cesta 57; s/d/tr €34/50/54; P ☐)
The Bit Center offers one of the best-value
deals in Ljubljana, although at 3km east of the
centre (bus 5, 9 or 13 to Emona stop) it's a bit
far from the action. Its 33 rooms are spartan
but bright and comfortable.

Park Hotel (Map pp62-3; ☎ 300 25 00, 433 00 88;
www.hotelpark.si; Tabor 9; s €39-55, d €48-71; P ☒ ☐)
A partial face-lift inside and out has turned
this 145-room tower-block hotel into an
even better-value midrange choice in central
Ljubljana. Pleasant, well-renovated standard
rooms are bright and unpretentiously well
equipped. Cheaper rooms have en suite toilet
but share showers on the corridor. Students
with ISIC cards get a 10% discount. The staff
are very friendly.

Hotel Emonec (Map pp66-7; ☎ 200 15 20; www
.hotel-emonec.com; Wolfova ulica 12; s €53, d €60-70, tr €83;
P ☒ ☐) The décor is simple and coldly
modern at this 26-room hotel, but everything
is spotless and you can't beat the central location – only steps away from Prešernov trg at
the back of a courtyard.

Vila Minka (Map pp62-3; ☎ 583 00 80; www.vila
minka.si; Kogovškova ulica 10; s/d €55/75, apt for 1/2/3/4

€70/85/100/120; P ☒ ☒ ☐ ⟨⟩) This welcoming
pension, some 4km northwest of Center in Ko-
seze, has about a dozen rooms and apartments.
It's a good choice for families or small groups
with their own wheels (though it can be reached
on bus 5 in just 20 minutes). Apartments are
positively huge, very bright and well equipped.
The glassed-in atrium, art on the walls and
tranquil surrounds are bonuses.

Pri Mraku (Map pp66-7; ☎ 421 96 00; www.daj-dam
.si; Rimska cesta 4; s €60-74.50, d €95-112, tr €116-125, ste
from €159; P ☒ ☒ ☐) Although it calls itself a
gostilna (innlike restaurant), the 'At Twilight'
is really just a smallish hotel (36 rooms) in
an old building with no lift. Almost opposite
the Križanke on Trg Francoske Revolucije,
it's ideally located for culture vultures. Only
some rooms have air-con. The welcome here
isn't always warm.

M Hotel (Map pp62-3; ☎ 513 70 00; www.m-hotel.si;
Derčeva ulica 4; s €62-83, d €95-115; P ☒ ☐ ⟨⟩) This
hotel 2km northwest of Center and set back
from noisy Celovška cesta (bus 1, 5, 8 or 15 to
Kino Šiška stop) is not much to look at from
the outside, but the 154 rooms are comfortable and airy, with all the basic mod-cons.
Park Tivoli is just round the corner.

Top End

Hotel Slon Best Western (Map pp66-7; ☎ 470 11 00;
www.hotelslon.com; Slovenska cesta 34; s €93-127, d €133-
166, tr €198, ste from €190; P ☒ ☒ ☐ ⟨⟩). In the
thick of things is the 174-room 'Hotel Elephant', with a history going back more than
four centuries. It is said that this was the spot
where a pachyderm presented to the Habsburg
emperor by an African king tarried on its
way to Vienna, although the present hotel
dates from the 20th century and has a certain Eastern Bloc elegance. There are several
categories of rooms, some with a Jacuzzi in
the bathroom.

Grand Hotel Union Executive (Map pp66-7; ☎ 308
12 70; www.gh-union.si; Miklošičeva cesta 1; s €149-191, d
€177-212, ste from €350; P ☒ ☒ ☐ ⟨⟩) This 187-
room hotel, the Art Nouveau southern wing
of a two-part hostelry, was built in 1905 and
remains the most desirable address for visitors
to Ljubljana. It has glorious public areas, including a cellar restaurant called the Unionska
Klet, which moves to the Unionski Vrt (Union
Garden) restaurant in summer. Guests get to
use the indoor swimming pool, sauna and
fitness centre on the 8th floor of the adjacent
133-room **Grand Hotel Union Business** (Map pp66-7;

THE AUTHOR'S CHOICE

Antiq Hotel (Map p66-7; ☎ 421 35 60; www.antiqhotel.si; Gornji trg 3-5; s €53-142, d €70-185; ✗ ✗ 🖳)
Well, it had to happen…Ljubljana now has its very own boutique hotel, and it's a corker. Cobbled together from a series of townhouses on the site of a Roman workshop in the heart of the Old Town, the Antiq has 14 rooms and apartments (most of which are very spacious), a small wellness centre and pretty back garden. The decor – kitsch with a smirk – may not be to everyone's taste. However, there are so many fabulous nooks and nice touches: glassed-in medieval courtyard, vaulted ceilings, two antiallergenic floors, bath towels trimmed with Slovenian lace. Among our favourite rooms are No 4 on the 2nd floor, measuring almost 42 sq metres with swooningly romantic views of the Hercules Fountain, and No 9, an even bigger two-room suite on the top floor with a terrace and fleeting glimpses of Ljubljana Castle. The two cheapest rooms have their own bathrooms on the corridor.

☎ 308 11 70; www.gh-union.si; Miklošičeva cesta 3; s €129-168, d €164-197, ste from €279; P ✗ ✗ 🖳 🖳 🖳), the Grand Union's recently renovated modern wing to the north. It caters to the business (not romance) minded.

EATING

Although there are many quality top-end restaurants, it is still possible to eat well in Ljubljana at moderate cost; even the more expensive restaurants offer an excellent-value three-course *dnevno kosilo* (set lunch) for as little as €6. For even cheaper options try the dull but functional snack bars around the stations and at the shopping mall below Trg Ajdovščina. For self-catering there are the markets and plenty of branches of the Mercator supermarket chain.

Restaurants

SLOVENIAN

Triglav (Map pp66-7; ☎ 430 10 21; Mala ulica 5; salads & soups €2.80-3.75, mains €5-9.60; ☯ 7am-10pm Mon-Fri) Primarily a lunch place, Triglav has stopped serving a mishmash of cuisines and dishes – from ramen soup and curries to tortillas – and embraced its name. It now serves traditional Slovenian dishes only.

Gostilna Pri Pavli (Map pp66-7; ☎ 425 92 75; Stari trg 21; starters €4.10-5.40, mains €5.80-10.85; ☯ 8am-11pm) A wonderful holdover from the socialist era, 'Paula's Place' is an attractive, country-style inn in an enviable location that has managed to retain its old-school style and prices. The Farmer's Feast (€22.10) is a two-person blowout.

Sokol (Falcon; Map pp66-7; ☎ 439 68 55; Ciril Metodov trg 18; starters €4.15-9.60, mains €5.80-11.20; ☯ 7am-11pm Mon-Sat, 10am-11pm Sun) In this old vaulted house near the Central Market, traditional Slovenian food is served on heavy tables by costumed waiters. Pizza is available if traditional dishes like *obara* (veal stew; €5.40) and Krvavica sausage with cabbage (€5.80) don't appeal.

Pri Škofju (At the Bishop's; Map p75; ☎ 426 45 08; Rečna ulica 8; starters €4.20-6.25, mains €4.60-13.35; ☯ 8am-midnight Mon-Fri, noon-midnight Sat & Sun) This wonderful little place in tranquil Krakovo south of the centre serves some of the best prepared local dishes and salads in Ljubljana, with an ever-changing menu. Set lunches are a bargain at €5 to €6.75.

Breskvar (Map p75; ☎ 283 88 33; Cesta na Loko 28; starters €6.25-12.50, mains €7.50-21.70; ☯ noon-10pm Mon-Fri, noon-5pm Sun) This cosy *gostilna* in Trnovo serves some of the finest home-cooking in town. The shady garden is a delight when the warmer months roll around, but we also love the retro dining room with scenes and memories of old Ljubljana.

SOUTH SLAV

Pod Rožnikom (Under Mt Rožnik; Map pp62-3; ☎ 251 34 46; Cesta na Rožnik 18; starters €2.30-4, mains €5.45-7; ☯ 10am-11pm Mon-Fri, 11am-11pm Sat & Sun) This place 'Under Mt Rožnik' (sort of) and just downwind from the zoo in Park Tivoli serves southern Slav-style grills, like *pljeskavica* (spicy meat patties) with *ajvar* (roasted red peppers, tomatoes and eggplant cooked into a purée) and starters such as *prebranac* (onions and beans cooked in an earthenware pot). Worth the trip.

Harambaša (Map p75; ☎ 041-843 106; Vrtna ulica 8; dishes €2.70-4; ☯ 10am-10pm Mon-Fri, noon-10pm Sat, noon-6pm Sun) At this small place in Krakovo you'll find authentic Bosnian – Sarajevan to be precise – cuisine served at low tables in a charming modern cottage atmosphere with quiet Balkan music and a lively crowd.

AUTHOR'S CHOICE

Aska in Volk (Map p66-7; ☎ 251 10 69; Gornji trg 4; starters €5.50-7.80, mains €7.60-18; ☒ noon-10pm Sun-Thu, noon-11pm Fri & Sat) The 'Lamb and Wolf', which takes its name from a novel by Bosnian Nobel Prize-winner Ivo Andrić (1892–1975), is an excellent choice for South Slav specialities. Effectively a café-cum-restaurant, the decor runs the gamut from 'colourful Bosnian village' to stylishly humorous, including fully laid tables suspended upside-down from the ceiling in the main dining room. The speciality here is the €12.30 lamb (there's no wolf in sight) roasted in the traditional way; it's a guaranteed winner.

Sofra (Map pp62-3; ☎ 565 68 00; Dunajska cesta 145; starters €3.35-5.85, mains €5.85-10.85; ☒ 11am-11pm Mon-Fri, noon-midnight Sat) Often touted as the most authentic Bosnian restaurant in town, there's also live music every night from September to June, when your fellow diners are likely to provide as much entertainment as those performing.

INTERNATIONAL

Pen Club (Map pp62-3; ☎ 251 41 60; Tomšičeva ulica 12; starters €2/7.50, mains €5.85-12.50; ☒ noon-11pm Mon-Fri) This artsy restaurant, at the top of old wooden steps in the headquarters of the national journalists' association, is a favourite with Slovenian literati. It just has to be one of the cosiest and most romantic eateries in town; try to bag a table on the terrace balcony.

Smrekarjev Hram (Smrekar's House; Map pp66-7; ☎ 308 19 07; Nazorjeva ulica 2; starters €5-11,80, mains €14.60-18.80; ☒ noon-11pm Mon-Fri Sep-late Jun) This Art Nouveau jewel run by the Grand Hotel Union and named after artist and illustrator Hinko Smrekar (1883–1942), famed (in certain circles) for his 'pan-Slavic' playing cards, has always been considered the poshest international restaurant in Ljubljana. It closes in summer.

Lunch Café (Map pp66-7; ☎ 425 01 18; Stari trg 9; starters €5-6.70, mains €5.85-16.30; ☒ 10am-10pm Mon Sat, noon-10pm Sun) More New York than Ljubljana, this café, from the people who brought you Pri Vitezu, is the perfect spot for a late breakfast (around €2.50), even later brunch (€7.50) and nosh until late. Pasta dishes (€3.75 to €6.70) are notable.

Manna (Map p75; ☎ 283 52 94; Eipprova ulica 1a; starters €6.70-10.40, mains €10-17.50, ☒ noon-midnight Mon-Sat) Festooned across the front of this canal-side restaurant in Trnovo is the slogan 'Manna – Bžanske Jedi na Zemlji' (Manna – Heavenly Food on Earth). It didn't feel quite like paradise the last time we visited, but the decor is stylish, there's a wonderful covered inner courtyard for dining almost al fresco and the setting is pretty nice.

Pri Vitezu (Map pp66-7; ☎ 426 60 58; Breg 18-20; starters €6.70-14.20, mains €11.70-20; ☒ noon-11pm Mon-Sat) Located on the left bank of the Ljubljanica River, 'At the Knight' is the place for a special meal (Mediterranean-style grills and Adriatic fish dishes), whether in the vaulted cellar dining rooms or adjoining wine bar.

JB (Map pp62-3; ☎ 433 13 58, 474 72 19; Miklošičeva cesta 17; starters €8.35-12.50, mains €16-25; ☒ 11am-midnight Mon-Fri, 6pm-midnight Sat) Old-world charm, a hybrid Slovenian-Mediterranean-French menu, a top-notch wine list and very stylish decor have made this restaurant one of the most popular in town for a fancy meal.

ITALIAN & MEDITERRANEAN

Mirje (Map pp62-3; ☎ 426 60 15; Tržaška cesta 5; starters €3.35-6.25, mains €5.40-8.35; ☒ 10am-10pm Mon-Fri, noon-10pm Sat) Just a few blocks southwest of the centre, this little trattoria serves a wide range of pizzas and pastas (€3.75 to €6.25), as well as a few more ambitions main courses. The decor – light wood furniture, checked tablecloths and blue-and-white trim – is upbeat and welcoming.

Julija (Map pp62-3; ☎ 425 64 63; Stari trg 9; starters €5-7.50, mains €7.50-15.85; ☒ 8am-midnight Mon-Thu & Sat, 8am-1am Fri, 10am-11pm Sun) Julija serves up decent risottos and pastas either outside on the pavement terrace or in a Delft-tiled backroom behind a café decorated with 1920s prints.

Like most European capitals nowadays, Ljubljana is awash in pizzerias, but the pick of the crop include the following:

Ljubljanski Dvor (Ljubljana Court; Map pp66-7; ☎ 251 65 55; Dvorni trg 1; pizza €4-9.60; ☒ 10am-midnight Mon-Sat, noon-11pm Sun) Overlooks the Ljubljanica.

Pizzerija Foculus (Map pp66-7; ☎ 251 56 43; Gregorčičeva ulica 3; pizza €4-6.65; ☒ 10am-midnight Mon-Fri, 11am-midnight Sat & Sun) Boasts a vaulted ceiling painted with spring and autumn leaves.

Trta (Grapevine; Map p75; ☎ 426 50 66; Grudnovo nabrežje 21; pizza €4.40-7.35; ☒ 11am-10.30pm Mon-Fri, noon-10.30pm Sat) On the right bank of the Ljubljanica opposite Trnovo.

Tramvaj Ekspress (Map pp62-3; ☎ 425 47 82; Trg Mladinskih Delovnih Brigad 10; pizza €3.35-6.70; ⏰ 10am-9pm Mon-Fri Jun-Jul, 10am-5pm Mon-Fri Aug-May) Eat your pizza in a vintage (c 1958) tramcar from Prague.

FRENCH

Chez Eric (Map pp66-7; ☎ 251 28 39; Mestni trg 3; starters €5.75-11.50, €15.65-19.40; ⏰ noon-4pm & 7-11pm Mon-Sat) This tastefully decorated restaurant has a short but well chosen menu. The three-course set dinner is €25.

SPANISH & MEXICAN

Cantina Mexicana (Map pp66-7; ☎ 426 93 25; Knafljev prehod 3; starters €2.70-3.75, mains €7.10-13.80; ⏰ 11am-midnight Sun-Thu, 11am-1am Fri & Sat) The capital's most stylish Mexican restaurant has an eye-catching red-and-blue exterior and hacienda-like decor, with sofas and lanterns inside. The fajitas (€7.50 to €11.70) are great.

Don Felipe (Map pp62-3; ☎ 434 38 62; Streliška ulica 22; tapas €3.85-5.40, mains €7-8.25; ⏰ noon-midnight) Southeast of Krekov trg, Don Felipe was Ljubljana's first Spanish restaurant and it remains the best. It specialises in tapas and paella (€8.25) and has some striking decor.

Mexico 1867 (Map pp62-3; ☎ 438 24 50; Medvedova cesta 18; mains €8.35-13.35; ⏰ noon-midnight Mon-Sat, noon-midnight Sun Sep-May) Mexico 1867's lurid colours, unappetizing scenes of civil war scenes and sombreros notwithstanding, the huge menus offers some authentic Mexican favourites, including nachos (€5 to €5.85), *chimichangas* (€6.70 to €7.50), tacos and fajitas.

MIDDLE EASTERN

Yildiz Han (Map p75; ☎ 426 57 17; Karlovška cesta 19; starters €2.70-5, mains €6.90-10.20; ⏰ noon-midnight Tue-Sun) If Turkish is your thing, head for this mom and pop-run restaurant, which features belly dancing and/or live Turkish music on Friday night.

Ali Baba (Map pp62-3; ☎ 230 17 87, 051-234 066; Poljanska cesta 11; mains €7.10-7.75; ⏰ 7am-11pm Mon-Fri, 10am-10pm Sat) Carpets and low brass tables decorate this cosy little restaurant, whose Iranian and Indian dishes are popular with journalists and students.

CHINESE & JAPANESE

Kitajska Zvezda (Map p75; ☎ 425 88 24; Hrenova ulica 19; starters €1.50-2.45, mains €5-6.45; ⏰ 11am-11pm) If you're looking for a fix of rice or noodles, try the 'Chinese Star' on the river just south of

the Old Town. Szechuan dishes, including the *mapo doufu* (tofu with garlic and chilli) are quite good.

Shanghai (Map pp62-3; ☎ 234 71 36; Poljanska cesta 14; starters €1.50-2.50, mains €6-9.60; ⏰ 11am-11pm) Shanghai has authentic Sichuan and Cantonese dishes – no Shanghainese ones that we could find – and a user-friendly picture menu. It's pretty toned-down fare so aficionados should stick with rice and noodle dishes (€4.20 to €5.45).

Sushimama (Map pp66-7; ☎ 426 91 25, 040-702 070; Wolfova ulica 12; mixed sushi €10.75-15, mixed sashimi €12-16.25; ⏰ 11am-11pm Mon-Sat) Ljubljana's only Japanese sushi restaurant has simple, restful decor and very fresh fish.

SEAFOOD

Taverna Tatjana (Map pp66-7; ☎ 421 00 87, 041-707 900; Gornji trg 38; starters €5-8.35, mains €8.35-20.90; ⏰ 5pm-midnight) Looking like an old-world wooden-beamed cottage pub with a nautical theme, this is actually a rather exclusive fish restaurant with a lovely (and protected) back courtyard for the warmer months.

Gostilna As (Map pp66-7; ☎ 425 88 22; Čopova ulica 5a, enter from Knafljev prehod; starters €7.50-16.70, mains €16.70-24.60; ⏰ noon-midnight) The 'Ace Inn', in the passage linking Wolfova ulica and Slovenska cesta, is the place for a special occasion, with seafood, a good wine list, and a few classic Slovene dishes dominating the menu. You can also enter from Slovenska cesta 30. The **As Lounge** in both the cellar and a glassed-in terrace is much more informal, with sandwiches (€4.15 to €6.25), salads (€4.15 to €7), and a few less elaborate main courses (€8.30 to €12.50).

VEGETARIAN

Ajdovo Zrno (Map pp66-7; ☎ 230 16 15, 041 690 478; Trubarjeva cesta 7; soups & sandwiches €1.60-2, set lunch €3.75-5.75; ⏰ 10am-7pm Mon-Fri) A relatively recent arrival on the Ljubljana dining scene, 'Buckwheat Grain' serves soups, sandwiches, fried vegetables and lots of different salads (self-service: €2.40 to €3). And they have terrific, freshly squeezed juices, including the unusual rose-petal juice with lemon. Enter from Mali trg.

Vegedrom (Map pp66-7; ☎ 513 26 42; Vodnikova cesta 35; soups & salads €2.10-3.35, dishes €4.20-9.80; ⏰ 9am-10pm Mon-Fri, noon-10pm Sat) Most eating places (including pizzerias) in Ljubljana have at least a couple of veggie dishes on the menu, but the only specialist vegetarian restaurant in town is this appealing if somewhat pricey vegan place at the northeastern edge of Park Tivoli. The platters for two are good value at €17.50 to €21, and there's a salad bar and some Indian-inspired dishes (€3.35 to €4.10).

Quick Eats

Delikatesa Ljubljanski Dvor (Map pp66-7; ☎ 426 93 27; Kongresni trg 11; pizza slices €1.20-1.70; ☺ 9am-midnight Mon-Sat) Locals queue for huge, bargain slices of pizzas, salads, and grilled vegetables sold by weight to take away or eat on the spot.

Paninoteka (Map pp66-7; ☎ 059-018 445, 041-529 824; Jurčičev trg 3; soups & toasted sandwiches €2.10-3.35; ☺ 8am-1am Mon-Sat, 9am-11pm Sun) Healthy sandwich creations on olive ciabatta are sold here to take away or to eat outside. Located in a lovely little square which has scenic views of the castle.

Restavracija 2000 (Map pp62-3; ☎ 476 68 00; Trg Republike 1; dishes €2.30-3, set lunch €6.25; ☺ 9am-7pm Mon-Fri, 9am- 4pm Sat) In the basement of the Maximarket department store, this glass and chrome self-service eatery is surprisingly upbeat, and just the ticket if you want something quick while visiting Ljubljana's main museums.

Hot Horse Trubarjeva (Map pp62-3; Trubarjeva cesta 31; snacks & burgers €2.50-3.35; ☺ 8am-1am Mon-Sat, noon-1am Sun); Park Tivoli (Park Tivoli; ☺ 24hr) These two places exist to supply Ljubljančani with a favourite treat: horse burgers. The branch in Park Tivoli is just down the hill from the Museum of Contemporary History (p74).

Ribca (Map pp66-7; ☎ 425 15 44; Adamič-Lundrovo nabrežje 1; dishes €2.70-6.70; ☺ 7am-4pm Mon-Fri, 7am-2pm Sat) This basement seafood bar below the Plečnik Colonnade in Pogačarjev trg serves tasty fried squid, sardines and herrings to hungry market-goers.

Kebapči (Map pp62-3; Trubarjeva cesta 47; döner €3.15-3.75, döner plate €4.40-5; ☺ 9am-1am Mon-Sat, 3pm-1am Sun) For a taste of the Middle East, try this little hole-in-the-wall up an alley off Trubarjeva cesta.

The **burek stand** (Map pp62-3; Pražakova ulica 2; burek €1.90; pizza slice €1.50; ☺ 24hr) southwest of the train and bus stations serves some of the best cheese, meat and apple *burek* in town. Another good spot for the same thing is **Nobel Burek** (Miklošičeva cesta 30; burek €1.90, pizza €1.50; ☺ 24hr).

Markets & Self-Catering

Convenient supermarkets include **Mercator** (Map pp62-3; Slovenska cesta 55; ☺ 7am-9pm) and **Maxi-market** (Map pp62-3; basement, Trg Republike 1; ☺ 9am-9pm Mon-Fri, 8am-5pm Sat) below the department store of that name. The latter has the largest selection of food and wine in the city centre as well as a bakery. Opposite the train and bus stations, **Noč in Dan** (Map pp62-3; Trg OF 13; ☺ 24hr) is a variety store open 'Day and Night'.

Ljubljana's adjoining **open-air markets** (Map pp66-7; Pogačarjev trg & Vodnikov trg; ☺ 8am-6pm Mon-Fri, 6am-5pm Sat Jun-Sep, 6am-4pm Mon-Sat Oct-May) opposite the cathedral sell mostly fresh fruit and vegetables, though some also sell seasonal goods such as wild mushrooms, honey, chestnuts, beeswax and fresh herbs.

To the west the **covered market** (Map pp66-7; Pogačarjev trg 4; ☺ 7am-2pm Mon-Wed & Sat, 7am-4pm Thu-Fri) on the ground floor of the Seminary has a superb range of meats, charcuterie, fish and dairy products. The nearby **fish market** (Map pp66-7; Adamič-Lundrovo nabrežje 1; ☺ 7am-4pm Mon-Fri, 7am-2pm Sat) is on the lower level of the Plečnik Colonnade overlooking the river.

DRINKING

Few European cities of comparable size to Ljubljana offer such a dizzying array of drinking options, whether your poison is beer, wine and spirits or tea and coffee. In Ljubljana there's a fine line between cafés, most of which serve food as well as drinks, and pubs and bars, particularly in the warmer months, when tables of both line the pavements.

Cafés & Teahouses

Kavarna Zvezda (Map pp66-7, ☎ 421 90 90; Kongresni trg 4 & Wolfova ulica 14; ☺ 7am-11pm Mon-Sat, 10am-8pm Sun) The 'Star Café' is celebrated for its shop-made cakes, especially *skutina pečena* (€2), an eggy cheesecake.

Café Antico (Map pp66-7; ☎ 425 13 39; Stari trg 17; ☺ 10am-midnight Mon-Sat, 11am-10pm Sun) With frescoed ceilings and retro-style furniture, this is the place for a quiet tête-à-tête over a cup of coffee or glass of wine.

Čajna Hiša (Map pp66-7; ☎ 421 24 44; Stari trg 3; ☺ 9am-11pm Mon-Fri, 9am-3pm & 6-10pm Sat) If you take your cuppa seriously come here; the appropriately named 'Teahouse' offers a wide range of green and black teas and fruit tisanes for €1.60 to €3.15 a pot; it sells the leaves, too.

Le Petit Café (Map pp66-7; ☎ 251 25 75; Trg Francoske Revolucije 4; ☻ 7.30am-3am Sun-Thu, 9am-midnight Fri & Sat) Just opposite the Križanke, this pleasant, studenty place offers great coffee and a wide range of breakfast goodies (€2.90 to €4.20), lunches and light meals.

Kafeterija Lan (Map pp66-7; Gallusovo nabrežje 27; ☻ 9am-midnight Mon-Thu, 9am-1am Fri & Sat, 10am-1am Sun) This little greener-than-green café-bar on the river below Cobbler Bridge is something of a hipster/gay magnet.

Slaščičarna Pri Vodnjaku (Map pp66-7; ☎ 425 07 12; Stari trg 30; ☻ 8am-midnight) For all kinds of chocolate of the-ice cream and drinking kind, the 'Confectionery by the Fountain' will surely satisfy – there are 32 different flavours (€0.85 per scoop) as well as teas (€1.50) and fresh juices (€1.05 to €3.35).

Trubadur (Map pp66-7; ☎ 434 35 30; Trubarjeva cesta 31; ☻ 7.30am-10pm Mon-Fri, 7.30am-3pm Sat) This little *sladki bar* (sweet bar) with the badly punned name (see street name) serves some of the best cakes on the left bank.

Café Galerija (Map pp66-7; ☎ 426 03 27; Mestni trg 5; ☻ 9am-1am Mon-Sat, 9am-10pm Sun) This Arabesque-style café, with brass tables, coloured glass and cosy nooks is hidden behind the City Gallery (p73).

Grajska Kavarna (Map pp66-7; ☎ 439 41 40; Ljubljana Castle, Grajska planota 1; 9am-midnight May-Sep, ☻ 9am-11pm) You wouldn't go out of your way to reach the 'Castle Café', but if you're on the hill and thirsty or peckish, it's a decent pit stop. Think 1970s concrete café.

Abecedarium Cafe (Map pp66-7; ☎ 426 95 14; Ribji trg 2; ☻ 7am-1am) Ensconced in the oldest house (1528) in Ljubljana and one-time residence of the writer Primož Trubar (p34), this place oozes atmosphere.

Slamič KavaČaj (Map pp62-3; ☎ 433 82 33; Kersnikova ulica 1; ☻ 7.30am-10pm Mon-Thu, 7.30am-9pm Fri, 9am-2pm Sun) This gem of a place serves excellent tea and coffee, and sells the stuff (and accoutrements) as well. There's a smokers' area upstairs.

Ambiente (☎ 430 27 56; Čufarjeva ulica 2; ☻ 7am-11pm Mon-Fri, 9am-11pm Sat) This stylish café-cum-bistro, hidden down a narrow side street just east of Miklošičeva cesta, caters to a diverse crowd throughout the day. Food is good too.

Pubs & Bars

Kavarna Pločnik (Map pp66-7; Prešernov trg 1; ☻ 7am-1am Apr-Oct) With the distinctive name of 'Pavement', this roped-off café-bar on the southern side of Prešernov trg is one of the most popular places for a drink. Sit outside and watch the passing parade or listen to some live music (most nights).

Maček (Map pp66-7; ☎ 425 37 91; Krojaška ulica 5; ☻ 9am-1am) *The* place to be seen on a sunny summer afternoon, the 'Cat' is Pločnik's rival on the right bank of the Ljubljanica. Happy hour is between 4pm and 7pm daily.

Cutty Sark (Map pp66-7; ☎ 425 14 77; Knafljev prehod 1; ☻ 9am-1am Mon-Sat, noon-1am Sun) A pleasant and well-stocked nautically themed pub in the courtyard behind Wolfova ulica 6, the Cutty Sark is a congenial place for a *pivo* (beer) or glass of *vino* (wine).

Dvorni Bar (Map pp66-7; ☎ 251 12 57; Dvorni trg 1; ☻ 8am-1am) This wine bar is an excellent place to taste Slovenia vintages; they've got 100 different types in stock and frequently schedule promotions and wine tastings.

Pr'skelet (Map pp66-7; ☎ 252 77 99; Ključavničarska ulica 5; ☻ 10am-3am) OK, it might be something of a one-joke wonder but you'll shake, rattle and roll at this skeleton-themed basement bar, where cocktails are two for one throughout the day.

Salon (Map pp66-7; ☎ 439 87 64; Trubarjeva cesta 23; ☻ 9am-1am Mon & Tue, 9am-3am Wed-Sat, 10am-1am Sun) Salon is a dazzling designer-kitsch cocktail bar featuring gold ceilings, faux leopard armchairs, heavy burgundy and gold drapes, and excellent cocktails (€4.20 to €6.25) and shooters (€3.75 to €4.20).

Žmavc (Map pp62-3; ☎ 251 0324; Rimska cesta 21; ☻ 7.30am-1am Mon-Sat, 8am-1am Sun) A super-popular student hangout west of Slovenska cesta, it has comic strip scenes and figures running halfway up the walls.

Šank Pub (Map p75; ☎ 281 11 71; Eipprova ulica 19; ☻ 6am-midnight Sun-Thu, 7am-1am Fri & Sat) Down in studenty Trnovo, this raggedy little place has pleasant outdoor tables beside the canal. It's just down from the Sax (p87).

Klub Metropol (Map pp62-3; ☎ 438 03 00; Kersnikova ulica 6; ☻ 8am-10pm Mon-Fri) This ultramodern bar with multicoloured comfy chairs and a groovy glass bar is almost too good for the students who frequent it and the hackers from Kiber Pipa (p64) downstairs.

Vinoteka Movia (Map pp66-7; ☎ 425 54 48; Mestni trg 2; ☻ noon-midnight Mon-Sat) If you're more interested in the grape than the grain, hop over to this excellent wine bar where, with due ceremony and ritual, you can taste your way through some award-winning Slovenian wines (€3.75 to €8.35 for 0.1L). They do retail as well: buy a bottle of their white Veliko Belo (€23) or red Veliko Rdeče (€27), a blend of Cabernet Sauvignon, Merlot and Pinot Noir.

BiKoFe (Map pp66-7; Židovska steza 2; ☼ 7am-1am Mon-Fri, 10am-1pm Sat, 6pm-1am Sun) A favourite with the hipster crowd, this small, smoky bar has mosaic tables, student art on the walls, soul and jazz on the stereo, and a giant water pipe on the menu for that long, lingering smoke (€3.50). Cool but a bit pretentious. There's a shady outdoor patio.

If you're looking to continue bending your elbow into the wee hours, head for **Čarli** (Map pp66-7; ☎ 232 81 83; Petkovškovo nabrežje 21; ☼ 9am-3am), a convivial, socialist-era boozer along the river east of Prešernov trg that its regulars treat like a second home; **Pod Skalco** (Under the Rock; Map pp66-7; ☎ 426 58 20; Gosposka ulica 19; ☼ 6.30am-3am Mon-Thu, 5pm-3am Fri-Sun) due south of the City Museum; or **Druga Pomoč** (Map pp62-3; ☎ 431 32 77; Šmartinska cesta 3; ☼ 6am-3am), a quintessential dive bar called 'Second Aid' and just north of the city's emergency hospital.

ENTERTAINMENT

Ljubljana Life (www.ljubljanalife.com) is a free quarterly magazine with practical information and listings. It's distributed free at the airport and in hotels and the tourist offices. *Where to? in Ljubljana*, available from the tourist offices, lists cultural and sporting events.

Nightclubs

D'Place (Map pp62-3; ☎ 040-626 901; www.club-dplace .com, in Slovene; Šmartinska cesta 152, BTC Shopping Centre; ☼ 10pm-6am Thu-Sat) This new club with different themed evenings (eg hip-hop and R'n'B on Saturday) in the Kolosej multiplex cinema at BTC City Shopping Centre has been making quite a splash since it opened in mid-2006.

Funfactory (Map p75; ☎ 428 96 90; Industrijska Cona Rudnik, Jurčkova cesta 224; ☼ 9pm-dawn Thu-Sat) Ljubljana's biggest club is hidden in a shopping centre opposite the Leclerc Hypermarket (bus 3 to the end) in the far southeast suburbs.

Global (Map pp66-7; ☎ 426 90 20; www.global.si, in Slovene; Tomšičeva ulica 2; ☼ 9am-5pm Mon-Sat) This retro cocktail bar on the 6th floor of the Nama department store becomes a popular dance venue nightly and attracts a chi-chi crowd. Take the bouncer-guarded lift in the passageway linking Cankarjeva ulica and Tomšičeva ulica.

Klub K4 (Map pp62-3; ☎ 438 03 04; www.klubk4 .org in Slovene; Kersnikova ulica 4; ☼ 10pm-4am) This evergreen club in the basement of the Student Organisation of the University of Ljubljana (Študentska Organizacija Univerze Ljubljani; ŠOU) features rave-electronic music Friday and Saturday, with other styles of music weeknights, and a popular gay and lesbian night on Sunday (p87). It closes when university breaks up.

Bachus Center Club (Map pp66-7; ☎ 241 82 44; www .bachus-center.com; Kongresni trg 3; ☼ 10pm-5am Mon-Sat) There's something for everyone at Bachus, it also has a restaurant and bar-lounge and attracts a mixed crowd.

As Pub (Map pp66-7; ☎ 425 88 22; Čopova ulica 5a but enter from Knafljev prehod; ☼ 7am-3am Wed-Sat) DJs transform this candle-lit basement bar, hidden beneath an upmarket fish restaurant, into a pumping, crowd-pulling nightclub four nights a week.

KUD France Prešeren (Map p75; ☎ 283 22 88; www .kud-fp.si; Karunova ulica 14; ☼ 9am-up to 1am) This 'noninstitutional culture and arts society' in Trnovo stages concerts as well as performances, literary events, exhibitions, workshops and so on, on most nights.

Slovenia, which cannot (it must be said) boast a truly rich tradition of indigenous music often looks to its former co-tenants, and music of the republics of the late Yugoslavia is all the rage at two clubs: **Tramontana** (Map pp66-7; ☎ 041-767 447; Nazorjeva ulica 6; ☼ 10am-5am Wed, 9pm-5am Thu-Sat), celebrated for its *Balkan žur* (Balkan party), and **Katastrofa** (Map pp62-3; ☎ 431 51 55; www.petica.si, in Slovene; Celovška cesta 25; ☼ 8pm-5am Fri & Sat) in the Tivoli Recreation Centre in Park Tivoli.

For an evening of alternative entertainment and partying, try **Metelkova Mesto** (Map pp62-3; btwn Metelkova ulica & Maistrova ul; www.metelkova.org). 'Metelkova Town', an ex-army garrison taken over by squatters after independence, is now a free-living commune – a miniature version of Copenhagen's Christiania. In this two-courtyard block, half a dozen idiosyncratic venues hide behind gaily tagged doorways, coming to life generally after midnight Thursday to Saturday. Entering the main 'city gate' from Masarykova cesta, the building to the right houses **Gala Hala** (www.galahala.com, in Slovene) with live bands and club nights, **Channel Zero** (punk, hardcore) and **100% Mizart**. Easy to miss in the first building to the left are **Tiffany** (below) for gay men and **Monokel** (below) for lesbians. Beyond the first courtyard to the southwest, well-hidden **Klub Gromka** (folk, live concerts) is beneath the bodyless heads. Next door is **Menza pri Koritu** (performance) and the idiosyncratic **Čajnica pri Mariči** (psycho-blues). Details are usually thin on the ground, the venues change and opening times are erratic; visit the Metelkova website or just show up.

Gay & Lesbian Venues

Ljubljana may not be the most gay-friendly city in Central Europe, but there are a few decent options. For general information and advice, ring **K4 Roza** (☎ 430 47 40; Kersnikova ulica 4), which is made up of the gay and lesbian branches of Škuc (Študentski Kulturni Center or Student Cultural Centre) or the gay and lesbian hotline **GALfon** (☎ 432 40 89; ⏰ 7-10pm).

K4 Roza (☎ 431 70 10, 438 03 04; Kersnikova ulica 4; ⏰ 10pm-6am Sun Sep-Jun) A popular spot for both gays and lesbians alike is this Sunday night disco at Klub K4 (p86). The music takes no risks, but the crowd is lively and friendly.

Tiffany (Map pp62-3; www.ljudmila.org/siqrd/tiffany in Slovene); Masarykova cesta 24; ⏰ 10pm-1am Wed & Thu, 10am-4pm Fri & Sat, 10pm-midnight Sun). This friendly gay and lesbian café-bar is in the small building to the left (east) as you enter Metelkova Mesto.

Monokel (Map pp62-3; www.klubmonokel.com, in Slovene; ⏰ 9pm-1am Fri) For lesbians, Monokel is in the same building as Tiffany.

Classical Music, Opera & Dance

Cankarjev Dom (Cankar House; Map pp62-3; ☎ 241 71 00; www.cd-cc.si; Prešernova cesta 10) Ljubljana's premier cultural and conference centre has two large auditoriums (the Gallus Hall has perfect acoustics) and a dozen smaller performance spaces offering a remarkable smorgasbord of performance arts (up to 1000 cultural events a year). The **ticket office** (☎ 241 72 99; ⏰ 11am-1pm & 3-8pm Mon-Fri, 11am-1pm Sat & 1hr before performance) is in the subway below Maximarket supermarket on the opposite side of Trg Republike.

Philharmonic Hall (Filharmonija; Map pp66-7; ☎ 241 08 00; www.filharmonija.si; Kongresni trg 10). Home to the Slovenian Philharmonic Orchestra, this smaller but more atmospheric venue stages concerts and hosts performances of the **Slovenian Chamber Choir** (Slovenski Komorni Zbor; ☎ 231 18 92), which was founded in 1991. Buy tickets from the **ticket office** (☎ 241 08 10; Hribarjevo nabrežje;

⏰ 4-6pm Mon-Sat) in the rear of the building facing the river.

Slovenian National Opera and Ballet Theatre (Slovensko Narodno Gledališče Opera in Balet; Map pp62-3; ☎ 241 17 40, box office 241 17 64, 031-696 600; www.operainbalet-lj.si; Župančičeva ulica 1; ⏰ 1-5pm Mon-Fri, 11am-1pm Sat & 1hr before performance) This historic theatre stages both opera and ballet.

Križanke (Map pp66-7; ☎ 241 60 00, box office 241 60 28; www.festival-lj.si; Trg Francoske Revolucije 1-2; ⏰ 10am-1.30pm & 4-8pm Mon-Fri, 10am-1pm Sat & 1hr before performance) The outdoor theatre at this sprawling 18th-century monastery hosts the events of the Ljubljana Summer Festival (p78). The smaller **Knights Hall** (Viteška Dvorana) is the venue for chamber concerts.

Rock, Pop & Jazz

Orto Bar (Map pp62-3; ☎ 232 16 74; www.orto-bar.com; Grabolličeva ulica 1; ⏰ 6pm-4am Mon-Thu, 5pm-6am Fri & Sat, 6pm-2am Sun) A popular bar for late-night drinking and dancing with occasional live music, Orto is just five minutes' walk from Metelkova.

Jazz Club Gajo (Map pp66-7; ☎ 425 32 06; Beethovnova ulica 8; www.jazzclubgajo.com; ⏰ 11am-2am Mon-Fri, 7pm-midnight Sat & Sun) Just up from the Parliament building, Gajo is the city's premier venue for live jazz and attracts both local and international talent, usually midweek or on Friday at 8.30pm. Jam sessions are at 8.30pm Monday.

Sax Pub (Map p75; ☎ 283 90 09; Eipprova ulica 7; ⏰ noon-1am Mon, 10am-1am Tue-Sat, 4-10pm Sun) In Trnovo and decorated with colourful murals and graffiti inside and out, Sax has live jazz at 9.30pm on Thursday.

Kavarna Geonavtik (Map pp66-7; ☎ 252 70 27; Kongresni trg 1; ⏰ 7am-2am Mon-Fri, 8am-2am Sat) This café-bar, behind the bookshop of the same name (p61), sometimes has jazz sessions.

Cinemas

Slovenska Kinoteka (Slovenian Cinematheque; Map pp62-3; ☎ 434 25 20; www.kinoteka.si in Slovene; Miklošičeva cesta 28) shows archival art and classic films whereas its sister-cinema **Kino Dvor** (Court Cinema; Map pp62-3; ☎ 434 25 48; www.kinodvor.si, in Slovene; Kolodvorska ulica 13) nearby more contemporary films. Screenings are usually at 6pm, 8pm and 10pm and cost €4.

Foreign films are never dubbed into Slovene but are shown in their original language with subtitles. For the latest films (€3.75 to €4.60), head for any of the cinemas listed below.

Kolosej (Map pp62-3; ☎ 520 55 00; www.kolosej.si, in Slovene; Šmartinska cesta 152) Twelve-screen multiplex in BTC City shopping centre 3.5km northeast of Center with more than 3300 seats.

Kino Komuna (Map pp66-7; ☎ 421 84 00; Cankarjeva cesta 1) In the passageway.

Kinoklub Vič (Map pp62-3; ☎ 241 84 10; Trg Mladinskih Delovnih Brigad 6) Southwest of Center.

Theatre

Ljubljana has half a dozen theatres so there should be something on stage for everyone. Slovenian theatre is usually quite visual with a lot of mixed media, so you don't always have to speak the lingo to enjoy the production. In addition to concerts and other musical events, **Cankarjev Dom** (p87) regularly stages theatrical productions.

Slovenian National Drama Theatre (Slovensko Narodno Gledališče Drama; Map pp66-7; ☎ 252 14 62, box office 252 15 11; www.sngdrama-lj.si; Erjavčeva cesta 1; box office 2-5pm & 6-8pm Mon-Fri, 6pm-time of performance Sat) Built as a German-language theatre in 1911, this wonderful Art Nouveau building is home to the national theatre company.

Slovenian Youth Theatre (Slovensko Mladinsko Gledališče; Map pp62-3; ☎ 231 06 10, 230 12 86; www .mladinsko-gl.si; Festivalna Dvorana, Vilharjeva cesta 11; box office 10am-noon & 3.30-5.30 Mon-Fri, 10am-noon Sat) Established in 1955 as the first professional theatre for children and youth in Slovenia, this company has staged some highly acclaimed contemporary productions in the Festival Hall north of the train station.

Glej Theatre (Gledališče Glej; Map pp66-7; ☎ 421 92 40, 251 66 79; Gregorčičeva ulica 3) Glej has been Ljubljana's foremost experimental theatre, working with companies that include Betontanc (dance) and Grejpfrut (drama). It stages about five productions a year.

Ljubljana Puppet Theatre (Lutkovno Gledališče Ljubljana; Map pp62-3; ☎ 300 09 70, box office 300 09 82; www.lgl.si; Krekov trg 2; box office 4-6pm Tue-Fri, 10am-noon Sat & 1hr before performance) The Ljubljana Puppet Theatre stages its own shows throughout the year and hosts Lutke, the biennial International Puppet Festival (Mednarodni Lutkovni Festival), in September.

Sport

Now that Ljubljana's Central Stadium (Centralni Stadion; Vodovodna cesta 20) just off Dunajska cesta in Bežigrad and designed by Jože Plečnik in 1925 has closed, matches are held at the nearby **ŽSD Ljubljana Stadium** (Map pp62-3; ☎ 438 64

70; Milčinskega ulica 2). Those wanting to watch the national team play, however, must now travel to Celje (p248) and the spanking new Celje Sport Park (Športni Park) multiuse stadium there. The capital's First Division team is NK Factor Ljubljana. For basketball, ice hockey and volleyball, the venue is the **Hala Tivoli** (Tivoli Hall; Map pp62-3; ☎ 431 51 55; Celovška cesta 25) sport centre in Park Tivoli.

SHOPPING

Ljubljana has plenty on offer in the way of folk art, antiques, music, wine and, increasingly, fashion. If you want everything under one roof, head for **BTC City** (☎ 585 11 00; www.btc.si; Šmartinska cesta 152; 9am-8pm Mon-Sat), a sprawling mall with scores of shops in Moste, northeast of Center. It can be reached on bus 2, 7 and 17.

Art & Antiques

Worth checking out is the weekly **antiques flea market** (Cankarjevo nabrežje; Map pp66-7; 8am-12pm Sun) held year-round on the embankment between Triple and Cobbler Bridges. A summer art market called **Ljubljana Montmartre** (Pogačarjev trg; 9am-4pm Sat Jun-Sep) near the Central Market has paintings and ceramics.

Antika Ferjan (Map pp66-7; ☎ 426 18 15; 1st fl, Mestni trg 21; 9am-7pm Mon-Fri, 10am-2pm Sat) Ferjan is a large shop with Slovenian and other European art and antique glass, furniture and clocks.

Carniola Antiqua (Map pp66-7; ☎ 231 63 97; Trubarjeva cesta 9; 10am-1pm & 4-7pm Mon-Fri, 10am-1pm Sat) This is among the best small antique galleries in town.

Galerija Fortuna (☎ 425 01 87; Gornji trg 1; 10am-1pm & 4-8pm Mon-Fri, 10am-1pm Sat) Packed into this lovely shop are some really beautiful antiques, especially glassware from the 1920s and other delightful Art Nouveau treasures. Prices are pretty reasonable too.

Trubarjev Antikvariat (Map pp66-7; ☎ 244 26 83; Mestni trg 25; 8.30am-1.30pm & 3.30-7.30 Mon-Fri, 8.30am-1.30pm Sat) Come here for antiquarian and second-hand books.

Clothing & Fashion

Almira Sadar (Map pp62-3; ☎ 430 13 29; Tavčarjeva ulica 6; 9am-7pm Mon-Fri, 9am-1pm Sat) On offer here are uniquely patterned women's foundation pieces and accessories in natural materials from one of Slovenia's leading designers.

Torbice Grošelj (Map pp62-3; ☎ 231 89 84; Tavčarjeva ulica 6; 8.30am-12.30pm & 3.30-7pm Mon-Fri, 8.30am-

12.30pm Sat) This shop just next door sells handbags by designer Marjeta Grošelj in top-quality leather.

Recently, the southern reaches of the Old Town have seen a number of high-quality fashion boutiques open up, including the four listed below.

Akultura (Map pp66-7; ☎ 425 17 00; www.akultura .si; Stari trg 11a; ☼ 10am-7pm Mon-Fri, 10am-1pm Sat) Skirts, jackets and gloves in multicoloured, butter-soft leathers. In summer, silk makes an appearance.

Devetka (Map pp66-7; ☎ 426 95 90; Gornji trg 1; ☼ 10am-1pm & 4-7pm Mon-Fri, 10am-1pm) Women's foundation pieces and bed linens in bold geometrical prints.

Katarina Silk (Map pp66-7; ☎ 425 00 10; Gornji trg 5; ☼ 10am-7pm Mon-Fri, 10am-2pm Sat) Silk scarves so fine they'll pass through a ring and unique costume jewellery.

Butanoga (Map pp66-7; ☎ 425 98 88; Levstikov trg 8; ☼ 1-8pm Mon-Fri, 9.30am-1.30pm Sat) Now we've seen shoes and we've worn shoes but we've never – ever – seen anything like these kind by Matjaž Vlah.

Folk Art & Gifts

Darila Rokus (Rokus Gifts; ☎ 234 77 17; www.darila.com; Gosposvetska cesta 2; ☼ 9am-noon & 2-7pm Mon-Fri, 9am-noon Sat) This stunning shop is the main outlet for a company manufacturing high-end glassware and crockery designed by the likes of Oskar Kagoj and Zora Stančič, reproductions of Plečnik's sketches and Trubar's original catechism, fine folk art and vintage wines.

Skrina (Trousseau; Map pp66-7; ☎ 425 51 61; www .skrina.si; Breg 8; ☼ 9am-7pm Mon-Fri, 9am-1pm Sat) This is the best shop – bar none – for distinctly Slovenian (and affordable) folk craft, like Prekmurje black pottery, Idrija lace, beehive panels with folk motifs, decorated heart-shaped honey cakes, painted Easter eggs, Rogaška glassware, colourful bridal chests and colourful stepped stools.

Studio Irma Vončina (☎ 425 00 51; Mestni trg 17; ☼ 10am-8pm Mon-Fri, 10am-1pm Sat Jun-Aug; 10am-4pm Mon-Fri, 10am-1pm Sat Sep-May) This gallery in the Old Town stocks some of the finest lace you'll find in Slovenia outside Idrija.

Ljubljanček (Map pp66-7; ☎ 308 19 40; Miklošičeva cesta 1; ☼ 8am-2pm & 3.30-7.30pm Mon-Fri, 8am-1pm Sat, 8am-noon Sun) This small souvenir shop in the Grand Hotel Union Executive specialises in products and souvenirs with distinct Ljubljana motifs. It also stocks local guides and English-language newspapers and periodicals.

ArtGlass Atelje (Map pp66-7; ☎ 031-717 458; Dvorni trg 2; ☼ 10am-7.30pm Mon-Fri, 9am-1pm Sat) This shop specialises in stunning functional and glass pieces by master craftsman Tomaž Miletič.

Piranske Soline (Map pp66-7; ☎ 472 01 90; Mestni trg 19; ☼ 9am-8pm Mon-Fri, 9am-4pm Sat & Sun) This shop in the Old Town sells bath sea salts and other products from Sečovlje (p180).

Rustika (Map pp66-7; ☎ 031-383 247, 041-859 666; ☼ 9am-7.30pm Jun-Sep, 10am-7pm Oct-May) This attractive gallery and shop, with wooden floors and a really 'rustic' feel, is conveniently located in Ljubljana Castle and is good for folk art.

Music

MCD Shop (Map pp66-7; ☎ 425 17 06; Miklošičeva cesta 2; ☼ 9am-8pm Mon-Fri, 9am-2pm Sat) This is Ljubljana's best music shop, with informed and very helpful staff.

Musikalje (Map pp66-7; ☎ 426 70 36; Trg Francoske Revolucije 6; ☼ 9am-6pm Mon-Fri, 9am-1pm Sat) This atmospheric shop near the Križanke is the place in Ljubljana for classical music, scores and instruments.

Spin Vinyl (Map pp66-7; ☎ 251 10 18; www.spinvinyl.si; Gallusovo nabrežje 13; ☼ 10.30am-7pm Mon-Fri, 10am-2pm Sat & Sun) A sizeable collection of old vinyl and CDs complements the newer stuff, which is a mix of alternative rock and dance music, both local and international.

Sporting Goods

Annapurna (Map p75; ☎ 426 34 28; Krakovski nasip 4; ☼ 9am-7pm Mon-Fri, 9am-1pm Sat) If you've forgotten your sleeping bag, ski poles, hiking boots, climbing gear or rucksack, this shop in Krakovo can supply you with most (or all) of it.

Lovec (Map pp62-3; ☎ 231 73 87; Gosposvetska cesta 12; ☼ 8am-7pm Mon-Fri, 8am-1pm Sat) For those into ridin', fishin' and shootin', 'Hunter' has all the kit and equipment you'll need.

Wine

The most central place to buy (and taste) Slovenian wine is **Vinoteka Movia** (p85).

Wine Cellars of Slovenia (Vinske Kleti Slovenije; Map pp62-3; ☎ 431 50 15; Jurček Pavilion, Ljubljana Fairgrounds, Dunajska cesta 18; ☼ 10am-7pm Mon-Fri, 9am-1pm Sat) If you're serious about wine this enormous wine cellar and restaurant north of Center is for you. It has a selection of 800 wines, most of which are Slovenian.

Vino Boutique (Map pp66-7; ☎ 425 26 80; Slovenska cesta 38; ☼ 10am-7pm Mon-Fri, 10am-1pm Sat) This small shop in a narrow passageway may not have as much choice as the Wine Cellars of Slovenia but it's more central, and but the owners are well informed and helpful.

GETTING THERE & AWAY
Air
For details of flights to and from Ljubljana, see p286.

Bus
Buses to destinations both within Slovenia and abroad leave from the same shedlike **bus station** (Map pp62-3; ☎ 234 46 01, information ☎ 090 42 30; www.ap-ljubljana.si; Trg OF 4; ⏲ 5.30am-10.30pm Mon-Sat, 8am-8pm Sun) opposite the train station. Next to the ticket windows are bilingual information phones and touch-screen computers. The posted timetable is useful once you get the hang of it.

You do not usually have to buy your ticket in advance; just pay as you board the bus. But for long-distance trips on Friday, just before the school break and public holidays, you are running the risk of not getting a seat. Book one the day before and reserve a seat (€1/3.60 domestic/international).

You can reach virtually anywhere in the country by bus – as close as Kamnik (€3, 45 minutes, 23km, every half-hour) or as far away as Brežice (€9.60, three hours, 109km, four a day). Here are some sample one-way fares (return fares are double), travel times, distances and frequencies from the capital: Bled (€6.15, 1¼ hours, 57km, hourly), Bohinj (€8, two hours, 86km, hourly), Koper (€10.75, 2½ hours, 122km, up to 11 daily), Maribor (€11.20, three hours, 127km; between two and eight daily), Murska Sobota (€15.70, 4¼ hours, 187km, one or two a day), Novo Mesto (€7, two hours, 72km, seven to 10 a day), Piran (€11.70, three hours, 140km, up to seven daily) and Postojna (€5.75, one hour, 53km, up to 24 daily).

For details of international bus services from Ljubljana, see p288.

Car & Motorcycle
All the big international car-rental firms have offices in Ljubljana, including **Avis** (Map pp62-3; ☎ 430 80 10; www.avis.si; Čufarjeva ulica 2; ⏲ 8am-6pm Mon-Fri, 8-11am & 6-8pm Sat, 8-11am Sun), **Budget** (Map pp66-7; ☎ 421 73 40; www.budget-slovenia.com; Grand Hotel Union Business, Miklošičeva cesta 3; ⏲ 8am-4pm Mon-Fri, 9am-noon Sat) and **Hertz** (Map pp62-3; ☎ 434 01 47; www .hertz.si; Trdinova ulica 9; ⏲ 8am-6pm Mon-Fri, 8am-1pm Sat,

8am-noon Sun). However, you should get a better deal at one of the local firms listed below.
ABC Rent a Car Cityhotel Turist (Map pp66-7; ☎ 510 43 20, 031-382 051; infoabc@siol.net; Cityhotel Turist, Dalmatinova ulica 15, enter from Tavčarjeva ulica; ⏲ 8am-4pm Mon-Fri, 8-11am & 6-8pm Sat, 8-11am Sun); airport (☎ 04-236 79 90; Brnik Airport; ⏲ 8am-9pm) Has its own fleet and acts as an agent for **Europcar** (www.europcar.si).
Atet Rent a Car (Map pp62-3; ☎ 513 70 17; www .atet.si; Derčeva ulica 4; ⏲ 8am-6pm Mon-Fri, 8am-noon Sat) In the M Hotel.
AutoRent (Map pp62-3; ☎ 234 46 50; www.renta carslo.com; Trg OF 5; ⏲ 8am-6pm Mon-Fri, 8am-1 Sat, 8am-noon Sun) Next to the post office.

For sample rates and information on conditions, see p293.

Hitching
If you are leaving Ljubljana by way of thumb, take one of the following city buses to the terminus and begin hitching there.
Bled, Jesenice & Austria (Salzburg) Bus 1 northwest (Vižmarje stop)
Maribor & Austria (Vienna) Bus 6 northeast (Črnuče stop)
Novo Mesto & Croatia (Zagreb) Bus 3 southeast (Rudnik stop)
Postojna, Koper, Croatian Istria and Italy (Trieste) Bus 6 southwest (Dolgi Most stop)

Train
Domestic and international trains arrive at and depart from central Ljubljana's lone **train station** (Map pp62-3; ☎ 291 33 32; www.slo-zeleznice .si; Trg OF 6; ⏲ 5am-10pm). You can get rail information from window no 10. Buy domestic tickets from window nos 1 to 8 and international ones from nos 9 and 10. You'll also find a branch of the Ljubljana Tourist Information Centre here.

The following are some one-way 2nd-class domestic fares, travel times, distances and frequencies from Ljubljana: Bled (€3.90 to €5.30, 55 minutes, 51km, up to 17 a day), Koper (€7.30 to €8.70, 2½ hours, 153km, four times a day), Maribor (€7.30 to €12.40, 1¾ hours, 156km, up to 25 a day), Murska Sobota (€9.90 to €14.50, 4¼ hour, 216km, up to eight a day) and Novo Mesto (€5, 1½ hours, 75km, up to 14 daily). Return fares are double the price, and there's a surcharge of between €1.45 to €1.80 on domestic InterCity (IC) train tickets.

For more information on international trains leaving Ljubljana, see p288.

GETTING AROUND
To/From the Airport

The cheapest way to Brnik Airport is by **public airport bus** (Map pp62-3; €3.70, 50 minutes, 27km) from stop no 28 at the bus station. These run hourly, from 6.10am to 8.10pm Monday to Friday; at the weekend there's a bus at 6.10am then one every two hours from 9.10am to 7.10pm.

A **private airport van** (Map pp62-3; ☎ 04-252 63 19, 041-792 865; €8) also links Trg OF near the bus station with the airport up to 10 times daily between 5.20am and 10.30pm, and is a 30 minute trip. They go from the airport to Ljubljana nine times a day between 5.45am and 11pm.

A taxi from the airport to Ljubljana will cost about €32.

Bicycle

Ljubljana is a city of cyclists, and there are bike lanes and special traffic lights everywhere. It's a real pleasure.

Ljubljana Bike (☎ 051-441 900; 2hr/1 day €0.85/4.20; 🕒 8am-8pm Apr-Oct) has bikes available from some 10 locations around the city, including the train station (Map pp62-3), the Slovenian Tourist Information Centre (p68), the Celica Hostel (p80), and at the at the start of Miklošičeva cesta (Map pp66-7).

Car & Motorcycle

You can **street park** (per hr €0.40-0.50; 🕒 8am-6pm Mon-Fri, 8am-1pm Sat) in Ljubljana, though not always very easily, especially in the museum area and close to the Old Town. There are enclosed car parks throughout the city, and their locations are indicated on most maps. The one below Trg Republike Miklošičev Park, for example, charges €1.25 for the first hour and €1per hour after that; a 12-hour stretch costs €13.

Public Transport

Ljubljana's public transport system, run by **LPP** (Ljubljanski Potniški Promet; ☎ 582 24 20; www.lpp .si in Slovene; Celovška cesta 160; 🕒 6.45am-7pm Mon-Fri,

6.45am-1pm Sat), is very user-friendly. There are a total of 21 lines numbered 1 to 22 (no 4 doesn't exist), and half a dozen of them (nos 1, 2, 3, 6, 8 and 11) are considered main lines. nos 2, 6 and 11 start at 3.15am and finish at midnight; the rest begin their runs at 5am and stop any time between 9pm and 10.30pm. Buses on the main lines run about every five to 15 minutes; service is less frequent on other lines and on Sunday and holidays.

You can pay the flat fare (€1.25) on board with exact change or use a tiny metal *žeton* (€0.80) available at many newsstands, kiosks and post offices.

Bus passes (as well as tokens, of course) can be purchased from three LPP locations, including the company's head office. More central is the **LPP Information Centre** (Map pp62-3; ☎ 430 51 75; Slovenska cesta 56; 🕒 6.45am-7pm Mon-Fri, 6.45am-1pm Sat) near the Borza (Ljubljana Stock Exchange) and the **LPP kiosk** (Map pp66-7; Slovenska cesta 55; 🕒 6am-8pm Mon-Fri, 7am-8pm Sat) at the system's central stop (Bavarski Dvor). Passes are available for a day (*dnevna vozovnica*, €3.75) or a week (*tedenska vozovnica*, €14.20).

From the bus or train stations, bus 2 will take you down Slovenska cesta to Mestni trg (Magistrat stop) in the Old Town. To reach Trnovo, catch bus 9 to the terminus (Trnovo stop). In general the central area of Ljubljana is perfectly walkable, so buses are really only necessary if you're staying out of town

Taxi

Metered taxis can be hailed on the street or hired from ranks near the train station, on Prešernov trg, at the Ljubljana Tourist Information Centre (p67), on Stritarjeva ulica, in front of Hotel Slon (p80) on Slovenska cesta, or on Mestni trg. Flagfall is €0.65 to €1 and the per-kilometre charge is €0.75 to €1.50, depending on whether you call ahead or hail a taxi on the street. You can call a taxi on any of the following numbers: ☎ 031-311 311, ☎ 041-445 406, and ☎ 051-809 908.

Gorenjska

If you're into adventure sport, Gorenjska (Upper Carniola) is the province to head for. Less than an hour from the capital you'll find yourself surrounded by mountains, lakes and high plateaus. Indeed, the Kamnik-Savinja Alps and its ski fields begin just a short drive away from Ljubljana, and Triglav National Park, with hiking and biking trails galore as well as Slovenia's share of the Julian Alps, is just around the corner. The lakes at Bled and Bohinj are popular centres for any number of outdoor activities. A mountain trek is an excellent way to meet other Slovenes in a relaxed environment so take advantage of this opportunity if you're in Gorenjska during the hiking season.

But Gorenjska is not just about shimmering lakes and mountain majesties; it also contains some of the country's most attractive and important historical towns. Škofja Loka, Kamnik, Kranj and Radovljica – to name just a few – are treasure-troves of Gothic, Renaissance and baroque art and architecture, and they are wonderful bases from which to explore this diverse and visually spectacular province.

Because of the difficulty of eking out a living in mountainous areas, the people of Gorenjska have a reputation in Slovenia for being on the, well, let's just say 'thrifty' side. You probably won't see evidence of this yourself, but you'll surely hear a fair few jokes similar to the ones made about the Scots. A rather sophomoric joke reported by Ljubljana-based American Erica Johnson Debeljak in her memoir *And the Distance Smells of Apples: A Story of Migration* (p31) was that `…we'd know we were entering Gorenjska when we'd see toilet paper fluttering on the clothes lines'.

HIGHLIGHTS

- Enjoy the hair-raising views from **Mt Triglav** (p128), Slovenia's tallest peak
- Hammer away in the delightful iron-mongering village of **Kropa** (p109)
- Drive or bike over the spectacular **Vršič Pass** (p131) in the Julian Alps
- Learn more about the boards and bees at the fabulous **Beekeeping Museum** (p106) in Radovljica
- Take a 'flight' back in time via cable car to **Velika Planina** (p96) near Kamnik

★ Vršič Pass

★ Mt Triglav ★ Radovljica

★ Kropa ★ Velika Planina

KAMNIK

☎ 01 / pop 12,800 / elev 382m

In the bosom of the mountains just 23km northeast of Ljubljana, Kamnik is often given a miss by travellers en route to sexier Bled or Bohinj. But the town's tidy and attractive medieval core, with its houses and portals of hewn stone, balconies and arcades, is well worth a visit, as is the nearby arboretum.

Kamnik competed with Ljubljana and Kranj for economic and cultural dominance in Kranjska (Carniola) throughout the Middle Ages. For centuries it controlled the pass in the Tuhinj Valley to the east, which was indispensable for moving goods from the coastal areas inland to Štajerska and Koroška. But when the route was redirected via Trojane to the southeast in the 1600s, Kamnik fell into a deep sleep and awakened only in the late 19th century when the town was linked by rail to Ljubljana.

Orientation

Kamnik lies on the west bank of the Kamniška Bistrica River and to the south of the Kamnik Alps. The Old Town consists of medieval Glavni trg and its southern extension, Šutna.

Kamnik's bus station lies beside the river east of Glavni trg and at the end of Prešernova ulica. The town has three train stations. The main station is on Kranjska cesta, southwest of Šutna. Kamnik-Mesto, which is convenient for the Old Town and its sights, is on Kolodvorska ulica west of the Little Castle. Kamnik Graben station, the terminus of the Ljubljana–Kamnik line, is northwest of Glavni trg on Tunjiška cesta.

Information

Kamnik Alpine Society (Planinsko Društvo Kamnik; ☎ 839 13 45; Šutna 42; ⏰ 9am-noon Mon & Fri, 1-4pm Wed) Advice and guides for walking in the Kamnik Alps.

Nova Ljubljanska Banka (Glavni trg 10; ⏰ 8am-noon & 2.30-4.30 Mon-Fri)

Post office (Glavni trg 27)

SKB Banka (Glavni trg 13; ⏰ 8.30am-noon & 2-5pm Mon-Fri)

Tourist Information Centre Kamnik (TIC; ☎ 839 14 70; Glavni trg 2; http://turizem.kamnik.si; ⏰ 9am-7pm daily Jul & Aug; 10am-6pm daily May, Jun & Sep; 8am-4pm Mon-Fri, 8am-noon Sat Oct-Apr) Has internet access (per 10 min/1hr €0.40/2.10).

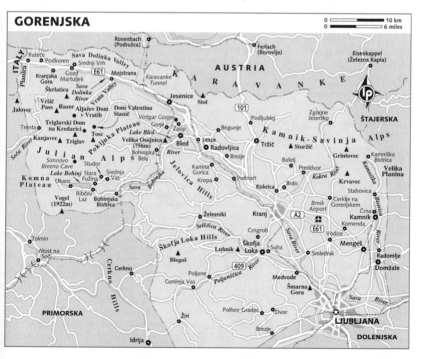

GORENJSKA

Sights
GLAVNI TRG & SURROUNDS
The **Franciscan monastery** (Frančiškanski Samostan; ☎ 831 80 37; Frančiškanski trg 2; ⊙ by arrangement), a short distance to the west of Glavni trg, was built in 1492. It has a rich library of theological, philosophical and scientific manuscripts and incunabula dating from the 15th to 18th centuries (including an original copy of the Bible translated by Jurij Dalmatin in 1584). Next door is the **Church of St James** (Cerkev Sv Jakoba; Frančiškanski trg), which has a chapel designed by Jože Plečnik. He also did the attractive beige-and-orange **house with loggia** on the eastern side of the square; it's now the R Bar (p96).

The **Little Castle** (Mali Grad; ⊙ 9am-7pm), on a low hill above the southern end of Glavni trg, has

foundations going back to the 11th century and is Kamnik's most important historical sight. Behind the castle stand the ruins of a unique two-storey **Romanesque chapel** (adult/child €1.25/0.42; ⊙ 10am-7pm mid-Jun–mid-Sep), which has 15th-century frescoes in its lower nave, wall paintings by Janez Potočnik (1749–1834) in the presbytery and a Gothic stone relief of a cross flanked by two angels above the main entrance. There are excellent views of the Old Town and surrounding countryside from here.

The **Miha Maleš Gallery** (Galerija Mihe Maleša; ☎ 839 16 16, 839 75 04; Glavni trg 2; adult/child €2.10/1.25; ⊙ 8am-1pm & 4-7pm Tue-Fri) contains some 2600 works by the eponymous painter and graphic artist, who was born in Kamnik in 1903. Enter from the north side of the tourist office.

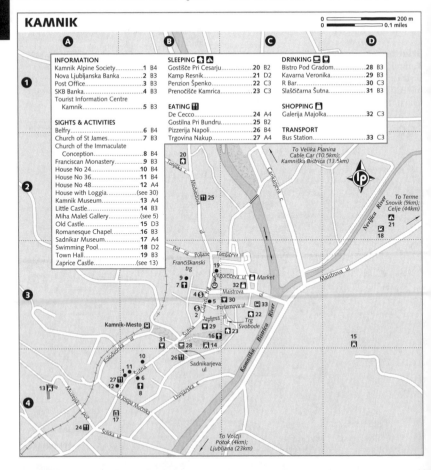

KAMNIK

0 — 200 m
0 — 0.1 miles

INFORMATION
Kamnik Alpine Society................1 B4
Nova Ljubljanska Banka 2 B3
Post Office......................................3 B3
SKB Banka.......................................4 B3
Tourist Information Centre
Kamnik..5 B3

SIGHTS & ACTIVITIES
Belfry...6 B4
Church of St James.......................7 B3
Church of the Immaculate
Conception..................................8 B4
Franciscan Monastery..................9 B3
House No 24..................................10 B4
House No 36..................................11 B4
House No 48..................................12 A4
House with Loggia...............(see 30)
Kamnik Museum.........................13 A4
Little Castle...................................14 B3
Miha Maleš Gallery..............(see 5)
Old Castle......................................15 D3
Romanesque Chapel...................16 B3
Sadnikar Museum........................17 A4
Swimming Pool............................18 D2
Town Hall.......................................19 B3
Žaprice Castle......................(see 13)

SLEEPING 🏠 🏕
Gostišče Pri Cesarju..................20 B2
Kamp Resnik................................21 D2
Penzion Špenko..........................22 C3
Prenočišče Kamrica....................23 C3

EATING 🍴
De Cecco..24 A4
Gostilna Pri Bundru...................25 B2
Pizzerija Napoli...........................26 B4
Trgovina Nakup...........................27 A4

DRINKING 🍷 🍸
Bistro Pod Gradom.....................28 B3
Kavarna Veronika........................29 B3
R Bar...30 C3
Slaščičarna Šutna........................31 B3

SHOPPING 🛍
Galerija Majolka..........................32 C3

TRANSPORT
Bus Station....................................33 C3

To Velika Planina
Cable Car (10.5km);
Kamniška Bistrica (13.5km)

To Terme
Snovik (9km);
Celje (44km)

To Volčji
Potok (4km);
Ljubljana (23km)

HELL HATH NO FURY

The Little Castle is home to Veronika, a legendary countess who was turned partly into a snake when she refused to help the Christian faithful build a church. The old gal was not only mean but spiteful, too. In her rage at having been asked to contribute, she struck the entrance to the castle with her fist. If you look to the right of the portal to the main courtyard as you go in, you'll see the imprint of her hand (sort of). Veronika continues to rule the treasure of the Little Castle and, in a way, the community of Kamnik too. She appears both on the town seal and on the license plate of every car registered here.

ŠUTNA

A walk along the quiet and attractive 500m-long main street of **Šutna** is a trip back in time: check the fine neoclassical house with columns at **No 24**, the stone relief of the Paschal Lamb above the door at **No 36** and the medieval fresco indicating a butcher's shop sign at **No 48** (now a grocery store).

In the centre of Šutna, opposite Šutna 36, stands the **Church of the Immaculate Conception** (Cerkev Marijinega Brezmadežnega Spočetja), erected in the mid-18th century but with a detached **belfry** (*zvonik*) that shows an earlier church's Gothic origins.

The **Sadnikar Museum** (Sadnikarjev Muzej; ☎ 839 13 62; Šutna 33; admission €1.25; ☼ by appointment), the first private museum to open in Slovenia (1893), exhibits Gothic artwork, period furniture and paintings from the 18th century amassed by pack-rat Josip Nikolaj Sadnikar (1863–1952), a local veterinarian and painter.

KAMNIK MUSEUM

Zaprice Castle (Grad Zaprice; Muzejski pot 3), with towers, ancient stone walls and an interesting chapel, was built in the 16th century but converted a century later into a baroque manor house. Today it houses the **Kamnik Museum** (Kamniški Muzej; ☎ 831 76 47; adult/child €2.10/1.25; ☼ 8am-1pm & 4-7pm Tue-Fri, 10am-1pm & 4-6pm Sat, 10am-1pm Sun), with dullish exhibits connected with Kamnik's glory days and 18th-century furniture by German designer Michael Thonet (1796–1871). More interesting are the **granaries** outside, from the 18th and 19th centuries, which have been brought here from the Tuhinj Valley, and the **lapidarium** in the courtyard with stone bits and bobs from the 15th to 18th centuries.

OTHER SIGHTS

The **Old Castle** (Stari Grad), a 13th-century ruin on Bergantov Hill (585m) east of the centre, can be reached on foot from the end of Maistrova ulica in about 20 minutes; the brochure *Tourist Sights in Kamnik and Vicinity* includes a map of the walking trail.

About 4km south of Kamnik is **Volčji Potok** (☎ 831 23 45; www.arboretum-vp.si; Volčji Potok 3; adult/child/senior & student/family €4.20/2.75/3.35/10.50; ☼ 8am-8pm Apr-Aug, 8am-7pm Sep, 8am-6pm Mar & Oct), Slovenia's largest and most beautiful arboretum. With the heart-shaped park of a former castle as its core, the 85-hectare arboretum has more than 2500 varieties of trees, shrubs and flowers from all over the world. There are five buses from Kamnik (€1.30, 10 minutes) to the arboretum on weekdays (at 6am, 8am, 1.15pm, 2.45pm and 7.10pm) and one daily at the weekend (at 4.50pm on Saturday, 4pm on Sunday). A lot more buses go to Radomlje, which is 1.5km south of the arboretum.

Activities

The arrow-straight 14km road north to Kamniška Bistrica is tailor-made for **cycling**.

There's an outdoor **swimming pool** (☎ 839 12 92; Maistrova ulica 15; adult/child €4.20/3.35; ☼ 10am-6pm Mon-Fri, 10am-8pm Sat & Sun mid-Jun–Aug) near the camping ground.

On a warm day you might be tempted by **Terme Snovik** (☎ 830 86 31; www.zarja-kovis.si/snovik /terme.htm; adult/child/student from €6.30/4.60/5.45 Mon-Fri, from €7.10/5.45/6.30 Sat & Sun; ☼ 9am-8pm Sun-Tue & Thu, 9am-10pm Wed, Fri & Sat), a spa and water park with enormous covered and open-air pools and a gaggle of saunas in Potok, 9km northeast of Kamnik. Buses from Kamnik (€1.70, 15 minutes) go to the spa at 10.30am and 12.30pm weekdays and at 10.30am on Saturday and Sunday.

Festivals & Events

Major events in Kamnik (infocenter.kamnik@siol.net for information) are the **Medieval Days** (Srednjeveški Dnevi), also called **Venerina Pot** (Path of Venus) on the second weekend in July and the **National Costumes Festival** (Dnevi Narodnih Noš) held on the second weekend in September. But the biggest event by far is Kamfest (www.kamfest.org), the so-called

'Festival with a View', held in the Little Castle in August with two-dozen cultural events over three weeks.

Sleeping

Kamp Resnik (☎ 831 73 14, 041-435 380; Maistrova ulica 32; per person/car/tent/caravan €2/2/2/4; ☯ May-Sep; **P** **㉄**) This tiny 1-hectare camping ground with 100 sites for 200 guests is northeast of the Old Town on the Nevljica River. There's a tennis court, and the public swimming pool and a popular pub are close by.

Penzion Špenko (☎ 831 73 30; romanspenko@email .si; Prešernova ulica 14c; s/d €30/50) This pension above a little bistro offers basic but very central accommodation in 10 rooms.

Gostišče Pri Cesarju (☎ 839 29 17, 041-629 846; fax 839 11 96; Tunjiška cesta 1; s/d €30/50; **P**) This 10-room guesthouse 500m north of Glavni trg is an excellent choice but the mansard rooms on the 2nd floor are rather cramped.

Prenočišče Kamrica (☎ 831 77 07, 041-222 700; kam rica.kamnik@siol.net; Trg Svobode 2; per person €32; **P**) The Kamrica is even more central than the Špenko but half the size with only five rooms. It's a cosy, flower-bedecked place; ask for the charming room in the back with views (just) of the Little Castle and use of the kitchen.

Eating

Pizzerija Napoli (☎ 839 27 44; Sadnikarjeva ulica 5; pizza €4.15-5.85, pasta €2.50-6; ☯ 11am-11pm Mon-Sat, noon-10pm Sun) South of the Little Castle in Šutna, this homey pizzeria, one of the few places for a meal in central Kamnik, has a great terrace and does takeaway as well.

De Cecco (☎ 831 74 47, 031-667 139; Šutna 68, meals from €6.50; ☯ 10am-midnight Mon-Thu, 10am-1am Fri & Sat) South of Kamnik Museum at the end of Muzejski pot, this pasta and pizza place is housed in a rather poshly done-up old village house.

Gostilna Pri Bundru (☎ 839 12 35, 041-679 457; Medvedova ulica 24; meals from €10; ☯ 9am-1am Mon-Fri, 10am-1am Sat) This popular inn 200m north of Glavni trg is a good place for a lunch or dinner of traditional Slovene fare.

There's a small supermarket called **Trgovina Nakup** (Šutna 48; ☯ 7am-9pm Mon-Fri, 7am-7pm Sat, 7-11.30am Sun) in the centre of the Old Town.

Drinking

Kavarna Veronika (☎ 839 11 43; Glavni trg 6; ☯ 8am-1am) This old-style café with a terrace, on the corner of Japljeva ulica, is a good place to cool

your heels over a cup of something warm and a slice of cake.

Slaščičarna Šutna (☎ 831 97 30; Šutna 2; ☯ 7am-10pm Mon-Sat, 8am-10pm Sun) A pleasant café-bar on the old main street, this place has good cakes and ice cream.

R Bar (Maistrova ulica 2; ☯ 7am-9pm Mon-Fri, 8am-2pm Sat, 8am-1pm Sun) This bar in the house that Plečnik built keeps early-bird hours but has big plate-glass windows from which to observe the action on Glavni trg.

Bistro Pod Gradom (Sadnikarjeva ulica 1a; ☯ 9am-midnight) This café-bar just below the castle attracts the young bloods of Kamnik throughout the day.

Entertainment

Slovenia's first choir, **Lira**, founded in 1882 and still going strong, occasionally gives local concerts. Ask the tourist-office staff for information.

Shopping

Galerija Majolka (☎ 839 10 81, 041-791 411; Maistrova ulica 11; ☯ 9am-noon & 3-7pm Mon-Fri, 9am-noon Sat) This shop just west of the bus station has a nice range of antiques, paintings, porcelain and souvenirs.

Getting There & Around

Buses from Ljubljana (€3, 45 minutes, 23km) run almost every 30 minutes on weekdays and hourly at the weekend. You can also reach Gornji Grad (€3, 40 minutes, 23km) on five buses a day (one daily at weekends) and Kamniška Bistrica (€2.20, 30 minutes, 14km) on three (two daily at weekends). From June to September there's a bus leaving for Logarska Dolina (€7.60, two hours, 81km) in Štajerska at 6.55am weekdays, returning at 4.55pm from the Rinka Waterfall.

Kamnik is on a direct rail line to/from Ljubljana (€2, 40 minutes, 23km, up to 16 a day) via Domžale.

You can book a taxi on ☯ 041-791 411.

VELIKA PLANINA

☎ 01 / elev to 1666m

Reaching a height of almost 1700m, the Velika Planina (Great Highlands) is a wonderful place to explore and is accessible to 1418m by cable car from the lower station just 11km north of Kamnik.

Velika Planina is where traditional dairy farmers graze their cattle between June and

September. If you follow the road from the upper station up the hill for about 2km, you'll reach a highland plain filled with more than 50 shepherds' huts and the tiny **Church of Our Lady of the Snows** (Cerkev Sv Marije Snežne) modelled after traditional local dairies. The low-lying rounded buildings with conical roofs are unique to Velika Planina, but they are replicas; the originals dating from the early 20th century were burned to the ground by the Germans in WWII.

Velika Planina is also an excellent spot for hiking and mountain biking. Ask the tourist office (p93) in Kamnik for the brochure *Velika Planina: A Treasure of Nature*, which outlines biking trails of up to 30km and hiking ones of up to 3½ hours. A circular walk of the plain and **Mala Planina** (1569m) to the south, for example, will take about three hours. In summer, the friendly shepherds in their big black hats will sell you curd, sour milk and white cheese.

The popular **Velika Planina ski grounds** (☎ 839 71 77; www.velikaplanina.si; day pass €11/10/8) have 4km of ski slopes and 10km of cross-country trails. When the slopes are skiable, a chairlift ferries skiers up to Gradišče from the upper cable-car station daily between December and April, where three T-bar tows should be running.

Sleeping & Eating

Domžalski Dom na Mali Planini (☎ 721 57 14, 051-340 730 ☺ daily Jun-Sep, Sat & Sun Oct-May) This Category II lodge at 1534m, with 13 rooms of three to eight beds, is one of a handful of mountain huts and lodges with accommodation in the area.

Okrepčevalnica Pri Žičnici (☎ 832 55 66; Kamniška Bistrica 2; ☺ 7.30am-5/9pm) This place is just what it says it is: a 'Snackbar at the Lower Cable-car Station'. There are picnic tables and barbecue pits here too.

Okrepčevalnica Zeleni Rob na Veliki Planini (☎ 041-678 266; ☺ 9am-3.30pm Mon-Thu, 9am-8am Fri, 8am-10pm Sat, 8am-4pm Sun) The snack bar and pub at Zeleni Rob (Green Edge) is about 1km up the hill from the upper cable-car station.

Getting There & Around

The cable-car station can be reached from buses bound for Kamniška Bistrica. The **cable car** (žičnica; ☎ 839 71 77, 832 55 66; www.velikaplanina .si; adult/child return €9.20/6.70; ☺ hourly 8am-6pm Mon-Thu, 8am-8pm Fri-Sun, mid-Jun–mid-Sep; 8am, noon & 4pm Mon-Thu, 9am & hourly noon-6pm Fri, hourly 8am-6pm Sat &

Sun mid-Sep–mid-Dec, Apr–mid-Jun; hourly 8am-6pm daily mid-Dec–Mar) runs year-round.

KAMNIŠKA BISTRICA
☎ 01 / pop 20 / elev 580m

This pretty little settlement in a valley near the source of the Kamniška Bistrica River is 3km north of the Velika Planina lower cable-car station, and the Category II **Dom v Kamniški Bistrici** (☎ 832 55 44; info.pdljmatica@siol.net; ☺ year-round) offers hostel-like accommodation in 11 rooms of two to five beds with a total of 36. Check-in is from 8am to 10pm in summer, 8am to 8pm in winter.

Kamniška Bistrica is the springboard for some of the more ambitious and rewarding Kamnik Alps treks, such as the ones to **Grintovec** (2559m; 11 hours return), **Brana** (2252m; eight hours) and **Planjava** (2394m; 10 hours). Information is available from the tourist office in Kamnik (p93).

The most popular hikes, however, are the easier, 3½-hour ones northwest to the mountain pass or saddle at **Kokra Saddle** (Kokrsko Sedlo; 1791m), with accommodation at the Category I **Zoisova Koča na Kokrskem Sedlu** (☎ 839 13 45, 051-635 549; pdkamnik@siol.net; ☺ mid-Jun–mid-Oct), with 135 beds, and north to **Kamnik Saddle** (Kamniško Sedlo; 1903m), where you'll find the Category I **Koča na Kamniškem Sedlu** (☎ 839 13 45, 051-611 367; ☺ mid-Jun–mid-Oct) mountain lodge with 142 beds.

Kamniška Bistrica can be reached from Kamnik (€2.20, 20 minutes, 14km) on three buses a day, leaving at 7am, 11.30am and 4.35pm Monday to Friday, at 7.20am and 4.45pm on Saturday, and at 7.50am and 4.55pm on Sunday.

ŠKOFJA LOKA
☎ 04 / pop 12,000 / elev 354m

Among the most beautiful settlements in Slovenia, Škofja Loka (Bishop's Meadow) has an Old Town protected as a historical and cultural monument since 1987. When the castle and other old buildings are illuminated on weekend nights, Škofja Loka takes on the appearance of a fairy-tale village.

History

Škofja Loka, like Ptuj and Piran, is among the oldest settlements in Slovenia. In 973 German Emperor Otto II presented the Bavarian Bishops of Freising with the valleys along the Poljanščica and Selščica Rivers. The point

GORENJSKA

where the two tributaries merge to form the Sora River began to develop as a town.

In the Middle Ages Škofja Loka developed as a trade centre along the Munich–Klagenfurt–Trieste route, doing particularly well in iron, linen and furs. A circular wall with five gates protected by guard towers was built around the town in 1318 to ensure that this success continued.

But it was all for naught. An army of the Counts of Celje breached the wall and burned the town to the ground in 1457; two decades later the Turks attacked. Then natural disasters struck: an earthquake in 1511 badly damaged the town, and several great fires at the end of the 17th century reduced most of Škofja Loka's finest buildings to ashes.

In 1803 the Habsburgs took possession of the town, and the advent of the railway later in the century put Škofja Loka on the road to industrialisation.

Orientation

The newer part of Škofja Loka and central Kapucinski trg lie to the north of the Selščica River. The Old Town to the south of the river consists of two long squares, Mestni trg, which runs south from Cankarjev trg and the river, and to the east the rat-run that is busy Spodnji trg.

Škofja Loka's bus station is on Kapucinski trg. The train station is 3km to the northeast at the end of Kidričeva cesta in the industrial suburb of Trata.

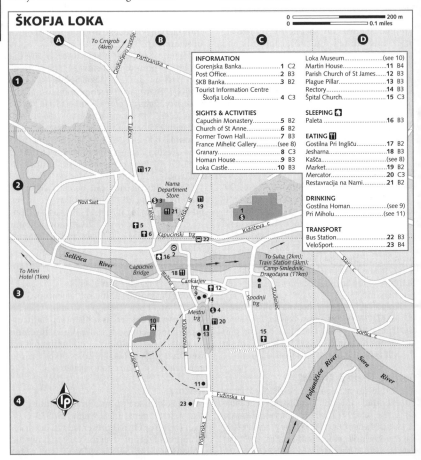

ŠKOFJA LOKA

| 0 | 200 m |
| 0 | 0.1 miles |

INFORMATION
Gorenjska Banka..........................1 C2
Post Office..................................2 B3
SKB Banka..................................3 B2
Tourist Information Centre
    Škofja Loka.............................4 C3

SIGHTS & ACTIVITIES
Capuchin Monastery....................5 C3
Church of St Anne........................6 B2
Former Town Hall........................7 B3
France Mihelič Gallery.............(see 8)
Granary......................................8 C3
Homan House..............................9 B3
Loka Castle...............................10 B3

Loka Museum.........................(see 10)
Martin House.............................11 B4
Parish Church of St James..........12 B3
Plague Pillar...............................13 B3
Rectory.....................................14 B3
Špital Church.............................15 C3

SLEEPING
Paleta..16 B3

EATING
Gostilna Pri Ingliču.....................17 B2
Jesharna....................................18 B3
Kašča...................................(see 8)
Market......................................19 B2
Mercator...................................20 C3
Restavracija na Nami..................21 B2

DRINKING
Gostilna Homan......................(see 9)
Pri Miholu.............................(see 11)

TRANSPORT
Bus Station...............................22 B3
VeloSport..................................23 B4

To Crngrob (4km)
Partizanska c
Grohaljevo naselje
C Talcev
To Mini Hotel (1km)
Selščica River
Novi Svet
Nama Department Store
Kapucinski trg
Capuchin Bridge
Blaževa ul
Sora ul
Kidričeva c
To Suha (2km); Train Station (3km); Camp Smlednik; Dragočajna (17km)
Studenec
Stara c
Cankarjev trg
Spodnji trg
Mestni trg
Klobovsova ul
Cesta Pot
Poljanska c
Fužinska ul
Sorška c
Poljanščica River
Sora River

Information

Gorenjska Banka (Kapucinski trg 7; 8am-6pm Mon-Fri, 8am-noon Sat) Diagonally opposite the bus station.

Post office (Kapucinski trg 14)

SKB Banka (Kapucinski trg 4; 8.30am-noon & 2-5pm Mon-Fri) In the Nama department store.

Tourist Information Centre Škofja Loka (512 02 68; td-skofja.loka@siol.net; Mestni trg 7; 8.30am-7pm Mon-Fri, 8.30am-12.30pm & 5-7.30pm Sat & Sun mid-Jun–mid-Sep; 8.30am-7pm Mon-Fri, 8.30am-12.30pm Sat mid-Sep–mid-Jun)

www.skofjaloka.si Useful website courtesy of city hall.

Sights

CANKARJEV TRG

Some parts of the **Parish Church of St James** (Župnijska Cerkev Sv Jakoba; Cankarjev trg) date back to the 13th century, but its most important elements – the nave, the presbytery with star vaulting (1524) and the tall bell tower (1532) – were added over the next three centuries. On either side of the choir are black marble altars designed in about 1700. On the vaulted ceiling are bosses with portraits of the Freising bishops, saints, workers with shears and a blacksmith; two crescent moons in the presbytery are reminders of the Turkish presence. The dozen or so distinctive ceiling lamps and the baptismal font were designed by Jože Plečnik.

On the south side of the church is the **rectory** (*župnišče*), part of a fortified aristocratic manor house built in the late 16th century. Below the rounded projection on the corner are curious consoles of animal heads.

MESTNI TRG

The group of colourful **16th-century burgher houses** on this square have earned the town the nickname 'Painted Loka'. Almost every one is of historical and architectural importance, but among the more impressive is **Homan House** (Homanova Hiša; Mestni trg 2), dating from 1511 with sgraffiti and bits of frescoes of St Christopher and of a soldier. The **former town hall** (stari rotovž; Mestni trg 35) is remarkable for its stunning three-storey Gothic courtyard and the 17th-century frescoes on its facade. Further south, **Martin House** (Martinova Hiša; Mestni trg 26) leans on part of the old **town wall**. It has a wooden 1st floor, a late Gothic portal and a vaulted entrance hall. The **plague pillar** in Mestni trg was erected in 1751.

SPODNJI TRG

This square to the east of Mestni trg was where the poorer folk lived in the Middle Ages; today it is a busy thoroughfare. The 16th-century **granary** (kašča; Spodnji trg 1) at the northern end is where the town's grain stores, collected as taxes, were once kept. It now contains the Kašča restaurant and wine bar. On the 1st floor is the **France Mihelič Gallery** (Galerija Franceta Miheliča; 517 04 00; adult/child €1.25/0.85; 1-5pm Tue-Sat), which displays the works of the eponymous artist born in nearby Virmaše in 1907. The **Špital Church** (Spodnji trg 9) was built in 1720 around the town's almshouse, and the poor lived in the cells of the courtyard building behind.

LOKA CASTLE

Overlooking the town from a grassy hill west of Mestni trg, the **castle** (Loški Grad; Grajska pot 13) was built in the early 13th century but extensively renovated after the earthquake in 1511. Today it houses the **Loka Museum** (Loški Muzej; 517 04 00; adult/child €3/2.10, with guide €3.35/2.50; 9am-6pm Tue-Sun Apr-Oct, 9am-5pm Sat & Sun Nov-Mar), which has one of the best ethnographical collections in Slovenia spread over two-dozen galleries that extend over two floors. The area around Škofja Loka was famous for its smiths and lace-makers, and there are lots of ornate guild chests on display. And don't miss the spectacular **Golden Altars** in the castle chapel. They were taken from a church destroyed during WWII in Dražgoše, northwest of Škofja Loka.

OTHER SIGHTS

The 18th-century **Capuchin monastery** (Kapucinski Samostan; 512 09 70; Kapucinski trg 2; by appointment), west of the bus station, has a priceless **library** of medieval manuscripts, as well as the *Škofja Loka Passion,* a processional with dramatic elements, from around 1720.

The stone **Capuchin Bridge** (Kapucinski Most) leading from the monastery's **Church of St Anne** (1710) dates from the 14th century and is an excellent vantage point for the Old Town and castle as well as the river with its deep gorge, dams, abandoned mills and 18th-century barracks.

Activities

The Škofja Loka Hills to the west, a region of steep slopes, deep valleys and ravines, is an excellent area for **walks** or **hikes**, and there are several huts with accommodation in the area. Before you set out, buy a copy of the 1:50,000 hiking map *Škofjeloško in Cerkljansko Hribovje* (Škofja Loka and Cerkno Hills; €8.20) and ask the tourist office for the pamphlet

Škofja Loka Walk around the Town and Surroundings, which will direct you to both Suha and Crngrob on foot (opposite).

One of the easiest trips in the brochure is to **Lubnik**, a 1025m peak northwest of the Old Town, which can be reached on foot in two hours via Vincarje or the castle ruins near Gabrovo. Start the walk from Klobovsova ulica in Mestni trg. A mountain hut near the summit, Category II **Dom na Lubniku** (☎ 512 05 01, 512 06 67; pd.skofjaloka@volja.net; ☾ daily Mar-Dec, Sat & Sun Jan & Feb), has seven triple rooms.

A hike to 1562m **Blegoš** further west would be much more demanding, but it takes only about three hours from Hotavlje, a village about 2km from Gorenja Vas and accessible by bus from Škofja Loka. There are two huts in the area. Category II **Koča na Blegošu** (☎ 512 06 67, 041-212 612; ☾ daily late Apr-Oct, Sat & Sun Nov-late Apr), at 1391m, has 61 beds. **Zavetišče GS na Jelencih** (☎ 518 11 28, 041-541 997; pd.gorvas@volja.net; ☾ Sat & Sun Nov-early May), about 2km to the southwest and at 1185m, has 20 beds.

This area is also superb for **cycling**. Ask the tourist office for *In the Shade of Lubnik*, which outlines the new 50km circular cycle route around Škofja Loka.

The **Stari Vrh ski centre** (☎ 518 80 39; matej.demsar@krajnik.net; half-day pass adult/child €12.50/11.30, day pass €16.30/13), 12km west of Škofja Loka, is situated at altitudes of 580m to 1216m and covers 10km of ski slopes and trails. There are five T-bar tows and a chairlift.

Festivals & Events

A music festival called **Pod Homanovo Lipo** takes place under the big linden tree in front of Homan House on Mestni trg on certain nights in July and August. **Venerina Pot** (Path of Venus; http://venera.skofjaloka.si) is a medieval-inspired festival held on the last weekend in June. In recent years the *Škofja Loka Passion* has been staged during this time.

Sleeping

Camp Smlednik (☎ 01-362 70 02; www.dm-campsmlednik.si; Dragočajna 14a; per adult/child €6.25/3.15, 2-/3-/4-person bungalows €40/50/60; ☾ May–mid-Oct) This 4-hectare camping ground in Dragočajna, 11km to the east, is the closest one to Škofja Loka. It is situated on the left bank of the Sava River and beside Lake Zbilje. There is also a beach with separate facilities set aside for naturists. The bungalows measure 36 sq metres and are like little cottages.

Pri Marku farmhouse (☎ 513 16 26, 041-711 260; www.pri-marku-porenta.si; Crngrob 5; per person €17-24; P ✗) This idyllic farmhouse in Crngrob (opposite), within praying distance of the Church of the Annunciation, has eight doubles, an apartment for five and, for those looking for a roll in the hay, there's accommodation in the barn.

Paleta (☎ 512 64 00, 041-874 427; paleta.art@siol.net; Kapucinski trg 17; s/d/tr/q €30/54/81/108; ❄ ✗ ⌨) This colourful and upbeat new place above an art-supplies shop (thus the name) just over Capuchin Bridge has four Ikea-standard but comfortable rooms with exceptional bathrooms. Room No 3 has views of the river *and* the castle.

Mini Hotel (☎ 515 05 40; www.minihotel.si; Vincarje 47; s/d/tr/q €40/60/75/90; P ⌨ ☎) This brand-new guesthouse is in the suburb of Vincarje, about 1km west of the bus station, and has eight sparkling rooms, an outdoor swimming pool, squash and tennis courts, a sauna and a gym.

Eating

Restavracija na Nami (☎ 512 50 19; Kapucinski trg 4; set lunch €3.35-5, pizza €5; ☾ 9am-8pm Mon-Sat) This self-service restaurant is on the 2nd floor of the Nama department store (enter from Cesta Talcev).

Jesharna (☎ 512 25 61; Blaževa ulica 10; pizza & pasta €3.35-7.20; ☾ 9am-11pm Mon-Fri, 10am-11pm Sat, 11.30am-10pm Sun) This very friendly, very upbeat *picerija in špageterija* (pizzeria and spaghetti house) overlooking the river has free internet access. It's more or less opposite the post office.

Gostilna Pri Ingliču (☎ 512 66 30; Cesta Talcev 4a; starters €4.20-5.85, mains €5.85-10, pizza €4-5.85; ☾ 9am-11pm Thu-Tue) This popular *gostilna* just a wee bit out of the centre serves standard Slovenian dishes as well as pizza and has both a big courtyard and an inviting terrace

Kašča (☎ 512 43 00, 041-688 597; Spodnji trg 1; starters €4.40-7.30, mains €5-11.50; ☾ noon-11pm Mon-Sat) This attractive pub and wine bar in the cellar of the town's 16th-century granary also serves good Slovenian dishes, including ones peculiar to the Škofja Loka area.

The covered **market** (Šolska ulica; ☾ 7am-1pm Thu & Sat) is northeast of the Nama department store. You'll find a **Mercator** (Mestni trg 9; 8am-7pm Mon-Fri, 7am-1pm Sat, 8am-noon Sun) supermarket in the Old Town.

Drinking

Gostilna Homan (☎ 512 30 47, 041-635 162; Mestni trg 2; ☼ 8am-11pm Mon-Thu, 8am-2am Fri & Sat, 8am-11pm Sun) This ground pub and café in historical Homan House is always busy, especially in the warm weather when tables are set out on Mestni trg under the giant linden trees.

Pri Miholu (☎ 512 00 59; Mestni trg 26; ☼ 9am-11pm Mon-Thu, 9am-midnight Fri, 10am-3pm Sat) This old-style pub is in historic Martin House and is built into part of the defence walls at Poljane Gate.

Getting There & Away

Count on at least hourly buses between 7.10am and 10.15pm to Kranj (€2.60, 20 minutes, 16km) and between 5.10am and 9.10pm to Ljubljana (€3, 30 minutes, 21km).

Škofja Loka can be reached on up to 12 trains a day from Ljubljana (€1.45, 30 minutes, 20km) via Medvode. An equal number continue on to Jesenice (€3.30, 50 minutes, 44km) via Kranj, Radovljica and Lesce-Bled. Up to eight of these cross the border for Villach, 87km to the north in Austria.

Getting Around

Local buses make the run between the train station in Trata and the bus station on Kapucinski trg. You can order a taxi on ☎ 041-625 875. **VeloSport** (☎ 512 32 00; Poljanska cesta 4; 9am-1pm & 3-7pm Mon-Fri, 9am-noon Sat) rents mountain bikes (per day/week €5.50/25).

AROUND ŠKOFJA LOKA
Suha

☎ 04 / pop 158 / elev 338m
The 15th-century **Church of St John the Baptist** (Cerkev Sv Janeza Krstnika) at Suha, about 2.5km east of Škofja Loka, is unexceptional except for the presbytery, which has an interior completely covered with amazing frescoes painted by Bartholomew of Loka in the 16th century. The paintings on the vaults show various Apostles, the coronation of Mary and scenes from the life of Christ. The panels below depict the five wise and five foolish virgins (the latter forgot to put oil in their lamps, according to the Gospel of St Matthew). Inside the arch facing the altar is a frightening scene from the Last Judgment.

If the church is locked, request the key from the house at No 32, the first building on the left as you enter Suha village and about 150m beyond the church.

Crngrob

☎ 04 / pop 35 / elev 420m
The **Church of the Annunciation** (Cerkev Marijinega Oznanenja; adult €1.25/0.85; ☼ by appointment) at Crngrob, about 4km north of Škofja Loka, has one of the most treasured frescoes in Slovenia. Look for it on the outside wall under a 19th-century portico near the church entrance. Called Holy Sunday (Sveta Nedelja) and produced in the workshop of Johannes de Laibaco (John of Ljubljana) in 1460, it explains in pictures what good Christians do on Sunday (pray, go to Mass, help the sick) and what they do not do (gamble, drink, play bowls or fight). The consequence of doing any of the latter is damnation – vividly illustrated with souls being swallowed whole by a demon. On the south wall there's a large fresco of St Christopher from the same era.

The interior of the church, which was built and modified between the 14th and 17th centuries, contains more medieval frescoes on the north wall as well as a huge gilded altar built in 1652. The colourful star vaulting of the presbytery has a number of bosses portraying the Virgin Mary, the Bishops of Freising, and a man on horseback, probably a church benefactor.

Crngrob is easily accessible on foot or by bicycle (p99) from Škofja Loka via Groharjevo naselje, which runs north from the Capuchin monastery and Cesta Talcev. An alternative is to take the bus bound for Kranj, get off at the village of Dorfarje and walk northwest for about 1.5km.

KRANJ

☎ 04 / pop 34,840 / elev 386m
Backed by a battalion of mountain peaks, including snow-capped Storžič (2132m), the Old Town in Kranj, Slovenia's fourth-largest and most industrialised city, looks most picturesque when seen from across the Sava River, looking to the northeast. This is a view you'll enjoy briefly from the right-hand windows of buses headed from Ljubljana to Bled or Kranjska Gora, between gaps in the light-industrial foreground.

History

A secondary Roman road linking Emona (Ljubljana) and Virunum (near today's Klagenfurt in Austria) ran through Kranj until about the 5th century; a hundred years later the marauding Langobards established a base

GORENJSKA

here. They were followed by tribes of early Slavs, whose large burial grounds can be partly seen below the floor of the Gorenjska Museum in the old town hall.

In the 11th century, Kranj was an important border stronghold of the Frankish counts in their battles with the Hungarians, and the town gave its name to the entire region – Kranjska (Carniola in English). It was also an important market and ecclesiastical centre, and within 200 years Kranj was granted town status by the new rulers, the Bavarian Counts of Andechs. More wealth came with the development of iron mining and foundries, and when the progressive Protestant movement reached Gorenjska, it was centred in Kranj. The city grew faster after the arrival of the railway in 1870.

Orientation

The attractive Old Town, sitting on an escarpment above the confluence of the Sava and Kokra Rivers, barely measures 1km by 250m and contains everything of interest in Kranj. It is essentially composed of three pedestrian streets running north to south. The main one begins as Prešernova ulica at Maistrov trg and changes its name to Cankarjeva ulica at Glavni trg, the main square and market place in medieval times. Cankarjeva ulica ends at Pungert, the 'Land's End' at the tip of the promontory.

Kranj's bus station is about 600m north of Maistrov trg on the corner of Bleiweisova cesta and Stošičeva ulica. The train station is on Kolodvorska cesta below the Old Town to the west.

Information

Gorenjska Banka Bleiweisova cesta (Bleiweisova cesta 1; ☽ 8am-6pm Mon-Fri, 8am-noon Sat); Old Town branch (Prešernova ulica 6; ☽ 9-11.30am & 2-5pm Mon-Fri, 8-11am Sat)

Mladinska Knjiga (☎ 201 58 35; Maistrov trg 1; ☽ 8.30am-7pm Mon-Fri, 8.30am-1pm Sat) Sells regional maps.

Post office (Poštna ulica 4)

SKB Banka (Koroška cesta 5; ☽ 8am-3.30pm Mon-Thu, 8am-2.30pm Fri) In the Hotel Creina building.

Tourist Information Centre Kranj (☎ 236 30 30; www.tourism-kranj.si; Koroška cesta 29; ☽ 8am-7pm Mon-Fri) Has internet access (per hour €2).

Sights

MAISTROV TRG

The gateway to the Old Town, this was the site of the upper town gates in the 15th cen-

tury. It was the most vulnerable part of Kranj; the steep Kokra Canyon protected the town on the eastern side and thick walls did the trick on the west from Pungert as far as the square. The **Špital Tower** (Špitalski Stolp; Maistrov trg 3), one of seven along the wall, now forms part of a butcher shop. The best view of the cone-shaped tower is from Kokrški breg. The unusual Art Deco building with the three statues facing the square to the north is the **former post office** (stara pošta; Koroška cesta 1), which dates from the 1930s. It has four Atlases on the south side.

The restored **Prešeren House** (Prešernova Hiša; Prešernova ulica 7) was home to the poet France Prešeren (1800–49) for the last two years of his life; he died in the front bedroom. It now contains the **Prešeren Memorial Museum** (Prešernov Spominski Muzej; ☎ 201 39 80; adult/child/student & senior/family €2/1/1.25/4.20; ☽ 10am-6pm Tue-Sun) in five rooms, two of them with original furnishings. Unfortunately, most of the explanatory notes next to the poet's letters, diaries and manuscripts are in Slovene only. Prešeren is buried in the parish cemetery, now called **Prešeren Grove** (Prešernov Gaj), about 500m to the north.

GLAVNI TRG

A beautiful plaza, Glavni trg (Main Square) is populated by Gothic and Renaissance buildings; the ones on the western side with their painted facades, vaulted hallways and arched courtyards are masterpieces. The 16th-century one opposite is the **former town hall** (mestna hiša; Glavni trg 4), which now contains most of the collection of the **Gorenjska Museum** (Gorenjski Muzej; ☎ 201 39 80; www.gorenjski-muzej.si; adult/child/student & senior/family €2/1/1.25/4.20; ☽ 10am-6pm Tue-Sun). Among the eye-catching bits and bobs lying around is a large porcelain stove topped with a Turk's turbaned head, an embroidered sheepskin coat called a *kožuh* and a child's toy consisting of a devil sharpening a gossip's tongue on a grindstone. Below the floor of the vaulted vestibule at the entrance to the museum, Slavic tombs (complete with bones) from the 9th and 10th centuries can be seen through glass panels.

The **Parish Church of St Cantianus** (Župnijska Cerkev Sv Kancijana), which was built on to part of an older church starting in about 1400, is the best example of a hall church (ie one with a nave and aisles of equal height) in Slovenia. The Mount of Olives relief in the arch above the main portal dating from 1450 is well worth a look before entering, as is the modern altar (1934) designed by Ivan Vurnik. Below the north side of the church there are more old bones from early Slavic graves and a medieval ossuary. On the south wall is a lapidarium of tombstones dating from the Middle Ages and nearby the **Fountain of St John Nepomuk**, with a stone statue of the 14th-

century Bohemian martyr complete with a doleful-looking octopus in the water.

PUNGERT

Another 300m further south, the Old Town dead-ends behind the **Plague Church**, built during a time of pestilence in 1470 and dedicated to the three 'intercessors against the plague' –

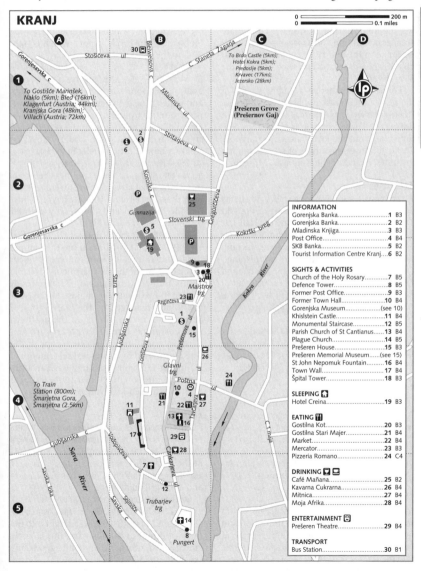

KRANJ

GORENJSKA

Sts Rok, Fabian and Sebastian. It is now used by Serbian Orthodox Christians. The three-storey **defence tower** (*obrambni stolp*) beside the church was built in the 16th century.

OTHER SIGHTS
At the end of Tomšičeva ulica northwest of Pungert is the **Church of the Holy Rosary** (Roženvenska Cerkev), built in the 16th century. It was a Protestant sanctuary during the Reformation. Beside the church are arcades, a fountain and a **monumental staircase** designed in the late 1950s by Jože Plečnik to give Kranj a dramatic entrance up from the Sava River.

To the north of here is a lengthy section of the restored **town wall** and **Khislstein Castle** (Grad Khislstein; Tomšičeva ulica 44), part of which was built during the Turkish invasions of the 15th century; check out the lovely arcaded courtyard. Today it houses the offices of several cultural institutes, including the Gorenjska Museum.

Activities
A very easy destination for a walk is **Šmarjetna Gora**, a 643m hill 3km northwest of the Old Town, where a fort stood during the Hallstatt period. The reconstructed **Church of St Margaret** is atop the hill. The views from here of Kranj, the Alps and the Sava River are astonishing.

Another easy walk follows the left bank of the **Kokra River** north from the eastern end of Poštna ulica for 8km and then back again. Ask the tourist office for the *Kokra River Gorge* brochure.

The Hotel Kokra sells **fishing licences** (per day €83.50) for use in the dozen-odd lakes on the hotel grounds and rents rods for €12.50 a day. They also offer **horse riding** (€10.50 to €18.80).

Festivals & Events
If you're in Kranj on the second Sunday in August, follow the flocks to Jezersko, on the Austrian border 28km northeast of Kranj, for the annual **Shepherds' Ball** (Ovčarski Bal). It's a day and evening of folk music, dancing and drinking *žganje* (brandy) – the ovine alternative to the bovine event in Bohinj (p122).

Sleeping
Most of the private rooms available within striking distance of Kranj are in Naklo, 5km northwest of the centre, including those at **Drinovec** (☎ 257 27 45; Ulica Bratov Praprotnik 9; per person €17; P)

Gostišče Marinšek (☎ 257 22 20, fax 257 11 15; Glavna cesta 2; s/d €25/49) This B&B in Naklo is above a popular restaurant and pub that sells its own homemade beer.

Hotel Creina (☎ 281 75 00; www.hotel-creina .si; Koroška cesta 5; s/d €60/80; P) This central brick-and-timber hotel with 87 rooms, the only game in town if you want to stay central, is popular with Austrian business people, tour groups headed for the Alps and airline crews who don't want to travel all the way to Ljubljana from Brnik airport, which is only 7km to the southeast.

Hotel Kokra (☎ 260 10 00; www.brdo.com; s/d/ste €34/54/80; P) Although it's hardly castle quality, this four-star hotel with 80 rooms and suites is near the entrance to Brdo and is surrounded by lovely parkland, plus a protected 478-hectare forest and a dozen lakes stocked with trout, carp and pike. While Kokra's new addition **Vrelec Brdo** (Brdo Spring; ☎ 260 18 16; open 5pm to midnight Monday to Friday, 4pm to midnight Saturday and Sunday) wellness centre is one of the most attractive in Slovenia. Don't miss the superb *toplar* (double hayrack) just outside the hotel and the nearby painted beehive.

Brdo Castle (☎ 260 10 00; www.brdo.com; apt from €547; P) If you have more than ample funds and you really want to treat yourself, check into one of the six apartments available at this 16th-century castle on 72 hectares of garden in Predoslje, about 5km northeast of Kranj, and managed by the State Protocol Service. It has two towers on the northern side, corridors crammed with artwork and a library containing a priceless copy of the Bible translated by Protestant reformer Jurij Dalmatin (1547–89). Nonguests can only view the interior by guided tour (€6.25 to €7.50) organised in advance.

Eating
Pizzeria Romano (☎ 236 39 00; Tavčarjeva ulica 31a; pizza €4-5.25, grills €4.40-6; 7am-11pm Mon-Thu, 7am-midnight Fri & Sat, 4-11pm Sun) This simple place northeast of the post office and perched precariously above the Kokra River Gorge has pizza, pasta and great grilled dishes.

Gostilna Kot (Corner Inn; ☎ 202 61 05; Maistrov trg 4; starters €2.10-7.10, mains €4-13.80; 7am-10pm Mon-Thu, 7am-11pm Fri, 7am-6pm Sat) Squeezed right into the thick of things in Maistrov trg, this is justly famed for its affordable and quite good daily specialities (€3.25 to €4).

Gostilna Stari Majer (☎ 280 00 20; Glavni trg 16; starters €5-6.25, mains €5.25-10.80; ☺ 9am-10pm) The stick-to-the-ribs Slovenian dishes at this old-style eatery will keep you going for longer than you'd think.

The large **market** (Tavčarjeva ulica; ☺ 6am-6pm mid-Mar–mid-Oct, 7am-3pm mid-Oct–mid-Mar) northeast of the Parish Church of St Cantianus sells mostly fruit and vegetables. You'll find a branch of **Mercator** (Maistrov trg 11; ☺ 7am-7pm Mon-Fri, 7am-1pm Sat) supermarket in the Old Town

Drinking

Kavarna Cukrarna (☎ 281 82 90; Tavčarjeva ulica 9; ☺ 8am-11pm Mon-Thu, 8am-midnight Fri & Sat, 8am-10pm Sun) This café with a balcony overlooking the dramatic Kokra River Gorge is a great place for a drink and a slice of something sweet.

Mitnica (☎ 040-678 778; Tavčarjeva ulica 35; ☺ 7am-11pm Mon-Wed, 7am-1pm Thu, 7am-3am Fri & Sat) This lovely and very welcoming *kavarna*, in the basement of a 16th-century toll house with a huge covered terrace backing onto the river, is just the place to relax in Kranj on a warm afternoon.

Moja Afrika (My Africa; ☎ 202 55 95; Cankarjeva ulica 3; ☺ 9am-midnight Mon-Thu, 9am-2am Fri & Sat, 5pm-midnight Sun) Tastefully decorated with African masks, bamboo, vines and contemporary sculptures, this attractive café-bar, turns into a club with DJ and/or live music at the weekend.

Café Mañana (☎ 236 41 21; Slovenski trg 7; ☺ 6am-midnight Mon, 6.30am-1am Tue & Wed, 6.30am-4am Thu & Fri, 9am-4am Sat, 1pm-midnight Sun) This enormous pub next to the Storžič cinema is popular with a very young crowd and is about the only place worth mentioning in 'new' Kranj. It's a dance club from 10pm on Friday and Saturday nights.

Entertainment

Prešeren Theatre (☎ 280 49 00; Glavni trg 6) This provincial theatre is very active, staging four plays and up to 200 performances a year. Note the rather dashing statue of Prešeren out front.

Concerts – both classical and popular – are held in the courtyard of Khislstein Castle in summer and sometimes at the Parish Church of St Cantianus during the year.

Getting There & Away

Buses depart from Kranj at least hourly for Bled (€3.50, 40 minutes, 26km), Bohinjska Bistrica (€5.10, 1½ hours, 45km), Ljubljana (€3, 40 minutes, 23km), Radovljica (€2.60,

30 minutes, 19km) and Škofja Loka (€2.60, 20 minutes, 16km). You can also reach Bovec via Kranjska Gora (€6.20, two hours, 57km) and the Vršič Pass on one bus a day in July and August. There's also a bus to Varaždin (€18, four hours, 201km) in Croatia at 5.50am on Saturday and Sunday.

Up to 15 trains a day pass through Kranj from Ljubljana (€2, 30 minutes, 29km) via Medvode and Škofja Loka. They continue to Radovljica, Lesce-Bled and Jesenice (€4, 40 minutes, 35km), where up to eight cross the border for Villach, 72km to the north in Austria.

Getting Around

Local buses make the run from the train station to the bus terminus on Stošičeva ulica.

You can ring a local taxi on ☎ 202 61 00.

KRVAVEC
☎ 04 / elev to 1971m

The **Krvavec ski centre** (☎ 252 59 30; www.rtc-krvavec.si; half-day pass adult/child/senior & student €20.50/13.30/18.40, day pass €23.40/14/21), 17km northeast of Kranj and easily done as a day trip from Ljubljana, is one of the most popular (and crowded) in Slovenia. A cable car transports you up to the centre at 1450m, and seven chairlifts and four T-bar tows serve the 33km of slopes and 3km of cross-country runs. Krvavec is also an excellent starting point for hikes in summer to **Kriška Planina** or **Jezerca**, about an hour's walk from the cable car's upper station.

RADOVLJICA
☎ 04 / pop 5935 / elev 496m

A charming town full of historic buildings, Radovljica enjoys an enviable position atop an outcrop 75m above a wide plain called the Dežela, literally 'Country' in Slovene.

Radovljica was settled by the early Slavs and grew into an important market town by the early 14th century. With increased trade on the river and the iron forgeries at nearby Kropa and Kamna Gorica, Radovljica expanded. The town was built around a large rectangular square fortified with a wall and defence towers. Radovljica's affluence in the Middle Ages can be seen in the lovely buildings still lining Linhartov trg today.

Orientation

The centre of old Radovljica is Linhartov trg; the new town extends primarily north and northwest along Gorenjska cesta towards

GORENJSKA

Lesce. Radovljica's bus station is 500m north-west of Linhartov trg on Kranjska cesta. The train station is below the Old Town on Cesta Svobode.

Information

Gorenjska Banka (Gorenjska cesta 16; ⏰ 8am-6pm Mon-Fri, 8am-noon Sat)

Post office (Kranjska cesta 1; ⏰ 7am-7pm Mon-Fri, 7am-noon Sat)

SKB Banka (Gorenjska cesta 10; ⏰ 8.30am-noon & 2-5pm Mon-Fri)

Tourist Information Centre Radovljica (☎ 531 53 00; tdradovljica@siol.net; Gorenjska cesta 1; ⏰ 8am-6pm Mon-Fri, 8am-noon Sat May-Sep; 9am-4pm Mon-Fri, 9am-1pm Sat Oct-Apr)

Sights

BEEKEEPING MUSEUM

Although it might not sound like a crowd-pleaser, this **museum** (Čebelarski Muzej; ☎ 532 05 20; www.muzeji-radovljica.si; Linhartov trg 1; adult/child/family €2.10/1.70/5; ⏰ 10am-1pm & 3-6pm Tue-Sun May-Oct; 10am-noon & 3-5pm Wed, Sat & Sun Mar, Apr, Nov & Dec) is one of the most interesting in the country, and there's not a whole lot you won't know about things apiarian after buzzing around for an hour or so inside. The museum is housed (together with a music school) in **Thurn Manor**, which began life as Ortenburg Castle in the early Middle Ages but was rebuilt with a large hall on the ground floor after the earthquake of 1511. The cream-and-white structure has interesting reliefs and stucco work on its facade.

The museum's exhibits take a close look at the history of beekeeping in Slovenia (which was at its most intense in the 18th and 19th centuries), the country's unique contribution to the industry with the development of the Carniolan grey bee species (Apis mellifera carnica) and the research of men such as Anton Janša (1734–73), who set up a research station in the Karavanke and is considered around the world as the 'father of modern beekeeping'. And the museum doesn't fail to pass on a few fun facts to know and tell. Did you realise that bees cannot see the colour red but go gaga over yellow? The museum's collection of illustrated beehive panels (panjske končnice) from the 18th and 19th centuries, a folk art unique to Slovenia, is the largest in the country.

Bees are still kept in Slovenia for their honey and wax but much more lucrative are such by-products as pollen, propolis and royal jelly used as elixirs and in homoeopathic medicine. Propolis is a brownish, waxy substance collected from certain trees by bees and used to cement or caulk their hives. Royal jelly, so beloved by the European aristocracy of the 1920s and 1930s and by the Chinese today, is the substance fed to the queen bee by the workers.

RADOVLJICA

0 _____ 200 m
0 _____ 0.1 miles

To Camping Radovljica & Swimming Pool (400m); Sport Penzion Manca (2.5km); Bled (6km)

Kranjska c

Ljubljanska c

Gorenjska c

To Mošje (4km); Grad Podvin (4km); Restavracija JB Podvin (4km)

Gorenjska c

Grub eva ul

Kolodvorska ul

To Camping Šobec Ground (2.5 km)

Train Station

Linhartov trg

C Svobode

Gradiška pot

Na Mlaki

INFORMATION	
Gorenjska Banka	1 A2
Post Office	2 A1
SKB Banka	3 A2
Tourist Information Centre Radovljica	4 A2

SIGHTS & ACTIVITIES	
Beekeeping Museum	(see 10)
Gallery	(see 9)
Koman House	5 B3
Mali House	6 B3
Parish Church of St Peter	7 B3
Rectory	8 B3
Šivec House	9 B3
Thurn Manor	10 B3
Vidič House	11 B3

SLEEPING	
Hotel Grajski Dvor	12 A2

EATING	
Gostilna Augustin	13 B3
Grajska Gostilnica	(see 12)

SHOPPING	
Kamen Gallery	14 B2
Vinoteka Sodček	15 B2

TRANSPORT	
Bus Station	16 A1

THE BOARDS & THE BEES

The keeping of honeybees (species *Apis*) has been an integral part of Slovenian agriculture since the 16th century when *ajda* (buckwheat) was first planted on fallow ground to allow the more intensive use of farm land. Bees favour buckwheat, so Slovenia, especially the alpine regions of Carniola (Kranjska), was soon awash in honey for cooking and beeswax for candles.

Originally bees were kept in hollow logs or woven baskets, but the entire hive was damaged when the honeycomb was removed. The invention of the *kranjič* hive, with removable boxes that resembled a chest of drawers, solved the problem by creating individual hives. It also led to the development of Slovenia's most important form of folk art.

Kranjič hives have *panjske končnice* (front boards) above the entrance, and painting and decorating these panels with religious motifs soon became all the rage. Ethnographers are still out to lunch over whether the illustrations were appeals to protect the hives from fire or disease, meant to guide the bees (they can distinguish colour) back home or to help beekeepers identify their hives.

The first panels (from the mid-18th century) were painted in a 'folk baroque' style and the subjects were taken from the Old and New Testaments (Adam and Eve, the Virgin May, Sts Florian and George, and especially patient Job, the patron of beekeepers) and history (the Turkish invasions, Napoleon, the Illyrian Provinces and the Counter-Reformation with Martin Luther being driven to hell by a devil). The most interesting panels show the foibles, rivalries and humour of the human condition. A devil may be sharpening a gossip's tongue on a grindstone or two women fighting over a man's trousers (ie his hand in marriage). A very common illustration shows the devil exchanging old wives for nubile young women – to the delight of the husbands. Another – in a 'world turned upside down' – has gun-toting deer and bears laying the hunter in his grave.

The painting of beehive panels in Slovenia enjoyed its golden age between about 1820 and 1880; after that the art form went into decline. The introduction of a new and much larger hive by Anton Žnidaršič at the end of the 19th century obviated the need for small illustrations, and the art form degenerated into kitsch.

Nowadays you'll see the best examples of painted beehive panels in museums, such as the ones at Radovljica and Maribor, but there are still a few traditional – and protected – ones around, such as those at Muljava in Dolenjska. An interesting twist is the beehive at Brdo Castle (p104) near Kranj painted in the 1970s by some of Slovenia's most outstanding artists. Nowadays the most common hives are the large box ones painted bright yellow (a colour bees like) and the 'hives on wheels', which can be moved into the sun or to a promising meadow.

LINHARTOV TRG

Radovljica's main square is named in honour of Slovenia's first dramatist and historian, Anton Tomaž Linhart (1756–95), who was born here. It is lined with houses mostly from the 16th century and has been described by the National Tourist Office as 'the most homogeneous old town core in Slovenia'.

Several lovely buildings are opposite the Beekeeping Museum, including **Koman House** (Komanova Hiša; Linhartov trg 23), which has a baroque painting on its front of St Florian, the patron saint of fires (he douses, not sets, them) and **Mali House** (Malijeva Hiša; Linhartov trg 25), which has a barely visible picture of St George slaying the dragon. The 17th-century **Vidič House** (Vidičeva Hiša; Linhartov trg 3) has a corner projection and is colourfully painted in red, yellow and blue, while **house No 17** has a fresco of Martin of Tours sharing his cloak with a beggar.

The most important house here is 16th-century **Šivec House** (Šivčeva Hiša; ☎ 532 05 20; Linhartov trg 22; ☖ 10am-noon & 6-8pm Tue-Sun Jul & Aug; 10am-noon & 5-7pm Tue-Sun Jun & Sep; 10am-noon & 4-6pm Tue-Sun Oct-May), which is an interesting hybrid: Renaissance on the outside and Gothic within. On the ground floor there is a vaulted hall, which now serves as a **gallery**, and on the 1st floor there is a wood-panelled late-Gothic drawing room with a beamed ceiling used as a wedding hall. There is also a chimneyless 'black kitchen' and an interesting collection of children's book illustrations by celebrated Slovenian artists. There fresco on the exterior that shows the Good Samaritan performing his work of mercy.

East of the square is the Gothic **Parish Church of St Peter** (Župnijska Cerkev Sv Petra), a hall church modelled after the one in Kranj. The three portals are flamboyant Gothic, and the sculptures inside were done by Angelo Pozzo in 1713. The building with the arcaded courtyard south of the church is the **rectory** (*župnišče*).

Activities
There is a public **swimming pool** (☎ 531 57 70; Kopališka cesta; ☼ 9am-9pm Jun–mid-Sep) near the camping ground open in summer, with tennis courts nearby.

The **Sport Riding Centre** (☎ 532 52 00) at Grad Podvin (Podvin Castle; right), about 4km southeast of Radovljica, has horses (€10.50 to €19) available for riding individually or with an instructor.

Festivals & Events
The biggest event of the year is the two-week **Festival Radovljica** (http://festival-radovljica.amis.net), one of the most important festivals of ancient classical music in Europe, held in mid-August.

Sleeping
Camping Radovljica (☎ 531 24 57, fax 531 57 70; Kopališka cesta 9; per person/car/caravan €6.70/1.50/ 2.10/1.50; ☼ Jun–mid-Sep; P) The town's smallish camping ground (1.5 hectares) is next to the public swimming pool, and the daily rate includes use of it.

Camping Šobec (☎ 535 37 00; www.sobec.si; Šobčeva cesta 25; camping per adult €9.50-11, child €7-8.50, bungalows for 2 €76-90, for 3-6 €98-115; ☼ late Apr-Sep; P) The largest (15 hectares with 500 sites) and arguably the best-equipped camping ground in Slovenia is in Lesce, about 2.5km northwest of Radovljica. Situated on a small lake near a bend of the Sava Dolinka River, the camping ground can accommodate 1500 people in tents and bungalows.

Hotel Grajski Dvor (☎ 531 55 85; www.hotel-grajski -dvor.si; Kranjska ulica 2; s €40-42, d €60-64; P) Radovljica's only hotel, the five-floor, 55-room 'Castle Courtyard' is central but certainly not luxurious. The attached Grajska Gostilnica restaurant is worth a visit.

Sport Penzion Manca (☎ 531 40 51; www.manca-sp.si; Gradnikova cesta 2; s €43-50, d €68-76, tr €84-96; P) This excellent-value pension about 2.5km north of Linhartov trg has 17 spic-and-span modern rooms and all sorts of sports facilities – from swimming pool and sauna to bicycles. Some rooms have views of the Karavanke range, others of Mt Triglav itself.

Grad Podvin (☎ 532 52 00; www.grad-podvin.si; Mošnje 1; s €44-51, d €60-68; P) If you missed out on (or couldn't afford) staying at Brdo Castle (p104), this 17-room hotel might be some compensation. It's a rather boxy Italianate affair about 4km southeast of Radovljica in the village of Mošnje but, hey, it's still a castle. Podvin Castle is surrounded by a lovely park and has tennis courts, an outdoor pool and a popular horse riding centre. The Restavracija JB Podvin next door is another draw.

Eating
Grajska Gostilnica (☎ 531 44 45; Kranjska ulica 2; starters €4.10-6.25, mains €7.75-12.50; ☼ 11am-11pm) The flagship at the Hotel Grajski Dvor, this place has become popular for its pasta (€5 to €6.70) and Dalmatian dishes, a great wine list and an atmospheric cellar below. All the metalwork was produced by UKO (p110) in Kropa.

Restavracija JB Podvin (☎ 532 52 80; Mošnje 1; starters €8.35-12.50, mains €14.60-18.80; ☼ 11am-11pm) This sister-restaurant of the similarly named establishment in Ljubljana has raised the standards of dining in Gorenjska in one fell swoop. It's next door to the Grad Podvin hotel.

Shopping
Vinoteka Sodček (☎ 531 50 71; Linhartov trg 8; ☼ 9am-7pm Mon-Fri, 8am-noon Sat) This shop has an excellent selection of Slovenian wines and tastings too.

Kamen Gallery (☎ 531 00 61; Linhartov trg 4; ☼ 9am-noon & 3-7pm Mon-Fri, 9am-noon Sat) This shop specialises in quality Slovenian folk craft of ceramics, wood and glass. The selection of beehive panel reproductions is phenomenal.

Getting There & Away

Buses leave Radovljica for Bled (€1.70, 10 minutes, 7.5km) almost every 30 minutes between 6.15am and 10.15pm and for Ljubljana (€5, one hour, 43km) via Kranj between 7am and 8.15pm. There are also buses to Kranjska Gora (€4.60, one hour, 39km, three a day) and Kropa (€2.20, 20 minutes, 11km, five to eight a day).

Radovljica is on the rail line linking Ljubljana (€3.30, 55 minutes, 48km) with Jesenice (€1.45, 20 minutes, 16km) via Škofja Loka, Kranj and Lesce-Bled. Up to 15 trains a day pass through the town in each direction. About eight of the northbound ones carry on to Villach, 54km to the north in Austria.

BREZJE

04 / pop493 / elev 488m

The **Basilica of Our Lady of Perpetual Help** (Bazilika Marije Pomojaj; ☎ 537 07 00; www.brezje.si; Brezje 72) in this village about 5km southeast of Radovljica has been a centre of pilgrimage since the time of the Illyrian Provinces and today attracts some 300,000 Catholic faithful each year. It is to Slovenia what Lourdes is to France, Knock is to Ireland and Częstochowa is to Poland; indeed, this was Pope John Paul II's first port of call when he first visited Slovenia in 1996. Still, apart from Janez Vurnik's stunning main altar, the altar painting of May (the main focus of attention) by Leopold Layer and some works by Ivan Grohar, the neo-Moorish basilica dating from 1900 is unexceptional. Brezje can be reached by bus from Bled (€1.30, 10 minutes, 5km, three or four daily) via Radovljica.

KROPA

☎ 04 / pop 835 / elev 531m

While in Radovljica, don't miss the chance for an easy half-day trip to visit Kropa, a delightful little village tucked away in a narrow valley below the Jelovica Plateau 11km to the southeast. Kropa has been a 'workhorse' for centuries, mining iron ore and hammering out the nails and decorative wrought iron that can still be seen in many parts of Slovenia. Today Kropa has turned its attention to screws – the German-owned Novi Plamen factory is based here – but artisans continue their work, clanging away in the workshop on the village's single street. The work of their forebears is evident in weather vanes, shutters and ornamental street lamps shaped like birds and dragons.

Sights

BLACKSMITH MUSEUM

The fascinating collection at this **museum** (Kovaški Muzej; ☎ 533 72 00; www.muzeji-radovljica.si; Kropa 10; adult/child €1.70/1.25, with forge display €2.10/1.70, with forge display & film €2.50/2.10; ☺ 10am-1pm & 3-6pm Tue-Sun May-Oct; 10am-noon & 3-5pm Wed, Sat & Sun Mar, Apr, Nov & Dec) traces the history of iron mining and forging in Kropa and nearby Kamna Gorica from the 14th to the early 20th centuries. Nail and spike manufacturing was the town's main industry for most of that period; from giant ones that held the pylons below Venice together to little studs for snow boots, Kropa produced more than 100 varieties in huge quantities. You did not become a master blacksmith here until you could fit a horseshoe around an egg – without cracking the shell.

The museum has working models of forges, a couple of rooms showing how workers and their families lived in very cramped quarters (up to 45 people in one house) and a special exhibit devoted to the work of Jože Bertoncelj (1901–76), who turned out exquisite wrought-iron gratings, candlesticks, chandeliers and even masks. The museum shows two films, one on nail production and one on local customs.

The house itself was owned by a 17th-century iron baron called Klinar, and it contains some valuable furniture and paintings. Among the most interesting pieces is a 19th-century wind-up 'jukebox' from Bohemia. Ask the curator to insert one of the large perforated rolls and watch the piano, drums, triangle and cymbals make music.

OTHER SIGHTS

An 18th-century furnace called **Vice Forge** (Vigenj Vice) lies a short distance north of the museum behind **house No 56**, birthplace of the Slovenian painter Janez Krstnik Potočnik (1749–1834), whose work can be seen in the baroque **Church of St Leonard** (Cerkev Sv Lenarta) on the hill to the east, and in Kamnik. Below it is the **Kroparica**, a fast-flowing mountain stream that once turned the 50 water wheels that powered the furnaces for the forges. Kropa has many other lovely old houses, including several around **Trg Kropa** (also called Plac), the main square, which also has an interesting old wayside shrine. The scary-looking neo-Gothic pile up on the hill to the west is the **Church of the Mother of God** (Cerkev Matere Božje).

GORENJSKA

Sleeping & Eating

Gostilna Pr' Kovač (At the Smith's; ☎ 533 63 20, 041-414 046; Kropa 30; per person €20-25) This convivial and very popular *gostilna* (starters €1.70 to €8, mains €7.10 to €10; open 10am-11pm Tuesday to Sunday) in a lovely old house with outside seating just north of the Blacksmith Museum has three rooms available for between two and six people.

Gostilna Pri Jarmu (☎ At the Yoke; ☎ 533 67 50; Kropa 2; starters €2-3.75, mains €4.60-8, pizza €2.50-4.20; ✆ 10am-midnight daily May-Sep, 10am-midnight Fri-Tue Oct-Jun) This humble *gostilna* at the southern end of Kropa serves hearty Slovenian favourites as well as a decent range of vegetarian dishes (€2.50 to €5).

There's a **Mercator** (Kropa 3a; ✆ 8am-7pm Mon-Fri, 7am-1pm Sat) supermarket branch between Gostilna Pri Jarmu and the post office.

Shopping

UKO Kropa forgers' workshop (☎ 533 73 00; Kropa 7a; ✆ 7am-6pm Mon-Fri, 9am-noon Sat Jul & Aug; 7am-3pm Mon-Fri, 9am-noon Sat Sep-Jun) Across from the museum, this place has a shop selling all manner of articles made of wrought iron.

Getting There & Away

Between five and eight buses run to Radovljica (€2.20, 20 minutes, 11km) daily. They stop in front of the Mercator supermarket.

BLED

☎ 04 / pop 5250 / elev 501m

With its emerald-green lake, picture-postcard island church, cliff-topping medieval castle and its mountain backdrop, Bled is Slovenia's most popular resort and its biggest tourist money-spinner. Not surprisingly, it can be overpriced and swarming with tourists.

But as is the case with many popular destinations around the world, people come in droves – and will continue to do so – because the place *is* special. On a clear day you can make out Mt Stol (2236m) and Slovenia's highest peak, Mt Triglav (2864m), in the distance – and then the bells start ringing from the belfry of the little island church. You should visit Bled at least once. It's quite simply magical.

History

Bled was the site of a Hallstatt settlement in the early Iron Age, but as it was far from the main trade routes, the Romans gave it short shrift. More importantly, from the 7th century the early Slavs came in waves, establishing themselves at Pristava below the castle, on the tiny island and at a dozen other sites around the lake.

Around the turn of the first millennium, the German Emperor Henry II presented Bled Castle and its lands to the Bishops of Brixen in South Tyrol, who retained secular control of the area until the early 19th century when the Habsburgs took it over.

Bled's beauty and its warm waters were well known to medieval pilgrims who came to pray at the island church; the place made it into print in 1689 when Janez Vajkard Valvasor described the lake's thermal springs in *The Glory of the Duchy of Carniola*. But Bled's wealth was not fully appreciated at that time, and in the late 18th century the keeper of the castle seriously considered draining Lake Bled and using the clay to make bricks.

Fortunately, along came a Swiss doctor named Arnold Rikli, who saw the lake's full potential. In 1855 he opened baths where the casino now stands, taking advantage of the springs, the clean air and the mountain light. With the opening of the railway from Ljubljana to Tarvisio (Trbiž) in 1870, more and more guests came to Bled and the resort was a favourite of wealthy Europeans from the turn of the century right up to WWII. In fact, under the Kingdom of Serbs, Croats and Slovenes, Bled was the summer residence of the Karadžordževići, the Yugoslav royal family.

Orientation

'Bled' refers both to the lake and to the settlements around it, particularly the built-up area to the northeast where most of the hotels are located. This development is dominated by a modern shopping complex called the Bled Shopping Centre (Trgovski Center Bled). Bled's main road, Ljubljanska cesta, runs eastward from here. Footpaths and a road called Cesta Svobode (when south of the lake) and Kidričeva cesta (when to the north) circle the lake.

Bled's bus station is at the junction of Cesta Svobode and Grajska cesta, just up from the Hotel Jelovica. There are two train stations. Lesce-Bled is 4km to the southeast on the road to Radovljica and on the line linking Ljubljana with Jesenice and Austria. Bled Jezero station, on Kolodvorska cesta northwest of the lake,

BLED

0 ———— 500 m
0 ———— 0.3 miles

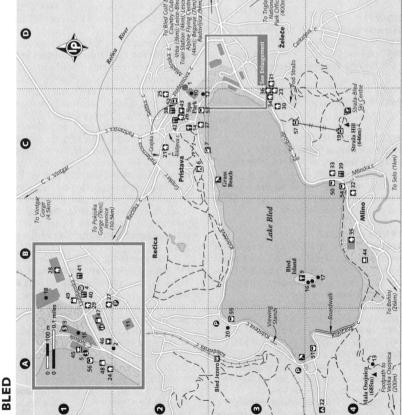

INFORMATION
3glav Adventures.......................(see 49)
À Propos Bar............................(see 47)
Bled School of Management...**1** D2
DZS..**2** A2
Globtour Bled...........................(see 28)
Gorenjska Banka.......................**3** A1
Kompas....................................(see 47)
Life Trek..................................(see 49)
News Kiosk..............................(see 18)
OSA..**4** B1
Post Office................................(see 47)
SKB Banka................................(see 47)
Tourist Information Centre
  Bled......................................**5** A1

SIGHTS & ACTIVITIES
Bled Castle...............................**6** C2
Castle Baths.............................**7** C2
Chaplain's House.......................**8** B4
Church of the Assumption..........**9** B3
Festival Hall.............................**10** C2
Golf Hotel Bled.........................**11** A2
Horse-Drawn Carriage Stand...**12** C2
Museum Collection...................(see 6)
Osojnica Viewing Point.............**13** A4
Parish Church of St Martin........**14** C2
Park Hotel...............................**15** A1
Provost's House.......................**16** B4
South Staircase........................**17** B4
Sport Hall................................**18** C2
Straža-Bled Ski Centre..............**19** C4
Tourist Train...........................(see 18)
Zaka Regatta Centre.................**20** A3

SLEEPING
Bledec Hostel..........................**21** C2
Camping Bled..........................**22** A4
Garni Hotel Berc......................**23** C3
Grand Hotel Toplice.................**24** A1
Hotel Astoria Bled....................**25** C2
Hotel Jelovica Bled...................**26** C2
Hotel Kompas Best Western......**27** B1
Hotel Krim Bled.......................**28** B1
Hotel Lovec..............................**29** B1

Jadran Hotel.............................**30** C3
Mayer Penzion..........................**31** D3
Penzion Mlino..........................**32** C4
Pletna Pension..........................**33** C4
Trst Hotel.................................**34** C3
Vila Bled...................................**35** B4
Vila Gorenka.............................**36** C3
Vila Prešeren............................**37** C2

EATING
Castle Restaurant......................(see 6)
Gostilna Pri Planincu................**38** C2
Mercator..................................**39** C4
Mercator..................................(see 46)
Ostarija Peglez'n......................**40** B1
Okarina...................................**41** B1
Peking.....................................(see 33)
Pizzeria Pletna.........................**42** C2
Slaščičarna Šmon......................**43** C2

DRINKING
Irish Pub.................................**44** B4
Kavarna Belvedere...................**45** A1
Kavarna Park...........................**46** A1
Pub Bled.................................(see 47)

SHOPPING
Bled Shopping Centre...............**47** A1
Fauna.....................................**48** A1
ProMontana.............................**49** B1

TRANSPORT
Avis...(see 47)
Boat Rentals.............................**50** C4
Boat Rentals.............................**51** A4
Boat Rentals.............................(see 7)
Budget....................................(see 47)
Bus Station..............................**52** C2
Europcar..................................**53** C3
Gondolas.................................**54** C4
Gondolas.................................**55** A3
Gondolas.................................**56** A1
Hertz......................................(see 27)
Straža Chairlift.........................**57** C3

Reka River

To Bled Golf &
Country Club
(3km); Lesce-Bled
Train Station (4km); Lesce
Alpine Flying Centre
(4km); Begunje (7km);
Radovljica (9km)

To Triglav
National
Park Office
(400m)

To Ribno (1km)

Želeče

See Enlargement

Pod Stražo

Straža-Bled
Ski Centre

Straža Hill
(646m)

To Vintgar
Gorge
(4.5km)

To Pokljuka
Gorge (7km);
Jesenice
(16.5km)

Pristava

Grass
Beach

Rečica

To Selo (1km)

Mlino

Lake Bled

Bled
Island

Viewing
Stands

Boardwalk

Bled Jezero

To Bohinj
(26km)

Mala Osojnica
(685m)

Footpath to
Velika Osojnica
(200m)

100 m
0.1 miles

C. v. Vintgar

connects Jesenice to the north with Nova Gorica, Sežana and Italy to the southwest.

Information

BOOKSHOPS & NEWSSTANDS

DZS (☎ 574 56 51; Cesta Svobode 19; ☯ 8.30am-7pm Mon-Fri, 8.30am-1pm Sat) Has some regional maps and guides in English.

News kiosk (Ljubljanska cesta 4; ☯ 7am-1pm & 2-7pm Mon-Sat, 8am-1pm & 2-6pm Sun) English-language newspapers at the eastern end of Bled Shopping Centre.

INTERNET ACCESS

À Propos Bar (☎ 574 40 44; apropos@g-kabel.si; Ljubljanska cesta 4; per 15/30/60 min €1.25/2.10/4.20; ☯ 8am-midnight) In Bled Shopping Centre (with wireless connection).

Bled School of Management (☎ 579 26 10; www.iedc .si; Prešernova cesta 33; access free; ☯ 8.30am-12.30pm & 4-8pm) Free internet access at one of the best small business schools in Europe.

MONEY

Gorenjska Banka (C Svobode 15; ☯ 9-11.30am & 2-5pm Mon-Fri, 8-11am Sat)

SKB Banka (Ljubljanska cesta 4; ☯ 8.30am-noon, 2-5pm Mon-Fri) In Bled Shopping Centre.

POST

Post office (Ljubljanska cesta 10; ☯ 7am-7pm Mon-Fri, 7am-noon Sat)

TOURIST INFORMATION

Tourist Information Centre Bled (☎ 574 11 22; www.bled.si; Cesta Svobode 10; ☯ 8am-10pm Mon-Sat, 10am-10pm Sun Jul & Aug; 8am-8pm Mon-Sat, 10am-6pm Sun Jun & Sep; 8am-7pm Mon-Sat, 9am-5pm Sun Oct & Mar-May; 9am-5pm Mon-Sat, 9am-2pm Sun Nov-Feb) Has probably the best website in Slovenia.

TRAVEL AGENCIES

3glav Adventures (☎ 041-683 184; www.3glav-adve ntures.com; Ljubljanska cesta 1; ☯ 9am-noon & 4-7pm Apr-Oct) The number one extreme-sport specialists in Bled, offering adventure trips throughout the area lasting six to 10 hours for individuals and groups.

Globtour Bled (☎ 575 13 00; www.globtour-bled.com; Ljubljanska cesta 7; ☯ 8am-8pm Mon-Sat, 8am-noon & 4-8pm Sun Jul & Aug; 8am-7pm Mon-Fri, 9am-2pm Sat Sep-Jun) In the eastern wing of the Hotel Krim Bled.

Kompas (☎ 572 75 00; www.kompas-bled.si; Bled Shopping Centre, Ljubljanska cesta 4; ☯ 8am-8pm Mon-Sat, 8am-noon & 4-7pm Sun Jul & Aug; 8am-7pm Mon-Sat, 8am-noon & 4-7pm Sun Sep-Jun)

Life Trek (☎ 578 06 62; www.lifetrek-slovenia.com; Ljubljanska cesta 1; ☯ 9am-8pm Jun-Sep, 9am-4pm Oct-May) Adventure-sport agency attached to the ProMontana sporting-goods shop (p117).

OSA (☎ 576 85 85, 040-984 150; www.osa.si; Ljubljanska cesta 5 ☯ 9am-8pm Jun-Sep, 9am-noon & 3-6pm Oct-May) In the Sport Hall.

Triglav National Park Office (☎ 578 02 00; www .tnp.si; Ljubljanska cesta 27; ☯ 8am-3pm Mon-Fri) Information about Slovenia's only national park.

Sights

BLED CASTLE

Perched atop a steep cliff more than 100m above the lake, **Bled Castle** (Blejski Grad; ☎ 578 05 25; Grajska cesta 25; adult/child/student €5/3.10/4.60; ☯ 8am-8pm May-Oct, 8am-5pm Nov-Apr) is how most people imagine a medieval fortress to be – with towers, ramparts, moats and a terrace offering magnificent views on a clear day. The castle, which is built on two levels, dates back to the 11th century (although most of what stands here now is from the 16th century) and for 800 years was the seat of the Bishops of Brixen.

The baroque southern wing houses a **museum collection** that traces the history of Lake Bled and its settlements from the Bronze Age to the mid-19th century. None of the furniture is original to the castle, but it helps give you an idea of how the leisured class lived in the Middle Ages. There's a large collection of armour and weapons (swords, halberds and firearms from the 16th to 18th centuries), jewellery found at the early Slav burial pits at Pristava, a few interesting carvings, including a 16th-century one of the overworked St Florian dousing yet another conflagration, as well as tapestries and ancient tiled stoves. The smallish 16th-century Gothic **chapel** contains paintings of castle donor Henry II and his wife Kunigunda on either side of the main altar.

Admission to the castle includes entry to the rather touristy **Castle Printworks** (Grajska Tiskarna) and **Castle Wine Cellar** (Grajska Klet), which is essentially a shop. The terrace of the castle restaurant affords wonderful views of the lake and surrounding mountains.

You can reach the castle on foot via one of three trails signposted 'Grad'. The first trail starts from the car park behind the Bledec Hostel; the second is a tortuous path up from the Castle Baths; and the third starts just north of the neo-Gothic **Parish Church of St Martin** (Farna Cerkev Sv Martina; Riklijeva cesta). This churc was designed by Friedrich von Schmidt in 1905, who also did the city hall and Votive Church in Vienna. Outside there's a small shrine designed by Jože Plečnik.

BLED ISLAND

The tiny, tear-shaped Bled Island (Blejski Otok), the only true island in Slovenia, has been the site of a Christian church since the 9th century. But excavations have shown that the early Slavs worshipped at a pagan temple here at least a century before that.

Getting to the island by a piloted **gondola** (pletna; ☎ 041-293 424; per person return €10) is the archetypal tourist experience; there are jetties below the tourist office, below Spa Park (Zdravilíški Park) to the north, in Mlino on the south shore and near Zaka Regatta Centre. You get about half an hour to explore the island. In all, the trip takes about 1½ hours. Alternatively, you can rent a rowing boat at the Castle Baths, at Mlino or at the large beach at the southwest end of the lake.

The boat sets you down on the island's south side at a monumental **South Staircase** (Južno Stopnišče) built in 1655. As you walk up you'll pass the **Chaplain's House** (Meznarija) and the **Provost's House** (Stavba Proštije) from the 17th and 18th centuries, with the Brixen bishops' coat of arms on the facade.

The baroque **Church of the Assumption** (Cerkev Marijinega Vnebovzetja; ☼ 7am-dusk), dating from the 17th century, contains some fresco fragments from the 14th century, a large gold altar and, under the floor of the nave, part of the apse of a **pre-Romanesque chapel**, the only one in Slovenia. Outside is a 15th-century **belfry** with a 'wishing bell' that visitors can ring if they want to ask a favour. Naturally everyone and their grandmother does it – again and again and again.

LAKE BLED

This lake is not a very large body of water – it measures only 2km by 1380m – and the second-best way to see it is from the shore. A walk around the lake (6km) shouldn't take but a couple of hours at the most, including the short (but steep) climb to the brilliant **Osojnica viewing point**. Along the way, you'll pass linden, chestnut and willow trees hanging over the water, boat slips, wooden walkways, anglers, the start of several hikes and a couple of interesting sights.

On the south shore you'll pass through the hamlet of Mlino, then leave the main road for a path that passes beneath the grand edifice of the Hotel Vila Bled. Around the far end of the lake, beyond a 300m stretch of boardwalk over the lake and past the camping ground, is the **Zaka Regatta Centre**, where an international rowing competition is staged in late June and a Slovenia-wide one in September. The **Castle Baths** are a bit further on.

The lazy or infirm can jump aboard the **tourist train** (adult/child €2.50/1.70; ☼ 9.30am-9.30pm May–mid-Oct) for the 45-minute twirl around the lake. It departs from in front of the **Sport Hall** (Športna Dvorana; Ljubljanska cesta 5) up to 20 times a day in season. Romantics will prefer one of the **horse-drawn carriages** (fijaker; ☎ 041-710 970) from the stand near the **Festival Hall** (Festivalna Dvorana; Cesta Svobode 11). A spin around the lake for five people costs €25, and it's the same price for two people to the castle. You can even get a carriage for four to Vintgar; the two-hour return trip costs €62.50.

Activities

ADVENTURE SPORTS

Agencies such as 3glav, Life Trek and OSA (opposite) organise a wide range of outdoor activities in and around Bled, including trekking, mountaineering, rock climbing, ski touring, cross-country skiing, mountain biking, rafting, kayaking, canyoning, caving, horse riding and paragliding.

The 3glav agency's most popular trip is the Emerald River Adventure (€55), an 11-hour **hiking** and **swimming** foray into Triglav National Park and along the Soča River. A two-day guided ascent of Triglav from Pokljuka, the Vrata Valley or Kot Valley costs €148. More challenging mountaineering traverses lasting between three and five days cost between €248 and €498. If you don't fancy scaling summits, a day-long trek through the alpine meadows of the Triglav Lakes Valley costs €68.

A 2½-hour **rafting** trip down the Sava Bohinjka/Soča River costs €23/30, and a three-hour **canyoning** descent is €45. Kayak trips lasting three hours cost €38. **Paragliding** is €70. **Horse riding** starts at €40 for a two-hour outing.

A half-day tour of the (easy) **Bobji Zob cave** near Bohinjska Bela is €20, while the more challenging **Simnovo Brezno cave**, just below Triglav and north of Lake Bohinj, costs €12 including equipment rental. It takes all day and has a 50m abseil descent.

You can hire a kayak and accessories from ProMontana (p117) for €5/15 per hour/day and mountain bikes, which are replaced annually, for €4/8/12 per hour/half-day/day.

OSA (p112) has **quad trips** of 20km (€39) and 45km (€58.50) lasting two and four hours respectively.

BOATING

You can rent **rowing boats** (per hr up to 4/6 people €10.50/15; mid-Apr–Oct) for getting to the island or just pottering about (motor boats are banned on the lake) from the Castle Baths (right). Boats for up to four people are also available from the Pension Pletna in Mlino or further west near the entrance to the camping ground for €10.50 per hour.

FISHING

The tourist office sells **fishing permits** valid for a day on the lake (€23), the Radovna River (€51) and the Sava Bohinjka River (€46 to €51, depending on location and catch). Fauna (p117) sells equipment and has a guide service.

FLYING

The **Lesce Alpine Flying Centre** (Alpski Letalski Center Lesce; ☎ 532 01 00; www.alc-lesce.si; Begunjska cesta 10) 4km to the southeast has panoramic flights in Cessna 172s over Bled (€70 for three people), Bohinj (€120) and even Triglav (€170), or anywhere you want for €108 an hour. You can even rent a glider here for €150 a day.

GOLF

The 18-hole, par-73 King's Course at the **Bled Golf & Country Club** (☎ 537 77 11; www.golf.bled.si; Mon-Fri €51, Sat & Sun €62; 8am-7pm Apr-Oct), about 3km to the east of the lake near Lesce, is Slovenia's best golf course and, with its dramatic mountain backdrop, one of the most beautiful in Europe. This club also has the nine-hole, par-36 **Lake Course** (Mon-Fri €35, Sat & Sun €44) open the same hours. You can rent a set of clubs for €15, and there's a PGA pro who gives lessons from €18.

HIKING

There are many short and easy signposted hikes around Bled (numbered signs correspond to numbered routes on the local hiking maps). One of the best is trail No 6 from the southwest corner of the lake to the summit of Velika Osojnica (756m). The view from the top – over the lake, island and castle, with the

peaks of the Karavanke in the background – is stunning, especially towards sunset. The climb to the first summit is steep, but the round trip, returning via Ojstrica (610m), takes only three hours or so. For details of longer treks see p113.

SKIING

Beginners will be content with the tiny (6-hectare) **Straža-Bled ski centre** (☎ 578 05 30; www.bled .si; half-day pass adult/child/student & senior €5.40/4.20/4.60, day pass €10.50/6.70/8.30), southwest of the Grand Hotel Toplice. A chairlift takes you 634m up the hill in three minutes; you'll be down the short slope in no time. Rental skis and poles are available from ProMontana (p117) and Kompas (p112). In summer it becomes a **summer tobogganing track** (poletno sankanje; per 1/2/3 rides adult €4.20/6.30/8.40, child €2.50/4.20/5.85), on which you wend your way down a metal chute sitting on a mini 'bobsled'.

SWIMMING

Bled's warm (23°C at source) crystal-clear water – it now rates a Blue Flag – makes it suitable for swimming well into the autumn, and there are decent beaches around the lake, including a big gravel one near the camping ground and a grass one on the northern side. Just east of the latter is the large **Castle Baths** (Grajsko Kopališče; ☎ 578 05 28; Kidričeva cesta 1; adult/child/student €5/3/3.35; 7am-7pm Jun-Sep), with an indoor pool and protected enclosures in the lake itself with huge water slides.

Hotels with indoor swimming pools filled with thermal water and saunas that are open to nonguests include the **Grand Hotel Toplice** (☎ 579 10 00; www.hotel-toplice.com; Cesta Svobode 12; €6.26), the **Park Hotel** (☎ 579 18 00; Cesta Svobode 15; Mon-Fri €6.26, Sat & Sun €7.52), **Hotel Jelovica Bled** (☎ 579 60 00; www.hotel-jelovica.si; Cesta Svobode 8; €11.27) and the **Golf Hotel Bled** (☎ 579 20 00; Cankarjeva ulica 4; under/over 3 hr 1600/2800).

Tours

In summer the **Old Timer Train** (Muzejski Vlak; adult/child return €33/19, with lunch & side trips €61/31; monthly May, Jul & Aug) offers excursions in vintage carriages hauled by a steam locomotive. Trains usually run between Jesenice, 13km to the northwest, and Most na Soči, stopping at Bled Jezero station and Bohinjska Bistrica. Ask the tourist office about departure times; there have been fewer trips scheduled for individuals in recent years, amounting to only about one a month in summer. You can buy tickets from most travel agencies in Bled, including Kompas (p112) or through the organiser **ABC Rent a Car** (☎ 01-510 43 20; abc-tourism@europcar.si; Ulica Jožeta Jame 16) in Ljubljana.

Festivals & Events

A number of special events take place during the summer in Bled, including the **International Rowing Regatta** in late June, the **International Music Festival** of violinists in early July, **Bled Days** (Blejski Dnevi) in late July, a multimedia festival where there are fireworks and the entire lake is illuminated by candlelight, and the **Okarina Etno Festival**, a two-day international festival of folk and world music in August. For information, visit www.bled.si.

Summertime concerts take place at the castle and the parish church, which houses one of the finest organs in Slovenia. In winter, the Pokljuka Plateau west of Bled is the venue for the **Biathlon World Cup** championship of cross-country skiing and rifle shooting.

Sleeping

Befitting a resort of such popularity, Bled has a wide range of accommodation – from Slovenia's first real hostel to a five-star hotel in a villa that was once Tito's summer retreat.

BUDGET

Camping Bled (☎ 575 20 00; www.camping.bled.si; Kidričeva cesta 10c; adult €8.50-11, child €6-7.70; ☼ Apr–mid-Oct; ℗ ▣) This popular 6.5-hectare site fills a rural valley behind a waterside restaurant at the western end of the lake about 2.5km from the bus station. There's space for 900 campers. It is strictly forbidden to camp elsewhere on the lake, and the law is enforced.

Vila Gorenka (☎ 051-369 070; vila.gorenka@siol.net; Želeška cesta 9; per person €16-20; ℗ ▣) This new budget establishment has 10 double rooms with washbasins in a charming old two-story villa just next to the Mayer Pension. Toilets and showers are shared and internet access is free. Some rooms on the 2nd floor have balconies overlooking the lake.

Bledec Hostel (☎ 574 52 50; www.mlino.si; Grajska cesta 17; HI members/nonmembers dm high season €17.50/20, low season €15.50/18, d high season €23.50/26, low season €21.50/24; ℗ ☒ ▣) This well-organised HI-affiliated hostel in the shadow of the castle has 13 rooms of three to five beds with attached bathrooms. It also has a bar, an inexpensive restaurant, a laundry room

(per load €8.35) and internet access (per half-hour €2.10).

Private rooms are offered by dozens of homes in the area. Both Kompas (p112) and Globtour Bled (p112) have extensive lists, with prices for singles/doubles at around €24/38. Apartments, which only require a minimum stay of three nights, cost from €45/87 a night for two/four people.

MIDRANGE

Penzion Mlino (☎ 574 14 04; www.mlino.si; Cesta Svobode 45; per person €25-30; ℗ ☒) This 15-room pension, perhaps better known for its restaurant than its accommodation, is just about as close as you'll get to the lake at this price. The same owners operate the Bledec Hostel

Hotel Astoria Bled (579 44 00; www.hotelastoria-bled .com; Prešernova cesta 44; s €39-55, d €54-86; ℗ ☒) This 72-room hotel near the bus station is run in cooperation with Bled's Vocational College for Catering and Tourism, so staff are generally young, enthusiastic and, well, new. It's just got a much-needed overhaul; choose one of the rooms on the south side, as they face the lake.

Hotel Jelovica Bled (☎ 579 60 00; www.hotel-jelovica .si; Cesta Svobode 8; s €40-70, d €50-110; ℗ ▣ ▣) Close to the bus station, the 100-room Jelovica fronts Spa Park above the lake and has a fully equipped health and spa centre and a swimming pool.

Garni Hotel Berc (☎ 576 56 58; www.berc-sp.si; Pod Stražo 13; s €40, d €65-70; ℗ ☒ ▣) Just opposite the Mayer, this new, purpose-built pension reminiscent of a Swiss chalet has 15 rooms on two floors and gets good reviews from readers.

Hotel Krim Bled (☎ 579 70 00; www.hotel-krim.si; Ljubljanska cesta 7; s €40.50-55, d €61-90; ℗ ☒ ▣) This sprawling 115-room hotel charges a lot less than most for its singles and doubles, but its location – up from the lake along busy Ljubljanska cesta – is not the best.

Pletna Pension (☎ 574 37 02; pletna@bled.net; Cesta Svobode 37; s & d €48-53, tr €57-62; ℗) This friendly little pension with attached shop and pizzeria has a couple of pleasant rooms fronting the lake.

Vila Prešeren (☎ 578 08 00; www.vila.preseren.s5.net; Kidričeva cesta 1; s lake view €58-64, park view €50-55, d lake view €78-88, park view €67-72, ste €112-154; ℗) A positively charming mini-hotel, this place has just six rooms and two suites in a lovely old villa dating from 1865 facing the lake just west of Spa Park.

Mayer Penzion (☎ 574 10 58; www.mayer-sp.si; Želeška cesta 7; d/q €70/90, apt €65-75; ℗ ☒ ▣) This delightful 13-room inn in a renovated 19th-century

THE AUTHOR'S CHOICE

Vila Bled (☎ 579 15 00; www.vila-bled.com; Cesta Svobode 26; s €130-150, d €170-190, ste lake view €210-240, park view €190-210; P 🖳 🖳) Now a Relais & Chateaux property, this 30-room hotel is where Tito and his foreign guests once put their feet up and their heads down. The 10 rooms and 20 suites (one with Jacuzzi) are furnished in retro-style 1950s decor. The hotel is surrounded by a large park with a tennis court, and it has its own covered lido and private boat dock. Guests can use the indoor pool at the Grand Hotel Toplice.

house is in a quiet location above the lake. Even if you're not staying here, have a meal at Mayer's excellent restaurant.

TOP END

Hotel Kompas Best Western (☎ 578 21 00; www.kh-bled.si; Cankarjeva ulica 2; s €78-110, d €98-130, ste €140-170; P 🍽 🍽 🖳 🖳 🖳) This rather bizarrely designed 95-room hotel – the atrium staircase is dizzying – has everything, including a huge pool under a glass dome. Some rooms have balconies overlooking the lake.

Hotel Lovec (☎ 576 86 15; www.lovechotel.com; Ljubljanska cesta 6; s €108-144, d €129-165, ste €206-246; P 🍽 🍽 🖳 🖳 🖳) A new favourite, the Lovec has been completely overhauled and now boasts 60 of the most attractive rooms in town. We love the rooms with blond-wood walls, red carpet, and bath with Jacuzzi in front of a massive window facing the lake. It has a pool and sauna.

Grand Hotel Toplice (☎ 579 10 00; www.hotel-toplice.com; Cesta Svobode 12; s €105-170, d €130-210, ste €220-260; P 🍽 🖳 🖳 🖳) With a history that goes back to the mid-19th century, the 87-room Toplice is Bled's 'olde worlde' hotel, with attractive public areas, rooms renovated in 2002 and superb views of the lake on its northern side.

The Toplice's two extensions – the **Trst Hotel** (Cesta Svobode 19; s €46-81, d €62-96) just opposite and the more attractive **Jadran Hotel** (Cesta Svobode 23; s €46-81, d €62-96) up on the hill – are half the price.

Eating

Pizzeria Pletna (☎ 576 72 11; Cesta Svobode 37; pizza €4.50-5.85, grills €5-6.70; ☽ noon-11pm) If you just want something cheap, cheerful and fast, head

for this simple pizzeria with a wood-fired oven above the main road in Mlino.

Peking (☎ 574 17 16; Ulica Narodnih Herojev 3; rice & noodles €3.60-4.80, mains €5.25-12.50; ☽ noon-11pm) This Chinese eatery opposite the Hotel Krim Bled has such favourites as *hui guo rou* (twice-cooked pork) and *ma po doufu* (spicy bean curd). They ain't exactly what you'd get in Chengdu, but this is Slovenia, after all.

Gostilna Pri Planincu (At the Mountaineer's; ☎ 574 16 13; Grajska cesta 8; starters €4.20-8, mains €5.85-15; ☽ noon-10pm) In situ since 1903, this is a homely pub-restaurant just down the hill from the Bledec Hostel. It offers simple Slovenian mains and grilled Balkan specialities like *čevapčiči* (spicy meatballs of beef or pork; €5.65) and tasty *pljeskavica z kajmakom* (Serbian-style meat patties with mascarpone-like cream cheese; €6.25).

Mayer Penzion (☎ 574 10 58; Želeška cesta 7; starters €7-8, mains €9.20-18.80; ☽ 5pm-midnight Tue-Fri, noon-midnight Sat & Sun) The restaurant at this delightful inn serves such tasty Slovenian fare as sausage, trout, roast pork and *skutini štruklji* (cheese curd pastries). The list of Slovenian wines (only) is a cut above.

Castle Restaurant (☎ 574 16 07, 041-337 696; Grajska cesta 25; starters €5-10.85, mains €10.85-18.80; ☽ 10am-10pm) The fabulous views are 'free' from the superbly situated terrace of the restaurant in the castle. It's run by the Bled's catering and tourism school and staffed by its charming students.

Okarina (☎ 574 14 58; Ljubljanska cesta 8; starters €6-12, mains €9-22; ☽ noon-midnight) This very upmarket restaurant has lost its parklike location just northwest of the Pri Planincu and is now in a modern dining room next to the post office. Still, the ethnic decorations and traditional musical instruments (an *okarina* is a small clay flute) remain, and along with well-pre-

THE AUTHOR'S CHOICE

Ostarija Peglez'n (☎ 574 42 18; Cesta Svobode 19a; starters €4.60-7.50, mains €6.30-16.30; ☽ 11am-midnight) A new favourite restaurant in Bled, the 'Iron Inn' is just opposite the landmark Grand Hotel Toplice. It has fascinating retro décor with lots of old household antiques and curios (including the eponymous iron) and wooden floors. It serves some of the best fish dishes in town. What's more, it is nonsmoking throughout.

pared Slovenian and international favourites, the Okarina's tandoor oven produces decent Indian dishes like chicken *tikka* and *rogan josh*. There are a fair few vegetarians choices.

Slaščičarna Šmon (☎ 574 16 16; Grajska cesta 3; ☯ 7.30am-9pm) Bled's culinary speciality is *kremna rezina* (cream cake; €1.70), a layer of vanilla custard topped with whipped cream and sandwiched neatly between two layers of flaky pastry, and while Šmon may not be its place of birth, it remains the best place in which to try it.

You'll find a **Mercator** (Ljubljanska cesta 4; ☯ 7am-7pm Mon-Sat, 8am-noon Sun) supermarket at the eastern end of Bled Shopping Centre and a smaller **Mercator** (Mlinska cesta 1; ☎ 8am-6pm Mon-Fri, 7am-1pm) branch on the south side of the lake.

Drinking
Kavarna Park (☎ 579 18 00; Cesta Svobode 10; ☯ 10am-10pm) The lovely 'Park Café' above the Casino Bled has a commanding position over the lake's eastern end.

Kavarna Belvedere (☎ 579 15 00; ☯ 2pm-midnight Mon-Fri, 11am-midnight Sat & Sun May-Oct) This delightful café-bar just southwest from (and part of) the Vila Bled is perched atop a 30m concrete tower overlooking the lake and has a great period-piece socialist mosaic on the back wall of the front room.

Pub Bled (☎ 574 26 22, 041-755 265; Cesta Svobode 19a; ☯ 9am-2am Sun-Thu, 9am-3am Fri & Sat) This friendly pub above the Ostarija Peglez'n restaurant has great cocktails and a DJ most nights.

Irish Pub (☎ 041-672 069; Cesta Svobode 8a; ☯ 7am-2am Mon-Fri, 9am-2am Sat & Sun) This raucous boozer next to the Hotel Jelovica is the pub of choice among locals and visitors alike.

Shopping
ProMontana (☎ 578 06 62; www.promontana.com; Ljubljanska cesta 1; ☯ 8am-8pm Mon-Fri, 8am-1pm & 3-7pm Sat & Sun Jun-Sep; 8am-7pm Mon-Fri, 8am-1pm & 3-7pm Sat & Sun Oct-May) This shop next to Life Trek sells and rents all kinds of sporting equipment including skis.

Fauna (☎ 574 26 31, 041-633 147; www.faunabled.com; Cesta Svobode 12; ☯ 8am-noon & 3-7pm Mon-Fri, 8am-noon Sat, 8-10am Sun) This shop sells fishing tackle and has a guiding service.

Getting There & Away
BUS
There are buses every 30 to 40 minutes to Radovljica (€1.70, 15 minutes, 7.5km) via

both Lesce and Begunje and at least one an hour to Bohinjska Bistrica (€3.50, one hour, 26km), Kranj (€3.50, 40 minutes, 26km) and Ljubljana (€6.10, 1¼ hours, 57km). Other destinations served from Bled include Bovec (€7, three hours, 74km) via Kranjska Gora and the Vršič Pass. A bus leaves daily at 7.50am in July and August, and on Saturday and Sunday only in June and September. Note that three bus lines operate between Bled and Bohinj, and if you buy a return ticket from one bus line, you will not be able to make your return journey on either of the other buslines.

CAR
All the big rental-car agencies have offices in Bled, including the following:

Avis (☎ 576 87 00; Ljubljanska cesta 4; ☯ 9am-5pm Mon-Fri, 8am-noon Sat & Sun) In the Bled Shopping Centre.

Budget (☎ 578 03 20; Ljubljanska cesta 4; ☯ 8am-noon & 5-7pm Mon-Fri, 8am-noon Sat, 9-11am Sun) In the Bled Shopping Centre.

Europcar (☎ 236 79 90, 031-382 051; Ljubljanska cesta 7; ☯ 8am-2pm Mon-Fri, 8am-noon Sat) In the Hotel Krim Bled.

Hertz (☎ 574 55 88; Cankarjeva cesta 2; ☯ 8am-7pm Mon-Fri, 8am-1pm Sat) In the Hotel Kompas Best Western.

TRAIN
Bled has no central train station. Trains for Bohinjska Bistrica (€1.45, 20 minutes, 18km, seven a day), Most na Soči and Nova Gorica (€5.05, 2¼ hours, 79km, seven a day) use little Bled Jezero station, which is 2km west of central Bled – handy for the camping ground but little else. From there you can make connections for Sežana, 40km to the southeast, and Italy. This mountain railway is one of the most picturesque in Slovenia. If you are headed southwest to Nova Gorica, sit on the right-hand side of the train to view the valley of the cobalt-blue Soča River.

Trains for Ljubljana (€3.90 to €5.30, 55 minutes, 51km, up to 17 a day) via Škofja Loka, Kranj and Radovljica use Lesce-Bled station, 4km to the east of town.

Getting Around
You can order a local taxi on mobile ☎ 041-631 629 or ☎ 041-597 935. Bicycles and mountain bikes can be rented from Kompas and Globtour for €3.75/6.25/10 per hour/half-day/day.

AROUND BLED
Vintgar Gorge

One of the easiest and most satisfying day trips from Bled is to **Vintgar Gorge** (Soteska Vintgar; adult/child/student €3/2.10/2.50; ☺ 8am-7pm late Apr-Oct), some 4km to the northwest. The highlight is the 1600m wooden walkway, built in 1893 and continually rebuilt since. It criss-crosses the swirling Radovna River four times over rapids, waterfalls and pools before reaching 13m-high **Šum Waterfall**. The entire walk is spectacular, although it can get pretty wet and slippery. There are little snack bars at the beginning and the end of the walkway and picnic tables at several locations along the way.

It's an easy walk to the gorge from Bled. Head northwest on Prešernova cesta then north on Partizanska cesta to Cesta v Vintgar. This will take you to Podhom, where signs show the way to the gorge entrance. To return, you can either retrace your steps or, from Šum Waterfall, walk eastward over Hom (834m) to the ancient pilgrimage **Church of St Catherine**, which retains some 15th-century fortifications. From there it's due south through Zasip to Bled. Count on about three hours all in.

Those unable or unwilling to walk all the way can take the train from Bled Jezero station to Podhom (€1, five minutes, 2km, seven a day). From there it's a 1.5km walk westward to the main entrance. From mid-June to September, a **tourist bus** (☎ 578 04 20; www.alpetour.si in Slovene; one-way/return €2.50/4.50) leaves Bled bus station daily at 10am and heads for Vintgar, stopping at the Krim and Grand Toplice Hotels, Mlino, the far end of the lake and Bled Castle, arriving at 10.30am. It returns from Vintgar at noon.

Pokljuka Plateau

The area around Bled offers endless possibilities for excursions, notably the forests and meadows of the Pokljuka Plateau below Triglav to the west. Here you can go exploring in the 2km-long Pokljuka Gorge (Pokljuška soteška), some 7km west of Bled and 2km from Gorje (€1.30, 10 minutes, 5km), which is served by up to two dozen buses a day from Bled on weekdays and up to nine at the weekend. Well-marked trails crisscross the plateau from town and are outlined on the 1:30,000 map *Bled* (€7.10) GZS and the 1:50,000-scale *Triglavski Narodni Park* (Triglav National Park; €7.50) PZS map, both available from the tourist office in Bled. You can also begin an ascent of Triglav from Pokljuka (p130).

BOHINJ

☎ 04 / pop 5260 / elev 523m

Bohinj, a larger and much less developed glacial lake 26km to the southwest, is a wonderful place to chill out after experiencing the tourist hordes at Bled in season. OK, it doesn't have a romantic little island or a castle looming high on a rocky cliff. But it does have Triglav, itself visible from the lake when the weather clears, and it lies entirely within the borders of Triglav National Park (p128) and has a wonderful naturalness that doesn't exist at Bled. The Bohinj area's handful of museums and historical churches will keep culture vultures busy during their visit, and for action types there are activities galore – from kayaking and mountain biking to scaling Triglav via one of the southern approaches (p130).

History

Bohinj was densely settled during the Hallstatt period due to the large amounts of iron ore in the area, and a trade route linked the lake with the Soča Valley and the Adriatic Sea via a pass at Vrh Bače southeast of Bohinjska Bistrica. During the Middle Ages, when the area fell under the jurisdiction of the Bishops of Brixen at Bled, Bohinj was known for its markets and fairs, which were held near the Church of St John the Baptist. Here peasants from the Friuli region around Trieste traded salt, wine and foodstuffs with their Slovenian counterparts for iron ore, livestock and butter. As the population grew, herders went higher into the Julian Alps in search of pasture land while charcoal burners cleared the upper forests for timber to fuel the forges. Triglav was 'conquered' from Bohinj for the first time in the late 18th century.

Orientation

Lake Bohinj, 4.5km long and up to 45m deep, lies in a valley basin on the southern edge of Triglav National Park. The Savica River flows into the lake from the west and the Sava Bohinjka flows out from the southeastern corner.

There is no town called Bohinj; the name refers to the entire valley, its settlements and the lake. The largest town in the area is Bohinjska Bistrica (population 1775), 6km to the east of the lake. Small villages on or near the southern and eastern shores include Ukanc; Ribčev Laz, where you can find everything of a practical nature; Stara Fužina at the mouth of the Mostnica Gorge; Studor, a veritable

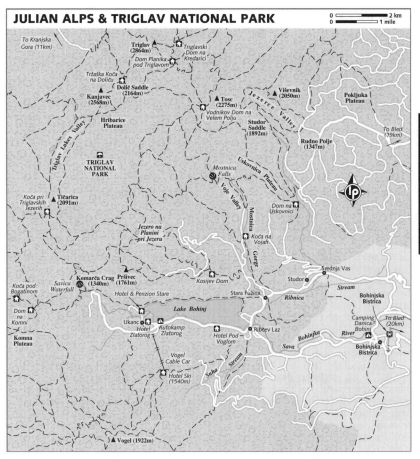

JULIAN ALPS & TRIGLAV NATIONAL PARK

0 —————— 2 km
0 —————— 1 mile

To Kranjska Gora (11km)
Triglav (2864m)
Triglavski Dom na Kredarici
Dom Planika pod Triglavom
Tržaška Koča na Doliću
Dolič Saddle (2164m)
Kanjavec (2568m)
Tosc (2275m)
Višević (2050m)
Pokljuka Plateau
Vodnikov Dom na Velem Polju
Hribarice Plateau
Studor Saddle (1892m)
Rudno Polje (1347m)
To Bled (19km)
Triglav Lakes Valley
TRIGLAV NATIONAL PARK
Uskovnica Plateau
Jezerce Valley
Mostnica Falls
Koča pri Triglavskih Jezerih
Tičarica (2091m)
Voje Valley
Dom na Uskovnici
Jezero na Planini pri Jezeru
Koča na Vojah
Mostnica Gorge
Srednja Vas
Komarča Crag (1340m)
Pršivec (1761m)
Kosijev Dom
Studor
Stream
Savica Waterfall
Koča pod Bogatinom
Hotel & Penzion Stare
Stara Fužina
Ribnica
Bohinjska Bistrica
Dom na Komni
Lake Bohinj
Ukanc
Hotel Zlatorog
Autokamp Zlatorog
Hotel Pod Voglom
Ribčev Laz
Bohinjka
Camping Danica Bohinj
To Bled (20km)
Komna Plateau
Sava
Bohinjska Bistrica
Vogel Cable Car
Suha Stream
Hotel Ski (1540m)
Vogel (1922m)

GORENJSKA

village of hayracks; and Srednja Vas. There are no settlements on the northern side.

In Ribčev Laz, buses stop near the tourist office and in Bohinjska Bistrica at the combination police station/town hall (*občina*) on Triglavska cesta and at the train station, 700m northeast of the town at Triglavska cesta 1.

Information

Alpinsport (☎ 572 34 86; www.alpinsport.si; Ribčev Laz 53; 9am-7pm Jun-Aug, 10am-6pm Sep-May) In a kiosk at the stone bridge over Sava Bohinjka.

Bohinjska Bistrica post office (Triglavska cesta 35; 8am-6pm Mon-Fri, 8am-noon Sat)

Gorenjska Banka (Trg Svobode 2b; 9-11.30am & 2-5pm Mon-Fri, 8-11am Sat) In Bohinjska Bistrica 100m east of the post office.

PAC Sports Hotel Pod Voglom (☎ 574 65 11, 041-698 523; www.pac-sports.com; Hotel Pod Voglom, Ribčev Laz 60; 10am-6pm); Penzion Rožič kiosk branch (Ribčev Laz 42; 8.30am-8pm Jul & Aug; 10am-6pm late Jun & early Sep; 10am-1pm & 5-7pm early Sep-late Jun)

Ribčev Laz post office (Ribčev Laz 47; 8-9.30am, 10am-3.30pm & 4-6pm Mon-Fri, 8am-noon Sat) ATM outside.

Tourist Information Centre Bohinj (☎ 574 60 10; www.bohinj.si; Ribčev Laz 48; 8am-6pm Mon-Sat, 9am-3pm Sun Sep-Jun; 8am-8pm daily Jul & Aug) Sells Bohinj Guest Card (€10) with discounts to museums, activities, accommodation and restaurants.

Sights
CHURCH OF ST JOHN THE BAPTIST

The **church** (Cerkev Sv Janeza Krstnika; 9am-noon & 3-6pm mid-Jun-mid-Sep, by appointment mid-Sep-mid-Jun),

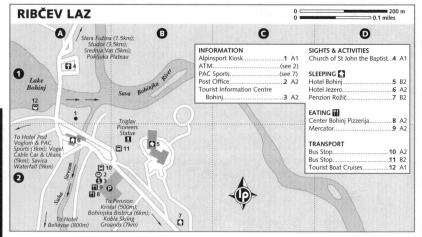

RIBČEV LAZ

INFORMATION		
Alpinsport Kiosk	1	A1
ATM	.........(see 2)	
PAC Sports	............(see 7)	
Post Office	2	A2
Tourist Information Centre		
Bohinj	3	A2

SIGHTS & ACTIVITIES		
Church of St John the Baptist	...4	A1

SLEEPING		
Hotel Bohinj	5	B2
Hotel Jezero	6	A2
Penzion Rožič	7	B2

EATING		
Center Bohinj Pizzerija	8	A2
Mercator	9	A2

TRANSPORT		
Bus Stop	10	A2
Bus Stop	11	B2
Tourist Boat Cruises	12	A1

on the northern side of the Sava Bohinjka just across the stone bridge, is what every medieval church should be: small, on a reflective lake and full of exquisite frescoes. It is the most beautiful and evocative church in all of Slovenia, with the possible exception of the Church of the Holy Trinity at Hrastovlje in Primorska. Unfortunately it was under renovation at the time of research.

The nave of the church is Romanesque, but the Gothic presbytery dates from about 1440. A large portion of the latter's walls, ceilings and arches are covered with 15th- and 16th-century frescoes. As you face the arch from the nave, look for the frescoes on either side depicting the beheading of the church's patron saint. On the opposite side of the arch, to the left, is Abel making his offering to God and, to the right, Cain with his inferior one. Upon the shoulder of history's first murderer sits a white devil – a very rare symbol. Behind you on the lower walls of the presbytery are rows of angels with vampire-like teeth; look for the three men above them singing. They have goitres, once a common affliction in mountainous regions due to the lack of iodine in the diet. The carved wooden head of St John the Baptist on one of the side altars dates from 1380. The poet Valentin Vodnik (1758–1819), who lived and worked in nearby Gorjuše, left his name in pencil on the back of the high altar.

Several paintings on the outside southern wall, one dating back to the early 14th century, depict St Christopher. In the Middle Ages

people believed they would not die on the day they had gazed upon an icon of the patron saint of travellers. No fools, our ancestors – they painted them on churches near roads and villages – but apparently they forgot to look at least once in their lives. They're all now dead, of course.

MUSEUMS

The **Alpine Dairy Museum** (Planšarski Muzej; ☎ 577 01 56; Stara Fužina 181; adult/child €1.85/1.50; ✆ 11am-7pm Tue-Sun Jul & Aug; 10am-noon & 4-6pm Tue-Sun Jan-Jun, Sep & Oct) in Stara Fužina, about 1.5km north of Ribčev Laz, has a small collection related to alpine dairy farming in the Bohinj Valley, once the most important such centre in Slovenia. Until the late 1950s large quantities of cheese were still being made on 28 highland pastures, but a modern dairy in nearby Srednja Vas does it all now. The four rooms of the museum – a cheese dairy itself once upon a time – contain a mock-up of a mid-19th-century herder's cottage, fascinating old photographs, cheese presses, wooden butter moulds, copper rennet vats, enormous snowshoes and sledges, and wonderful hand-carved crooks.

While you're in Stara Fužina, take a walk over to the village of **Studor**, just 2km to the east. **Oplen House** (Oplenova Hiša; ☎ 572 35 22; Studor 16; adult/child €1.85/1.50), which keeps the same hours as the Alpine Dairy Museum, is a typical old peasant's cottage with a chimneyless 'smoke kitchen' that has been turned into a museum focusing on the domestic life of peasants in the Bohinj area at the turn of the 20th century.

But Studor's real claim to fame is its many **toplarji**, the double-linked hayracks with barns or storage areas at the top. Look for the ones at the entrance to the village; they date from the 18th and 19th centuries.

SAVICA WATERFALL

One of the reasons people come to Bohinj is to hike to the magnificent **Savica Waterfall** (Slap Savica; adult/child €2/1, parking €2.50; ⊗ 9am-6pm Jul & Aug; 9am-5pm Apr-Jun, Sep & Oct), which cuts deep into a gorge 60m below.

The waterfall, the source of Slovenia's longest and mightiest river, is 4km from the Hotel Zlatorog in Ukanc and can be reached by footpath from there. Cars (and the bus in summer) continue via a paved road to a car park beside the Savica restaurant, from which it's a 20-minute walk up 510 steps and over rapids and streams to the falls.

The falls are among the most impressive sights in the Julian Alps, especially after a heavy rain, but bring something waterproof or you may be soaked by the spray. Two Category I huts with accommodation and food to the west are **Dom na Komni** (☎ 572 14 75, 040-695 783; info.pdljmatica@siol.net; ⊗ year-round) with 84 beds at 1520m and **Koča pod Bogatinom** (☎ 572 3213, 040-645 865; planinsko-drustvo-srednja-vas@siol.net; ⊗ late Jun-Sep) with 53 beds at 1513m. Both can be reached in about 2½ hours.

Activities

ADVENTURE SPORTS

Alpinsport (p119) and PAC Sports (p119) offer a wide range of activities, including **canyoning** (€37 to €55), **rafting** (€23 to €30) on the lake and Sava Bohinjka River, **hydrospeed** (€30), and **tandem paraglider flights** (€75 to €98) – even from the top of Vogel! PAC Sports can arrange visits to **Bohinj Adrenalin Park** (Adrenalinski Park Bohinj; adult/child/student €29/23/25; ⊗ 10am & 5pm Jul & Aug, by appointment Jun & Sep), featuring high rope courses and walkways, giant swings and so on behind the Hotel Pod Voglom (under renovation).

BOATING

PAC Sports and Alpinsport rent **kayaks** (1hr/3hr/day €4/9.20/14.20) and **canoes** (1hr/3hr/day €5/11.70/20.50).

In season, the cunningly named **Tourist Boat** (Turistična Ladja; ☎ 041-434 986; one-way €6.25/4.60, return €7.50/5.50; ⊗ hourly 10am-6pm early Jun–mid-Sep; 10am, 11.30am, 1pm, 2.30pm, 4pm & 5.30pm mid-Apr–early Jun; 11.30am, 1pm, 2.30pm & 4pm mid-Sep–Oct) sails between Ribčev Laz and Kamp Zlatorog at Ukanc. You can buy tickets at the tourist office.

FISHING

Lake Bohinj is home to lake trout and char, and the jade-coloured Sava Bohinjka River is rich in brown trout and grayling. You can buy **fishing licences** (lake €25, river as far as Bitnje catch/catch & release €80/33.50) valid for a day from the tourist office and hotels. The season runs from March to late October.

HIKING

A circular walk around the lake (12km) from Ribčev Laz should take between three and four hours. Otherwise you could just do parts of it by following the hunters' trail in the forest above the south shore of the lake to the Hotel Zlatorog and taking the bus back, or walking along the more tranquil northern shore under the cliffs of Pršivec (1761m). Much more strenuous is the hike up to **Vogel** (1922m) from the cable car's upper station. Take a map and compass, and don't set out if it looks stormy; Vogel is prone to lightning strikes. The whole trip should take about four hours. Another excellent hike, readers tell us, is the two-hour one north from Stara Fužina through the Motnica Gorge to the **Mostnica Falls** (Motniški Slapovci), which rival Savica Waterfall after a heavy rain.

The 1:25,000 *Bohinjsko Jezero z Okolico* (Lake Bohinj & Surrounds; €6.30) map available at the tourist office lists a dozen excellent walks. Also useful is the 1:15,000 *Bohinj* (€5) map with as many walks outlined.

HORSE RIDING

The **Mrcina Ranč** (☎ 041-790 297; www.bombagroup .com; per hr/half-day/day €16/43/50) in Studor offers a range of guided tours lasting one hour to three days on sturdy Icelandic ponies.

SKIING

The main station at Bohinj is **Vogel ski centre** (☎ 572 97 12; www.vogel.si; half-day pass adult/child/senior & student €14.60/10.50/12.50, day pass €21/14.60/18), 1535m above the lake's southwestern corner and accessible by cable car. With skiing up to 1800m, the season can be long, sometimes from late November to early May. Vogel has 18km of ski slopes and 8km of cross-country runs served by four chairlifts and four T-bar tows.

The lower station of the **cable car** (adult/child €10/7; every 30min 7am-7pm Jul & Aug, 8am-6pm Sep-Jun) is about 250m uphill south of the Hotel Zlatorog in Ukanc, about 5km west of Ribčev Laz.

The lower (up to 1480m) **Kobla ski centre** (☎ 574 71 00; www.bohinj.si/kobla; day pass adult/child/student €18.50/13.40/15.60) is about 1km east of Bohinjska Bistrica. It has 23km of slopes and 13km of cross-country runs served by three chairlifts and three T-bars.

STEAM TRAIN
The Old Timer Train (p114) passes through Bohinjska Bistrica on its way to and from Jesenice and Most na Soči several times in summer. Ask the tourist office for its current schedule.

SWIMMING
Some of the beaches on Lake Bohinj's northern shore are reserved for naturists in summer. Nonguests can use the indoor swimming pool at the **Hotel Zlatorog** (☎ 572 33 81; Ukanc 65; pool/pool & sauna Mon-Fri €6/7, Sat & Sun €8/9; 4-10pm) should Bohinj's infamous early morning fog drive you inside.

Aqua Park Bohinj (☎ 577 02 10; www.vodni-park -bohinj.si; Triglavska cesta 17; adult 3hr €7.50-8.40, day €9.70-10.60; child 3hr €4.90-5.30, day €7.10-7.50; 9am-10pm Jan-Mar, Jul & Aug; 9am-9pm Apr-Jun & Sep-Dec), a new water park in Bohinjska Bistrica, has 380 sq metres of pools with slides as well as saunas and fitness and wellness centres. Entry fees vary according to the season.

Festivals & Events
The **Cows' Ball** (Kravji Bal) is a wacky weekend of folk dance, music, eating and drinking to mark the return of the cows from their high pastures to the valleys. On **Bonfire Night** (Kresna Noč), celebrated on the weekend closest to the Feast of the Assumption (15 August), candle-lit flotillas go out on the lake, and there are fireworks. For details on both events, go to www.bohinj.si.

Sleeping
BUDGET
Camping Danica Bohinj (☎ 572 10 55, 572 17 02; www .bohinj.si/camping-danica; Triglavska cesta 60; per person €5.70-8; May-Sep) The Danica camping ground, which has space for 650 campers, is located in a small wood 200m west of the bus stop in Bohinjska Bistrica on the road to the lake.

Autokamp Zlatorog (☎ 572 34 82, 577 80 00; www.al pinum.net; Ukanc 2; per person €6-10; May-Sep; P) This pine-shaded 2.5-hectare site accommo-

dating 500 guests is on the lake at its western end near the Hotel Zlatorog.

The tourist office can arrange **private rooms** (per person €9.20-13.20) and **apartments** (apt for 2 €29.30-38.70, apt for 4 €43.20-68.80) in Ribčev Laz, Stara Fužina and neighbouring villages

MIDRANGE
Pension Planšar (☎ 572 30 95, 041-767 254; www.plansar .com; per person €16-20) This welcoming place in Stara Fužina, better known for its fabulous cheeses (opposite), has two cosy rooms and an apartment for rent.

Penzion Rožič (☎ 572 91 00; www.penzion-rozic .com; Ribčev Laz 42; per person €20-25; P) This unpretentious chalet-style guesthouse with 20 rooms and a popular restaurant is just 200m east of the tourist office.

Penzion Kristal (☎ 577 82 00; www.hotel-kristal-slov enia.com; Ribčev Laz 4a; per person €20-30; P) This exceedingly friendly, family-run pension is about 500m south of the Pension Rožič. Its restaurant is very popular in the area.

Pri Andreju (☎ 572 35 09; info@priandreju-sp.si; Studor 31; per person apt for 2/4 people low season €28/47, high season €32/56) This farmhouse in picturesque Studor has three apartments for between two and five people.

Hotel Bellevue (☎ 572 33 31; www.alpinum.net; Ribčev Laz 65; s €30-48, d €40-76; P) The shabby, 59-room Bellevue has a beautiful (if somewhat isolated) location on a hill about 800m south of the Hotel Jezero. Whodunnit fans take note: Agatha Christie stayed here for three weeks in 1967. Thirty-eight of the rooms are in the unattractive Savica Annexe.

Hotel & Penzion Stare (☎ 574 64 00; www.impel -bohinj.si; Ukanc 128; s €35-48, d €50-86; P) This isolated 10-room pension, north of the Hotel Zlatorog on the Sava Bohinjka River, is surrounded by lovely gardens. If you really want to get away from it all without having to climb mountains, this is your place. Prices depend on whether or not you want a balcony.

TOP END
Hotel Jezero (☎ 572 91 00; www.bohinj.si/alpinum/jezero; Ribčev Laz 51; s €52-86, d €69-141; P) This recently renovated 63-room place is the closest hotel to the lake, just opposite the stone bridge in Ribčev Laz. It has a lovely indoor swimming pool, two saunas and a fitness centre but no lift.

Hotel Bohinj (☎ 577 60 00; www.alpinum.net; Ribčev Laz 45; s €48-65, d €76-110; P) This 52-room hotel overlooks the lake from a hill above the road to Bohinjska Bistrica 100m northeast of the post office. It has a couple of rooms adapted for disabled travellers.

Hotel Zlatorog (☎ 572 33 81; www.alpinum.net; Ukanc 65; s €50-75, d €72-122; P ⊠ ⚊) Out of the way and pleasant for that reason, this lakeside hotel just under 5km west of Ribčev Laz has 43 rooms in its main hotel building and another 31 in a villa annexe. It's Slovenia's first official organic hotel; no synthetic pesticides or fertilizers were used to grow anything on offer here.

Hotel Ski (☎ 572 16 91; www.alpinum.net; Vogel Ski Centre; s €41-55, d €62-100) Rates at this recently renovated 29-room hotel at 1540m are at their highest during the skiing season.

Eating

Center Bohinj Pizzerija (☎ 572 31 70; Ribčev Laz 50; pizza €4.60-6.50, grills €5.70-10.50; ☼ 9am-10pm Dec-Oct) This jack-of-all-trades just down from the tourist office is the only eatery in the centre of Ribčev Laz. It can satisfy all tastes (except very demanding ones).

Penzion Rožič (starters €3.80-7.50, mains €5.80-11.70; ☼ noon-10pm) The restaurant at this popular pension in Ribčev Laz has a lovely covered terrace, although the views of the main road are not very special.

Gostilna Mihovc (☎ 572 33 90; Stara Fužina 118; dishes €4-7; ☼ 10am-midnight) This place in Stara Fužina is a popular place – not least for its homemade brandy. Try the *pasulj* (bean soup) with sausage (€5) or the beef *golač* (goulash; €4.40).

Planšar (☎ 572 30 95; Stara Fužina 179; ☼ 10am-8pm Tue-Sun Jun-Oct, 10am-8pm Sat & Sun Dec-May) If you want something light and incredibly tasty, head for the 'Herder', just opposite the Alpine Dairy Museum – appropriately enough. It specialises in home-made dairy products: hard Bohinj cheese, a soft, strong-tasting cheese called *mohant* (not to everyone's taste), cottage cheese, curd pie, sour milk and so on. You and a friend can taste a variety of them for €5.50 or make a meal of cheese and different types of grain dishes such as *žganci* (buckwheat) and *ješprenj* (barley). Other dishes available include *štruklji* (cheese dumplings) and *jota* (a thick soup of beans and salt pork).

Two country-style restaurants make a trip to Srednja Vas, the next village over from Studor and about 5km from Ribčev Laz,

worthwhile. The first restaurant is **Gostišče Rupa** (☎ 572 34 01; Srednja Vas 87; meals from €15; ☼ 10am-midnight Jul & Aug, 10am-midnight Tue-Sun Sep-Jun), which serves excellent home-cooked food, including spectacular Bohinj trout and *ajdova krapi*, crescent-shaped dumplings made from buckwheat and cheese. The second is **Pri Hrvatu** (☎ 572 36 70; Srednja Vas 76; meals from €15; ☼ noon-11pm late Jun–mid-Sep, noon-11pm Wed-Mon mid-Sep–late Jun), an equally popular place that can trace its pedigree back eight decades.

There's a **Mercator** (Ribčev Laz 49; ☼ 7am-7pm Mon-Fri, 7am-5pm Sat) supermarket next to the tourist office.

Shopping
The traditional craft of Bohinj is the *gorjuška čedra*, a small hand-carved wooden pipe with a silver cover for smoking tobacco or whatever. The tourist office sells the real thing and can tell you which masters are still making them in the area.

Getting There & Away
Buses run regularly from Ukanc to Ljubljana (€8.5, two hours, 91km, hourly) via Ribčev Laz, Bohinjska Bistrica and Bled (€4, one hour, 34km), with six extra buses daily between Ukanc and Bohinjska Bistrica (€2.20, 20 minutes, 12km) via Stara Fužina, Studor and Srednja Vas. Buses headed as far as Ukanc are marked 'Bohinj Zlatorog'. Note that three bus lines operate between Bled and Bohinj, and if you buy a return ticket from one bus line, you will not be able to make your return journey on either of the other buslines.

The lake itself is not on a train line. From Bohinjska Bistrica, passenger trains to Novo Gorica (€4.50, 1½ hours, 61km, up to seven a day) make use of a century-old, 6327m tunnel under the mountains that provides the only direct option for reaching the Soča Valley. In addition there are five daily auto trains (*avtovlaki*) to Podbrdo (€7.10, eight minutes, 7km) and three to Most na Soči (€10.85, 25 minutes, 28km).

Getting Around
From late June to late September, buses make the run daily from Bohinjska Bistrica train station to the Savica Waterfall car park (€2) via Hotel Jezero in Ribčev Laz. There are daily departures at 8.35am and 10.25am and on Saturday and Sunday an extra departure at 7.05am.

You can rent bicycles and mountain bikes from Alpinsport and PAC Sports for €4/8.80/13.40 per one hour/three hours/day.

KRANJSKA GORA
☎ 04 / pop 1420 / elev 803m

Forty kilometres northwest of Bled, in the Sava Dolinka Valley, is Kranjska Gora (Carniolan Mountain), the largest and best-equipped ski resort in the country. Somehow, though, it just doesn't seem Slovenian. The fact that the Italian *and* the Austrian borders are a half-dozen kilometres to the west and northwest might help explain that impression.

The Sava Dolinka Valley separates the Karavanke range from the Julian Alps. It has been an important commercial route between Gorenjska and Koroška for centuries; the 853m pass at Rateče is the lowest Alpine link between the Sava and Drava Valleys. The first railway in Gorenjska – from Ljubljana to Tarvisio (Trbiž) in Italy – made use of this pass when it opened in 1870.

Kranjska Gora was just a small valley village called Borovška Vas until the late 19th century, when skiing enthusiasts began to flock here. Planica (south of Rateče), the cradle of ski jumping, helped put the town on the world map earlier in the 20th century.

Kranjska Gora is at its best under a blanket of snow, but its surroundings are wonderful to explore in warmer months as well. The possibilities for hiking and mountaineering are endless in Triglav National Park on the town's southern outskirts, and there aren't many travellers who won't be impressed by a trip over the Vršič Pass (1611m), the gateway to the Soča Valley and the province of Primorska.

Orientation

Kranjska Gora sits at the foot of Vitranc (1631m) and in the shadow of two higher peaks (Razor and Prisank) that rise above 2600m. Rateče and Planica, famous for ski-jumping championships, are 6km to the west, while Jasna Lake, Kranjska Gora's doorway to Triglav National Park, is 2km to the south.

Kranjska Gora is a very small town with some unattractive modern buildings around its periphery and a more atmospheric (and older) core along Borovška cesta. The chairlifts up to the ski slopes on Vitranc are at the western end of town off Smerinje ulica.

Buses stop along Koroška cesta about 250m west of the big TGC shopping centre at the main entrance to the town from the motorway.

Information

Globtour (☎ 582 02 00; www.globtour-kranjskagora .com; Borovška cesta 92; ⏰ 9am-7pm Jul, Aug, Dec-Mar; 9am-7pm Mon-Sat Sep-Nov & Apr-Jun)

Gorenjska Banka (Borovška cesta 95; ⏰ 9-11.30am & 2-5pm Mon-Fri, 8-11am Sat)

Post office (Borovška cesta 92) Next to Mercator supermarket.

SKB Banka (Borovška cesta 99a; ⏰ 8.30am-noon & 2-5pm Mon-Fri) Beside the ski school.

Tourist Information Centre Kranjska Gora (☎ 588 17 68; www.kranjska-gora.si; Tičarjeva cesta 2; ⏰ 8am-7pm Mon-Sat, 9am-6pm Sun Jun-Sep & mid-Dec–Mar; 8am-3pm Mon-Fri, 9am-6pm Sat, 9am-1pm Sun Apr, May, Oct–mid-Dec)

Sights

One of the very few sights in Kranjska Gora, the endearing late-18th-century **Liznjek House** (Liznjekova Hiša; ☎ 588 19 99; Borovška cesta 63; adult/child €2.30/1.70; ⏰ 10am-6pm Tue-Sat, 10am-5pm Sun May-Oct & Dec-Mar) contains quite a good collection of household objects and furnishings peculiar to this area of Gorenjska. Among the various exhibits here are some excellent examples of trousseau chests covered in folk paintings, some 19th-century icons painted on glass and a collection of linen tablecloths (the valley was famed for its flax and its weaving).

Antique carriages and a sledge are kept in the massive barn out the back, which once housed food stores as well as pigs and sheep. The stable reserved for cows below the main building now contains a **memorial room** dedicated to the life and work of Josip Vandot (1884–1944). Vandot was a writer born in Kranjska Gora who penned the saga of Kekec, the do-gooder shepherd boy, who, together with his little playmate Mojca and his trusty dog Volkec, battles the evil poacher and kidnapper Bedanec. It's still a favourite story among Slovenian kids (and has been made into several popular films).

Activities
SKIING

The snow-covered slopes of the Sava Dolinka Valley, running for almost 11km from Gozd Martuljek all the way to Rateče and Planica, are effectively one big piste. However, the

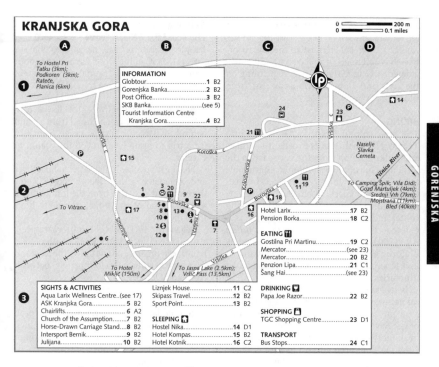

KRANJSKA GORA

0 _____ 200 m
0 _____ 0.1 miles

INFORMATION
Globtour.................................1 B2
Gorenjska Banka.....................2 B2
Post Office..............................3 B2
SKB Banka...........................(see 5)
Tourist Information Centre
   Kranjska Gora.....................4 B2

To Hostel Pri
Tatku (3km);
Podkoren (3km);
Rateče,
Planica (6km)

Koroška

Naselje
Slavka
Černeta

To Camping Špik; Vila Didi;
Gozd Martuljek (4km);
Srednji Vrh (7km);
Mojstrana (11km);
Bled (40km)

To Vitranc

To Hotel
Miklič (150m)

To Jasna Lake (2.5km);
Vršič Pass (13.5km)

Hotel Larix.............................17 B2
Pension Borka........................18 C2

EATING
Gostilna Pri Martinu...............19 C2
Mercator.............................(see 23)
Mercator................................20 B2
Penzion Lipa..........................21 C1
Šang Hai............................(see 23)

SIGHTS & ACTIVITIES
Aqua Larix Wellness Centre..(see 17)
ASK Kranjska Gora.................5 B2
Chairlifts................................6 A2
Church of the Assumption......7 B2
Horse-Drawn Carriage Stand...8 B2
Intersport Bernik.....................9 B2
Julijana.................................10 B2

Liznjek House........................11 C2
Skipass Travel.......................12 B2
Sport Point...........................13 B2

SLEEPING
Hostel Nika..........................14 D1
Hotel Kompas.......................15 B2
Hotel Kotnik.........................16 C2

DRINKING
Papa Joe Razor.....................22 B2

SHOPPING
TGC Shopping Centre............23 D1

TRANSPORT
Bus Stops.............................24 C1

main areas are the **Kranjska Gora ski centre** (☎ 580 94 00, 588 14 14; www.kr-gora.si; half-day pass adult/child/ senior & student €21.30/14.60/18.40, day pass €28/17/23) and Podkoren, 3km to the west, with ski jumping concentrated at Planica. The season usually lasts from mid-December to early March.

Skiing in Kranjska Gora is on the eastern slopes of Vitranc, and some runs join up with those at Podkoren – site of the Men's World Cup Slalom and Giant Slalom Competition (Vitranc Cup) in late December – on Vitranc's northern face to an altitude of 1570m. Together Kranjska Gora and Podkoren have five chairlifts and 15 tows. Generally, skiing is easier at Kranjska Gora than at Podkoren, where two of the most difficult slopes – Rutež (761m) and Zelenci (398m) – are located. In all, the two centres have 20km of pistes and 40km of cross-country courses.

The ski-jumping centre at **Planica** (www .planica.si), 6km to the west and across the motorway from Rateče, has six jumps with lengths of 25m, 120m and 180m. The short lift near the Dom Planica hut reaches an altitude of 900m. There are also some good possibilities at Planica for tobboganing and

for cross-country skiing in the Tamar Valley. The Ski Jumping World Championships are held here every year in March. The 100m mark was reached here by Austrian Josef Bradl in 1934 and the 200m one by the Finn Toni Nieminen in 1994. Another Finn, Janne Ahonen, set a new world record here in 2005 by jumping 240m.

Needless to say, there are quite a few places offering ski tuition and renting equipment, but it's best to stick with the tried and true. **Intersport Bernik** (☎ 588 14 70; info@intersport-bernik .com; Borovška cesta 88a; ☟ 8am-8pm mid-Dec–mid-Mar; 8am-2pm mid-Mar–mid-Dec), **ASK Kranjska Gora** (☎ 588 53 02; www.ask-kg.com; Borovška cesta 99a; ☟ 9am-4pm Mon-Sat, 10am-6pm Sun mid-Dec–mid-Mar; 9am-2pm Mon-Fri mid-Mar–mid-Dec), which shares the same building as SKB Banka, and **Skipass Travel** (☎ 582 10 00; www.skipasstravel.si; Borovška cesta 95; ☟ 7.30am-3pm Mon-Sat, 7.30am-noon Sun mid-Mar–mid-Dec; 7am-9pm mid-Dec–mid-Mar) all offer skiing and snowboarding instruction, with alpine and cross-country tuition in groups and individually. For one-on-one instruction, expect to pay from €25/40 for one/two hours (from €38/55 for two people). These establishments also rent equipment, as does **Sport Point** (☎ 588 48 83; famatrend@siol.net; Borovška cesta 93a; ☺ 8am-8pm mid-Dec–mid-Mar, 7am-7pm mid-Mar–mid-Dec) next to the tourist office. Skis and poles should cost €13.50 to €19 a day or €62 to €90 per week, depending on the style and class. Snowboards cost from €13/63 a day/week.

HIKING

The area around Kranjska Gora and into Triglav National Park is excellent for hikes and walks ranging from the very easy to the difficult. One of the best references available is *Walking in the Julian Alps* (2005) by Justi Carey and Roy Clark, published by Cicerone Press in the UK; it includes some 50 walking routes and short treks. Another option is *A Guide to Walks and Scrambles in the Julian Alps* (2003) by Mike Newbury. Published by Zlatorog Publications in Perth, Scotland, it uses Kranjska Gora as a base for its suggested itineraries.

Between Podkoren and Planica is a beautiful nature reserve called **Zelenci** (837m), with a turquoise-coloured lake that is the source of the Sava River. You can easily walk here in about two hours, on a path from Kranjska Gora via Podkoren and on to **Rateče**. These attractive alpine villages are notable for their medieval churches, rustic wooden houses and traditional hayracks. Then, if you want to continue on your journey, there's a well-marked trail via Planica to the Category II 128-bed **Dom v Tamarju** (☎ 587 60 55, 041-448 830) at 1108m in the **Tamar Valley**, 6km to the south. The walk is spectacular, and lies in the shadow of **Mojstrovka** (2366m) to the east and **Jalovec** (2645m) to the south. From here, the **Vršič Pass** is less than three hours away on foot.

Another great walk from Kranjska Gora – and quite an easy one – takes you north and then east through meadows and pasture land to the traditional village of **Srednji Vrh** and **Gozd Martuljek** in a couple of hours. The views of the Velika Pisnica Valley and the Martuljek range of mountains to the south are breathtaking. From Gozd Martuljek, it's only 9km east to **Mojstrana**, the starting point for the northern approaches to Triglav. In Mojstrana, the **Triglav Museum Collection** (Triglavska Muzejska Zbirka; ☎ 589 10 35; Triglavska cesta 50; adult/child €1.25/0.85; ☺ 10am-noon & 2-5pm Tue-Sun May-Oct), housed in an old inn, shows the history of mountaineering in Slovenia.

OTHER ACTIVITIES

The **Aqua Larix Wellness Centre** (☎ 588 45 00; www.htp-gorenjka.si; Borovška cesta 99; nonguests pool €9-10, pool & sauna €13-16.50) in the Hotel Larix is an indoor water park with pools, saunas and treatment centres and a great place to relax after a day on the slopes.

Horse-drawn carriages (☎ 588 12 41; Borovška cesta) seating four people can be hired from a stand behind SKB Banka. Prices range from €10 for a trip to Jasna Lake to €30 for a jaunt to Planica.

Fishing is possible in the Sava Dolinka River and Jasna Lake. A day **fishing licence** (€17) for the river and available from the tourist office allows a total of three fish, the daily limit from the Sava.

Julijana (☎ 588 13 25, 041-623 701; www.sednjek.si), a small travel agency in a kiosk south of SKB Banka, can organise **rafting tips** on the Sava and Soča for €30 (minimum four people) between April and October.

Sleeping

Accommodation costs in Kranjska Gora peak from December to March and in midsummer. April is the cheapest time to visit, though some hotels close for renovations and redecorating at this time.

BUDGET

Camping Špik (☎ 587 71 00; recepcija.spik@hitholidays-kg.si; Jezerci 21; per person €6-9.60; ☺ Jun-Sep; P ⊠) The closest camping ground to Kranjska Gora is this 2.5-hectare site for 500 guests near the Hotel Špik in Gozd Martuljek, 4km east of Kranjska Gora. It's on the left bank of the Sava Dolinka below the peaks of the Martuljek range, and there's an outdoor swimming pool in the grounds.

Hostel Nika (☎ 588 10 00; zvone.oreskovic@s5.net; Čičare 2; dm/s/d €11/16/28; P ⊠ ⊠) This somewhat institutional hostel with 66 beds on Čičare is about 800m northeast of the centre and just across the main road from the TGC Shopping Centre.

Hostel Pri Tatku (☎ 588 15 19; Podkoren 72; pritatku@gmail.com; per person 4-/6-bed dm €14/15) We've heard excellent things about this four-room, 15-bed hostel in a traditional old farmhouse in Podkoren, 3km to the west of Kranjska. There's a decent-sized common kitchen.

Both the tourist office and Globtour have **private rooms** (s €15.50-22.50, d €21-35) and **apartments** (apt for 2 €29-42, apt for 4 €48-78), with prices depending on the category and the time of year. There are a lot of houses with rooms available in the development called Naselje Slavka Černeta, south of the TGC shopping centre.

MIDRANGE

Pension Borka (☎ 587 91 00, 031-536 288; darinka .tasic@siol.net; Borovška cesta 71; per person €25) This central but very frayed property has some three-dozen rooms – mostly doubles and triples – in desperate need of upgrading. It has a large cellar restaurant and a TV room.

Vila Didi (☎ 588 08 54, 041-344 003; www.vila didi-oitzl.si; Jezerci 10; s & d €37-60; **P**) The eight guestrooms at this very attractive pension at the foot of the mountains in Gozd Martuljek are furnished with antiques. Prices depend on the size of the room and whether it has a balcony.

Hotel Kotnik (☎ 588 15 64; www.hotel-kotnik.si; Borovška cesta 75; s €48-62, d €56-84; ✗) If you're not into the big high-rise hotels with hundreds of rooms, choose this charming, bright-yellow property. It has 15 cosy rooms, a great restaurant and pizzeria, and you couldn't be more central.

TOP END

Hotel Miklič (☎ 588 16 35; www.hotelmiklic.com; Vitranška ulica 13; s €45-66, d €70-112; **P** ✗ 💻) This pristine 35-bed pension south of the centre is surrounded by luxurious lawns and flowerbeds and boasts an excellent restaurant and a small fitness room with sauna. It's definitely a cut above most other accommodation in Kranjska Gora.

Hotel Kompas (☎ 588 16 61; www.hitholidays-kg.si; Borovška cesta 100; s €63-80, d €96-128; **P** 🐾) With 149 rooms, the four-star Kompas is Kranjska Gora's biggest hotel. It's a pleasant enough place, recently renovated and set back in its own grounds. It boasts an indoor pool, tennis courts and the chairlifts are just over the road.

Hotel Larix (☎ 588 44 77; www.hitholidays-kg.si; Borovška cesta 99; s €63-80, d €96-128; **P** ✗ 💻 ♿ 🐾) Even closer to the lifts, and now in the same stable as the Kompas, is the 118-room Larix. It boasts the wonderful Aqua Larix Wellness Centre, with sauna, steam and a pool that seems to go on forever.

Eating & Drinking

Gostilna Pri Martinu (☎ 582 03 00; Borovška cesta 61; starters €4.20-5.85, mains €5.85-10, ☻ 10am-11pm) This atmospheric tavern-restaurant in an old house opposite the fire station is one of the best places in town to try local specialities such as venison, trout and *telečja obara* (veal stew; €3.75).

Šang Hai (☎ 588 13 46; Naselje Slavka Černeta 34; starters €2-3, mains €6.20-8.70; ☻ noon-midnight) If you fancy a change from local fare and pizza, try this Chinese restaurant, on the ground floor of the TGC Shopping Centre and facing the car park on the north side.

Hotel Kotnik (☎ 588 15 64; starters €5-8.80, mains €7.20-14; ☻ 11am-10pm) One of Kranjska Gora's better eateries, the restaurant in this stylish inn, with bits of painted dowry chests on the walls, serves grilled meats (pepper steak a speciality; €10) that should keep you going for a while. The adjoining pizzeria (pizza €4.80 to €6; open noon to 10pm) is for something quicker.

Penzion Lipa (☎ 582 00 00; Koroška cesta 14; starters €4.20-7.80, mains €11.70-19.20; ☻ 11am-11pm) This pension has an attractive, family-style restaurant just across from where the buses stop. They also do decent pizzas and pasta dishes (€4.80 to €6).

Papa Joe Razor (☎ 588 15 26; Borovška cesta 86; ☻ 9am-1am) Based in the old Razor Hotel dating from 1902, Papa Joe's is Kranjska Gora's most popular late-night and *après ski* venue, with live music at the weekend. It also does fast food like hamburgers (€2 to €3.80) and pizza (€4.60 to €6.20).

There's a **Mercator** (Borovška cesta 92; ☻ 7am-7pm Mon-Fri, 7am-7pm Sat, 8am-noon Sun) supermarket in the centre of the village and a **Mercator** (Naselje Slavka Černeta 33; ☻ 7am-7pm Mon-Fri, 7am-5am Sat) branch on the 1st floor of the TGC shopping centre.

Getting There & Around

Buses run hourly to Ljubljana (€8.5, two hours, 91km) via Jesenice (€3, 30 minutes, 23km), where you should change for Bled (€2.60, 20 minutes, 16km). There are just two direct departures to Bled (€4.90, one hour, 40km) on weekdays at 9.15am and 1.10pm. Daily in July and August and on Saturday and Sunday in June and September there's a service to Bovec (€5.50, two hours, 46km) via the spectacular Vršič Pass.

Intersport Bernik and Sport Point (opposite) and Julijana (opposite) all rent bicycles and mountain bikes (hour/half-day/day from €3.50/6.30/10). Juliana also rents motor scooters (half-day/day €18.80/27.30).

TRIGLAV NATIONAL PARK

☎ 04 & 05 / elev to 2864m

Triglav National Park (Triglavski Narodni Park), with an area of almost 84,000 hectares (4% of Slovenian territory), is one of the largest national reserves in Europe. It is a pristine, visually spectacular world of rocky mountains – the centrepiece of which is Triglav (2864m), the country's highest peak – as well as river gorges, ravines, canyons, caves, rivers, streams, forests and alpine meadows. It is a popular weekend destination for all manner of activity, from hiking and mountain biking to fishing and rafting. And there are approaches from Bohinj,

Kranjska Gora and, in Primorska, Trenta – to name just a few gateways.

Marked trails in the park lead to countless peaks and summits besides Triglav. Favourite climbs include **Mangart** (2679m) on the Italian border (the 12km road that descends to the Predel Pass is the highest road in Slovenia), the needlepoint of **Jalovec** (2645m) in the north, and the sharp ridge of **Razor** (2601m) southeast of Vršič. But Triglav National Park is not only about climbing mountains. There are easy hikes through beautiful valleys, forests and meadows, too. Two excellent maps are the PZS 1:50,000-scale *Triglavski Narodni Park* (Triglav National Park; €7.50) and

CLIMBING THE BIG ONE

The 2864m limestone peak called Triglav (Three Heads) has been a source of inspiration and an object of devotion for Slovenes for more than a millennium. The early Slavs believed the mountain to be the home of a three-headed deity who ruled the sky, the earth and the underworld. No one managed to reach the summit until 1778 when an Austrian mountaineer and his three Slovenian guides climbed it from Bohinj. Under the Habsburgs in the 19th century, the 'pilgrimage' to Triglav became, in effect, a confirmation of one's Slovenian identity, and this tradition continues to this day: a Slovene is expected to climb Triglav at least once in his or her life.

You can climb Slovenia's highest peak too, but despite the fact that on a good summer's day more than a hundred people will reach the summit, Triglav is not for the unfit or faint-hearted. In fact, its popularity is one of the main sources of danger. On the final approach to the top, there are often dozens of people clambering along a rocky, knife-edge ridge in both directions, trying to pass each other and kicking loose stones down on those below.

If you are fit and confident, and have a good head for heights, then by all means hire a guide and go for it. Guides can be hired through 3glav (p112) or Life Trek (p112) in Bled, Alpinsport (p119) or PAC Sports (p119) in Bohinj and the Triglav National Park Information Centre (p132) in Trenta, or book in advance through the Alpine Association of Slovenia (PZS; p43). Only experienced mountain walkers with full equipment – including good hiking boots, warm clothes and waterproofs, map and compass, whistle, head torch, first-aid kit, and emergency food and drink – should consider making the ascent without a guide. Take care – people die on Triglav every year.

Triglav is usually inaccessible to hikers from late October to early June. June and July are the rainiest (and sometimes snowiest) summer months, so August and particularly September and early and mid-October are the best times to make the climb. Patches of snow and ice can linger in the higher gullies until late July, and the weather can be very unpredictable at altitudes above 1500m, with temperatures varying by as much as 20°C and violent storms appearing out of nowhere.

Before you attempt the climb, see if you can find a copy of the dated but still useful *How to Climb Triglav* (Planinska Založba; €7), a superb, 63-page booklet that describes a dozen of the best routes, which may be available in bookshops and tourist offices in Slovenia. The most useful map for the ascent of Triglav is the PZS 1:25,000 *Triglav Planinska Karta* (€7.50), with all the trails and huts clearly marked. The PZS also publishes a two-sheet 1:50,000-scale map of the Julian Alps; for Triglav and the park you want the eastern part: *Julijske Alpe – Vzhodni Del* (€7.50).

It is park tradition in Slovenia to greet (or at least smile at) everyone you pass while climbing. And don't be surprised when you've reach the top and you find yourself being turned over and having your bottom beaten with a birch switch. It's a long-established tradition for Triglav 'virgins'. Once at the summit, you too can tell yourself with pride: 'Today I am a Slovene'.

ZLATOROG AND HIS GOLDEN HORNS

The oft-told tale of Zlatorog, the mythical chamois (*gams* in Slovene) with the golden horns who lived on Mt Triglav and guarded its treasure, almost always involves some superhuman (or, in this case, superantelopine) feat that drastically changed the face of the mountain. But don't let Slovenes convince you that their ancient ancestors passed on the tale. The Zlatorog story first appeared in the *Laibacher Zeitung* (Ljubljana Gazette) in 1868 during a period of Romanticism and national awakening. This one tells of how the chamois created the Triglav Lakes Valley, a wilderness of tumbled rock almost in the centre of Triglav National Park.

Zlatorog roamed the valley (at that time a beautiful garden) with the White Ladies, good fairies who kept the mountain pastures green and helped humans whenever they found them in need.

Meanwhile, down in the Soča Valley near Trenta, a greedy plot was being hatched. It seemed that an innkeeper's daughter had been given jewels by a wealthy Venetian merchant. The girl's mother demanded that her daughter's suitor, a poor but skilled hunter, match the treasure with Zlatorog's gold hidden under Mt Bogatin and guarded by a multiheaded serpent. If not, he was at least to bring back a bunch of Triglav 'roses' (actually pink cinquefoils) in mid-winter to prove his fidelity – an impossible task.

The young hunter, seething with jealousy, climbed the mountain in search of the chamois, figuring that if he were to get even a piece of the golden horns, the treasure of Bogatin – and his beloved – would be his. At last the young man spotted Zlatorog, took aim and fired. It was a direct hit.

The blood gushing from Zlatorog's wound melted the snow, and up sprang a magical Triglav rose. The chamois nibbled on a few petals and – presto! – was instantly back on his feet. As the chamois leapt away, roses sprang up from under his hooves, luring the hunter onto higher and higher ground. But as they climbed, the sun caught Zlatorog's shiny horns. The hunter was blinded, lost his footing and plunged into a gorge.

The once kind and trusting chamois was enraged that a mere mortal would treat him in such a manner. In his fury he gored his way through the Triglav Lakes Valley, leaving it much as it looks today. He left the area with the White Ladies, never to return.

And the fate of the others? The innkeeper's daughter waited in vain for her lover to return home. As spring approached, the snow began to melt, swelling the Soča River. One day it brought her a sad gift: the body of her young swain, his lifeless hand still clutching a Triglav rose. As for the innkeeper's rapacious wife, we know nothing. Perhaps she learned Italian and moved to Venice.

Observant (and thirsty) travellers will see the face of Zlatorog everywhere they go in Slovenia. It's on the label of the country's best beer (p52).

Freytag & Berndt's 1:50 000 *Julische Alpen* €8.14. The English-language *Triglav National Park: The Two-in-One Guide* (Založba Mladinska Knjiga; €16.70), which comes as a 104-page booklet with a map, is also worth consideration.

Although Slovenia counts 44 country (or 'landscape') parks and three regional ones, this is the country's only gazetted national park, and it includes almost all of the Alps lying within Slovenia. The idea of a park was first mooted in 1908 and realised in 1924, when 14 hectares of the Triglav Lakes Valley were put under temporary protection. The area was renamed Triglav National Park in 1961 and expanded 20 years later to include most of the eastern Julian Alps. Today the park stretches from Kranjska Gora in the north to Tolmin in the south and from the Italian border in the west almost to Bled in the east. The bulk of the park lies in the Gorenjska province, but once you've crossed the awesome Vršič Pass – at 1611m Slovenia's highest – and begun the descent into the Soča Valley, you've entered Primorska.

Triglav National Park is especially rich in fauna and flora, including blossoms such as the pink Triglav rose, blue Clusi's gentian, yellow hawk's-beard, Julian poppy and purple Zois bellflower. For details on park behaviour and etiquette, see p42.

FOUR ROUTES TO THE TOP

There are about 20 different ways to reach the top of Triglav, with the main approaches being to the south (Bohinj and Pokljuka) and the north (Mojstrana and the Vrata Valley). They offer varying degrees of difficulty and have their pluses and minuses. Experienced hikers tend to go for the more forbidding northern approaches, descending via one of the gentle southern routes. Novices usually ascend and descend near Bohinj. The western route from Trenta in the Soča Valley is steep and less frequented due to its relatively remote start. Most treks require one or two overnight stays in the mountains.

Mojstrana is the easiest trailhead to get to from Ljubljana (€7.30, 1¾ hours, 77km) by public transport – hourly buses between Kranjska Gora and the capital stop here. The Savica Waterfall at Bohinj is also walkable from Ukanc, which is served by bus (p123). If you're driving, there are parking areas at Rudno Polje and at the head of the Vrata Valley near Aljažev Dom, though the latter can only be reached on an unsurfaced road with gradients up to 1:4.

From Pokljuka

The approach to Triglav from Rudno Polje (1347m) on the Pokljuka Plateau, 18km southwest of Bled, is the shortest way to reach the peak – a round trip of 25km, with 1500m of ascent. A very fit and experienced mountain walker could do this in around eight to 10 hours of continuous hiking, but most mortals stay overnight at a hut. The route follows a well-marked trail under Viševnik (2050m) and over the Studor Saddle (1892m), before contouring around the slopes of Tosc to the Category I **Vodnikov Dom na Velem Polju** (☎ 04-572 32 13, 051-607 211; planinsko-drustvo-srednja-vas@siol.net; ☼ late Jun-early Oct), with 58 beds at 1817m (three hours). Another two hours' climbing leads to Category I **Dom Planika pod Triglavom** (☎ 04-574 40 69, 051-614 773; ☼ Jul-Sep) with 123 beds at 2401m, from which a further hour of steep climbing and scrambling along the summit ridge takes you to the top of Old Mr Three Heads.

From Bohinj

The approaches to Triglav from Bohinj (523m) are longer and involve more ascent than those in the north and the west but are more gently graded. They are more often used for descent. However, the following route would make a good three-day loop.

From the Savica Waterfall a path zigzags up the steep Komarča Crag (1340m), with an excellent view of the lake. Three to four hours hike north from the falls is the Category I **Koča pri Triglavskih Jezerih** (☎ 01-231 26 45, 040-620 783; info.pdljmatica@siol.net; ☼ mid-Jun–mid-Oct) at 1685m, a 200-bed hut at the southern end of the fantastic Triglav Lakes Valley where you spend the first night. If you want a good view over the valley and its seven permanent lakes (the others fill up in spring only), you can climb to Tičarica (2091m) to the northeast in about an hour. An alternative – although longer – route from the waterfall to the Triglav Lakes Valley is via Category I **Dom na Komni** (☎ 5/2 14 75, 040-695 783; info.pdljmatica@siol.net; ☼ year-round) and the Komna Plateau, a major battlefield in WWI.

On the second day you hike north along the valley, which the immortal chamois Zlatorog (p129) is said to have created, then northeast to the desert-like Hribarice Plateau (2358m). You then descend to the Dolič Saddle (2164m) and the Category I **Tržaška Koča na Doliču** (☎ 574 40 69, 051-614 780; ☼ late Jun-Sep) with 144 beds at 2151m and about four hours from Koča pri Triglavskih

Kranjska Gora to Soča Valley

One of the most spectacular – and easy – trips in Triglav National Park is simply to follow the paved road, open from May to October only, from Kranjska Gora via the Vršič Pass to Bovec, about 50km to the southwest. Between July and September, you can do the trip by bus. At other times, you'll need your own transport – be it a car, motorbike or mountain bike.

The first stop from Kranjska Gora is **Jasna Lake** (Jezero Jasna), about 2km south of town. It's a beautiful, almost too-blue glacial lake with white sand around its rim and the little Pivnica River flowing alongside. Standing guard is a bronze statue of that irascible old

Jezerih. You could well carry on to **Dom Planika pod Triglavom** at 2401m and about 1½ hours to the northeast, but this hut is often packed. It's better to stay where you're sure there's a bed unless you've booked ahead. From Dom Planika it's just over an hour to the summit of Triglav.

You could return the way you came, but it's far more interesting to go back to Bohinj via Stara Fužina. This way passes the **Vodnikov Dom na Velem Polju** at 1817m – less than two hours from Dom Planika – where there are two routes to choose from: down the Voje Valley, or along the Uskovnica ridge, a highland pasture to the east. The former takes about four hours; the route via Uskovnica is a little longer but affords better views. The trail to Rudno Polje and the road to Bled branches off from the Uskovnica route.

From Mojstrana

This approach, which is dominated by the stupendous northern face of Triglav, is popular with experienced climbers, and is often combined with a leisurely descent along the Triglav Lakes Valley to Bohinj. From the village of Mojstrana, which has **Kamp Kamne** (☎ 589 11 05; http://campingkamne .com; Dovje 9; per person €5-6; ☺ year-round) and a **Mercator** (Dunjaska cesta 10; ☺ 7am-7pm Mon-Fri, 7am-5pm Sat, 8am-noon Sun) supermarket, a mostly unsurfaced road leads in 11km to the Category II **Aljažev Dom v Vratih** (☎ 04-589 51 00, 031-384 013; pd.dovje-mojstrana@siol.net; ☺ late Apr-late Oct) with 138 beds at 1015m. Walking here should take about three hours, including time for a look at Peričnik Waterfall on the way. You'll probably want to spend the night here, as it is among the most beautiful sites in the park, with a perfect view of Triglav's north face, the third largest rock wall in Europe. Nearby is a 10m boulder called Mali Triglav (Little Triglav), where you can practise your ascent of the Big One.

From here, the steep and exposed Tominšek Trail leads via the northwest flank of Cmir and below Begunjski Vrh to Begunjski Studenec, a spring with excellent drinking water at 2100m (three hours). Much of this trail is a *via ferrata* (iron way) protected with iron spikes and cables.

From the spring you can choose to walk to either Category I **Dom Valentina Staniča** (☎ 051-614 772; pd.jav.kor.bela@s5.net; ☺ Jul–mid-Sep), 30 minutes to the southeast with 136 beds at 2332m, or to Category I **Triglavski Dom na Kredarici** (☎ 04-202 31 81; info.pdljmatica@siol.net; ☺ mid-Jun–mid-Oct), an hour to the south. The latter is the main hut serving the northern routes and at 2515m is the highest accommodation in the land; the summit is two hours away. Although Triglavski Dom has 140 beds in 30 rooms and another 160 beds in eight dormitories, it is often full; the best idea is to spend the night at Dom Staniča and make the ascent in the morning (two hours from hut to summit).

From Trenta

Because Trenta is more difficult to reach from the population centres of Ljubljana and southern Austria, the western approach to Triglav is quieter than the other routes. It's a long climb, though, starting from an altitude of just over 600m.

From Trenta, an hour's hike eastward along the Zajdnica Valley leads to the foot of Triglav's massive western face, where you begin zigzagging monotonously up an easy but seemingly endless trail for four more hours to the Dolič Saddle and the **Tržaška Koča na Doliču** at 2151m. From here, you can follow the normal route to the summit via **Dom Planika pod Triglavom** at 2401m or take the slightly more difficult west ridge (2½ hours), passing the ruined Morbegna barracks built by the Italian army in WWII at 2500m.

goat **Zlatorog** (p129), the mythical chamois with the golden horns.

As you zigzag up to just over 1100m, you'll come to the **Russian Chapel** (Ruska Kapelica), a little wooden church erected on the site where hundreds of Russian prisoners of war were buried in an avalanche in March 1916 while building the road you are travelling on.

The climbing then begins in earnest as the road meanders past a couple of huts and corkscrews up the next few kilometres to **Vršič Pass** (1611m), about 13km from Kranjska Gora. The area was the scene of fierce fighting during WWI, and a high percentage of the dead lay where they fell (at 1525m there's a **military cemetery** to the east of the road). The Tičarjev

GORENJSKA

Dom mountain hut is also east of the road, just before it begins to drop down the far side. To the west is **Mojstrovka** (2366m), to the east **Prisank** (2547m) and to the south the valley of the Soča River points the way to Primorska. A hair-raising descent of about 10km ends just short of the **monument to Julius Kugy**, a pioneer climber and writer (1858–1944) whose books eulogise the beauty of the Julian Alps.

From here you can take a side trip along the **Soča Trail** (Soška Pot) of about 2.5km northwest to the **source of the Soča River** (Izvir Soče). Fed by an underground lake, the infant river bursts from a dark cave before dropping 15m to the rocky bed from where it begins its long journey to the Adriatic. The trail then continues for another 18km in 16 stages along the cobalt Soča as far as Bovec.

Not long after joining the main road again, you'll pass the entrance to the **Alpinum Juliana** (admission free; ☉ 8.30am-6.30pm May-Sep), a 2.5-hectare botanical garden established in 1926 that showcases the flora of all of Slovenia's Alps (Julian, Kamnik-Savinja and Karavanke) as well as the Karst. The elongated mountain village of **Trenta** (population 110; elevation 620m) is just south.

Trenta has a long tradition of mountain guides. Shepherds and woodsmen made the first ascents of the Julian Alps possible in the 19th century, and their bravery and skill are commemorated in a plaque just below the botanical garden. Na Logu, in the upper part of Trenta, is the gateway to the western approach to Triglav, a much less frequented and steeper climb than most of the others (p130).

In Spodnja Trenta (Lower Trenta) the **Dom Trenta** (☎ 05-388 93 30, 388 93 06; Trenta 31; ☉ 10am-6pm late Apr-Oct) contains the **Triglav National Park Information Centre** (www.tnp.si) and the **Trenta Museum** (Trentarski Muzej; adult/child/student €3.80/2.30/2.50), which focuses on the park's geology and natural history as well as the Trenta guides and pioneers of Slovenian alpinism.

The equally long village of **Soča** (population 145; elevation 480m) is another 8.5km downriver. The **Church of St Joseph** (Cerkev Sv Joža) from the early 18th century has paintings by Tone Kralj (1900–75). Completed in 1944 as war still raged in central Europe, one of the frescoes on the ceiling depicts Michael the Archangel struggling with Satan and the foes of humanity, Hitler and Mussolini.

Bovec (p134), the recreational centre of the Upper Soča Valley (Gornje Posočje), is 12km west of Soča.

SLEEPING

The staff at Dom Trenta (left) in Trenta can book private rooms (per person €14) and apartments (for four from €50) in summer.

There are several mountain huts on or near the Vršič road. All of them serve very basic dishes three times day. Category II **Koča na Gozdu** (☎ 041-682 704; info@prezlc.si; Vršiška cesta 86; ☉ daily late Apr-Sep, Sat & Sun Oct-late Apr) with 43 beds is at 1226m, whereas **Erjačeva Koča na Vršiču** (☎ 04-586 60 70, 051-399-226; plan.drustvo@siol.net; Vršiška cesta 90; ☉ year-round), also Category II with 99 beds, is at 1525m. Category II **Tičarjev Dom na Vršiču** (☎ 04-586 60 70, 051-634 571; plan.drustvo@siol.net; Trenta 85; ☉ May–mid-Oct) with 91 beds and berths sits right on the pass.

Above Tičarjev Dom is Category II **Poštarski Dom na Vršiču** ☎ 041-610 029; Vršiška cesta 91; ☉ mid-Jun–Sep) with 65 beds at 1688m. Near the source of the Soča River at 886m is the Category III **Koča pri Izviru Soče** (☎ 04-586 60 70, 041-603 190; plan.drustvo@siol.net; ☉ late Apr-late Oct) with 34 beds.

Camping grounds abound in the park. In Trenta there's 45-site **Kamp Trenta** (☎ 041-615 966; www.campingtrenta.o-f.com; Trenta 60a; per person €5.50-6.50; ☉ May-Sep) and the smaller **Kamp Triglav** (☎ 05-388 93 11; marija.kravanja@volja.net; Trenta 18; per person €5.50; ☉ Apr-Sep) with 40 sites. In Soča you'll find **Kamp Soča** (☎ 05-388 93 18; Soča 8; per person €5.50-6.50; ☉ Apr-Sep), with 170 sites, and **Kamp Korita** (☎ 05-388 93 38; Soča 38; per person €5; ☉ May-Oct).

The lovely **Kekečeva Domačija** (Kekec Homestead; ☎ 05-381 1088, 041-413 087; www.kekceva-domacija.si; Trenta 76; per person €40), about 2.5km off the main road heading for the source of the Soča, has four apartments named after characters in the Kekec tales (p124) as the eponymous movie (1951) was filmed nearby.

GETTING THERE & AWAY

Two buses (6.30am and 3pm) a day in July and August and on Saturday and Sunday only in June and September link Ljubljana with Bovec (€12.50, 3¾ hours, 146km) in Primorska via Kranj, Lesce-Bled, Kranjska Gora, the Vršič Pass and Trenta. The afternoon bus then carries on to Kobarid, Tolmin and Nova Gorica.

Primorska

It may come as a surprise to many that the name of the long, slender province that forms Slovenia's western frontier means 'by the sea' or 'littoral'. Yes, there is a coastline, though it's only 47km long. And there's a whole lot more to Primorska than just that.

Like Gorenjska, its smaller and squatter neighbour to the east and northeast, Primorska offers travellers an endless list of activities and sights; it really can claim to be 'Europe in miniature'. There are mountains to climb and rivers to raft in the Soča Valley, wines to taste in the vineyards of the Vipava Valley and Brda Hills near Nova Gorica, expansive caverns at Škocjan and white stallions to ride at Lipica in the Karst and beaches on which to while away the hours on fine summer days at Piran and Portorož. And most of those activities can be enjoyed on the same day.

At the same time, Primorska can claim some of the most important and historic places in the country. Koper, Piran and Izola – three erstwhile Venetian ports full of Gothic architecture and art – will keep even the most indefatigable of sightseers busy, and there are hilltop churches, ancient monasteries and richly endowed museums sprinkled throughout the province.

Primorska enjoys some of the finest weather in Slovenia, with warm coastal winds affecting the valleys as far as Kobarid and Bovec and inland. As a result, the climate and the flora here are distinctly Mediterranean right up to the foothills of the Alps.

PRIMORSKA

HIGHLIGHTS

- Enjoy a fresher-than-fresh seafood meal along the coast at **Izola** (p168) or **Piran** (p171)
- Raise the adrenaline by **canyoning**, **hydrospeeding** or **rafting** (p135) the Soča River from Bovec
- Be reminded of where you come from (and where you are going) at the **Church of the Holy Trinity** (p163) in Hrastovlje
- Enter into the world of Jules Verne's *A Journey to the Centre of the Earth* by touring the **Škocjan Caves** (p151)
- Sample some of the world-class red wines (especially the Merlots) from the **Vipava** (p150) and **Brda** regions (p144)

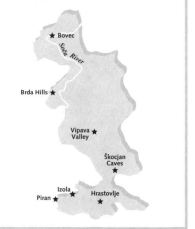

SOČA VALLEY

The region of the Soča Valley (Posočje) stretches from Triglav National Park to Nova Gorica. Its most dominant feature is the 136km Soča River, which can widen to 500m and narrow to less than a metre but always stays a deep, almost unreal aquamarine colour. The valley has more than its share of historical sights, but most people come here for rafting, hiking and skiing.

The Soča Valley has been an important trade route between the Friulian Plain and the alpine valleys since the earliest times. It was the site of several Hallstatt settlements, evidenced by the rich archaeological finds unearthed at Most na Soči, Tolmin and Kobarid. Under the Romans the valley was on the important road between Noricum and the province of Histria.

The proximity of Venice and the Napoleonic wars of the late 18th and early 19th centuries restored the valley's strategic role. The railway to Bohinj brought modern transport between the Sava Valley and Gorica for the first time in 1906, and during WWI millions of troops were brought here to fight on the battle front stretching from the Karst to Mt Rombon. Between the wars, Primorska and the Soča Valley fell under Italian jurisdiction. Many Italians were expelled or left the province voluntarily after WWII.

PRIMORSKA

0 — 10 km
0 — 6 miles

BOVEC

☎ 05 / pop 1635 / elev 451m

The effective capital of the Upper Soča Valley (Gornje Posočje), Bovec has a great deal to offer adventure-sports enthusiasts. With the Julian Alps above, the Soča River below and Triglav National Park at the back door, there's an abundance to choose from. If you have the time you could spend a week hiking, kayaking, mountain biking and, in winter, skiing at Mt Kanin, Slovenia's highest ski station.

History

The area around Bovec is first mentioned in documents dating back to the 11th century. At that time it was under the direct rule of the Patriarchs of Aquileia but was later transferred to the Counts of Gorica and, in about 1500, to the Habsburgs. The Turks passed through the basin on their way to the Predel Pass in the 15th century, and on two occasions (in 1797 and again in 1809) Napoleon's army attacked Austria from here.

Bovec suffered terribly in the fighting around the Soča Valley during WWI. Much of the town was destroyed, but its reconstruction by the architect Maks Fabiani in the 1920s gave Bovec an interesting combination of traditional and modern buildings. Further reconstruction took place after severe earthquakes in 1976 and again in 1998.

Orientation

Bovec lies in a broad basin called the Bovška Kotlina at the meeting point of the Soča and Koritnica Valleys. Towering above are several peaks of well over 2000m, including Rombon (2208m) and Kanin (2587m). The Soča River flows past Bovec 2km to the south at Čezsoča. The Italian border is 16km to the southwest via the pass at Učeja and 17km north at Predel.

The centre of the town is Trg Golobarskih Žrtev, one of the few named streets here. Actually, it's a long square that forms the main east–west drag and runs northward to the neo-Romanesque church of St Urh. Buses stop on Trg Golobarskih Žrtev in front of the Letni Vrt restaurant.

Information

Abanka (Trg Golobarskih Žrtev 18; 8.30-11.30am & 2-5pm Mon-Fri) Opposite the tourist office.

Bar Kavarna (☎ 388 63 35; Trg Golobarskih Žrtev 25; 20 min €1.50; 7am-10pm) Internet access.

Nova KBM Banka (Trg Golobarskih Žrtev 47; 8am-6pm Mon-Fri, 8am-noon Sat)

Post office (Trg Golobarskih Žrtev 8; 8-9.30am, 10am-3.30pm & 4-6pm Mon-Fri, 8am-noon Sat)

Tourist Information Centre Bovec (☎ 384 19 19; www.bovec.si; Trg Golobarskih Žrtev 8; 9am-8pm Jul & Aug, 9am-5pm Mon-Fri, 9am-noon & 4-6pm Sat, 9am-noon Sun Sep-Jun) Next door to the post office.

Sights

The **Kluže Fortress** (Trdnjava Kluže; ☎ 384 19 00; www .kluze.net; adult/student & child €1.70/1.25; 9am-9pm Jul & Aug; 10am-5pm Sun-Fri, 10am-7pm Sat Jun & Sep), built by the Austrians in 1882 on the site of a 17th-century fortress and above a deep ravine on the Koritnica River, is 4km northeast of Bovec and worth the trip just to see its awesome location. There's a small exhibition devoted to the Soča Front and other local WWI battles. There's also a bar with hot and cold drinks. You can reach the fortress on the main road from Bovec towards Log pod Mangartom and the Predel Pass into Italy.

Activities

ADVENTURE SPORTS

There are up to a dozen outfits organising all kinds of adventure sports. Among the better known half-dozen are **Avantura** (☎ 041-718 317; info@avantura.org; Trg Golobarskih Žrtev 19; 9am-9pm Jun-Aug); **Bovec Rafting Team** (☎ 388 61 28, 041-338 308; www.brt-ha.si; Mala Vas 106; 9am-7pm May-Sep), in a kiosk opposite the Martinov Hram restaurant; **Outdoor Freaks** (☎ 389 64 90, 041-553 675; www .freakoutdoor.com; Trg Golobarskih Žrtev 38; 9am-7pm May-Sep), in the Rombon building on the main square; **Soča Rafting** (☎ 389 62 00; www.socarafting .si; Trg Golobarskih Žrtev 48; 9am-7pm Jun-Sep, 9am-4pm Oct-May), about 100m uphill from the tourist office; **Sport Mix** (☎ 389 61 60, 031-871 991; www .dir.si; Trg Golobarskih Žrtev 18; 9am-7pm May-Jun & Sep, 8am-9pm Jul-Aug); and **Top Extreme** (☎ 330 00 90, 041-620 636; www.top.si; Trg Golobarskih Žrtev 19; 9am-9pm Jun-Aug).

PRIMORSKA

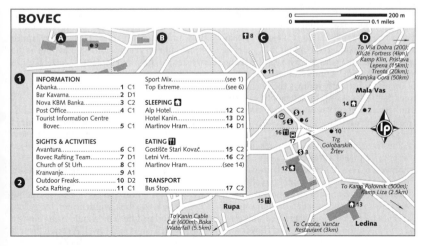

BOVEC

INFORMATION	
Abanka 1 C1	
Bar Kavarna 2 D1	
Nova KBM Banka 3 C2	
Post Office 4 C1	
Tourist Information Centre	
Bovec 5 C1	
SIGHTS & ACTIVITIES	
Avantura 6 C1	
Bovec Rafting Team 7 D1	
Church of St Urh 8 C1	
Kranvura 9 A1	
Outdoor Freaks 10 D2	
Soča Rafting 11 C1	

Sport Mix ....(see 1)	
Top Extreme ....(see 6)	
SLEEPING	
Alp Hotel 12 C2	
Hotel Kanin 13 D2	
Martinov Hram 14 D1	
EATING	
Gostišče Stari Kovač 15 C2	
Letni Vrt 16 C2	
Martinov Hram ....(see 14)	
TRANSPORT	
Bus Stop 17 C2	

To Vila Dobra (200); Kluže Fortress (4km); Kamp Klin, Pristava Lepena (15km); Trenta (20km); Kranjska Gora (50km)

Mala Vas

Trg Golobarskih Žrtev

To Kamp Polovnik (500m); Kamp Liza (2.5km)

Rupa

Ledina

To Kanin Cable Car (600m); Boka Waterfall (5.5km)

To Čezsoča; Vančar Restaurant (3km)

0   200 m
0   0.1 miles

FISHING

Hotel Alp and Kamp Klin both sell fishing licences for hooking the famous Soča trout. There are two types: one for the area east of Čezsoča, as well as the Lepenjica River (€70.50), and another for the Soča below Bovec (€60), where there is a lot more kayaking and boating. The season lasts from April to October.

HIKING & CYCLING

The 1:25,000-scale map called *Bovec z Okolico* (Bovec with Surroundings; €7.20) lists a number of walks and hikes ranging from a two-hour stroll south to **Čezsoča** and the protected gravel deposits in the Soča to an ascent of **Rombon** (2208m), which would take a good five hours one way. The smaller-scaled 1:40,000 Bovec (€7.20) also has walks in the area. Ask the tourist office for the pamphlet *Kolesarske Poti/Cycle Tracks*, which lists a half-dozen trips of various degrees of difficulty.

The **Kanin Mountain Bike Path** (www.mtbpark kanin.com, in Slovene) is just 2km from the cable car's station B. From the uppermost stop (station D) hikers could make the difficult three-hour climb of Kanin (2587m) or reach the **Prestreljenik Window** (2498m) in about an hour.

The tourist offices and some of the sports agencies listed above can organise **guided walks**, such as the one costing €140 to the **Mangart Saddle** (2072m) along the highest road in Slovenia, where you'll find accommodation at the Category I **Koča na Mangartskem Sedlu** (☎ 041-954 761; erik_cuder@siol.net; ﾂ daily mid-Jun–Sep, Sat & Sun Oct) with 53 beds at 1906m, and to the **Krn Lake** 1340m above the Lepena Valley, where you'll find the Category I **Planinski Dom pri Krnskih Jezerih** (☎ 302 30 30; planinskod .novagorica@siol.net; ﾂ Jun–Sep) with 170 beds and berths at 1385m. A mountain-walking tour of medium difficulty follows the Soča Front lines (p139), passing trenches, old caverns, bunkers and observation posts. It takes between eight and 10 hours and costs about the same.

The most popular do-it-yourself walk in the area is to **Boka Waterfall**, 5.5km to the southwest of Bovec. The waterfall drops 106m from the Kanin Mountains into the valley and is almost 30m wide – it's an impressive sight, especially in late spring when the snow melts. To get there on foot, follow marked walkways B2 and S1 on the *Bovec z Okolico* (Bovec and Surroundings) map; mountain-bike track No 1 on the map will also take you there. The trip up to the falls (850m) and back takes about 1½ hours, but the path is steep in places and can be very slippery.

Sport Mix, Soča Rafting, Bovec Rafting Team and Outdoor Freaks all rent **bicycles** and **mountain bikes** (hr/day/5 days €5/15/60).

PARAGLIDING

In winter you can take a tandem paraglider flight (ie as a passenger accompanied by a qualified pilot) from the top of the Kanin cable car, 2000m above the valley floor. The cost of a flight ranges from €100; ask the Avantura agency for details. Paragliding is at its best from the Mangart Saddle (2072m) between June and September.

SKIING

The **Kanin ski centre** (☎ 388 60 98; www.bovec.si; day pass adult/child/senior & student €22/16/18) in the mountains northwest of Bovec has skiing up to 2200m – the only real altitude alpine skiing in Slovenia. As a result, the season can be long, with good spring skiing in April and even May. The ski area – 17km of pistes and 15km of cross-country runs served by four chairlifts and three T-bars – is reached by a cable car in three stages. The bottom station is 600m southwest of the centre of Bovec on the main road. You can rent a complete kit (skis, poles, boots) from an outfit called **Kravanje** (☎ 041-719 314; Kaninska Vas 7; ﾂ 8-noon & 4-7pm Dec-May) at Kaninska Vas reception for about €16.50 a day.

The **cable car** (one-way/return €8.35/11.30) runs continuously during the skiing season; in July and August it runs hourly from 7am to 4pm and every hour from 8am to 3pm at the weekend in June and September. Several walks lead from the upper station.

WATER SPORTS

Rafting, kayaking and canoeing on the beautiful Soča River (10% to 40% gradient; Grades I to VI) attract many people to Bovec. The season lasts from April to October, and organised excursions are available daily.

Rafting trips for two to eight people on the Soča over a distance of 10km cost €27 to €37 and for 21km €34.60 to €42, including neoprene long johns, windcheater, life jacket, helmet and paddle. You should bring along a swimsuit, T-shirt and towel. A canoe for two is €50 for the day, and a single kayak is €27. A number of kayaking courses are also on offer (eg a one/two-day course for beginners costs €60/77, with equipment rental another €27). A guided 10km kayak/canoe trip costs from €30/28.50 per person

A 3km, two-hour **canyoning** trip near the Soča, in which you descend through gorges and jump over falls attached to a rope, costs from €34. **Hydrospeed**, which is like riding down a river on a boogie board, costs €30 to €35 for 8km to 10km.

Sleeping

Private rooms (per person €12-25) are easy to come by in Bovec, and the tourist office and other agencies have hundreds on their lists.

Kamp Polovnik (☎ 389 60 07, 031-344 417; www .kamp-polovnik.com; per adult/child €6.70/4.80; ☼ Apr-Oct) About 500m southeast of the Hotel Kanin, this is the closest camping ground to Bovec. It is small but in an attractive setting.

Kamp Liza (☎ 389 63 70; per person €8; ☼ Apr-Oct) This little site is further afield in Vodenca, 2.5km southeast of the town centre at the point where the Koritnica and Soča Rivers meet.

Kamp Klin (☎ 388 95 13; kampklin@volja.net; Lepena 1; per person €7-9.10; ☼ Apr-Oct) This large and quite lovely camping ground is in Lepena on the idyllic Lepenjica River, about 15km southeast of Bovec.

Martinov Hram (☎ 388 62 14; sara.berginc@volja.net; Trg Golobarskih Žrtev 27; per person €24-39) This lovely guesthouse just 100m east of the centre has 14 beautifully furnished rooms and an excellent restaurant with an emphasis on specialities from the Bovec region.

Pristava Lepena (☎ 388 99 00; www.pristava-lepena .com; Lepena 2; per person €42-58; ☼ Apr–mid-Oct) This positively idyllic 'holiday village' is set in an alpine meadow 15km southeast of Bovec. There are 13 apartments in six traditional houses, a lovely restaurant, and fishing and riding opportunities.

Alp Hotel (☎ 388 60 40; www.alp-chandler.si; Trg Golo-barskih Žrtev 48; s €37-48, d €56-78; P X ▣) This 103-room hotel, with a bit of landscaped garden around it, is fairly good value and as central as you are going to find in Bovec.

Hotel Kanin (☎ 388 60 21; hoteli.bovec@siol.net; Ledina 9; s €42-57, d €64-93; P X ▣ ▣) About 150m southeast of the Alp Hotel, this 124-room property has much quieter surrounds, a large indoor swimming pool and a sauna.

THE AUTHOR'S CHOICE

Dobra Vila (☎ 389 64 00; www.dobra-vila-bovec .com; Mala Vas 112; s/d €71.50/110; P X ▣ 🛠) This absolute stunner of a 12-room boutique hotel is housed in the former telephone-exchange building, which dates back to 1932. It has its own small cinema, a library and wine cellar and a fabulous restaurant. The place is peppered with interesting artefacts; we love the 1932 Bianchi Freccia d'Oro 175T motorcycle in one of the windows. One of the two quads is attractively laid out on two levels.

The rooms are not as nice as those at the Alp, though some have balconies.

Eating

Gostišče Stari Kovač (☎ 388 66 99; Rupa 3; pizza €4.50-6.80; ☼ noon-11pm Tue-Sun) The 'Old Blacksmith', just west of the Alp Hotel, is a good choice for pizza cooked in a wood-burning stove.

Letni Vrt (☎ 389 63 83, 041-775 127; Trg Golobarskih Žrtev 12; meals from €10; ☼ 11am-10pm Wed-Mon) Opposite the Alp Hotel, the 'Summer Garden' has pizza, grilled dishes and trout at affordable prices. Its garden is lovely in summer – as it would be.

Martinov Hram (☎ 388 62 14; Trg Golobarskih Žrtev 28; mains €5.35-14.60; ☼ 10am-10pm Wed-Mon) This restaurant in an attractive inn specialises in seafood and grills and during the winter season serves pizzas as well. There is a lovely roadside terrace in front.

Vančar (☎ 389 60 76, 389 60 77; Čezsoča 43; meals from €15; ☼ 11am-10pm Jul & Aug, 11am-10pm Wed-Sun Sep-Jun) If you want to eat where local people do, head for this place about 3km south of Bovec. Expect huge portions.

Dobra Vila (☎ 389 64 00; www.dobra-vila-bovec.com; Mala Vas 112; starters €5-7.50, mains €9.20-15.85; ☼ noon-10pm) This spectacular restaurant at the Soča Valley's first boutique hotel specialises in game dishes and has a wonderful winter garden and outdoor terrace.

Getting There & Away

Buses to Kobarid (€3, 30 minutes, 21km) and Tolmin (€4.50, one hour, 37km) are frequent, with up to six departures a day (a lot fewer at the weekend). There are also buses to Ljubljana (€12, 2½ hours, 142km, three a day) via Tolmin and Most na Soči and to

Nova Gorica (€7, two hours, 72km, three a day). In July and August there are up to four daily buses to Kranjska Gora (€4, 1½ hours, 33km) via Vršič Pass, one of which carries on to Bled (€7, 2½ hours, 74km).

KOBARID
☎ 05 / pop 1240 / elev 235m

The charming town of Kobarid is a lot quainter than Bovec, 21km to the northwest, and the woodland scenery somewhat tamer. Despite being surrounded by mountain peaks higher than 2200m, Kobarid feels more Mediterranean than alpine and the architecture retains its Italianate look. The Italian border at Robič is only 9km to the west.

Indeed, on the surface not a whole lot has changed in this sleepy hollow since the American writer Ernest Hemingway described Kobarid (then Caporetto) in his novel *A Farewell to Arms* (1929), depicting the horror and suffering of WWI. It was 'a little white town with a campanile in a valley,' he wrote, 'a clean little town and there was a fine fountain in the square'. The bell in the tower still rings on the hour, but the fountain has disappeared.

Kobarid did have a history before WWI and things have happened here since. It was a military settlement during Roman times, was hotly contested in the Middle Ages and was hit by a devastating earthquake in 1976, which destroyed some historical buildings and farmhouses with folk frescoes. But the world will always remember Kobarid as Caporetto, the site of the decisive battle of 1917 in which the combined forces of the Central Powers defeated the Italian army.

Orientation
Kobarid lies in a broad valley on the west bank of the Soča River. The centre of town is Trg Svobode, dominated by the Gothic Church of the Assumption and that famous bell tower. Buses stop in front of the Bar Kramar on the eastern side at Trg Svobode 9.

Information
Abanka (Markova ulica 16; ⌚ 8.30–noon & 2.30–5pm Mon-Fri, 8am–noon Sat)

Nova KBM Banka (Trg Svobode 2; ⌚ 8–11.15am & 2–5.15pm Mon-Fri)

Post office (Trg Svobode 2; ⌚ 8–9.30am, 10am–3.30pm & 4–6pm Mon-Fri, 8am–noon Sat)

Tourist Information Centre Kobarid (☎ 380 04 90; www.lto-sotocje.si; Gregorčičeva ulica 8; ⌚ 9am-8pm Mon-Fri, 9am–12.30pm & 3.30–8pm Sat & Sun Jul & Aug; 9am-12.30pm & 1.30-7pm Mon-Fri, 9am–1pm Sat Sep-Jun) Next door to the award-winning Kobarid Museum.

X Point (☎ 388 53 08, 041-692 290; www.xpoint.si; Trg Svobode 6; ⌚ 9.30am-5pm Apr-Oct) An extreme-sports agency that organises rafting, canyoning, kayaking, canoeing, paragliding and trekking in and around Kobarid and Tolmin.

Sights & Activities
KOBARID MUSEUM
Located in 18th-century Mašera House, this **museum** (Kobariški Muzej; ☎ 389 00 00; Gregorčičeva ulica 10; adult/child/student & senior €4/2.50/3; ⌚ 9am-6pm Mon-Fri, 9am-7pm Sat & Sun Apr-Oct; 10am-5pm Mon-Fri, 10am-

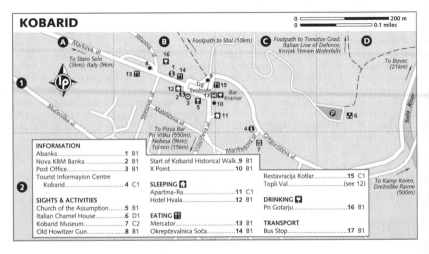

KOBARID

0 ————— 200 m
0 ————— 0.1 miles

INFORMATION	
Abanka	1 B1
Nova KBM Banka	2 B1
Post Office	3 B1
Tourist Informayion Centre Kobarid	4 C1

SIGHTS & ACTIVITIES	
Church of the Assumption	5 B1
Italian Charnel House	6 D1
Kobarid Museum	7 C2
Old Howitzer Gun	8 B1

Start of Kobarid Historical Walk	9 B1
X Point	10 B1

SLEEPING	
Apartma-Ra	11 C1
Hotel Hvala	12 B1

EATING	
Mercator	13 B1
Okrepčevalnica Soča	14 B1

Restavracija Kotlar	15 C1
Topli Val	(see 12)

DRINKING	
Pri Gotarju	16 B1

TRANSPORT	
Bus Stop	17 B1

PRIMORSKA

6pm Sat & Sun Nov-Mar) is devoted almost entirely to the Soča Front (below) and deals with the tragedy of the 'war to end all wars'.

The museum is divided into about a dozen rooms on three floors. The rooms on the 1st and 2nd floors have themes: the **White Room** describes the particularly harsh conditions of waging war in the mountains in the snow and fog; the **Hinterland Room** explains what life was like for soldiers during pauses in the fighting and also for the civilian population that was uprooted by war and famine; the **Black Room** displays horrific photographs of the dead and dying.

On the 3rd floor the **Battle of Kobarid Room** deals with the events over three days – 24 to 27 October 1917 – when the combined Austrian and German forces met up near Kobarid and launched the offensive that defeated the Italian army.

Among the collection are photographs documenting the horrors of the front, military charts, diaries and maps, and two large relief displays showing the front lines and offensives through the Krn Mountains and the positions in the Upper Soča Valley the day before the decisive breakthrough. There's also a 20-minute presentation of slides with commentary.

KOBARID HISTORICAL WALK

A free brochure from the tourist office describes the 5km Kobarid Historical Walk (Kobariška Zgodovinska Pot). From the Kobarid Museum walk to the north side of Trg Svobode, a winding road lined with the Stations of the Cross climbs up a hill called Gradič to the **Italian Charnel House** (Italijanska Kostnica), which contains the bones of more than 7000 Italian soldiers killed on the Soča

---

THE SOČA/ISONZO FRONT

The breakthrough in the Soča Front (more commonly known as the Isonzo Front) by the combined Austro-Hungarian and German forces near Caporetto (Kobarid) in October 1917 was one of the greatest military campaigns fought on mountainous terrain and one of the costliest ever fought in terms of human life. By the time the fighting had stopped 17 days later, hundreds of thousands of soldiers lay dead or wounded, writhing and screaming in the blood-drenched earth, gassed and mutilated beyond recognition.

In May 1915, Italy declared war on the Central Powers and their allies and moved its army across the southwestern border of Austria to the strategically important Soča Valley. From there, they hoped to move eastward to the heart of Austria-Hungary. By then, however, the Austrians had fortified the lines with trenches and bunkers for 80km from the Adriatic and the Karst to the mountain peaks overlooking the Upper Soča Valley as far north as Mt Rombon. The First Offensive launched by the Italians was successful in the first month, and they occupied Kobarid and Mt Krn to the northeast, where they would remain for some 29 months.

The Italians launched another 11 offensives over the next 2½ years, but the difficult mountain terrain meant a war of attrition between two entrenched armies. Territorial gains were minimal, but the fighting in the mountains and the limestone plateau to the south was horrific.

On 24 October 1917 the stalemate was broken when the Austro-Hungarians and Germans formulated an unusual plan of attack based on surprise and moved hundreds of thousands of troops, arms and material (including seven German divisions) into the area between Bovec and Tolmin, with Kobarid as the first target. The 12th Offensive – the 'miracle of Kobarid' – routed the Italian army and pushed the fighting back to the Friulian Plain, where the war continued for another year. The sketches of the breakthrough by one Lieutenant Erwin Rommel, who would become known as the 'Desert Fox' while commanding Germany's North African offensive in WWII, are invaluable for understanding the battle. But no account is more vivid than the description of the Italian retreat in Hemingway's *A Farewell to Arms*. The novelist himself was wounded on the Gorica battlefield in the spring of 1917 while driving an Italian ambulance.

The 12th Offensive was the greatest breakthrough in WWI, and it employed some elements of what would later be called 'lightning war' (blitzkrieg). The Italians alone lost 500,000 soldiers, and another 300,000 were taken prisoner. Casualties on the Soča Front for the entire 1915–17 period, including soldiers on the battlefields and men, women and children behind the lines, number almost a million.

PRIMORSKA

Front. Benito Mussolini attended the dedication in September 1938. The charnel house is topped with the 17th-century **Parish Church of St Anthony** (Župnijska Cerkev Sv Anton), which was moved here in 1935.

From the ossuary, a path leads north (take the left-hand fork after a minute's walk) for just over 1km to **Tonočov Grad**, an ancient fortified hill where an archaeological project has uncovered the remains of houses and churches dating from the 5th and 6th centuries.

The path then descends through the remains of the **Italian Defence Line** (Italijanska Obrambna Črta) built in 1915, past cleared trenches, gun emplacements and observation posts, before crossing the Soča over **Napoleon Bridge** (Napoleonov Most), a replica of a bridge built by the French in the early 19th century and destroyed in May 1915. On the far side of the river, the path leads up a side valley to a series of walkways that take you to the foot of the spectacular **Kozjak Stream Waterfalls** (Slapovi Potoka Kozjak). The route then returns to Kobarid along the east bank of the Soča. Allow three hours for a leisurely circuit.

Sleeping

Kamp Koren (☎ 389 13 11; www.kamp-koren.si; Drežniške Ravne 33; per person €6.50-8.50; ☉ mid-Mar–Oct; P ▯ &) The oldest camping ground in the Soča Valley, this small, 1-hectare site is about 500m north of Kobarid on the left bank of the Soča River and just before the turn to Drežniške Ravne, a lovely village with traditional farmhouses.

Apartma-Ra (☎ 389 10 07; apartma-ra@siol.net; Gregorčičeva ulica 6c; per person €15-25; P ✂ ✗) This welcoming little place with 25 beds between the Kobarid Museum and Trg Svobode (enter via the driveway from Volaričeva ulica) is entirely nonsmoking. Some rooms have terraces and bicycles are available for rent to guests for €6/9 per half-day/day.

Hotel Hvala (☎ 389 93 00; wwww.hotel-hvala.si; Trg Svobode 1; s €54-65, d €78-100; P ✗ ▯) The only hotel in town is the delightful 'Hotel Thanks' (actually it's the family's name), which has 32 rooms, a bar, a superb restaurant and a Mediterranean-style café in the garden open in summer. It even sells **fishing permits** (per day €51-59, for 3 days €136-159) for the Soča River.

Hiša Franko (☎ 389 41 20; www.hisafranko.com; Staro Selo 1; s & d €90-119; P ✗ ▯) This guesthouse in an old farmhouse 3km west of Kobarid in Staro Selo, halfway to the Italian border, has 13

themed rooms – we love the Moja Afrika (My Africa) one – some of which have terraces and Jacuzzis. Guests can hire mountain bikes for €7 a day. The restaurant here is legendary.

Nebesa (☎ 384 46 20, 041-769 484; www.nebesa .si, Livek 39; d €176-220; P) The 'Paradise' compound, with its four two-person modern 'cabins' and its scenic location 900m up in the mountains about 9km southeast of Kobarid on the road to Tolmin, is one of the few places to stay in Slovenia that is a 'destination' onto itself. Self-contained, with kitchen, fireplace and open terraces, the cabins measure more than 50 sq metres and are among the most dramatic (and romantic) places to stay in Slovenia.

Eating & Drinking

Okrepčevalnica Soča (☎ 389 05 00; Markova ulica 10; pizza €3.20-6; ☉ 11am-10pm) The simple 'Soča Snack Bar' opposite the Hotel Hvala has drinks and snacks.

Pizza Bar Pri Vitku (☎ 389 13 34; Pri Malnih ulica 41; pizza & pasta €3.35-6.20; ☉ 11am-midnight Mon-Fri, noon-midnight Sat & Sun) This upbeat little pub-restaurant is about 500m south of the town centre and serves decent pizza and pasta dishes as well as more ambitious grilled dishes.

Restavracija Kotlar (☎ 389 11 10; Trg Svobode 11; starters €5.40-10.40, mains €6.25-16.70; ☉ noon-11pm Thu-Mon) This attractively decorated place is a good choice for a fast and affordable lunch when touring the nearby Kobarid Museum.

Hiša Franko (starters €6.70-11.40, mains €11.70-16; ☉ noon-3pm & 6-10pm Tue-Sun) Kobarid's 'other' slow-food phenomenon is this gourmet restaurant in a guesthouse of the same name in

---

THE AUTHOR'S CHOICE

Topli Val (starters €7.50-10, mains €6.75-25; ☉ noon-10pm) With a name like 'Warm Wave' and owners originally from Portorož, this excellent restaurant at the Hotel Hvala is bound to specialise in seafood. It's excellent – from the mixed shellfish starter (€14.60) and carpaccio of sea bass (€7.50) to the Soča trout and signature lobster with pasta (€26.70). Expect to pay about €40 per person with a decent bottle of wine, such as Četrtič Ferdinand Belo from Brda (€17), although the house wine is a snip at €7.50 a bottle. There's a lovely front terrace and back garden open in warmer months.

Staro Selo just west of town. Tasting menus, which change according to the season, cost €37.50/46 for five/seven courses.

Mercator (Markova ulica 1; ☉ 8am-7pm Mon-Fri, 8am-noon Sat) This large branch of the popular supermarket chain is just west of Trg Svobode.

Pri Gotarju (☎ 388 57 43; Milanova ulica; ☉ 6am-11pm Sun-Thu, 6am-midnight Fri & Sat) This café-pub in a shady garden is a pleasant place for a drink – especially in the courtyard in summer. In the grassy area near the petrol station opposite is a rusting 150mm howitzer that weighs more than 5000kg and was built by Krupp in 1911.

Getting There & Around

There are three to four buses a day to the northwest and Bovec (€3, 30 minutes, 21km) and to the southeast and Tolmin (€2, 30 minutes, 16km). Other destinations include Ljubljana (€10, 2½ hours, 115km, up to four a day) via Cerkno and Idrija (€6.20, two hours, 58km) and Nova Gorica (€5.80, two hours, 55km, five a day). Daily in July and August and at the weekend in June and September, a bus crosses over the spectacular Vršič Pass to Kranjska Gora (€5.80, two hours, 52km).

NOVA GORICA

☎ 05 / pop 12,600 / elev 93m

Nova Gorica is a green university town straddling the Italian border and an easy entry and exit point from the rest of the EU to the west.

When the town of Gorica, capital of the former Slovenian province of Goriška, was awarded to the Italians under the postwar Treaty of Paris in 1947 and became Gorizia, the new socialist government in Yugoslavia set about building a model town on the eastern side of the border. They called it 'New Gorica' and erected a chain-link barrier between the two towns.

This 'mini-Berlin Wall' was finally pulled down to great fanfare on 30 April 2004 after Slovenia joined the EU, leaving Piazza Transalpina (Trg z Mozaikom) straddling the border right behind Nova Gorica train station. With no barrier remaining there's really nothing to stop you wandering across to the Italian side, where the Italian bus 1 will whisk you to Gorizia train station. However, this is still not a legal border crossing and won't become one

until Slovenia joins the Schengen Convention (October 2007).

With Italy behind them and a couple of flashy casino-hotels dominating the place, most people arrive here to try their luck or move on. But Nova Gorica is worth a pause. Its immediate surrounds – the Franciscan monastery at Kostanjevica and Gorico to the south and the ancient settlement of Solkan in the north – offer some startling contrasts.

Orientation

Nova Gorica sits on a broad plain south of the Soča River. Across the Italian region of Goriziano to the northwest are the vineyards of the Brda Hills (Goriška Brda). The Vipava Valley (Vipavska Dolina), an even more important wine-growing area, lies to the southeast. The Karst region is south and southeast of Nova Gorica.

Nova Gorica itself is an unusually long town, running about 5km from the border at Rožna Dolina (Casa Rossa) in the south to Solkan in the north. The bus station is in the centre of town at Kidričeva ulica 22, 400m southwest of the Hotel Perla. The train station is at Kolodvorska ulica 6, about 1.5km to the west.

Information

Bar Evropa (www.go.net; Delpinova ulica 20; per hr €2; 5pm-2am Sun-Thu, 5am-3am Fri & Sat Jul & Aug; 7am-1am Mon-Thu, 7am-3am Fri, noon-3am Sat, noon-1am Sun Sep-Jun) Internet access south of Bevkov trg.

Nova KBM Banka (Kidričeva ulica 11; ☉ 7.30am-6pm, 7.30am-noon Sat) Near the Hotel Perla.

Nova Ljubljanska Banka (Bekov trg 3; ☉ 9am-1pm & 3-5pm Mon-Fri) In the central square.

Post office (Kidričeva ulica 19; ☉ 7am-7pm Mon-Fri, 7am-1pm Sat) Opposite the bus station.

Tourist Information Centre Nova Gorica (☎ 333 46 00; www.novagorica-turizem.com; Bekov trg 4; ☉ 8am-8pm Mon-Fri, 9am-1pm Sat & Sun Jul & Aug; 8am-6pm Mon-Fri, 9am-1pm Sat & Sun Sep-Jun) In the lobby of the Kulturni Dom (Cultural House). Free internet access.

Sights

In the train station, the rather esoteric **Goriška Border Museum** (Muzej Državna Meja na Goriškem; ☎ 333 44 00; Kolodvorska ulica 6; admission free; ☉ 1-5pm Mon-Fri, 9am-7pm Sat, 10am-7pm Sun), which traces the story of divided Gorica/Gorizia from 1945 to that pivotal day in April 2004 when the walls came a-tumblin' down, is not going to hold

PRIMORSKA

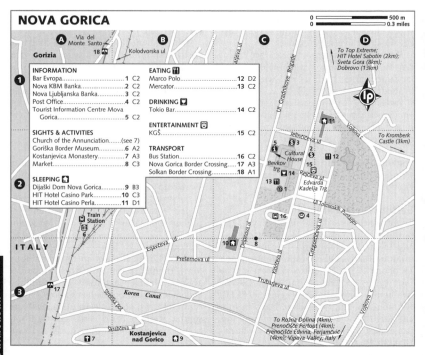

NOVA GORICA

INFORMATION	**EATING**
Bar Evropa..........................1 C2	Marco Polo.......................12 D2
Nova KBM Banka.................2 C2	Mercator..........................13 C2
Nova Ljubljanska Banka.......3 C2	
Post Office.........................4 C2	**DRINKING**
Tourist Information Centre Mova	Tokio Bar..........................14 C2
Gorica.............................5 C2	
	ENTERTAINMENT
SIGHTS & ACTIVITIES	KGŠ..................................15 C2
Church of the Annunciation......(see 7)	
Goriška Border Museum..........6 A2	**TRANSPORT**
Kostanjevica Monastery..........7 A3	Bus Station........................16 C2
Market..............................8 C3	Nova Gorica Border Crossing...17 A3
	Solkan Border Crossing.........18 A1
SLEEPING	
Dijaški Dom Nova Gorica..........9 B3	
HIT Hotel Casino Park.............10 C3	
HIT Hotel Casino Perla............11 D1	

your attention for long. And neither the neo-baroque **Basilica of Our Lady of the Assumption** (Bazilika Marije Venbovzete), built in 1927 on the site of a 16th-century apparition of Mary, nor the **Museum of the Soča Front** (Muzej Doške Fronte; ☎ 333 11 40; adult/child €1.25/0.85; ◷ 10am-6pm Sat & Sun Apr-Sep, 10am-4pm Sat & Sun Oct-Mar) at the **Franciscan monastery** (Frančiškanski Samostan; ☎ 330 40 20) compound perched atop 682m-high **Sveta Gora** (Monte Santo) 8km north of Nova Gorica is worth the trip; you can see the church from most of the town anyway.

The **Kostanjevica Monastery** (Samostan Kostanjevica; ☎ 330 77 50; Šrabčeva 1; admission €1.25; ◷ 9am-noon & 3-5pm Mon-Sat, 3-5pm Sun), on another hill 800m south of the train station, was founded by the Capuchin Franciscans in the early 17th century and has a wonderful library that can be visited. The narrow, single-nave **Church of the Annunciation** (Cerkev Marijinega Oznanenja) nearby has interesting stuccos. In the spooky crypt is the **tomb of the Bourbons** (grobnica bourbonov), which contains the mortal remains of the last members of the French house of Bourbon, including Charles X (1757–1836).

Three kilometres east of the town, 17th-century **Kromberk Castle** (Grad Kromberk; Grajska ulica 1) houses the **Goriško Museum** (Goriški Muzej; ☎ 335 98 11; www2.arnes.si/~dpogac1/muzej; adult/child €1.25/0.85; ◷ 8am-3pm Mon-Fri, 1-5pm Sun). It features important archaeological, ethnological and fine-arts collections. You'll also find the fabulous Grajska Klet restaurant located here.

Activities

Top Extreme (☎ 330 00 90, 041-620 636; www.top.si; Vojkova ulica 9) in Solkan, north of the centre, has, among other active pursuits on offer, **bungee jumping** (jump €37; ◷ 11am-2.30pm Sat & Sun May-Oct) from the 55m-high Solkan Bridge over the Soča. It's available at the weekend in season, but make sure you book ahead. They also organise rafting, kayaking and canyoning on the river (p135).

Ask the tourist office for the pamphlet *Peš Poti na Goriškem* (Footpaths in Goriška), which outlines about a dozen **hiking trails** of between 3km and 20km (1½ hours to six hours) around Nova Gorica, including Kostanjevica and Sveta Gora.

Sleeping

The tourist office has a list of **private rooms** (per person €20-25), but most are located a ways out of town.

Dijaški Dom Nova Gorica (☎ 335 48 00; www.hostel -ng.si; Streliška pot 7; dm per person €14.50, d €41; ☼ late Jun-Aug) This student dormitory at the southern end of Kidričeva ulica has 377 beds but accepts foreign guests in summer only.

Prenočišče Edvina (☎ 333 01 80, 031-885 656; prenoc isca.edvina@siol.net; Vipavska cesta 134; s/d/tr €21/33.50/46) This two room B&B is also in Rožna Dolina, a stone's throw from the more established Pertout hostelry.

Prenočišče Pertout (☎ 330 75 50, 041-624 452; www.prenociscepertout.com; Ulica 25 Maja 23; s/d/tr €22.50/32/47.50) This five-room hostelry with singles, doubles and triples in Rožna Dolina, south of the centre, is scarcely 200m from the Italian border at Cassa Rossa.

Ferjančič (☎ 333 31 36, 041-754 562; alma.ferjancic@sil .net; Vipavska cesta 144; per person €25) Still in Rožna Dolina, this small hostelry with two rooms (one double and one quad) is almost next door to Prenočišče Edvina.

HIT Hotel Sabotin (☎ 336 50 00; www.hit.si; Cesta IX Korpusa 35; s €42-59, d €64-78, tr €87-96; P X □) This 63-room hotel in an old baroque manor house in Solkan, about 2km north of the bus station, is the best-value hotel in Nova Gorica. Rates depend on the season and whether you are in an old or newly renovated room.

HIT Hotel Casino Perla (☎ 336 30 00; www.hit.si; Kidričeva ulica 7; s €78-85, d €107-116.50, tr €127.50-135.50; P X X □ X) The bigger of the two central HIT hotels, the 105-room Perla is a favourite with Italians, who can't get enough of the casino. It's in a big glass and steel modern structure that could be anywhere – Hong Kong, Las Vegas, Disneyland. For a cheesy, Austin Powers-style treat, ask for a room with a waterbed.

HIT Hotel Casino Park (☎ 336 20 00; www.hit .si; Delpinova ulica 5; s €78-102, d 108-142, tr €129-168; P X □ &) This flashy 82-room hotel, surrounded by lots of trees and lawn, is convenient to the bus station. Not to be outdone, they too have rooms with waterbeds.

Eating & Drinking

Marco Polo (☎ 302 97 29; Kidričeva ulica 13; starters €5.85-11.50, mains €7.50-12.50; ☼ 11am-11pm Sun-Thu, 11am-midnight Fri, noon-midnight Sat) This large, very popular restaurant does all manner of great Italian victuals, including pizza (€3.75 to €6.25). There's a lovely terrace overlooking a park and a pond.

Grajska Klet (☎ 302 71 60, 041-692 237; Grajska ulica 1; per person €30; ☼ noon-10pm Fri-Tue) If you've won big at the casino or just want to treat yourself, the place to go is the 'Castle Cellar' on the ground floor of Kromberk Castle, one of the best restaurants in the region. It specialises in using fresh local produce, including Adriatic seafood and Soča trout, and will happily cater for vegetarians.

Tokio Bar (Bevkov trg 1; ☼ 7am-midnight Sun-Thu, 8am-2am Fri & Sat) This über-decorated bar with a naff name is central and very popular with students.

The Sabotin and Perla hotels both have several decent restaurants. The **Sabotin** (☎ 336 52 81; meals from €20; ☼ 7am-3pm & 6-11pm Mon-Sat, 7am-11pm Sun) regularly hosts international chefs who try their hands at Slovenian, Mediterranean or Šumadijan (Serbian regional) cuisine. The Perla's **Mediterraneo** (☎ 336 31 49; meals from €25; ☼ noon-midnight Sun-Thu, noon-1am Fri & Sat) has Italian-ish cuisine.

There's a large **Mercator** (Delpinova ulica 22; ☼ 7am-7pm Mon-Sat) in the shopping centre south of Bevkov trg. The outdoor **market** (Delpinova ulica) is east of the Hotel Park.

Entertainment

KGŠ (☎ 333 38 71; Trg Edvarda Kardelja 1; ☼ 8am-midnight Mon-Thu, 8am-3am Fri, 3pm-midnight Sat & Sun) This popular student bar and club in the town hall has DJs on Friday and Saturday nights.

HIT Casino Perla (☎ 336 30 00; Kidričeva ulica 7; admission free Mon-Fri, €5 Sat & Sun; ☼ 24hr) and **HIT Casino Park** (☎ 336 26 33; Delpinova ulica 5; admission free Mon-Fri, €5 Sat & Sun; ☼ 24hr) are the company store – nothing makes more money in Nova Gorica, and it's all from the Italians from across the border. Both casinos offer all the usual games – American and French roulette, blackjack, several types of poker, baccarat – and there are almost 1500 slot machines between them.

Getting There & Away
BUS

From Nova Gorica you can expect buses every two hours or so to Ljubljana (€9.60, 2½ hours, 106km), Postojna (€6.20, 1½ hours, 58km) and Tolmin (€4.50, one hour, 39km). Other destinations include Bovec (€7, two hours, 72km, three a day), Idrija (€6.20, 1½ hours, 60km, one or two) via Tolmin or Ajdovščina, Koper (€7.60, two hours, 84km, one daily in

PRIMORSKA

July and August) and Piran (€9, 2¼ hours, 97km, one daily at 7am). Daily in July and August and at the weekend in June and September, a bus crosses over the spectacular Vršič Pass to Kranjska Gora (€10.50, three hours, 118km).

There's a use shuttle bus (€1, 25 minutes, hourly) between the train stations in Nova Gorica and Gorizia in Italy.

TRAIN
About a half-dozen trains head northeast each day for Jesenice (€5.35, 2¼ hours, 89km) via Most na Soči, Bohinjska Bistrica (€4.50, 1¼ hours, 61km) and Bled Jezero (€5, 1¾ hours, 79km) on what is arguably the country's most beautiful train trip. In the other direction, an equal number of trains go to Sežana (€2.65, one hour, 40km), where you can change for Ljubljana or Trieste in Italy.

Nova Gorica is linked to Ajdovščina (€1.85, 40 minutes, 26km) to the southeast by two trains a day (at 5.36am and 2.25pm) on weekdays only from September to late June.

Getting Around
Local buses serve Solkan, Rožna Dolina, Šempeter and Vrtojba from the main station. You can order a taxi on ☎ 303 51 11 or 041-632 428.

AROUND NOVA GORICA
If you want to have a look at **Goriška Brda** (Brda Hills), the hilly wine region that stretches from Solkan west to the Italian border, start in **Dobrovo**, 13km to the northwest of Nova Gorica. The Renaissance-style **Dobrovo Castle** (Grad Dobrovo; ☎ 333 11 40, 335 98 11; Grajska cesta 10; adult/child €1.25/0.85; ⏰ 10am-6pm Tue-Sun), dating from about 1600, is filled with elegant period furnishings and exhibits on the wine industry. In the cellar there is a **vinoteka** (☎ 395 92 11, 031-342 369; ⏰ 11.30am-9pm Tue-Sun) where you can sample the local vintages (white Rebula and Chardonnay or the Pinot and Merlot reds), which go nicely with the cheese, air-cured *pršut* and salami on offer. There's also an excellent **restaurant** (☎ 395 95 06; meals from €20; ⏰ noon-11pm Tue-Sun) in the castle. In addition to its grapes and wine, Goriška Brda is celebrated for its fabulous cherries available in early June.

Southeast from Nova Gorica is **Vipava Valley**, famous for its wines, especially red Teran. For details see p150.

CENTRAL PRIMORSKA

Central Primorska is a land of steep slopes, deep valleys and innumerable ravines with plenty of good hiking, the magical Idrijca River and a couple of interesting towns. The region is dominated by the Cerkno and Idrija Hills, foothills of the Julian Alps that eventually join the Škofja Loka Hills in Gorenjska to the east. It's an area often overlooked by travellers heading for the sexier Alps, Karst or beaches – and is all the more attractive for that reason.

Nowhere else in Slovenia are fields found on such steep slopes and houses in such remote locations as in the regions around Idrija and Cerkno. The ravines and valleys were very useful to the Partisans during WWII, and the region is dotted with monuments testifying to their presence: the Franja hospital near Cerkno, the Slovenija Partisan printing house at Vojsko, 14km northwest of Idrija, and the Pavl hospital, 20km southeast of Idrija.

IDRIJA
☎ 05 / pop 5765 / elev 340m

Idrija sits snugly in a deep basin surrounded by hills at the confluence of the Idrijca and Nikova Rivers. When most Slovenes think of Idrija, three things come to mind: *žlikrofi*, lace and mercury. The women of Idrija have been taking care of the first two for centuries, stuffing the crescent-shaped 'Slovenian ravioli' with a savoury mixture of bacon, potatoes and chives as fast as they spin their web-like lace (*čipka*). The men, on the other hand, went underground to extract the 'quicksilver' (*živo srebro*) that made this town one of the richest in medieval Europe.

The first mine opened at Idrija in 1500, making it the second oldest mercury mine in the world after the one in Almadén in central Spain. By the 18th century, Idrija was producing 13% of the world's mercury, thought to be the purest. All that meant money – for both Idrija and the imperial court in Vienna. And because of the toxic effects of mercury, doctors and lawyers flocked here to work. The Idrija miners faced many health hazards, but the relatively high wages attracted workers from all over the Habsburg Empire. In the 18th century, Idrija was second in size only to Ljubljana among the towns of Carniola.

The mercury market bottomed out in the 1970s, and the production of this once precious element has ceased altogether in Idrija. But the mine has left the town a difficult and expensive legacy. Idrija sits on something like 700km of shafts that go down 15 levels to 32m below sea level. The first four have now been filled with water and more have to be loaded with hard core and concrete to stabilise the place. Otherwise, they say, the town will sink.

Orientation

The centre of Idrija is Mestni trg, but everything of a practical nature is to the southeast over the Nikova River on or just off Lapajnetova ulica, where you'll find the bus station wedged between Vodnikova ulica and Prešernova ulica.

Information

Abanka (Lapajnetova ulica 47; ⏰ 8.30am-noon & 2-5pm Mon-Fri)
Nova KBM Banka (Lapajnetova ulica 43; ⏰ 7.30am-6pm Mon-Fri, 7.30am-noon Sat)
Post office (Vodnikova ulica 1)
Tourist Information Centre Idrija (☎ 374 39 16; www.idrija-turizem.si; Vodnikova ulica 3; ⏰ 9am-6pm Mon-Fri, 10am-6pm Sat & Sun Apr-Oct, 9am-4pm Mon-Fri, 10am-4pm Sat Nov-Mar) On the 1st floor behind the new purpose-built post office.

Sights

MUNICIPAL MUSEUM

This excellent **museum** (Mestni Muzej; ☎ 372 66 00; www.muzej-idrija-cerkno.si; Prelovčeva ulica 9; adult/student & child €3/2.50; ⏰ 9am-6pm) is housed in the enormous Gewerkenegg Castle on top of the hill to the west of Mestni trg. The collections, which deal with mercury, lace and local history, are exhibited in three wings centred on a courtyard. The **rococo frescoes** of plants, scrolls and columns framing the windows and arcades date from the 18th century.

Mercury (Hg) is the only metal that exists in a liquid state at room temperature. The silvery metal is extracted from the mercury ore – a bright-red mineral called cinnabar – by smelting at a high temperature. Mercury is a very heavy metal, much denser than iron, and in the castle's north wing, amid a jungle of minerals and fossils, is a large cauldron of mercury with an iron ball floating on the top.

Part of the **ethnographical collection** in this wing shows rooms in a typical miner's house at various times in history. A miner's job carried status, and they earned more than double the average wage in this part of Slovenia. The miners were well organised, and socialism was popular in the late 19th and early 20th centuries.

In the Rondel Tower of the east wing there's a mock-up of the 'call man', the unspeakable so-and-so who summoned miners to work every day at 3.30am by hitting a hollow log with a mallet in the town centre. At the bottom of the **Mercury Tower** at the start of the south wing is a Plexiglas cube filled with drops of mercury and 15 halogen lights on tracks, representing the number of levels in the mercury mine here.

One large room in the south wing is given over entirely to the **bobbin lace** (*klekljana čipka*)

PRIMORSKA

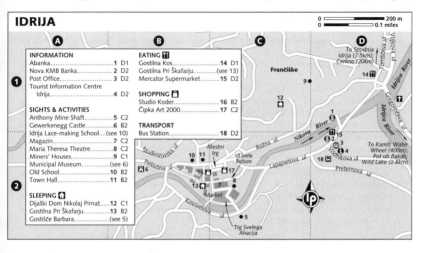

woven here in broad rings with distinctive patterns. Some 40 different motifs run the gamut from the usual hearts and flowers to horseshoes, crescents and lizards. Check out the tablecloth that measures 3m by 1.80m. It was designed for Madame Tito and took 5000 hours to make.

An exhibition on the 2nd floor of the south wing traces Idrija history in the 20th century – from WWI and the Italian occupation to WWII and the birth of socialist Yugoslavia. Take a look at the enormous, bright-red hammer and sickle in the last room; it once adorned the entrance to the mercury mine.

ANTHONY MINE SHAFT

The **mine** (Antonijev Rov; ☎ 377 11 42, 031-810 194; www.rzs.idrija.si; Kosovelova ulica 3; adult/child €4.60/3.35; ☽ tour 10am & 3pm Mon-Fri, 10am, 3pm & 4pm Sat & Sun), a 'living museum' in the Šelštev building south of Trg Svetega Ahacija, allows you to get a feeling for the working conditions of mercury miners in Idrija.

The tour, lasting about 1¼ hours, begins in the 'call room' of an 18th-century building where miners were selected each morning and assigned their duties by the *obergutman* (supervisor). There's an excellent 20-minute video in several languages (including English) describing the history of Idrija and the mine.

Before entering the shaft, which was sunk in 1500 and led to the first mine measur-

ing 1.5km long, 600m wide and 400m deep, you must don green overcoats and helmets with the miners' insignia and wish each other 'Srečno!' (Good luck!), the traditional miners' farewell.

As you follow the circular tour, you'll see samples of live mercury on the walls that the miners painstakingly scraped to a depth of about 5cm, as well as some cinnabar ore. The 18th-century **Chapel of the Holy Trinity** (Cerkev Sv Trojice) in the shaft contains statues of St Barbara, the patroness of miners, and St Ahacius, on whose feast day (22 June) rich deposits of cinnabar were discovered.

OTHER SIGHTS

There are several fine neoclassical buildings on Mestni trg, including the **town hall** (mestna hiša; Mestni trg 1), built in 1898. To the west of the square is the **Idrija Lace-Making School** (Čipkarska Šola Idrija; ☎ 373 45 72; Prelovčeva ulica 2; adult/child €2.50/2.10; ☽ by appointment) in the Stara Šola (Old School), built in 1876. Lace-making is still a popular elective course of study in elementary schools in Idrija.

In Trg Svetega Ahacija – the centre of town in the Middle Ages – the large 18th-century building on the north side is the **Magazin** (Trg Svetega Ahacija 4), a granary and warehouse where the miners, who were paid in food as well as in cash, kept their stores. To the east is the **Maria Theresa Theatre** (Gledališče Marije Terezije; Trg Svetega Ahacija 5), built in 1770 and the oldest in the country.

ON THE WINGS OF MERCURY

Alchemists in the Middle Ages were convinced that all metals originated from mercury and tried to use the metal, named after the fleet-footed messenger of the Roman gods, to obtain gold from other metals. The biggest boon came in the 16th century, when it was discovered that mercury, which bonds as an alloy to many metals, could separate gold or silver from rock or ore.

Mercury was used as an early antidote to syphilis. The Venetians needed it to make their famous mirrors, and later milliners used it to lay felt for making hats. Mercury is a highly toxic substance and can affect behaviour; occupational mercurialism from vapours and absorption by the skin is a serious disorder. As a result, many milliners went crazy, and this was the inspiration for the Mad Hatter in *Alice's Adventures in Wonderland* by Lewis Carroll (1865). In modern times, mercury has been used in the drug, paper and electrical industries, in dentistry and in some detonators and bombs.

Mercury mining in Idrija came to an end both because the use of heavy metals had been largely abandoned by many industries in favour of more environmentally friendly substances and for economic reasons. A 2.5L flask (about 34kg) of mercury that went for US$800 in the 1970s was worth only $100 a decade later. A European Union resolution approved in 2006 calls for a ban on EU mercury exports by 2008.

Laid out across the slopes encircling the valley are Idrija's distinctive **miners' houses**. Large wooden A-frames with cladding and dozens of windows, they usually had four storeys with living quarters for three or four families.

One of the most interesting examples of mining technology that still exists is the **Kamšt** (☎ 372 66 00; Vodnikova ulica; adult/child €1.70/1.25; ⏰ 9am-4pm by appointment), a 13.6m water wheel made of wood that was used to pump the water out of flooded mines from 1790 until 1948. It is about 1.5km southeast of Mestni trg.

Activities

An excellent 3km trail called **Pot ob Rakah** follows the Idrijca River Canal from the Kamšt to **Wild Lake** (Divje Jezero), a tiny, impossibly green lake fed by a karst spring more than 80m under the surface. After a heavy rainfall, water gushes up from the tunnel like a geyser and the lake appears to be boiling (although the surface temperature never exceeds 10°C).

The lake was declared a natural monument in 1967, and little signboards around the shore identify the plants and trees and point out the lake's unique features. The body of water flowing from Wild Lake into the Idrijca just happens to be the shortest river in Slovenia. The **Jezernica River** is a mere 55m long.

If you were to follow the canal for 15km to the southwest, you'd come to the first of the **barriers** (*klauže*) of stacked wood and stones that dammed the Idrijca and Belca Rivers to float timber in the 18th century. They were once called 'Slovenian pyramids' because of their appearance. Wood was an important resource here, both to support the 700km of mine shafts and because the heat needed to extract mercury from cinnabar required a lot of fuel. The dams continue for 12km down the Belca River.

Festivals & Events

The big event in Idrija is the annual **Lace-making Festival** (Festival Idrijske Čipke; www.idrija-turizem.si) in late June, which includes a contest with up to a hundred competitors.

Sleeping

The tourist office has a list of **private rooms** (per person €20-25) available.

Dijaški Dom Nikolaj Pirnat (☎ 373 40 70; info@ciu-np.si; Ulica IX Korpusa 6; per person €13; ⏰ Jul & Aug;

(P ⊡) This student dormitory 300m northeast of Mestni trg has 56 beds available in multibed rooms in summer only.

Gostilna Pri Škafarju (☎ 377 32 40; gostilnaskafar@s5.net; Ulica Svete Barbare 9; s/d €35/50; (P) In addition to food, this popular gostilna also offers accommodation in three smallish mansard rooms for between one and three people. You can't beat the location.

Gostišče Barbara (☎ 377 11 62, 041-716 701; joze.medle@siol.net; Kosovelova ulica 3; s/d/tr €45/54.50/71; (P ⊠ ⊠ ⊡) A seven-room inn above the Anthony Mine Shaft, Barbara also boasts an excellent restaurant with rather limited opening hours.

Hotel Kendov Dvorec (☎ 372 51 00; www.kendov-dvorec.com; s €75-135, d €95-155, tr €177; (P ⊠ ⊡) If you're looking for somewhere romantic in the area, this 'castle hotel' in Spodnja Idrija, 4km north of Idrija, has 11 rooms in a converted mansion, the oldest part of which dates from the 14th century. It's fitted with 19th-century antique furniture and enjoys stunning views along the Idrijca Valley. Its restaurant is worth the journey in itself.

Eating

Gostilna Pri Škafarju (☎ 377 32 40; gostilnaskafar@s5.net; Ulica Svete Barbare 9; starters €3.35-5.50, mains €5.65-12; ⏰ 10am-10pm Mon, Wed & Thu, 10am-11pm Fri & Sat, noon-8pm Sun) Pizza (€3.80 to €5.50) baked in a beautiful wood-burning tile stove is why most people come to this friendly gostilna, but there are plenty of other things on the menu such as *žlikrofi* (€5 to €8).

Gostilna Kos (☎ 372 20 30; Tomšičeva ulica 4; starters €2.50-5.80, mains €5.50-12.50; ⏰ 7am-3pm Mon, 7am-10pm Tue-Sat) Pri Škafarju does acceptable *žlikrofi*, but the best place to have this most Idrijan of specialities (€4.20 to €7.50), especially the mushroom ones, is at the 'Blackbird'.

Gostišče Barbara (☎ 377 11 62, 041-716 701; joze.medle@siol.net; Kosovelova ulica 3; meals from €15; ⏰ 4-9pm Mon-Fri) This restaurant in the inn of that name serves 'slow food' and many consider it to be the best restaurant in town.

Hotel Kendov Dvorec (☎ 372 51 00; www.kendov-dvorec.com; 4-7 course menus €30-42; ⏰ noon-midnight) This excellent restaurant in the very stylish Hotel Kendov Dvorec in Spodnja Idrija has an excellent list of Slovenian wines and a lovely garden.

There's a large **Mercator** (Lapajnetova ulica 45; ⏰ 7am-7pm Mon-Fri, 7am-1pm Sat) supermarket opposite the bus station.

Shopping

Idrija lace is among the finest in the world, and a small piece makes a great gift or souvenir. There are two places almost side by side in the main square worth a look, including **Studio Koder** (☎ 377 13 59; Mestni trg 16; ☯ 10am-noon & 4-7pm Mon-Fri, 10am-noon Sat), a very stylish shop diagonally across the lace-making school, and **Čipka Art 2000** (☎ 372 25 73; Mestni trg 14; ☯ 7am-4pm Mon, Tue, Thu & Fri, 7am-6pm Wed, 9am-noon Sat), a larger place but with a smaller selection of lace.

Getting There & Away

There are hourly buses to Cerkno (€2.60, 30 minutes, 20km) and Ljubljana (€6.20, 1½ hours, 58km), between one and three to Tolmin (€5, one hour, 44km), one or two to Bovec (€7.30, two hours, 77km) and one at 5.45am to Nova Gorica Idrija (€6.20, 1½ hours, 60km) via Ajdovščina.

CERKNO

☎ 05 / pop 1670 / elev 355m

Cerkno is a quiet town in the Cerknica River Valley with only a third as many people as its neighbour 20km to the south, Idrija. Still, it has an important museum as well as the remains of a secret Partisan hospital from WWII. Just before Lent Cerkno becomes an important destinations for ethnologists and party-goers alike when the Laufarija, the ancient Shrovetide celebration (opposite), takes place.

Orientation & Information

Glavni trg, where the buses stop, is the main square. There is no tourist office in Cerkno, but the helpful and knowledgeable staff at the Hotel Cerkno will provide information.

Nova KMB Banka (Glavni trg 5; ☯ 8am-6pm Mon-Fri, 8am-noon Sat)

Post office (Bevkova ulica 9) In the *občina hiša* (council house) diagonally opposite Cerkno Museum.

Sights

CERKNO MUSEUM

The **museum** (Cerkljanski Muzej; ☎ 372 31 80; www.muzej-idrija-cerkno.si; Bevkova ulica 12; adult/child €1.70/1.25; ☯ 10am-1pm & 2-6pm Tue-Sun) is about 150m southwest of Glavni trg. The permanent exhibit called 'Cerkljanska through the Centuries' traces the development of the region from earliest times up to the end of the 20th century. Most people, however, come to see the museum's collection of **Laufarija masks**.

FRANJA PARTISAN HOSPITAL

The **hospital** (Partizanska Bolnišnica Franja; ☎ 372 31 80; www.muzej-idrija-cerkno.si; adult/child €3/2.50; ☯ 9am-6pm Apr-Sep; 9am-4pm Mar, Oct & Nov; 9am-4pm Sat & Sun Dec-Feb), hidden in a canyon near Dolenji Novaki about 5km northeast of Cerkno, treated

---

THE LAUFARIJA TRADITION

Ethnologists believe that the Laufarija tradition and the masks came from Austria's South Tyrol hundreds of years ago. *Lauferei* means 'running about' in German, and that's just what participants do as they nab their victim. The masks with the crazy, distorted faces on display here are originals bought from one of the Laufarji clubs.

Groups of boys and young men (and now a few girls and women) belonging to Laufarji societies (not unlike the Mardi Gras krewes in New Orleans) organise the event every year and about two dozen perform. Those aged 15 and over are allowed to enter, but they must prove themselves as worthy apprentices by sewing costumes. These outfits – though not ornate – must be made fresh every year because many of them are made out of leaves, pine branches, straw or moss stitched onto a burlap (hessian) backing and take quite a beating during the festivities.

The action takes place on the Sunday before Ash Wednesday and again on Shrove Tuesday (Pustni Torek). The main character is the Pust, whose mask is horned and who wears a moss costume weighing up to 100kg. He's the symbol of winter and the old year – he must die.

The Pust is charged by people with a long list of grievances – a bad harvest, inclement weather, lousy roads – and, of course, is found guilty. Some of the other two dozen Laufarji characters represent crafts and trades – the Baker, the Thatcher, the Woodsman – while the rest have certain character traits or afflictions such as the Drunk and his Wife, the Bad Boy, Sneezy and the Sick Man, who always plays the accordion. The Old Man wearing Slovenian-style lederhosen and a wide-brimmed hat executes the Pust with a wooden mallet, and the body is rolled away on a caisson.

STONE AGE MUSIC

The image of our Neanderthal ancestors sitting around a campfire making beautiful music together is not an easy one to conjure up. But it's whole lot easier now following a major discovery made in a mountain cave near Cerkno.

Palaeontologists were messing around in the area in 1995 collecting Stone Age tools when a local pundit who happened to pass by told them he knew where they'd find lots more like that. He led them to Divje Babe, a cave some 200m above the main road linking Cerkno with the Tolmin–Idrija highway, and they began digging. Among the buried tools was a piece of cave bear femur measuring 10cm long and perforated with four aligned holes – two intact and two incomplete at either end. It looked exactly like a, well, flute.

Because objects of such antiquity cannot be dated by the usual radiocarbon techniques, the flute was sent to the City University of New York to undergo electron spin resonance, which measures the small amounts of radiation absorbed by objects from the time of their burial. And the verdict? According to researchers, the flute is anywhere between 45,000 and 82,000 years old, depending on how much moisture – which inhibits the absorption of radiation – the cave floor has been exposed to. One thing is certain, however: Slovenia can now claim the oldest known musical instrument on earth. And – just in case you were wondering – it still works.

---

wounded Partisan soldiers from Yugoslavia and other countries from late 1943 until the end of WWII. Franja Hospital has nothing to do with political or economic systems; it is a memorial to humanity, courage and self-sacrifice. It is a moving and very worthwhile place to visit.

The complex, named after its chief physician, Dr Franja Bojc-Bidovec, was built in December 1943 for the needs of IX Corps, which accounted for 10,000 soldiers. By May 1945 it had more than a dozen buildings, including treatment sheds, operating theatres, X-ray rooms and bunkers for convalescence. More than 500 wounded were treated here, and the mortality rate was only about 10%.

The complex, hidden in a ravine by the Pasica Stream with steep walls riddled with caves and recently shored up, had an abundance of fresh water, which was also used to power a hydroelectric generator. Local farmers and Partisan groups provided food, which was lowered down the steep cliffs by rope; medical supplies were diverted from hospitals in occupied areas or later air-dropped by the Allies. The hospital came under attack by the Germans twice – once in April 1944 and again in March 1945 – but it was never taken.

Activities

The English-language *Cerkno Map of Local Walks*, available from the Hotel Cerkno, lists eight walks in the Cerkno Hills (Cerkljansko Hribovje), most of them pretty easy and lasting between 1½ and five hours return. Walk

No 7 goes to the **Franja Partisan Hospital** (3½ hours) and back. The highest peak in the area is **Porezen** (1632m) to the northeast, which has a mountain hut called **Dom Andreja Žvana-Borisa na Poreznu** (☎ 377 51 35, 051-615 245; daily Jul & Aug; Sat & Sun May, Jun, Sep & Oct) at 1590m with 44 beds and berths.

The **Cerkno Ski Centre** (☎ 374 34 00; www.hotel-cerkno.si; half-day pass adult/child/senior & student €19.70/13/17.60, day pass €22.50/15/18.80), 10km northeast of Cerkno, is atop Črni Vrh (1291m) and covers 18km of ski slopes and 5km of trails. There are six chairlifts and two tows and cannons for making artificial snow.

Festivals & Events

The **Laufarija festival** (http://laufarija.cerkno.net in Slovene) in late February/early March takes place in Glavni trg and in Sedejev trg near the Hotel Cerkno. See opposite.

Sleeping & Eating

Gačnk v Logu (☎ 372 40 05, 041-753 524; gacnk@cerkno.com; per person €21) This B&B and restaurant in Dolenji Novaki (house No 1), not far from the Franja Partisan Hospital, has nine rooms with between two and four beds. The renovated restaurant (meals from €12, open 9am to 11pm) is very popular with local people, particularly for lunch at the weekend.

Želinc farmhouse (☎ 372 40 20; www.zelinc.com; Želin 8; per person €22; P) This very green farmhouse with 13 singles and doubles and two apartments for three is near Straža, 5km southwest of Cerkno on route No 102 to Idrija.

Hotel Cerkno (☎ 374 34 00; www.hotel-cerkno.si; Sedejev trg 8; s/d €51/76; P ⏸ ☎) This 75-room partially renovated hotel is in a modern building just south of Glavni trg. It's a comfortable enough place with a large indoor pool (nonresident adult/child €5.60/4.60), sauna, gym and three clay tennis courts (per hour €4.20).

There's a **Mercator** (Sedejev trg 8; ⏰ 8am-7pm Mon-Fri, 7am-noon Sat, 8-11am Sun) supermarket next to the Hotel Cerkno.

Getting There & Away

There are hourly bus departures to Idrija (€2.60, 30 minutes, 20km) on weekdays, with between four and six at the weekend, up to four a day to Ljubljana (€7.30, two hours, 77km) and one to Bovec (€6.50, 1¾ hours, 66km) via Most na Soči, Tolmin and Kobarid. Another four (two on Saturday, one on Sunday) go just to Tolmin (€4, one hour, 33km), where you can change for Nova Gorica and the coast.

KARST REGION

The Karst region (www.kras-carso.com) is a limestone plateau stretching from Nova Gorica southeast to the Croatian border, west to the Gulf of Trieste and east to the Vipava Valley. Because it was the first such area to be researched and described in the 19th century, it is called the Classic, Real, True or Original Karst and always spelled with an upper-case 'K'. Other karst areas (from the Slovene word *kras*) around the world only get a lower-case 'k'.

The thick layers of limestone deposits were laid down millions of years ago. Earth movements then raised the limestone above sea level, where it could be attacked by mildly acidic rainwater. Over hundreds of thousands of years, this slow, chemical erosion has produced limestone pavements, dry valleys, sinkholes, springs and, of course, vast subterranean networks of caves and tunnels.

Rivers, ponds and lakes can disappear and then resurface in the porous limestone through sinkholes and funnels. Some rivers have created large underground caverns like the caves at Škocjan. Calcium carbonate dissolved in the water dripping from the roofs of caves creates stalactites and stalagmites. When these underground caverns collapse – and

they do periodically – they form a depression (*polje*) that collects soil (mostly red clay, the *terra rossa* of the Karst) and then vegetation. These fertile hollows are cultivated by local farmers, but because of the proximity of underground rivers, they tend to flood quickly after heavy rain.

The Karst, with its olives, ruby-red Teran wine, *pršut* (air-dried ham), old stone churches and red-tiled roofs, is some people's favourite region of Slovenia. But although the weather is very pleasant for most of the year, with lots of sun and low humidity, don't be fooled. The *burja*, a fiercely cold northeast wind, can do a lot of damage in winter, although it is said to give the *pršut* its distinctive taste.

VIPAVA VALLEY

05 / elev up to 100m

This wide and fertile valley stretches southeast from Nova Gorica into the Karst. Some of the red wines produced here are world class, and Vipava Merlot is among the best wines of Central Europe. It's an excellent place to tour by car or bike; ask the tourist office in Nova Gorica for the brochure *Wine Road of the Lower Vipava Valley*.

The Vipava Valley is where the Romans first launched their drive into the Danube region, and it was overrun by the Goths, Huns and Langobards from the 4th to 6th centuries before the arrival of the early Slavs. Along the way though the valley, about 22km southeast of Nova Gorica, is **Vipavski Križ** (Santa Croce), a walled medieval village with a ruined castle, a Gothic church and a 17th-century monastery with some wonderful illuminated medieval manuscripts.

Another 4km to the west is **Ajdovščina** (Aidussina). This was the site of Castra ad Fluvium Frigidum, a Roman fort on the River Frigidus (Vipava) and the first important station on the road from Aquileia to Emona (Ljubljana).

The town of **Vipava**, in the centre of the valley some 33km southeast of Nova Gorica, is full of stone churches below **Mt Nanos**, a karst plateau from which the Vipava River springs. Be sure to make a side trip 2km north to Dornbeck and **Zemono Manor** (Dvorec Zemono; ☎ 366 51 29; Prešernova ulica 6), a summer mansion built in 1680 by one of the Counts of Gorica as a hunting lodge. Today the mansion, built in the shape of a cross inside a square with arcaded hallways and a raised central area, houses the **Gostilna Pri Lojzetu** (☎ 368 70 07; meals from €20; noon-10pm Wed-Sun), a luxurious restaurant in the manor's wine cellar. Have a peek at the baroque murals near the entrance. They portray a phoenix and a subterranean cave, symbols of fire and water.

Further afield, you can explore **Rihemberk Castle** (☎ 333 43 10, rihemberk@siol.com; Cesta IX Korpusa 46; 2.30-7pm Sat & Sun May-Sep), which dates back to the 13th century and has a dominant cylindrical tower in the centre at Branik. Alternatively, visit the walled village of Štanjel with its own castle and magnificent Ferrari Gardens to the north, but the areas with the most to see and do are to the south. About 10km southwest of Štanjel and 12.5km northwest of Sežana is the fabulous **Mladinski Hotel Pliskovica** (☎ 764 02 50; 041-947 327; www.hostelkras .com in Slovene; Pliskovica 11; per person from €18), a hostel with six rooms and 45 beds purpose-built into a 400-year-old Karst house. It has a kitchen and laundry room and is open year-round.

Getting There & away
Buses departing from Nova Gorica for Postojna every two hours or so pass through Ajdovščina (€3, 45 minutes, 24km) and Vipava (€4, one hour, 31km). Trains between Nova Gorica and Sežana serve Štanjel (€2, 40 minutes, 24km) and Dutovlje (€2.65, 50 minutes, 31km), 4.5km east of Pliskovica, seven times a day on weekdays and twice at the weekend.

ŠKOCJAN CAVES
☎ 05 / elev 425m

The immense karst caves at Škocjan, a Unesco World Heritage site since 1986, are far more captivating than the larger one at Postojna, 33km to the northeast in Notranjska, and for many travellers, a visit here will be one of the highlights of their trip to Slovenia.

The Škocjan Caves (Škocjanske Jame), 5.8km long and 250m deep, were carved out by the Reka River, which originates in the foothills of Snežnik, a 1796m mountain to the southeast. The Reka enters the caves in a gorge below the village of Škocjan and eventually flows into the Dead Lake, a sump at the end of the cave where it disappears. It surfaces again – this time as the Timavo River – at Duino in Italy, 40km to the northwest, before emptying into the Gulf of Trieste.

Unesco included the surrounding 413-hectare **Škocjan Caves Regional Park** (Regijski Park Škocjanske Jame; ☎ 763 28 40; www.park-skocjanske-jame

.si) in its World Heritage Sites list in 1996. Today, visitors can explore about 2km of these spectacular caves.

Orientation
The caves lie about 1.5km east of the main Ljubljana–Koper highway. The closest town of any size is Divača (population 1300), about 5km to the northwest. Divača's train station, where buses stop as well, is at Trg 15 Aprila 7, about 500m west of this highway.

Information
Banka Koper (Kolodvorska ulica 2; 8.30am-noon, 3-5pm Mon-Fri, 8.30am-noon Sat) In Divača west of the Penzion Risnik.

Kraški Turist (☎ 041-573 768; kraskiturist@gmail.com; 8am-5pm Apr-Oct) Next to the small café at the train station.

Post office (Kraška cesta 77; 8-9.30am, 10am-3.30pm, 4-6pm Mon-Fri, 8am-noon Sat) In Divača opposite the Penzion Risnik.

Sights
ŠKOCJAN CAVES
Visiting the **caves** (☎ 763 28 40, 708 21 10; www.park -skocjanske-jame.si; Škocjan 2; adult/child/senior & student €10.85/4.20/7.50; 1½-hr tours hourly 10am-5pm Jun-Sep; 10am, 1pm & 3.30pm Apr, May & Oct; 10am & 1pm Mon-Sat, 10am, 1pm & 3pm Sun Nov-Mar) involves a shepherded two-hour walking tour that includes hundreds of steps and ends with a rickety funicular ride.

The **ticket office** (9am-last tour) sells all kinds of literature, including the 1:6000 *Regijski Park Škocjanske Jame* (Škocjan Caves Regional Park; €3) map and *The Škocjan Caves* (€4.30) guide. If you have time before your tour, follow the path leading north and down some steps from the reception area for 200m to the lookout (signposted 'Razgledišče/Belvedere'). Extending before you is a superb vista of the Velika Dolina (Big Valley) and the gorge where the Reka starts its subterranean journey.

Visitors to the caves assemble around the picnic tables in front of the souvenir shop or restaurant, and the guides will separate you into five groups according to language spoken. You then walk with your him or her for about 500m down a gravel path to the main entrance in the Gločak Valley. Through a tunnel built in 1933, you soon reach the head of **Silent Cave** (Tiha Jama), a dry branch of the underground canyon that stretches for

500m. The first section, called **Paradise**, is filled with beautiful stalactites, stalagmites and flow stones; the second part (called **Calvary**) was once the river bed. The Silent Cave ends at the **Great Hall** (Velika Dvorana), 120m wide and 30m high. It is a jungle of exotic dripstones and deposits; keep an eye out for the mighty stalagmites called the Giant and the Organ.

The sound of the Reka River, as it rushs through cascades and whirlpools below, heralds your entry into the astonishing **Müller Hall**, with walls 100m high. To get over the Reka and into long, narrow **Svetina Hall** you must cross **Hanke Canal Bridge**, 45m high, narrow and surely the highlight of the trip. Only experienced speleologists are allowed to explore the 5km of caves and halls that extend to the northwest of the bridge ending at Dead Lake (Mrtvo Jezero).

From Svetina Hall you climb up a path hewn into the stone to **Bowls Hall**, remarkable for its rare bowl-like potholes that were formed when water flooding the cave churned and swirled up to the ceiling. They look like troughs or even rice terraces.

Schmidl Hall, the final section, emerges into the Velika Dolina. From here you walk past **Tominč Cave**, where finds from a prehistoric settlement have been unearthed, and over a walkway near the **Natural Bridge** to the funicular, which carries you 90m up the rock face to near the reception area.

You might be surprised to learn that the Škocjan Caves are home to an incredible amount of flora and fauna: 250 varieties of plants and five different types of bats. The temperature in the caves is constant at 12°C so you should bring along a light jacket or sweater. Good walking shoes (the path can get pretty wet and slippery in the high humidity) and a torch (flashlight) are also recommended.

VILENICA & DIVAČA CAVES

The 803m-long **Vilenica Cave** (Jama Vilenica; ☎ 734 42 59, 051-648 711; www.vilenica.com; adult/child €5/3.35; ☼ 10am, 3pm & 5pm Sun May-Sep; 3pm Sun Oct-Apr) is 2km northwest of Lokev, halfway between Divača and Lipica. It was the first karst cave to open to the public in the early 19th century and still welcomes guests every Sunday year-round.

Divača Cave (Divaška Jama; ☎ 031-522 785, 041-671 183; divaška.jama@divaca.net; adult/child €5/3.35; ☼ 3pm Sun May-Oct), about 3km northeast on the road to Divača, is only 672m long but has excellent dripstones and rock formations.

Sleeping & Eating

Avtokamp Kozina (☎ 680 26 11; www.hotelitabor-kozina .com; Bazoviška cesta 23; per person €6.70; ☼ May-Sep) This camping ground, 7km south of Divača, is the closest there is to the caves. It has 25 sites for trailers and caravans and 60 for tents.

Gostilna Malovec (☎ 763 02 00; Kraška cesta 30a; s/d/tr €20/40/60) The Malovec, in Divača, has a half-dozen basic but comfortable renovated rooms in a building beside its popular restaurant (starters €3.35 to €5.85, mains €5 to €9.10, open 8am to 10pm), which serves Slovenian favourites (including first-rate *gibanica*) to an appreciative crowd.

Pr' Vncki (☎ 763 30 73; pr.vncki@gmail.com; Matavun 10; per person €20-22) This place in Matavun is just steps south of the caves and as close as you are going to get. It has four traditionally styled rooms with a total of 10 beds in a charming old farmhouse.

Gostilna Pri Jami (☎ 763 29 61, 051-360 604; starters €3.35-4.60, mains €5-9.20; ☼ 9am-10pm Apr-Sep, 9am-8pm Oct-Mar) 'By the Caves' is just that – a restaurant next to the ticket office to the caves.

Gostilna Malovec Orient Express (☎ 763 30 10; Kraška cesta 67; pizza €5-10.85; ☼ 11am-11pm Sun-Fri, 11am-2am Sat) For something a bit more, well, 21st century, cross the road from the Malovec for this lively pizzeria and pub with great salads (€1.70 to €3.35) and a large back terrace.

There's a **Mercator** (Kraška cesta 32; ☼ 7am-7pm Mon-Sat, 8-11am Sun) supermarket near Gostilna Malovec in Divača.

Getting There & Away

The Škocjan Caves are about 5km by road southeast of the Divača train station. Staff at both the train station and at helpful Kraški Turist (p151) at the station can provide you with a photocopied route map for walking to the caves. In any case the way is clearly signposted from the station through the village of Dolnje Ležeče to Matavun. Alternatively, the Kraški Turist in Divača rents bicycles (per hour/day/weekend €1.25/8.35/12.50) and can arrange transport for around €5 per person. Ask them for the pamphlet *Discover the Treasures of the Karst and Brkini*, which includes a map with cycling and hiking routes in the area.

Buses from Ljubljana to Koper and the coast stop at Divača (€7.60, 1½ hours, 82km, half-hourly). For Croatia, there are also daily

(Continued on page 161)

RICHARD I'ANSON

Ljubljana Castle and the Old Town (p69)

Triple Bridge and the Franciscan Church of the Annunciation (p68), Ljubljana

RICHARD I'ANSON

JONATHAN SMITH

Cafe-culture (p84), Ljubljana

RICHARD I'

Bronze door at the
Cathedral of St Nicholas
(p69), Ljubljana

RICHARD I'ANSON

Nightlife (p86), Ljubljana

Stalls at Central Market (p69), Ljubljana

RICHARD I'ANSON

NEIL WILSON

Mt Triglav (p128), Gorenjska

Lake Bled and Bled Island (p113)

GRANT DIXON

Local dwelling on the shores of Lake Bled (p113)

JON DAVISON

MARTIN MOOS

Lake Bohinj with the Church of St John the Baptist (p119) in the background, Gorenjska

Triglav Lakes Valley, Triglav National Park (p128), Gorenjska

GRANT DIXON

Titov trg in Koper (p166), Primorska

CRAIG PERS

CRAIG PERSHOUSE

Tartinijev trg (p173) and surrounding rooftops in Piran, Primorska

The basin at Bovec (p134), Primorska

A. FEVŽER / WWW.SLOVENIJA-TOURISM.SI

The Cows' Ball (p122) in Bohinj, Gorenjska

MARTIN MOOS

JON DAVISON

Stalactites inside the Postojna Caves (p184), Notranjska

Pivka River (p183), Notranjska

NEIL WILSON

Veliki Naravni Most (natural bridge) at Rakov Škocjan (p189) in Cerknica, Notranjska

NEIL WILSON

Krka River (p198), Dolenjska

B. KLADNIK / WWW.SLOVENIJA-TOURISM.SI

ARHIV KRKA ZDRAVILIŠČA / WWW.SLOVENIJA-TOURISM.SI

Thermal spa (p201) at Dolenjske
Toplice, Dolenjska

The murals and frescoes of Posavje Castle (p212) in Brezice, Dolenjska

NEIL WILSON

Podsreda Castle (p228), Štajerska

NEIL WILSON

MARTIN

MARTIN MOOS

View from Ptuj Castle (p234), Štajerska

Town house on Glavni trg (p242) in Maribor, Štajerska

Logarska Valley (p256), Štajerska

B. BAJŽELJ / WWW.SLOVENIJA-TOUR

(Continued from page 152)

buses to Zagreb (€19.20, 4½ hours, 213km) at 5.40am and 7.06am and to Poreč and Rovinj (€9.30, three hours, 103km) at 3.07pm from June to September in Croatia.

Divača is on the rail line linking Ljubljana (€5.90, 1½ hours, 104km, hourly) with Sežana (€1, 10 minutes, 9km). Around 20 trains a day run in each direction. Divača is also the railhead for up to five trains a day to Koper (€3.30, 50 minutes, 49km) via Hrpelje-Kozina, and there are two or three daily connections to Buzet and Pula, 122km to the south in Croatia.

LIPICA

☎ 05 / pop 95 / elev 403m

Lipica, a tiny village 9km southwest of Divača and just 2km northeast of the Italian border, lives for and on and through one commodity only: horseflesh. In this case, it's the snow-white beauties called Lipizzaners, which were first bred here for the Spanish Riding School in Vienna in the late 16th century.

Although very much part of the region, Lipica feels like Eden after all that limestone. Indeed, the word '*lipica*' in Slovene means 'little linden', after the trees that grow in such profusion here.

History

In 1580 Austrian Archduke Charles, son of Ferdinand I, founded a stud farm here to breed and train horses for the imperial court in Vienna. He was looking for a lighter, more elegant breed for parades and military purposes, and when he coupled Andalusian horses from Spain with the local Karst breed, the Lipizzaner was born. But they weren't quite the sparkling white beauties we know today. Those didn't come about for another 200 years when white Arabian horses got into the act.

The stud farm remained the property of the court in Vienna until the end of WWI when the Italians took control of Primorska and the horses were moved to Hungary and then Austria. In 1943, with WWII still raging, the Germans moved more than 200 horses to the Sudetenland in Bohemia (now the Czech Republic). When the area was liberated by American forces in 1945, most of the horses and the stud farm's archives were shipped off to Italy. Sadly, only 11 horses returned when operations resumed at Lipica in 1947; the all-important studbooks and 80 other horses, including five stallions, that had been confiscated by the Germans during the war, were assigned to Italy.

Today about 400 Lipizzaners remain at the original stud farm while Lipizzaners are also bred in various locations around the world, including Piber, northeast of Graz in Austria, which breeds the horses for the Spanish Riding School. And of course everyone claims theirs is the genuine article. Indeed, in a bid to get its

---

DANCING HORSES OF LIPICA

Lipizzaners are the finest riding horses in the world, much sought after for *haute école* dressage. And with all the trouble that's put into producing them, it's not surprising. They are very intelligent, sociable horses, quite robust and graceful.

Breeding is paramount – as they say. Just four equine families with 16 ancestors can be traced back to the early 18th century, and their pedigrees read like those of medieval royalty. When you walk around the stables at Lipica you'll see charts on each horse stall with complicated figures, dates and names like 'Conversano' and 'Neapolitano'. It's all to do with the horse's lineage.

Lipizzaners foal between January and May, and the colts and fillies suckle for six or seven months. They remain in the herd for about three years. They are then separated for training, which takes another four years.

Lipizzaners are not white when they are born but grey, bay or even chestnut. The celebrated 'imperial white' does not come about until they are between five and 10 years old, when their hair loses its pigment. Their skin remains grey, however, so when they are ridden hard enough to sweat, they become mottled.

A fully mature Lipizzaner measures about 15 hands (about 153cm) and weighs between 500kg and 600kg. They have long backs, short, thick necks, silky manes and expressive eyes. They live for 25 to 30 years and are particularly resistant to disease. They will nuzzle you out of curiosity if you approach them while they graze.

case across, Slovenia has put a pair of Lipizzaners on the reverse side of its new €0.20 coin.

Orientation & Information

The centre of everything in Lipica is the stud farm in the southwest corner of the village and the two hotels nearby. The **tourist office** (☎ 739 15 80; lipica@siol.net; 8.15am-6pm Apr-Oct, 9am-4pm Nov-Mar) is at the main ticket office facing the stud.

Sights

LIPICA STUD FARM

The 311-hectare **stud farm** (Kobilarna Lipica; ☎ 739 15 80; www.lipica.org; Lipica 5; 8am-6pm) can be visited on a **guided tour** (adult/student €7/3.50; hourly 9-11am & 1-6pm daily Jul-Aug; 10-11am & 1-5pm Mon-Fri, 9-11am & 1-6pm Sat & Sun Apr-Jun, Sep & Oct; 11am & hourly 1-3pm Mon-Fri, hourly 10-11am & hourly 1-4pm Sat & Sun Mar, 11am & hourly 1-3pm daily Nov-Feb). The tours begin opposite the information and ticket office; wait by the sign bearing the name of the language you want to hear the commentary in (including English). A visit covers the stables (the one called Velbanca dates from the early 18th century) and the riding halls to give you an idea of what it's like to learn dressage and control a very large animal.

The highlight of a visit (if you time it right) is the **exhibition performance** (adult/child incl stud farm tour €14/7; 3pm Tue, Wed, Fri & Sun Apr-Oct) of these elegant horses as they go through their complicated paces with riders *en costume*. It's not as complete a show as the one at the Spanish Riding School in Vienna or in such ornate surroundings, but watching great white horses pirouetting and dancing to Viennese waltzes sort of makes up for it. You can also attend a once-a-week **training performance** (adult/child incl stud farm tour €9/4.50; noon Thu Apr-Oct).

If you miss the performances, try to be around when the horses are moved from the stables to pasture (usually between 9am and 10am) and again in the afternoon (around 5.30pm to 6pm).

Activities

Sixty horses are available for **riding** (per hr from €16; 9am, 10am, 4pm & 5pm Sun-Fri Apr-Oct; 9am, 10am, 2pm & 3pm Nov-Mar) both in the ring and in the open countryside at two levels. There is also a large choice of one-hour lessons, including individual (€20 to €34) and group classes (€22) for beginners and intermediate riders and individual dressage classes (€42). There are week-long courses (€240) of six two-hour

lessons for beginners and advanced riders and dressage instruction (6 hours €230). You can also have a jaunt in a horse-drawn, four-person **carriage** (30/60 min €19/38; 3.30pm & 4.30pm Mon-Fri, 11am-2pm & 3.30-6pm Sat & Sun Apr-Oct).

The **Lipica Golf Course** (☎ 734 63 73; www.lipica.org; 9/18-hole Mon-Fri from €20/27.50, Sat & Sun €24.50/35.50, half-set clubs €9.50) behind the Maestoso has nine holes for a par 37, a driving range (€3) and a couple of putting greens.

Near the Hotel Maestoso are five **tennis courts** (per hr from €5, racquet €3.50) available for hire.

Sleeping & Eating

There are just two hotels in Lipica, both managed by the **Lipica Stud Farm** (☎ 739 15 80; www.lipica.org). Rates depend on the season and are heavily discounted for stays of a week or more if you are taking a riding course.

Hotel Klub (☎ 739 15 70; s €43-53.50, d €62-79, ste for 2 €68-87; P) The 80-roomer is generally for those staying for longer periods. It has a sauna and fitness centre and is slightly closer to the stud farm.

Hotel Maestoso (☎ 739 17 90; s €53-68, d €82-106, ste for 2 €126-152; P) This 68-room hotel has most of the amenities, including an indoor swimming pool, a sauna and nearby tennis courts.

Letni Vrt (dishes €5.85-8; 11am-8pm Apr-Sep) The 'Summer Garden' is a self-service place with terrace east of the Maestoso serving simple meals and Balkan grills. It is open in the warmer months only.

Maestoso (€3.75-7, mains €6.25-15.80; 7am-11pm) This café-restaurant with a terrace is the better of the two places to eat in Lipica and is open year-round.

Getting There & Around

Most people visit Lipica as a day trip from Sežana, 4km to the north, or Divača, 13km to the northeast, both of which are on the Ljubljana–Koper rail line. There is no public transport from the train stations in Sežana and Divača to Lipica, though you can rent bicycles in Divača (p152). In Lipica itself bicycles are available for hire from the fitness centre at the Hotel Klub for €5/14 per hour/day.

HRASTOVLJE

☎ 05 / pop 140 / elev 164m

The Romanesque church in this tiny Karst village is the Istrian equivalent of St John the Baptist's Church in Bohinj. OK, so it's not on a lake. But it is small, surrounded by medieval walls with corner towers and covered inside with extraordinary 15th-century frescoes. This is the reason to make the trip here – as difficult as it can be.

Hrastovlje lies near the source of the Rižana River, whose valley effectively forms the boundary between the Karst and the coast. From here northward to the village of Črni Kal and on to Osp, a row of fortresses were built below the limestone plains during the Bronze Age, which the Illyrian tribe of Histrians later adapted to their needs. The valley and surrounding areas would prove to be safe havens for later inhabitants during the Great Migrations and the Turkish invasions.

Sights

The **Church of the Holy Trinity** (Cerkev Sv Trojica; ☎ 031-432 231; adult/student & child €1.70/0.85; ⌚ 8am-noon & 1-5pm), which has a nave and two aisles, was built between the 12th and 14th centuries in the southern Romanesque style. The fortifications were added in 1581 in advance of the Ottomans.

The sombre exterior does not prepare you for what's inside. The complete interior of the church is festooned with **narrative frescoes** painted by Johannes de Castuo (John of Kastav near Rijeka) in around 1490. The paintings are a *Biblia pauperum* – a 'Bible of the poor' – to help the illiterate understand the Old Testament stories, the Passion of Christ and the lives of the saints. Spare the 20 minutes it takes to listen to the taped commentary (in four languages, including English) that will guide you around the little church.

Facing you as you enter the church is the main altar, carved in the 17th century, and the central apse with scenes from the Crucifixion on the ceiling and portraits of the Trinity and the Apostles. On the arch, Mary is being crowned Queen of Heaven. To the right of the central aisle are episodes from the seven days of Creation, and to the left is the story of Adam and Eve, as well as the murder of Abel by Cain and the latter's banishment.

On the ceilings of the north (left) and south (right) aisles are scenes from daily life (sowing, hunting, fishing, making wine etc) as well as the liturgical year and its seasonal duties. Christ's Passion is depicted at the top of the southernmost wall, including his descent into hell, where devils are attacking him with blazing cannons.

Below the scenes of the Passion is what attracts most people to this little church: the famous **Dance of Death** (Mrtvaški Ples), or Danse Macabre, fresco showing 11 skeletons leading the same number of people forward to a freshly dug grave, a pick and shovel at the ready. A twelfth skeleton holds open the lid of a coffin. The line-up includes a child, a cripple, a young man, a moneylender (who is trying to bribe his skeletal escort with a purse), a merchant, a monk, a bishop, a cardinal, a queen, a king and a pope. On the cardinal's cassock you can still see graffiti left by a visitor in 1640. The message is as subtle as a sledge hammer: we are all equal in the eyes of God no matter how important we (or others) think we are in this mortal life.

Getting There & Away

Hrastovlje is 24km southwest of Divača off the main highway to the coast; Koper is 18km to the northwest. Any bus travelling this road in either direction will drop you off just west of Črni Kal, where a massive flyover has cut travel time to the coast substantially, but it's still another 8km south to Hrastovlje. Without a car or bicycle the only sure way of making it to Hrastovlje is by a single daily train.

A train leaves Divača (€2.65) at 7.47am daily, arriving at Hrastovlje station at 8.20am; the church is about 1km to the northwest. The next train of any kind through this backwater is the 7.12pm from Koper (€1.45), which gets into Hrastovlje 15 minutes later. The train carries on to Divača, Postojna and Ljubljana, arriving there at 9.43pm.

If you're driving south to the coast on route No A1, take the first exit after Črni Kal, which is for route No 208 heading south for Buzet and Pula in Croatia. The road to Hrastovlje runs just off it.

THE COAST

Slovenia's short coast (47km) on the Adriatic Sea (Jadransko Morje) is an area of both history and recreation. Three seaside towns – Koper, Piran and Izola – are full of important Venetian Gothic architecture and art, and there are clean beaches, boats for rent and rollicking clubs.

But the Slovenian coast is not everybody's cup of tea. It is fairly overbuilt, jammed from May to September and the water is not especially

PRIMORSKA

inviting, though there are some decent beaches at Portorož. Also, bear in mind that many of the hotels, camping grounds, tourist offices and restaurants here close or severely curtail their opening times during the off-season, which is from November to March or April.

The Koper wine-producing area is known for its white Malvazija and Chardonnay and red Refošk. Concerts, theatre and dance events take place during the **Primorska Summer Festival** (www.portoroz.si) in Koper, Izola, Piran and Portorož in July and the first half of August.

KOPER

☎ 05 / pop 23,270 / elev 4m

By far the largest town on the coast, Koper at first glance appears to be a workaday port city that scarcely gives tourism a second thought. It is much less crowded and more down to earth than its ritzy cousin Piran, 17km down the coast, but despite the industry, container ports and high-rise buildings, Koper has managed to preserve its compact medieval centre. Its recreational area, the seaside resort of Ankaran, is to the north across Koper Bay.

PRIMORSKA

History

Koper has been known by many names during its long and turbulent history. As an island separated from the mainland by a canal, it was called Aegida by ancient Greek sailors, Capris by the Romans (who found it being used to raise goats) and Justinopolis by the Byzantines. The Patriarchs of Aquileia (p22), who took over the town in the 13th century and made it the base for their estates on the Istrian peninsula, renamed it Caput Histriae – Capital of Istria – from which its Italian name Capodistria is derived. They fortified the town and erected some of Koper's most beautiful buildings, including its cathedral and palaces.

Koper's golden age came during the 15th and 16th centuries under the Venetian Republic. Trade increased and Koper became the administrative and judicial centre for much of Istria. It also had a monopoly on salt, which Austria so desperately needed. But when Trieste, 20km to the northeast, was proclaimed a free port in the early 18th century, Koper lost its importance.

Between the world wars Koper was controlled by the Italians, who launched a programme of Italianisation. After the defeat of Italy and Germany in WWII the disputed Adriatic coast area – the so-called Free Territory of Trieste – was divided into two zones. Under the 1954 London Agreement, Zone B and its capital, Koper, went to Yugoslavia while Zone A, including Trieste, fell under Italian jurisdiction.

Up to 25,000 Italian-speaking Istrians fled to Trieste, but 3000 stayed on in Koper and other coastal settlements. Today Koper is the centre of the Italian ethnic community of Slovenia, and Italian is widely spoken here.

Orientation

The centre of Koper's semicircular Old Town is Titov trg, a marvellous Gothic-Renaissance square with Venetian influences. The marina and tiny city beach are to the northwest. The joint bus and train station is 1.4km to the southeast at Kolodvorska cesta 11.

Information

BOOKSHOP

Mladinska Knjiga (☎ 663 38 80; Pristaniška ulica 5a; 8.30am-7pm Mon-Fri, 8am-1pm Sat)

INTERNET ACCESS

Pina (☎ 627 80 72; Kidričeva ulica 43; adult/student per hr €3.75/1.25; 9am-9pm Mon-Fri) Internet café with 10 terminals.

MONEY

Banka Koper (Kidričeva ulica 14; 8.30am-noon & 3-5pm Mon-Fri, 8.30am-noon Sat)

Maki Exchange Bureau (☎ 627 25 44; Pristaniška ulica 13; 7.30am-7.30pm Mon-Fri, 7.30am-1pm Sat)

Nova Ljubljanska Banka (Pristaniška ulica 45; 8.30am-1pm & 3.30-5pm Mon-Fri)

POST

Post office (Muzejski trg 3)

TOURIST INFORMATION

Tourist Information Centre Koper (☎ 664 64 03; www.koper-tourism.si; Titov trg 3; 8am-9pm Jul & Aug; 9am-5pm Mon-Sat, 1-5pm Sun Sep-Jun); summer branch (☎ 663 20 10; Ukmarjev trg 7; 8am-9pm Jul & Aug) The main centre is in the Praetorian Palace.

TRAVEL AGENCIES

Kompas (☎ 663 05 82; Pristaniška ulica 17; 8am-7.30pm Mon-Fri, 8am-1pm Sat)

Palma Travel Agency (☎ 663 36 60; Pristaniška ulica 21; 8am-7pm Mon-Fri, 8am-noon Sat)

Sights

The easiest way to see most everything of interest in Koper's Old Town is simply to walk from the marina on Ukmarjev trg east along Kidričeva ulica to Titov trg and then south down Čevljarska ulica, taking various detours along the way.

KIDRIČEVA ULICA
One of the most colourful streets in Koper, Kidričeva ulica starts at Carpacciov trg, where the **Column of St Justina** (Steber Sv Justine) com-

memorates Koper's contribution – a galley – to the Battle of Lepanto in which Turkey was defeated by the European powers in 1571. Nearby is a large Roman covered basin that now serves as a fountain. At the southern end of the square is the arched **Taverna**, a one-time salt warehouse dating from the 15th century.

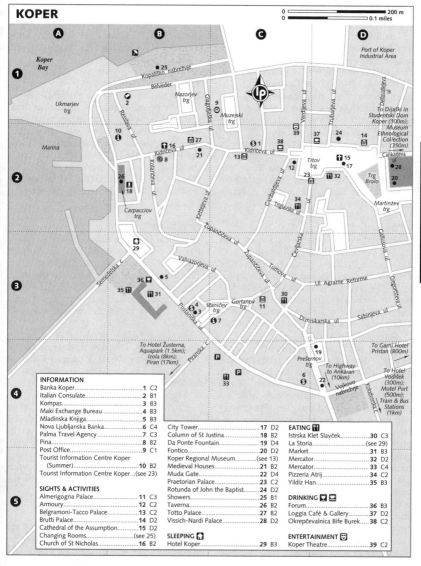

PRIMORSKA

On the north side of Kidričeva ulica there are several disused churches from the 16th century, including the **Church of St Nicholas** (Cerkev Sv Nikolaja; Kidričeva ulica 30), and the 18th-century baroque **Totto Palace** (Palača Totto; Kidričeva ulica 22a), with a relief of the winged lion of St Mark taken from Koper's medieval fortress. Opposite the palace are some wonderful old **medieval town houses** (Kidričeva ulica 33), with protruding upper storeys painted in a checked red, gold and green pattern.

The **Belgramoni-Tacco Palace** (Palača Belgramoni-Tacco; Kidričeva ulica 19), dating from the early 17th century, houses the **Koper Regional Museum** (Pokrajinski Muzej Koper; ☎ 663 35 70; adult/child €1.70/1.25; ☽ 10am-6pm Tue-Fri, 9am-1pm Sat & Sun), with displays of old maps and photos of the port and coast, Italianate sculptures and paintings dating from the 16th to 18th centuries, and copies of medieval frescoes. Note the wonderful bronze knocker on the front door of Venus arising from a seashell. The museum's **ethnological collection** (etnološka zbirka; ☎ 627 20 28; Gramšijev trg 4; ☽ 10am-6pm Tue-Fri, 9am-1pm Sat) is in a 17th-century building in the eastern section of the Old Town.

TITOV TRG
In almost the exact centre of old Koper, Titov trg is a beautiful square full of interesting buildings; mercifully, like much of the Old Town's core, it is closed to traffic. On the north side is the arcaded Venetian Gothic **Loggia** (Loža; Titov trg 1) built in 1463. It now contains an elegant yet affordable café and the **Loggia Gallery** (Loža Galerija; ☎ 627 41 71; adult/child €1.70/0.85; ☽ 11am-5pm Tue-Sat, 11am-1pm Sun).

To the south, directly opposite, is the gleaming white and recently renovated **Praetorian Palace** (Pretorska Palača; Titov trg 3; admission free; ☽ 8am-9pm Jul & Aug; 9am-5pm Mon-Sat, 1-5pm Sun Sep-Jun), a mixture of Venetian Gothic and Renaissance styles dating from the 15th century and the very symbol of Koper. It now contains the town hall, with a reconstructed old pharmacy and the main branch of the tourist office on the ground floor and exhibits on the history of Koper and a ceremonial hall for weddings on the 1st floor. The facade of the palace, once the residence of Koper's mayor who was appointed by the doge in Venice, is chock-a-block with medallions, reliefs and coats of arms.

On the square's western side, the **Armoury** (Armeria; Titov trg 4) was a munitions dump four

centuries ago. Opposite is the **Cathedral of the Assumption** (Stolnica Marijinega Vnebovzetja; ☽ 7am-9pm) and its 36m-tall belfry, now called the **City Tower** (Mestni Stolp; adult/child €1.70/1.25; ☽ 10am-1pm & 3-5pm). The cathedral, partly Romanesque and Gothic but mostly dating from the 18th century, has a white classical interior with a feeling of space and light that belies the sombre exterior.

Behind the cathedral to the north is a circular Romanesque **Rotunda of John the Baptist** (Rotunda Janeza Krstnika), a baptistery dating from the second half of the 12th century with a ceiling fresco.

TRG BROLO
Linked to Titov trg to the east, **Trg Brolo** is a wide and peaceful square of fine old buildings, including the late-18th-century baroque **Brutti Palace** (Palača Brutti; Trg Brolo 1), now the central library, to the north. On the eastern side is the **Fontico** (Fontiko; Trg Brolo 4), a granary where the town's wheat was stored in the late 14th century, and the **Vissich-Nardi Palace** (Palača Vissich-Nardi; Trg Brolo 3), containing government offices.

ČEVLJARSKA ULICA
Historical **Čevljarska ulica** (Cobbler Street), a narrow pedestrian street, runs south from Titov trg. As you walk under the arch of the Praetorian Palace, have a look to the right. The little hole in the wall with the Italian inscription 'Denontie' was where anonymous denunciations of officials and others could be made.

At the end of Čevljarska ulica and down the stone steps is the **Almerigogna Palace** (Palača Almerigogna; Gortanov trg 13), a painted Venetian Gothic palace and arguably the most beautiful building in Koper.

The 17th-century Italian family who erected the **fountain** in Prešernov trg, 200m to the southeast, was named Da Ponte; thus it is shaped like a bridge (*ponte* in Italian). At the southern end is the **Muda Gate** (Vrata Muda). Erected in 1516, it's the last of a dozen such entrances to remain standing. On the south side of the archway you'll see the city seal: the face of a youth in a sunburst.

Activities
Koper's tiny **beach** (☎ 627 18 41; Kopališko nabrežje 1; adult/child €2.30/1.50, after 2pm €1.70/1.25; ☽ 8am-7pm May-Sep), on the northwest edge of the Old

Town, has a small bathhouse with showers and changing rooms, toilet, grassy area for lying in the sun and café-bar. Frankly you'd do better to visit the **Aquapark** (☎ 663 80 00; adult/child all day Mon-Fri €10.50/6.70, Sat & Sun €14.20/8.80; 9am-9pm), which has 3700 sq metres of open and covered swimming pools, at the Hotel Žusterna. Alternatively, you could travel to Ankaran, about 10km to the north by road, and swim at the sand-and-pebble beach there or in one of the two seawater **swimming pools** (adult all day €9.40, child €6.60, senior & student €8.60; 8am-9pm May-Sep) at the Adria Ankaran holiday resort (below).

Sleeping

Camp Adria Ankaran (☎ 663 73 50; www.teni.si/adria; Jadranska cesta 25; adult €8.80-11, child €3.50-4.40; late Apr-Sep; P ◻ ♿ ♨) This enormous camping ground (the closest one to Koper) with 500 sites for 1200 guests in Ankaran extends over 7 hectares on the eastern side of the Adria Ankaran holiday resort and down to the sea. There is any number of sporting facilities, and the camping charge includes use of the two swimming pools.

Motel Port (☎ 639 32 60; motel.port@siol.net; Ankaranska cesta 7; dm €14, rm for up to 3/4 €46/65; P ✕ ◻) Hidden on the top floor of a Mondrianesque shopping centre south of the Old Town, this place has excellent en suite rooms as well as HI-affiliated dormitory rooms, but its location beside a truck terminal results in a constant traffic rumble.

Dijaški in Študentski Dom Koper (☎ 662 62 50; www.d-dom.kp.edus.si in Slovene; Cankarjeva ulica 5; dm €15; late Jun-Aug) This modern 350-bed five-storey dormitory about 150m east of Trg Brolo rents beds in triple rooms primarily in summer. However, there are about three rooms available year-round.

Kompas (p164) and the Palma Travel Agency (p164) can arrange **private rooms** (s €12.50-14.60, d €20.85-25) and **apartments** (apt for 2 €29.20-35.40, apt for 4 €43.80-54.20). Most rooms and apartments are in the new town beyond the train station, however.

MIDRANGE

Hotel Vodišek (☎ 639 24 68; www.hotel-vodisek.com; Kolodvorska cesta 2; s/d/tr/q €40/60/75/88; ✕ ✕ ◻) This tiny hotel with 32 reasonably priced rooms is in a shopping centre halfway between the Old Town and the train and bus stations. Use of bicycles is free for guests.

Garni Hotel Pristan (☎ 614 40 00; www.pristan-koper.si; Ferrarska ulica 30; s €55-61, d €82-91, ste €74-108; P ✕ ✕ ◻) This 16-room property in a modern boat-shaped building above a shopping mall about 700m east of Titov trg is close to many of the large Slovenian and international shipping companies based in Koper and is most suited for business travellers.

TOP END

Hotel Žusterna (☎ 663 80 00; www.terme-catez.si; Istrska cesta 67; s €60-68.50, d €99-116; P ♨) This 117-room sister-hotel of the Koper, about 1.5km to the west on the main coastal road, is not convenient for touring the Old Town, but its Aquapark (left) is a major draw for those seeking recreation.

Hotel Koper (☎ 610 05 00; www.terme-catez.si; Pristaniška ulica 3; s €60, d €100-110; ✕ ♿ ♨) This pleasant, 65-room property on the edge of the historic Old Town is the only really central hotel in town. Rates include entry to the Aquapark at the Hotel Žusterna.

Eating

Okrepčevalnica Bife Burek (☎ 271 347; Kidričeva ulica 8; snacks & light bites €1.50-3.50; 7am-10pm) This place servies good-value *burek* and pizza slices, which you can carry to Titov trg and eat there.

Istrska Klet Slavček (☎ 627 67 29; Župančičeva ulica 39; dishes €3.35-10.85; 7am-10pm Mon-Fri) The 'Istrian Cellar', situated in the 18th-century Carli Palace, is one of the most colourful places for a meal in the Old Town. Filling set lunches go for less than €10, and there's Malvazija and Teran wine available straight from the barrel.

Pizzerija Atrij (☎ 626 28 03; Triglavska ulica 2; pizzas €4.20-6.05; 9am-10pm Mon-Fri, 10am-10pm Sat) This old favourite down an alleyway no wider than your average fullback's shoulder spread serves decent pizzas and has a small back garden.

La Storia (☎ 031-769 079; Pristaniška ulica 3; starters €4.80-6.70, mains €5-10; 11am-9pm Mon-Fri, noon-5pm Sat & Sun) This Italian-style trattoria in the same building as the Hotel Koper focuses on pasta and salads and has outside seating in the warmer months. The salad bar (small/large €2.30/3.35) is good value.

Yildiz Han (☎ 626 14 60; Pristaniška ulica 2; starters €2.70-5, mains €6.90-10.20; noon-midnight) 'Star House', a branch of a similarly named establishment in Ljubljana, has all our Turkish favourites, including *sigara böreği* (filo parcels

PRIMORSKA

filled with cheese), *yaprak dolmasi* (stuffed vine leaves) and kebabs.

There's an outdoor **market** (Pristaniška ulica; ☺ 7am-2pm Mon-Sat) in the open courtyard of the shopping centre. A short distance to the southeast is a huge **Mercator** (Pristaniška ulica 8; ☺ 7am-8pm Mon-Fri, 7am-1pm Sat) supermarket with a smaller **Mercator** (Titov trg 2; ☺ 7am-8pm Mon-Fri, 7am-1pm Sat, 8am-noon Sun) in the Old Town open on Sunday.

Drinking

Loggia Café (☎ 621 32 13; Titov trg 1; ☺ 7.30am-10pm Mon-Sat, 10am-10pm Sun) This lovely café in the exquisite 15th-century Loggia is the best vantage point for watching the crowds on Titov trg.

Forum (☎ 627 20 94; Pristaniška ulica 2; ☺ 7am-10pm) This café-bar at the northern side of the market, next to the Yildiz Han Turkish restaurant and facing a little park and the sea, is a popular local hangout.

Entertainment

Koper Theatre (Gledališče Koper; ☎ 663 13 81; Verdijeva ulica 3) Just north of Titov trg, the city's theatre stages plays as well as concerts and dance performances.

Getting There & Away

BUS

Although train departures are limited, the bus service to and from Koper is good. Buses go to Izola, Strunjan, Piran (€2.60, ½ hour, 18km) and Portorož every half-hour on weekdays and every 40 minutes at the weekend. The buses start at the train and bus station and stop at the market on Pristaniška ulica before continuing on to Izola. Up to 15 buses daily make the run to Ljubljana (€10.35, 1¾ to 2½ hours, 120km).

Buses to Trieste (€3, one hour, 23km, up to 13 a day) run along the coast via Ankaran and Muggia weekdays only. Destinations in Croatia include Rijeka (€7.60, two hours, 84km, 10.10am Monday to Friday), Rovinj (€11.10, 129km, three hours, 3.55pm daily July and August) via Poreč (€8, two hours, 88km), plus two or three to Poreč only, notably at 8.30am Monday to Friday.

TRAIN

Koper is on a minor rail line linking it with Ljubljana (2¼ hours, 153km) via Postojna and Divača. There are local services (€7.30, 2½ hours) at 10.03am and 7.12pm and faster IC services (€8.70, 2¼ hours) at 5.55am and 2.45pm. To get to Buzet and Pula in Croatia from Koper, you must change at Hrpelje-Kozina (€4, 30 minutes, 37km, five daily) for any of three trains a day.

Getting Around

Local buses 1, 2 and 3 go from the main bus and train stations to the eastern edge of Cankarjeva ulica in the Old Town, with a stop near Muda Gate.

Parking in much of the Old Town is restricted – or banned altogether – between 6am and 8pm. Generally, you must leave your vehicle in the pay car parks along Pristaniška ulica.

To order a taxi in Koper ring ☎ 041-554 770 or ☎ 031 386 000.

IZOLA

☎ 05 / pop 10,425 / elev 2m

Izola, a somewhat scruffy fishing port 7km southwest of Koper, is the poor relation among the historical towns on the Slovenian coast. As a result, it is often bypassed by foreign visitors. But Izola does have a certain Venetian charm, a few narrow old streets, and some nice waterfront bars and restaurants where you might tarry for a while.

History

The Romans built a port called Haliaetum at Simon's Bay (Simonov Zaliv) southwest of the Old Town, and under the control of Venice in the Middle Ages, Izola – at that time an island (*isola* is Italian for 'island') – flourished, particularly in the trading of olives, fish and its celebrated wine. But a devastating plague in the 16th century and the ascendancy of Trieste as the premier port in the northern Adriatic destroyed the town's economic base. During the period of the Illyrian Provinces in the early 19th century, the French pulled down the town walls and used them to fill the channel separating the island from the mainland. Many of the medieval churches and buildings were also razed at that time.

After several fish canneries were opened at Izola in the 20th century, the town began to industrialise. It remains the country's foremost fishing port, but Izola's glory days seem a million years ago as you walk through the narrow streets whose houses look like they could topple over in the slightest of winds.

Orientation

Almost everything of a practical nature is located around Trg Republike. Buses stop in front of the Bela Skale travel agency at Cankarjev drevored 2 on the square's southeastern edge. To reach the Old Town and its main square, Veliki trg, walk north along the waterfront promenade called Sončno nabrežje.

Information

Abanka (Pittonijeva ulica 1; ☼ 9am-1pm & 3.30-7pm Mon-Fri) In a side street just to the bus stops.
Banka Koper (Drevored 1 Maja 5; ☼ 8.30am-noon, 3-5pm Mon-Sat, 8.30am-noon Sat)
Post office (Cankarjev drevored 1)
Tourist Information Centre Izola (TIC; ☎ 640 10 50; tic.izola@izola.si; Sončno nabrežje 4; ☼ 9am-9pm Mon-Sat, 10am-5pm Sun Jun-Sep; 8am-7pm Mon-Fri, 8am-5pm Sat Oct-May)

Sights & Activities

Izola isn't overly endowed with important historical sights; Napoleon and his boys took care of that. Those that survive include the striking, orange-striped 16th-century **Parish Church of St Maurus** (Župnijska Cerkev Sv Mavra; Garibaldijeva ulica) and its detached bell tower on the hill above the town, the **Municipal Palace** (Mestna Palača; Veliki trg), which now houses offices of the local council, and the renovated Venetian Gothic **Manzioli House** (Manziolijev trg) behind the Municipal Palace, which was built in 1470 and was the residence of an Istrian chronicler in the 16th century.

Izola's most beautiful building, however, is the rococo **Besenghi degli Ughi Palace** (cnr Gregorčičeva ulica & Ulica Giordano Bruno) below the church, which is sadly no longer open to the public. Built between 1775 and 1781, the mansion has windows and balconies adorned with stuccos and wonderful wrought-iron grilles painted light blue.

Izola can now make its superlative claim to fame with the **Parenzana Museum** (☎ 640 10 50, 041-613 299; 1st fl, Ulica Alme Vivode 3; admission free; ☼ 9am-noon & 6-9pm Tue-Sun), a branch of the Pomorski Museum Sergej Mašera in Piran. It has both train and ship models and is the largest such collection in the world.

There are pebble **beaches** to the north and southeast of the Old Town, but the best one

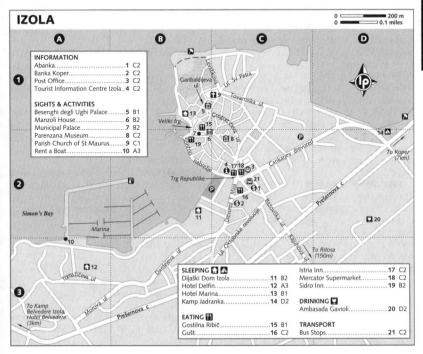

is at **Simon's Bay** about 1.5km to the southwest. It has a grassy area for sunbathing.

The *Prince of Venice* is a 39m high-speed catamaran that makes day trips between Izola and Venice and can be used recreationally or as a way to get to or from Italy. See p291 for details.

You can rent speedboats from **Rent a Boat** (041-618 099, 041-348 077; 8-10am & 6-8pm) at the marina. Bookings by telephone can be made between 8am and 2pm Monday to Friday.

Sleeping
BUDGET
Kamp Jadranka (☎ 640 23 00; Polje cesta 8; per person €6.30-8.40; ☾ Apr-Oct; P) This small site on the waterfront 1km east of the Old Town is just off the busy coastal road and fills up quickly in summer.

Kamp Belvedere Izola (☎ 660 51 00, 660 41 00; www.belvedere.si; Dobrava ulica 1a; adult €6.50-8.50, child €3.80-5; ☾ Apr-Sep; P ☎) This 3-hectare camping ground on a bluff 3km west of Izola has wonderful views of the town and the Adriatic and a large swimming pool.

Dikaški Dom Izola (☎ 662 17 40; www.s-sgtsi.kp.edus .si in Slovene; Prekomorskih Brigad ulica 7; dm €20; ☾ Jul & Aug) This 174-bed hostel in the Srednja Gostinska in Turistična Šola (Middle School of Catering and Tourism) overlooks the marina and welcomes foreign guests in summer only.

MIDRANGE
Hotel Belvedere (☎ 660 51 00; www.belvedere.si; Dobrava ulica 1a; s €39-64, d €52-85, apt for 2 €46-79, apt for 4 €68-100; P ☎ ☎ ☎) As well as its singles and doubles, this large hotel beside the Belvedere camping ground 3km west of town has apartments for between two and four people, although some have to be booked for at least three nights.

Hotel Delfin (☎ 660 70 00; www.hotel-delfin.si; Tomažičeva ulica 10; s €39-50.50, d €65-88; P ☎ ☎) Hard by Izola's marina complex, the Delfin is a bit out of the centre but still near the water. It's a pleasant enough place on a hill about 1km southwest of Trg Republike and has its own swimming pool. But it's a big place, with 225 rooms, and caters largely to tour groups.

Hotel Marina (☎ 660 41 00; www.belvedere.si; Veliki trg 11; s €42-81, d €56-108, ste €102-148; P ☎ ☎ ☎ ☎) The 52-room Hotel Marina couldn't be any more central: it's right on the main square and fronting the harbour. Rates depend on

the season and whether your room faces the water and has a balcony. There's a new and very attractive spa and wellness centre here.

Eating
Izola is the best place on the coast to enjoy a seafood meal. Be careful when you order, however, and ask the exact price of the fish. As seafood is sold by decagram (usually abbreviated as *dag* on menus), you might end up eating (and paying) a lot more than you expected. And be sure to have a glass of Malvazija, the pale-yellow local white that is light and reasonably dry.

Istria Inn (☎ 641 80 50, 031-384 243; Trg Republike 1; dishes €3-5.50; ☾ 6am-midnight) This place on the main road into the Old Town has good-value set lunches (€5.50) and stays open most of the day. Try the gnocchi with *pršut* in a red Refošk wine sauce.

Gušt (☎ 041-650 333; Drevored 1 Maja 3; pizza & pasta €4.40-6; ☾ 8am-1am) This *picerija* and *špageterija* opposite the Banka Koper has decent pizza, pasta and salads (from €3).

Sidro Inn (☎ 641 47 11; Sončno nabrežje 24; starters €5.85-10, mains €6.30-20; ☾ 8am-midnight) One of Izola's best restaurants, Sidro is an old standby on the waterfront just up from the tourist office.

Gostilna Ribič (☎ 641 83 13; Veliki trg 3; starters €4.20-8.75, mains €8-17.50; ☾ 8am-1am) Another of the town's top restaurants, this is an eatery on the inner harbour that's much loved by locals and specialises in turbot.

There's a **Mercator** (Trg Republike 4; ☾ 7am-8pm Mon-Fri, 7am-1pm Sat) supermarket opposite the bus stops.

Entertainment
Ambasada Gavioli (☎ 641 82 12; www.ambasada-gavioli .com; Industrijska cesta; ☾ midnight-6am Sat) In the industrial area southeast of the port, the Ambasada Gavioli still holds the crown as queen of Slovenia's rave clubs.

Getting There & Away
Frequent buses between Koper (€1.70, 15 minutes, 6km) and Piran (€1.70, 20 minutes, 9.5km) go via Izola. Other destinations from Izola (via Koper) include Ljubljana (€9.60, 2½ hours, 105km, five a day, with up to nine in July and August) and Nova Gorica (€7.60, 1¾ hours, 84km, one or two a day).

International routes include six buses a day (five on Saturday) to Trieste (€2.10, 40 minutes, 23km) in Italy and two departures to Umag (€3.70, one hour, 41km) and Pula (€8.50, 2½ hours, 94km) at 2.12pm daily and at 7.42am Monday to Saturday. There's also a daily bus to Zagreb (€22, 6½ hours, 243km) at 4.44am in Croatia.

For getting to/from Italy by boat see p291.

Getting Around

From June to August a minibus does a continuous loop from the Belvedere Izola holiday village west of the Old Town to Simon's Bay, Izola Marina, Trg Republike and the Jadranka camping ground and back.

Order a taxi in Izola on ☎ 040-602 602.

You can rent bicycles at **Ritosa** (☎ 640 12 40; Kajuhova ulica 28; per day €10; ⏰ 8am-7pm Mon-Fri, 8am-1pm Sat).

STRUNJAN

☎ 05 / pop 560 / elev up to 116m

For centuries past the people who lived at Strunjan, a peninsula halfway between Izola and Piran, were engaged in making salt; you'll see the disused pans spread out before you on the descent along the main road (route No 111) from the Belvedere tourist complex. Today the area is protected, and this is because of the expanded 429-hectare **Strunjan Country Park** (Krajinski Park Strunjan), which contains the saltpans and the contiguous **Stjuža Lagoon**, both classified as natural monuments.

Although there has been much development around Strunjan Bay to the southwest, much of the peninsula is remarkably unspoiled. It is bounded by a high cliff, **Cape Ronek** (Rtič Ronek; 116m), at its northernmost point; below it is Moon Bay (Mesečec Zaliv), the prettiest inlet on the coast, which can be seen from the footpath along the cape.

The **Strunjan Health Resort** (Zdravilišče Strunjan; ☎ 676 41 00; www.krka-zdravilisca.si; Strunjan 148; s €50-55, d €72-85, ste €100-110) has all types of accommodation on offer, but the **Salinera** (☎ 676 31 00; www.hoteli-piran.si; Strunjan 14; Ⓟ ⌧ ⌧ ⌧ ⌧), a new resort on the opposite side of the bay, with a 101-room hotel as well as villas and apartments is a lot nicer. Along with a beach, the resort has an indoor pool filled with heated sea water as well as tennis courts and

other sport facilities, including the curiously named Bioenergy Park (Bioenergijski Park) with 12 'energy points' or *chakras* meant to stimulate and improve the metabolism. At the resort's wellness centre much use is made of *fango* – the salty mud found nearby for beauty and therapeutic purposes. **Avtokamp Strunjan** (☎ 678 20 76; amd-piran@siol.net; per person €6.70-9.20) has an area of 1.5 hectares and space for 500 campers.

Frequent bus services link Strunjan with Izola (€1.70, 15 minutes, 6km), Koper, Piran (€1.30, 10 minutes, 3.5km) and Portorož.

PIRAN

☎ 05 / pop 4050 / elev 23m

Picturesque Piran (Pirano in Italian), sitting at the tip of a narrow peninsula, is everyone's favourite town on the Slovenian coast. Its Old Town is a gem of Venetian Gothic architecture and full of narrow atmospheric streets, but it can be a mob scene at the height of summer.

History

Piran has been settled since ancient times, and it is thought that the town's name comes from the Greek word for fire *(pyr)*. In those days, fires were lit at Punta, the very tip of the peninsula, to guide ships to the port at Aegida (now Koper). The Romans established a settlement here called Piranum after their victory over the Illyrians and Celts. They in turn were followed by the early Slavs, the Byzantines, the Franks and the Patriarchs of Aquileia.

Venetian rule began in the late 13th century and lasted in one form or another for more than 500 years. Unlike Koper and Izola, whose citizens rose up against the Venetians time and time again, Piran threw its full support behind Venice in its struggles with Aquileia and Genoa. (The fact that Venice was Piran's biggest customer for the salt it produced was certainly an incentive.) The Venetian period was the town's most fruitful, and many of its beautiful buildings and its fortifications were erected then.

Economic stagnation under Austrian and then Italian rule from the early 19th century until after WWII meant that Piran was able to preserve – at a price to the affluence of its citizens – its medieval character. Today it is one of the best preserved historical towns anywhere on the Adriatic and is protected in its entirety as a cultural monument.

PRIMORSKA

Orientation

Piran's Old Town rests on the westernmost point of Slovenian Istria. Strunjan Bay lies to the north; Piran Bay and Portorož, Slovenia's largest beach resort, are located to the south.

Tartinijev trg, north of Piran Harbour and the small marina, is the centre of the Old Town today, but in the Middle Ages the focal point was Trg 1 Maja (also written Prvomajski trg) to the northwest. The bus station is along the waterfront, about 350m south of Tartinijev trg, at Dantejeva ulica 6.

Information

Banka Koper (Tartinijev trg 12; ☉ 8.30am-noon & 3-5pm Mon-Fri, 8.30am-noon Sat)

Cyber Point Piran (☎ 671 00 22; http://cyberpoint.ksop -cscp.si in Slovene; 4th fl, Študentek Bldg, Župančičeva ulica 14; per hr €4.20; ☉ 1-9pm Mon-Fri) Internet access on five terminals.

Maona Tourist Agency (☎ 673 45 20; www.maona.si; Cankarjevo nabrežje 7; ☉ 9am-7pm Mon-Fri, 10am-1pm & 5-7pm Sat, 10am-1pm Sun) Unstintingly helpful travel agency organising everything from private rooms to activities and cruises.

Post office (Cankarjevo nabrežje 5)

Tourist Information Center Piran (☎ 673 02 20; www.piran.si; Tartinijev trg; ☉ 9am-1.30pm & 3-9pm mid-Jun–mid-Sep, 10am-5pm mid-Sep–mid-Jun) In the impressive Municipal Hall.

Trafika (Tartinijev trg 15; ☉ 6.30am-8pm Mon-Sat, 8am-1pm Sun) Sells English-language newspapers beside the Hotel Tartini.

PRIMORSKA

PIRAN

0 _____ 200 m
0 _____ 0.1 miles

INFORMATION	
Banka Koper............................1	D2
Café Teater..........................(see 47)	
Cyber Point Piran....................2	D3
Maona Travel Agency.................3	D3
Post Office...........................4	D3
Tourist Information Centre Piran..5	C2
Trafika................................6	D2
Turist Biro............................7	C2

SIGHTS & ACTIVITIES	
Aquarium...............................8	C2
Baptistery.............................9	D2
Bell Tower............................10	D2
Cathedral of St George..............11	D1
Church of St Clement................12	B1
Church of St Francis Assisi.........13	D2
Church of St Peter...................14	D2
Cistern................................15	C2
Court House..........................16	C2
Dolphin Gate.........................17	C2
Gabrielli Palace....................(see 20)	
Minorite Monastery................(see 13)	
Municipal Hall.......................18	D2
Old Pharmacy........................19	C1
Parish Museum of St George....(see 11)	
Sergej Mašera Maritime	
Museum.............................20	D3
Sub-net..............................21	B1
Tartini House.........................22	D2
Tartini Statue........................23	D2
Venetian House......................24	D2

SLEEPING	
Alibi B14..............................25	B1
Alibi T60.............................26	C1
Hotel Piran...........................27	C2
Hotel Tartini.........................28	D2
Max...................................29	D2
Val Hostel............................30	B1

EATING	
Delfin.................................31	C2
Flora.................................32	B1

Galeb.................................33	B1
Market...............................34	C2
Mercator Supermarket..............35	C2
Noč in Dan..........................36	C4
Pavel.................................37	C2
Pavel 2..............................38	C2
Pri Mari.............................39	C4
Riva..................................40	B1
Santée Caffe........................41	D3
Stara Gostilna......................42	C2
Tri Vdove............................43	C2
Verdi.................................44	C2

DRINKING	
Galerija Tartini Café...............45	D2
Zižola Kantina......................46	D2

ENTERTAINMENT	
Tartini Theatre......................47	C3

SHOPPING	
Piranske Soline...................(see 24)	

TRANSPORT	
Bus Station.........................48	C4
Bus Stop.............................49	C2
Danoi Rent a Bike..................50	C2

Bathing Area

Punta
Lighthouse   Prešernovo

Gulf of
Trieste

Pebble
Beach

nabrežje

Trail to Beaches,
Fiesa, Hotel Fiesa,
Avtokamp Fiesa
(800m)

Piran
Bay

Bathing Area

Trg 1
Maja

Židovski
trg

Trubarjeva

Tomačičev
trg

Tartinijev
trg

Kajuhova
ul

Marina

Piran
Harbour

Customs
Wharf

Bidovčeva
ul

Gortanova ul

Trg
Bratsva

Bolniška ul

To Car Park (200m);
Portorož (5km)

Grudnova
ul

Turist Biro (☎ 673 25 09; www.turistbiro-ag.si; Tomažičeva ulica 3; ◷ 10am-1pm & 4-7pm Mon-Fri, 10am-1pm Sat & Sun) Opposite the Hotel Piran.

Sights

SERGEJ MAŠERA MARITIME MUSEUM

Located in the **Gabrielli Palace** (Palača Gabrielle; Cankarjevo nabrežje 3) on the waterfront, this **museum** (Pomorski Muzej Sergej Mašera; ☎ 671 00 40; www.pommuz -pi.si; adult/child €2.50/2, with guide €3.35/3; ◷ 9am-noon & 6-9pm Tue-Sun Jul & Aug, 9am-noon & 3-6pm Tue-Sun Sep-Jun) is named in honour of a Slovenian naval commander whose ship was blown up off the Croatian coast in WWI. The mid-19th-century palace, with its lovely moulded ceilings, parquet floors and marble staircase, is worth a visit in itself.

The museum's excellent exhibits focus on sea, sailing and salt-making – three things that have been crucial to Piran's development over the centuries. The salt pans at Sečovlje, southeast of Portorož, get most of the attention on the ground floor. There are some old photographs showing salt workers going about their duties in coolie-like straw hats, as well as a wind-powered salt pump and little wooden weights in the form of circles and diamonds that were used to weigh salt during the Venetian Republic.

The antique model ships upstairs are very fine (especially the 17th-century galleon and 18th-century corvette); other rooms are filled with old figureheads and weapons, including some very lethal-looking blunderbusses. The folk paintings are ex-voto offerings that were placed by sailors on the altar of the pilgrimage church at Strunjan for protection against shipwreck.

TARTINIJEV TRG

The **statue** of the nattily dressed gentleman in Tartinijev trg, an oval-shaped, marble-paved square that was the inner harbour until it was filled in 1864, is that of local boy composer and violinist Giuseppe Tartini (1692–1770). To the east is the **Church of St Peter** (Cerkev Sv Petra; 1818), which contains the restored 14th-century **Piran Crucifix**. Across from the church is **Tartini House** (Tartinijeva Hiša; ☎ 663 35 70; Kajuhova ulica 12; adult/child €1/0.65; ◷ 9am-noon & 6-9pm Tue-Sun Jul & Aug, 11am-noon & 5-6pm Tue-Sun Sep-Jun), the composer's birthplace and popular concert venue.

One of Piran's most eye-catching structures is the red 15th-century Gothic **Venetian House** (Benečanka; Tartinijev trg 4), with its tracery windows and balcony in the northeast of the square. There is a story attached to the stone relief between the two windows of a lion with a banner in its mouth and the Latin inscription *Lassa pur dir* above it. A wealthy merchant from Venice fell in love with a beautiful local girl, but she soon became the butt of local gossips. To shut them up (and keep his lover happy), the merchant built her this little palace complete with a reminder for his loose-lipped neighbours: 'Let them talk'.

The **Court House** (Sodnijska Palača; Tartinijev trg 1), which has two 17th-century doors, and the porticoed 19th-century **Municipal Hall** (Občinska Palača; Tartinijev trg 2) are to the south. The **Aquarium** (Akvarij; ☎ 673 25 72; Kidričevo nabrežje 4; adult/child €2.50/1.70; ◷ 10am-noon & 2-7pm late Mar–mid-Jun, Sep–mid-Oct, 9am-10pm mid-Jun–Aug), about 100m south of the square along the harbour, might be small, but there's a tremendous variety of sea life packed into its two-dozen tanks

CATHEDRAL OF ST GEORGE & SURROUNDS

The Renaissance and baroque **Cathedral of St George** (Stolna Cerkev Sv Jurija; Adamičeva ulica 2) stands on a ridge north of Tartinijev trg above the sea. To the east runs a 200m stretch of the 15th-century **town walls** complete with loopholes. They once ran from the sea all the way to the harbour, and seven crenellated towers are still intact.

The church was founded in 1344 and was rebuilt in baroque style in 1637. It is currently undergoing a massive rebuilding, and visitors are allowed only into the choir to view the magnificent marble altar and star-vaulted ceiling. Church plate, paintings and an unusual statue of St George slaying the dragon, with a woman curiously holding the monster by a lead, can be seen in the attached **Parish Museum of St George** (Župnijski Muzej Sv Jurija; ☎ 673 34 40; admission €1; ◷ 11am-5pm), which contains church plate, paintings and a **lapidary** in the crypt.

The cathedral's freestanding **bell tower** (zvonik; adult/child €1.25/0.85; ◷ 11am-5pm), built in 1608, was clearly modelled on the campanile of San Marco in Venice and can be climbed daily for excellent views of the town and harbour. Next to it, the octagonal 17th-century **baptistery** (*krstilnica*) contains altars, paintings and a Roman sarcophagus from the 2nd century later used as a baptismal font.

On your way up to Tartinijev trg are the **Minorite Monastery** (Minoritski Samostan; ☎ 673 44 17; Bolniška ulica 20) with a wonderful cloister and the **Church of St Francis Assisi** (Cerkev Sv Frančiška Asiškega) built originally in the early 14th century but enlarged and renovated over the centuries. Inside are ceiling frescoes, a giant clam shell for donations and the Tartini family's burial plot.

TRG 1 MAJA & PUNTA

Behind the market north of Tartinijev trg, medieval homes have been built into an ancient defensive wall along Obzidna ulica, which passes under the 15th-century **Dolphin Gate** (Dolfinova Vrata). **Židovski trg**, the centre of Jewish life in Piran in the Middle Ages, is about 100m to the northwest of here.

Trg 1 Maja (1st May Square) may sound like a socialist parade ground, but it was the centre of Piran until the Middle Ages, when it was called Stari trg (Old Square). The surrounding streets are a maze of pastel-coloured overhanging houses, vaulted passages and arcaded courtyards. The square is surrounded by interesting baroque buildings, including the former town **pharmacy** (lekarna; Trg 1 Maja 2) on the north side (now the Fontana restaurant). In the centre of the square is a large baroque **cistern** (*vodnjak*) that was built in the late 18th century to store fresh water; rainwater from the surrounding roofs flowed into it through the fish borne by the stone *putti* cherubs in two corners.

Punta, the historical 'point' of Piran, still has a **lighthouse**, but today's is small and modern. Just behind it, however, the round, serrated tower of the **Church of St Clement**, originally built in the 13th century but altered 500 years later, evokes the ancient beacon from which Piran got its name.

Activities

DIVING

Sub-net (☎ 673 22 18; www.sub-net.si; Prešernovo nabrežje 24; shore/boat dive €25/40; ☷ 9am-noon & 2-6pm Sun-Fri, 9am-noon & 2-7pm Sat) organises shore and boat-guided dives, gives PADI open-water courses (around €150) and rents equipment. Don't expect Red Sea–style corals in these parts, though; the most unusual underwater sight hereabouts is the wreck of a WWII seaplane in Portorož Bay.

SWIMMING

Piran has several 'beaches' – rocky areas along Prešernovo nabrežje – where you might get your feet wet. They are a little better on the north side near Punta, but as long as you've come this far keep walking eastward on the paved path for just under 1km to **Fiesa**, which has a very small but clean beach.

Tours

Maona Tourist Agency (p172) and several other travel agencies in Piran and Portorož can book you on any number of cruises – from a loop that takes in the towns along the coast to day-long excursions to Brioni National Park and Rovinj in Croatia, or Venice and Trieste in Italy.

The large, sleek **Marconi** (☎ 673 45 20; www.maona.si; ☷ 10.30am Tue, 10am Fri & Sun late May-Sep), which can carry up to 400 passengers, cruises down the Istrian coast of Croatia as far as the Brioni Islands (adult/child return €59/29.50) and the national park there on Friday, with a stop at Rovinj (return €28/14). The boat leaves at 10am and returns to Piran at 6.35pm. On Tuesday it does only as far as Rovinj and back and on Sunday to Poreč (€28/14), also with a stop at Rovinj.

For day trips to Venice from Piran with Venezia Lines see p291.

Festivals & Events

The **Tartini Festival** (www.tartinifestival.org) of classical music takes place in venues throughout Piran, including the vaulted cloister of the Minorite monastery, in mid-August.

Sleeping

BUDGET

Avtokamp Fiesa (☎ 674 62 30, 031-487 255; autocamp .fiesa@siol.net; adult €8.35-10, child €2.50; ☷ May-Sep; Ⓟ) The closest camping ground to Piran is at Fiesa, 4km by road but less than 1km if you follow the coastal trail east of the Church of St George. It's in a quiet valley by two small, protected ponds and close to the beach, but it becomes very crowded in summer. There are snack bars, a café and a small supermarket (open 8am to 2pm) here.

Val Hostel (☎ 673 25 55; www.hostel-val.com; Gregorčičeva ulica 38a; with/without HI card €20/24 Jun-Aug, €18/23 Sep-May; ✄ ▣) This central partially renovated hostel on the corner of Vegova ulica has 22 rooms (56 beds) with shared shower, free internet access, kitchen and washing machine. It's a great favourite with backpackers, but there's a surcharge of €2 for one night's stay in the high season.

Private rooms (s €15.85-25, d €23-35) and **apartments** (apt for 2 €36.30-44.20, for 4 €56-72) are available through Maona Tourist Agency (p172) and Turist Biro (p173) throughout the year, but the biggest choice is available during summer.

MIDRANGE & TOP END

Max (☎ 673 34 36, 041-692 928; www.maxpiran.com; Ulica IX Korpusa 26; s/d €50/60; ☒ ▣) Piran's most romantic accommodation has just six rooms, each named rather than numbered, in a delightful, very pink townhouse just down from the cathedral.

Hotel Fiesa (☎ 671 22 00, 031-619286; www.hotel-fiesa.com; Fiesa 57; s €53-70, d €75-98; ☒) Although not in Piran itself, this 22-room very pink hotel overlooking the sea near the Avtokamp Fiesa camping ground is unquestionably one of the most atmospheric places to stay in the area. Among the best sea-facing rooms are Nos 1, 2, 7, 8 and 9, all of which have balconies.

Hotel Tartini (☎ 671 10 00; www.hotel-tartini-piran.com; Tartinijev trg 15; s €48-76, d €70-104, ste €122-185; ☒ ☒ ☒) This attractive, 45-room property faces Tartinijev trg and manages to catch a few sea views itself. The staff are especially friendly and helpful.

Hotel Piran (☎ 676 21 00; www.hoteli-piran.si; Stjenkova ulica 1; s €57-84, d €70-123, ste €131-181; ☒ ☒ ☒ ▣) One of Piran's only two central hotels, the Hotel Piran, with 80 rooms and 10 apartments, is right on the water.

Eating

Santeé Caffe (☎ 051-309 980; Cankarjevo nabrežje 11; ☒ 7am-midnight) This hyper-friendly place has sandwiches (€1.25 to €3.10) and salads (€4.20) and walls painted in colours as vivid as its excellent ice creams.

Flora (☎ 673 12 58; Prešernovo nabrežje 26; pizza €3.35-5.85; ☒ 8am-1am Jul & Aug, 10am-10pm Sep-Jun) The terrace of this simple pizzeria east of the Punta lighthouse has uninterrupted views of the Adriatic.

Stara Gostilna (☎ 673 31 65, 040-640 240; Savudrijska ulica 2; starters €4.20-7, mains €5.85-14.60; ☒ 9am-11pm) This delightful bistro in the Old Town serves both meat and fish dishes and has some of the best and most welcoming service in town.

Pri Mari (☎ 673 47 35, 041-616 488; Dantejeva ulica 17; starters €3.75-8.35, mains €6.25-14.60; ☒ noon-10pm Tue-Sat, noon-6pm Sun) This very stylish restaurant south of the bus station makes an ambitious (and successful) attempt at combining Mediterranean and Slovenian food.

There's an outdoor **market** (Zelenjavni trg; ☒ 7am-2pm Mon-Sat) in the small square behind the Municipal Hall. There's a small **Mercator** (Levstikova ulica 3; ☒ 7am-8pm Mon-Fri, 7am-1pm Sat, 8-11am Sun) supermarket in the Old Town and a **Noč in Dan** (☎ 671 57 52; Tomšičeva ulica 41; ☒ 7am-midnight daily) branch opposite the bus station.

One of Piran's attractions is its plethora of fish restaurants, especially along Prešernovo nabrežje, though don't expect any bargains. Most of them – including **Pavel** (☎ 674 71 01; Gregorčičeva ulica 3; ☒ 11am-11pm), **Pavel 2** (☎ 674 71 02; Kosovelova ulica 1; ☒ 11am-11pm) and **Tri Vdove** (Three Widows; ☎ 673 02 90; Prešernovo nabrežje 4; ☒ 11am-10pm) – cater to the tourist trade and are over-priced; expect to pay about €25 per person with house wine. Instead, try any of the following fish restaurants, which are very popular with Piranites:

Verdi (☎ 673 27 37; Verdijeva ulica 20; starters €6.30-12.50, mains €4-16.70) The tables at this place in the back streets of the Old Town spill out onto the nearby square on warm summer days. The seafood pasta is excellent.

Delfin (☎ 673 24 48; Kosovelova ulica 4; mains €6.30-16.70; ☒ 11am-11pm Mon-Fri, 11am-midnight Sat & Sun) This restaurant is housed in a 15th-century house facing Trg 1 Maja.

Riva (☎ 673 22 25; Gregorčičeva ulica 46; starters €5-8.35, mains €8.35-16.70; ☒ 9am-midnight) Our new favourite (and very classy) seafood restaurant on Prešernovo nabrežje has the best sea views and décor. There's a pizzeria (pizzas €4.20 to €5.40) next door for ichthyphobes.

PRIMORSKA

Galeb (☎ 673 32 25; Pusterla ulica 5; meals from €14.60; ⏱ 11am-4pm & 6pm-midnight Wed-Mon) An excellent family-run restaurant, Galeb is east of the Punta lighthouse and nonsmoking throughout.

Drinking & Entertainment

Galerija Tartini Café (☎ 673 33 81; Tartinijev trg 3; ⏱ 7am-midnight) This café in a classical building next to the Venetian House is a wonderful place for a cup of something hot and a slice of something sweet.

Café Teater (☎ 051-310 102, 041-638 933; Stjenkova ulica 1; ⏱ 7am-3am Mon-Fri, 9am-3am Sat & Sun), With a waterfront terrace and antique furnishings, this is where anyone who's anyone in Piran can be found.

Zižola Kantina (Tartinijev trg 10; ⏱ 9am-2am) This simple, nautically themed bar has tables right on the main and is popular with Piranites.

Tartini Theatre (Gledališče Tartini; ☎ 676 67 00; Kidričevo nabrežje) Built in 1910 and seating 300 spectators, this theatre hosts a program of classical concerts throughout the year.

Shopping

Piranske Soline (☎ 673 31 10; Tartinijev trg 4; ⏱ 9am-8pm Mon-Fri, 9am-4pm Sat & Sun) In the Venetian House, this place sells bath sea salts and other products from Sečovlje (p180).

Getting There & Away

From the bus station buses head for Koper (€2.60, 30 minutes, 18km) via Izola every 20 to 40 minutes. Other destinations that can be reached from here include Ljubljana (€11.70, 2½ to three hours, 140km, eight daily) via Divača and Postojna, and Nova Gorica (€9, 2¼ hours, 97km, one at 2.20pm Monday to Friday year-round and another at 4.50pm daily in July and August) and Sečovlje (€1.70, 15 minutes, 9.5km, eight a day).

Some five buses go to Trieste (€4.60, 1¾ hours, 36km) in Italy on weekdays only, and there is a daily departure for the Croatian capital Zagreb (€23, six hours, 259km) at 4.25am. One bus a day heads south for Croatian Istria from June to September, leaving at 4.25pm and stopping at the coastal towns of Umag, Poreč and Rovinj (€7, two hours, 74km).

From Tartinijev trg, I&I minibuses (€1) shuttle to Portorož and the camping grounds at Lucija (minibus 1) every half-hour from 5.30am to 10.45pm (11.45pm on Friday and Saturday) continuously year-round.

Piran and Izola despatch catamarans to Venice (p291) at least once a week.

Getting Around

CAR

Traffic is severely restricted here, and parking spaces are at an absolute premium. All vehicles are stopped at a tollgate 200m south of the bus station where the sensible choice is to use the huge municipal car park (€0.80 per hour, €7.75 per day) and walk or take a shuttle bus into the centre. You could take a ticket and drive into the centre (first hour free, then €2.70 per hour), but old Piran is so small, parking is so limited and its alleyways so narrow (mostly footpaths) that you're likely to regret it.

TAXI

For a taxi in Piran call ☎ 051-607 333 or ☎ 031-252 126.

BICYCLE

Bikes are available from **Danoi Rent a Bike** (Prešernovo nabrežje; per hr/6 hr/day €2.50/10.50/18; ⏱ 8am-1am May-Sep), a small kiosk wedged between the two Pavel restaurants along the waterfront.

PORTOROŽ

☎ 05 / pop 2760 / elev to 90m

Every country with a sea coast has got to have a honky-tonk beach resort – a Blackpool, a Bondi or an Atlantic City – and Portorož is Slovenia's very own. The 'Port of Roses' skirts a sandy bay about 5km southeast of Piran. Obala (Beach Rd), the main drag, is essentially a strip of high-rise hotels, restaurants, bars, travel agencies, shops, parked cars and small beaches, and it is not to everyone's liking.

But Portorož isn't all bad. Its sandy beaches are the largest on the coast and are relatively clean, there are pleasant spas and wellness centres where you can take the waters or cover yourself in curative mud, and the list of other activities is endless. At the same time, the vast array of accommodation makes Portorož a useful fall back if everything's full in nearby Piran.

History

Portorož may look as if it was born yesterday, but that's not the case. Though most of the development along Obala dates from the late 1960s and 1970s, the settlement was first mentioned in the 13th century, and its sheltered bay was fiercely contested over the next 200 years.

Portorož achieved real fame in the 19th century when Austro-Hungarian officers came here to be treated with *fango*, the mud collected from the salt pans at Sečovlje (p180). Word spread quickly and in 1912 the luxurious Palace hotel (under protracted renovation) was established.

Orientation

Portorož's main development looks on to the bay from Obala, but there are satellite resorts and hotel complexes to the northwest at Bernardin and south near the Portorož Marina at Lucija. Buses stop opposite the main beach on Postajališka pot.

Information

INTERNET ACCESS

Kapelca Bar (☎ 674 42 36; Obala 16a; 20 min €1.70; ⏰ 7am-1am Mon-Sat, 11am-1am Sun) Pub with internet access.

MONEY

Banka Koper (Obala 33; ⏰ 8.30am-noon & 3-5pm Mon-Fri, 8.30am-noon Sat)

POST

Post office (K Stari cesti 1)

TOURIST INFORMATION

Tourist Information Centre Portorož (☎ 674 02 31; www.portoroz.si; Obala 16; ⏰ 9am-1.30pm & 3-9pm mid-Jun–mid-Sep, 10am-5pm mid-Sep–mid-Jun)

TRAVEL AGENCIES

Atlas Express (☎ 674 67 72; atlas.portoroz@siol.net; Obala 55; ⏰ 8am-7pm Mon-Fri, 9am-1pm Sat) Local rep for American Express.
Istriana Tourist Service (☎ 674 03 60; www.istriana .si; Postajališka pot 2; ⏰ 8am-10pm Jul & Aug, 9am-6pm Mon-Sat Sep-Jun) At the main bus stop.
Kompas (☎ 617 80 00; Obala 41; ⏰ 9am-8pm Mon-Fri, 9am-1pm & 4-7pm Sat & Sun Jul & Aug; 9am-7pm Mon-Fri, 9am-1pm Sat & Sun Sep-Jun)
Maona Tourist Agency (☎ 674 03 63; Obala 14b; ⏰ 9am-8pm daily Jul & Aug; 9am-7pm Mon-Fri, 10am-7pm Sat, 10am-1pm Sun Sep-Jun) Branch of the excellent agency in Piran.

Sights

Forma Viva atop the Seča Peninsula near the Lucija camping ground is an outdoor sculpture garden with more than a hundred works of

art carved in stone. This is just one of several such parks in Slovenia. They were international exhibitions where sculptors worked with local materials: stone at Portorož, wood at Kostanjevica na Krki in Dolenjska, iron at Ravne na Koroškem in Koroška and – God help us – concrete in Maribor. The real reason for coming is the fantastic view of Portorož and Piran Bays. The salt pans at Sečovlje are a short walk to the south.

Activities

BOATING & CRUISES

Maona Tourist Agency rents out boats, and you can also hire them on the grassy beach area directly west of the Metropol Hotel.

Spinaker (☎ 674 54 20, 041-281 133; www.spinaker.si; Sončna pot 8; 1/2/4hr €38/67/112; ⏰ 10am-6pm May-Sep) can take five of you sailing along the coast to Piran and beyond from the main pier in Portorož. There are also cruises on the **Solinarka** (☎ 031-653 682, 040-648 376; poropat@siol .net; adult/child €6.70/4.20; ⏰ varies) tour boat from Portorož to Piran and Strunjan and back and a circular one on the **Svetko** (☎ 041-623 191; €13; ⏰ 9.40am) from Bernardin to Izola.

Jonathan Yachting (☎ 677 89 30, 041-644 533; www .jonathan-yachting.si; Cesta Solinarjev 4) in Portorož has a range of boats for hire: a 10m Elan 333 sailing yacht with four to six berths costs from €990 a week from mid-October to mid-April and as much as €1750 a week in July and August. An 11m, six-berth Dufour 34 is €1200 and €2200 respectively.

Atlas Express (left) and others can book day trips to Venice aboard the *Prince of Venice* and with Venezia Lines (p291).

PANORAMIC FLIGHTS

Sightseeing by ultra-light plane is available at the **Portorož airport** (☎ 672 25 25; info@solinair.si; Sečovlje 19; ⏰ 8am-8pm Apr-Sep, 3-5pm Oct-Mar). Flights over Portorož and Piran or the whole coast (15 minutes) cost about €35.

SPAS

Terme & Wellness Centre Palace (☎ 696 50 11; www .lifeclass.net; Obala 43; ⏰ 7am-7pm), a large spa connected with the Grand Hotel Palace that you can also enter from K Stari cesti, is famous for thalassotherapy (treatment using sea water and by-products like mud from the salt flats). The spa offers various types of warm sea-water and brine baths (€35.50 to €44), Sečovlje mud baths (€23), massage (€35 for 40

PORTOROŽ

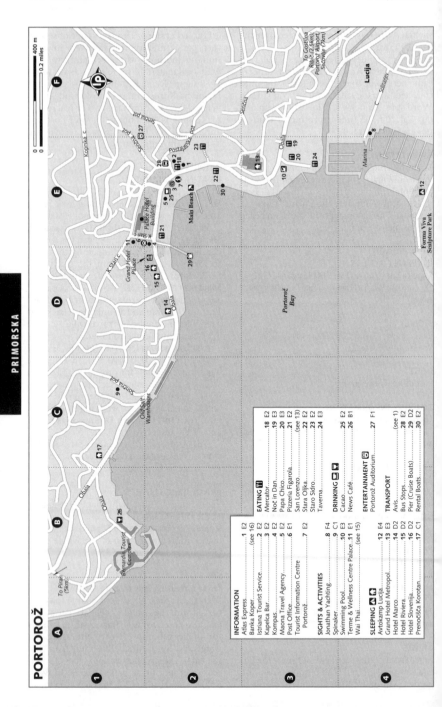

INFORMATION
Atlas Express.................................1 E2
Banka Koper...........................(see 16)
Istriana Tourist Service.................2 E2
Kapelca Bar..................................3 E2
Kompas.......................................4 E2
Maona Travel Agency....................5 E2
Post Office...................................6 E1
Tourist Information Centre
   Portorož...................................7 E2

SIGHTS & ACTIVITIES
Jonathan Yachting........................8 F4
Spinaker......................................9 C1
Swimming Pool...........................10 E3
Terme & Wellness Centre Palace..11 E1
Wai Thai..................................(see 15)

SLEEPING
Avtokamp Lucija.........................12 E4
Grand Hotel Metropol..................13 E3
Hotel Marco...............................14 D2
Hotel Riviera..............................15 D2
Hotel Slovenija...........................16 D2
Premočísta Korotan.....................17 C1

EATING
Mercator....................................18 E2
Noč in Dan.................................19 E3
Papa Chico.................................20 E3
Pizzeria Figarola..........................21 E2
San Lorenzo...........................(see 13)
Stara Oljka.................................22 E2
Staro Sidro.................................23 E2
Taverna......................................24 E3

DRINKING
Cacao...25 E2
News Café...................................26 B1

ENTERTAINMENT
Portorož Auditorium....................27 F1

TRANSPORT
Avis.......................................(see 1)
Bus Stops...................................28 E2
Pier (Cruise Boats).......................29 D2
Rental Boats...............................30 E2

minutes) and a host of other therapies and beauty treatments. The palatial indoor **swimming pool** (nonguests 4hr pass €9.60/12.20 Mon-Fri/Sat & Sun; ☯ 1-9pm Mon-Fri, 11am-9pm Sat & Sun).

Wai Thai (☎ 692 70 70; Obala 33; 50-min massage €46-52; ☯ 9am-10pm Thu-Tue, 2-10pm Wed) begs the question, why Thai? The answer: it's Slovenia's most sumptuous wellness centre. Located in the Hotel Riviera, the spa's decor suggests a provincial *wat*, and there are Thai masseuses to help you relax and lots of other treatments, too.

SWIMMING

The lifeguard-patrolled **beaches** (☯ 8am-8pm Apr-Sep) at Portorož, including the main one, which accommodates 6000 fried and bronzed bodies, have water slides and outside showers, and beach chairs (€3.80) and umbrellas (€3) are available for rent. Beaches are off-limits between 11pm and 6am and camping is strictly forbidden.

The large outdoor **swimming pool** (adult/child €3.80/2.50; ☯ 10am-6pm May-Sep), south of the Grand Hotel Metropol and owned by the same people, is open in summer.

Festivals & Events

An unusual local event involving a lot of pageantry is the **Baptism by Neptune** (Neptunov Krst) of new recruits to the naval school held in early September.

Sleeping
BUDGET

Avtokamp Lucija (☎ 690 60 00; www.metropolgroup.si; Seča 204; adult €7.20-11.70, child €3; ☯ early Apr-Sep; P ⌨ ☎) This 6-hectare camping ground is below the Seča Peninsula and south of the marina about 2km from the bus station. It offers all sorts of sporting facilities and can (and often does) accommodate 1000 guests.

Prenočišča Korotan (☎ 674 5400; www.sd.upr.si/sdp/prenocisca; Obala 11; s/d/tr €29/41/55; ☯ Jul & Aug; ⌨) Just off the main road between Piran and the centre of Portorož (take I&I minibus 1), this unusually upmarket summer-only hostel in Korotan has en suite rooms and computers for internet access.

The Maona (p177) and Istriana (p177) travel agencies have **private rooms** (s €13-27, d €22-35) and **apartments** (apt for 2 €27-47, apt for 4 €50-87), with prices varying widely and depending on both the category and the season. Some of the cheapest rooms are up on the hillside, quite a walk from the beach. Getting a room

for fewer than three nights (for which you must pay a supplement) or a single any time can be difficult, and in winter many owners don't rent at all.

MIDRANGE & TOP END

Portorož counts upwards of 20 hotels, not including the Palace, the Art Nouveau hotel that put Portorož on the map (currently undergoing a long-overdue renovation and set to reopen in 2008), and very little budget accommodation. Hotel rates in Portorož can be very high during the summer months. Many hotels close for the winter in October or November and do not reopen until April or even May.

Hotel Marko (☎ 617 40 00; www.hotel-marko.com; Obala 28; s €54-83, d 67-104; P ⌨ ☒ ⌨) Much of Portorož is high-rise city. For something on a more human scale, check out this lovely 48-room hotel with scenic gardens just opposite the main beach.

Grand Hotel Metropol (☎ 690 10 00; www.metropolgroup.si; Obala 77; s €110-165, d €160-240; P ⌨ ⌨ ⌨ ⌨) Currently the only five-star hotel in town, the 104-room Metropol is up on a hill overlooking the beach. It boasts a casino, huge indoor and outdoor swimming pools and the excellent San Lorenzo restaurant on the ground floor.

Hotel Riviera & Hotel Slovenija (☎ 692 00 00; www.lifeclass.net; Obala 33; s €125-164, d €166-224; P ⌨ ☒ ⌨ ⌨ ⌨) The sister properties are joined at the hip and are good choices if you want to stay someplace central. The Riviera has 160 rooms, three fabulous swimming pools and the Wai Thai spa. The Slovenija is somewhat bigger with 183 rooms. Both have four stars.

Eating

Taverna (☎ 690 50 00; Obala 22; starters €6.25-7.50, mains €7.30-14.60; ☯ noon-11pm) Part of the group that owns the Grand Hotel Metropol, Taverna serves so-so meat and better fish dishes, but the location – at the end of a slip road overlooking the marina and the bay – is superb.

Stara Oljka (☎ 674 85 55; Obala 20; starters €6.20-7.50, mains €7-16; ☯ 10am-midnight) The 'Old Olive Tree' specialises in grills (Balkan, steaks etc) and you'll often see something large being roasted on a spit here. There's a large and very enticing sea-facing terrace.

Pizzeria Figarola (☎ 674 22 00; Obala 14a; pizza €5.65-7.50; ☯ 10am-10pm) There are dozens of decent

PRIMORSKA

pizzerias all along Obala but Figarola, with a huge terrace just up from the main pier, is the place of choice.

Staro Sidro (☎ 674 50 74; Obala 55; starters €4.20-10, mains €7.10-16; ☒ 11am-11pm) A tried-and-true favourite in Portorož, the 'Old Anchor' is next to the lovely Vila San Marco. Its garden has seafood and a lovely terrace overlooking Obala and Portorož Bay. Try the crayfish soup and the blackened rice with prawns.

Papa Chico (☎ 677 93 10; Obala 26; starters €3.75-5.45, mains €4.60-8.75; ☒ 9am-2am Mon-Sat, 10am-2am Sun) This pleasant cantina serves 'Mexican fun food' (go figure), including hysterical fajitas (€7.50 to €9.20).

San Lorenzo (☎ 690 10 00; Obala 77; starters €5.40-9, mains €7.90-20.50; ☒ noon-11pm) Located on the ground floor of the Grand Hotel Metropol, this Italian/Mediterranean restaurant is among the finest in Portorož. The wine selection is superb.

You'll find a branch of the **Mercator** (Obala 53; ☒ 7am-8pm Mon-Sat) supermarket chain next to where the buses stop and a **Noč in Dan** (☎ 671 57 63; Obala 26; ☒ 24hr) branch open round the clock near the open-air swimming pool.

Drinking & Entertainment

Cacao (☎ 674 10 35; Obala 14; ☒ 8am-3am) This über-designer café wins the award as the most stylish on the coast. It has a fabulous terrace.

News Café (☎ 674 10 04; Obala 4f; ☒ 8am-2am) The News is not exactly central (it's in the Bernadin tourist complex), but it's a comfortable café and an 'American bar' with food and is handy to the Korotan hostel.

Portorož Auditorium (Portorož Avditorij; ☎ 676 67 00; www.avditorij.si; Senčna pot 12; box office ☒ 8-10am & 10.30am-2pm Mon-Fri) The main cultural venue in Portorož, with two main indoor theatres and a huge open-air amphitheatre, the auditorium is 200m behind where the buses stop. Some of the events of the Primorska Summer Festival (www.portoroz.si) in July and part of August take place here.

Getting There & Away
BUS

Buses leave Portorož for Piran, Strunjan and Izola (€2.20, 20 minutes, 12km) about every 20 to 40 minutes throughout the year. Other destinations from Portorož and their daily frequencies are the same as those for Piran (p176). The bus for Zagreb (€23, six hours, 255km) leaves at 4.31am.

I&I minibuses (p176) make the loop from the Lucija camping grounds through central Portorož to Piran throughout the year.

CAR & MOTORCYCLE

The main car-rental companies, including **Avis** (☎ 674 05 55) at Atlas Express (p177), are all represented in Portorož. Atlas Express rents motor scooters for six hours/day for €35/40.

Getting Around
CAR

Parking space is tight in Portorož, and you must 'pay and display' to park in Portorož. One hour costs €0.85, a full day €8.35.

TAXI

For a local taxi in Portorož ring ☎ 674 55 55 or ☒ 673 07 00.

BICYCLE

Atlas Express (p177) rents bicycles per six hours/day for €12/18.

SEČOVLJE
☎ 05 / pop 580

The disused salt pans at Sečovlje, covering an area of 724 hectares from Seča to the Dragonja River on the Croatian border, have been turned into **Sečovlje Saltworks Country Park** (Krajinski Park Sečoveljske Soline; www.kpss.soline.si) and a **nature reserve**, which attracts some 270 bird species. The area, crisscrossed with dikes, channels, pools and canals, was once a hive of activity and one of the biggest money-spinners on the coast in the Middle Ages. Today, it looks like a ghost town with its empty grey-stone houses and pans slowly being taken over by hardy vegetation.

In the centre of the reserve is the wonderful **Saltworks Museum** (Muzej Solinarstva; ☎ 672 13 30, 671 00 40; www.pommuz-pi.si; adult/child/student €3.35/2/2.50; ☒ 9am-8pm Jun-Aug, 9am-6pm Apr, May, Sep & Oct) housed in two buildings. The exhibits relate to all aspects of salt-making and the lives of salt workers and their families: tools, weights, water jugs, straw hats, baking utensils and the seals used to mark loaves of bread baked communally. Out among the pans south of the museum is a **wind-powered pump** (just follow the earthen dikes to reach it) that still twirls in the breeze. The museum staff make use of it and other tools to produce a quantity of salt every year in the traditional way. In all about 2000 tonnes of salt are produced at Sečovlje annually.

SALT OF THE SEA

Although salt-making went on for centuries along the Slovenian coast at places like Sečovlje and Strunjan, the technique changed very little right up to 40 years ago when harvesting on a large scale all but ended.

Sea water was channelled via in-flow canals – the 'salt roads' – into shallow ponds separated by dikes, which were then dammed with small wooden paddles. Wind-powered pumps removed some of the water, and the rest evaporated in the sun and the wind as the salt crystallised from the remaining brine. The salt was collected, drained, washed and, if necessary, ground and iodised. It was then loaded onto a heavy wooden barge called a *maona* and pulled to salt warehouses (*skladišča soli*).

Salt harvesting was seasonal work, lasting from 24 April (St George's Day) to 24 August (St Bartholomew's Day), when the autumn rains came. During that time most of the workers lived with their families in rented houses lining the canals at Sečovlje. They paid the landlord with their 'salt funds' – the pans around each house.

The set-up of each house was pretty much the same. The large room downstairs served as a storehouse while upstairs there were two bedrooms and a combination living room and kitchen. All the windows and doors opened on both sides so that workers could observe changes in the weather. Rain and wind could wipe out the entire harvest if the salt was not collected in time.

In September the workers returned to their villages to tend their crops and vines. Because they lived both on the land and 'at sea', Slovenian salt workers were said to 'sit on two chairs'.

Sečovlje is right on the border with Croatia, and to reach it you must pass through Slovenian immigration and customs first, so don't forget your passport. Before you cross the Croatian checkpoint, however, you make a sharp turn to the right (east) and continue along an unsealed road for just under 3km. The two museum buildings stand out along one of the canals.

Buses from Portorož stop at the town of Sečovlje, about 1.5km north of the border, so it's best to catch a bus heading into Istria if you can time it right and get off just before the Croatian frontier.

The best way to visit the salt pans in summer is on the **Solinarka** (☎ 031-653 682, 040-648 376; poropat@siol.net; adult/child 10.85/6.30; ☼ twice daily Jul & Aug) tour boat, which departs the Bernadin complex at about 9.30am and 4pm, Piran at 9.45am and 4.15pm and Portorož at 10.15am and 4.45pm. (To avoid disappointment, double-check these times.) The trip lasts two hours, and the price includes entry to the Saltworks Museum.

PRIMORSKA

Notranjska

In a country where more than half of the land mass is covered in forest, Notranjska takes the cake. It is for the most part wooded and, as a result, communications have always been poor and development slow in 'Inner Carniola'. Today, much of the province is given over to logging, especially on the Bloke Plateau and in the Lož Valley.

But forests are hardly the most distinguishing physical characteristic of the province. Slovenia counts more than 6000 karst caves and sinkholes created by ponor (or 'disappearing') rivers and 10 of these caverns, most of them in Notranjska, are open to visitors.

If you can imagine much of the land surface as a great Swiss cheese, you'll get the picture. Notranjska's abundant rain and snow vanishes into the holes of this 'cheese', and then resurfaces on the fringes of karst fields called polje. As a result, certain lakes, such as those at Cerknica and Planina, are 'intermittent', meaning they only appear at certain times of the year. Below the surface course a number of important underground rivers, including the Unica, Pivka, Ljubljanica and Rak.

Notranjska's isolated setting has spawned some of Slovenia's most cherished myths and legends, notably that of the Turk-slayer Martin Krpan, made famous in Fran Levstik's book of the same name. Today the region is fast becoming a centre of outdoor activity, especially with the opening of Notranjska Regional Park, which encompasses a large portion of the province, and the country parks at the Rakov Škocjan gorge and around Snežnik Castle.

HIGHLIGHTS

- Repeat history and throw cherries from **Erazem's Nook** (p187) in Predjama Castle
- Get forked by Uršula at Cerknica's **Pustni Karneval** (p189)
- Feast on dormice (eek!) on **Polharska Noč** (Dormouse Night; p191) in late September at Snežnik Castle
- Be inspired by the mimelike **Live Christmas Crib** (p185) at the Concert Hall in Postojna Cave

POSTOJNA

☎ 05 / pop 8665 / elev 555m

The karst cave at Postojna, one of the largest in the world, is among Slovenia's most popular attractions. As a result, it is very commercialised and jammed most of the year with tour groups. It must be said, however, that Postojna's stalagmite and stalactite formations are unequalled.

The Postojna Cave (Postojnska Jama) system, a series of caverns, halls and passages some 20.5km long and two million years old, was hollowed out by the Pivka River, which enters a subterranean tunnel near the cave's entrance. The river continues its deep passage underground, carving out several series of caves, and emerges again as the Unica River.

The Unica meanders through a sunken field of porous limestone – the Planinsko Polje (Planina Polje) – which becomes Lake Planina in the rainy season. But, as is the nature of what is called a ponor river, it is soon lost to the underground. It reappears near Vrhnika as the Ljubljanica River and continues its journey northward to the capital.

History

Postojna Cave has been known – and visited – by residents of the area for centuries; you need only look at the graffiti dating back seven centuries in the Gallery of Old Signatures by the entrance. But people in the Middle Ages knew only the entrances; the inner parts were not explored until April 1818, just days

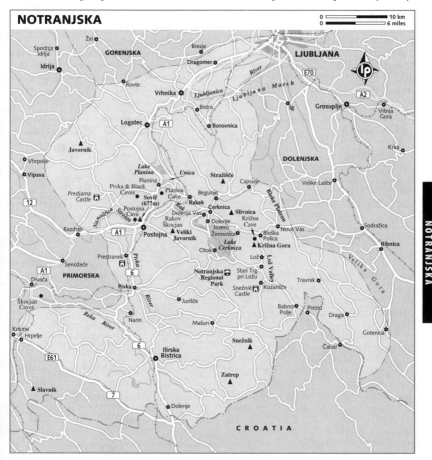

NOTRANJSKA

before the arrival of Habsburg Emperor Franz I (r 1792–1835). The following year the Cave Commission accepted its first organised tour group, including Archduke Ferdinand, and Postojna's future as a tourist destination was sealed. Since then more than 30 million people have visited Postojna.

Orientation

The town of Postojna lies in the Pivka Valley at the foot of Sovič Hill (677m). The Pivka River and the entrance to the cave are about 1.5km northwest of Titov trg in the town centre.

Postojna's bus station is at Titova cesta 36, about 250m southwest of Titov trg. The train station is on Kolodvorska cesta about 1km to the southeast of the square.

Information

Banka Koper (Tržaška cesta 2)

DZS (☎ 720 07 40; Titov trg 3; ☺ 8.30am-7pm Mon-Fri, 8.30am-1pm Sat) Bookshop with maps next door to Kompas.

Kompas Postojna (☎ 721 14 80; info@kompas-postoj na.si; Titov trg 2a; ☺ 8am-8pm Mon-Fri, 9am-1pm Sat Jun-Aug; 8am-7pm Mon-Fri, 9am-1pm Sat May, Sep & Oct; 8am-5pm Mon-Fri, 9am-1pm Sat Nov-Apr) This travel

agency is the best source of information in town. Also has private rooms and changes money (3% commission).

Post office (Ulica 1 Maja 2a)

SKB Banka (Ljubljanska cesta 5a)

Tourist Information Centre Postojna (☎ 728 25 11; td.tic.postojna@siol.net; Jamska cesta 28; ☺ same as Postojna Cave) In a kiosk just south of the Postojna Cave entrance.

Sights & Activities

POSTOJNA CAVE

Visitors get to see about 5.7km of the **cave** (Postojnska Jama; ☎ 700 01 00; www.postojnska-jama.si; adult/child/student €17.50/11.50/13.30; ☺ tours hourly 9am-6pm May-Sep; 10am, noon, 2pm & 4pm Apr & Oct; 10am, noon & 2pm Mon-Fri, 10am, noon, 2pm & 4pm Sat & Sun Nov-Mar) on 1½-hour tours; some 4km of this is covered by an electric train, which runs as far as the **Big Mountain** (Velika Gora) cavern. Here you stand under one of the five signs identifying your language, and a guide escorts you through halls, galleries and caverns.

These are dry galleries, decorated with a vast array of white stalactites shaped like needles, enormous icicles and even fragile spaghetti. The stalagmites take familiar shapes – pears, cauliflower and sand castles – but there are

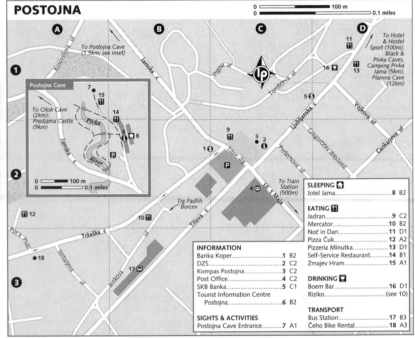

POSTOJNA

INFORMATION	
Banka Koper	1 B2
DZS	2 C2
Kompas Postojna	3 C2
Post Office	4 C2
SKB Banka	5 C1
Tourist Information Centre	
Postojna	6 B2

SIGHTS & ACTIVITIES	
Postojna Cave Entrance	7 A1

SLEEPING	
Jotel Jama	8 B2

EATING	
Jadran	9 C2
Mercator	10 B2
Noč in Dan	11 D1
Pizza Čuk	12 A2
Pizzeria Minutka	13 D1
Self-Service Restaurant	14 B1
Zmajev Hram	15 A1

DRINKING	
Boem Bar	16 D1
Riziko	(see 10)

TRANSPORT	
Bus Station	17 B3
Čeho Bike Rental	18 A3

THE HUMAN FISH

Proteus anguinus is one of the most mysterious creatures in the world. A kind of salamander, but related to no other amphibian, it is the largest known permanent cave-dwelling vertebrate. The blind little fellow lives hidden in the pitch black for up to a century and can go for years without food.

The chronicler Valvasor wrote about the fear and astonishment of local people when an immature 'dragon' was found in a karst spring near Vrhnika in the late 17th century, but he judged it to be 'an underground worm'. Several other reports about this four-legged 'human fish' (*človeška ribica* as it's called in Slovene) were made before a doctor in Vienna realised its uniqueness in 1768. In announcing its existence to the scientific world, he called it *'Proteus anguinus'*, after the protector of Poseidon's sea creatures in Greek mythology and the Latin word for 'snake'.

Proteus anguinus is 25cm to 30cm long and a bundle of contradictions. It has a long tail fin that it uses for swimming, but can also propel itself with its four legs (the front pair have three small 'fingers' and the back have two 'toes'). Although blind, with atrophied, almost invisible eyes, *Proteus anguinus* has an excellent sense of smell and is sensitive to weak electric fields in the water. It uses these to move around in the dark, locate prey and communicate. It breathes through frilly, bright-red gills at the base of its head when submerged, but also has rudimentary lungs for breathing when outside the water. The humanlike skin has no pigmentation whatsoever, but looks pink in the light due to blood circulation.

The question that scientists have asked themselves for three centuries is: how do the beasties reproduce? The creatures' reproduction has never been witnessed in a natural state, and they haven't been very cooperative in captivity. It is almost certain that they hatch their young from eggs and don't reach sexual maturity until the (almost human) age of 16 or 18.

---

also bizarre columns, pillars and translucent curtains that look like rashers of bacon.

From the Velika Gora cavern you continue across the **Russian Bridge**, built by prisoners of war in 1916, through the 500m-long **Beautiful Caves** (Lepe Jame) that are filled with wonderful ribbon-shaped stalactites and stalagmites two million years old (it takes 30 years to produce 1mm of stalactite). The halls of the Beautiful Caves are the furthest point you'll reach; from here a tunnel stretches to the Black Cave (Črna Jama) and Pivka Cave (p186).

The tour continues south through the Winter Hall (Zimska Dvorana), past the Diamond Stalagmite and the Pillar Column, which have become symbols of the cave. You then enter the Concert Hall (Koncertna Dvorana), which is the largest in the cave system and can accommodate 10,000 people for musical performances. In the week between Christmas and New Year, the Live Christmas Crib (Jaslice) – the Nativity performed by actors – also takes place in the cave.

The bizarre pink creatures you'll see in a tank at the end of the tour are *Proteus anguinus,* unique 'human fish' first described by Janez Vajkard Valvasor (see above).

Postojna Cave has a constant temperature of between 8°C and 10°C with a humidity of 95%, so a waterproof jacket is essential. Green felt cloaks can be hired at the entrance for €2. Check the website for package deals including combination tickets.

Two hundred species of fauna (including cave beetles, bats, hedgehogs, and the 'human fish') found in the cave are studied at **Proteus Vivarium** (adult/child/student €7/4.30/5, incl Postojna Cave €21/12.70/15.85; ⏰ 8.30am-6.30pm May-Sep; 9.30am-4.30pm Apr & Oct; 9.30am-2.30pm Mon-Fri, 9.30am-4pm Sat & Sun Nov-Mar), part of a speleobiological research station located in the cave. It is open to visitors and has a video introduction to underground zoology. A 45-minute tour then leads you into a small, darkened cave to peep at some of the shy creatures you've just learned about.

OTHER CAVES

For more information about other caves north of Postojna ask at the Tourist Information Centre Postojna at Postojna Cave, or at Kompas Postojna (opposite) in town.

Otok Cave (Otoška Jama; admission €7.10; ⏰ by appointment), some 1.5km northwest of Postojna Cave, is very small (632m in length) and the tour only takes about an hour, but its stalagmites and stalactites are very impressive. There's no electric lighting, so you'll need a torch, and the temperature is 8°C.

NOTRANJSKA

Pivka Cave (Pivka Jama) and **Black Cave** (Črna Jama; admission €7.10; ☺ by appointment) – the most popular caves after Postojna – are about 5km to the north. The entrance is in the Pivka Jama camping ground. You reach the 4km-long system by descending more than 300 steps. A walkway has been cut into the wall of a canyon in Pivka Cave, with its two siphon lakes and a tunnel, and a bridge leads to Black Cave. This is a dry cavern and, as the name implies, its dripstones are not white. A tour of both caves takes about two hours.

Planina Cave (Planinska Jama; ☎ 041-338 696; admission €7.10; ☺ tours 5pm Mon-Fri Jul & Aug; 3pm & 5pm Sat, 11am, 3pm & 5pm Sun Apr-Sep), 12km to the northeast near the unpredictable Lake Planina, is the largest water cave in Slovenia and a treasure-trove of fauna (which includes *Proteus anguinus*). The cave's entrance is at the foot of a 100m rock wall. It's 6.5km long, and you are able to visit about 900m of it in an hour. There are no lights so take a torch. Many parts of the cave are accessible only in low water or by rubber raft.

MOUNTAIN BIKING & CAVING

True to its name, the Hotel & Hostel Sport (right) can arrange all sorts of activities, including weekend packages with mountain-biking trips in nearby Notranjska Regional Park, and caving under Predjama Castle starting at €140 per person with room and half-board. They rent mountain bikes for €8.40/14.60 per half/full day.

Sleeping

Kompas (p184) can organise private rooms (per person €13.90 to 15.80) in town and farmhouse stays (per person €21) further afield in Narin (15km southwest) and Razdrto (11km west). The most central rooms are at Jamska cesta 21 and Vilharjeva ulica 17.

Camping Pivka Jama (☎ 720 39 93; www.venus-trade .si; Veliki Otok 50; camping €9.40-10.30, child €7.20-8.10, 4-bed bungalow €66.80-77.20, 4-bed bungalow with kitchen €83.50-91.80; ☺ Mar-Oct; P Ⓡ Ⓖ) This 7-hectare site is in a pine forest near the entrance to Pivka and Black Caves. Some of the little stone-and-wood bungalows have kitchens and there's a swimming pool.

Hotel Jama (☎ 728 24 00; www.postojna-cave.com; Jamska cesta 28; s €40-50, d €60-80; P ⊠ Ⓡ) This 267-bed property 200m southeast of the entrance to Postojna Cave has had something of a facelift in recent years, but there is little

reason to stay out here unless you want to be the first person in the cave in the morning.

Eating & Drinking

Pizza Čuk (☎ 720 13 00; Pot k Pivki 4; pizza €3.90-5.45; ☺ 10am-10pm Mon-Thu, 10am-11pm Fri, noon-11pm Sat, noon-10pm Sun) More central but not as good as Pizzeria Minutka, Čuk is southwest of Titov trg just off Tržaška cesta.

Pizzeria Minutka (☎ 720 36 25; Ljubljanska cesta 14; pizza €4.20-5.85, mains €5.85-8.35) A pizzeria with a terrace, Minutka is a favourite with locals and also does more ambitious main courses.

Jadran (☎ 720 39 00; Titov trg 1; starters €3.35-5.45, mains €5.85-10; ☺ 9am-10pm) This central, old-style restaurant has a good selection of reasonably priced fish dishes and friendly – if not silver – service.

Zmajev Hram (☎ 700 01 81; set menus €8-28; ☺ 9am-6pm May-Dec, 9am-3pm Jan-Apr) Housed in a stunning (and totally revamped) 1920s-style building next to the cave entrance, the 'Cave Restaurant' has a dozen set menus from which to choose. There's also a much cheaper self-service restaurant (dishes €4) nearby, open from 8am to 6pm.

There are a couple of central places for self-catering in Postojna town, including **Mercator** (Tržaška cesta 9; ☺ 7am-8pm Mon-Fri, 7am-1pm Sat, 8am-noon Sun) and the almost round-the-clock **Noč in Dan** (Ljubljanska cesta 13; ☺ 5am-midnight Mon-Fri, 24hr Sat & Sun).

Two places worth heading for if the whistle is dry include central **Boem Bar** (☎ 726 13 11; Ljubljanska cesta 11; ☺ 6am-midnight), a comfortable place near the Hotel & Hostel Sport, and **Riziko** (Tržaška cesta 9; ☺ 7am-11pm Mon-Thu, 7am-midnight Fri, 8am-3am Sat, 8am-11pm Sun) above Mercator, which attracts a very young (think skateboarders) crowd.

Getting There & Around

Buses from Ljubljana to the coast as well as Nova Gorica stop in Postojna (€5.75, one hour, 53km, half-hourly). Other destinations include Cerknica (€3, 30 minutes, 24km, four on schooldays), Koper (€6.15, one hour, 56km, four to six a day), Nova Gorica (€6.15, one hour, 58km, five to eight a day), Piran (€6.65, 1¼ hours, 69km, three or four a day), and Snežnik and Stari Trg pri Ložu (€8, two hours, 88km, one on schooldays at 2.10pm).

International destinations include Zagreb (€16.50, three hours, 195km, one daily at 6.07am) in Croatia, and Trieste (€5.75, 1½ hours, 51km, one at 6.50am Monday to Saturday) in northern Italy.

Postojna is on the main train line linking Ljubljana (€5.90, one hour, 67km) with Sežana and Trieste via Divača (€2.65 to €4.30, 40 minutes, 37km), and is an easy day trip from the capital. As many as 20 trains a day make the run from Ljubljana to Postojna and back. You can also reach here from Koper (€5.35 to €6.75, 1½ hours, 86km) on one of up to seven trains a day.

Čeho Bike Rental (☎ 040-169 401; Tržaška cesta 23; 9am-noon & 3-7pm Mon-Fri, 9am-noon Sat) has bicycles for rent; they cost €5 for three hours or €10 per day.

If you need a taxi in Postojna, call ☎ 031-777 974.

PREDJAMA CASTLE

☎ 05 / elev 490m

Situated in the gaping mouth of a cavern halfway up a 123m cliff just 9km northwest of Postojna, **Predjama Castle** (Predjamski Grad; ☎ 751 60 15; www.postojna-cave.com; adult/child/student €7/4.30/5; 9am-7pm May-Sep, 10am-6pm Apr & Oct, 10am-4pm Nov-Mar) has a dramatic setting. Although a castle has stood on the site since 1202, the one you see today dates from the 16th century. Then – as now – the four-storey fortress looked unconquerable.

The castle's eight rooms contain little of interest – oil paintings, weapons, a 15th-century pietà – but the castle does have a drawbridge over a raging river, holes in the ceiling of the entrance tower for pouring boiling oil on intruders, a very dank dungeon, a 16th-century chest full of treasure (unearthed in the cellar in 1991), and an eyrie-like hiding place at the top called Erazem's Nook.

The **cave** (Jama pod Predjamskim Gradom; adult/child/student €5/3.30/4; tours 11am, 1pm, 3pm & 5pm May-Sep) below Predjama Castle is a 6km network of galleries spread over four levels. Much of it is open only to speleologists, however casual visitors can see about 900m of it. Longer tours that go to the end of the cave's **Eastern Passage** (€42, six hours) or **Erazem's Gallery** (Erazmov Rov, €16, one hour) are available by prior arrangement only.

Gostilna Požar (☎ 751 52 52; Predjama 2; meals from €14.50; 10am-10pm Thu-Tue) is a simple restaurant conveniently located next to the ticket kiosk and in full heart-stopping view of the castle.

The closest you'll get by local bus to Predjama from Postojna is Bukovje (€1.70, 15 minutes, 9km, five a day weekdays), and buses run during the school year only. Bukovje is a village about 2km northeast of Predjama. A taxi from Postojna, including an hour's wait at the castle, will cost €25, which staff at Kompas Postojna (p184) can arrange.

DEATH ON THE THRONE

Erazem Lueger was a 15th-century robber baron who, like Robin Hood, waylaid wagons in the deep forest, stole the loot and handed it over to the poor. During the wars between the Hungarians (under 'good' King Matthias Corvinus) and the Austrians (behind 'wicked' Frederick III), Lueger (naturally) supported the former. He holed up Predjama Castle and continued his daring deeds with the help of a secret passage that led out from behind the rock wall.

In the autumn of 1484 the Austrian army under Gašpar Ravbar, the governor of Trieste, attacked the castle, but it proved impregnable for months. All the while Erazem mocked Ravbar and his soldiers, even showering them with fresh cherries to prove that he came and went as he pleased.

But Erazem proved to be too big for his breeches and met an ignoble fate. Having gone 'to where even the sultan must go on foot' (as Valvasor described it), Erazem was hit by a cannon ball as he sat on the toilet. It seems a turncoat servant had betrayed him, by marking the location of the water closet with a little flag, for Ravbar and his men.

CERKNICA

☎ 01 / pop 3540 / elev 559m

Cerknica is the largest town on a lake that isn't always a lake – one of Slovenia's most unusual natural phenomena. It's close to Notranjska Regional Park and the gorge at Rakov Škocjan.

The area around Lake Cerknica has been settled since prehistoric times, and a trade route once ran over the Bloke Plateau to the east, linking Slovenia and Croatia. During the Roman period, Cerknica was a stopover on the road leading from Emona (Ljubljana) to the coast. Cerknica was given town status in the 11th century.

But Cerknica is a good example of how important communication lines are for the development of a town. The railway linking Trieste and Ljubljana opened in 1857, but it dodged Cerknica in favour of Rakek, 5km to the northwest. The highway from Ljubljana towards the coast follows the same route, and Cerknica remains something of a backwater.

Orientation

Cerknica lies about 3km north of Lake Cerknica. Cesta 4 Maja is the main street in the centre of town. The bus station is on Čabranska ulica about 100m to the southwest and behind the post office.

Information

Notranjska Regional Park (Notranjski Regijski Park; ☎ 031-655 993; www.notranjski-park.si in Slovene; Tabor 42; ☉ by appointment) Headquarters of the new 22,810-hectare park 100m north of the tourist office.

Nova Ljubljanska Banka (Cesta 4 Maja 64) In the Imam shopping centre.

Post office (Cesta 4 Maja 52; ☉ 8am-7pm Mon-Fri, 8am-noon Sat) Next door to the tourist office.

SKB Banka (Partizanska cesta 1) Next door to Valvasor Hram.

Tourist Information Centre Cerknica (☎ 709 36 36, 041-510 047; tdrustvo@volja.net; Cesta 4 Maja 51; ☉ 8am-3pm Mon-Fri)

Sights

PARISH CHURCH OF OUR LADY

Sitting atop a gentle slope 200m north of Cesta 4 Maja, the Parish Church of Our Lady (Župnijska Cerkev Sv Marije) is the only real attraction right in Cerknica. To reach it, walk up the street called simply Tabor, which runs to the east of the shopping centre.

The church sat in the middle of a fortified settlement; the ramparts and two towers, built to withstand Turkish raids in the late 15th century, remain intact. On the Latin plaque in the wall, the number four of the year 1472 is written with a loop – the top half of an eight – because four was considered unlucky in the Middle Ages.

Completed in the early 16th century, this is a hall church – with nave and aisles of equal height – and not unlike the church (p102) in Kranj in Gorenjska. In the 18th century two side chapels were added, and the bell tower was given its baroque dome.

LAKE CERKNICA

Since ancient times periodic Lake Cerknica (Cerniško Jezero) has baffled and perplexed people, including the Greek geographer and historian Strabo (63 BC–AD 24), who called the mysterious body of water Lacus Lugeus (Mourning Lake). It wasn't until Valvasor explained how the water system worked at the end of the 17th century that it was fully understood.

Cerknica is a polje, a field above a collapsed karst cavern full of sinkholes, potholes, siphons and underground tunnels, which can stay dry for much of the year but then floods. From the south, the polje is fed by a disappearing river, the Stržen, and to the east and west it collects water underground from the Bloke Plateau and the Javornik Mountains. During rainy periods in the autumn and spring, all this water comes rushing into the polje. Springs emerge and the water begins to percolate between the rocks. The sinkholes and siphons cannot handle the outflow underground, and the polje becomes Lake Cerknica – sometimes in less than a day.

The surface area of Lake Cerknica can reach 24 sq km, but it is never more than a few metres deep. At that time it is an important wetland, attracting some 200 species of birds each year. During dry periods (usually July to September or later), farmers drive cattle down to the polje to graze.

The lake really begins at the village of Dolenje Jezero (population 225), about 2.5km south of Cerknica, where you will find the **Lake House Museum** (Muzej Jezerski Hram; ☎ 709 40 53, 041-561 870; www.jezerski-hram.si; adult/child €3/2; ☉ demonstration 3pm Sat), with a 5m by 3m, 1:2500 scale working model of Lake Cerknica, showing how the underground hydrological system

lonelyplanet.com

NOTRANJSKA •• Cerknica **189**

BIG MEN FOR BIG TIMES

Slovenian folk tales are rife with fairies, witches and things that go bump in the night, but among the most common stories are those describing the derring-do of 'super heroes', whose strong wills and unusual strength enabled them to overcome evil and conquer their brutish enemies.

The legends are not limited to one geographical area. Peter Klepec, who swept away his enemies using trees uprooted with his bare hands, lived on the Kolpa River and is associated with Bela Krajina. Another hero called Kumprej ruled the Upper Savinja Valley in Štajerska with his mighty voice and fearsome blade. His shoes were five times larger than those of the average person and when he disappeared shoeless a poor couple made footwear for their entire family from the clodhoppers.

But perhaps the most popular stories revolve around the feats of one Martin Krpan, the hero of the Bloke Plateau in Notranjska. Krpan's traits and characteristics are familiar. He was an outlaw with a big heart hunted by the imperial guard for smuggling salt. When he was arrested, Martin Krpan proved his super-human strength to the emperor in Vienna by picking up and carrying his own horse.

Realising his fortune at having such a powerful giant under his control, the emperor set Martin Krpan on Berdavs, the local scourge and personification of the marauding Turk. Martin Krpan defeated Berdavs and chopped off his head with his magic axe – complete with a handle made of Slovenian linden wood. For his pains the imperial court allowed him to freely transport and sell salt.

The tales of Martin Krpan are traditional but reached a wider audience when the writer Fran Levstik collected and published them under the title *Martin Krpan* in 1858.

actually works. There's also an ethnological collection.

RAKOV ŠKOCJAN

Protected Rakov Škocjan is a 6km-long gorge lying some 5km west of Cerknica. The Rak River, en route to join the Pivka River at Planina Cave, has sculpted 2.5km of hollows, caves, springs and **Veliki** and **Mali Naravni Most**, the Big and Little Natural Bridges. There are lots of hiking and biking trails through and around the gorge and the area surrounding it is a protected country park. To the south lies the Snežnik-Javornik Massif, including its tallest peak, **Veliki Javornik** (1268m).

From Rakek train station (p190), you can reach the gorge on foot in about an hour.

Activities

The tourist office sells **fishing licences** (lake/Rak River/Unica River fly-fishing per day €96/10/10) and has **boat rentals** on the lake.

The **Kontrabantar farmhouse** (☎ 709 22 53; Dolenja Vas 72; per hr €8; noon–10pm Thu–Sun) in Dolenja Vas, 2km southwest of Cerknica, has horses and offers riding lessons, as well as tours by coach around the lake.

The staff at the **Hotel Rakov Škocjan** (p190) can organise any number of activities, from hiking (from €20 per person) and caving

(from €23) to cycling and fishing in the surrounding park. They offer packages such as one that includes accommodation, half-board, a bicycle and a trip to Križna Cave (p191) for €38 per person per day in a double . Ask them for the free English-language booklet *Rakov Škocjan and the Nature Trail*.

The **Cerknica Mountain Trail** heads southwest from Cerknica to thickly forested **Veliki Javornik** (1268m). From here you can take a side trip of about two hours to the gorge at Rakov Škocjan (left). Otherwise the trail skirts the southern shore of Lake Cerknica and carries on northeast to **Križna Gora** (857m) and its nearby **cave** (p191). It continues northwest to **Slivnica** (1114m), home of the witch Uršula and other sorcerers, where you will find the mountaintop guesthouse Dom na Slivnici (p190). The next day you walk north northwest to **Stražišče** (955m) and then south along the main road for 3km to Cerknica.

Festivals & Events

Cerknica is famous for its pre-Lenten carnival called **Pustni Karneval** (www.cerknica.net/pust), which takes place for four days over the weekend before Ash Wednesday (late February/early March). Merrymakers wearing masks of Uršula, who makes her home on Mt Slivnica, and other legendary characters parade up and

NOTRANJSKA

down Cesta 4 Maja while being provoked by upstarts with pitchforks.

Sleeping & Eating

Domačija Zigmund (☎ 709 15 25, 041-601 661; Žerovnica 54; r/apt per person €16.70/14.60; **P**) This farmhouse at the end of Žerovnica, an idyllic village some 6km southeast of Cerknica, has rooms as well as a four-person apartment. You'll need your own transport.

Dom na Slivnici (☎ 709 41 40, 041-518 108; per person €18.50; ☽ daily May-Sep, Sat & Sun Oct-Apr; **P**) This splendidly positioned five-room guesthouse (with 12 beds) atop Mt Slivnica is accesible by foot, or by road 8km east of Cerknica.

TeLiCo (☎ 709 70 90, 041-711 088; Brestova ulica 9; s/d €23/35.50; **P** ☻) This small seven-bed B&B on the eastern edge of town, with two double rooms with shared bathroom and WC, has stunning views and its own swimming pool.

Valvasorjev Hram (☎ 709 37 88; Partizanska cesta 1; dishes €2.50-3.10; ☽ 8am-11pm Mon-Fri, 10am-11pm Sat & Sun) This very basic place opposite the tourist office serves hearty dishes like *jota* (bean soup) and *klobasa* (sausage) as well as pizza, and has its own wine cellar.

Pizzeria Glaž'k (☎ 709 33 44; Partizanska cesta 17; ☽ 7am-11pm Mon-Fri, 7am-midnight Sat) This basic pizzeria is up a gentle slope 200m north of Cesta 4 Maja and across from the 16th-century Parish Church of Our Lady. Set lunch is a bargain at €3.

You'll find a large **Mercator** (Cesta 4 Maja 64; ☽ 7am-8pm Mon-Fri, 7am-1pm Sat, 8am-noon Sun) in the Imam shopping centre west of the centre, and a smaller **Mercator** (Cesta 4 Maja 50; ☽ 7am-9pm Mon-Sat, 8am-noon Sun) diagonally opposite the tourist office.

THE AUTHOR'S CHOICE

Hotel Rakov Škocjan (☎ 709 74 70, 051-310 477; www.h-rakovskocjan.com; Rakov Škocjan 1; s/d/tr €42/70/98; **P** ✗ ☐) In the heart of Rakov Škocjan Country Park and surrounded by deep forest ribboned with hiking and cycling trails, this 13-room guesthouse 7km west of Cerknica is the ideal spot for a no-holds-barred active holiday (p189). It has a sauna and an excellent game restaurant (meals from €12; open 7am to 10pm) that serves nonguests as well, with outdoor grill and terrace seating in the warmer months.

Getting There & Around

Buses run between Cerknica and Ljubljana (€5.50, one hour, 49km, six to eight a day) and Postojna (€3, 30 minutes, 24km, four on schooldays). In addition about half a dozen go to Rakek (€1.70, 10 minutes, 8km) and Stari Trg pri Ložu (€6.50, 1½ hours, 64km). Three buses a day cross the Croatian border to Previd (€3.50, one hour, 30km) at 5.17am, 6.22am and 3.37pm.

Rakek, about 8km northwest of Cerknica, is on the rail line that connects Ljubljana with Sežana. About 10 trains a day to and from the capital stop at Rakek (€3.90 to €5.30, one hour, 55km). Heading south, all stop at Postojna (€1.50, 15 minutes, 12km) and Pivka, but only about half continue on to Divača (€3.30, 50 minutes, 49km) and Sežana.

The Hotel Rakov Škocjan (left) rents bicycles for €2/4.50/15 per hour/day/week.

SNEŽNIK CASTLE
☎ 01 / elev 593m

Just south of the village of Kozarišče (population 240), in the secluded Lož Valley (Loška Dolina) some 21km southeast of Cerknica, stands 16th-century Renaissance **Snežnik Castle** (Grad Snežnik; ☎ 705 78 14; www.postojna-cave .com). Surrounded by a large and protected park, it is one of the loveliest and best-situated fortresses in Slovenia. The entrance to the castle, formerly the property of the Schönburg-Waldenburg family, who used what they called Schneeberg as a summer residence and a hunting lodge until WWII, is through a double barbican with a drawbridge and moat. Unfortunately the castle is currently undergoing massive renovations and remains closed to the public.

In the 19th-century dairy building adjacent to the castle, resides the rather esoteric **Dormouse Museum & Hunting Collection** (Polharska Muzej in Lovska Zbirka; ☎ 705 75 16, 031-288 470; Kozarišče 70; adult/child €1.25/1; ☽ 10am-1pm & 3-6pm Wed-Fri, 10am-1pm & 2-6pm Sat & Sun mid-Apr–Oct). The dormouse (p50) or loir *(polh)* is a favourite food in Notranjska and the hunting and eating of it is tied up with a lot of tradition, which the museum explores. The fur is used to make the *polhovka*, the distinctive fur cap worn by Božiček, Slovenia's version of Santa Claus, and dormouse *mast* (fat) is a much-prized machine oil. According to popular belief, the dormouse is shepherded by Lucifer himself and thus deserves its fate in the cooking pot.

The hunting part of the museum is a nightmare of stuffed animals, antlers and other 'trophies' from the Snežnik-Javornik Massif and Cerknica Lake areas

The big occasion in these parts of Notranjska is **Dormouse Night** (Polharska Noč) when it's open season for trapping the incredible edible *polh*. It's held on the first Saturday after 25 September.

Snežnik Castle's isolation makes it tough to reach by public transport. Without a car, bicycle or horse, you'll have to take a bus from Cerknica to Stari Trg pri Ložu (€6.50, 1½ hours, 64km, up to six a day) and walk 4km. Staff at the Hotel Rakov Škocjan (opposite) in the country park, some 30km to the northwest, can arrange transport to and from the castle.

Križna Cave (www.kovinoplastika.si/gsk/krizna-jama; adult/child €5/2.50; ☉ 3pm Sun May-Oct), about 7km north of Snežnik Castle and a kilometre or so after you turn off the main road from Cerknica, is one of the most magnificent water caves in the world.

It is 8.8km long and counts 22 underground lakes filled with green and blue water as well as a unique 'forest' of ice stalagmites near the entrance. The dry part of the cave, which includes a short boat ride, can be toured without booking in advance. To go as far as the Kalvarija chamber by rubber raft via 13 lakes (€25 to €29), you must contact the guide named Alojz Troha (☎ 041-632 153; krizna_jama@yahoo.com), in Bloška Polica (house No 7) near Grahovo, in advance. It's a four-hour tour if you elect to do the entire cave, and the price includes all equipment.

A stage of the E6 European Hiking Trail (p43) leads south from near Snežnik Castle for about 15km to **Snežnik** (1796m), the highest non-Alpine mountain in Slovenia, whose peak remains covered in snow until well into the spring. There is accommodation at the Category I PZS-maintained hut **Koča Draga Karolina na Velikem Snežniku** (☎ 041-333 198, 041-447 339; ☉ Sat & Sun May-Jul, Sep & Oct; daily Aug).

Dolenjska &
Bela Krajina

'Lower Carniola' is a gentle area of rolling hills, vineyards, forests and the Krka River flowing southeastward into Croatia. Those white hilltop churches with their red-tile roofs you'll see everywhere once protected the people from the marauding Turks and other invaders; the ones on the flat lands are newer – built in the baroque style and painted the mustard colour ('Maria Theresa yellow') so common in Central Europe.

There's something of a dichotomy in the way the rest of Slovenia views Dolenjci, the natives of the charming Dolenjska province. On the one hand they are portrayed in comic sketches and literature as being unsophisticated, even dull-witted, country bumpkins. On the other hand, many people say that the 'purest' Slovene is spoken in Dolenjska – around the village of Rašica, south of the town of Krka, to be precise.

The E6 and E7 European Hiking trails pass through Dolenjska, and there are lots of chances to do some kayaking or canoeing on the Krka. The province is also the cycling centre of Slovenia and famous for its thermal spas.

Bela Krajina, the 'White March' of southeastern Slovenia, is separated from Dolenjska by the scenic Gorjanci mountain range. The province, which takes its name from the countless stands of birch trees dotting the province, is a treasure trove of Slovenian folklore, and, if you're lucky, you'll see more traditional dance and hear more music here than anywhere else in the country, particularly around Črnomelj and Adlešiči.

HIGHLIGHTS

- Go cycling along the picturesque **valley** (p198) of the Krka River
- Go on safari with a camera in the virgin forests of **Kočevski Rog** (p202)
- Walk back in time at **Bogenšperk Castle** (p197), especially in the late great Janez Vajkard Valvasor's study
- Make a pilgrimage to the **Three Parishes** (p218) churches in Rosalnice near Metlika
- Enjoy the almost medieval merrymaking of the **Jurjevanje** (p220) festival in Črnomelj in mid-June

History

Dolenjska was settled early on and is well known for its Hallstatt (early Iron Age) ruins, especially near Stična, Šmarjeta and Novo Mesto. The Romans made the area part of the province of Upper Pannonia (Pannonia Superior) and built roads connecting Emona (Ljubljana) with smaller settlements.

In the Middle Ages, the people of Dolenjska clustered around the many castles along the Krka (eg at Žužemberk and Otočec), and monasteries sprang up at Stična, Kostanjevica na Krki and near Šentjernej. Dolenjska declined after the Middle Ages and progress only came in the late 19th century when a railway line linked Novo Mesto with Ljubljana.

Like Dolenjska, Bela Krajina is famous for its Hallstatt and Roman sites; a 3rd-century shrine to the god Mithra near the village of Rožanec (p221) is one of the best preserved in Europe. In the Middle Ages, Bela Krajina was the remotest part of Slovenia, and in some ways it still feels like that. Many of the peasant uprisings of the 15th and 16th centuries started here or across the border in Croatia.

DOLENJSKA

The castles along the Krka River in Dolenjska are some of the best preserved in Slovenia, as are the many monasteries and abbeys. Keep an eye out for Dolenjska's distinctive *toplarji* (double hayracks).

RIBNICA

☎ 01 / pop 3490 / elev 489m

Though Ribnica is the oldest and most important settlement of western Dolenjska and just over the hills from the border with Notranjska, people in this region have traditionally affiliated with neither province. As far as they are concerned, this is Kočevsko, a forested, sparsely inhabited area with a unique history.

Ribnica was an important feudal centre during the Middle Ages and was ruled by a succession of lords, including the Counts of Celje, before the Habsburgs arrived. Like neighbouring Notranjska and Bela Krajina to the southeast, Kočevsko suffered greatly from the Turkish invasions of the 15th century.

Orientation

Ribnica's main street, Škrabčev trg, lies on the east bank of the tiny Bistrica River and runs parallel to it. Buses stop in front of the Parish Church of St Stephen.

Information

Nova Ljubljanska Banka (Škrabčev trg 9b; ☺ 8.30am-noon & 2.30-4.30pm Mon-Fri) Southeast of the Church of St Stephen.
Post office (Kolodvorska ulica 2)
Tourist Information Centre Ribnica (☎ 836 93 35, 051-415 429; turizem.ribnica@siol.net; Škrabčev trg 23; ☺ 9am-4pm Mon-Fri, 8am-noon Sat)

Sights

On the west bank of the Bistrica, **Ribnica Castle** (Ribniški Grad; Gallusovo nabrežje 1) was originally built in the 11th century but was transformed and expanded over the centuries. Only a small section – a Renaissance wall and two towers – survived bombings during WWII. Today the castle houses a small **ethnographic collection** (☎ 835 03 76, 041-390 057; adult/child/student €1.70/0.85/1.25; ☺ 10am-1pm & 4-7pm Tue-Sun) showcasing the traditional woodcrafts and pottery made in the area. The castle, set in an attractive semicircular park with memorial statues and markers to Slovenian greats, is a popular venue for weddings.

The **Parish Church of St Stephen** (Župnijska Cerkev Sv Štefana; Škrabčev trg), built in 1868 on the site of earlier churches, would not be of much interest were it not for the two striking towers added by Jože Plečnik in 1960 to replace the ones toppled during WWII.

Opposite the church is **Šteklíček House** (Šteklíčkova Hiša; Škrabčev trg 16); the plaque attached to it explains that the 19th-century poet and patriot France Prešeren spent two years here (1810–12) in what was then the region's best-known school.

The gallery at **Mikel House** (Miklova Hiša; ☎ 835 03 76; Škrabčev trg 21; admission free; ☺ 10am-noon & 4-6pm), a lovely cream-and-white building dating from 1858, is renowned for its cutting-edge exhibitions of contemporary art.

Activities

Ribnica is the base for many excellent walks. A well-marked 'science education trail' leads north of the town for about 4.5km to the summit of **Stene Sv Ana** (963m), with fantastic views over the Ribnica Valley; ask the tourist office for a copy of the *Natural Heritage of Ribnica* pamphlet. Along the way you'll pass the entrance to France Cave and the hilltop Church of St Anne (930m).

DOLENJSKA & BELA KRAJINA

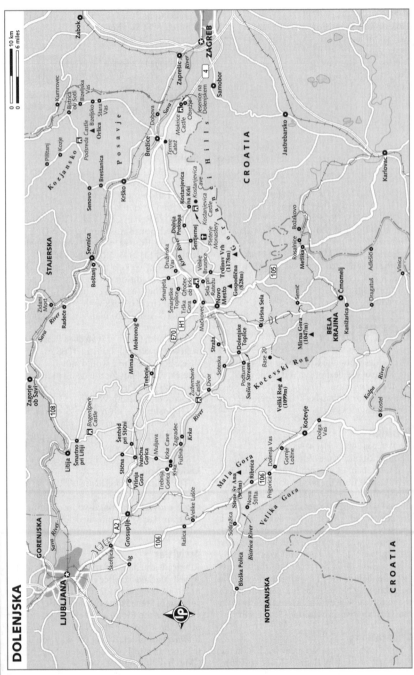

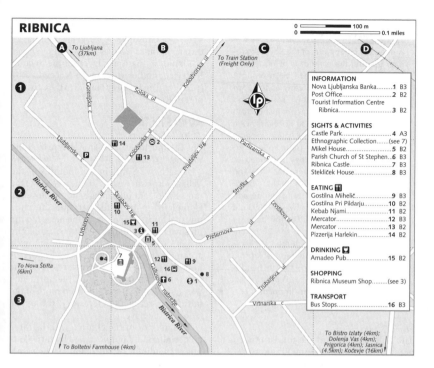

RIBNICA

INFORMATION	
Nova Ljubljanska Banka	1 B3
Post Office	2 B2
Tourist Information Centre Ribnica	3 B2

SIGHTS & ACTIVITIES	
Castle Park	4 A3
Ethnographic Collection	(see 7)
Mikel House	5 B2
Parish Church of St Stephen	6 B3
Ribnica Castle	7 B3
Steklíček House	8 B3

EATING	
Gostilna Mihelič	9 B3
Gostilna Pri Pildarju	10 B2
Kebab Njami	11 B2
Mercator	12 B3
Mercator	13 B2
Pizzerija Harlekin	14 B2

DRINKING	
Amadeo Pub	15 B2

SHOPPING	
Ribnica Museum Shop	(see 3)

TRANSPORT	
Bus Stops	16 B3

From the Jasnica recreational centre (on the way to Kočevje), where horses are available for hire, a more difficult path leads north about 6km to the junction with the Ribnica Alpine Trail. This joins up with the E7 European Hiking Trail about 5km west of Velike Lašče.

A trail into the Velika Gora ridge west of Ribnica that leads to a comfortable mountain hut is more easily accessible from Nova Štifta (p196).

Festivals & Events

Ribnica's main event is the **Dry Goods and Pottery Fair** (Ribniški Semenj Suhe Robe in Lončarstva; www.ribnica.si) held on the first Sunday in September, though most of the weekend is given over to music, drinking and, of course, buying and selling.

Sleeping

Bistro Izlaty (☎ 836 40 45; Prigorica 115; s/d €18/28; P) This small eatery 4km southeast of Ribnica on the road to Kočevje and less than 1km from the pottery village of Dolenja Vas has basic but comfortable accommodation.

Boltetni Farmhouse (☎ 836 02 08, 041-898 034; Dane 9; per person €21; May-Sep; P X) This engaging

farmhouse at Dane, an 'end-of-the-line' village 4km west of Ribnica, offers accommodation in three rooms and is about the best place to stay in the area.

Eating & Drinking

Kebab Njami (Škrabčev trg 36; dishes €1-2.80; 8am-11pm Mon-Sat, 10am-midnight Sun) This little hole-in-the-wall that stays awake while the rest of Ribnica sleeps sells kebabs and burgers.

Pizzerija Harlekin (☎ 836 15 32; Gorenjska cesta 4; pizzas €3.10-4.60; 10am-midnight Mon-Fri, 10am-11pm Sat) North of the centre, this convenient night owl serves pizzas and salads.

Gostilna Mihelič (☎ 836 31 31; Škrabčev trg 22; set menus €4.50-18.60; 9am-10pm Tue-Sat, 8am-4pm Sun) This place opposite the Church of St Stephen is one of the very few central places for a proper meal in Ribnica.

Gostilna Pri Pildarju (☎ 836 25 49; Škrabčev trg 27; meals from €12; 8am-3pm & 5-10pm Mon-Sat, 8am-2pm Sun) A few doors up from the tourist office, this cosy *gostilna* (innlike restaurant) is the most salubrious place for a meal in Ribnica.

Amadeo Pub (Škrabčev trg 25; 7am-11pm Mon-Thu, 7am-midnight Fri & Sat, 9am-midnight Sun) This convivial

DOLENJSKA & BELA KRAJINA

café-pub next door to the tourist office is a popular hang-out for young Ribničani.

There's a large **Mercator** (Kolodvorska ulica; 8am-5pm Mon-Fri, 8am-noon Sat) supermarket next to the post office. A more central **Mercator** (Škrabčev trg 19; 7am-7.30pm Mon-Fri, 7am-1pm Sat, 7-11am Sun) with extended hours is just up from the Church of St Stephen.

Shopping
Ribnica Museum Shop (Muzejska Trgovina Ribnica; 041-786 935; Škrabčev trg 23; 9am-noon & 4-7pm, 9am-6pm Sat) This long-overdue shop sharing space with the tourist office sells all manner of *suha roba* (wooden products) produced in the area, as well as clay pottery and whistles from nearby Dolenja Vas. The tourist office can help you arrange visits to master craftspeople in the area, including wood carvers at Sajevec (house No 16) and Kot (house No 26) and pottery throwers in Prigorica and Dolenja Vas.

Getting There & Around
Buses run at least hourly north to Ljubljana (€5, one hour, 44km), and south to Kočevje (€2.60, 30 minutes, 19km). The infrequent bus to Sodražica (€1.70, 15 minutes, 9km) is good for stopping in Nova Štifta.

Ribnica is no longer served by passenger train. The Grosuplje–Kočevje line that passes through Ribnica handles freight only.

Ribnica is 16km northwest of the town of Kočevje, another gateway to Kočevski Rog (p202), and on highway No 106 to the Croatian port of Rijeka.

NOVA ŠTIFTA
01 / elev 300m
The **Church of the Assumption of Mary** (Cerkev Marije Vnebovzete; 836 99 43, 041-747 188; 10am-noon & 2-6pm) at Nova Štifta, in the foothills of the Velika Gora 6km west of Ribnica, is one of the most important pilgrimage sites in Slovenia. Completed in 1671, the baroque church is unusual for its shape – both the nave and the presbytery are in the form of an octagon. The arcade on the west side fronting the entrance accommodated extra pilgrims on important holy days. The church proved so popular that the enclosed stairway on the north side was added in 1780 to allow even more of the faithful to reach the clerestory, the upper storey of the nave.

The interior of the church, with its three golden altars and pulpit carved by Jurij Skarnos, is blindingly ornate. Look for the painting of an aristocratic couple on stained glass on the north side of the presbytery. In the courtyard opposite the Franciscan monastery (where the church key is kept) stands a linden tree, planted in the mid-17th century, complete with a tree house that has been there for over a century.

Dom na Travni Gori (836 63 33; Ravni Dol 10; per person €15), a guesthouse 890m up with restaurant and accommodation, can be reached in about 1½ hours on a marked trail heading southwest from Nova Štifta.

STIČNA
01 / pop 710 / elev 357m
The abbey at Stična is the oldest monastery in Slovenia and one of the country's most important religious and cultural monuments. At only 35km from Ljubljana, Stična can be visited on a day trip from the capital or en route to Novo Mesto, the valley of the lower Krka or Bela Krajina.

Orientation
The village of Stična is about 2.5km north of Ivančna Gorica (population 1570), where you'll find the train station (Sokolska

ulica 1). Long-distance buses stop in front of the station.

Sights

Stična Abbey (Stiški Samostan; ☎ 787 71 00, 787 72 95; www2.pms-lj.si/sticna in Slovene; Stična 17; adult/student & child €3/1.70; ☼ 8am-noon & 2-5pm Tue-Sat, 2-5pm Sun, tours 8.30am, 10am, 2pm & 4pm Tue-Sat, 2pm & 4pm Sun) was established in 1136 by the Cistercians, a branch of the Benedictines who worked as farmers and observed a vow of silence. It became the most important religious, economic, educational and cultural centre in Dolenjska, but it was abandoned in 1784 when Emperor Joseph II dissolved all religious orders in the Habsburg Empire.

The Cistercians returned in 1898, and today almost the entire complex is again in use. There are currently some 15 priests and monks in residence.

The entrance to the walled monastery, an incredible combination of Romanesque, Gothic, Renaissance and baroque architecture, is on the east side across a small stream. On the north side of the central courtyard is the Old Prelature, a 17th-century Renaissance building, which contains the **Slovenian Religious Museum** (Slovenski Verski Muzej). Its permanent collection (History of Christianity in Slovenian) is on the 2nd floor. The museum is a hotchpotch of antique clocks, paintings, furniture and farm implements, mixed with chalices, monstrances and icons. There are a few 16th-century missals and medical texts in Latin and German, but all the medieval documents are facsimiles of the originals carted off to libraries in Vienna and Ljubljana when the order was disbanded.

On the west side of the courtyard the **Abbey Church** (1156) was built as a buttressed, three-nave Romanesque cathedral, but it was rebuilt in the baroque style in the 17th and 18th centuries. Look inside for the Renaissance red-marble tombstone of Abbot Jakob Reinprecht in the north transept and the blue organ cupboard with eight angels (1747) in the choir loft. The greatest treasures here are the Stations of the Cross painted in 1766 by Fortunat Bergant, who spelled his surname with a 'W' on the last one.

South of the church is Stična's celebrated vaulted cloister, which mixes Romanesque and early Gothic styles. The cloister served as an ambulatory for monks in prayer and connected the church with the monastery's other wings. The arches and vaults are decorated with frescoes of the prophets and Old Testament stories as well as allegorical subjects such as the Virtues and the Four Winds. Look for the carved stone faces on the west side that were meant to show human emotions and vices – upon which the clergy were expected to reflect.

On the south side of the cloister is a typically baroque monastic refectory, with an 18th-century pink ceiling and decorative swirls and loops made of white stucco. **Neff's Abbey**, built in the mid-16th century by Abbot Volbenk Neff, runs to the west. The arches in the vestibule on the ground floor are painted with a dense network of leaves, blossoms, berries and birds.

The Cistercians sell their own products (honey, wine, herbal teas, liqueurs) in a small **shop** (☼ 8am-4pm Mon-Fri, 8am-1pm Sat) at the abbey entrance.

Sleeping & Eating

Grofija (☎ /fax 787 81 41; Vir pri Stični 30; per person €21; P ✗) This 19th-century farmhouse called 'County' has four rooms and is 2km along a circuitous route southeast of the abbey.

Krjavel (☎ 787 71 10; Ljubljanska cesta 38; pizza €3.35-5.80, mains €4.60-6.70; ☼ 10am-11pm Jun-Sep, 8am-10pm Oct-May) This little place in Ivančna Gorica, about 150m northeast of the train station and just off the road to the abbey, serves local favourites and quite decent pizza.

You'll find a small **Tuš** (Stična 27a; ☼ 7am-7pm Mon-Fri, 7am-3pm Sat) supermarket just up the hill from the abbey. There's a much larger **Mercator** (Trg OF 1; ☼ 7am-7pm Mon-Fri, 7am-1pm Sat) in Ivančna Gorica just east of the train station.

Getting There & Away

Stična is served by up to a dozen buses a day from Ljubljana (€4.55, one hour, 38km) on weekdays, reducing to five on Saturday.

Ivančna Gorica is on the rail line linking Ljubljana with Novo Mesto, Črnomelj and Metlika. Up to 14 trains a day arrive from the capital (€2.65, one hour, 37km) with as many heading for Novo Mesto (€2.65, 45 minutes, 38km).

BOGENŠPERK CASTLE

☎ 01 / elev 172m
Just under 20km to the northeast of Stična is 16th-century **Bogenšperk Castle** (Grad Bogenšperk; ☎ 898 78 67, 041-703 992; www.bogensperk.si; Bogenšperk 5; adult/child/student €3/2.30/2.50; ☼ tours hourly 10am-

DOLENJSKA & BELA KRAJINA

5pm Tue-Sat, 10am-6pm Sun Apr-Oct; 9am-5pm Sat & Sun Nov-Mar). Here the celebrated Slovenian polymath Janez Vajkard Valvasor spent the most productive two decades of his life, writing and eventually publishing *The Glory of the Duchy of Carniola* (1689), his encyclopaedic work on Slovenian history, geography and culture.

Valvasor bought the Renaissance-style castle from the aristocratic Wagen family in 1672, and installed his printing press, engraving workshop and extensive library here. But due to the enormous debts incurred in getting his magnum opus published, he was forced to sell up 20 years later.

The castle, with its rectangular courtyard and three towers (the fourth was struck by lightning and burned down in the 19th century), houses a museum devoted to the great man, his work and Slovenian culture. Valvasor's library is now used as a wedding hall (complete with a cradle, as is traditional in Slovenia), but his study, with its beautiful parquetry, black limestone columns and painted ceiling, is pretty much the way he left it when he performed his last alchemy experiments here. Other rooms contain examples of Valvasor's original cartography and etching, an original four-volume set of his famous work, a printing press similar to the one he used himself and a collection of hunting trophies, including a 362kg brown bear shot at Banjaloka in Kočevski Rog in 1978. The most interesting exhibits, however, are the ones that deal with folk dress (life-size mannequins sport costumes modelled exactly on Valvasor's illustrations), superstition and folk medicine.

Bogenšperk is accessible from Ivančna Gorica only by car or bicycle. Trains link Ljubljana with Litija (€2.65, 30 minutes, 31km, up to two dozen a day), but it's still another 7km south to Bogenšperk – much of it uphill.

KRKA VALLEY

The Krka River springs from a karst cave southwest of Stična, near the village of Trebnja Gorica, and runs to the southeast and east until it joins the mightier Sava River near Brežice. At 94km it is Dolenjska's longest and most important waterway.

If you are continuing on to other towns in Dolenjska and/or Bela Krajina and have your own transport – car, bicycle or four-legged beastie – the ideal way to go is to follow route No 216 along the Krka River, which cuts a deep and picturesque valley along its upper course. Infrequent buses from Ljubljana to Novo Mesto via Dolenjske Toplice follow this route.

VALVASOR, SLOVENIA'S RENAISSANCE MAN

Most of our knowledge of Slovenian history, geography, culture and folklore before the 17th century comes from the writings of one man, Janez Vajkard Valvasor, and more specifically his book *The Glory of the Duchy of Carniola*.

Valvasor, whose name comes from the *valvassores* (the burghers who lived in the towns of the Holy Roman Empire in the early Middle Ages), was born to a noble family from Bergamo in 1641, in Ljubljana's Old Town – a plaque marks the spot in Stari trg. After a Jesuit education there and in Germany, he joined Miklós Zrínyi, the Hungarian count and poet, in the wars against the Turks and travelled widely, visiting Germany, Italy, North Africa, France and Switzerland. He collected data on natural phenomena and local customs as well as books, drawings, mineral specimens and coins.

In 1672 Valvasor installed himself, his books and his precious collections at Bogenšperk Castle, where he conducted scientific experiments (including alchemy) and wrote. In 1689 he completed his most important work. Published in German at Nuremburg under the title *Die Ehre des Herzogthums Crain* it ran to four volumes, comprising 3500 pages with 535 maps and copper engravings. *The Glory of the Duchy of Carniola* remains one of the most comprehensive works published in Europe before the Enlightenment, a wealth of information on the Slovenian patrimony that is still explored and studied to this day.

As is so often the case with great men and women in history, Valvasor did not live to enjoy the success of his labour. Publishing such a large work at his own expense ruined him financially and he was forced to leave Bogenšperk in 1692. Valvasor died a year later at Krško, a town 65km to the east on the Sava River.

Muljava

☎ 01 / pop 270 / elev 320m

This picturesque town of double hayracks and beehives is about 5km south of Ivančna Gorica. Muljava was the birthplace of Josip Jurčič (1844–81), whose book *The 10th Brother* is considered the first novel in Slovene.

The **Church of the Assumption** (Cerkev Marijinega Vnebovzetja; ☎ 780 60 32) lies east of the main road at the start of the village; seek the key from the vicarage opposite and to the north at No 39. Not all of the paintings in the presbytery and on the vaulted arches (Cain and Abel making their sacrifices, symbols of the Apostles and St Margaret) are very clear, but the fresco depicting the death of the Virgin Mary on the south wall is still vibrant. The frescoes are signed by Johannes de Laibaco (John of Ljubljana) and dated from 1456.

The **Josip Jurčič Museum** (Muzej Josipa Jurčiča; ☎ 787 65 00; Muljava 11; adult/child/student €2.70/2.30/2.50; ☺ 8am-noon & 2-5pm Tue-Fri, 2-5pm Sat & Sun) is housed in the author's birthplace, a small cottage 250m west of the main road. South of the house is a well-preserved *kozolec* (hayrack), and a beehive with 28 still-vibrant painted *panjske končnice* (front panels) from the 19th century.

Gostilna Pri Obrščaku (☎ 787 63 81; Muljava 22; meals from €10; ☺ 7am-9pm Mon, Tue & Thu-Sat, 8am-8pm Sun) is a roadside *gostilna* in Muljava with a covered terrace, which serves up hearty Slovenian fare like *klobasa in zelje* (sausage with sauerkraut).

There's a **Mercator** (Muljava 21; ☺ 7am-6pm Mon-Fri, 7am-1pm Sat) supermarket in the heart of Muljava.

Krka Cave

☎ 01 / elev 268m

Two kilometres from the main road and just west of the village of Trebnja Gorica, **Krka Cave** (Krška Jama; ☎ 780 60 72, 041-276 252; Krka 4; adult/child/student €1.25/1/0.65; ☺ 5-7pm Mon-Fri, 10am-1pm & 3-7pm Sat & Sun) isn't in the same league as Postojna or Škocjan Caves, but along the 1.9km route (a bit more than half the total length) you get to see some stalactites shaped like ribbons and fragile-looking 'spaghetti' and a siphon lake that is the source of the Krka River. The usual depth of the lake is 17m, but in winter – depending on the rain and the snowfall – the lake can rise almost as high as the ceiling. The cave temperature is 8°C to 9°C.

There are a number of farmhouses offering accommodation in the valley for between €15 and €18 per person, including **Magovac** (☎ 780 60 49, Krka 13), which has 11 beds.

Žužemberk

☎ 07 / pop 1085 / elev 220m

About 17km from Muljava, this is the site of mighty **Žužemberk Castle** (☎ 388 51 81, 041-324 710; Grajski trg 1; ☺ by arrangement), which is perched on a cliff overlooking the Krka River. First mentioned in 1295, the castle was completely rebuilt and the old walls fortified with round towers in the 16th century, only to be all but flattened during air raids in WWII. Five squat towers have been rebuilt or partially reconstructed, and renovations continue apace. The Castle Cellar (Grajska Klet) is the venue for the **Summer Castle Performances** (Poletne Grajske Prireditve), a series of concerts held from June to September.

ACTIVITIES

The 9km stretch of the Krka from its mouth to Zagradec, about halfway to Žužemberk, is one of Slovenia's most popular **fishing** spots. The season lasts from March to late October, and permits, available from Gostilna Pri Gradu, cost €25 a day.

The fast-flowing Krka offers excellent **kayaking** and **canoeing**, and Žužemberk is a good spot from which to set out. Any of the following outfits can kit you out:

Carpe Diem (☎ 780 60 11; Krka 27) In Krka.

Rafting Klub Gimpex Straža (☎ 384 75 36, 031-723 922; www.rafting-gimpex.com in Slovene; Stara Cesta 1) In Straža, 12km to the southeast of Žužemberk.

Žužemberk Kayak and Canoe Club (☎ 308 70 55, 031-556 641; Prapreče 1a) 1km northwest of Žužemberk.

SLEEPING & EATING

Koren (☎ 308 72 60; www.turizem-koren.si; Dolga Vas 5; per person €15) This farmhouse in Dolga Vas near Žužemberk has accommodation for 14 people in five rooms and one apartment.

Gostilna Pri Gradu (☎ 308 72 90; Grajski trg 4; starters €3.75-7.50, mains €8-10.80; ☺ 6am-11pm Sun-Thu, 6am-midnight Fri & Sat) This old-style eatery under a linden in front of the castle has a terrace open in the warmer months.

There's a **Mercator** (Grajski trg 26; ☺ 7am-7pm Mon-Fri, 7am-1pm Sat, 8-11am Sun) wedged between the Gostilna Pri Gradu and the castle.

GETTING THERE & AWAY

The bus stop is in front of the post office at Grajski trg 28. Up to four buses a day go to

Ljubljana (€5.80, 1½ hours, 53km) on weekdays, with one on Saturday and Sunday. From Monday to Friday two buses a day depart at 4.55am and 8.15am for Novo Mesto (€3, 30 minutes, 22km), but there's only one at 9.15am on Saturday.

DOLENJSKE TOPLICE

☎ 07 / pop 740 / elev 176m

Within striking distance of Novo Mesto (13km to the northeast), this thermal resort is the oldest and one of the few real spa towns in Slovenia. Located in the karst valley of the Krka River below the wooded slopes of Kočevski Rog, Dolenjske Toplice is an excellent place to hike, cycle, fish or simply relax.

History

Although the curative powers of the thermal springs were known as early as the 14th century, the first spa was not built here until 1658 when Ivan Vajkard, a member of the aristocratic Auersperg family, opened the Prince's Bath. The Kopališki Dom (Bathers' House), complete with three pools, was built in the late 18th century when the first

chemical analysis of the thermal waters was done. Within a century, Dolenjske Toplice (Strascha Töplitz) had 30 rooms, basic medical facilities and its very own guidebook, but tourism did not really take off until 1899, with the opening of the Zdravilíški Dom (Health Resort House).

Orientation

Dolenjske Toplice lies about 1.5km south of the Krka River on an undulating stream called the Sušica. Virtually everything – including the two hotels of the thermal resort – are on or just off the main street, Zdravilíški trg. Buses stop here just south of or opposite the post office. Dolenjske Toplice is not on a rail line.

Information

Dolenjska Health Resort (Zdravilíšče Dolenjske Toplice; ☎ 391 94 00; www.krka-terme.si) Central contact for hotel and camping-ground bookings, beauty and medical treatments and so on.

K2M (☎ 306 68 30, 041-887 362; www.k2m.si; Pionirska cesta 3; ✆ 9am-6pm Mon-Fri, 9am-noon Sat) Travel agency with private rooms, guides and local maps.

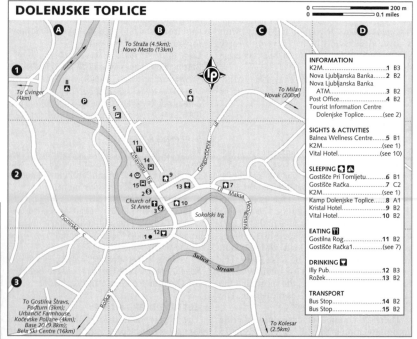

DOLENJSKE TOPLICE

| 0 | 200 m |
| 0 | 0.1 miles |

To Straža (4.5km); Novo Mesto (13km)

To Cvinger (4km)

To Milan Novak (200m)

Zdravilíški trg

Gregorčičeva ul

Ul Maksa Henigmana

Church of St Anne

Sokolski trg

Pionirska c

Sušica Stream

Rožca c

To Gostilna Stravs, Podtrum (3km); Urbančič Farmhouse, Kočevske Poljane (4km); Base 20 (9.8km); Bela Ski Centre (16km)

To Kolesar (2.5km)

INFORMATION
K2M.....................................1 B3
Nova Ljubljanska Banka.......2 B2
Nova Ljubljanska Banka
   ATM............................3 B2
Post Office............................4 B2
Tourist Information Centre
   Dolenjske Toplice...........(see 2)

SIGHTS & ACTIVITIES
Balnea Wellness Centre........5 B1
K2M.................................(see 1)
Vital Hotel......................(see 10)

SLEEPING
Gostišče Pri Tomljetu...........6 B1
Gostišče Račka...................7 C2
K2M.................................(see 1)
Kamp Dolenjske Toplice......8 A1
Kristal Hotel.......................9 B2
Vital Hotel.........................10 B2

EATING
Gostilna Rog......................11 B2
Gostišče Račka1...............(see 7)

DRINKING
Illy Pub.............................12 B3
Rožek...............................13 B2

TRANSPORT
Bus Stop............................14 B2
Bus Stop............................15 B2

DOLENJSKA & BELA KRAJINA

Nova Ljubljanska Banka (Zdravili ški trg 8; ⏰ 8am-noon & 2.30-4.30pm Mon-Fri) Shares a building with the tourist office; ATM south of the Church of St Anne.

Post office (Zdravili ški trg 3; ⏰ 8-9.30am & 10am-5pm Mon-Fri, 8am-noon Sat)

Tourist Information Centre Dolenjske Toplice (☎ 384 51 88; www.dolenjske-toplice.si; Zdravili ški trg 8; ⏰ 9am-noon & 2-7pm Mon-Sat, 9am-noon Sun mid-Jun–Sep; 9am-3pm Mon-Fri, 9am-noon Sat & Sun Oct–mid-Jun)

Activities
THERMAL SPA

Taking the waters is the *sine qua non* of Dolenjske Toplice: the warm mineral water (32°C to 38°C) gushing from 1000m below the two covered thermal pools at the **Vital Hotel** (☎ 391 94 00; www.krka-terme.si; Zdravili ški trg 11; nonguests Mon-Fri €8.35-9.60, Sat & Sun €9.20-10.50; ⏰ 7am-8pm) is ideal for such ailments as rheumatism, and can avert backache. The health resort also offers any number of other therapies, from underwater massage (€14.30) to detox aromatherapy (€21).

The indoor and outdoor thermal pools in the **Laguna** (Lagoon; ☎ 391 97 50; day pass Mon-Fri adult/child €8.75/6.70, Sat & Sun €10.50/8.35) section of the large **Balnea Wellness Centre** (⏰ 9am-9pm Sun-Thu, 8am-11pm Fri & Sat) are 300m north of the hotels, reached via a lovely park. In the **Oaza** (Oasis; day pass Mon-Fri/Sat & Sun €13/14.60) section of the centre are a host of indoor and outdoor saunas and steam baths. The **Aura** section has massage and treatments. Hotel guests pay €4.20/7 for Laguna/Oaza and there are combination tickets available.

HIKING

A number of walks and bike paths of less than 5km can be accessed from Dolenjske Toplice, or you might consider hiking in the virgin forests of Kočevski Rog (p202).

Marked paths listed on the free *Tourist Map of the Municipality of Dolenjske Toplice* include a 4km **archaeological walk** west to Cvinger (263m), where Hallstatt tombs and iron foundries have been unearthed. Nature lovers may be interested in the **nature trail** in the forest just west of Podturn (3km), which also takes in a small cave and the ruins of 13th-century Rožek Castle. Further afield is the 2km **Dormouse Trail** (Polharska Pot), which makes a loop from Kočevske Poljane about 4.5km southwest of Dolenjske Toplice and could be combined with a hike to Base 20 (p202). Ask the tourist office for a brochure about the trail.

OTHER ACTIVITIES

Horse riding is available at the **Urbančič farmhouse** (☎ 306 53 36, 040-608 969; Kočevske Poljane 13; per hr €10.50) in Kočevske Poljane, 4km to the southwest. Horse-drawn carriages accommodating three people can be hired from **Milan Novak** (☎ 041-590 877; Gregorčičeva ulica 52; €10 per hour).

K2M (☎ 306 68 30, 041-887 362; www.k2m.si; Pionirska cesta 3; ⏰ 9am-6pm Mon-Fri, 9am-noon Sat) can organise kayak, canoe and rafting trips on the Krka. Renting a canoe/kayak from K2M or the Balnea Wellness Centre costs €12.50 to €16.70 a day.

The **Bela Ski Centre** (Smučarski Center Bela; ☎ 384 92 00; vladka.asnic@iskra-semic.si; half-day pass adult/child €6.30/5, day pass €8.25/6.30), formerly called the Rog-Črmošnjice ski centre, is located 16km south of Dolenjske Toplice. It has 6km of slopes and 7km of cross-country trails on the slopes of Mt Gače at altitudes between 700m and 965m. They are served by a chairlift and five T-bar tows.

Sleeping
Kamp Dolenjske Toplice (☎ 391 94 00; www.krka-terme .si per person €2.10-8, incl 3hr pool pass €8.80-12.10; ⏰ year-round; Ⓟ ☒) This renovated 3-hectare camping ground accommodating 100 people is just off the northern end of Zdravili ški trg, more or less opposite the Balnea complex.

Gostišče Pri Tomljetu (☎ 306 50 23, 031-643 345; Zdravili ški trg 24; d/tr without bathroom €21/31; Ⓟ) None of the eight rooms in this leafy guesthouse behind the Balnea complex has its own bathroom, but each has a sink, and cooking facilities are available.

K2M (☎ 306 68 30, 041-887 362; www.k2m.si; Pionirska cesta 3; d/apt €25/42; ⏰ reception 9am-6pm Mon-Fri, 9am-noon Sat) Has private rooms and an apartment for four to seven people available.

Gostišče Račka (☎ 306 55 10; www.giostinstvo-luzar .si; Ulica Maksa Henigmana 15; s/d €27/46; Ⓟ) This modernised and attractive village house to the east of the centre has rooms and apartments for up to six people (33 beds) that are 10% cheaper after two nights' stay.

Vital & Kristal Hotels (☎ 391 94 00; www.krka -terme.si; Zdravili ški trg 11; s €61-66, d €102-112; Ⓟ ☒ ▣ ☐ ♿) The health resort's pair of four-star hotels face one another and share the same facilities, including three indoor thermal pools, two saunas and a fitness centre. Both offer discounted weekend and week-long packages.

Eating & Drinking

Gostišče Račka (☎ 306 55 10; www.giostinstvo-luzar.si; Ulica Maksa Henigmana 15; pizza & pasta €3.80-5.85; ☺ 8am-11pm Sun-Thu, 8am-midnight Fri & Sat Jul & Aug; 8am-10pm Sun-Thu, 8am-11pm Fri & Sat Sep-Jun) This B&B does double duty as a restaurant and is a popular place for pizza and pasta.

Gostilna Rog (☎ 391 94 12; Zdravilíški trg 22; meals from €10; ☺ 9am-10pm Sun-Thu, 9am-11pm Fri, 9am-midnight Sat) On the edge of the park, the 'Horn' serves traditional Slovenian dishes and has folk music from 8pm on Friday and Saturday.

Rožek (☎ 391 94 00; ☺ 7am-10pm) This small, glassed-in café-bar at the end of the pretty plaza between the Vital and Kristal Hotels is a lovely place to relax after a soak.

Illy Pub (☎ 306 58 51, 041-331 898; Pionirska cesta 1; ☺ 7am-11pm Mon-Fri, 8am-midnight Sat & Sun) Dolenjske Toplice's young bloods tend to congregate at this boozer just across the bridge.

Two *gostilna* a short distance out of town but definitely worth the distance are **Gostilna Štravs** (☎ 306 53 90; Podturn 28; meals from €15; ☺ 8am-11pm) – 3km southwest in Podturn and specialising in freshwater fish and game – and our current favourite **Kolesar** (☎ 306 50 03; Dolenje Sušice 22; meals from €12), 2.5km to the southeast.

Getting There & Around

There are hourly buses to Novo Mesto (€2.20, 20 minutes, 11km) between 6.30am and 6.30pm Monday to Saturday, and two weekday buses to Ljubljana (€7, 1½ hours, 73km) via Žužemberk (€2.60, 30 minutes, 18km) at 5.35am and 10.29am.

You can hire bicycles from the K2M tourist agency for €3.35/10.50 per hour/day.

KOČEVSKI ROG

☎ 07 / elev to 1099m

One of the most pristine areas in Slovenia, Kočevski Rog has been a protected nature area for more than a century, and six virgin forests, covering an area of more than 200 hectares, are preserved here. Brown bears, as many as 700 of them, are said to live here and constitute the only sizeable bear populations extant in Europe.

The region was – and still is – so remote and filled with limestone caves that during the early days of WWII the Partisans, under the command of Marshal Tito, headquartered here, building bunkers, workshops, hospitals,

schools and even printing presses. The nerve centre was the so-called **Base 20** (Baza 20; ☎ 306 60 25; www.dolmuzej.com), about 10km southwest of Dolenjske Toplice at 708m, which was reconstructed and turned into a national monument after the war.

Once a favourite 'pilgrimage' spot for many Slovenes and Yugoslavs, Base 20 is now a shadow of its former self – its 26 buildings are deteriorating and the indicator maps are all but illegible. A plaque erected near the site in 1995 diplomatically pays homage to everyone involved in the 'national liberation war', presumably including the thousands of Domobranci (Home Guards) murdered here by the Partisans in 1945. The site is always open, but a **tourist guide** (☎ 306 60 25, 041-315 165; 90-min tour adult/child & student €2/1.35 ☺ 8am-4pm Tue-Fri Apr-Sep) is on hand in season, near the start of the trail.

The range's tallest peak, **Veliki Rog** (1099m), is about 5km to the southwest.

There is no scheduled bus service, but Base 20 is easily reached by sealed road on foot or bicycle from Podturn, 7km to the northeast. From the car park and Gostišče Pri Bazi 20, it's a 650m walk up a well-maintained mountain path to the site.

NOVO MESTO

☎ 07 / pop 22,425 / elev 189m

Situated on a sharp bend of the Krka River, the inappropriately named 'New Town' is the political, economic and cultural capital Dolenjska, and one of the prettiest towns in the province. But – Janus-like – today's Novo Mesto shows two faces to the world. The Old Town, perched high up on a rocky promontory above the left bank of the Krka, is filled with interesting things to see. The new town, to the north and south, thrives on the business of Krka, a large pharmaceutical and chemical company, and Revoz, which produces Renault cars.

For Slovenes, Novo Mesto is synonymous with the painter Božidar Jakac (1899–1989), who captured the spirit of the place on canvas, and the writer Miran Jarc (1900–42) who did the same in prose with his autobiographical novel *Novo Mesto*. For the traveller, Novo Mesto is both a destination and an important gateway to the historical towns and castles along the lower Krka River, the karst forests of the Gorjanci Hills to the southeast, Bela Krajina and Croatia.

History

Novo Mesto was settled during the late Bronze Age around 1000 BC, and helmets and decorated burial urns unearthed in surrounding areas suggest that Marof Hill, above the Old Town, was the seat of Hallstatt princes during the early Iron Age. The Illyrians and Celts came later, and the Romans maintained a settlement here until the 4th century AD.

During the early Middle Ages, Novo Mesto flourished as a market because of its location and later became the centre of the estates owned by the Cistercian abbey at Stična. In 1365 Habsburg Archduke Rudolf IV raised it to the status of a town, naming it Rudolphswert. By the 16th century some 15,000 loads of freight passed through Novo Mesto each year. But plague, fires, and raids by the Turks on their way to Vienna took a toll on the city and, within a hundred years, Novo Mesto's main square had become grazing land for cattle.

Prosperity returned in the 18th and 19th centuries: a college was established in 1746, Slovenia's first National Hall (Narodni Dom) opened here in 1875 and a railway line linked the city with Ljubljana in the 1890s.

Orientation

Almost everything of interest in Novo Mesto is in the toe-shaped Old Town. Its centre is Glavni trg, a large, cobbled square lined with arcaded shops and public buildings.

The bus station is at Topliška cesta 1, southwest of the Old Town across Šmihel Bridge. Novo Mesto has two train stations: the main one on Kolodvorska ulica about 2km northwest of the Old Town and little Novo Mesto-Center on Ljubljanska cesta at the western edge of the Old Town.

Information

Abanka (Rozmanova ulica 40; 8am-noon & 2-5pm Mon-Fri)

Knjigarna Goga (☎ 393 08 02; Glavni trg 6; 9am-7pm Mon-Fri, 9am-1pm Sat) Lovely bookshop with regional maps, guides and café with music; in the arcade.

Kompas Novo Mesto (☎ 393 15 20; www.robinson-sp.si; Novi trg 10; 8am-6pm Mon-Fri, 9am-noon Sat) Organises excursions and adventure sports in Dolenjska through its Robinson arm.

Post office (Novi trg 7)

SKB Banka (Novi trg 3; 8.30am-noon & 2-5pm Mon-Fri)

Tourist Information Centre Novo Mesto (☎ 393 92 63; www.novomesto.si; Novi trg 6; 9am-6pm Mon-Fri, 9am-noon Sat Jun-Sep; 8am-3pm Mon & Tue, 8am-5pm Wed, 8am-2pm Thu & Fri Oct-May) On the ground floor of an office building west of Novi trg.

Sights

CHAPTER CHURCH OF ST NICHOLAS

Perched above the Old Town, this Gothic **church** (Kapiteljska Cerkev Sv Nikolaja; Kapiteljska ulica) is Novo Mesto's most visible historical monument. And, with a 15th-century vaulted (and very floral) presbytery and crypt, painted ceiling, a belfry that had once been a medieval defence tower, and an altar painting of the church's eponymous saint supposedly painted by the Venetian master Jacopo Tintoretto (1518–94), it is also the city's most important.

If the church is locked, you'll find the key at the **Provost's House** (Proštija; Kapiteljska ulica 1), the yellow building to the northwest built in 1623. Just south of this is a section of the **medieval town walls** erected in the 14th century.

DOLENJSKA MUSEUM

Below the Chapter Church about 100m to the southeast is the enormous **Dolenjska Museum** (Dolenjski Muzej; ☎ 373 11 30; www.dolmuzej.com; Muzejska ulica 7; incl Jakac House adult/student & child €3/2; 9am-5pm Tue-Sat, 9am-1pm Sun Apr-Sep; 9am-4pm Tue-Fri, 9am-1pm Sat & Sun Oct-Mar). The oldest building, which once belonged to the Knights of the Teutonic Order, houses a valuable collection of archaeological finds unearthed in the southern suburb of Kandija in the late 1960s. Don't miss the Hallstatt helmet dating from the 4th century BC with two enormous axe blows on top, the fine bronze situla (or pail) from the 3rd or 4th century BC embossed with battle and hunting scenes, and the Celtic ceramics and jewellery (particularly the bangles of turquoise and dark-blue glass).

Other collections in the complex include one devoted to recent history and an excellent ethnographic collection with farm implements, commemorative jugs presented at weddings, decorated heart-shaped honey cakes, and icons painted on glass.

The museum also administers **Jakac House** (Jakčev Dom; ☎ 373 11 31; Sokolska ulica 1; adult/child €1.50/1; same as museum), which exhibits some of its 830-odd works by the prolific painter Božidar Jakac. The artist visited dozens of countries in the 1920s and 1930s, painting and sketching such diverse subjects as Parisian dance halls, Scandinavian port towns, African villages and American city skylines. But his best works are of Novo Mesto's markets, people, churches and rumble-tumble wooden riverside houses.

GLAVNI TRG

The neo-Renaissance **town hall** (rotovž; Glavni trg 7), out of step with the square's other arcaded buildings, ostentatiously calls attention to itself at all hours with its bells and odd facade. The coat of arms on the front is that of Archduke Rudolf IV, the town's founder.

Southeast of the town hall is the **Church of St Leonard** (Frančiškanska Cerkev Sv Lenarta; Frančiškanska ulica), which was originally built by Franciscan monks fleeing the Turks in Bosnia in 1472, and the attached, bright yellow **Franciscan monastery** (Frančiškanski Samostan; Frančiškanska ulica 1), whose library contains some 12,000 volumes,

including important 12th-century incunabula. The **Gymnasium** (Jenkova ulica 1), founded by Maria Theresa in 1746, is to the north.

Activities

FLYING

The **Novo Mesto Aeroclub** (☎ 334 82 22; www.aero klub-nm.si; 9am-7pm) at Prečna (house No 46), 4.5km northwest of Novo Mesto and served by bus, has sightseeing flights over Novo Mesto and the Krka Valley in Cessna 172s. A 15-minute flight costs €63 for up to three passengers.

HORSE RIDING

About 3km south of Prečna, the **Novo Mesto Sport Equestrian Centre** (☎ 337 30 40, 041-554 265;

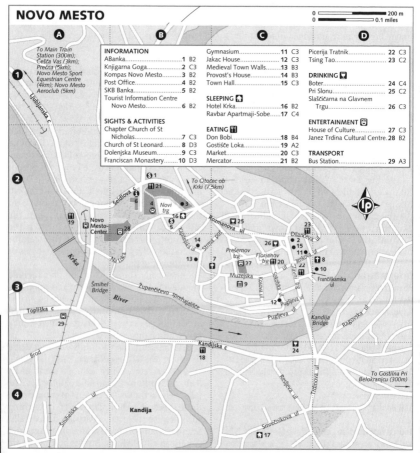

konji.cescavas@siol.net; per hr from €10; ⏱ by appointment) at house No 55 in the village of Češča Vas, has Holsteiners and Arabians for riders of all levels. You can ride on any day, but you should book first.

Sleeping

Ravbar Apartmaji-Sobe (☎ 373 06 80; www.ravbar.net; Smrečnikova ulica 15-17; s €24-29, d €39.50-42, 2-person apt €37.50-50; P 🖳) This family-run guesthouse has rooms and modern, spotlessly clean apartments in a leafy and quiet suburban area south of the river. You might even get to visit their *zidanica* (cottage with wine cellar) in the Luben vineyards.

Gostilna Pri Belokranjcu (☎ 302 84 44; www.pri belokranjcu-vp.si; Kandijska cesta 63; s/d/tr €32/48/65; P) Further afield – about 1.5km from the Old Town – this *gostilna* with 14 rooms is on a busy road but is a decent option given its proximity to Novo Mesto and its popular restaurant.

Hotel Krka (☎ 394 21 00; www.krka-terme.com; Novi trg 1; s/d/ste €75/112/150; P ✕ ♿ 🖳 ♿) The only place to stay in the centre of town is this 53-room business hotel, with modern, comfortable rooms, some of which are adapted for disabled guests. Oddly, in a hotel of this class, guests have to pay for internet access (€1.70/6.70 for 20 minutes/two hours).

The tourist office has a list of private rooms (from €21 per person). The closest camping grounds are at Otočec, 7.5km to the northeast, and Dolenjske Toplice, 12km to the southwest.

Eating

Tsing Tao (☎ 332 43 88; Dilančeva ulica 7; mains €5.20-8.30) Tucked away in a cellar north of Glavni trg, this friendly restaurant named after China's favourite beer has main courses such as chicken with chilli and peanuts (€5.65). A number of set menus is available.

Gostilna Pri Belokranjcu (starters €3.70-5.85, mains €6.70-17.50; ⏱ 8am-11pm Mon-Sat) This popular inn a short distance from the Old Town serves hearty Slovenian favourites and has good-value set menus (€6.70 and €9.60).

Gostišče Loka (☎ 332 11 08; Župančičevo sprehajališče; meals from €12; ⏱ noon-10pm Mon-Fri, noon-11pm Sat, noon-8pm Sun) Situated right on the Krka River, just beyond the small footbridge linking the two banks, the 'Meadow' serves decent fish dishes and is the place to try Cviček, the uniquely Slovenian light (9%) red wine from

Dolenjska. There's garden seating available in the warmer months.

As everywhere in Slovenia, Novo Mesto has a surfeit of pizzerias. Nothing could be more central than **Picerija Tratnik** (☎ 332 15 51; Glavni trg 11; pizza €4.20; ⏱ 6am-10pm Mon-Fri, 6am-11pm Sat, 7am-10pm Sun), below a coffee shop of the same name, but head south of the river to **Don Bobi** (☎ 338 24 00; Kandijska cesta 14; pizza €4.50; ⏱ 9am-11pm Mon-Sat) if you want better quality pizza and pasta.

There is an outdoor **market** (Florjanov trg; ⏱ Mon & Fri) selling fruit and vegetables in the centre of the Old Town. Enter the large **Mercator** (Novi trg 5; ⏱ 7am-7pm Mon-Fri, 7am-1pm Sat) supermarket from Seidlova cesta.

Drinking

Pri Slonu (☎ 332 14 95; Rozmanova ulica 22; ⏱ 7am-11pm Mon-Fri, 6pm-midnight Sat) This intimate café-bar attracts Novo Mesto's Bohemian types.

Slaščičarna na Glavnem Trgu (☎ 332 12 47; Glavni trg 30; ⏱ 7am-8pm) The 'Inn on the Square' has a pleasant old-style café on the ground floor with a sidewalk terrace and an ice-cream parlour.

Boter (☎ 041-213 466; Kandijska cesta 9; ⏱ 7am-midnight Mon-Sat, 9am-11pm Sun) This waterfront café-pub on the south side of the Krka has views of the Old Town from across the river that could be straight out of a Jakac painting.

Entertainment

The municipal **House of Culture** (Dom Kulture; ☎ 332 12 14; Prešernov trg 3) has a studio cinema with screenings at 8.30pm, and it sponsors occasional theatrical and musical performances in conjunction with the **Janez Trdina Cultural Centre** (Kulturni Center Janeza Trdine; ☎ 393 03 90; Novi trg 5). Ask the staff about concerts held in the courtyard of the Provost's House during the **Novo Mesto Summer Nights** (Novomeški Poletni Večeri; tic@novomesto .si) festival in July and August.

Getting There & Away

BUS

There are between three and six daily departures to Dolenjske Toplice (€2.20, 15 minutes, 11km), Otočec ob Krki (€1.70, 10 minutes, 7.5km), Šentjernej (€3, 30 minutes, 21km) and Šmarješke Toplice (€2.20, 20 minutes, 12km), and seven to 10 buses a day to Brežice (€5, one hour, 44km), Kostanjevica na Krki (€4.50, one hour, 39km) and Ljubljana (€7, two hours, 72km) via Trebnje or Žužemberk.

DOLENJSKA & BELA KRAJINA

Two or three buses a day go to Črnomelj (€5, one hour, 43km), and you can also reach Zagreb (€7.80, 2½ hours, 77km) on the daily bus, which departs at 8.50am.

TRAIN
Up to 14 trains a day serve Novo Mesto from Ljubljana (€5, 1½ hours, 75km) via Ivančna Gorica and Trebnje Gorica. Ten of these continue on to Črnomelj (€2.65, 45 minutes, 32km) and Metlika (€3.30, one hour, 47km), where there are connections to Karlovac in Croatia.

Getting Around
You can call a taxi in Novo Mesto on ☎ 332 57 77 or 041-625 108.

OTOČEC OB KRKI
☎ 07 / pop 680 / elev 173m

The castle at Otočec, on a tiny island in the middle of the Krka River, 7.5km northeast of Novo Mesto, is one of Slovenia's loveliest and most complete fortresses. The first castle here stood on the right bank of the river, but during the Mongol onslaught in the mid-13th century, a canal was dug on the south side, creating an artificial island. Today the castle, which dates from the 16th century, houses a five-star hotel. The area around Otočec, the gateway to the lower Krka and the Posavje region, has become something of a recreational (especially cycling) centre.

Orientation & Information
The castle – now Hotel Grad Otočec – is 1km east of Otočec village on a secondary road running parallel to highway H1 (E70) and the river. You reach the castle via a wooden bridge. The cheaper Hotel Šport, owned by the same group, is up the hill a few steps north of the bridge. The camping ground is southwest of the island on the south bank.

Staff at the reception of the **Hotel Grad** (☎ 384 89 00, Grajska cesta 2) can provide information about recreational facilities and equipment rentals. You can change money here, at the reception of the Hotel Šport or at the post office in Otočec village. There's an ATM at the petrol station next to the Hotel Šport.

Sights
Even if you're not staying at the hotel, there's no harm in having a look around **Otočec Castle** (Otoški Grad) and, if the weather is warm, en-

joying a drink or a coffee at the terrace café in the courtyard. The castle, with elements of late Gothic and Renaissance architecture, consists of two wings and entrance block connected by a pentagonal wall. There are four squat, rounded towers with very thick walls, narrow windows and conical roofs at each end.

Activities
The **sport centre** just east of the Hotel Šport rents bicycles and mountain bikes (1 hour/5 hours/1 day €8.35/14.60/20.50). The **tennis centre** has three indoor courts (per hour €16.70 to €21, for guests €16.70 to €17.50; open 8am-11pm) and six outdoor courts (€5 to €6.70, for guests €6.30; open 8am-11pm). There's also a sauna and steam room (€7.50), and fitness centre (per hour €4.20), which guests get to use for free.

Rent canoes, rowing boats and rafts from the **camping ground** (☎ 384 89 00, 384 86 00; per day €12.50-16.70); the best areas for boating on the Krka are downstream from Struga.

The Krka River around Otočec is a popular **fishing spot** for pike, perch and carp, and fishing permits (per day €13.50) are available from the castle hotel.

Slovenia's newest golf course, the nine-hole, par-36 **Golf Grad Otočec** (☎ 384 89 05, 041-304 444; www.terme-krka.com; 9 holes Fri/Sat & Sun €25/30), opened along the Krka just 800 metres from the castle hotel in the summer of 2006. Hiring a set of clubs costs €10 and a pull car is €4.

Sleeping & Eating
Kamp Otočec (☎ 384 86 00, 384 89 00; www.krka-terme .com; per person/car/tent/caravan €5/2/1.50/3; ☼ mid-May-Sep; P ☒) This camping ground, with 50 sites accommodating 200 guests, is on a 2-hectare strip of land running along the south bank of the Krka River. To reach it from the castle, cross the second bridge, turn left (east) and walk for 300m. It has its own tennis court and pool, and there's a 'beach' along the river.

Šeruga farmhouse (☎ 334 69 00; turist.kmetija .seruga@siol.net; per person €22) If your budget won't extend to accommodation at the Hotel Grad Otočec and you want something a bit more rural, this farmhouse in the village of Sela pri Ratežu (house No 15), about 2km south of Otočec village, has nine double rooms (some with kitchen), an apartment for three and a recommended restaurant (open 6am to 10pm) specialising in trout and štruklji (dumplings made with cheese) of various types.

THE AUTHOR'S CHOICE

Hotel Grad Otočec (☎ 384 89 00; www.krka -terme.com; s €104-113, d €148-164; P ✗ 🖳) The five-star Castle hotel is one of the most atmospheric places to stay in Slovenia. Many (but not all) of its two-dozen rooms of varying sizes have polished parquet floors, Oriental carpets, marble-topped tables and large baths; in fact, a few are in dire need of renovation. There are lots of packages on offer as well. This is not the place where you want to spend the night alone – for many different reasons. Guests may use the pools at the Šmarješke Toplice spa (p208) free of charge.

Hotel Šport (☎ 384 86 00; www.krka-terme.com; s €62.50-70.50, d €84-100; P ✗ 🖳) This hotel, housed in a concrete-and-glass box opposite the island and the castle, has 78 rooms as well as a separate 37-room motel (singles €32 to €37, doubles €50 to €62) and 24 more attractive bungalows (singles €40 to €46, doubles €64 to €78) in the adjacent holiday centre.

Tango (☎ 384 86 00; meals from €10; 🕚 11am-10pm Sun-Thu, 11am-1am Fri & Sat) This flagship restaurant diagonally opposite the Hotel Šport building should be a distant second choice to the Grad, but given how fast the Grad fills up with nonguests and wedding parties you may have no choice.

Grad (☎ 384 8702, 384 8700; starters €5.40-11.70, mains €8-15.50; 🕚 8am-midnight) At the Hotel Grad Otočec, this restaurant seats 76 people and the smaller Hunter's Room accommodates two dozen more. With ancient stone walls, chandeliers and stained glass, it's loaded with atmosphere though the service is not very good. Specialities are game and fish; try the unusual red trout with a glass of Dolenjska Cviček. The four-course set menu is excellent value at €14.60.

Getting There & Away

The buses linking Novo Mesto (€1.70, 15 minutes, 7.5km) and Šmarješke Toplice (€1.70, 15 minutes, 7km) stop at the bridge leading to the castle between three and six times a day.

AROUND OTOČEC OB KRKI

The vineyards of **Trška Gora** (428m) can be reached by road and trail from Mačkovec, about 5km southwest of Otočec on the road

to Novo Mesto. From Mačkovec follow the road north for 1km to Sevno and then continue along the winding track for 2km until you reach Trška Gora and the **Church of St Mary**. From here there are wonderful views of the Gorjanci Hills, Kočevski Rog and the Krka Valley.

Further afield is **Gospodična** (828m) in the Gorjanci Hills and **Dom Vinka Paderšiča na Gorjancih** (☎ 041-682 469, 031-456 293; 🕚 mid-Apr–mid-Oct Wed-Mon, mid-Oct–mid-Apr Sat & Sun), a Category III mountain lodge with a restaurant and 49 beds. Gospodična and the lodge are about 13km southeast of Otočec in the shadow of **Trdinov Vrh** (1178m), the highest peak in the Gorjanci, on the Croatian border. The route from Otočec goes for 5km southeast to **Velike Brusnice**, famous for its cherries and cherry festival (☎ 041-354 455) in mid-June, then to Gabrje (4.5km) and to Gospodična (3.5km).

ŠMARJEŠKE TOPLICE

☎ 07 / pop 490 / elev 258m

If all that Cviček wine is taking its toll on you, consider taking a break at Šmarješke Toplice, a spa town in a small, lush valley about 5km north of Otočec. While it doesn't have anything close to the history or atmosphere of Dolenjske Toplice, 25km to the southwest, it has lovely grounds and more than enough facilities to keep you busy and help recharge those batteries.

The three natural pools that once stood on the site of the spa were used by local people as far back as the 18th century and were collectively known as the Lake Spa. Development did not come until 1950, when the first hotel was built, but even that remained a rather exclusive facility reserved for the *nomenklatura* (communist honchos). Only in the last decade has Šmarješke Toplice really made it onto the map. It is now well known as both a serious therapy centre for those with cardiovascular problems, as well as a haven for relaxation and healthy living.

Orientation & Information

The spa complex and its hotels are north of the tiny village of Šmarješke Toplice. Buses stop in front of and opposite the Tuš supermarket, where an ATM can be found out the front. You can change money at the **post office** (🕚 8-9.30am & 10am-5pm Mon-Fri, 8am-noon Sat) next door.

Activities

The spa counts six thermal pools fed by 32°C spring water rich in carbon dioxide and minerals. The two **indoor pools** (nonguests Mon-Fri €4.80-8.35, Sat & Sun €7.30-9.20) are in the hotel complex and used for therapy.

Nearby is the **Vitarium Centre** (☎ 384 34 00; www.vitarium.si), a health spa with treatments, a sauna, solarium and fitness centre. Here you'll also find the **Centre for Nordic Walking** (Center Nordijske Hoje; nordiccenter-st@email.si), which can provide you with walking sticks (€4.20) not unlike cross-country ski poles and a guide or brochure with nine self-led walks of between 2.8km and 11km around Šmarješke Toplice. The wine-growing areas surrounding Šmarješke Toplice make for some excellent walking, and there are trails and footpaths southwest to Trška Gora and northeast to Vinji Vrh.

The largest of the four **outdoor pools** (nonguests Mon-Fri €5.85, Sat & Sun €6.70) is below the sports centre; there's a children's pool nearby. The basin of an older (and smaller) pool directly above the hot spring is made of wood. As a result the water temperature is 2°C warmer.

The **sports centre** has four clay tennis courts (one illuminated at night) available for hire, and racquets are available. There are also facilities for table tennis, minigolf and lawn bowls.

Sleeping & Eating

Domen farmhouse (☎ 784 30 10, 041-890 901; domen .zorko@email.si; Družinska Vas 1; s/d €18/30; P 🖳) A budget alternative to staying at the spa is this 18-room pension in Družinska Vas, about 1.5km southeast of Šmarješke Toplice. The Domen also has a tennis court and a decent restaurant (mains €5 to €8.35; open noon to 8pm Saturday and Sunday), with simple but tasty Slovenian home-style dishes available at the weekend.

Apartmaji na Dobravi (☎ 384 41 00; www.apartmaji nadobravi.si; Šmarješke Toplice 240; 2-/5-person apt May-Oct €66/101, Nov-Apr €55.50/91; P ✗ 🖳) This villa, about 1km east of the main complex on the road to Bela Cerkev, has 15 luxury apartments for two to five people, with kitchens. It has its own steam bath, sauna, solarium and massage pool.

Šmarješke Toplice spa complex (☎ 384 34 00; www .terme-krka.com; P ✗ 🖳 🖳 🖳) The complex has three hotels and a villa with two apartments.

Vila Ana (Šmarješke Toplice spa complex; s & d €46-57) These two attractive apartments are in a luxury villa opposite the Tuš supermarket and post office. They're a bit far from the action, though.

Toplice (Šmarješke Toplice spa complex; s €63-66, d €102-108) The Toplice is in the middle section of the complex and was built in 1983. Some of its 47 rooms have small balconies with views of the nearby hills and forests.

Šmarjeta (Šmarješke Toplice spa complex; s €69.50-72.50, d €104-120) This hotel, which was totally renovated in 2006, has 100 rooms and is the largest hotel in the complex. Some of the rooms also have balconies.

Vitarium (Šmarješke Toplice spa complex; s €71.50-74.50, d €118-124) This new 72-room hotel offers the best (and most expensive) accommodation in Šmarješke Toplice.

Tuš (Šmarješke Toplice 116; 🕐 7.30am-7pm Mon-Fri, 7.30am-5pm Sat) This supermarket is next to the post office in Šmarješke Toplice village.

Getting There & Around

There are four to five buses a day to Novo Mesto (€2.20, 20 minutes, 12km) and Otočec (€1.70, 15 minutes, 7km) from the village of Šmarješke Toplice.

The sports centre rents bicycles for €4.20 per hour. You can call a taxi on ☎ 307 56 50 or 041-625 108.

KOSTANJEVICA NA KRKI

☎ 07 / pop 700 / elev 180m

The glory days of Kostanjevica have long since passed, and today the town is so sleepy it is almost comatose. Though it is dubbed 'the Venice of Dolenjska' by the tourist industry, as well as being under full protection as a cultural monument, many of its buildings are in poor condition with the exception of the former Cistercian monastery a kilometre south of town. Still, it remains an important art centre and its location is magical.

Kostanjevica, situated on an islet just 500m long and 200m wide enclosed by the Krka River, was an important commercial centre in the Middle Ages. In 1563 after repeatedly attacking the town, the Turks were defeated by Ivan Lenkovič, supreme commander of the Military March.

Orientation

Although most of Kostanjevica's historical sights are on the island, some other interesting

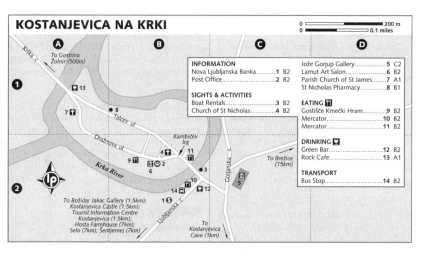

places as well as things of a more practical nature are on the mainland to the northwest or southeast, reached by two small bridges. Buses stop outside and opposite the Green Bar.

Information

Nova Ljubljanska Banka (Ljubljanska cesta 6; ☽ 8am-noon & 2.30-4.30pm Mon-Fri) Near the bus stops on the main road into town.

Post office (Kambičev trg 5; ☽ 8-9.30am & 10am-5pm Mon-Fri, 8am-noon Sat)

Tourist Information Centre Kostanjevica (☎ 498 71 08; tic-gbj@galerija-bj.si; Grajska cesta 45; ☽ 9am-6pm Tue-Sun Apr-Oct; 9am-4pm Tue-Sun Nov-Mar) In a wonderful old mill to the right, after the main entrance of Kostanjevica Castle.

Sights

OLD TOWN

No-one is going to get lost or tired touring Kostanjevica – walk 400m up Oražnova ulica and 400m down Talcev ulica and you've seen the lot.

On Kambičev trg, across the small bridge from the bus stop, stands the **Church of St Nicholas** (Cerkev Sv Miklavža) a tiny late-Gothic structure dating from the late 16th century. In the presbytery the brightly coloured frescoes of scenes from the Old and New Testaments were painted by Jože Gorjup (1907–32). You can see more of this expressionist's work, including the wonderful *Bathers* series, at the **Jože Gorjup Gallery** (☎ 486 60 13; Gorjanska cesta 2; ☽ 8am-2pm Mon-Fri) in the primary school back over the same bridge.

If you walk northwest along Oražnova ulica for about 200m, you'll reach a 15th-century manor house that now contains the **Lamut Art Salon** (Lamutov Likovni Salon; ☎ 498 74 06; Oražnova ulica 5; ☽ during exhibitions 9am-6pm Mon-Fri, 9am-4pm Sat), a branch of the Božidar Jakac Gallery (p210). The painter and graphic artist Vladimir Lamut (1915–62) completed a large portion of his work here.

Continue along Oražnova ulica, passing a lovely *fin-de-siècle* house (No 24), to the **Parish Church of St James** (Župnijska Cerkev Sv Jakoba), a 13th-century Romanesque building with a mostly baroque interior, at the island's northwestern tip. Above the carved stone portal on the western side are geometric designs and decorative plants and trees. On the south side is a 15th-century depiction of Jesus rising from the tomb.

Talcev ulica, the island's other street, is lined with attractive 'folk baroque' houses, including the 200-year-old **St Nicholas Pharmacy** (Talcev ulica 20).

KOSTANJEVICA CASTLE

About 1.5km southwest of town, this former Cistercian monastery, which most people call **Kostanjevica Castle** (Kostanjeviški Grad; ☎ 498 70 08; www.galerija-bj.si; Grajska cesta 45; adult/student & child €2.50/1.25; ☽ 9am-6pm Tue-Sun Apr-Oct, 9am-4pm Tue-Sun Nov-Mar), was established in the mid-13th century and remained a very wealthy institution in the Middle Ages. It was abandoned in 1785 when monastic orders were dissolved. Today it houses a large and important art gallery.

FORMA VIVA

The Kostanjevica Castle grounds are used to exhibit more than a hundred large wooden sculptures from Forma Viva, an international exhibition that was held in several places in Slovenia from 1961 to 1988, whereby sculptors worked with materials associated with the area. Here it was oak, in Portorož stone, iron at Ravne in Koroška and (shudder) concrete in Maribor. In 1998 Forma Viva was revived at Kostanjevica and it is once again an annual event.

The beautifully painted main entrance through two squat painted towers leads to an enormous courtyard enclosed by a cloister with 260 arcades on three floors. To the west stands the disused **Church of the Virgin Mary** containing elements from the 13th to 18th centuries; it is now used as exhibition space.

The **Božidar Jakac Gallery** upstairs contains 16th-century frescoes taken from the church, with works by such Slovenian artists as the impressionist Božidar Jakac (1899–1989) and brothers France (1895–1960) and Tone Kralj (1900–75). There is also a permanent collection of Old Masters from the Carthusian monastery at Pleterje (opposite). Much of Jakac's work here consists of lithographs and etchings done while documenting the underground Partisan movement in 1943, although some of his oils and pastels (eg *Before the Storm* and *Midnight on Hradčani*), are outstanding. The expressionist France Kralj was incredibly versatile and prolific, turning out hundreds of works in oil, ink, bronze and wood; don't miss his sculptures *The Reapers, Mother and Child* and *Stallion*. Some of Tone Kralj's early work (like *Veined Sunset* and *Evening of Life*) is almost surreal, but his later move to a kind of socialist realism obliterates all traces of it. The collection from Pleterje features works by French, German, Italian and Flemish artists of the 16th to 18th centuries and is pretty sombre stuff.

KOSTANJEVICA CAVE

This tiny **cave** (Kostanjeviška Jama; ☎ 498 70 88, 041-297 001; adult/child/student €4.20/1.25/3.35; ☯ tours 10am, noon, 2pm, 4pm & 6pm daily Jul & Aug; 10am, noon, 2pm, 4pm & 6pm Sat & Sun mid-Apr–Jun, Sep & Oct), on a partly unsealed road about 1.5km southeast of town, has half-hour tours in spring, sum-

mer and autumn. The guide will lead you 300m in (only 750m of the cave has been fully explored), past a small lake and several galleries full of stalactites and stalagmites. The temperature is a constant 12°C.

Activities

The little ice-cream kiosk next to the bridge, just before you cross over to the island, rents **canoes** and **kayaks** (per hour €6.25) from April to September for excursions on the Krka.

The **Hosta farmhouse** (☎ 308 1034, 041-690 066; Sela 6) in the village of Sela near Šentjernej, 7km west of Kostanjevica, has horses for hire and even boasts a riding school.

Sleeping & Eating

Gostilna Žolnir (☎ 498 71 33; www.zolnir-sp.si; Krška cesta 4; s/d €27/43.50; ℗ ☒) This old-style *gostilna*, about 700m northwest of the island, has 12 double rooms and a wonderful restaurant (starters €4.60 to €7.10, mains €5.58 to €10.80) open from 7am to 10pm. The owners are very serious about the food and wine they serve. A speciality of Kostanjevica is duck served with *mlinci* (pancakes) and, of course, Cviček wine.

Gostišče Kmečki Hram (☎ 498 70 78; Oražnova ulica 11; meals from €10; ☯ 7am-11pm Tue-Thu, 7am-midnight Fri & Sat, 8am-8pm Sun) This wonderful old-style inn, which recently received a tarting-up, really looks like the 'Peasant House' it calls itself and offers good home cooking. Note the old wine press outside.

There's a **Mercator** (Ljubljanska cesta 4a; ☯ 7am-7pm Mon-Fri, 7am-1pm Sat, 7-11am Sun) supermarket next to the bus stop and a smaller but more central **Mercator** (Kambičev trg 2; ☯ 7am-7pm Mon-Fri) just over the bridge at the eastern end of the town.

Drinking

Green Bar (☎ 041-586 576; Ljubljanska cesta 3; ☯ 6am-midnight) This bar in an attractive old baroque building next to the bus stop is a pleasant place for a drink.

Rock Cafe (☎ 041-233 312; Talcev ulica 28; ☯ 6am-11pm Mon-Fri, 6am-1am Sat, 7am-midnight Sun) At the northeastern end of the island, the Rock attracts a relatively raucous (for a comatose town) crowd.

Getting There & Away

There are one or two daily buses from Kostanjevica to Novo Mesto (€4.55, one hour, 39km),

Brežice (€3, 45 minutes, 24km), Šentjernej (€1.70, 15 minutes, 7.5km) and Ljubljana (€9.30, three hours, 104km) and two or three to Krško (€2.20, 30 minutes, 16km).

PLETERJE MONASTERY

Located 9km southwest of Kostanjevica na Krki, the enormous **Pleterje Monastery** (Samostan Pleterje; ☎ 308 12 25; admission free; ⏰ 7.30am-6pm) belongs to the Carthusians, the strictest of all Roman Catholic monastic orders. The Gothic **Holy Trinity Church** (also called the Old Gothic Church or Stara Gotska Cerkev), 250m up a linden-lined path from the car park, is the only part of the complex open to the general public. But the monastery's location in a narrow valley between slopes of the Gorjanci Hills is so attractive and peaceful that it's worth a visit. The **Pleterje Trail** (Pleterski Pot) is a 1½-hour walk in the hills around the complex.

Pleterje was founded in 1407 by Herman II, one of the Counts of Celje, and its construction was supervised by an English abbot called Prior Hartman. The complex was fortified with ramparts, towers and a moat during the Turkish invasions, and all but abandoned during the Protestant Reformation, which swept Dolenjska in the 16th century. The Carthusian order, like all monastic communities in the Habsburg Empire, was abolished in 1784. When the monks returned to Pleterje more than a century later, they rebuilt the complex according to the plans of the order's charterhouse at Nancy in France.

You may catch a glimpse of the dozen or so white-hooded monks quietly going about their chores – they take a strict vow of silence – or hear them singing their offices in the Gothic church at various times of the day. But the ubiquitous signs reading *Klavzura – Vstop Prepovedan* (Seclusion – No Entry) and *Območnje Tišine* (Area of Silence) remind visitors that everything apart from the church is off limits.

Above the ribbed main portal of the austere church (1420) is a fresco depicting Mary and the Trinity. Inside, the rib-vaulted ceiling with its heraldic bosses and the carved stone niches by the simple stone altar are worth a look, but what is most interesting is the medieval rood screen, the low wall across the aisle that separated members of the order from lay people.

There's a monastery **shop** (⏰ 7.30am-5.30pm Mon-Sat) at the new reception building to the left as you enter the complex, where the monks sell some of their own products, including packs of beeswax candles (€3), honey (€5.40), propolis (€1.90 for a small flask), Cviček wine (€2.50 a litre) and various brandies, including *sadjevec* (fruit; €5), *brinjevec* (juniper; €14.20), *slivovka* (plum; €5.85) and everyone's favourite: *hruška* (pear; €17.50). If you're wondering how they got that pear into the seamless bottle, well, the explanation is simple. An empty glass bottle is placed upside-down over the immature fruit while it is still on the tree. When the pear ripens inside, the bottle and pear are 'picked' and filled with brandy. Drink too much of this stuff and you'll see visions of that place the monks warn us all about.

To the west of the monastery car park is the **Pleterje Open-Air Museum** (Pleterski Muzej na Prostem; ☎ 337 76 81, 031-639 191; Drča 1; adult/child/family €1.90/1.25/5; ⏰ 9am-6pm Apr-Sep), with 10 structures dating from the 19th century – thatched peasant houses, a pigsty, hayracks and even an outhouse – moved here from the areas around Šentjernej.

Šentjernej (population 1350), 3km north of Pleterje and 7km west of Kostanjevica, can be reached on one of five Novo Mesto (€3, 30 minutes, 21km) buses; return to Kostanjevica (€1.70, 15 minutes) on one of up to five buses headed for Brežice. Buses stop in Trg Gorjanskega Bataljona, the main square, from where you'll have to make your way to Pleterje on foot.

POSAVJE REGION

Most of what is called Posavje, the area 'on the Sava River' that extends as far as the border with Croatia, is in Štajerska. Historically and geographically, however, Posavje is closely tied to Dolenjska and easily accessible from many of its towns.

History

Like Dolenjska, Posavje was settled early and is rich in archaeological finds from the Hallstatt, Celtic and Roman periods. The Sava River, of course, was paramount, and the Romans built a major port here called Neviodunum near today's Drnovo.

Posavje took centre stage during the Turkish invasions starting in the 15th century – which explains the large number of heavily fortified castles in the region – and again a century later during the Slovenian-Croatian peasant uprisings and the Protestant Reformation. River traffic increased in the 19th century after a 20km stretch of the Sava was regulated, and the arrival of the railway in 1862 linking Ljubljana and Zagreb helped the region develop industrially.

Posavje had more than its share of suffering during WWII. In a bid to colonise the area the occupying German forces engaged in a brutal programme of 'ethnic cleansing' and expelled more than 15,000 Slovenes.

Brežice

☎ 07 / pop 6265 / elev 158m

Brežice is not the largest town in Posavje – that distinction goes to Krško, 12km upriver – but from a traveller's point of view it is certainly the most interesting. The town lies between the Orlica Hills to the north and the Gorjanci Hills to the south, and opens onto a vast plain to the east.

HISTORY

Situated in a basin just north of where the Krka flows into the Sava, Brežice was an important trading centre in the Middle Ages and was granted a town charter in 1354. Brežice's most dominant feature has always been its castle, mentioned in documents as early as 1249, with a strategic position some 400m from the Sava. In the 16th century the original castle was replaced with a Renaissance fortress to strengthen the town's defences against the Turks.

The castle was built with the help of Italian masters and is not dissimilar in design to the ones at Otočec and Mokrice. Over a century later, the castle's new owners, the Counts of Attems, renovated the building in the baroque style and added several sumptuous rooms, including the largest function room in Slovenia. Today the castle houses the Posavje Museum.

ORIENTATION

Brežice's main street is Cesta Prvih Borcev. Heading south it becomes Prešernova cesta and crosses the Sava. Going north it changes its name to Trg Izgnancev and Cesta Bratov Milavcev. The main artery going eastward is Bizeljska ulica.

The bus station is behind the big shopping centre on Cesta Svobode, 200m north of Bizeljska ulica and about 1km from the Posavje Castle. The train station is further afield on Trg OF, about 2.5km north of the town centre.

INFORMATION

There is no tourist office in Brežice. Seek help from the staff at the **Posavje Museum** (☎ 496 12 71) or try the **Čatež Tourist Office** (☎ 493 67 77; www .visitbrezice.com; Topliška cesta 35, Čatež ; ☉ 9am-5pm) opposite the wellness centre.

Nova Ljubljanska Banka (Cesta Prvih Borcev 40; ☉ 8.30am-noon & 2-5pm Mon-Fri)

Post office (Trg Izgnancev 1a) In a lovely Art Nouveau building.

SKB Banka (Cesta Prvih Borcev 39; ☉ 8.30am-noon & 2-5pm Mon-Fri)

SIGHTS

Housed in the Renaissance Posavje Castle, the **Posavje Museum** (Posavski Muzej; Cesta Prvih Borcev 1; ☎ 466 05 11; www.posavski-muzej.si; adult/student & child €2/1; ☉ 8am-2.30pm Mon-Fri, 10am-2pm Sat & Sun) is one of provincial Slovenia's richest museums, particularly for its archaeological and ethnographic collections.

From the courtyard you ascend a staircase whose walls and ceiling are illustrated with Greek gods, the four Evangelists and the Attems family coat of arms. Rooms on the 2nd floor contain bits and pieces from early times to the arrival of the Slavs; don't miss the skeletons from the 9th century BC unearthed near Dobova, the 5th-century BC bronze bridle and the Celtic and Roman jewellery. In the ethnographic rooms, along with the carved wooden bowls, decorated chests and plaited loaves of bread, is a strange beehive in the shape of a soldier from the early 1800s.

Other rooms in the museum cover life in the Posavje region in the 16th century (focusing on the peasant uprisings in the area and the Protestant Reformation) and during the two world wars, with special emphasis on the deportation of Slovenes by the Germans during WWII. But the museum's real crowd-pleaser is the Knights' Hall (Viteška Dvorana), an Italian baroque masterpiece where everything except for the floor is painted with landscapes, gods and heroes from Greek and Roman mythology, allegories, the Muses and so on.

ACTIVITIES

Rheumatics have been bathing in the thermal spring near Čatež ob Savi (population 320), 3km southeast of Brežice, since the late 18th century. Today, while the huge **Terme Čatež** (☎ 493 67 00, 493 50 00; www.terme-catez.si; Topliška cesta 35) complex still attracts those suffering from such aches and pains, it is every bit as much a recreational area. The spa counts 10 thermal-water (27°C to 36°C) **outdoor pools** (3hr/day pass Mon-Fri €5.85/8, Sat & Sun €7/8.75; ◷ 9am-8pm Jun-Aug; 9am-7pm Apr, May & Sep), with huge slides,

fountains and artificial waves over an area of 10,000 sq m. The indoor **Zimska Termalna Riviera** (Winter Thermal Riviera; Terme Čatež; 3hr/day pass Mon-Fri €6.70/8.80, Sat & Sun €8.80/10.80; ◷ year-round) complex measures 1800 sq m with a water temperature of about 32°C. The spa also has eight different saunas, a steam room, Roman bath, solarium, gym, a jogging track along the river and tennis courts.

You can rent a **bicycle** (per day €6.25) at the Kamp Terme Čatež.

FESTIVALS & EVENTS

The **Festival Brežice** (www.festivalbrezice.com) is a month-long series of concerts featuring ancient music and is held from late June to late July in various venues around the region, including the Knights' Halls in the castles at Bizeljsko and Mokrice.

SLEEPING

Gostilna Les (☎ 496 11 00; www.gostilna-les.com; Rimska cesta 31; s/d/tr €28/44/56; P ⌨) This attractive B&B with seven rooms and one five-person apartment is about 1.5km south of Brežice at the confluence of the Krka and Sava Rivers. It's about the same distance west of Terme Čatež.

Gostilna Splavar (Raftman's Inn; ☎ 499 06 30; www .splavar.si; Cesta Prvih Borcev 40; s/d €45/66; P ⌨) This welcoming 15-room *pension* on Brežice's high street is above the Splavar restaurant and popular Rafter's Pub. The staff are friendly.

Ošterija Debeluh (☎ 96 10 70, 041-565 859; Trg Izgnancev 7; s/d €45/66) Not as nice as the Splavar but still in central Brežice, this 18-room guesthouse is above a popular restaurant of the same name.

Terme Čatež spa complex (☎ 493 50 00, 493 67 00; www .terme-catez.si; Topliška cesta 35) The complex has three hotels as well as a huge camping ground. There are also 400 apartments (one to three people €59 to €95, four to five people €70.50 to €104).

Kamp Terme Čatež (Terme Čatež; ☎ 493 50 00; www .terme-catez.si; Topliška cesta 35, Čatež; per person €12.50-14; ◷ year-round; P ⛽) The daily rate at this 3.5-hectare camping ground accommodating 555 guests at the Terme Čatež spa complex includes two daily entrances to the outdoor swimming pools or one to the Winter Thermal Riviera.

Hotel Čatež (Terme Čatež; s 73-75, d €117-120; P ⌨ ⛽ ⛽ ⛽ ⛽) A three-star place with some 60 rooms and a new addition generally reserved for those who are taking the spa seriously.

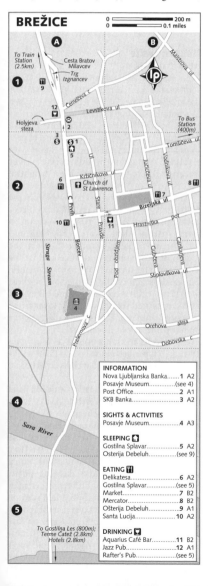

BREŽICE

DOLENJSKA & BELA KRAJINA

Hotel Toplice (Terme Čatež; s €94-96, d €146-149; P X X 🔲) This 131-room hotel with four stars has a new and an old (1925) wing.

Hotel Terme (Terme Čatež; s 101-104, d €160-166; P X X 🔲) The nicest of the three properties, this four-star hotel in a somewhat isolated section of the complex has 146 rooms.

EATING

Santa Lucija (☎ 499 25 00, 041-624 596; Cesta Prvih Borcev 15; pizza €4.20-5, grills €4.40-6.90; � 6.30am-midnight) This pizzeria with an over-the-top ceiling fresco does a roaring a trade in takeaway, as it does in eat-in pizza.

Gostilna Splavar (starters €5-8, mains €7-11.70; � 6am-midnight Mon-Sat, 8am-10pm Sun) A popular B&B, this *gostilna* is also a fine restaurant with a winter garden and summer terrace. The Laški Rizling, a slightly fruity, medium-dry wine from Bizeljsko, is not a bad accompaniment to the fish dishes on offer. It's also celebrated for the homemade ice cream (one/two/three scoops for €0.75/1.35/1.85).

Ošterija Debeluh (☎ 496 10 70, 496 67 52; Trg Izgnancev 7; grills €4.60-7.50, mains €7.50-10.80; � 8am-10pm Mon-Sat) This attractive eatery, whose name roughly translates as 'Fatty's', serves Balkan specialities.

There's a supermarket called **Delikatesa** (Cesta Prvih Borcev 23; � 7am-7pm Mon-Fri, 7am-noon Sat) diagonally opposite the Church of St Lawrence. You'll find a much larger **Mercator** (Bizeljska ulica 23; � 7am-8pm Mon-Fri, 7am-1pm Sat, 7-11am Sun) beyond the produce **market** in the direction of the bus station.

DRINKING

Rafter's Pub (� 8am-midnight Mon-Sat, 8am-10pm Sun) This popular English-style pub is at the Gostilna Splavar.

Jazz Pub (Trg Izgnancev 2; � 6am-midnight Mon-Fri, 7am-midnight Sat, 8am-midnight Sun) The very attractive and friendly drinking spot is popular with students.

Aquarius Café Bar (☎ 499 25 05; Bizeljska cesta 4; � 6am-1am Mon-Sat, 8am-1am Sun) Housed on three levels of Brežice's unmistakeable pink water tower (1914), this café-bar is decorated with old photos of the town and antiques.

GETTING THERE & AROUND

Buses make the run to Terme Čatež (€1.30, 10 minutes, 4.5km) at least once an hour. There are some four buses a day to Bizeljsko (€2.60, 30 minutes, 18km) and Ljubljana (€9.60, three

hours, 109km), and six to Kostanjevica (€3, 45 minutes, 24km) and Novo Mesto (€5.10, one hour, 44km).

As many as 15 trains a day serve Brežice from Ljubljana (€6, 1¾ hours, 107km) via Zidani Most, Sevnica and Krško (€1, 10 minutes, 9km). Many of these trains then cross the Croatian border near Dobova and carry on to Zagreb.

You can order a taxi on ☎ 041-611 391 or 041-790 842.

Mokrice Castle

☎ 07 / elev 148m

Near Jesenice na Dolenjskem, about 10km southeast of Brežice, renovated **Mokrice Castle** is the loveliest in the Posavje region and is now a 29-room luxury hotel. With one of Slovenia's few 18-hole golf courses, a 20-hectare 'English park' full of rare plants, a large orchard of pear trees and a small disused Gothic chapel with a vaulted ceiling and wedding-cake plaster tracery, a trip to the castle makes a delightful excursion from Brežice.

The castle as it stands today dates from the 16th century, but there are bits and pieces going back to Roman times (inscription stones, part of a tower and so on) built into the structure. Like many other castles in the region, it was built as a defence against the Turks and later turned into a baronial manor. The castle is supposedly haunted by the ghost of a 17th-century countess named Barbara, who committed suicide after her lover failed to return from sea. She is particularly active on her name day (4 December).

The greens fee for a round at Mokrice's 18-hole, 71-par **golf course** is €37/45.50 weekdays/weekends. A half-set of clubs costs €12.50 to rent.

The 11 rooms at the **Mokrice Castle Golf Hotel** (☎ 457 42 40; www.terme-catez.si; s €94-101.50, d 138.50-153, ste €276-304; P X 🔲) have beamed ceilings and period furniture, and some of the eight suites – one measures 240 sq m – have fireplaces. The **Grad** (starters €5.85-9.20, mains €8.35-18.80; � 7am-11pm) restaurant is a gorgeous venue with fancy game and fish dishes, and classical music. The cellar has dozens of different Slovenian wines available by the glass or bottle. Try some *viljamovka*, Mokrice's famous pear brandy.

You can reach Mokrice from Čatež ob Savi on the infrequent bus to Obrežje (€1.30, 10 minutes, 5km) – though some Zagreb-bound buses stop here too – but the ideal way to go would be by bicycle from Čatež, following the secondary road running parallel to route No 1 (E70).

Bizeljsko-Sremič Wine District

☎ 07 / elev to 175m

Cycling the 18km from Brežice to **Bizeljsko** (population 670) is a great way to see the Bizeljsko-Sremič wine country, but there are buses, allowing you to get off whenever you see a *gostilna, vinska klet* (wine cellar) or *repnica* (flint-stone cave for storing wine) that takes your fancy. In Bizeljsko, try some of the local medium-dry whites and reds at the **Vinska Klet Pinterič** (☎ 495 12 66, 041-520 481; Bizeljska cesta 115; ✆ 10am-7pm) or at **Gostilna Šekoranja** (☎ 495 13 10; Bizeljska cesta 72; ✆ 8am-11pm Tue-Sun). In the nearby village of **Stara Vas** visit the **Vinoteka Pri Peču** (☎ 452 01 03; ✆ 10am-midnight Wed-Mon) or **Repnica Pudvoi** (☎ 495 12 28, 031-484 003; ✆ 11am-7pm Sat & by appointment) cellars at house No 58 and No 89 respectively.

From Bizeljsko you can either return to Brežice or continue north for 7km past Bizeljska Vas and the ruins of the 15th-century **Bizeljsko Castle** to Bistrica ob Sotli. From here, buses head northwest to Kozje via the village of Podsreda, the site of the oldest castle in Slovenia (p228).

BELA KRAJINA

Bela Krajina has countless opportunities for active pursuits and relaxing stops along the heritage trails and wine roads. Ask the tourist office in Metlika or Črnomelj for the brochure packet *S Kolesom po Beli Krajini* (By Bike in Bela Krajina), with cycling trails – many of them circular – outlined on 10 separate maps. Bela Krajina contains two important parks: the 275-hectare Lahinja Country Park and a large part of the 6500-hectare Kolpa Country Park.

METLIKA

☎ 07 / pop 3245 / elev 167m

One of Bela Krajina's two most important towns, Metlika lies in a valley at the foot of the Gorjanci range of hills. It is surrounded by Croatia on three sides, and the Kolpa River lies about 1km to the south. There was a major Hallstatt settlement here during the early Iron Age, and the Romans established an outpost in Metlika on the road leading to the important river port of Sisak in Croatia. During the Turkish onslaught of the 15th and 16th

centuries, Metlika was attacked 17 times and occupied in 1578.

Orientation

Metlika's Old Town, consisting of three main squares, stands on a ridge between a small stream called the Obrh and the main street, Cesta Bratstva in Enotnosti (Avenue of Fraternity and Unity). The modern bus station is 650m south of the Old Town on Cesta XV Brigade opposite the large shopping centre (Naselje Borisa Kidriča; NBK). The train station is on Kolodvorska ulica, another 600m southeast along Cesta XV Brigade.

Information

Metlika Public Library (Ljudska knjižnica Metlika; ☎ 369 15 20, 305 83 70; Cesta Bratstva in Enotnosti 23; 10am-6pm Mon, Wed & Fri, 10am-3pm Tue & Thu, 9-11am Sat) Free internet access on three terminals.

Nova Ljubljanska Banka Trg Svobode (Trg Svobode 7; ✆ 8.30am-noon & 2.30-5pm Mon-Fri); shopping centre (NBK 2; ✆ 8am-noon & 2.30-4.30pm Mon-Fri)

Post office (NBK 2) In the same shopping centre as the bank branch.

Tourist Information Centre Metlika (TIC; ☎ 363 54 70; www.metlika.si; Mestni trg 1; ✆ 9am-4pm Mon-Fri, 9am-noon Sat Jun-Oct; 8am-3pm Mon-Fri, 9am-noon Sat Nov-May)

Sights

TRG SVOBODE

Housed in **Metlika Castle** (Metliški Grad; Trg Svobode 4) with its splendid arcaded courtyard, the **Bela Krajina Museum** (Belokranjski Muzej; ☎ 306 33 70; adult/

DOLENJSKA & BELA KRAJINA

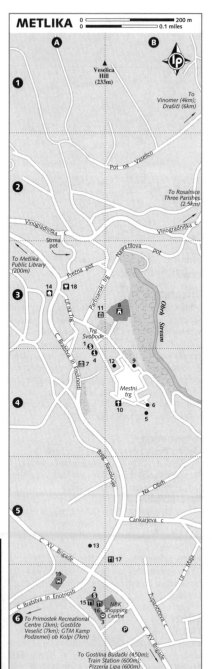

student & child €2.50/1.70; ⊙ 9am-5pm Mon-Sat, 10am-2pm Sun) houses a permanent collection of archaeological finds taken from the area. There are Hallstatt buckles, bracelets and amulets from Pusti Gradac (p221) south of Črnomelj, and an early plaster cast of the Mithraic relief from the Roman period found at Rožanec (p221) near Črnomelj, as well as items relating to the area's ethnology and agriculture: beekeeping, fruit cultivation, viniculture, fishing and animal husbandry. The artist and sculptor Alojzij Gangl (1859–1935), who was born in Metlika, is given pride of place.

Metlika was the first town in Slovenia to have its own fire brigade, and the small building west of the castle entrance contains the **Slovenian Fire Brigades Museum** (Slovenski Gasilski Muzej; ☎ 305 86 97; Trg Svobode 5; admission free; ⊙ 9am-1pm). There are old fire trucks with enormous wheels, ladders and buckets.

MESTNI TRG

This colourful, leafy square of 18th- and 19th-century buildings, includes the neo-Gothic **town hall** (Mestni trg 24) dating from 1869 and **old cottages** at Nos 20 and 21. At the southern end of the square is the so-called **Commandery** (Komenda; Mestni trg 14), which once belonged to the

Knights of the Teutonic Order (note the stone relief of a Maltese cross above the entrance). Its **defence tower** dates from the 16th century. To the northwest the **Parish Church of St Nicholas** (Farna Cerkev Sv Nikolaja; Mestni trg 14) was built in 1759 and modelled on the Križanke's Church of the Virgin Mary in Ljubljana. On the ceiling are sobering frescoes of the Day of Judgment by Domenico Fabris, with some satyrlike devils leading sinners to damnation.

CESTA BRATSTVA IN ENOTNOSTI

Along this busy main street is the **Kambič Gallery** (Galerija Kambič; ☎ 305 83 32; Cesta Bratstva in Enotnosti 51; admission free; ⌚ 10am-4pm Tue-Sat, 10am-1pm Sun), which shows some 200 artworks donated by a university professor and stages cutting-edge temporary exhibits.

Activities

The Kolpa River is clean and very warm (up to 28°C to 30°C in summer), so you might want to go **swimming** at the Primostek or Podzemelj camping grounds.

The Kolpa is known for its grayling, carp and brown trout, but the area around Vinica, further south, is richer for **fishing**. You can purchase daily fishing licences at all camping grounds.

There are a lot of **hikes** and **walks** in the surrounding areas, including the 6.5km-long **St Urban's Trail** (Urbanova Pot) to Grabrovec and back via **Veselica**, a 233m-high small hill less than 1km north of Metlika, with great views over the town. Another is the Učna Pot Zdence Vidovec from the village of Božakovo just east of Rosalnice (below) to the Zdence and Vidovec karst caves. Ask the TIC for brochures outlining the walks. They also have pamphlets outlining **bike trails**.

Ask the tourist information centre about organised wine tastings at the **Vinska Klet** (☎ 363 70 52; www.kz-metlika.si; Cesta XV Brigade 2; per person €2.50-8.35; ⌚ by appointment), the 'Wine Cellar' run by the local wine cooperative.

Festivals & Events

Metlika's main event is the **Vinska Vigred** (www .melika.si) wine festival held the third weekend of May.

Sleeping

Primostek Recreational Centre (Rekreacijski Centre Primostek; ☎ 384 92 88, 305 81 23; camping adult/child €5/3.35; bungalow per person from €9.50; ⌚ May-Sep; P) This

camping ground 2km southwest of Metlika has sites for tents and caravans as well as five bungalows with eight beds each.

GTM Kamp Podzemelj ob Kolpi (☎ 305 81 23, 363 52 80; gostinstvo-turizem@gtm-metlika.si; Podzemelj 16b; camping adult/child €6.25/5; ⌚ May–mid-Sep; P) A larger and better-equipped camping ground on the Kolpa 7km southwest of Metlika measures 2.5 hectares in size and can accommodate 50 tents and 200 guests. Without wheels the only way to reach here is by train from Metlika. It's a 2km walk from the station at Gradac.

Gostišče Veselič (☎ 306 91 56; veselic1966@hotmail .com; per person €17; P) This *gostilna* in Podzemelj (house No 17), not far from the camping ground, has four rooms. Its restaurant is a favourite of locals.

Bela Krajina Hotel (☎ 363 52 80, 305 81 23; Cesta Bratstva in Enotnosti 28; s/d without bathroom €15.30/29, with bathroom €22.80/37.20; P) The Bela Krajina has 24 fairly shabby rooms but is as central as you are going to get – it's the only hotel in town.

Eating

Julija Pizzeria (☎ 305 9487; NBK 9; pizza from €4.50; ⌚ 7am-midnight Sun-Thu, 7am-1am Fri & Sat Jun-Aug; 7am-11pm Sun-Thu, 7am-midnight Fri & Sat Oct-May) This pizzeria with a popular bar (open from 9am to 11pm daily) is in the large shopping centre opposite the bus station.

Pizzeria Lipa (☎ 363 51 30; Cesta Bratstva in Enotnosti 83; pizza from €5; ⌚ 7am-10pm Mon-Wed, 7am-11pm Fri-Sun) If you want something lighter, head for this decent pizzeria southeast of the bus station.

Gostilna Budački (☎ 363 52 00; Ulica Belokranjskega Odreda 14; meals from €10; ⌚ 8am-10pm Mon-Thu, 8am-midnight Fri & Sat, noon-3pm Sun) One of the very few 'real' places to eat in Metlika, this *gostilna* 450m south of the centre gets good reviews for its home-style cooking.

Gostišče Veselič (meals from €10; Podzemelj; ⌚ 8am-10pm Thu-Tue) This B&B has an excellent restaurant and is well worth the 7km trip down from Metlika.

There's a large **Mercator** (NBK 2; ⌚ 6.30am-7pm Mon-Fri, 6.30am-3pm Sat, 8-11am Sun) supermarket branch in the shopping centre opposite the bus station.

Drinking

Bar Salon 1 (⌚ 040-309 970; Cesta Bratstva in Enotnosti 45; ⌚ 6am-11pm Mon-Thu, 6am-1am Fri, 7am-1am Sat, 8am-11pm Sun) Opposite the Bela Krajina Hotel, this enormous place is popular among Metlika's young bloods.

Grajska Točilnica (☎ 305 89 99; ☺ 7am-11pm Mon-Thu, 7am-midnight Fri, 8am-midnight Sat, 8am-noon Sun) If you want to try some Bela Krajina wine but don't have the time to get out into the country, head for this café-bar in the castle courtyard. You can sample Pinot Blanc, Chardonnay, the Rieslings and sweet Gold Muscatel.

Bacchus (☺ 041-346 291; NBK 2; ☺ 10pm-5am Thu-Sat) This club on the 1st floor of the shopping centre opposite the bus station is patronised by people from around the region.

Getting There & Away

Destinations served by bus from Metlika include Črnomelj (€2.60, 30 minutes, 16km, three a day, with more during school term), Novo Mesto (€3.50, one hour, 30km, six daily) and Vinica (€5.50, 1½ hours, 46km, two to three a day).

Metlika is served by up to eight trains daily from Ljubljana (€6.50, 2¾ hours, 122km) via Novo Mesto and Črnomelj (€1.45, 20 minutes, 15km). Three trains a day head for Karlovac, 33km to the south in Croatia.

AROUND METLIKA
Rosalnice
☎ 07 / pop 365 / elev 138m

The **Three Parishes** (Tri Fare) in Rosalnice, 2.5km east of Metlika, is a row of three graceful little Gothic churches that have been important pilgrimage sites for seven centuries. Although they were originally built in the late 12th century by the Knights Templar, today's churches date from the 14th and 16th centuries. The one to the north – the largest and oldest of the three – is the **Church of Our Lady of Sorrows** and has a Gothic presbytery. The church in the middle, **Ecce Homo**, has a large tower rising above its porch. The one on the south with the buttresses and another Gothic presbytery is the **Church of Our Lady of Lourdes**. The churches do not keep fixed opening hours. Seek the key from **house No 44** (☎ 306 00 51).

There is a train from Metlika to Rosalnice (€1, two minutes, 1km, daily at 3.21pm) south of the Three Parishes, but it is just as easy to walk from Metlika; begin in the Old Town, head northeast along Navratilova pot and follow Ulica Janka Brodariča eastward for 600m, then turn south. After 200m turn east and continue straight on to the churches.

Metlika Wine District
☎ 07 / elev to 235m

The hills to the north and northeast of Metlika are one of Bela Krajina's most important wine-producing areas and produce such distinctive wines as Metliška Črnina, a very dark– almost black – red wine and a late-maturing sweet 'ice wine' called Kolednik Ledeno Vino. They are also superb areas for easy walking.

On the way to **Vinomer** and **Drašiči**, two important wine towns about 4km and 6km respectively from Metlika, you'll walk through *steljniki*, stands of birch trees growing among ferns in clay soil. They are the very symbol of Bela Krajina.

Drašiči is famous for its folk architecture, and you can sample local wines at several places, including the **Kostelec farmhouse** (☎ 305 90 93, 041 788 938; Drašiči 13) and the **Simonič farmhouse** (☎ 305 81 85, 041-572 596; Drašiči 56). Be sure to phone ahead. Ask the tourist office in Metlika about wine tastings at the 250-year-old **Soseska Zidanica** (☎ 041-788 938; ☺ by appointment), a vineyard cottage next to the Church of St Peter in the centre of Drašiči.

ČRNOMELJ
☎ 07 / pop 5850 / elev 156m

The capital of Bela Krajina and its largest town, Črnomelj (pronounced cher-*no*-mel) is situated on a promontory in a loop where the Lahinja and Dobličica Rivers meet. The town is not overly endowed with important sights, but it is Bela Krajina's folk 'heart', and its popular Jurjevanje festival attracts hundreds of dancers and singers from around the region.

Legend has it that Črnomelj (a corruption of the words for 'black mill') got its name when a beggar, dissatisfied with the quality of the flour he'd been given, put a curse on the local miller.

Črnomelj was settled very early on, and the Roman presence is evident from the Mithraic shrine at Rožanec (p221), about 4km northwest of the town. During the Turkish invasions in the 15th and 16th centuries, the town was attacked incessantly, but due to its strong fortifications and excellent hilltop lookouts at Stražnji Vrh and Doblička Gora to the west, it was never taken. Črnomelj played an important role during WWII. After Italy's surrender in 1943, the town functioned for a time as Slovenia's capital and was the centre

of the Slovenian National Liberation Council
and of Partisan activity.

Orientation

Buses stop on Trg Svobode in the heart of
the Old Town, in front of Črnomelj Castle
and near the Posojilnica, the old savings and
loan bank building. The train station is about
200m north of the Hotel Bojana at Kolodvorska cesta 1.

Information

Nova Ljubljanska Banka Kolodvorska cesta (Kolodvor-
ska cesta 32b; ⊙ 8.30am-noon & 2.30-4.30pm Mon-Fri);
Posojilnica (Trg Svobode 2; ⊙ 8am-noon & 2.30-4.30pm
Mon-Fri)

Post office (Kolodvorska cesta 30; ⊙ 7am-7pm Mon-
Fri, 7am-noon Sat)

Tourist Information Centre Črnomelj (☎ 305
65 30, 040-726 014; tic-crnomelj@ric-belajrajina.si; Trg
Svobode 3; ⊙ 8am-3.30pm Mon-Fri, 9am-noon Sat) On
the ground floor of Črnomelj Castle.

Sights & Activities

Črnomelj Castle (Črnomeljski Grad; Trg Svobode 3), parts
of which date from the mid-12th century,
houses the **Town Museum Collection** (Mestna Muzejska Zbirka; ☎ 305 65 30, 306 11 00; adult/child €0.80/0.40;
⊙ 8am-3.30pm Mon-Fri, 9am-noon Sat) on the 1st floor,
with items and documents related to the history of Črnomelj and Bela Krajina from the
5th century AD.

The foundations of **Stonič Castle** (Stoničev Grad;
Ulica Staneta Rozmana 4) to the south also go back
nine centuries; this is where the town's original castle stood. The **Commandery** (Komenda; Trg
Svobode 1) of the Teutonic Knights, the grey
building across the square to the southeast,
is a more recent structure, originally built
in 1655 and altered 200 years later. On it is a
stone relief of two knights and an inscription
in German.

The history of the **Parish Church of St Peter**
(Cerkev Sv Petra; Ulica Staneta Rozmana), almost opposite Stonič Castle, also goes back more than
seven centuries, but what you'll see today is a
standard-issue baroque structure with a single
spire. You can still see Roman tombstones
built into the walls, and on the western exterior above the main entrance is a fresco of St
Christopher, the patron saint of travellers.

The decrepit **Church of the Holy Spirit** (Cerkev
Sv Duha; Ulica Mirana Jarca) at the southeastern end
of the Old Town was built in 1487 and is still
undergoing extensive renovations. Opposite,

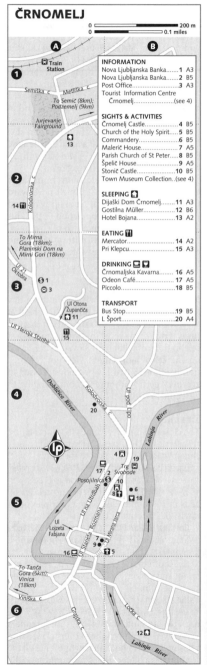

ČRNOMELJ

0 — 200 m
0 — 0.1 miles

INFORMATION	
Nova Ljubljanska Banka........1	A3
Nova Ljubljanska Banka........2	B5
Post Office.........................3	A3
Tourist Information Centre	
Črnomelj......................(see 4)	

SIGHTS & ACTIVITIES	
Črnomelj Castle.................4	B5
Church of the Holy Spirit.....5	B5
Commandery......................6	B5
Malerič House....................7	A5
Parish Church of St Peter....8	B5
Špelič House.....................9	A5
Stonič Castle...................10	B5
Town Museum Collection...(see 4)	

SLEEPING	
Dijaški Dom Črnomelj.........11	A3
Gostilna Müller................12	B6
Hotel Bojana....................13	A2

EATING	
Mercator.........................14	A2
Pri Klepcu.......................15	A3

DRINKING	
Črnomaljska Kavarna.........16	A5
Odeon Café......................17	A5
Piccolo...........................18	B5

TRANSPORT	
Bus Stop.........................19	B5
L Šport..........................20	A4

DOLENJSKA & BELA KRAJINA

in **Špelič House** (Špeličeva Hiša; ☎ 306 11 90; Ulica Mirana Jarca 20; admission free; ☺ 9am-2pm & 5-7pm Mon-Fri, 9-11am Sat), there is a gallery of Bela Krajina art, and next door **Malerič House** (Maleričeva Hiša; Ulica Mirana Jarca 18; ☺ 8am-3.30pm Mon-Fri, 9am-noon Sat) has local arts and crafts on display and for sale; contact the tourist office if it is shut.

One of the most popular hikes in this part of Bela Krajina starts at the northern end of Ulica 21 Oktobra; it goes for 18km northwest to Mirna Gora (1047m), where you can stay 100m up at Category III **Planinski Dom na Mirni Gori** (☎ 306 85 73, 041-910 357; ☺ Wed-Sun), with 50 beds in nine rooms and three dorms.

A wine road *(vinska cesta)* runs from Tanča Gora, 5km southwest of Črnomelj, northward through Doblička Gora, Stražnji Vrh and Ručetna Vas to **Semič** (population 750). This attractive little town, 9km north of Črnomelj, has the ruins of a 13th-century castle and church, and to the southeast lies the source of the Krupa River.

Festivals & Events

Jurjevanje (www.jurjevanje.si in Slovene), a three-day festival of music, dance and bonfires held at the fairground near the train station in mid-June, is one of the most important and oldest celebrations of folklore in Slovenia. It is based on the **Zeleni Jurij** (Green George) celebration held on 23 April, when boys dressed in greenery go from house to house singing to welcome in spring.

Sleeping

The closest camping grounds to Črnomelj are at **Podzemelj** (p217), 9km northeast of Črnomelj, and at **Vinica** (p222), 18km to the south.

Dijaški Dom Črnomelj (☎ 306 21 60; www.d-crnomelj .nm.edus.si; Ulica Otona Župančiča 7; per person €12; ☺ year-round; ⓟ ⌨) This HI-affiliated hostel has 50 beds in 10 doubles and as many triples open to visitors throughout the year.

Gostilna Müller (☎ 356 72 00, 041-689 056; Ločka cesta 6; per person €23; ⓟ) With four rooms and a decent restaurant, this B&B is across the river to the south of the Old Town. The rooms are bright and attractive, and it's an easy walk into central Črnomelj.

Hotel Bojana (☎ 306 29 00, fax 306 29 03; info@redex .si; Kolodvorska cesta 60; s/d/tr €65/85/100; ⓟ ⌨) The decrepit old Hotel Lahinja has undergone a major overhaul and has been transformed into a flashy, 10-room hotel that, while it has all the comforts, is a bit too gilded for our tastes. Still,

a place to stay in central Črnomelj is a rarely spotted species and very much welcome.

Eating

Pri Klepcu (☎ 356 74 70; Ulica Otona Župančiča 6; pizza €2-4.60; ☺ 9am-10pm Mon-Thu, 9am-11pm Fri, noon-11pm Sat, 4-10pm Sun) For pizza, try this place just southeast of the bank and post office. It's not the most authentic but it's cheap and central.

Gostilna Müller (starters €4.20-7, mains €4.60-10.85; ☺ 8am-11pm Tue-Fri, 9am-midnight Sat, 11am-10pm Sun) The restaurant at this B&B is among the best places to go for a meal in Črnomelj. Try one of the fish or traditional Slovenian dishes.

There is a branch of the **Mercator** (Kolodvorska cesta 53; ☺ 7am-7pm Mon-Fri, 7am-1pm Sat) supermarket 200m north of the post office.

Drinking

Odeon Café (Ulica na Utrdbah 2; ☺ 6am-11pm) This wonderful little place in a renovated old building just west of Črnomelj Castle overlooks the Dobličica River and has outside seating in the warmer months. The music is very well chosen. The café is owned by one of Bela Krajina's most popular radio stations.

Črnomaljska Kavarna (☎ 305 36 06; Ulica Lojzeta Fabjana 7; ☺ 6.30am-10pm Mon-Thu, 6.30am-11pm Fri & Sat, 7am-noon Sun) Known locally as 'the mayor's place' (now you know who's involved), the 'Črnomelj Café' is an upmarket pub-café serving hot and cold drinks just below the bridge spanning the Lahinja River.

Piccolo (☎ 305 32 96; Trg Svobode 1a; ☺ 7am-2am Mon-Thu, 10am-4am Fri & Sat, 10am-2am Sun) Below a small shopping centre, this bar, complete with pool table, is a popular place for a drink and becomes something of a club at the weekend.

Getting There & Around

Bus service is not very good to and from Črnomelj, although there are up to nine daily departures to Vinica (€2.60, 30 minutes, 18km) via Dragatuš depending on the season, two daily buses at 10.25am and 14.30pm to Adlešiči (€2.20, 30 minutes, 11km), two or three daily buses to Novo Mesto (€5.05, one hour, 43km) and a bus on Friday and Sunday to Ljubljana (€10, 2½ hours, 113km) via Muljava and Žužemberk.

Črnomelj is served by up to nine trains a day from Ljubljana (€5.90, 2¼ hours, 107km) via Novo Mesto and Semič. Three to five daily trains also depart Črnomelj for Karlovac, 45km to the south in Croatia.

You can hire bicycles from **L Šport** (☎ 305 24 81, 040-657 657; Kolodvorska cesta 13; half-day €6.25-8.35; ☽ 8am-7pm Mon-Fri, 8am-noon Sat).

AROUND ČRNOMELJ
Rožanec
☎ 07 / pop 60 / elev 195m
About 4km northwest of Črnomelj just off the old Roman road (now route No 216) is the little village of Rožanec; to reach it turn west just after Lokve. From a parking lot in the village centre, a sign points the way along a trail that leads about 400m to the **Mithraeum** (Mitrej), a temple dedicated to the god Mithra, dating from the 2nd century AD. At first it appears to be no more than a natural hollow in the limestone set on a wooded hillside. But on one of the exposed limestone faces is a 1.5m-high carved relief of Mithra sacrificing the sacred bull, watched by Sol (the sun, at top left) and Luna (the moon, at top right), with a dog, serpent and scorpion at his feet.

Lahinja Country Park
☎ 07 / elev to 242m
This 275-hectare park, about 9km south of Črnomelj, is a protected karst area and the source of the Lahinja River, with trails crisscrossing the area. Two small swamps are home to a number of endangered plants and animals, especially birds like orioles, nightingales and kingfishers. The area around **Pusti Gradac** is a treasure-trove of prehistoric finds and caves. The **park information centre** (☎ 305 74 28, 031-705 519) is in Veliki Nerajec at house No 18a.

KOLPA VALLEY
☎ 07 / elev to 264m
The 113km-long Kolpa, which forms Slovenia's southeastern border with Croatia, is the warmest and one of the cleanest rivers in the country. As a result, it has become a popular recreational area for swimming, fishing and boating, especially around the village of **Vinica**. To the northeast (and downstream) is **Adlešiči**, known for its folk culture and easy walks.

Sights
In Vinica (population 210) the **Oton Župančič Memorial Collection** (Spomninska Zbirka Otona Župančiča; ☎ 364 61 14, 040-630 365; Vinica 9; adult/child €1.25/0.85; ☽ by arrangement), a branch of the Bela Krajina Museum in Metlika, is housed in the cottage where the celebrated Slovenian poet was born in 1878.

While passing through the village of **Purga** just north of Adlešiči (population 130), visit the **Čebelar Adlešič** (Adlešič Beekeepers; ☎ 307 02 37; Purga 5). The family will be happy to show you their hives, explain all things apiarian and sell you their honey, There's a tasting of their *domača medica* (homemade mead) for €2.50. The ruins of **Pobrežje Castle**, about 1km northeast of Purga, are worth exploring.

Activities
Much of the Slovenian riverbank of the Kolpa from Fučkovci, just north of Adlešiči, as far southwest as Stari Trg ob Kolpi forms the 6500-hectare **Kolpa Country Park**, a protected area of natural wonders and cultural monu-

---

MITHRA & THE GREAT SACRIFICE
Mithraism, the worship of the god Mithra, originated in Persia. As Roman rule extended into the west, the religion became extremely popular with traders, imperial slaves and mercenaries of the Roman army, and spread rapidly throughout the empire in the 1st and 2nd centuries AD. In fact, Mithraism was the principal rival of Christianity until Constantine came to the throne in the 4th century.

Mithraism was a mysterious religion and its devotees (mostly male) were sworn to secrecy. What little is known of Mithra, the god of justice and social contract, has been deduced from reliefs and icons found in temples, such as the ones at Rožanec near Črnomelj and at Ptuj in Štajerska. Most of them portray Mithra clad in a Persian-style cap and tunic sacrificing a white bull in front of Sol, the sun god. From the bull's blood sprout grain and grapes and from its semen animals grow. Sol's wife Luna, the moon, begins her cycle and time is born.

Mithraism and Christianity competed strongly because of a striking similarity in many of their rituals. Both religions involved the birth of a deity on winter solstice (25 December), shepherds, death and resurrection and a form of baptism. Devotees of Mithraism knelt when they worshipped and a common meal – a 'communion' of bread and water – was a regular feature of the liturgy.

ments. **Žagar Zvonko** (☎ 306 44 41, 041-609 920), a company based in Damelj (house No 11), southwest of Vinica and in the heart of the park, rents canoes and rafts (€13 to €16 per day) and organises river excursions on water scooters. The ambitious, however, will look into the rapid-water kayak run from Stari Trg, 20km upriver (and still in the park), to Vinica costing about €20. Contact either **Grand Kolpa** (☎ 305 51 01, 041 740 798; www.grandkolpa-sp.si; Stari Trg ob Kolpi 15) in Stari Trg or **Dol** (☎ 01-894 36 77; 031-381 133; Dol 7) in Dol (house No 7) near Stari Trg. **Fishing** is especially good around Dol; you can buy a daily fishing licence at Camping Kolpa Vinica.

From Adlešiči, two easy **hikes** to nearby hills afford great views of the Kolpa, vineyards and surrounding towns. To get to Mala Plešivica (341m), walk south along a marked trail for about half an hour. A short distance to the west is a sinkhole with a water source called Vodenica; steps lead down to the source, where you'll find a large stone vault. Velika Plešivica (363m), topped with a 12th-century church dedicated to St Mary Magdalene, is about an hour's walk northwest of Adlešiči.

Sleeping & Eating

Camping Kolpa Vinica (☎ 306 16 50, 041- 615 560; Vinica 19; per adult/child €5/3.75; ☼ May-Sep; P) This camping ground hard by the Kolpa River and just metres from the Croatian border covers an area of about 1.5 hectares and has 150 tent and caravan sites.

Avtokamp Katra Vinica (☎ 364 60 34, 041-368 312; Vinica 33; per person €5; ☼ May-Sep; P) Next to Camping Kolpa Vinica on the river, this small camping ground has sites for 40 tents and caravans.

Grabrijanovi farmhouse (☎ 307 00 70, 040-391 286; Adlešiči 5; per person €14.60-17.50; ☼ Mar–mid-Jan; P) This farmhouse, with three rooms and four apartments on the main road 500m from the Kolpa in Adlešiči, is one of the better choices in the area and the food gets rave reviews. Bikes are available for guests.

Pri Štefaniču farmhouse (☎ 305 73 47; www.pri -stefanicu.com/; Dragatuš 22; per person €18-25; P) This farmhouse, with the popular Župančičev Hram restaurant (meals from €10), has ac-commodation in eight rooms and is an excellent starting point for walks in Lahinja Country Park.

Raztresen farmhouse (☎ 307 05 16, 041-736 587; www.rim.si; Jankoviči-Rim 16-18; half-board €23-27; P ▫) Along with accommodation, this dynamic place 400m from the crossroads in Dolenjci, north of Adlešiči, offers courses in traditional crafts and trades (weaving, basketry, beekeeping), a shop and a gallery.

Gostilna Balkovec (☎ 305 76 32; starters €3.35-5.45, mains from €5; ☼ 8am-11pm) This little *gostilna* in Mali Nerajec (house No 3), on the edge of Lahinja Country Park. specialises in *pečenka* (roast meat), especially *jagenjček* (roast lamb), which costs €15 per person.

Gostilna Milič (☎ 307 00 19; Adlešiči 15; meals €8.50; ☼ 11am-midnight Tue-Thu, 11am-1am Fri & Sat, 9am-10pm Sun) In the centre of Adlešiči, Milič is one of the oldest eateries in Bela Krajina. Its drawcard is a large baker's oven that produces anything and everything from pizza to roast suckling pig.

Gostilna Kapušin (☎ 369 91 50; Krasinec 55; meals from €10; ☼ 8am-11pm Tue-Sun) This popular *gostilna*, about 6km north of Adlešiči, has excellent fish dishes and is highly recommended by locals.

Shopping

At the **Čebelar Adlešič** farmhouse (p221) you can buy honey, mead, beeswax, pollen and propolis, the sticky substance collected from certain trees by bees to cement their hives and considered an elixir.

The **Raztresen farmhouse** (above) contains a gallery of locally produced crafts for sale, including hand-woven linen from flax grown on the farm, painted Easter eggs, wicker baskets, even bee colonies. A visit to the gallery with demonstrations is €5.70 per person. It also has a range of local wines (including the sweet 'ice' variety) and brandies in beautifully crafted hand-blown bottles.

Getting There & Around

Depending on the season up to nine buses a day link Vinica with Črnomelj (€2.60, 30 minutes, 18km) via Dragatuš. There are a couple of buses a day from Adlešiči to Črnomelj (€2.20, 30 minutes, 11km).

Štajerska & Koroška

Štajerska (Styria in English), far and away Slovenia's largest province, gets a bum rap from other Slovenes. They dismiss the province as one huge industrial farm and tease the locals for being country bumpkins who drink too much. It's true that Štajerska has more big farms than any other part of Slovenia. And, along with wheat and potatoes, hops for making beer are an important crop, as are grapes for the province's excellent wines (which may partly explain the Štajerci's reputation for overindulgence). But Štajerska is not the flat, seemingly endless plain that is Prekmurje. Indeed, to the west Štajerska is overlooked by the Savinja Alps and to the north by the Pohorje Massif, an adventure-land of outdoor activities. Those in search of culture and the past will be drawn by three of the country's most historical cities and towns: Maribor, Celje and that little gem, Ptuj.

In stark contrast is tiny Koroška (Carinthia in English), to the north of Štajerska and a mere shadow of what it once was. Indeed, until the end of WWI, Carinthia included an area much larger than the three valleys in now encloses. A region of dark forests, mountains and highland meadows, Koroška is tailor-made for outdoor activities, including skiing, mountain biking and horse riding, but especially hiking.

There is a reason why Koroška is so small. In the plebiscite ordered by the victorious allies after WWI, Slovenes living on the other side of the Karavanke, the 120-km-long rock wall that separates Slovenia from Austria, voted to put their economic future in the hands of Vienna while the mining region of the Mežica Valley went to Slovenia. As a result, the Slovenian nation lost 90,000 of its nationals (7% of the population) as well as the cities of Klagenfurt (Celovec) and Villach (Beljak) to Austria.

HIGHLIGHTS

- Walk the narrow back streets of medieval **Ptuj** (p232), the jewel of Štajerska
- Sample some of the nightlife in the water-front Lent district of **Maribor** (p243)
- Go native on a farm holiday in the **Central Pohorje Region** (p246)
- Pedal underground (and above!) at the spectacular **Mountain Bike Park** (p262) at Črna na Koroškem near Dravograd
- Sober up (metaphysically, mate) viewing the scary 15th-century frescoes of the Final Judgement in the **Church of the Holy Spirit** (p262) in Slovenj Gradec

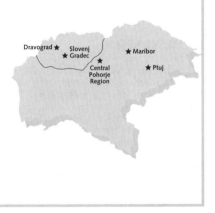

History

Štajerska has been at the crossroads of Slovenia for centuries and virtually everyone has 'slept here' – at least for a time: Celts, Romans, early Slavs, Habsburgs and Nazi German occupiers. In the 14th century the Counts of Celje were among the richest and most powerful feudal dynasties in Central Europe and they challenged the Austrian monarchy's rule for 100 years. Štajerska suffered more than most of the rest of Slovenia under the black leather boot of Nazism in WWII, and many of its inhabitants were murdered, deported or forced to work in labour camps.

Despite its current size, Koroška holds a special place in the hearts and minds of most Slovenes. The Duchy of Carantania (Karantanija), the first Slavic state dating back to the 7th century, was centred here, and the word 'Carinthia' is derived from that name. The region was heavily fortified with castles during the Middle Ages and, from the 12th century onward, was an important cultural and artistic centre. Development came to western Koroška in the early 19th century with the opening of the iron mines at Prevalje and Ravne na Koroškem.

ŠTAJERSKA

Some Slovenian guidebooks divide Štajerska up simply as the 'Maribor area' and the 'Celje area'. Here we've split it into many more sections: the Kozjansko region in the southeast; the spa town of Rogaška Slatina above Kozjansko; historic Ptuj; Maribor, Slovenia's second-largest city; the Pohorje Massif; the central city of Celje; and the Upper Savinja Valley bordering Gorenjska.

KOZJANSKO REGION

Kozjansko is a remote region along the eastern side of the Posavje Mountains and the 80km-long Sotla River, which forms the border with Croatia. It is an area of forests, rolling hills, vineyards, scattered farms and the site of one of Slovenia's three regional parks, with much to offer visitors in the way of spas, castles, hiking, cycling and excellent wine.

In the Middle Ages Kozjansko became the frontier region between Austrian Styria and Hungarian Croatia, which accounts for the important castles at Podsreda, Podčetrtek and Bistrica ob Sotli.

Podčetrtek

☎ 03 / pop 560 / elev 224m

Most people make their way to this village on a little bump of land extending into Croatia to relax at the ever-expanding Terme Olimia thermal spa just a short distance from the centre. Looming overhead are the remains of a castle originally built in the 11th century and an important fortification during the wars with the Hungarians 300 years later.

In case you were wondering, the town's seemingly unpronounceable name comes from the Slovenian word for 'Thursday' – the day the market took place and the district court sat.

ORIENTATION

The centre of Podčetrtek is at the junction of four roads: to the west is Cesta Slake and the village of Olimje; to the north and northwest, Trška cesta, Cesta Škofja Gora and the castle; and to the northeast, Zdraviliška cesta and the spa complex.

All buses stop at the crossroads as well as at the spa and the camping ground. There are three train stations. For the village centre and the castle, get off at Podčetrtek. Atomske Toplice Hotel is good for Terme Olimia, the spa hotels and Lipa Village. Podčetrtek Toplice is the correct stop for the camping ground and Aqualuna water park.

INFORMATION

Banka Celje (Cesta Slake 1; ⏰ 8.30-11.30am & 2-5pm Mon-Fri) Next to Mercator supermarket.

Post office (Trška cesta 23; ⏰ 8am-9.30am, 10am-3.30pm & 4-6pm Mon-Fri, 8am-noon Sat) Some 200m north of the crossroads.

Tourist Information Centre Podčetrtek (☎ 810 90 13; www.turizem-podcetrtek.si; Cesta Škofja Gora 1; ⏰ 8am-4pm Mon-Sat May-Sep, 9am-noon Sun; 8am-3pm Mon-Sat, 9am-noon Sun Oct-Apr) Usually closes for a half-hour at 10am.

SIGHTS

The enormous **Podčetrtek Castle** (Grad Podčetrtek) on the hill-top (335m) to the northwest of town is not the 11th century original built by the Krško bishops; that one was razed in the 15th century during the wars with the Hungarians. The present Renaissance-style castle went up some time in the mid-16th century but was badly damaged by an earthquake in 1974. The castle, which is in very bad repair and not open to the public,

ŠTAJERSKA

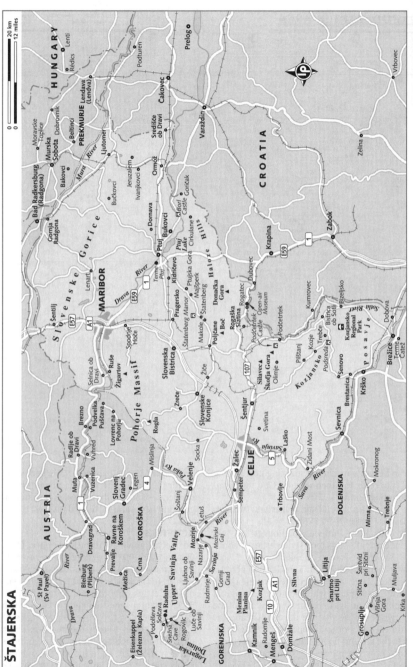

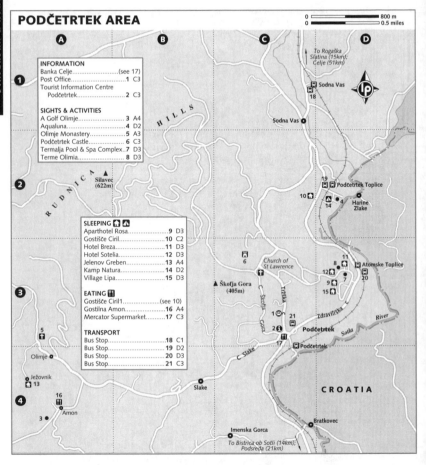

PODČETRTEK AREA

can be easily reached by walking north along Trška cesta and then west on Cesta na Grad for about 2km.

The Minorite **Olimje monastery** (Minoritski Samostan Olimje; ☎ 582 91 61; Olimje 82; ⏰ 8am-7pm Mon-Sat), 3km southwest of Podčetrtek, was built as a Renaissance-style castle in about 1550. When Pauline monks took over what was then called Wolimia in German about a century later, they added the baroque **Church of the Assumption**, which boasts its original ceiling paintings in the presbytery, one of the largest baroque altars in the country and the unbelievably ornate **Chapel of St Francis Xavier**. On the ground floor of one of the four corner towers is the monastery's greatest treasure: a 17th-century **pharmacy** (adult/child €1.25/0.85;

⏰ 10am-noon & 1-6pm) painted with religious and medical scenes. The Franciscan monks in residence continue the monastic tradition of growing herbs and medicinal plants.

ACTIVITIES

Formerly known as Atomske Toplice, **Terme Olimia** (☎ 829 70 00; www.terme-olimia.com; Zdraviliška cesta 24; nonguests adult €8.80-10, child €6.70-7.90; ⏰ 8am-10pm Sun-Fri, to midnight Sat), about 1.2km northeast of Podčetrtek, has thermal water (28°C to 35°C) full of magnesium and calcium, which is recommended for those recovering from surgery or trying to cure rheumatism. These days, however, it places most of the emphasis on recreation. The eight indoor and outdoor pools connected by an underwater passage at the **Termalija** pool and spa complex alone cover an area of 2000 sq metres, and there's sauna, steam room, solarium and sports facilities. Next to the camping ground, about 1km north of the main Terme Olimia complex, is **Aqualuna** (adult €12.50-13.80, child €9.20-10.40; 9am-8pm Mon-Fri, 8am-8pm Sat & Sun May-Sep), a water park with another eight outdoor pools over 3000 sq metres and the requisite slides, Adrenaline Tower, wave machines and so on.

Some of the most rewarding **hikes** and **bike** trips in Slovenia can be made in this area, and the free 1:18,000-scale *Podčetrtek–Terme Olimia* tourist maps lists dozens of excursions for walkers, cyclists and mountain bikers. The easiest walks on marked trails take an hour or two (although the circuitous one northeast to the hill-top Church of St Emma at 345m lasts about four hours), and there are bicycle routes all the way to Kozje (37km), Podsreda (41km) and Rogaška Slatina (31km).

The Jelenov Greben farmhouse (below) offers 50-minute sightseeing flights in a hot-air **balloon** for €100 per person.

A Golf Olimje (810 90 66; http://agolf.podcetr tek.si; Olimje 24; 18 holes adult/child Mon-Fri €24.20/17.50, Sat & Sun €29.20/20.50) is a nine-hole, 31-par golf course owned by and just south of the Gostilna Amon (right). Hiring half a set of clubs costs €6.25.

SLEEPING

Kamp Natura (829 78 33; www.terme-olimia.com; camp site per person €6.90-7.90, with pools €12.10-13.80; late Apr–mid-Oct) Owned and operated by Terme Olimia, this small camping ground is about 1km north of the main spa complex on the edge of the Sotla River; if you've checked in and you've got a guest card, you can take the shortcut to the spa through Croatia! More expensive rates include daily entry to the Aqualuna water park next door as well as the Termalija complex pool

Gostišče Ciril (582 91 09; www.ciril-youthhostel -bc.si; Zdraviliška cesta 10; per person €12.50-16; P) Hostel-like accommodation above this very popular restaurant on the main road is in 15 basic rooms with two and three beds. It's just across from the entrance to the camping ground and the Aqualuna water park.

Jelenov Greben (Deer Ridge; 582 90 46; www.jel enov-greben.si; Olimje 90; s €33.50-37.50, d €59-66, apt €58.50-67; P) This spectacular property, set on a ridge some 500m south of Olimje at Ježovnik, has 12 cosy rooms (some have balco-

nies), four-person apartments and a popular restaurant (starters €3 to €8, mains €5.50 to €11.70, picnic lunches from €6.25) that is open daily from 9am and celebrated for its venison and wild mushroom dishes. There is also a shop selling farm products and souvenirs that is open 9am to 7pm. 'Deer Ridge' is a working farm and a hundred head of deer roam freely on the eight hectares of land.

Terme Olimia (829 70 00; www.terme-olimia.com; P) Along with its camp site to the north, the spa complex offers accommodation in two hotels, an apartment complex and a tourist village. Package deals are endless at this place and those staying at any of the Terme Olimia properties may use all the pools for free.

Its cheapest accommodation is **Village Lipa** (Vas Lipa; 2-/4-bed bungalow €66/83), a tourist 'village' at the southern end of the complex that does not look unlike a cookie-cutter American suburban housing development. If that's what you're after, there are 25 houses with 136 apartments. **Aparthotel Rosa** (apt for 2/4 €99.50/166) just west of the spa complex has 94 apartments with living room, bedroom, kitchen, bathroom and satellite TV. The 154-room **Hotel Breza** (s/d €71.50-118) is housed in a rather strange, five-storey structure with roofs sloping off every which way. Still, it has direct access to the Termalija complex and its very own pool.

The new kid on the block is the 145-room **Hotel Sotelia** (s/d €91.50/153), a luxurious and very 'green' hotel whose undulating design and colours seem to make it blend into the forest behind it.

The tourist office has a list of families offering **private rooms** (per person €10.50 to €25) in Podčetrtek and Sodna Vas, 2km north of the spa complex on the main road.

EATING

Gostišče Ciril (starters €4.20-5.40, mains €5.40-6.20; 9am-9pm Mon-Fri, to 10pm Sat & Sun) This grill restaurant above the popular hostel is frequented by local Slovenes and their Croatian neighbours. The vine-covered terrace is lovely on a warm evening. They also do pizza (€3.10 to €4.60)

Gostilna Amon (818 24 80; Olimje 24; meals from €15; 11am-10pm Sun-Thu, to 11pm Fri & Sat) This Maison de Qualité establishment up in the hill south of Olimje is simply the best place for miles around. It offers high-quality food and organic wines. Set lunch is excellent value at €8.

There's a branch of **Mercator** (Cesta Slake 1; ☉ 7am-7pm Mon-Fri, 7am-1pm Sat, 8am-noon Sun) supermarket beside Banka Celje in Podčetrtek village.

GETTING THERE & AROUND

Between two and five buses a day on weekdays pass by Podčetrtek and Terme Olimia on their way to Bistrica ob Sotli (€2.20, 20 minutes, 14km) and Celje (€4, one hour, 35km). During the school term there's two buses on weekdays to Rogaška Slatina (€2.60, 30 minutes, 18km) and Maribor (€7, 1½ hours, 73km)

Podčetrtek is on the rail line linking Celje (via Stranje) with Imeno. Up to six trains leave the main Podčetrtek station every day for Celje (€2.65, 45 minutes, 35km) and Imeno (€1, three minutes, 3km).

You can call a taxi on ☎ 041-614 847.

Kozjansko Regional Park
☎ 03 / elev to 686m

Protected under the old regime as far back as 1981 and established by parliament in 1999, 20,760-hectare **Kozjansko Regional Park** (Kozjanski Regijski Park; ☎ 800 71 00; www.gov.si/kp in Slovene; Podsreda 45; ☉ 8am-4pm Mon-Fri), one of only three so designated in the country, stretches along the Sotla River, from the border with Dolenjska and Bizeljsko in the south to Podčetrtek in the north. It encompasses several communities, including Bistrica ob Sotli (population 282), just over the border from the Croatian village of Kumrovec, where Tito was born in 1892 to a Slovenian mother and a Croatian father.

The forests and dry meadows of the park harbour a wealth of flora and fauna, notably butterflies, reptiles and birds, including corncrakes, kingfishers and storks. There are a number of trails in the park, including the 32km-long **Podsreda Trail** (Pešpot Podsreda), which begins next to one of the best-preserved Romanesque castles in Slovenia.

Podsreda Castle
☎ 03 / elev 415m

Perched on a hill south of the village of Podsreda (population 205), **Podsreda Castle** (Grad Podsreda; ☎ 580 61 18; adult/child €2.50/1.90; ☉ 10am-6pm Tue-Sun Apr-Oct) looks pretty much the way it did when it was built as Hörberg in about 1200. A barbican on the southern side, with walls 3m thick, leads to a central courtyard with a sgraffito of a knight; in the barbican is a medieval kitchen and a dungeon hidden beneath a staircase. The rooms in the castle wings, some with beamed ceilings and ancient chandeliers, now contain a glassworks exhibit (crystal from Rogaška Slatina, vials from the Olimje pharmacy, green Pohorje glass). However, the tiny Romanesque chapel is worth the visit, and there's a wonderful collection of prints of Štajerska's castles and monasteries taken from *Topographii Ducatus Stiria* (1681) by Georg Mattäus Vischer (1628–96). The fabulous wood-panelled Renaissance Hall hosts exhibitions, classical concerts and, of course, weddings.

A rough, winding 5km-long road leads to the castle, but you can also reach it via a relatively steep 2km trail from Stari Trg, less than 1km southeast of Podsreda village. If you've built up an appetite climbing up and down those hills, there's a small *gostilna* (inn-like restaurant) called **Pri Martinu** (☎ 580 61 20; Podsreda 47; meals from €10) in the village, which has a vine-covered terrace and rooms for rent (€12.50 per person).

Getting to Podsreda from Podčetrtek is tricky if you don't have your own wheels. The only option is to catch the one daily bus to Kozje and there wait for the one headed for Bistrica ob Sotli, which passes through Podsreda village.

ROGAŠKA SLATINA
☎ 03 / pop 4730 / elev 228m

Rogaška Slatina is Slovenia's oldest and largest spa town, a veritable 'cure factory' with almost a dozen hotels and treatments and therapies ranging from 'pearl baths' to dreadful-sounding 'lymph drainage'. It's an attractive place set among scattered forests in the foothills of the Macelj range, and hiking and cycling in the area is particularly good.

Although the hot spring here was known in Roman times, Rogaška Slatina didn't make it on the map until 1574, when the governor of Styria, one Wolf Ungnad, took the waters on the advice of his physician. A century later a publication entitled *Roitschocrene* examined the curative properties of the springs and claimed they had helped the ailing viceroy of Croatia. The news spread to Vienna, visitors started to arrive in droves and inns were opened. By the early 19th century Rogaška Slatina was an established spa town.

Orientation

The heart of Rogaška Slatina is the spa complex, an attractive – and architecturally important – group of neoclassical, Secessionist and Plečnik-style buildings surrounding a long landscaped garden called Zdraviliški trg (Health Resort Square). The hotels and central Terapija building to the north and northeast are late 1960s and '70s vintage and not in keeping with the rest of the lovely square.

Rogaška Slatina's bus station is south of Zdraviliški trg on Celjska cesta. The train station is 300m further south on Kidričeva ulica.

Information

Post office (Kidričeva ulica 3; ⏳ 8am-6pm Mon-Fri, to noon Sat)

SKB Banka (Kidričeva ulica 11)

Srečko exchange office (Kidričeva ulica; ⏳ 8am-5pm Mon-Fri, to noon Sat) In the little pavilion opposite SKB Banka.

Tourist Information Centre Rogaška Slatina (☎ 581 44 14; tic.rogaska@siol.net; Zdraviliški trg 1; ⏳ 9am-7pm Mon-Fri, 11am-5pm Sat & Sun Jul & Aug; 9am-4pm Mon-Fri, to noon Sat Sep-Jun) Less-than-helpful tourist office at the southern end of the square.

Activities

The mineral water (called Donat Mg) found at the spa complex **Terme Rogaška** (☎ 811 70 10; www.terme-rogaska.com) contains the richest amount of magnesium in the world and is primarily for drinking. The stuff is sold throughout Slovenia for both curative and

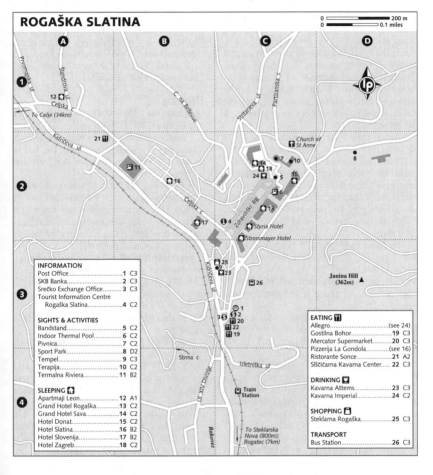

ROGAŠKA SLATINA

0   200 m
0   0.1 miles

refreshment purposes, but you might find the real thing here tastes a little bit too metallic and salty. The water, which also contains calcium, sulphates, lithium and bromide, is said to eliminate stress, aid digestion and encourage weight loss. The magnesium alone, it is claimed, regulates 200 bodily functions.

You can engage in a 'drinking cure' of your own at the **Pivnica** (admission €1.50, 3-day pass €7.50; ☽ 7am-1pm & 3-7pm Mon-Sat, 7am-1pm & 4-7pm Sun), the round, glassed-in drinking hall where mineral water is dispensed directly from the springs. It's just beyond the gazebolike **bandstand** where concerts are staged in the warmer months.

The centre of real action at the spa is the 12-storey **Terapija** (www.rogaska-medical.com; Zdraviliški trg 9; ☽ 7.30am-6.30pm Mon-Fri, 8am-noon & 3-6.30pm Sat & Sun) building where those pearl baths (€16) are being taken and all those lymph glands are being drained (€23). At the Hotel Donat opposite the bandstand there's an **indoor thermal pool** (€8; ☽ 8am-8pm Sun-Thu, to 11pm Fri & Sun), sauna, steam room and gym. A 30-minute body massage costs €20. Most of the larger hotels have their own wellness centres, including the Grand Hotel Rogaška's Vis Vita and the Lotus Terme at the Sava.

The so-called **Termalna Riviera** (☎ 819 19 50; Celjska cesta 7; 3-hr pass adult/senior & student/child €6.25/4.60/4.20, 1-day pass €7.50/5.85/5; ☽ 9am-8pm Sun-Thu, to 11pm Fri & Sat) next to the Sonce shopping centre has one indoor and two outdoor swimming pools that are all connected. There's also a whirlpool and saunas. Terme Rogaška hotels include free entry to these pools in their rates.

The **Sport Park** (☎ 581 56 16; ☽ 10am-noon & 4-9pm), a couple of hundred metres east of the Hotel Donat and up the hill, has six outdoor and four indoor **tennis courts** (per hr €4.20 to €10.85; racquet & balls €6.25) and a **squash court** (€4.25) available for hire.

South of the sports centre on Janina Hill (362m) is a tiny **ski slope** (day/night pass €5/6.25), where you can also rent equipment. Terme Rogaška guests get to ski for free.

There are **walking trails** marked on the 1:25 000 *Rogaška Slatina* PZS map (€2.10) available from the TIC; they range from 2km to 15km and fan out from Rogaška Slatina into the surrounding hills and meadows. One leads 15km to the **Church of St Florian**, on a hill northeast of the spa, and to Ložno, from where you can continue on another 4km to **Donačka Gora**. If

you want to do it an easier way, take a bus or train to Rogatec, then walk to Donačka Gora in about two hours. Accommodation there is at the Category III **Rudljev Dom na Donački Gori** (☎ 582 79 79, 031 730 466; ☽ mid-Apr–Oct; Sat & Sun Nov–mid-Apr) at 590m, which has 40 beds in 24 rooms.

The walk to **Boč** northwest of Rogaška Slatina takes about four hours though you can drive as far as Category III **Dom na Boču** (☎ 582 46 17, 031 743 017; Drevenik 7; ☽ year-round), a mountain hut a couple of kilometres south of the peak at 658m with 47 beds in 15 rooms.

Festivals & Events

Rogaška Musical Summer is a series of some 40 concerts, from chamber music and opera to Slovenian folk music, which is held in and around the central bandstand from June to late September. The tourist office will provide you with a list of what's on. Concerts are sometimes held in the Grand Hotel Rogaška's Crystal Hall (Kristalna Dvorana), where Franz Liszt once tickled the ivories.

Sleeping

Apartmaji Leon (☎ 492 13 60; www.virgo-sp.si; Celjska cesta 28a; apt €40-80; P ♿) If you're in a group, you might try this pension with apartments measuring 40 and 60 sq metres for two to five people. It's 350m northeast of the Termalna Riviera.

Hotel Slatina (☎ 818 41 00; www.rogaska-medical .com, in Slovene; Celjska cesta 6; s/d €50/84, apt from €110; P ◻) This attractive 60-room hotel in a restored late-19th-century spa building has singles, doubles and apartments for two to four people with kitchenette.

Hotel Slovenija (☎ 811 50 00; hotel.slovenia@siol .net; www.terme-rogaska.com; Celjska cesta 1; s €52-60, d €84-100; P ✕ ◻) This flower-bedecked, 65-room hotel is one of the best deals for its price; it's the cheapest in town and central to everything. The service is especially friendly.

Grand Hotel Sava (☎ 811 40 00; www.rogaska.si; Zdraviliški trg 6; s €50.50-75.50, d €83-138.50, ste €128-232; P ✕ ✕ ◻ ♿) The modern Sava and the attached older (and cheaper) **Hotel Zagreb** (s €48.50-57.50, d €79-93.50; P ✕ ✕ ◻), each with four stars, are at the northwestern end of Zdraviliški trg and count a total of 276 rooms. It's certainly the most popular and active complex in town and another plus is the recent renovation at the Zagreb.

Hotel Donat (☎ 811 30 00; www.ghdonat.com; Zdraviliški trg 10; s €62-76, d €88-148, ste €198-278; P ✕ ☎) Despite the ugly modern exterior, the four-star Donat, with 250 beds, has some of the best facilities, including a large swimming pool open to nonguests

Grand Hotel Rogaška (☎ 811 20 00; www.terme -rogaska.com; Zdraviliški trg 10; s €69-104, d €108-188, ste €148-308) Along with its two branches, the contiguous Hotel Styria and Hotel Strossmayer (singles €46 to €66, doubles €68 to €108) on the eastern side of Zdraviliški trg with more than 350 beds among them, this four-star property is *la crème de la crème* of accommodation in Rogaška Slatina. The Grand, with its spectacular public areas (especially the Crystal Hall), dates from 1913 while the other two were added in the mid-19th century.

The TIC can arrange **private rooms** and **apartments** in the town and surrounding areas for between €14.60 and €20.80, depending on the season and room category.

Eating

Slaščičarna Kavarna Center (☎ 819 24 33; Kidričeva ulica 21; dishes from €2.50; ☉ 7am-11pm Mon-Thu, 7am-1am Fri & Sat, 8am-11pm Sun) Essentially an ice-cream shop and café, the Center serves döners and kebabs until relatively late.

Pizzerija La Gondola (☎ 818 41 00; Celjska cesta 6; dishes €3.35-4.60; ☉ noon-11pm Mon-Fri, to 1am Sat, to 11pm Sun) Beneath the Hotel Slatina, this delightful cubby-hole serves good pizzas, pastas and salads.

Ristorante Sonce (☎ 819 21 60; Celjska cesta 9; meals €10; ☉ 9am-11pm Mon-Sat, 11am-5pm Sun) This restaurant with impressive wine cellar near the shopping centre specialises in seafood.

Gostilna Bohor (☎ 581 41 00; Kidričeva ulica 23; pizza €3.35-4.60, mains €4.60-10.50; ☉ 8am-10pm Mon-Thu, 8am-11pm Fri & Sat, 10am-10pm Sun) For hearty Slovenian fare and better-than-average pizza, try this popular local eatery. The Kmečka Pizza ('Farmer's Pizza') has virtually everything from the barnyard on top.

Allegro (☎ 811 40 00; Zdraviliški trg 5; starters €3.75-7.10, mains €6.70-16.70; ☉ 7pm-midnight) This Italian/Mediterranean restaurant, with some Slovenian favourites thrown in for good measure, is accessible from the Sava and Zagreb hotels as well as the Kavarna Imperial. Look out for daily specials. Service is friendly but painfully slow.

There's a **Mercator** (Kidričeva ulica 13; ☉ 8am-7pm Mon-Fri, to 1pm Sat) next to the post office.

Drinking

Kavarna Attems (☎ 819 27 10; Zdraviliški trg 22; ☉ 8am-1am Mon-Thu, to 3am Fri & Sat, to 1pm Sun) Most visitors to Rogaška Slatina spend their evenings in the hotel bars and cafés; the Attems, in the stunning Art Nouveau Tempel building dating from 1904 and renovated in 2001 at the southern end of Zdraviliški trg, is popular with a younger crowd.

Kavarna Imperial (☎ 811 40 00; Zdraviliški trg 5; ☉ 11am-midnight) One of the most pleasant places for a drink in the spa complex is this café with a huge outside terrace attached to the Hotel Zagreb. There's live music by night.

Shopping

Rogaška Slatina is almost as celebrated for its crystal as it is for its mineral water.

Steklarna Rogaška (☎ 819 09 14; Zdraviliški trg 23; ☉ 9am-7pm Mon-Fri, to 6pm Sat, to 1pm & 3-6pm Sun) This showroom next to the Kavarna Attems has a large selection of stemware, vases and bowls.

Steklarska Nova (☎ 818 20 27; Steklarska ulica 1; ☉ 8am-7pm Mon-Fri, to 1pm Sat) This outlet attached to the school where the making (presumably not breaking) of Rogaška glass is taught, is 1km south of the town centre and has a wide range of leaded crystal on sale.

Getting There & Away

Buses to Celje (€4, 45 minutes, 34km) and Rogatec (€1.70, 10 minutes, 7km) leave Rogaška Slatina almost hourly. There are buses to Maribor (€7, 1½ hours, 75km, two or three daily) and Ljubljana (€9.30, two hours, 105km, 4.47am daily). Other destinations that can be reached by bus include Dobovec (€2.20, 30 minutes, 15km, up to four daily) and the Croatian border and Ptuj (€5.75, one hour, 53km, 6.50am daily).

Rogaška Slatina is on the train line linking Celje (€2.65, 50 minutes, 36km, up to seven daily) via Rogatec (€1, 10 minutes, 6km) and Dobovec with Zabok in Croatia, where you can change for Zagreb.

AROUND ROGAŠKA SLATINA
Rogatec Open-Air Museum

In Rogatec (population 1575), 7km east of Rogaška Slatina, this **outdoor museum** (Muzej na Prostem Rogatec; ☎ 818 62 00; www.muzej-rogatec.si; Ptujska cesta 23; adult/student/child €2.70/2.30/2.10; ☉ 8am-6m Tue-Fri, 10am-6pm Sat & Sun Apr-early Nov) is Slovenia's largest and most ambitions *skanzen* (open-air museum). Ten original structures or replicas have been relocated or built here to create a typical Styrian farm of the 19th and early 20th centuries. The large farmhouse, barn, *toplar* (double-linked hayrack) and vintner's cottage are particularly interesting.

Rogatec can be reached from Rogaška Slatina (€1.70, 10 minutes, 7km, almost hourly) by frequent bus.

PTUJ
☎ 02 / pop 18,145 / elev 229m

Ptuj, one of the oldest towns in Slovenia, equals Ljubljana in terms of historical importance. Ptuj's compact medieval core, with its castle, museums, monasteries and churches, can easily be seen in a day. But there are so many interesting side trips and a host of activities in the area that you may decide to base yourself here for a while.

History
Ptuj, whose name in English sounds not unlike someone spitting, began life as a Roman military outpost on the right (south) bank of the Drava River and later grew into a civilian settlement called Poetovio on the opposite side. Unlike so many other Slovenian towns, Ptuj doesn't have to put a spade into the ground to prove its ancient origins: Tacitus mentioned it by name in his *Historiae* as having existed as early as 69 AD.

By the 1st century AD the largest Roman township in what is now Slovenia, Poetovio lay on a major road linking Pannonia and Noricum provinces. In the 2nd and 3rd centuries, Ptuj was the centre of the Mithraic cult (p221), a new religion that had gained popularity among Roman soldiers and slaves, and several complete temples have been unearthed in the area. But all this came to a brutal end when the Goths attacked the town in the 5th century. They were followed by the Huns, Langobards, Franks and then the early Slavs.

Ptuj received its town rights in 977 and over the next several centuries it grew rich through trade on the Drava. By the 13th century it was competing with the 'upstart' Marburg (Maribor), 26km upriver, in both crafts and commerce. Two monastic orders – the Dominicans and the Franciscan Minorites – settled here and built important monasteries. The Magyars attacked and occupied Ptuj for most of the 15th century, though each of a half-dozen raids by the Turks was thwarted.

When the railroad reached eastern Slovenia from Vienna on its way to the coast in the mid-19th century, the age-old rivalry between Maribor and Ptuj turned one-sided: the former was on the line and the latter missed out altogether. Though Ptuj was rescued from oblivion in 1863 when the railway line to Budapest passed through it, the town remained essentially a provincial centre with a German majority and very little industry until WWI.

Orientation
Ptuj lies on the left (north) bank of the Drava River. The castle, with its irregular shape and ancient walls, dominates the town from a 300m hill to the northwest. Most sites of historical interest lie on or near Slovenski trg, but Minoritski trg is the gateway to the Old Town.

The bus station is about 300m northeast of Minoritski trg at Osojnikova cesta 11. The train station is another 250m further along at Osojnikova cesta 2.

Information
Ivan Potrč Library (☎ 771 48 01, 779 12 01; Prešernova ulica 33-35; per hr €0.85; ☺ 8am-7pm Mon-Fri, to 1pm Sat) Eight terminals with internet access.
Nova Ljubljanska Banka (Prešernova ulica 6) Next door to the Garni Hotel Mitra.
Post office (Vodnikova ulica 2)
Ptuj Alpine Society (☎ 777 15 11; Prešernova ulica 27; ☺ 5-7pm Tue & Fri) Information about hiking in the area.
SKB Banka (Trstenjakova ulica 2)
Tourist Information Centre Ptuj (☎ 771 60 11; www.ptuj-tourism.si; Slovenski trg 5; ☺ 8am-6pm Mon-Fri, 9am-1pm Sat Jun; 8am-7pm Mon-Fri, to 3pm Sat & Sun Jul & Aug; 8am-5pm Mon-Fri, to 1pm Sat Sep-May) In the 16th-century Ljutomer House.

Sights
Ptuj's Gothic centre, with its Renaissance and baroque additions, is a joy to explore on foot. The following sights can be done on a 'walking tour' if visited in the order which they appear.

MINORITSKI TRG & MESTNI TRG
On the east side of **Minoritski trg**, which has a 17th-century **plague pillar** of Mary and the Infant Jesus in the centre, is the massive **Minorite monastery** (Minoritski Samostan; ☎ 771 30 91; Minoritski trg 1; ☺ by appointment), which was built in the 13th century. Because the Franciscan Minorites dedicated themselves to teaching, the order was not dissolved under the edict issued by Habsburg Emperor Joseph II in the late 18th century, and it has continued to function in Ptuj for more than seven centuries.

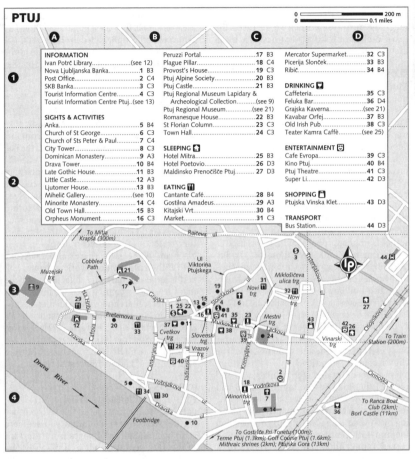

PTUJ

0 ————— 200 m
0 ————— 0.1 miles

The arcaded monastery, which dates from the second half of the 17th century, has a **summer refectory** on the 1st floor, with beautiful stucco work and a dozen ceiling paintings of Sts Peter (north side) and Paul (south side). One panel depicts the martyrdom of my namesake, poor St Stephen, who was stoned – as in with rocks thrown at him – to death by a group of pagans including Saul (later baptised as Paul). The monastery also contains a 5000-volume **library** of important manuscripts including part of a 10th-century codex used to cover a prayer book around 1590 and an original copy of the New Testament (1561) translated by Primož Trubar.

On the northern side of the monastery's inner courtyard, the **Church of Sts Peter and Paul** (Cerkev Sv Petra in Pavla), one of the most beautiful examples of early Gothic architecture in Slovenia, was reduced to rubble by Allied bombing in January 1945. It was painstakingly rebuilt over the decades and has now risen – phoenixlike – as a gem of modern architecture on the same spot.

About 150m west of the monastery is round **Drava Tower** (Dravski Stolp; Dravska ulica 4), a Renaissance water tower built as a defence against the Turks in 1551. It houses the **Mihelič Gallery** (Miheličeva Galerija; ☎ 787 92 50; admission free; ☺ 10am-1pm & 4-7pm Tue-Fri), which hosts temporary exhibits of modern art.

At the end of Krempljeva ulica, which runs north from Minoritski trg, is **Mestni trg**, a rectangular square once called Florianplatz in honour of the **St Florian Column** (1745) standing in the northwest corner. To the east is the neo-Gothic **town hall** (Mestni trg 1) designed by an architect from Graz in 1907.

SLOVENSKI TRG

Murkova ulica, which has some interesting old houses on it, leads westward from Mestni trg to funnel-shaped **Slovenski trg**, the heart of old Ptuj. In the centre, the **City Tower** (Mestni Stolp) was erected in the 16th century as a belfry and later turned into a watch tower. Roman tombstones and sacrificial altars from Poetovio were incorporated into the tower's exterior walls in 1830; you can still make out reliefs of Medusa's head, dolphins and a man on horseback.

In front of the City Tower stands the 5m-tall **Orpheus Monument** (Orfejev Spomenik), a Roman tombstone from the 2nd century with scenes from the Orpheus myth. It was used as a pillory in the Middle Ages; those found guilty of a crime were shackled to iron rings attached to the holes on the lower half. The colourfully decorated building to the south is **Ptuj Theatre** (Gledališče Ptuj; Slovenski trg 13), originally built in 1786. Until 1918 it staged plays in German only.

Behind the City Tower is the **Church of St George** (Cerkev Sv Jurija), which reveals an array of styles from Romanesque to neo-Gothic. The church contains some lovely late-14th-century choir chairs decorated with animals, a carved relief of the Epiphany dating from 1515 and frescoes in the middle of the south aisle and the restored **Laib Altar**, a three-winged altar painting by Konrad Laib (c 1410–60) completed in the mid-15th century. Near the entrance is a carved 14th-century statue under glass of St George slaying the dragon.

On the northern side of the square are several interesting buildings, including the 16th-century **Provost's House** (Slovenski trg 10) with medallions, the baroque **Old Town Hall** (Slovenski trg 6) and **Ljutomer House** (Slovenski trg 5), now housing the tourist office, whose Mediterranean-style loge was built in 1565 by Italian workers who had come to Ptuj to fortify it against the Turks.

PREŠERNOVA ULICA

Pedestrian **Prešernova ulica**, the town's market in the Middle Ages, leads westward from Slovenski trg. The arched spans that look like little bridges above some of the narrow side streets are to support older buildings. The **Late Gothic House** (Prešernova ulica 1), dating from about 1400, has an unusual projection held up by a Moor's

head. Opposite is the sombre **Romanesque House** (Prešernova ulica 4), the oldest building in Ptuj. The renovated yellow pile called the **Little Castle** (Mali Grad; Prešernova ulica 33-35) was the erstwhile home of the Salzburg bishops and a number of aristocratic families over the centuries.

MUZEJSKI TRG

Just past Sunny Park (Sončni Park) in Muzejski trg is the former **Dominican Monastery** (Dominikanski Samostan; Muzejski trg 1), which contains the **lapidary and archeological collections** of the **Ptuj Regional Museum** (☎ 778 87 80, 748 03 60; adult/child €3/1.70; ☽ 10am-5pm mid-Apr–Nov). The monastery was built in 1230 but abandoned in the late 18th century when the Habsburgs dissolved the Catholic religious orders. The beautiful eastern wing has a cross-ribbed Romanesque window and Gothic cloisters with 14th-century frescoes of Dominican monks in their black and white garb. There's also a **refectory** with 18th-century stucco work, a chapter hall and a large Roman coin collection. But the main reason for coming is to see the Roman tombstones, altars and wonderful mosaics unearthed in Ptuj and at the **Mithraic shrines** (☎ 778 87 80; adult/child €0.85/0.45, with guide €1.70/1; ☽ by appointment) at Spodnja Hajdina (key at house No 37a) and Zgornji Breg (key at Ulica K Mitreju 3), a couple of kilometres west of town.

PTUJ CASTLE

Parts of the **castle** (Grad Ptuj; Na Gradu 1; ☎ 748 03 60) date back to the first half of the 12th century (eg the west tower), but what you see here is an agglomeration of styles from the 14th to the 18th centuries put into place by one aristocratic owner after another. The castle houses the **Ptuj Regional Museum** (Pokrajinski Muzej Ptuj; ☎ 787 92 30, 778 87 80; www.pok-muzej-ptuj.si; adult/student & child €3/1.70, with guide €3.75/2.30; ☽ 9am-6pm daily May-Jun & Sep–mid-Oct; 9am-6pm Mon-Fri, to 8pm Sat & Sun Jul & Aug; 9am-5pm mid-Oct–Apr) on its three arcaded floors, but mostly worth the trip for the views of Ptuj and the Drava. The shortest way to the castle from here is to follow narrow Grajska ulica, which starts just west of the Garni Hotel Mitra and leads to a covered wooden stairway and the castle's Renaissance **Peruzzi Portal** dating from 1570.

As you enter the castle courtyard, look to the west at the red marble **tombstone of Frederick IX**, the last lord of Ptuj who died in 1438. The ground floor of one wing contains a fascinating **musical instruments collection** from the 17th to 19th centuries: some 300 flutes, horns, drums, lutes, violas, harps, clavichords and so on. As you approach each case, a tape plays the music the instruments make.

The 1st floor is given over to period rooms, each with its own style, as well as an impressive **Knights' Hall** (Viteška Dvorana). The rooms are treasure-troves of tapestries, painted wall canvases, portraits, weapons and furniture left by the castle's last owners, the Herbersteins (1873–1945) or brought from Dornava Castle, 8km to the northeast of Ptuj. You'll probably notice a coat of arms containing three buckles and the motto 'Grip Fast' in English. It belonged to the Leslies, a Scottish-Austrian family who owned the castle from 1656 to 1802.

Festival Hall contains Europe's largest collection of **Turkerie portraits**, but they are of historical rather than artistic interest. They are portraits are of Turkish and European aristocrats, generals and courtiers commissioned by Count Johann Herberstein in 1665 and painted in Štajerska. Partly because of these paintings, Turkish dress became all the rage for a time in the 18th century.

On the 2nd floor is the **Castle Gallery** of Gothic statues and oil paintings from the 16th to the 19th centuries. Have a look at the scene of Ptuj in winter by Franc Jožef Fellner (1721–70) and a painting from the early 19th century of the Church of St George, marred by graffiti in German. Two fine statues – one of St Catherine (with a wheel) and the other of St Barbara (with a tower) – carved from sandstone in about 1410 in the 'soft' Gothic style, are among the museum's most priceless possessions. There's also a large collection of **Kurent masks** on this floor as well as a collection of works of the graphic artist France Mihelič (1907–98) who worked here from 1936 to 1941. His gruesome *Mrtvi Kurent* (Dead Kurent) is memorable.

Activities

Terme Ptuj (☎ 749 41 00, 749 45 80; www.terme-ptuj.si; Pot v Toplice 9; adult €7.10-9.20, child €4.60-6.30; ☼ 7am-10pm Sun-Thu, to 11pm Fri & Sat), a thermal spa about 1.5km west of town on the south bank of the Drava, is primarily a huge recreational water park called Termalni Park, with seven outdoor swimming pools, six indoor thermal ones (water temperature 32°C to 36°C) and eight tennis courts. You can rent **bicycles** (1 hr/half-day/day €1.25/3.80/6.30) here.

About 300m west of Terme Ptuj is 18-hole, par-71 **Golf Course Ptuj** (☎ 788 91 10, 041-791 065; www.golf-ptuj.com; Mlinska cesta 13; 18 holes €35 Mon-Fri, €40 Sat & Sun, clubs hire €8; ☼ mid-Mar–mid-Nov), by all accounts the most attractive links in Slovenia.

Licences for **fishing** in the Drava are available from the Hotel Poetovio in Ptuj (p236) and **Anka** (☎ 749 05 00; Dravska ulica 10; ☼ 9am-noon & 2-4pm Mon-Fr), a travel agency near the Ribič restaurant.

You can rent **rowing** and **sailing** boats from the **Ranca Boat Club** (Brodarsko Društvo Ranca; ☎ 041-791 005; www.ranca-ptuj.com, in Slovene), about 2km southeast of the centre on the Drava.

Festivals & Events

Kurentovanje (www.kurentovanje.net) is a rite of spring celebrated for 10 days in February leading up to Shrove Tuesday; it's the most popular and best-known folklore event in Slovenia (below).

KURENT: PARTY TIME IN PTUJ

Ptuj – and many towns on the surrounding plain and in the hills – marks Shrovetide with Kurentovanje, a rite of spring and fertility that may date back to the time of the early Slavs. Such celebrations are not unique to Slovenia; they still take place at Mohács in Hungary and in Bulgaria and Serbia as well. But the Kurentovanje is among the most extravagant of these celebrations.

The main character of the rite is Kurent, god of unrestrained pleasure and hedonism – a 'Slovenian Dionysus'. The Kurents (there are many groups of them) are dressed in sheepskins with five cowbells dangling from their belts. On their heads they wear huge furry caps decorated with feathers, sticks or horns and coloured streamers. The leather face masks have eyeholes outlined in red, trunk-like noses and enormous red tongues that hang down to the chest.

The Kurents move from house to house in procession scaring off evil spirits with their bells and *ježevke* (wooden clubs) topped with quills taken from hedgehogs. A *hudič* (devil), covered in a net to catch souls, leads each group. Young girls present the Kurents with handkerchiefs, which they then fasten to their belts, and people smash little clay pots at their feet for luck and good health.

Three **traditional fairs** that take place in Novi trg in Ptuj are those dedicated to St George (Sv Jurij; 23 April), St Oswald (Sv Ožbalt; 5 August) and St Catherine (Sv Katarina; 25 November).

Sleeping

Camp Terme Ptuj (☎ 749 41 00, 749 45 80; www.terme -ptuj.si; Pot v Toplice 9; adult €12-13.30, child €6-9.35; year-round; P) This 1.5-hectare camping ground next to the thermal spa and water park has 120 sites. Rates include entry to the park and use of pools and other recreational facilities. Terme Ptuj also has what it calls camp cottages (€62.60 to €83.50), essentially stationary mobile homes for four people; attractive, cottagelike bungalows (singles €51 to €55, doubles €82 to €90) and modern apartments (singles €42 to €46.30, doubles €74 to €82) in larger villas.

Mladinsko Prenočišče Ptuj (MPP; ☎ 771 08 14; csod.yhptuj@guest.arnes.si; Osojnikova cesta 9; dm €15) This HI-affiliated dormitory near the bus station has 13 rooms with between two and six beds and is open all year. HI members get a discount of €2.

Gostišče Pri Tonetu (☎ 788 56 83; svensek.mar jeta@amis.net; Zadružni trg 13; s/d €17/34; P) This guest house with 24 beds in nine rooms and a popular restaurant (open 7am-11pm Mon-Sat, 8am-11pm Sun) just over the footbridge on the south bank of the Drava and a good springboard for cycling and walks. Ptuj's thermal baths and the golf course are nearby.

Hotel Poetovio (☎ 779 82 01; www.memoria.si; Vinarski trg 5; s/d/tr €28/39.60/49; P) The 29-room Poetovio has small but bright and airy rooms and is handy to the bus and train stations. The noisy club below has been replaced with a quieter casino, but the bus and train stations – and the huge Super Li club – are still too close for comfort. Still, the price is right.

Hotel Mitra (☎ 787 74 55; www.hotelptuj.com; Prešernova ulica 6; s €51-61, d €71-81, apt €111) This 23-room hotel is one of provincial Slovenia's more interesting hotels. Although the guestrooms are fairly ordinary, most of them are pretty big, though the ones on the top floor have mansard ceilings. You can't beat the location, but the rooms are on three floors and there is no lift.

The tourist office can arrange **private rooms** (per person €20 to €25) but most are on the other side of the Drava near Terme Ptuj or in the nearby village of Juršinci. If the tourist office is closed, a fairly central choice for rooms is **Mitja Krapša** (☎ 787 75 70; rozalija_k@hotemail.com; Maistrova ulica 19; per person €19), at the end of a 900m (as yet) unsealed track that starts west of Castle Hill.

Eating

Picerija Slonček (☎ 776 13 11; Prešernova ulica 19; pizza €3.50-4.20; 9am-10pm Mon-Fri, to 11pm Sat) The cosy 'Little Elephant', with an interesting marble fountain out front, serves pizza and some meatless dishes as well as grills.

Kitajski Vrt (☎ 776 14 51; Dravska ulica 7; starters €2-2.50; mains €5-6.25; 11am-10pm Tue-Sun, 2-10pm Mon) Ptuj's only Chinese restaurant is almost opposite the Ribič and has a fair few vegetable dishes on its menu. It's not especially authentic but if you crave noodles, you'll find them here.

Cantante Café (Cankarjeva ulica 5; sandwiches €1.60, dishes €2.50-5.40; 7am-midnight Sun-Thu, to 2am Fri & Sat) A branch of the popular Maribor bar/restaurant has now opened in Ptuj.

Gostilna Amadeus (☎ 771 70 51; Prešernova ulica 36; starters €5.50-7.50, mains €5.80-16.70; noon-10pm Mon-Thu, to 11pm Fri & Sat, to 4pm Sun) This very pleasant restaurant above a pub and near the foot of the road to the castle serves *štruklji* (dumplings with herbs and cheese; €3.30), steak and pork dishes and fish. Service is very warm and efficient.

The town's open-air **market** (Novi trg; 7am-3pm) sells fruit, vegetables and more. You'll find a large **Mercator** (Novi trg 3; 7.30am-7pm Mon-Fri, to 1pm Sat) supermarket in the same square.

THE AUTHOR'S CHOICE

Ribič (☎ 749 06 35; Dravska ulica 9; starters €5.70-7.50, mains €5.90-16.70; 11am-11pm Mon-Thu, to midnight Fri & Sat, 10am-11pm Sun) Arguably the best restaurant in Ptuj, the 'Angler' faces the river and the speciality here is – not surprisingly – fish, especially boiled or fried trout (€7.75). The seafood soup served in a bowl made of bread (€2.50) is exceptional. If the oil on the salad tastes odd (nutty, a little smoky), that's because it's *bučno olje* (pumpkin-seed oil), a speciality of the Drava Plain region. Make sure to have the dessert speciality: chocolate fondant with ice cream (€4). There's live Slovenian folk music some nights.

Drinking

Grajska Kavarna (Castle Café; ☎ 041-711 586; Na Gradu 1; ◷ same as castle) This pleasant little café in the castle courtyard serves sandwiches, cakes and hot and cold drinks.

Teater Kamra Caffè (☎ 787 74 55; Prešernova ulica 6; ◷ 8am-11pm) A café-cum-music pub attached to the Hotel Mitra with occasional live music, the Theatre Room Café attracts Ptuj's Bohemian set.

Caffeteria (☎ 041-349 609; Murkova ulica 6; ◷ 7.30am-10pm Mon-Thu, to 1am Fri) Ptuj can compete with Ljubljana in the earnestness stakes now that it has its own cosy teahouse serving a number of herbal concoctions and tisanes.

Kavabar Orfej (☎ 772 97 61; Prešernova ulica 5; ◷ 6am-10pm Mon-Thu, to 1am Fri & Sat, 10am-10.30pm Sun) The Orfej remains the anchor tenant on Prešernova ulica and is where everyone usually starts (or ends up).

Old Irish Pub (Murkova ulica 5; ◷ 9am-11pm Mon-Thu, to 1am Fri & Sat, 2pm-11pm Sun) This popular watering hole 100m east of Prešernova ulica has a good selection of beer.

Feluka Bar (☎ 771 14 87; Čučkova ulica 6a; ◷ 8am-11pm Mon-Sat, 9am-10pm Sun) This über-trendy designer bar is on the wrong side of the tracks from the centre but attracts the crowds with its wonderful décor and drinks.

Entertainment

Ptuj Theatre (Gledališče Ptuj; ☎ 749 32 50; Slovenski trg 13) Just beside the City Tower, the Ptuj Theatre stages a varied programme year-round.

Kino Ptuj (☎ 748 18 10; Cvetkov trg 3; screenings 6pm & 8pm) This wonderful Art Deco movie theatre has a couple of screenings a day.

Café Evropa (☎ 771 02 35; Mestni trg 2; ◷ 7am-11pm Mon-Thu, to 4am Fri, 8am-4am Sat, 2-11pm Sun) By day and evening a popular café, the Evropa turns into on on Ptuj's hottest clubs on Friday and Saturday nights.

Super Li (☎ 779 82 01; Vinarski trg 5; ◷ 9am-11pm Sun-Wed, to 1am Thu, to 4am Fri & Sat) If you're up for an old-fashioned disco scene head for this place neat to the Hotel Poetovio. There are live bands on Friday night.

Shopping

Ptujska Vinska Klet (Ptuj Wine Cellar; ☎ 787 98 10; Vinarski trg 1; ◷ 7am-7pm Mon-Fri, to noon Sat) One of the largest cellars in Slovenia, this is the place to go if you want to buy wine, especially local tipple such as Haloze Chardonnay, Šipon or Laški Rizling. The cellar also stocks Zlata Trta, the 'Golden Vine' sweet wine dating from 1917 and the oldest vintage in Slovenia.

Getting There & Around

Buses depart hourly for Maribor (€3.50, 40 minutes, 27km), Majšperk (€2.20, 30 minutes, 14km) and Ormož (€3.50, 40 minutes, 26km), but count on only about half a dozen departing on Saturday and far fewer (or none) on Sunday. Other destinations and their frequencies include: Rogaška Slatina (€5.80, one hour, 53km, 7.58am) via Majšperk and Radenci (€7, two hours, 75km, 3.45pm).

Two buses a week head for Stuttgart (€74, 11½ hours, 704km, 2.14am Monday and Friday) via Munich in Germany. There's one bus once a day to Varaždin and Zagreb (€8.75, 1½ hours, 97km, 8am Monday and Friday) and another just to Varaždin (€5.50, 1½ hours, 49km, 5.05pm Sunday).

You can reach Ptuj up to six times a day by train from Ljubljana (€7.30 to €12, 2½ hours, 155km) direct or via Zidani Most and Pragersko. Up to nine trains go to Maribor (€2.65 to €4, 45 minutes, 37km). Four trains a day head for Murska Sobota (€4.50 to €6, 1¼ hours, 61km) via Ormož.

Book a taxi on ☎ 031-842 227 or 041-798 788.

AROUND PTUJ
Ptujska Gora
☎ 02 / pop 335 / elev 345m

The pilgrimage **Parish Church of the Virgin Mary** (Županjska Cerkev Sv Marije; ☎ 794 42 31; www.ptujska-gora.si; Ptujska Gora 40; ◷ 8am-7pm May-Oct, by appointment Nov-Mar) in this village 13km southwest of Ptuj contains one of the most treasured objects in Slovenia: a 15th-century carved **Misericordia** of the Virgin Mary and the Child Jesus (p238).

The church itself, built at the start of the 15th century, is the finest example of a three-nave Gothic church in Slovenia. Among some of the other treasures inside is a small wooden **statue of St James** on one of the pillars on the south aisle and, under the porch and to the right as you enter, 15th-century **frescoes** of Christ's Passion and of several saints, including St Nicholas and St Dorothy with the Child Jesus. Look behind the modern tabernacle in the chapel to the right of the main altar for faint frescoes of St Peter and St Michael the Archangel.

The church, perched atop Black Hill (Črna Gora), is an easy 10-minute walk from where the bus headed for Majšperk will let you off.

GIMME SHELTER

The altar carving above the main altar in the church at Ptujska Gora, which dates from about 1410, portrays the images of 82 people from all walks of life taking shelter under Mary's enormous cloak. This is held aloft by seven angels; another two are crowning the Virgin. Below it people place small photographs of themselves and their loved ones in order to 'join' the throngs of the faithful. The carving is as important an historic document as it is a work of art. Among the lifelike faces looking up to Mary are the Counts of Celje (Frederick II and the three Hermans).

The protective mantle of the Madonna is a not-uncommon motif in Gothic art. Making use of her large enveloping cloak, Mary gives shelter to 'outlaws' and refugees and dispels fear and need among the faithful of all social classes. The mantle of Mary motif did not evolve into baroque and subsequent art styles, however, but more or less disappeared by the 16th century.

Dragica (☎ 725 02 70, 031-556 633; Ptujska Gora 37; ⏰ 8am-11pm Tue-Sun) at the foot of the hill is a small bar with snacks.

A road called the **Wind Rattle Route** (after the unusual wind-powered noisemaker called *klopotec* used here to scare the crows away from the crops) follows a 50km course from Ptujska Gora to Zavrč via Dolena, Gorca and the town of Cirkulane. Ask the tourist office in Ptuj for a map.

Wine Roads

Ptuj is within easy striking distance of two important wine-growing areas: the **Haloze** district and the **Jeruzalem-Ljutomer** district. They are accessible on foot, by car and, best of all, by bike; ask the tourist office in Ptuj for the pamphlet *Cycle Tracks in Haloze* (Kolesarske Poti po Halozah).

The Haloze Hills extend for about 30km from Makole, 18km southwest of Ptuj, to Goričak on the border with Croatia. The footpath taking in this land of gentle hills, vines, corn and sunflowers is called the **Haloze Highlands Trail** (Haloška Planina Pot). It is accessible from near **Štatenberg** (☎ 803 02 16; adult/child €1.70/1.25; ⏰ 11am-6pm Wed-Sun), an 18th-century manor at Makole, 9km southwest of Ptujska

Gora in the Dravinja Valley. The manor has fabulous stucco work and frescoes in eight enormous rooms; don't miss the impressive paintings of the four elements as well as Peace, the Sciences and the Arts in the Knights' Hall. There's a **restaurant** (⏰ 11am-10pm Wed-Sun) and **wine cellar** here, with tastings available.

It's much easier to pick up the Haloze trail near **Borl Castle** (www.borl.org), 11km southeast of Ptuj, however. Borl was originally built in the 13th century and fell to the Hungarians until the late 15th century. It changed ownership again and again, and was used as a detention centre first by the Nazis and then the communists after the war. It is undergoing a very slow renovation, though the roof has been replaced and the tower repaired.

The **Jeruzalem-Ljutomer wine road** begins at Ormož and continues for 18km north to Ljutomer (population 3385), the main seat in the area, via the hill-top village of Jeruzalem. There are quite a few cellars, small restaurants and pensions along this positively idyllic route where you can sample any of the region's local whites, especially around Ivanjkovci, including **Gostišče Taverna Jeruzalem Svetinje** (☎ 719 41 28; www.taverna-mn.si, in Slovene; Veličane 59; r per person €21, 4-person apt €50).

MARIBOR

☎ 02 / pop 87,950 / elev 275m
Although it is the nation's second-largest city, Maribor has only about a third the population of Ljubljana, and it often feels more like a large provincial town than northeast Slovenia's economic, communications and cultural hub. It has the country's only other university – founded in 1975 – outside the capital, an important museum, a number of galleries, a theatre founded in 1786 and an attractive Old Town along the Drava River. Maribor is also the gateway to the Maribor Pohorje, a hilly recreational area to the southwest, and the Mariborske and Slovenske Gorice wine-growing regions to the north and the east.

History

Maribor rose to prominence in the Middle Ages when a fortress called Marchburg was built on Piramida, a hill to the north of the city, to protect the Drava Valley from the Magyar onslaught. The settlement that later developed along the river grew wealthy through the timber and wine trade, financed largely by the town's Jewish community, and the waterfront landing (Pristan) in the Lent district became one of the busiest ports in the country.

The town was fortified with walls in the 14th century to protect it against first the Hungarians and then the Turks; four defence towers still stand along the Drava. Though its fortunes declined somewhat in later centuries, the tide turned in 1846 when the railroad from Vienna reached here – the first town in Slovenia to have train connections with the imperial capital. Maribor became the centre of Slovene-speaking Styria – a kind of counterbalance to German-speaking Graz in Austria – and began to industrialise.

Air raids during WWII devastated Maribor, and by 1945 two-thirds of it lay in ruin. New areas were opened up on the right (south) bank of the Drava, and in the 1950s Maribor was one of Slovenia's most 'proletarian' cities, which is still evident from the factory buildings and housing estates south of the river.

Orientation

Maribor sits on both sides of the Drava River, with the Lent waterfront district and other parts of the Old Town on the LEFT (north) bank. There are several main squares, although funnel-shaped Grajski trg is the historical centre.

Maribor's enormous bus station – built in the 1980s but decaying before our very eyes – is northeast of Grajski trg on Mlinska ulica. The train station is about 350m further north on Partizanska cesta. One of only three international airports in Slovenia, **Maribor airport** (Aerodrom Maribor; ☎ 629 11 75; www.maribor-airport.si; Letališka cesta 10) is at Orehova Vas, 8km southeast of the Old Town.

Information

BOOKSHOPS

Mladinska Knjiga (☎ 234 31 13; Gosposka ulica 28; 9am-6pm Mon-Fri, 8am-noon Sat) Sells Lonely Planet guides and maps, including the 1:50,000-scale map *Pohorje* (GZS).

MK Univerzitetna Knjigarna (☎ 238 05 50; Gospejna ulica 8; 8am-6pm Mon-Fri, 9am-noon Sat) Behind the university library.

INTERNET ACCESS

Kibla Cyber Café (☎ 229 40 12; www.kibla.org; Ulica Kneza Koclja 9; free; 9am-10pm Mon-Fri, 4-10pm Sat & Sun) Perhaps the flashiest internet café in the world, with 10 terminals.

MARKS (☎ 040-500 457; www.marksmb.net; Partizanska cesta 21; free; 7am-10pm Mon-Fri, 5pm-midnight Sat & Sun) Central youth club has free internet access on three terminals.

MONEY

Abanka (Glavni trg 18; 8am-5pm Mon-Fri, to 11am Sat) In the mall at the eastern end of Glavni trg.

Luna exchange office (☎ 250 00 40; Grajski trg 8; 8am-6.30pm Mon-Fri, to 1pm Sat)

Nova KBM Bank (Trg Svobode 2; 8-11.30am & 2-5pm Mon-Fri) Opposite Maribor Castle.

POST

Post office (Partizanska cesta 1) There's also another branch at Slomškov trg.

TOURIST INFORMATION

Tourist Information Centre Maribor (☎ 234 66 11; www.maribor-tourism.si; Partizanska 47; 9am-6pm Mon-Fri, to 1pm Sat) Opposite the train station.

Sights

GRAJKSI TRG

The centre of the Old Town, this square is graced with the 17th-century **Column of St Florian**, dedicated to the patron saint of fire fighters.

Maribor Castle (Mariborski Grad; Grajski trg 2), on the square's northeast corner, is a successor to the Piramida fortress of medieval times. The 15th-century castle contains a **Knights' Hall** (Viteška Dvorana) with a remarkably disproportionate ceiling painting, the baroque **Loretska Chapel** and a magnificent **rococo staircase** (1759), with pink walls, stucco work and figures arrayed on the banisters and visible though glass doors from the corner of Grajska ulica and Slovenska ulica.

The castle also contains the **Maribor Regional Museum** (Pokrajinski Muzej Maribor; ☎ 228 35 51; www.pmuzej-mb.si; adult/child €2.50/2; 9am-5pm Tue-Sat, 10am-2pm Sun Apr-Dec), one of the richest collections in Slovenia, which is arranged in 20 rooms. Be advised that at the time of research the museum was undergoing extensive renovations and parts (or all) of the permanent collection may be closed.

On the ground floor there are archaeological, clothing and ethnographic exhibits, including 19th-century beehive panels painted with biblical scenes from the Mislinja and Drava Valleys, models of Štajerska-style hayracks, Kurent costumes and wax ex voto offerings from the area around Ptuj. Upstairs there are rooms devoted to Maribor's history and its guilds and crafts (glassware, wrought

ŠTAJERSKA & KOROŠKA

MARIBOR

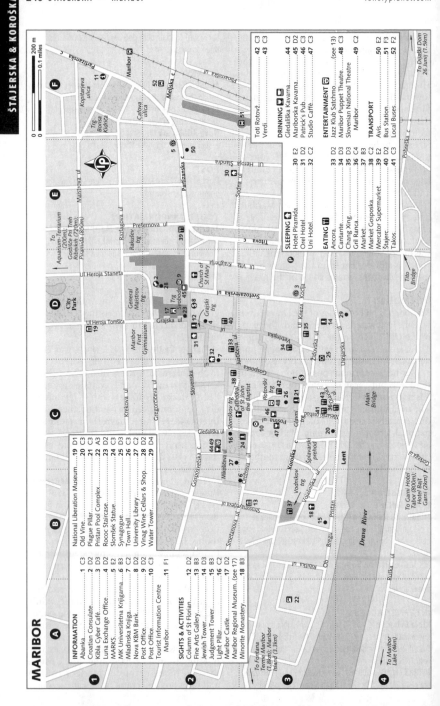

INFORMATION
Abanka.................................	1 C3
Croatian Consulate................	2 D2
Kibla Cyber Café...................	3 D3
Luna Exchange Office............	4 D2
MARKS.................................	5 E2
MK Universitetna Knjigarna....	6 B3
Mladinska Knjiga...................	7 C2
Nova KBM Bank....................	8 D2
Post Office...........................	9 C3
Post Office...........................	10 C3
Tourist Information Centre	
Maribor..........................	11 F1

SIGHTS & ACTIVITIES
Column of St Florian..............	12 D2
Fine Arts Gallery...................	13 B3
Jewish Tower........................	14 D3
Judgement Tower..................	15 B3
Light Pillar...........................	16 C2
Maribor Castle......................	17 D2
Maribor Regional Museum.....(see 17)
Minorite Monastery...............	18 B3

National Liberation Museum....	19 D1
Old Vine.............................	20 C3
Plague Pillar........................	21 C3
Pristan Pool Complex............	22 A3
Rococ Staircase....................	23 D2
Slomšek Statue.....................	24 C3
Synagogue...........................	25 D3
Town Hall............................	26 C3
University Library..................	27 C2
Vinag Wine Cellars & Shop....	28 D2
Water Tower........................	29 D4

SLEEPING 🛏
Hotel Piramida.....................	30 E2
Orel Hotel............................	31 D2
Uni Hotel.............................	32 C2

EATING 🍴
Ancora................................	33 D2
Cantante.............................	34 D3
Chang Xing..........................	35 D3
Gril Ranca...........................	36 C4
Market................................	37 B3
Market Gosposka..................	38 B3
Mercator Supermarket...........	39 E2
Štajerc...............................	40 D2
Takos.................................	41 C3

Toti Rotovž.........................	42 C3
Verdi..................................	43 C3

DRINKING 🍷 🍺
Gledališka Kavarna...............	44 C2
Mariborska Kavarna..............	45 D2
Patrick's Pub.......................	46 C3
Studio Caffè........................	47 C3

ENTERTAINMENT 🎭
Jazz Klub Satchmo................	(see 13)
Maribor Puppet Theatre.........	48 C3
Slovenian National Theatre	
Maribor..........................	49 C2

TRANSPORT
Avis...................................	50 E2
Bus Station.........................	51 F3
Local Buses........................	52 F2

ironwork, clock-making), a complete 18th-century pharmacy, and altar paintings and sculptures from the 15th to the 18th centuries. Taking pride of place among the sculptures are the exquisite **statues by Jožef Straub** (1712–56) taken from the Church of St Joseph in the southwestern suburb of Studenci.

Two blocks north of the castle is a stunning 19th-century mansion housing the **National Liberation Museum** (Muzej Narodne Osvoboditve; ☎ 235 26 00; www.muzejno-mb.si; Ulica Heroja Tomšiča 5; adult/ child €1.25/0.85; ⏰ 8am-6pm Mon-Fri, 9am-noon Sat), whose collections document Slovenia's struggle for freedom throughout the 20th century, with particular emphasis on work of the Pohorje Partisans during the Nazi occupation.

TRG SVOBODE
This square east of Maribor Castle, along with leafy Trg Generala Maistra and Rakušev trg to the north, would be unremarkable except for the honeycomb of **wine cellars** below that cover an area of 20,000 sq metres and can store seven million litres of plonk. The cellars, dating from the early 19th century, are managed by the wine export company **Vinag** (☎ 220 81 13, 031-313 841; www.vinag.si; Trg Svobode 3; ⏰ 9am-7pm Mon-Fri, 8am-1pm Sat). They are filled with old oak barrels, steel fermentation tanks and an 'archive' of vintage wine – all kept at a constant 15°C. There's a small cellar open to the public. The wine shop here has a large selection of local vintages, including Mariborčan, Laški Rizling, Chardonnay, Traminer and Gold Muscatel.

CITY PARK
North of Maribor's Old Town is City Park (Mestni Park): a lovely arboretum with three ponds, swans and a bandstand. It also contains a small **Aquarium-Terrarium** (Akvarij-Terarij; ☎ 234 96 63; Ulica Heroja Staneta 19; adult/senior & student/ child €3.50/3/2.50; ⏰ 8am-7pm Mon-Fri, 9am-noon & 2-7pm Sat & Sun) with 45 small tanks filled with tropical fish and reptiles. To the northeast is **Piramida** (386m), where the titans of Marchburg once held sway and a chapel now takes pride of place. There's some lovely residential architecture in the streets around the park.

SLOMŠKOV TRG
South of City Park is a square named after Anton Martin Slomšek (1800–62), the Slovenian bishop and politician who was beatified by the late Pope John Paul II in 1999, the first

Slovene to earn such distinction. That's him seated in front of the cathedral just southwest of the **light pillar**, a 16th-century lantern that once stood in the churchyard.

The imposing **Cathedral** (Stolna Cerkev) dedicated to St John the Baptist, dates from the 13th century and shows elements of virtually every architectural style from Romanesque to modern (including some inept 19th-century attempts to 're-Gothicise' it). Of special interest are the flamboyant Gothic sanctuary and the choir stalls with reliefs showing scenes from the life of the patron saint. The grand building across the park to the west is the **University Library** (Univerzitetna Knjižnica; ☎ 250 74 00; Gospejna ulica 10). On the northern side of the square is the **Slovenian National Theatre Maribor** (Slovensko Narodno Gledališče Maribor; ☎ 250 61 00; Slovenska ulica 27) housed in two mid-19th-century buildings and in a modern wing.

The **Fine Arts Gallery** (Umetnostna Galerija; ☎ 229 58 60; www.umetnostnagalerija.si; Strossmayerjeva ulica 6; adult/child €2/1.25; ⏰ 10am-6pm Tue-Sat, to 1pm Sun), southwest of Slomškov trg, has a relatively rich collection of modern works by Slovene artists.

LENT
South of the Fine Arts Gallery and across Koroška cesta is Maribor's **market** and the dilapidated remains of the 13th-century **Minorite monastery**, closed by Joseph II in 1784 and used as a military barracks until 1927. To the south along the riverfront is the round **Judgement Tower** (Sodni Stolp), the first of four defence towers still standing, with curious friezes on the south side.

About 150m east along the Pristan embankment is Maribor's most celebrated attraction, the so-called **Old Vine** (Stara Trta; Vojašniška ulica 8), which is still producing between 35kg and 55kg of grapes and about 25L of red wine per year after being planted more than four centuries ago. It is tended by a city-appointed viticulturist, and the dark red Žametna Črnina (Black Velvet) is distributed to visiting dignitaries as 'keys' to Maribor in the form of 0.25L bottles designed by the celebrated Slovenian artist Oskar Kogoj.

About 300m east is the pentagonal **Water Tower** (Vodni Stolp; Usnjarska ulica 10), a 16th-century defence tower. Just north of it a set of steps lead to **Židovska ulica** (Jewish St), the centre of the Jewish district in the Middle Ages. The 15th-century **synagogue** (☎ 252 78 36; Židovska ulica

4; ☻ 8am-2pm Mon-Fri) has been renovated, and the square **Jewish Tower** (Židovski Stolp; Židovska ulica 6) dating from 1465 is now a **photo gallery** (☎ 251 24 90; ☻ 10am-7pm Mon-Fri, to 1pm Sat).

GLAVNI TRG

Maribor's marketplace in the Middle Ages, **Glavni trg** is just north of the river and the main bridge crossing it. In the centre of the square is perhaps the most extravagant **plague pillar** found anywhere in Central Europe. Designed by Jožef Straub and erected in 1743, it includes the Virgin Mary surrounded by half a dozen saints. Behind it is the **town hall** (Glavni trg 14) built in 1565 by Venetian craftsmen living in Styria. Running north from Glavni trg is pedestrianised **Gosposka ulica**.

Activities

Maribor has several outdoor swimming pools, including several on **Maribor Island** (Mariborski Otok; ☎ 623 10 32; adult/senior & student/child €4.60/4.20/3.75; ☻ 9am-8pm Jun-Sep), a sand bank at the end of a dammed-off portion of the Drava River called **Maribor Lake** (Mariborsko Jezero), about 4km west of the Old Town. A sunbathing area is reserved for naturists. Local bus 15 from the train station will drop you off at the Kamnica stop, near the start of the footpath leading to the bridge and the island.

Fontana Terme Maribor (☎ 234 41 00; www.termemb.si; Koroška cesta 172; adult/child 4hr pass €8.35/5.85 Mon-Fri, Sat & Sun €9.20/6.70; ☻ 9am-10pm), a huge spa complex, is 2km west of the centre and accessible via bus 8 or 15. It offers thermal pools and whirlpools with a water temperature of 33°C to 37°C, sauna, solarium, fitness centre and massage.

A much less flash but more central bathing venue is the **Pristan Pool Complex** (Kopališče Pristan; ☎ 229 47 30; Koroška cesta 33; adult/senior & student/child €4.60/4.20/3.75; ☻ 7am-9pm Mon-Fri, 8am-9pm Sat, 8am-8pm Sun) complex on the river west of Lent, which you can also enter from Ob Bregu. It has a pool, sauna, gym and massage. Evening swimming from 7.30pm to 9pm costs €3.

Festivals & Events

Maribor hosts a lot of events throughout the year, including the **Borštnik Meeting** (www.borstnikovo.info), Slovenia's biggest theatre festival, in the second half of October. But the biggest event on the city's calendar is the **Lent Festival** (http://lent.slovenija.net), a two-week celebration of folklore, culture and music in

late June/early July, when stages are set up throughout the Old Town.

Among the most colourful (and unusual) ceremonies here is the **'christening' of the rafts** on the Drava in June and the **harvesting of the Old Vine** for wine in early October.

Sleeping

The tourist office can organise private rooms (singles/doubles from €25/38) and apartments.

Dijaški Dom 26 Junij (☎ 480 17 10; www.dd26junij.si, in Slovene; Železnikova ulica 12; s/d/tr €15/22/33; ☻ Jul-late Aug; ✗ 🖵) This 30-room college dormitory with triples in the southeastern suburb of Pobrežje accepts travellers in July and August only. From the train station take bus 3 and get off at the cemetery stop. Reception is open from 7am to 10am and again from 7pm to 11pm,

Uni Hotel (☎ 250 67 00; www.termemb.si; Grajski trg 3a; HI member/nonmember per person €19.60/25; ✗ 🖵) This very central, almost luxurious 53-room 'residence hotel' affiliated with Hostelling International is run by (and, following massive renovations, now attached to) the Hotel Orel, where you'll find reception. It's home to full-time students and visiting professors during the academic year but lets out beds in singles and doubles to visitors during holidays.

Hotel Bajt Garni (☎ 332 76 50; www.hotel-bajt.com; Radvanjska cesta 99; s €36-43.50, d €47-62; 🅿 ✗) About 1200m south of the Garni Hotel Tabor in Nova Vas but twice as nice, the 51-bed Bajt Garni is a modern-looking pension hotel with excellent breakfast and service. The chairlift to the Maribor Pohorje is a couple of kilometres to the southwest.

Garni Hotel Tabor (☎ 421 64 10, www.hoteltabor.podhostnik.si; Ulica Heroja Zidanška 18; s €37-42, d €56-70, tr €72; 🅿 ✗ ♿) This friendly, 42-room hotel is housed in an uninspiring concrete block in Tabor 3km to the southwest of the centre across the Drava. Reach it on bus 6, 12 or 18.

Hotel Orel (☎ 250 67 00; www.termemb.si; Grajski trg 3a; s €50-76, d €71-86, ste €96-180; 🅿 ✗ 🖵 ♿) After what seems like years of massive (and messy) renovations, Maribor's most central hotel has emerged all shiny and pretty and ready to kick ass. It's got 71 rooms; enter from Volkmerjev prehod 7.

Hotel Piramida (☎ 234 44 00; www.termemb.si; Ulica Heroja Šlandra 10; s €77-108, d €95-131, ste €124-148; 🅿 ✗ 🖵) Maribor's only four-star hotel, the 76-bed Piramida is essentially a former tourist hotel tarted up with a bit of paint and marble. Still, the facilities, such as the mini relaxation centre with sauna, solarium and gym, are more than adequate.

Eating

Gril Ranca (☎ 252 55 50; Dravska ulica 10; grills €3.50-5.60; ✷ 8am-11pm Mon-Sat) This place serves simple but scrumptious Balkan grills like *pljeskavica* and *čevapčiči* in full view of the Drava. Cool place on a hot night.

Štajerc (☎ 234 42 34; Vetrinjska ulica 30; starters €2-3.40, mains €5.20-6.70; ✷ 9am-10pm Mon-Thu, to midnight Fri & Sat) The 'Styrian' pub-restaurant is the place to head for if you're in the mood for reasonably priced local dishes. It has a lovely garden open in the warmer months.

Chang Xing (☎ 250 15 90; Ključavničarska ulica 2; starters €3.55-4.10, mains €5-8.70) The 'Long Prosperity' is the place to go for simple rice and noodle dishes.

Takos (☎ 252 71 50; Mesarski prehod 3; mains €6.25-9.20; ✷ 11am-midnight Mon-Thu, noon-2am Fri & Sat) This atmospheric Mexican restaurant in Lent serves excellent fajitas (€7.50 to €9.20) and quesadillas (€3.10 to €4.60) turns into a snappy little night spot after the 11pm happy hour on Friday and Saturday. Set menus are €6.25 and €8.40.

Cantante (☎ 242 53 12; Vetrinjska ulica 5; sandwiches €1.60, dishes €2.50-5.40; ✷ 9am-10pm Mon-Thu, to midnight Fri & Sat) This popular bar/restaurant with its Cuban/Hemingway feel and mojitos for days serves Cuban and South American dishes.

Toti Rotovž (☎ 228 76 50; Rotovški trg 9; meals from €15; ✷ 9am-midnight Mon-Thu, to 2am Fri & Sat) This peculiar place behind the town hall, with a wine cellar below and a terrace in a lovely arcaded square, tries (not altogether successfully) to serve Slovenian, Balkan grilled, Thai, Japanese, Italian, Greek and Mexican dishes. What is this? Fusion confusion? Set menus (don't ask) are from €6.25

Gostišče Pri Treh Ribnikih (☎ 234 41 70; Ribniška ulica 3; meals from €15; ✷ 11am-10pm Mon-Sat, to 9pm Sun) A great place for a meal if you want to get out of the city but don't feel like travelling is the 'Inn at the Three Fishponds' in City Park. Oddly, its specialities are cheese *štruklji* (dumplings) and stuffed pork ribs, with fish all but banished from the menu. There's quite a good wine card.

Two pizzerias worth consideration are **Ancora** (☎ 250 20 33; Jurčičeva ulica 7; pizza €2.60-4.25;

✷ 9am-1am Mon-Fri, 10am-1am Sat, 10.30am-10.30-pm Sun), on the 1st floor of a very popular bar/restaurant, and **Verdi** (☎ 250 81 20; Dravska ulica 8; pizza €4-6.25; ✷ 10am-midnight Sun-Thu, to 2am Fri & Sat), in a narrow alley just off Pristan; look for the sign with the three rats.

There's a **market** (Vodnikov trg; ✷ 6.30am-3pm Mon-Sat, to 12.30pm Sun) selling produce just north of the former Minorite monastery. **Mercator** (Partizanska cesta 7; ✷ 7am-7pm Mon-Fri, to 1pm Sat) supermarket has a branch on the corner of Prešernova ulica, but **Market Gosposka** (Gosposka ulica 21; ✷ 7am-8pm Mon-Sat, 7.30am-1pm Sun) is more central and keeps longer hours at the weekend.

Drinking

Gledališka Kavarna (☎ 252 37 20; Slovenska ulica 2; ✷ 8am-11pm Mon-Thu, 8am-midnight Fri, 10am-2pm & 7pm-1am Sat) The very upmarket 'Theatre Café' next to the Slovenian National Theatre (enter from Slomškov trg) attracts a bohemian crowd.

Mariborska Kavarna (Partizanska cesta 1; ✷ 6am-10pm Mon-Thu, 6am-midnight Fri, 8am-midnight Sat, 8am-10pm Sun) The olde-worlde 'Maribor Café' has been renovated to within an inch of its life and the outside and inside are now generations apart. Still, it's central.

Studio Caffè (Poštna ulica 3; ✷ 7am-10pm Mon-Thu, to 11pm Fri & Sat, to midnight Sun) This is one of the better terraced cafés of the many in the alleyways north of Glavni trg.

Patrick's Pub (☎ 251 18 01; Poštna ulica 10; ✷ 8am-midnight Mon-Thu, 8am-2am Fri & Sat, 4-11pm Sun) The pubs and restaurants along the Drava in Lent can get pretty lively on summer evenings and this pub on a pedestrian street is one of the liveliest.

Entertainment

Concerts are held in several locations, including the Knights' Hall in Maribor Castle and the cathedral. Ask the tourist office for a list.

Slovenian National Theatre Maribor (Slovensko Narodno Gledališče Maribor; ☎ 250 61 00, box office 250 62 26; www.sng-mb.si; Slovenska ulica 27; ✷ 10am-5pm Mon-Fri, to 1pm Sat & 2hr before performance) This branch of the SNG in Ljubljana has one of the best reputations in the country, and its productions have received critical acclaim throughout Europe. The city's ballet and opera companies also perform here. Enter from Slomškov trg.

Maribor Puppet Theatre (Lutkovno Gledališče Maribor; ☎ 228 19 70, 031-614 533; www.lg-mb.si; Ratovški trg 2) Maribor's second-most famous theatre has productions year-round at its base in the lovely arcaded courtyard north of Glavni trg.

Jazz Klub Satchmo (☎ 250 21 50; www.jazz-klub.si; Strossmayerjeva ulica 6; ☺ 9am-2am Mon-Thu, 9am-3am Fri, 7pm-3am Sat, 7pm-midnight Sun) Maribor's celebrated jazz club meets in a wonderful cellar in the Fine Arts Gallery building.

Getting There & Away
BUS
You can reach virtually any large town in Slovenia (and destinations in Austria, Croatia and even Germany) from Maribor. The bus station is huge, with 30 bays, as well as a few shops, bars and cafés.

Bus services are frequent to Celje (€5.80, 1½ hours, 55km, three to 10 daily), Dravograd (€6.50, two hours, 61km, six to 10 daily), Lendava (€10, three hours, 111km, one to three daily), Murska Sobota (€6.20, 1½ hours, 60km, seven to 12 daily), Ptuj (€3.50, 45 minutes, 27km, hourly) and Radenci (€5.50, one hour, 48km, hourly). For Ljubljana (€11.20, three hours, 127km) there are up to eight buses weekdays, five on Saturday and two on Sunday.

Other destinations include Gornji Grad (€9.30, three hours, 101km, one daily), Rogaška Slatina (€7, two hours, 75km, two daily Monday to Friday) and Slovenj Gradec (€7, two hours, 71km, three daily).

For destinations in Croatia expect two buses daily from to Varaždin and Zagreb (€10.75, two hours, 119km, 5.35pm Monday and 7pm Friday). There are daily buses from Maribor to Munich, Stuttgart and Frankfurt (€78, 12½ hours, 778km, 6.50pm and 9.50pm daily) and another at 8.12am Saturday.

CAR
Avis (☎ 228 79 10; www.avis.si; Partizanska cesta 24; ☺ 9am-5pm Mon-Fri) This central car-rental agency is opposite the train station. It has cars with unlimited kilometres and all insurance and taxes for €48/252 per day/week.

TRAIN
From Ljubljana (156km), you can reach Maribor on the ICS express service (€12.40, 1¾ hours, five trains daily), or any of 20 or so slower trains (€7.30, 2½ hours). About half a dozen trains a day, originating in Maribor,

go east through Pragersko to Ormož (€3.90 to €6, 1¼ hours, 59km, hourly), from where you can make your way into Croatia. Connections can be made at Ormož for trains to Murska Sobota (€4, one hour, 39km).

Three daily trains head west for Dravograd (€4.50, 1½ hours, 64km) and other stops in Koroška. These trains cross the Austrian border at Holmec, and one carries on to Klagenfurt (Celovec) on weekdays. There are also services from Maribor to Zagreb (€12, three hours, 119km, up to nine daily), Vienna (€38, 3½ hours, 257km, four daily), Belgrade (€44.30, 8½ hours, 518km, four daily), and Venice (€25, eight hours, 375km, three daily).

Getting Around
Maribor and its surrounds are well served by local buses. They depart from the stands south of the train station near Meljska cesta.

For a local taxi, ring ☎ 250 07 77 or 251 77 55.

MARIBOR POHORJE
☎ 02 / elev to 1346m
Maribor's green lung and its central playground, the eastern edge of the Pohorje Massif is known in these parts as the Maribor Pohorje (Mariborsko Pohorje). It can be easily reached by car, bus or cable car from town. The area has any number of activities on offer – from skiing and hiking to horse riding and mountain biking.

Information
Tourist Information Centre Bolfenk (☎ 603 42 11; www.maribor-tourism.si; Na Slemenu; ☺ 9.30am-4.30pm Wed-Sun Mar-Oct; 10.30am-3.30pm Wed-Sun Nov-Feb) In the Natural and Cultural Heritage Centre Bolfenk.

www.pohorje.org Useful website, especially for activities.

Sights
The **Natural and Cultural Heritage Centre Bolfenk** (Center Naravne in Kulturne Dediščine Bolfenk; ☎ 603 42 11; admission free; ☺ 9.30am-5.30pm Wed-Sun) shares space with the tourist office in a disused church (1501) 150m southwest of the cable-car upper station. It has exhibits related to the Maribor Pohorje's minerals, rocks, orchids and herbs (many of them used in local teas and tisanes). There is also a permanent exhibition on the history of skiing in Slovenia,

Activities

There are heaps of easy **walks** and more difficult **hikes** in Hotel Areh, but following a stretch of the marked Slovenian Alpine Trail, which originates in Maribor and goes as far as Ankaran on the coast, west and then southwest for 5km will take you to the two **Šumik waterfalls** and **Pragozd**, one of the very few virgin forests left in Europe. Another 6km to the southwest is **Black Lake** (Črno Jezero), the source of the swift-running Lobnica River, and **Osankarica**, where the Pohorje battalion of Partisans was wiped out by the Germans in January 1943. A massive monument marks the site of the battle.

The **Pohorje Sport Centre** (Športni Center Pohorje, ☎ 603 65 09, 220 88 41; www.pohorje.org; Mladinska ulica 29) in Maribor organises most of the activities in the Maribor Pohorje, from hiking and ski trips to paintball. They can also offer excursions to the **Pohorje Adrenaline Park** (Adrenalinski Park Pohorje; ☎ 220 88 43, 031-655 665; adult/student/child from €23.75/21.20/15.85), a recreational area with all manner of towers, high-rope courses, swings and beams near Koča Luka, midway between the two cable-car stations.

The sport centre also operates the excellent **Pohorje Bike Park** (☎ 051 692 797; adult/child with bike half-day €14.20/11.70 full day €16.70/14.20), which starts at 1050m next to the upper cable-car station and wends its way down 4km through the forests, with more than 30 different obstacles such as table tops, hips, banks, step-downs and jumps up to 6m.

Cycling is an ideal way to explore the back roads and trails of the Maribor Pohorje. Make sure to ask the tourist office for the very detailed *Pohorje Cycling Map* and the simple but useful *Kolesarske Poti na Mariborskem Pohorju* (Cycle Trials in the Maribor Pohorje). The sport centre rents **mountain bikes** (per hour/day €4.20/16.70) as does the Hotel Areh and other hotels.

The **Maribor Pohorje ski grounds** (☎ 603 65 53; www.pohorje.org; half-day pass adult/student/child €20.40/18/14.60, day pass €23.75/21.20/15.85) stretch from the Hotel Habakuk (336m) near the lower cable-car station to Žigartov Vrh (1346m) west of the Areh Hotel. With 80km of slopes (10km illuminated at night), 36km of cross-country runs and 20 ski lifts and tows (plus gondola), this is Slovenia's largest ski area, and long waits for tows are uncommon here. Ski equipment rentals (per day skis €8.75 to €12.50, snowboard €18.75) are available

from the upper cable-car station, and there's a ski and snowboarding school.

You can rent horses from the **Koča Koča** (☎ 603 65 41, 041-949 776), a restaurant hut 50m from the upper cable-car station, for €4.20 if you are content to sit in the paddock; it costs €8.35/35.40 per hour/five hours to take the a nag out on the trails. A three-hour trip in a horse-drawn coach costs €16.70 per hour.

Festivals & Events

The annual **Women's World Cup Slalom and Giant Slalom Competition** – the coveted Zlata Lisica (Golden Fox) trophy – takes place on the main piste of the Maribor Pohorje ski grounds in January.

Sleeping & Eating

There are plenty of places to stay in the Maribor Pohorje, including more than a dozen **mountain lodges** and **holiday homes**, many of them run by the Športni Center Pohorje. They can provide you with a list and basic map. Places close to main roads are the Category III **Ruška Koča pri Arehu** (☎ 603 50 46, 041-666 552; year-round) with 36 beds rooms at 1246m and the more swish Category III **Poštarski Dom pod Plešivcem** (☎ 822 10 55, 875 09 06; Hočko Pohorje 40) with 38 beds rooms at 805m.

Camp Pohorje (☎ 614 09 50; www.pohorje.org; Pot k Mlinu 57; adult/child €6.70/5; year-round) This tiny camping ground, with only 20 pitches for tents and 10 for caravans, is at the foothills of the Maribor Pohorje just next to the cable car's lower station.

Hotel Areh (☎ 603 50 40, 220 88 41; www.pohorje .org; Lobnica 32; s/d 28.50/46; P) At the summit of Areh peak (1250m), about 6km southwest of the upper cable-car station, this pleasant 84-bed ski lodge at 1050m has rustic, wood-panelled rooms, a pleasant restaurant and helpful staff. They rent ski equipment and mountain bikes.

Apartmaji Bolfenk (☎ 603 65 00, 220 88 41; info .scp@sc-pohorje.si; Hočko Pohorje 131; apt for up to 5/8 people €75/110; P) This well maintained property next to the landmark Bellvue Hotel (currently under renovation) has apartments for between four and 12 people that are actually quite grand. All have living room with fireplace and kitchen.

Hotel Zarja (☎ 603 60 00; www.hotel-zarja.si; Frajhajm 34; s/d €29/48, apt €80; P) Just east of the Hotel Are and the ski fields, the chaletlike Zarja has 15 comfortable and airy rooms.

Hotel Habakuk (☎ 300 81 00; www.termemb.si; Pohorska ulica 59; s €118-140, d €169-211, ste from €259; ⓟ ⓧ ⓧ ⓛ ⓡ ⓐ) This huge, five-star property, with 137 rooms near the lower cable-car station, offering luxurious accommodation along with an ample recreation and wellness centre with the indoor and outdoor thermal water pools. The high season runs from January to March.

Almost everyone takes their meals in their hotels in the Maribor Pohorje; there are almost no independent restaurants. Be on the lookout for dishes and drinks unique to the region, including *pohorski lonec* (Pohorje pot), a kind of goulash; *pohorska omleta,* a pancake filled with fruit; and *boroničevec,* a brandy made with berries harvested in the Pohorje.

Getting There & Away

You can drive or, if ambitious, cycle the 20km from the Old Town in Maribor south past the Renaissance-style Betnava Castle, turning west at Spodnje Hoče before reaching a fork in the road at a small waterfall. Go left and you'll reach the Areh Hotel after about 5km. A right turn and less than 4km brings you to the Natural and Cultural Heritage Centre and the upper cable-car station.

A much easier – and more exhilarating – way to get to the Bellevue and the heart of the Maribor Pohorje is to take the **cable car** (vzpenjača; ☎ 041-959 795; Pohorska ulica) from the station in Zgornje Radvanje, 6km southwest of Maribor's Old Town. There are clamps on the outside of each cabin for mountain bikes and skis.

From the train station in Maribor take local bus 6, which leaves about every 15 to 20 minutes, and get off at the terminus. On weekdays the cable car runs every hour from 8am till noon and 6pm to 8pm; from 12.30pm to 5.30pm they go every half-hour. At the weekend departures are at 8am, 9am, 6pm, 7pm and 8pm and half-hourly between 9.30am and 5.30pm. A one-way ticket for adults/children is €5.85/4.60, a return €7/5.85.

CENTRAL POHORJE REGION

☎ 03 / elev to 1517m

Travellers can easily sample Pohorje's recreational offerings along its eastern edge from Maribor and its western fringes from Slovenj Gradec and Dravograd in Koroška. But the pear-shaped massif's highest and most beautiful area is in the centre.

Although it's true that the Pohorje peaks can't hold a candle to those of the Julian and the Kamnik-Savinja Alps – most here barely clear the 1500m mark – this is the only part of the country where you can appreciate the sheer vastness of the mountains without feeling hemmed in or vertiginous. What's more, hiking and trekking in the winter here is as good as it is in the summer. Many of the hillsides have been cleared and are now given over to brush, pasture and meadows. Others have been planted with oak trees.

Zreče (population 2875), about 40km southwest of Maribor, is the springboard for the central Pohorje region; indeed, the region is also known as the Zreče Pohorje (Zreško Pohorje). Although certainly not Slovenia's most attractive town – it's dominated by the tool-manufacturing company Unior – Zreče has a modest spa and is within easy striking distance of the ski and sport centre around **Rogla** (1517m), 16km to the north, where teams – including the Slovenian Olympic one – come to train.

Information

Banka Celje (13b Cesta na Roglo, Zreče; ◷ 8-11.30am & 2-5pm Mon-Fri) In the Zreče Bazaar (Zreški Bazar) shopping centre above the bus station 150m from the spa's main entrance.

Post office (13b Cesta na Roglo, Zreče; ◷ 8am-6pm Mon-Fri, to noon Sat) To the southeast of the bank.

Tourist Information Centre Zreče (☎ 759 04 70; tic.zrece.lto@siol.net; Cesta na Roglo 11j, Zreče; ◷ 7am-3pm Mon-Wed & Fri, 7am-5pm Thu, 9am-noon Sat) In the modern market complex southeast of the Zreče Bazaar.

www.rogla.si Useful website, especially for activities.

Activities

HIKING & MOUNTAIN BIKING

The 1:50,000 GZS *Pohorje* (€7.50) map outlines various circular hiking trails that are as short as 2km (30 minutes) and as long as 32km (eight hours). The latter covers much of the hike described in the Maribor Pohorje section – Šumik waterfalls, Black Lake and Osankarica – but from the other side. Another good one is the 12km hike (three hours) that leads northwest to the **Lovrenc Lakes** (Lovrenska Jezera), a turf swamp with 19 lakes that are considered a natural phenomenon.

Mountain bikers should get hold of a copy of the excellent 1:100,000 *Pohorje Cycling Map*, with a dozen trails outlined from Maribor in the east to Slovenj Gradec and Dravograd in the west. A brochure produced by Terme Zreče called *Kolesarske Poti na Zreškem Pohorju* (Bike Trails in the Zreče Pohorje) is much more basic and limits its focus (eight trails) to the areas between Zreče and Rogla.

HORSE RIDING

The **Rogla Equine Centre** (Konjeniški Center Rogla; ☎ 041-612 456; riding per hr from €12.50, 45min lesson from €16.70; ☻ 11am-5pm) is about 3km northeast of Rogla next to the Dom na Pesku (p248). In winter it offers **husky sledge rides** (open 2pm to 4pm Fri).

SKIING & SNOWMOBILING

The **Rogla ski grounds** (☎ 757 61 61, 232 92 64; www .rogla.si; half-day pass adult/student/child €20.50/18.30/ 13.30, day pass €23.30/20.80/15) has 12km of ski slopes and 18km of cross-country trails served by two chairlifts and 11 tows. The season is a relatively long one – from the end of November to as late as April. There's also the **Rogla Ski School** (Smučarska Šola Rogla; ☎ 757 74 68; www.unior.si; ☻ 8.30am-4pm Mon-Fri, 5-8pm Sun), in a little wooden cabin at the base of the ski lift where you can also learn to snowboard. You can rent equipment from **Ski Servis** (☎ 757 74 89; per day skis €10.50-15; ☻ 8.15am-2pm) office at the Planja Hotel.

An outfit called **AALT** (☎ 041-624 131; www .aalt.si) based at the Pizzerija Planja (p248) has snowmobile rides and trips ranging from a single lap of 400m (€3) to a 120km 'safari' with overnight for €200 (second person €65). Most people will be satisfied with a 15km ride (€45, second person €19) lasting an hour.

THERMAL SPA

While **Terme Zreče** (☎ 757 62 68; www.terme-zrece .si; Cesta na Roglo 15) is a serious treatment centre for post-operative therapy and locomotor disorders (especially those involving sports injuries), it is also a place where you simply have fun. Along with an indoor **thermal pool** (water temperature is 32°C), there's a large covered recreational and two outdoor **swimming pools** (adult/child 3hr Mon-Fri €6.20/4.60, Sat & Sun €7.50/5.85 all day Mon-Fri €8/5.85, Sat & Sun €9.60-7.50; ☻ 9am-9pm) as well as a couple of **Jacuzzis**, **saunas** and **steam rooms** (pool, sauna & steam room adult weekday/weekend €11.70/13.30; ☻ 11am-9pm Mon-Thu, 10am-9pm Fri-Sun). There are a number of treatments (eg aromatic oil massage, medicinal mud treatment, milk bath for two) on offer.

OTHER ACTIVITIES

The **Rogla Sport Hall** (Športna Dvorana Rogla; ☎ 757 74 31) has a covered stadium for all kinds of team sports (including basketball and volleyball), jogging tracks, lawn bowls, a squash court (per 45 minutes €8.40) and a badminton court (one hour €10.50), and indoor and outdoor **tennis courts** (1hr €14.60; ☻ 9am-9pm). The Planja Hotel has an **indoor swimming pool** (adult/child €6.25/4.20, with sauna adult €10.40; ☻ 9am-9pm).

The **Bicycle Centre** (Kolesarski Center; ☎ 757 63 57; bicycles/mountain bikes 1hr 4.20/6.25, day €11.70/16.60) is at the Terme Zreče.

Sleeping

Garni Hotel Zvon (☎ 757 36 00; www.hotelzvon .biz, in Slovene; Slomškova ulica 2; s €36-62, d €58.50-71; P ☒ ☒ ☐) There's no particular reason for staying at Zreče; all the fun is up in Rogla. But if you're a serious disciple of things thermal, the pensionlike 'Bell' is just opposite the entrance to the spa and has 15 spotless rooms.

Dobrava 2000 Hotel (☎ 757 60 00; www.terme -zrece.si; Cesta na Roglo 15; s €71-118.50; P ☒ ☒ ☐ ☒ ☒) The spa's flagship hotel, this four-star place has 76 rooms in an unexceptional block at the entrance to the spa. Several rooms are adapted for guests with disabilities. Make sure you get one of the rooms with a balcony. The Dobrava Hotel (singles €66 to €109) is a slightly cheaper, three-star extension with 35 rooms. More pleasant still are the Terme Zreče Villas (singles €50 to €55, doubles €83 to €95) in a small wooded area 150m from the main spa building with 40 apartments and an equal number of double rooms.

Planja Hotel (☎ 757 71 00; www.terme-zrece.si; €52.50-66, d €83.50-111; P ☒ ☐ ☒) This four-star, 30-bed property, the poshest place to stay in Rogla, also has a three-star wing with 88 beds called the Rogla Hotel (singles €45 to €52, doubles €68.50 to €81). Its rooms, frankly, are brighter and more attractive than those in the main hotel. Hotel Brinje (singles €36 to €40, doubles €56 to €64) is essentially just a poky annexe of the Planja with 22 apartments. The hotel also has a couple of bungalows (singles €33 to €37, doubles €50 to €58.50) set off on their own.

The central Pohorje region abounds in farmhouses with rooms and apartments for rent, particularly along Cesta Kmečnega near Resnik, about 7km southwest of Rogla. One of the best is the four-room **Pačnik farmhouse** (☎ 576 22 02; Resnik 21; per person €22-27; ☻ Jul-Sep, mid-Dec–mid-Mar; P), a very isolated farmhouse where your humble author first 'discovered' Slovenia in the early 1990s and then wrote the 1st edition of this book. In the same settlement, the three-room **Kočnik-Kovše farmhouse** (☎ 576 11 28; Resnik 33; per person €20-24; P) stands next to a small wood and is open all year.

Eating

Špajza Inn (☎ 576 26 15; Cesta na Roglo 13b; pizza €3.75-5.40; ☺ 7am-9pm Mon-Thu, 7am-10pm Fri & Sat, noon-9pm Sun) If you feel like pizza in Zreče, try the 'Pantry' in the shopping centre.

Pizzerija Planja (☎ 757 72 50; pizza €3.85-5.60; ☺ 8.30am-5pm Sep-Jun; to 8pm Jul & Aug) Along with pizza this place – just north of the Planja Hotel in Rogla and near the ski lift – does breakfasts and Slovenian dishes.

Stara Koča (☎ 757 74 47; set lunch €8.75; ☺ 7am-11pm) The 'Old Hut' is the main restaurant at the Planja Hotel and is done up to look like a rustic mountain hut.

Dom na Pesku (☎ 759 27 61; meals from €10; ☺ 8am-8pm Apr-Oct; 7am-9pm Nov-Mar) Also called Dom Pesek, this mountain lodge 3km north of Rogla on the unsealed road to Koroša is a popular place for hearty Slovenian fare.

Gostilna Jančič (☎ 752 04 83; Cesta na Roglo 4b; starters €3.35-4.20, mains €4-6.70; ☺ 8am-11pm Mon-Fri, 9am-11pm Sat) This *gostilna* in Zreče on the main road to Rogla and opposite the shopping centre is a friendly place for a quick meal.

There's a **Mercator** (Cesta na Roglo 11; ☺ 8am-8pm Mon-Sat, to noon Sun) supermarket in the Zreče Bazaar shopping centre in Zreče.

Getting There & Away

There are regular connections from Zreče to Celje (€3.50, 45 minutes, 26km, eight buses on weekdays) via Slovenske Konjice (€1.30, 15 minutes, 5km, eight to 10 weekdays, two on Saturday). Two buses a day from Celje (and at least three from Slovenske Konjice) stop at Zreče and then carry on to Rogla (€9, 2½ hours, 97km). Local buses make the runs from Zreče bus station to Rogla and to Resnik.

In winter there are special ski buses from Zreče (five in each direction) as well as Celje and Slovenske Konjice. Terme Zreče runs buses hourly from 6am to 8.30pm or 9pm up to Rogla for its guests in winter, with up to eight a day in each direction departing during the rest of the year.

CELJE

☎ 03 / pop 36,950 / elev 238m

With its time-warp historical centre, fabulous architecture, excellent museums and enormous castle looming over the picturesque Savinja River, Celje might at first appear to have won the tourism sweepstakes. But tell that to the city fathers… Slovenia's third-largest city can be a dispiriting place after dark, with even the simplest of places to eat and drink at a premium.

History

Celj (then known as Celeia) was the administrative centre of the Roman province of Noricum between the 1st and 5th centuries, and roads linked the town with other Roman settlements at Virunum (near Klagenfurt in Austria), Poetovio (Ptuj) and Emona (Ljubljana). It was an affluent town, as is evident from the large baths, mosaics and temples unearthed in the area. In fact, it flourished to such a degree that it gained the nickname 'Troia secunda', the 'second Troy'. Celeia's glory days came to an end when it was sacked by the Huns in 452 and overrun by subsequent tribes during the Great Migrations.

Celje's second Camelot came in the mid-14th century when members of the Žonek family took control of the area. The Counts – later the Dukes – of Celje, one of the richest and most powerful feudal dynasties in Central Europe, were the last on Slovenian soil to challenge absolute rule by the Habsburgs, and they united much of Slovenia for a time. Under their rule, which lasted for just a century, Celje acquired the status of a town, and they built the castles, town fortifications and most of the churches still standing today. The counts left Celje and the nation an invaluable legacy, and a part of their emblem – three gold stars forming an inverted triangle – have been incorporated into the Slovenian state flag and seal.

Celje was never able to repeat those glory days, and plagues, flooding, invasions and revolts struck the town over the ensuing centuries. Celje was in fact more German than Slovene until the end of WWI, when the town government passed into local hands for the first time. Celje's most recent claim to fame is the opening in 2004 of the spanking new, 8600-seat Celje Sport Park (Športni Park Celje; Podjavošokva ulica) multiuse stadium in the northern suburb of Golovec, home ground of the local CMC Publikum football as well as where the national league plays.

Orientation

Celje's compact Old Town is bordered by Levstikova ulica and Gregorčičeva ulica to the north and northwest, the area around the Lower Castle to the west, the train tracks to the east and the Savinja River to the south.

The town has two main squares: Glavni trg at the southern end of Stanetova ulica, a pedestrian street, and Krekov trg opposite the train station. The main bus station is 300m north of the train station opposite the huge Celeia shopping mall on Aškičeva ulica. Local and suburban buses stop south of the train station on Ulica XIV Divizije.

Information

Abanka (Krekov trg 10; 8am-5pm Mon-Fri, to 11am Sat) Opposite the train station.

Banka Celje (Vodnikova ulica 2; 8.30-11.30am & 2-5pm Mon-Fri) In a building designed by Jože Plečnik in 1930.

Cyber Cafe Stane (492 41 69, 031-324 400; Stanetova ulica 17a; per hr €0.65; 8am-9pm Mon-Fri, 9am-9pm Sat, 2-8pm Sun) Internet access on seven terminals.

Kompas (428 03 08; Glavni trg 1; 8am-5pm Mon-Fri, to noon Sat) Accommodation and car hire; enter from Prešernova ulica.

Mladinska Knjiga (428 52 52; Stanetova ulica 3; 8.30am-7pm Mon-Fri, 8am-noon Sat) Sells regional maps and guides.

Post office (Krekov trg 9)

Tourist Information Centre Celje (428 79 36; tic@celje.si); Celje Hall (Krekov trg 3; 9am-5pm Mon-Fri, to 1pm Sat); Celje Castle (Cesta na Grad; 9-7pm late Apr-Sep)

Sights

KREKOV TRG

Opposite the train station is where you'll find mammoth neo-Gothic **Celje Hall** (Celjski Dom; Krekov trg 3), built in 1907 and erstwhile social centre for German-speaking *Celjani*, which now contains the year-round tourist office and the **Children's Art Gallery** (Galerija Likovnih Del Mladih; 548 17 71; admission free; 10am-6pm Tue-Sat), devoted to art produced by those under the age of 20 and the only such museum in all of Slovenia. Next door is the **Hotel Evropa** (Krekov trg 4), the oldest hotel in Celje. Just south of the hotel (and connected to it) is a medieval **defence tower**, and about 150m further on, the

Water Tower (Vodni Stolp; Razlagova ulica 19), part of the city wall and ramparts and built between 1451 and 1473. Many of the blocks used are of Roman origin. On the same street is the **Josip Pelikan Photo Studio** (Fotografski Atelje Josipa Pelikana; 548 58 91; www2.arnes.si/~cemnzc; Razlagova ulica 5; 10am-2pm Tue-Fri, 9am-noon Sat, 2-6pm Sun), the complete studio of an early 20th-century Celje photographer and part of the Museum of Recent History.

SLOMŠKOV TRG & GLAVNI TRG

A few steps to the northwest of the tower is the **Abbey Church of St Daniel** (Opatijska Cerkev Sv Danijela), dating from the early 14th century. The church has some magnificent frescoes and tombstones, but its greatest treasure is a 15th-century carved wooden **pietà** in the **Chapel of the Sorrowful Mother** to the left of the sanctuary. The chapel has carved stone walls and vaults with remnants of frescoes from the early 15th century and carved effigies of the Apostles. Parts of Celje's **medieval walls** and **ramparts** can be seen along Ulica na Okopih, west of the church.

Contiguous with Slomškov trg is **Glavni trg**, the heart of the Old Town. It is filled with lovely townhouses dating from the 17th and 18th centuries and, in the warmer months, outdoor cafés. In the centre of the square is the requisite **plague pillar** (1776) dedicated to Mary.

MUZEJSKI TRG

A birch-lined park along the Savinja River's northern embankment has an **open-air lapidary** of Roman remains unearthed in the Celje area. Overlooking it is the 16th-century **Old County Palace** (Stara Grofija; Muzejski trg 1), a lovely Renaissance building with a two-level arcade around a courtyard, which contains the renovated **Celje Regional Museum** (Pokrajinski Muzej Celje; 428 09 50; www2.arnes.si/~pokmuzce; adult/student/child €3.30/2.10/1.70; 10am-6pm Tue-Sun Mar-Oct; 10am-6pm Tue-Fri, to noon Sat Nov-Feb).

Needless to say, the museum places much emphasis on Celeia and the Counts of Celje, right down to exhibiting 18 of the nobles' skulls in glass cases. (They were taken from the Minorite Church of Mary on Prešernova ulica in 1956, and the one belonging to Ulric is particularly gruesome.) The museum has a dozen rooms, many of them done up in styles from different periods (eg baroque, neoclassical, Biedemeier, Secessionist), painted

ŠTAJERSKA & KOROŠKA

with various scenes and filled with fine furniture. Don't miss the 18th-century cabinet with hunting scenes inlaid with ivory, the 20-drawer 'bank' desk with a secret compartment and the neoclassical combined clock and music box that still works. But the museum's main attraction is the **Celje Ceiling** (Celjski Strop), an enormous trompe l'oeil painting

in the main hall of columns, towers, angels frolicking skyward, noblemen and ladies looking down at you looking up. Completed in about 1600 by a Polish artist, the mural was meant to lift the ceiling up to the sky, and it does just that. Other panels represent the four seasons and show scenes from Roman and Greek mythology.

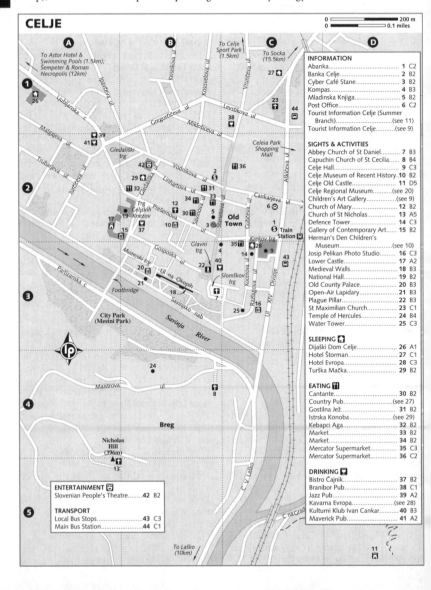

CELJE

INFORMATION	
Abanka	1 C2
Banka Celje	2 B2
Cyber Café Stane	3 B3
Kompas	4 B3
Mladinska Knjiga	5 B2
Post Office	6 C2
Tourist Information Celje (Summer Branch)	(see 11)
Tourist Information Celje	(see 9)

SIGHTS & ACTIVITIES	
Abbey Church of St Daniel	7 B3
Capuchin Church of St Cecilia	8 B4
Celje Hall	9 C3
Celje Museum of Recent History	10 B2
Celje Old Castle	11 D5
Celje Regional Museum	(see 20)
Children's Art Gallery	(see 9)
Church of Mary	12 B2
Church of St Nicholas	13 A5
Defence Tower	14 C3
Gallery of Contemporary Art	15 B3
Herman's Den Children's Museum	(see 10)
Josip Pelikan Photo Studio	16 C3
Lower Castle	17 A2
Medieval Walls	18 B3
National Hall	19 B2
Old County Palace	20 B3
Open-Air Lapidary	21 B3
Plague Pillar	22 B2
St Maximilian Church	23 C1
Temple of Hercules	24 B4
Water Tower	25 C3

SLEEPING	
Dijaški Dom Celje	26 A1
Hotel Štorman	27 C1
Hotel Evropa	28 C3
Turška Mačka	29 B2

EATING	
Cantante	30 B2
Country Pub	(see 27)
Gostilna Jež	31 B2
Istrska Konoba	(see 29)
Kebapci Aga	32 B2
Market	33 B2
Market	34 B2
Mercator Supermarket	35 C3
Mercator Supermarket	36 C2

DRINKING	
Bistro Čajnik	37 B2
Branibor Pub	38 C1
Jazz Pub	39 A2
Kavarna Evropa	(see 28)
Kulturni Klub Ivan Cankar	40 B3
Maverick Pub	41 A2

ENTERTAINMENT	
Slovenian People's Theatre	42 B2

TRANSPORT	
Local Bus Stops	43 C3
Main Bus Station	44 C1

TRG CELJSKIH KNEZOV

The funnel-shaped 'Square of the Celje Counts' leads north from Muzejski trg. At the start is the **Lower Castle** (Spodnij Grad) built in the 14th century for the Celje Counts and today containing the **Gallery of Contemporary Art** (Galerija Sodobne Umetnosti; ☎ 426 51 50; Trg Celjskih Knezov 8; admission free; 🕙 11am-6pm Tue-Fri, 10am-noon Sat, 2-6pm Sun). To the north is the **National Hall** (Narodni Dom; Trg Celjskih Knezov 9), the cultural and social centre for Celje's Slovenes at the end of the 19th century and now the city hall.

PREŠERNOVA ULICA

Walking eastward along this street from trg Celjskih Knezov, you'll pass the **Celje Museum of Recent History** (Muzej Novejše Zgodovine Celje; ☎ 428 64 10; www.muzej-nz-ce.si; Prešernova ulica 17; adult/senior & student/child €2.10/1.25/0.85; 🕙 10am-6pm Mon-Fri, 9am-noon Sat, 2-6pm Sun) in the former town hall building, which was built in 1830. The museum records the story of Celje ('Living in Celje: 1900-2000') from the late 19th century onwards and includes a re-creation of an early 20th-century street complete with tailor, hairdresser, clockmaker and goldsmith. It also contains the **Herman's Den Children's Museum** (Otroški Muzej Hermanov Brlog), the first children's museum in Slovenia.

BREG

On the south bank of the Savinja River a covered stairway with 90 steps at Breg 2 leads to the **Capuchin Church of St Cecilia** (Kapucinska Cerkev Sv Cecilije). The Germans used the nearby monastery (now apartments) as a prison during WWII. Between the church and **City Park** (Mestni Park; Partizanska cesta) is the reconstructed Roman **Temple of Hercules** (Heraklejev Tempelj; Maistrova ulica) dating from the 2nd century AD. Further south, you can walk up 396m-high **Nicholas Hill** (Miklavški Hrib), topped by the **Church of St Nicholas** (Cerkev Sv Miklavža), for a wonderful view of the castle, the Old Town and the Savinja.

CELJE OLD CASTLE

The largest fortress in Slovenia, the **Celje Old Castle** (Stari Grad Celje; ☎ 031-348 296; Cesta na Grad; admission free; 🕙 9am-9pm May-Sep; 9am-6pm Apr & Oct; 10am-5pm Nov-Mar), is perched on a 407m-high escarpment about 2km southeast of the Old Town; the walk up via a footpath from Cesta na Grad takes about half an hour. The castle was originally built in the early 13th century

and went through several transformations, especially under the Counts of Celje in the 14th and 15th centuries.

When the castle lost its strategic importance in the 15th century it was left to deteriorate, and subsequent owners used the stone blocks to build other structures, including parts of the Lower Castle and the Old County Palace. A surprisingly large portion remains intact, however, and has been restored, including the 35m-high **Frederick Tower** (Friderikov Stolp).

Activities

The tourist office has brochures listing a number of **walks** and **hikes** into the surrounding countryside lasting between one and four hours. The longest one (28km) leads southeast to **Mt Tovst** (834m) and the picturesque village of Svetina via the Category III **Celjska Koča** (☎ 577 41 15) mountain hut at 650m. This can also be done by car or bicycle. They also distribute the brochure Poti Primerne za Kolesarjenje (Trails Suitable for Cycling), with 10 routes outlined for Celje and settlements to the north.

There are a couple of open-air **swimming pools** (☎ 547 30 10; adult/child €4.20/3.35; Ljubljanska cesta 41; 🕙 noon-7pm Mon-Fri, 9am-7pm Sat & Sun Jun-Aug) on the Savinja just south of the Astor Hotel, about 1.5km west of the centre.

Sleeping

Dijaški Dom Celje (☎ 426 66 00, 041-621 266; mojca .golouh1@guest.arnes.si; Ljubljanska cesta 21; s/d/tr €18/33/44.50; 🕙 Jul & Aug) Northwest of the centre, this 600-bed dorm accepts travellers for the most part in summer only though between 60 and 100 beds are frequently available during the school year as well.

Turška Mačka (Turkish Cat; ☎ 548 46 11; turska .macka@siol.net; Gledališka ulica 7; s/d €32.50/51; P ✗) This evocatively named, 26-room hotel behind the Slovenian People's Theatre is the nicest small place to stay in Celje. It has small but comfortable rooms and a decent restaurant.

Hotel Evropa (☎ 426 90 00; www.hotel-evropa.si; Krekov trg 4; 1st & 2nd fl s/d €37/60, 3rd & 4th fl s/d/€34.50/55/64; P ✗) Located near the train station and in the centre of town, this 60-room historic hotel has pleasant, helpful staff. The rooms on the 1st and 2nd floors, with three stars, are renovated and relatively attractive; the two-star rooms on the 3rd and 4th floors are older and somewhat gloomy.

Astor Hotel (☎ 548 23 50; www.astor-hotel.net; Ljubljanska cesta 39; s/d/tr €37.50/58/70; P ⊠ ⊞) This modern, 32-room hotel is about 1.5km west of the Old Town but as close as you'll get to the Savinja River. It has its own swimming pool and casino.

Hotel Štorman (☎ 426 04 26; www.storman.si; Mariborska cesta 3; s €41-56.50, d €64-83, tr €74.50, ste from €100; P ⊠ ⊠ ⊞) The 52-room Štorman is in a canary-yellow, nine-storey block just north of the 15th-century Church of St Maximilian. The hotel is a favourite with businesspeople but eschew any of the rooms facing Mariborska cesta – it's a major highway.

Kompas can arrange **private rooms** and **apartments** (s/d/t €33.30/50.80/65).

Eating

Kebapci Aga (Prešernova ulica; dishes €3-4.60; ☯ 8am-1am Mon-Thu, 6pm-4am Fri & Sat, 5pm-1am Sun) This little kiosk opposite the National Hall attracts punters by the carload, but it's still not clear whether it's the kebabs or dearth of alternatives in Celje that attracts them.

Gostilna Jež (Linhartova ulica 6; dishes €3.25-4.60; ☯ 6am-10pm Mon-Fri, 7am-10pm Sat, 6am-4pm Sun) This very simple eatery is a great place for a cheap and filling lunch (as so many market-goers seem to think).

Cantante (☎ 490 01 36; Savinova ulica 9; sandwiches €1.60, dishes €2.50-5.40; ☯ 8am-midnight Mon-Fri, 8am-2am Sat, noon-midnight Sun) This popular bar/restaurant with branches in Maribor and Ptuj has portraits of Che, good music and even better cocktails. Food leans toward Tex-Mex.

Country Pub (☎ 426 04 14; salads €2.40-5.30, burgers €3.25-3.70, steaks €10.30-13.70; ☯ 6am-1am) It's not often that we recommend hotel outlets but this pleasant pub/restaurant on the ground floor of the Hotel Štorman is a viable option in a city with few choices.

Istrska Konoba (☎ 548 46 11; starters €5-8, mains €7.50-10.80; ☯ 7am-10pm Sun-Thu, to midnight Fri & Sat) The 'Istrian Cellar' restaurant at the Turška Mačka hotel is one of the few proper dining rooms in Celje open nightly. It was designed by Karst artist Lojze Spacal; check out the lovely stained-glass doors and windows.

There's an outdoor **market** (cnr Savinova ulica & Linhartova ulica; ☯ 6am-3pm) with fresh fruit, vegetables and other foodstuffs behind the Minorite Church of Mary. You'll find a large **Mercator** (Stanetova ulica 14; ☯ 7am-8pm Mon-Fri, 7am-3pm Sat, 8-11am Sun) supermarket almost opposite the Banka Celje to the northeast. There's a

more central **Mercator** (Prešernova ulica 1; ☯ 6am-7pm Mon-Fri, 7am-3pm Sat) branch next to the Hotel Evropa.

Drinking

Kavarna Evropa (☎ 496 90 00; ☯ 7am-11pm Mon-Sat, 8am-10pm Sun) This olde-worlde café in the Hotel Evropa – all dark wood panelling, gilt mouldings and fusty chandeliers – is a good place for a cup of coffee and a cake.

Bistro Čajnik (☎ 548 32 00; Trg Celjskih Knezov 3; ☯ 7am-10pm Mon-Fri, 8am-10pm Sat) If tea is your drink, head for the 'Teapot Bistro'. It's also worth a stop for a snack (cakes €1.50, sandwiches €2.10 to €3.50).

Kulturni Klub Ivan Cankar (Glavni trg 7; ☯ 8am-10pm) This ever-so-cool literary café attracts the thinking men and women of Celje. Retro décor and lots and lots of attitude.

Branibor Pub (☎ 492 41 44; Stanetova ulica 27; ☯ 6am-1am Mon-Thu, 6am-2.30am Fri, 7am-2am Sat, 8am-1am Sun) This is one of the best pubs in town, with jazz and other live music some nights.

There's a group of pubs bunched up opposite Gledališki trg, including **Maverick Pub** (Ljubljanska cesta 7; ☯ 6am-midnight Sun-Thu, 8am-2am Fri & Sat), a lively place with a large outdoor terrace for people-watching in the warmer months, and the more subdued **Jazz Pub** (Ljubljanska cesta 9; ☎ 6am-11pm Mon-Thu, 6am-midnight Fri, 3pm-midnight Sat, 3-11pm Sun) next door.

Entertainment

Slovenian People's Theatre (Slovensko Ljudsko Gledališče; ☎ 426 42 00, box office 426 42 08; Gledališki trg 5; ☯ 9am-noon Mon-Fri) The SLG, which encompasses part of a medieval tower on Vodnikova ulica, stages six plays a season.

Getting There & Away

BUS

Intercity buses, which leave from the main station, run at least once an hour (less frequently at weekends) to Mozirje (€4.60, one hour, 36km), Rogaška Slatina (€4, one hour, 34km) and Zreče (€3.50, 45 minutes, 26km). Count on up to six buses on weekdays and three at the weekend to Ljubljana (€7, 1½ hours, 71km) and Maribor (€5.80, 1½ hours, 55km). Other destinations accessible by bus from Celje and their frequencies include: Dravograd (€6.50, 1¾ hours, 65km, one daily), Gornji Grad (€5.80, 1½ hours, 53km, one or two daily), Logarska Dolina (€12.50, four hours, 149km, 9.10am Monday to Friday April to October), Murska Sobota (€10, three hours, 115km, two daily) and Podsreda (€4.60, one hour, 39km, six weekdays).

For destinations like such as Šempeter (€2, 20 minutes, 12km, hourly), Škofja Vas and Šentjur, go to the bus stops south of the train station on Ulica XIV Divizije.

TRAIN
Celje is one of the few rail hubs in all of Slovenia, and for once you have a real choice between taking the train or the bus. Celje is on the main line between Ljubljana and Maribor; from Ljubljana (€5.35 to €9.40, 1½ hours, 89km) you can reach Celje up to two dozen times a day by regular train and eight times a day by ICS express train.

Celje is also on the line linking Zidani Most (connections to and from Ljubljana and Zagreb) with Maribor (€4.50 to €6, one hour, 67km, half-hourly) and the Austrian cities of Graz and Vienna.

A spur line links Celje with Velenje (€2.65, 50 minutes, 38km) via Šempeter up to nine times a day Monday to Saturday in each direction. A third line connects Celje with Zabok in Croatia via Rogaška Slatina (€2.65, 50 minutes, 36km), Rogatec and Dobovec. Up to seven trains arrive and depart on weekdays but only a couple at the weekend.

Getting Around
For a local taxi ring ☎ 544 22 00 or ☎ 041-606 070.

ŠEMPETER
☎ 03 / pop 1900 / elev 257m
Twelve km west of Celje and accessible by bus and train, Šempeter is the site of a **Roman necropolis** (Rimska Nekropola; ☎ 700 20 56; www.td-sempeter.si; Ob Rimski Nekropoli 2; adult/student/child €3/2.10/1.70; ☷ 10am-6pm daily Apr-Sep; 10am-3pm Sat & Sun Oct-Mar) reconstructed between 1952 and 1966. The burial ground contains four complete tombs and scores of columns, stellae and fragments carved with portraits, mythological creatures and scenes from daily life. They have been divided into about two dozen groups linked by footpaths.

Tomb No I, the oldest of them all, was commissioned by Gallus Vindonius, a Celtic nobleman who lived on a nearby estate in the 1st century. The largest is the **Priscianus tomb** (No II), raised in honour of a Roman official and

his son. (Notice the kidnapping scene on the side relief.) The most beautiful is the **Ennius tomb** (No III), with reliefs of animals and, on the front panel, the princess Europa riding a bull. If you compare these three with the more recent tomb erected in about 250 AD in honour of Secundanius, it is obvious that Roman power and wealth was on the decline here in the mid-3rd century.

If you get hungry, **Gostišče Štorman** (☎ 703 83 00, www.storman.si; Šempeter 5a; meals from €18, set menus €8.70-20.50; ☷ 7am-midnight), one of the first private restaurants to open in Slovenia under the former regime, is about 2km east of the site on the road to/from Celje.

UPPER SAVINJA VALLEY
The Upper Savinja Valley (Zgornja Savinjska Dolina) refers to the drainage areas and tributaries of the Savinja River from its source in the eastern Savinja Alps to a gorge at Letuš, 12km northwest of Šempeter. Bounded by forests, ancient churches, traditional farmhouses and Alpine peaks higher than 2000m, the valley is a land of breathtaking beauty. There are activities here to suit every taste and inclination – from hiking, mountain biking and rock climbing to fishing, kayaking and swimming in the Savinja.

The Savinja begins its rapid flow above Rinka – at 90m Slovenia's highest waterfall – then it enters Logarska Dolina and continues past isolated hamlets and farmland. The region beyond the gorge at Ljubno is quite different, with a number of towns – really overgrown villages – of historical importance, including Radmirje, Gornji Grad, Nazarje and Mozirje.

The valley has been exploited for its timber since the Middle Ages, and until WWII the Savinja was used to power 200 sawmills. Rafters transported the timber from Ljubno to Mozirje and Celje and some of the logs travelled as far as Romania. The trade brought wealth and special rights to the valley, evident from the many fine buildings still standing here.

The free English-language brochure entitled *The Savinjska and Šaleška Valleys* is helpful if you intend spending a fair bit of time in the area. Serious hikers should pick up a copy of the 1:50,000 *Zgornja Savinjska Dolina* map (€7.30) by GZS.

The destinations mentioned in this section fall along the 45km valley road from Mozirje to the Rinka Waterfall, which can be done by bus or car but is tailor-made for bicycles.

THE HAYRACK: A NATIONAL ICON

Nothing is as Slovenian as the *kozolec,* the hayrack seen almost everywhere in the country except in Prekmurje and the Karst area of Primorska. Because the ground in Alpine and hilly areas can be damp, wheat and hay are hung from racks, allowing the wind to do the drying faster and more efficiently.

Until the late 19th century, the *kozolec* was looked upon as just another tool to make a farmer's work easier and the land more productive. Then the artist Ivan Grohar made it the centrepiece of many of his Impressionist paintings, and the *kozolec* became as much a part of the cultural landscape as the physical one. Today it is virtually a national icon, and a sure way to reduce Slovenian *izseljenci* (emigrants) or *zamejci* (ethnic Slovenes living outside the national borders) to nostalgic tears is to send them a postcard or Christmas card of a *kozolec* on a distant slope covered in snow.

There are many different types of Slovenian hayracks: single ones standing alone or 'goat hayracks' with sloped 'lean-to' roofs, parallel and stretched ones and double *toplarji* (hayracks), often with roofs and storage areas on top. Simple hayracks are not unknown in other parts of Alpine Central Europe, but *toplarji,* decorated or plain, are unique to Slovenia.

Hayracks were made of hardwood (usually oak) from the early 17th century. Today, however, the hayrack's future is in concrete, and the new stretched ones can go on forever.

Mozirje

☎ 03 / pop 1960 / elev 340m

The administrative centre of the Upper Savinja Valley lying on the Savinja's left bank, Mozirje is a town with a long history has little to show for its past except for a much rebuilt Gothic Church of St George at the at the western end of Na Trgu just after you cross the small Trnava Stream. Mozirje is really just a convenient stop on the way to Logarska Dolina though the town's botanical garden opposite the bus station is worth a look and there's skiing in winter.

INFORMATION

Nova Ljubljanska Banka (Na Trgu 9; ⊙ 8am-5pm Mon-Fri)

Post office (Savinjska cesta 3) About 200m southwest of the bank.

Tourist office (☎ 839 47 00; td.mozirje@siol.net; 1st fl, Savinjska cesta 7; ⊙ 9am-5pm Apr-Oct; 8am-2pm Mon-Fri Nov-Mar) In council building opposite Mercator.

SIGHTS & ACTIVITIES

Worth the short walk south of town and across the river is **Mozirski Gaj** (Savinja Grove; ☎ 583 27 19; www.mozirskigaj.com; Hribernikova ulica 1; adult/student/child €4.20/3.35/2.10; ⊙ 8am-7pm Apr-Sep), a seven-hectare botanical park and flower garden with a small **open-air ethnographic museum**.

In winter, a cable car runs from Žekovec, 4km northwest of Mozirje, to the **Golte ski centre** (☎ 839 12 00; www.golte.si; half-day pass adult/child €16.30/11.20, day pass €21.70/16), where there are

12km of slopes up to 1600m high and 5km of cross-country trails.

SLEEPING & EATING

Levc farmhouse (☎ 839 53 60; tklevc@volja.net; per person €17; **P**) About 800m southeast of Savinjski Gaj in Loke (house No 19) is this farmhouse with five guestrooms. The main activity here is cattle breeding.

Korošec farmhouse (☎ 583 11 22; www.turizemko rosec.com in Slovene; Ljubija 5; 2-/6-person apt from €32/60; **P**) At the eastern entrance to Mozirje is this attractive tourist farm with three apartments sleeping up to six people as well as sauna and Jacuzzi.

Kozorog (☎ 583 10 22; Na Trgu 32; meals from €8.50; ⊙ 7am-10pm Mon-Sat, 8am-7pm Sun) This is a simple and inexpensive restaurant in the centre of Mozirje that is a popular destination in these parts.

Gaj (☎ 839 51 56; mains €3.80-8; ⊙ 10am-10pm) This restaurant at the entrance to the Mozirski Gaj botanical garden also does pizza (€3.80 to €5).

Mercator (Savinjska cesta 4; ⊙ 7am-8pm Mon-Sat, 8am-3pm Sun) This branch of the supermarket chain is opposite the tourist office.

Nazarje

☎ 03 / pop 950 / elev 365m

The town of 'Nazareth', at the confluence of the Savinja and Dreta rivers 2km south of Mozirje, is dominated by a 15th-century double-towered 'castle' (manor house, really) that houses a museum, a music school and offices of the Glin logging company, the industry that built Nazarje. In fact, the town's coat of arms bears a stylised image of the castle and three fir trees. **Nova Ljubljanska Banka** (Savinjska cesta 2; ☺ 8.30-noon & 2.30-5pm Mon- Fri) is in the 1960s-styled Dom Kulture (Culture House), opposite Vrbovec Castle.

SIGHTS & ACTIVITIES

Vrbovec Castle (Grad Vrbovec; Savinjska cesta 4) contains the **Forestry and Woodworking Museum** (Muzej Gozdarstva in Lesarstva; ☎ 839 16 13; adult/child €1.70/0.85; ☺ 9am-5pm Tue-Sun Mar-Nov), which is the industry that has kept bread on the tables of Nazarje for centuries (witness the huge pulp-processing plant just across the road).

Towering above the town on a hill called Gradišče is the **Franciscan monastery** (Frančiškanski Samostan; ☎ 583 19 93; Samostanska pot 50) and its **Church of the Annunciation**, originally from the mid-17th century, all but flattened by Allied bombs in 1944 and now rebuilt. The twin-spired church has a choir loft with fine grill work; the original chapel, built by Bishop Tomaž Hren of Ljubljana in the early 17th century, now serves as the presbytery. The monastery has a lovely garden surrounded by an arcaded courtyard though most people make the drive up to the monastery or climb its 200-odd steps to see its **library** (by appointment) which has 16th-century manuscripts as well as priceless parchment incunabula dating from the 11th and 12th centuries.

The Hotel Burger Veniše (below) has **horses** for hire.

SLEEPING & EATING

Hotel Burger Veniše (☎ 839 25 50, 041-698 424; ven ise@siol.net; Lačja Vas 22; s/d €35/60) This 15-room hotel and riding centre is in a beautiful valley 3km southwest of Nazarje.

Three kilometres west of Nazarje, you'll find a couple of camping grounds on opposite sides of the river, including **Camping Menina** (☎ 583 50 27, 041-771 846; www.camping menina.com; Varpolje 105; adult €5-6.50, child €3.50-4.50; ☺ mid-Apr–mid-Nov), a 6.5-hectare site on the north bank of the Savinja with cottages (€60) for up to 10 people, and **Camping Savinja-Petrin** (☎ 583 54 72, 041-528 098; primozbitenc@siol.net; Spodnje Pobrežje 11; per person €5; ☺ May-Sep), with 80 sites on the south bank of the river.

Gostišče Grad Vrbovec (☎ 583 28 00; Savinjska cesta 4; starters €3-6.25, mains €4.80-8.20; ☺ 9am-10pm Mon-Fri, 11am-10pm Sat) This fine restaurant in Vrbovec Castle and overlooking the river is an excellent place to stop for lunch. Be sure to try the trout.

Ljubno ob Savinji to Solčava

Two kilometres before the town of Ljubno ob Savinji (population 1160), there's the option for a detour to two historical towns along route No 225. **Radmirje** (population 470), 1km to the southwest, is very picturesque with Štajerska-style hayracks and two important churches: the 16th-century **Church of St Michael** in the centre of town and the 18th-century pilgrimage **Church of St Francis Xavier** (☎ 584 10 96; Radmirje 50) on Straža Hill, containing a rich **treasury** of Mass vestments donated by the kings of Poland and France and a gold chalice from Habsburg empress Maria Theresa. Both can be easily reached from the main road. Five kilometres further on in the Zadrečka Valley is **Gornji Grad** (population 930). The **former Benedictine monastery** (Attemsov trg 2) contains the small **Gornji Grad collections** (☎ 584 34 47, 041-299 013; ☺ 3-5pm Sat, 9-11am & 3-5pm Sun), in the **Šteklo**, a 16th-century defence tower at the entrance to the complex. It contains everyday objects relating to life on the Menina Planina, an area of mountain pastures and slopes south of town. The large baroque **Cathedral of Sts Hermagoras and Fortunatus** (Katedrala Sv Mohorja in Fortunata) in the same complex was built in the mid-18th century (although parts go back to the 13th century) and modelled after the cathedral in Ljubljana. There's a **tourist information centre** (☎ 839 18 58, 584 3 072; tic@gornji-grad.si; Attemsov trg 3) in the nearby town hall that keeps very erratic hours.

Once you've passed Ljubno, the Upper Savinja Valley begins to feel – and smell – truly Alpine, with the mountains so close you can almost touch them, the houses built entirely of wood and the heady scent of pine in the air. The road continues along the winding Savinja, past wooden bridges, more hayracks and, in a gorge 4km beyond **Luče** (population 445) and visible from the main road, a curious rock tower called the **Igla** (Needle).

Just before **Rogovilc**, the usual starting point for canoeing and kayaking trips on the Savinja, there's a turn south to **Robanov Kot** (population 140), a pristine valley and protected park with trails and farmhouse accommodation.

To the northeast of Robanov Kot and below Mt Raduha (2062m) there's an ice cave called **Snežna Jama** (Snow Cave; ☎ 572 48 66, 041-424 091; silvo_ramsak@hotmail.com; admission €4.20; ☺ tour every 2hr 9am-5pm Sat & Sun Jun–mid-Jul; daily mid-Jul–Aug; 9am-4pm Sat & Sun Sep) is accessible by car via a forest road. Temperature ranges from 0°C to 3°C, so dress appropriately.

Solčava (population 240), at 642m the highest town in the Upper Savinja Valley, has some lovely road markers with folk icons and painted barns. Road No 926 north from Solčava to the Alpine village of **Podolševa** (population 70), which continues west and down into Logarska Dolina as the No 927, is one of the most picturesque in Slovenia.

Logarska Dolina

☎ 03 / elev to 1100m

Most of the glacial 'Forester Valley' (Logar Valley) – about 7.5km long and no more than 500m wide – has been a country park of just under 2438 hectares since 1987. This 'pearl of the Alpine region' with more than 30 natural attractions, such as caves, springs, peaks and waterfalls as well as endemic flora (golden slipper orchid) and rare fauna (golden eagles, peregrine falcons), is a wonderful place to explore for a few days. The **Tourist office** (☎ 838 90 04; www.logarska-dolina.si; Logarska Dolina 9; ☺ 9am-3pm Apr-Sep) is in a small wooden kiosk opposite the Plesnik Hotel car park.

SIGHTS & ACTIVITIES

Logarska Dolina Country Park (Krajinski Park Logarska Dolina) is open year-round, but from April to September (and at weekends in October) cars and motorcycles entering the park must pay €5 and €3 respectively; pedestrians and cyclists always get in free. A road goes past a chapel and through the woods to **Rinka Waterfall** (Slap Rinka), but there are plenty of trails to explore and up to 20 other waterfalls in the area.

The bottom of the Rinka Waterfall is a 10-minute walk from the end of the valley road. The climb to the top takes about 20 minutes. It's not very difficult, but it can get slippery. From the top to the west you can see three peaks reaching higher than 2200m: Kranjska Rinka, Koroška Rinka and Štajerska Rinka. Until 1918 they formed the triple border of

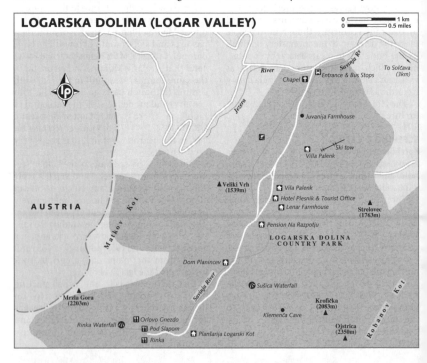

LOGARSKA DOLINA (LOGAR VALLEY)

0 — 1 km
0 — 0.5 miles

Savinja River

River

Chapel

Entrance & Bus Stops

To Solčava (3km)

Jezera

Juvanija Farmhouse

Ski tow

Villa Palenk

Veliki Vrh (1539m)

Vila Palenk

Hotel Plesnik & Tourist Office

Lenar Farmhouse

Strelovec (1763m)

AUSTRIA

Matkov Kot

Pension Na Razpotju

LOGARSKA DOLINA COUNTRY PARK

Dom Planincev

Savinja River

Sušica Waterfall

Mrzla Gora (2203m)

Klemenča Cave

Krofička (2083m)

Robanov Kot

Rinka Waterfall

Orlovo Gnezdo

Pod Slapom

Planšarija Logarski Kot

Ojstrica (2350m)

Rinka

Book accommodation online at lonelyplanet.com

KOROŠKA •• Dravograd **257**

ŠTAJERSKA & KOROŠKA

Carniola (Kranjska), Carinthia (Koroška) and Styria (Štajerska). Ask the tourist office for the *Trail around Logarska* brochure.

Opposite Dom Planincev (below) is a trail leading to **Sušica Waterfall** and **Klemenča Cave**.

Another magnificent and much less explored valley, the 6km-long **Matkov Kot**, runs parallel to Logarska Dolina and the border with Austria. You can reach here by road by turning west as you leave Logarska Dolina.

The tourist office can organise any number of activities: from horse riding (per hr €8.35 to €10.85) and coach rides (€20.80) for up to five people to paragliding (€50), guided mountaineering and rock climbing (€8.35 to €14.60). It also rents mountain bikes (1-/4-hour €2.10/8.35). Nonguests can use the Plesnik Hotel's swimming pool and sauna (per day €12.50). The valley also has some very basic ski grounds (day pass €8.35), including two small tows, 1km of slope and 15km of cross-country ski trails.

SLEEPING & EATING
Dom Planincev (☎ 584 70 06, 031- 269 785; Logarska Dolina 15a; per person €15.50; ☺ late Apr-Oct; P) This mountain hut 2.5km from Rinka has a relaxed, rustic feel to it and sleeps up to 32 people.

Planšarija Logarski Kot (☎ 383 90 30, 041-210 017; info@logarska.si; per person €15.50; ☺ late Apr-Oct; P) More isolated than the Dom Planincev but closer to the falls, this locally run hut has accommodation for two dozen hikers.

Juvanija farmhouse (☎ 838 90 80; juvanija@email.si; Logarska Dolina 8; per person €19; P) Just inside the entrance to the park, this farmhouse has four rooms sleeping up to 11 people.

Lenar farmhouse (☎ 838 90 06; ltk.lenar@siol.net; Logarska Dolina 11; per person €19, apt for 3 €42; P) Another farmhouse with four rooms and apartments, Lenar is a couple of kilometres further south from the entrance.

Pension Na Razpotju (☎ 839 16 50; razpotju@siol.net; Logarska Dolina 14; s/d €45/74; P ✗ ⬜) A spanking new, 24-bed pension set back from the main road is a nice alternative to the Palenk complex, a short distance to the north.

Hotel Plesnik (☎ 839 23 00; www.plesnik.si; Logarska Dolina 10; s €78-83, d €124-132; P ✗ ⬜ ⬛) A 30-room hotel in the centre of the valley with a pool, sauna, a fine restaurant (☺ 8am-10pm) and lovely public area, the Plesnik pretty much *is* Logarska Dolina. As a result it seems to be resting on its laurels, and both the standards of reception and service have dropped

dramatically in recent years. Its annexe, the Villa Palenk (singles/doubles €66/106), with 11 rooms done up in generic 'Alpine style', takes the overflow.

The closest **Mercator** (☺ 7am-7pm Mon-Fri, 7am-noon Sat, 8-11.30am Sun) supermarket is in Luče (house No 105).

In the Logarska Valley itself, along with the restaurants at the Plesnik Hotel and Dom Planincev, there are a couple of simpler places to grab a bite, including:

Pod Slapom (☎ 838 90 36; Logarska Dolina 15b; ☺ 10am-10pm) This attractive little snack bar and restaurant, with things like goulash and Balkan grills, is above the car park close to the Rinka Waterfall.

Orlovo Gnezdo (☎ 584 70 06; ☺ 10am-6pm) The 'Eyrie' is a simple eatery in a tall wooden tower overlooking the falls and reached by a steep set of steps.

Getting There & Away
From Mozirje, there is an hourly bus service to Celje (€4.50, one hour, 36km) on weekdays but only two on Saturday. Other destinations are Gornji Grad (€2.60, 30 minutes, 16km, up to six a day) and Solčava (€3.50, 45 minutes, 29km, five on weekdays).

From Gornji Grad, buses go to Ljubljana (€5.80, 1½ hours, 51km, four daily Monday to Friday, 4.38am Saturday and 12.01pm Sunday) and Kamnik (€3, 45 minutes, 23km, five, with one or two at the weekend). There's a 7.51am bus on Sunday to Logarska Dolina (€3.50, one hour, 30km) from June to September only.

KOROŠKA

The truncated province of Koroška is essentially just three valleys bounded by the Pohorje Massif on the east, the last of the Karavanke peaks, Mt Peca (where good King Matjaž is said to be resting), on the west and the hills of Kobansko to the north. The Drava Valley runs east to west and includes the towns of Dravograd, Muta and Vuzenica. The Mežica and Mislinja valleys fan out from the Drava; the former is an industrial area with such towns as Ravne, Prevalje and Črna na Koroškem while the latter's main centre is Slovenj Gradec.

DRAVOGRAD
☎ 02 / pop 3385 / elev 362m
Dravograd, situated on both sides of the Drava (which, at 144km, is Slovenia's second-longest river after the Sava), is a sleepy place with

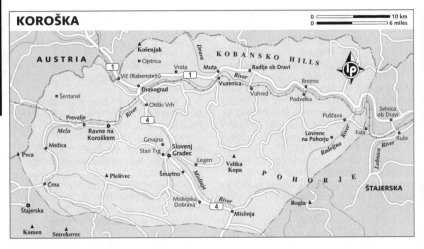

KOROŠKA

few sights of its own (though students of history might make a trip here for its infamous WWII connections). It is, however, an excellent springboard for exploring the Kobansko Hills to the north and the Drava Valley to the east.

The town whose name means 'Drava Castle' is much smaller than its sister city, Slovenj Gradec, 12km to the south. It is just as old, however, with a recorded history dating back to the 12th century. It was at this time that the castle, the ruins of which can be seen on the hill to the north of town, was built. Located on a bend in the Drava at the point where the smaller Meža and Mislinja Rivers flow into it, the castle and the town were of great strategic importance for centuries and at the beginning of the 20th century as many as 2000 rafts sailed between here and Maribor, 60km to the east, each year. The river traffic came to a grinding halt in 1943 when the Dravograd hydro-power plant opened.

Orientation

Dravograd's historical centre and its main street, Trg 4 Julija, are on the north bank of the Drava. The bus and train stations are about 1km southeast on the south bank.

Information

Koroška Banka (Trg 4 Julija 44; 8.30am-12.30pm & 2.30-5pm Mon-Fri) Two doors east of the Church of St Vitus.

Post office (Trg 4 Julija 1) At the eastern end of Trg 4 Julija just before the bridge over the Drava.

Tourist office (871 02 85; info@dravograd.si; Trg 4 Julija 57; 10am-6pm May-Oct)

Sights & Activities

The **Church of St Vitus** (Cerkev Sv Vida), at the western end of Trg 4 Julija and opposite No 47, is one of the most important Romanesque buildings extant in Slovenia. Built in the second half of the 12th century and only recently renovated, it is a solid structure of light-brown stone with a high tower between the nave and the small circular presbytery.

The basement of the **town hall** (878 30 11; Trg 4 Julija 7; admission €1; by arrangement) was used as a Gestapo prison and torture chamber during WWII, and can be visited; ask at the tourist office. The hydroelectric dam on the Drava nearest Dravograd was built by German soldiers during the war, and many of them were lodged in town.

It's an easy hike north from Dravograd to the **castle ruins** (not much more than a wall); just head up Pod Gradom, a lane just before Trg 4 Julija 22. The more energetic may want to carry on further into the **Kobansko Hills**, where you just might encounter some traditional charcoal burners. A circular section of the **Kozjak Mountain Trail** leads north past Goriški Vrh to Mt Košenjak (1522m) and returns to Dravograd via Ojstrica.

The tourist office can arrange three-hour **rafting trips** (871 0200; per person €16) on the Drava. The trip starts at Vrata, about 10km to the east, and carries on to Dravograd. The price includes food and drink.

Sleeping & Eating

Planinski Dom Košenjak (☎ 878 35 04, 041-887 4444; pd.dravograd@email.si; ❧ Thu-Sun Mar–mid-Nov; Sat & Sun year-round) If you don your hiking boots and set out for Mt Košenjak, there is accommodation at this 43-bed Category II mountain lodge situated at 1169m north of Dravograd.

Restavracija-Prenočišča Korošica (☎ 878 69 11; www.korosica.si; starters €3.70-5.75, mains €5.80-9.60; ❧ 7am-10pm, 11am-midnight, 11am-10pm) This popular restaurant in Otiški Vrh (house No 25a) about 3km southeast of Dravograd has 15 comfortable rooms (singles/doubles €34/60).

Hotel Hesper (☎ 878 44 40; www.hesper.si; Koroška cesta 48; s/d/tr €38/57/85; P ✗ ✗ ☐) About 1.5km northwest of Trg 4 Julija in the Traberg shopping centre, this 24-room property is the only place to stay in central Dravograd. One redeeming feature is its restaurant **Narodna** (National; ☎ 878 44 40; meals from €15; ❧ 7am-10pm), which is popular with *Avstrijci* from over the border.

There is a surfeit of **farmhouse** accommodation at Šentanel (p260), about 18km southwest of Dravograd.

Kaiser (☎ 878 31 04; 4 Trg Julija 27; meals from €8; ❧ noon-10pm) Light meals are served at this central café-restaurant.

Lovski Rog (☎ 878 32 88; Trg 4 Julija 37; meals from €10; ❧ 5.30am-11pm Mon-Thu, 5.30am-midnight Fri, 6am-10pm Sat, 7am-8pm Sun) Come to the 'Hunting Bugle' for stick-to-the-ribs Slovenian dishes. It's most popular at breakfast and lunch.

You'll find a **BA Center** (Trg 4 Julija 15; ❧ 7am-9pm) supermarket with extended hours in the centre of town and a much larger but less central **Mercator** (Koroška cesta 48; 7am-8pm Mon-Fri, 7am-3pm Sat, 8am-noon Sun) next to the Hotel Hesper.

Getting There & Away

Count on a bus every hour or so to Črna (€3.50, one hour, 27km), Maribor (€6.50, two hours, 61km) via Radlje ob Dravi and Slovenj Gradec (€1.70, 15 minutes, 10km). Buses also serve Celje (€6.50, two hours, 65km, one at 2.30pm), Gornji Grad (€6.65, two hours, 67km, one at 1.10 Monday to Saturday) and Ljubljana (€10.80, three hours, 121km, two or three daily).

Dravograd is on the rail line linking Maribor and Bleiburg (Pliberk) and Klagenfurt in Austria. Up to five trains a day on weekdays depart for Maribor (€4.50, 1½ hours, 64km) via Vuzenica and Vuhred. Four trains leave for Ravne na Koroškem and Prevalje

(€1.50, 20 minutes, 12km), one of which crosses the Austrian border and carries on to Klagenfurt.

AROUND DRAVOGRAD

An excellent bike trip follows the spectacular Drava Valley through the Pohorje and Kobansko Hills, 60km eastward to Maribor. The river, whose highest flow is reached at the start of the summer, is at its most scenic at Brezno and just above Fala, where it narrows into a gorge. Just before Maribor, the Drava widens into a lake with the help of a major dam.

You don't have to go that far to see some great scenery, however. Vuzenica and Muta, two very attractive villages, are just 14km from Dravograd and can be reached by train or on the Maribor bus.

Vuzenica

☎ 02 / pop 1625 / elev 366m

The **Church of St Nicholas** (Cerkev Sv Nikolaja; for key ☎ 876 40 34 or ☎ 040-858 236) in Vuzenica, on the Drava's right bank, was built in the 12th century and expanded later; note the Gothic buttresses outside. Its outstanding features include a fabulous baroque gold altar, a star-vaulted ceiling typical of Koroška, 15th-century frescoes in the porch and an original fortified wall surrounding the churchyard. The ruins of a 16th-century **castle** can be seen on Pisterjev Vrh northeast of town.

Muta

☎ 02 / pop 2410 / elev 369m

A two-tier village across the Drava from Vuzenica, Muta has churches on both levels, but you want the one in **Spodnja Muta** (Lower Muta) near the main road. The austere **Rotunda of St John the Baptist** (Rotunda Janeza Krstnika; for key ☎ 876 13 97, 040-959 491) is one of the oldest churches in Slovenia – it was built while Pope Leo IX (1002–54) toured Carinthia and Styria in the mid-11th century. Its round shape, wooden-shingled roof and steeple are typical of the province, and the tiny church appears quite content with itself sitting in a field with the hills far behind it. There are fragmented reliefs on the east side of the apse, and near the west entrance is a stone relief of an eagle dating from Roman times. If you can manage to get the rotunda opened, you'll see 14th-century frescoes in the choir and the painted wooden ceiling in the presbytery dating from

UNDER THE LINDEN TREES

If cities can have municipal animals – where would Rome be today without the she-wolf that suckled Romulus and Remus or Berlin without its bear – why can't a country have a national tree? Slovenia's is the linden (or common lime), and its heart-shaped leaf has become something of a symbol of Slovenia and Slovenian hospitality.

The stately linden (*lipa*) grows slowly for about 60 years and then suddenly spurts upward and outwards, living to a ripe old age. It is said that a linden grows for 300 years, stands still for another 300 and takes 300 years to die.

Linden wood was used by the Romans to make shields and, as it is easy to work with, artisans in the Middle Ages carved religious figures from it, earning linden the title *sacrum lignum*, or 'sacred wood'. Tea made from the linden flower, which contains aromatic oils, has been used as an antidote for fever and the flu at least since the 16th century.

More importantly, from earliest times the linden tree was the focal point of any settlement in Slovenia – the centre of meetings, arbitration, recreation and, of course, gossip. The tree, which could never be taller than the church spire, always stood in the middle of the village, and important decisions were made by town elders at a table beneath it.

In fact, so sacred is the linden tree to Slovenes that its destruction is considered a serious offence. In discussing the barbarous acts committed by the Italians during the occupation of Primorska between the wars, one magazine article passionately points out that 'Kobarid had to swallow much bitterness… The fascists even cut down the linden tree…'

In today's Slovenia, the linden represents not just hospitality but democracy too – something that has not been lost on seekers of high office. More than one politician facing an election has been known to waltz around Slovenia's oldest linden, the 800-year-old Najevska Lipa under Koroška's Mt Peca, which was featured on a commemorative stamp in 2002.

the late 16th century. The relief of an eagle at the entrance dates back to Roman times.

Šentanel
☎ 02 / pop 180 / elev 411m
This picturesque (and award-winning!) village in the Mežica Valley, 6km northwest of Prevalje, is not a destination in itself but if you have your own transport and would like to get away from it all, consider spending a night or two in one of the dozen or so farmhouses here. Prevalje is 12km southwest of Dravograd and easily accessible by bus and train.

Ploder farmhouse (☎ 823 11 04, 041-867 375; kmetijaplode@hotmail.com; per person €18) This farmhouse in Šentanel (house No 3) has 11 rooms, including one that has six beds with dormitory accommodation.

Marin-Miler farmhouse (☎ 824 05 50, 041-654 886; per person €19) A more isolated place at Šentanel 8 with 6 rooms, this farmhouse has views of Mt Peca.

SLOVENJ GRADEC
☎ 02 / pop 8030 / elev 410m
Slovenj Gradec is not the capital of Koroška – that distinction goes to the industrial centre of Ravne na Koroškem to the northwest – but it is certainly the province's cultural and recreational heart. A large number of museums, galleries and historical churches line its main square, while the sporting opportunities in the Pohorje Massif to the east are endless.

History
The history of Slovenj Gradec is closely tied to Stari Trg, a suburb southwest of the Old Town where there was a Roman settlement called Colatio that existed from the 1st to the 3rd centuries. At that time an important Roman road from Celeia (Celje) to Virunum (near Klagenfurt in Austria) passed through Colatio. Slovenj Gradec was an important trade centre in the Middle Ages and minted its own coins. Later it became an important cultural and artistic centre with many artisans and craft guilds. Among the prominent Habsburg nobles based in Slovenj Gradec over the centuries were members of the Windisch-Grätz family, a variant of the German name for the town (Windisch Graz). *Windisch* (or *wendisch*) was once the general German term for 'Slavic'; 'Gradec' is Slovene for 'Graz'.

Orientation

Slovenj Gradec's main street is Glavni trg, a colourful long 'square' lined with old town houses and shops. The bus station is at Pohorska cesta 15, about 500m northeast of the tourist office. Slovenj Gradec is not on a train line.

Information

Koroška Banka (Glavni trg 30; 🕑 8.30am-12.30pm & 2.30-5pm Mon-Fri)

Mladinska Knjiga (☎ 881 22 83; Glavni trg 12; 🕑 8am-7pm Mon-Fri, to 1pm Sat) Stocks regional maps and guides.

Post office (Francetova cesta 1) At the northern end of Glavni trg.

Tourist Information Centre Slovenj Gradec (TIC; ☎ 881 21 16; www.slovenj-gradec.si; Glavni trg 24; 🕑 8am-4pm Mon-Fri, 9am-noon Sat & Sun) On the ground floor of the former town hall.

Sights

MUSEUMS

The **former town hall**, where the tourist office is located, also contains two important museums. The **Koroška Regional Museum** (Koroški Pokrajinski Muzej; ☎ 884 20 55; Glavni trg 24; http://gostje .kivi.si/muzej; adult/student/child €2.10/1.70/1.50; 🕑 8am-6pm Tue-Fri, 9am-noon & 3-6pm Sat & Sun) has exhibits on the 2nd floor devoted to the history of Slovenj Gradec and the Koroška region – from local sport heroes' awards and farm implements to painted beehive panels and models of wartime hospital rooms and schools run by Partisans. There's also a very good archaeological collection focusing on the Roman settlement of Colatio. It includes jewellery and other effects taken from a Slavic burial ground at Puščava near Castle Hill (Grajski Grič) to the west.

The **Koroška Gallery of Fine Arts** (Koroška Galerija Likovnih Umetnosti; ☎ 884 12 83; www.glu-sg.si; adult/ student & child/family €2.10/1.25/4.20; 🕑 9-6pm Tue-Fri, 9am-noon & 3-6pm Sat & Sun) on the 1st floor of the former town hall has rotating exhibits but counts among its permanent collection African folk art, bronze sculptures by Franc Berneker (1874–1932) and naive paintings by Jože Tisnikar (b 1928). Tisnikar is among the most interesting and original artists in Slovenia, and his obsession with corpses, distorted figures and oversized insects is at once disturbing and funny. Don't miss *Rojstva in Smrt* (Birth and Death), *Ti, ki Ostanejo* (Those who Stay) and *Črička* (Crickets). The paintings are all very black and blue. Outside the

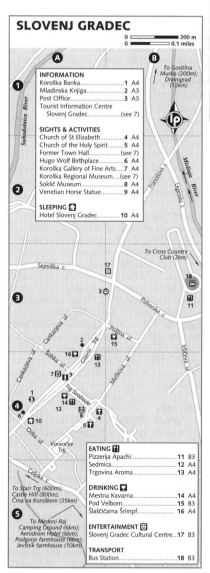

town hall is the **Venetian Horse**, a life-size work by contemporary sculptor/designer Oskar Kogoj. It has become something of a symbol for Slovenj Gradec.

The items on display at the **Soklič Museum** (Sokličev Muzej; ☎ 884 15 05; Trg Svobode 5; 🕑 by appointment) in the church rectory were amassed by Jakob Soklič (1893–1972), a priest who

---

SLOVENJ GRADEC

0   200 m
0   0.1 miles

INFORMATION
Koroška Banka.....................1 A4
Mladinska Knjiga................2 A3
Post Office...........................3 A3
Tourist Information Centre
   Slovenj Gradec................(see 7)

SIGHTS & ACTIVITIES
Church of St Elizabeth.........4 A4
Church of the Holy Spirit.....5 A4
Former Town Hall...............(see 7)
Hugo Wolf Birthplace..........6 A4
Koroška Gallery of Fine Arts...7 A4
Koroška Regional Museum....(see 7)
Soklič Museum.....................8 A4
Venetian Horse Statue..........9 A4

SLEEPING 🛏
Hotel Slovenj Gradec............10 A4

EATING 🍴
Pizzerija Apachi....................11 B3
Sedmica...............................12 A4
Trgovina Aroma....................13 A4

DRINKING
Mestna Kavarna...................14 A4
Pod Velbom.........................15 B3
Slaščičarna Šrimpf................16 A4

ENTERTAINMENT 🎭
Slovenj Gradec Cultural Centre...17 B3

TRANSPORT
Bus Station...........................18 B3

began squirreling away bits and bobs in the 1930s. Among the mediocre watercolours and oils of peasant idylls and the umpteen portraits of the composer Hugo Wolf (1860–1903), whose **birthplace** (Glavni trg 40) is nearby, are green goblets and beakers from nearby Glažuta (an important glass-manufacturing town in the 19th century), local embroidery and linen, religious artefacts and some 18th-century furniture. The statue of a saint holding a chalice with a snake coming out of it represents St John the Evangelist. (In quite a reversed role for a biblical reptile, a serpent once warned the apostle that he was about to quaff poisoned wine.)

CHURCHES

The sombre **Church of St Elizabeth** (Trg Svobode) was built in 1251 and is the town's oldest structure. But aside from the Romanesque nave and a couple of windows, almost everything here is baroque, including the massive gold altar and the altar paintings done by local artist Franc Mihael Strauss (1647–1740) and his son Janez Andrej Strauss (1721–82). Far more interesting is the 15th-century **Church of the Holy Spirit** (Trg Svobode) to the south with an interior covered with Gothic frescoes by Andrej of Otting. The 27 panels on the north wall represent the Passion of Christ; the scenes on the archway are of the Final Judgment.

Activities

The **Slovenian Alpine Trail** passes through Stari Trg and the centre of Slovenj Gradec before continuing up to Mala Kopa (1524m), where it meets the E6. There is a Category II 48-bed mountain hut at 1102m to the northwest called **Koča pod Kremžarjevim Vrhom** (☎ 884 48 83; 041-832 035; ⏰ Wed-Mon late Apr-Sep, Sat & Sun Oct-late Apr). The **E6** heads north through Vuhred and Radlje ob Dravi to Austria, and the Slovenian Alpine Trail carries on eastward to Rogla and Maribor. There is more accommodation on Velika Kopa at 1377m at the 68-bed **Grmovškov Dom pod Veliko Kopo** (☎ 883 98 60, 041-643 663; ⏰ year-round). If you are going to do a fair amount of hiking in the western Pohorje, pick up a copy of the 1:50,000-scale *Pohorje* GZS map (€7.50).

Koroša is becoming something of a centre for mountain biking. The adrenalin-pumping **Mountain Bike Park** (☎ 870 30 60; www.mtbpark .com; Center ulica 153) is situated at the Hotel Club Krnes in Črna na Koroškem, near Dravograd. It sits at the centre of a network of some

1000km of marked forest and mountain trails ranging in length from 20km to 350km – some of which climb up to 1690m – and a downhill racecourse. There's even a 5km trail through a 300-year-old Frederick Mine (Fridrihov Rov), which must be booked in advance. The hotel offers single or multiday guided mountain-bike tours and organises training camps and competitions. Mountain bikes cost per day €15/20 for front/full suspension and per week €84/133.

Three ski slopes are within striking distance of Slovenj Gradec, but the closest is **Kope** (☎ 882 27 40; www.pohorje.org; half-day pass adult/student/child €17/15/12.50, day pass €20.50/17.50/14.60), 1300m to 1520m above the Mislinja Valley on the western edge of the Pohorje Massif. The ski grounds have 8km of runs, 15km of cross-country trails and seven lifts on Mala Kopa and Velika Kopa peaks. To reach Kope, follow the Velenje road (No 4) for 3km south and then turn east. The ski area is another 13km at the end of the road.

Two farmhouses in the vicinity have horses and ponies for hire including the **Podgorje 91 farmhouse** (☎ 041-619 621) at house No 91 of Podgorje pri Slovenj Gradcu, 6km to the southwest, and the **Jevšnik farmhouse** (☎ 041-325 698; Straže 125) at Mislinja, 10km to the southeast.

Sleeping & Eating

Medeni Raj camping ground (☎ 885 0500; www.aero drom-sg.si; Mislinjska Dobrava 110; camp site per person €6.50, bungalows €25; ⏰ mid-Mar–mid-Oct) 'Sweet Paradise' is a small, friendly place with sites for 200 tents and caravans and six bungalows set among pine trees of Turiška Vas just beyond the Aerodrom hotel in Mislinjska Dobrava.

Hotel Slovenj Gradec (☎ 884 52 85; www.kope.si; Glavni trg 43; s/d €31/57.50; Ⓟ Ⓧ Ⓧ) The only hotel option in town is this depressing 68-room property with rather gloomy rooms and long, dark corridors that seem to go on forever. It still desperately needs a makeover.

Aerodrom (☎ 885 0500, 051-603 556; www.aero drom-sg.si; Mislinjska Dobrava 110; s/d €48/66; Ⓟ Ⓧ Ⓧ Ⓛ Ⓓ) It's a bit of a schlep 6km southeast of Slovenj Gradec but the four-star Aerodrom is head and shoulders above any other accommodation in the area.

Sedmica (☎ 884 51 09, 041-769 797; Trg Svobode 7; dishes €3.75-5; ⏰ 9am-10pm Mon-Sat, noon-midnight Sun) The 'Little Seven' is a pizzeria and *špageterija* in the centre of town with pizzas and all kinds of pasta dishes.

Pizzerija Apachi (☎ 883 17 84; Pohorska cesta 17b; pizza €3.75-4.80; ☙ 9am-midnight Mon-Thu, 9am-2am Fri & Sat, 3-10pm Sun) This pizzeria with a 'cowboys and Indians' theme (go figure) is next to the bus station.

Gostilna Murko (☎ 883 81 03; Francetova cesta 24; meals from €12; ☙ 8am-10pm) About 400m north of the centre on the Mislinja, Gostilna Murko is a roadside inn popular with Austrian tourists on the go.

There's a small **Trgovina Aroma** (Glavni trg 17; ☙ 6am-8pm Mon-Sat, 8am-6pm Sun) supermarket on the main square.

Drinking

Mestna Kavarna (☎ 884 51 09; Trg Svobode 7; ☙ 6.30am-midnight Mon-Thu, 8am-2am Fri & Sat, 8.30am-midnight Sun) This updated yet old-style café on the corner of Glavni trg is the most comfortable place in town to tip back a coffee or maybe even something stronger.

Šlaščičarna Šrimpf (☎ 884 14 82; Glavni trg 14; ☙ 8.30am-8pm) This long-established café draws the crowds with its fabulous cakes. Try the *zagrebska* (€1.35), a rich concoction of custard, cream, chocolate and flaky pastry.

Pod Velbom (☎ 884 28 00; Glavni trg 1; ☙ 6am-midnight Sun-Thu, 6am-2am Fri, 9am-2am Sat) If you're looking for some company, the best place for meeting people in the centre of Slovenj Gradec is this pub-café; enter from Poštna ulica.

Entertainment

Classical music concerts are sometimes held at the Church of St Elizabeth and the **Slovenj Gradec Cultural Centre** (Kulturni Dom Slovenj Gradec; ☎ 884 50 05; Francetova ulica 5).

Getting There & Away

There are hourly buses to Črna (€4, one hour, 35km), Dravograd (€1.70, 15 minutes, 10km) and Mislinja (€2.20, 30 minutes, 14km). Other destinations served by bus from Slovenj Gradec include Celje (€5.80, 1½ hours, 55km, 3.10pm daily), Gornji Grad (€6.20, 1½ hours, 57km, one at 1.31pm Monday to Saturday), Ljubljana (€10, three hours, 111km, two to three daily) and Maribor (€7, two hours, 71km, two or three daily).

You can call a taxi in Slovenj Gradec on ☎ 041-645 901.

Prekmurje

The head of the 'chicken' that is (almost) the shape of Slovenia, Prekmurje is a region apart. Neither mountainous nor bordering the sea, it consists largely of a broad plain extending for some 25km beyond the Mura River. Winters can be very cold on the Prekmurje plain, and summers extremely hot.

Prekmurje is marked by wide fields – it is the country's largest agricultural region – and rounded hills, floating watermills, hearty cuisine, a somewhat fiery-tempered people and very distinct dialects, which emerged and thrived due to the region's isolation. But most tourists are attracted to this forgotten corner of Slovenia by its thermal health resorts, especially the ones at Radenci, Moravske Toplice and Banovci.

The province's isolation is rooted in history – until 1924 not a single bridge spanned the sluggish Mura. As a result, Prekmurje retains much of its traditional folklore and distinctive architecture, which you can't help noticing as you travel around. The province's farmhouses are very similar to the *kerített házak* (fenced-in houses) found in Transdanubia across the border in Hungary; given the history of the area, this is not at all surprising. Until the end of WWI most of Prekmurje was ruled by Austria-Hungary, and a sizeable Magyar minority still lives here. In fact, in some ways Prekmurje looks and feels more like Hungary than Slovenia, emphasised by the abundance of white storks (p270), a relatively large Roma (Gypsy) population and the occasional Hungarian-style *čarda* (inn).

HIGHLIGHTS

- Take the waters *au naturel* at the **spa resort** (p267) of Banovci
- Visit Prekmurje's remaining **floating mill** (p267) on the Mura River near Veržej
- Admire the wonderful 14th-century **frescoes** (p267)at the Church of St Martin in Martjanci
- Satisfy that sweet tooth with a plate of **gibanica**, pastry with poppy seeds, walnuts, fruit, cheese and cream

MURSKA SOBOTA

☎ 02 / pop 12,400 / elev 189m

Slovenia's northernmost city, Murska Sobota is unusual in mostly alpine Slovenia because it is situated on a plain flatter than a *palačinka*, a pancake filled with jam or nuts and topped with chocolate that is so popular here. Today, the capital and administrative centre of Prekmurje has little to recommend it except for its odd architectural mix of neoclassical, Secessionist and 'socialist baroque' buildings. But it is an excellent base for day trips to the nearby potters' villages and thermal spas.

History

Murska Sobota was little more than a Hungarian market town – its name in both Slovene and Hungarian (Muraszombat) means 'Mura Saturday', indicating when the market took place – until two pivotal events last century. The first was the opening of the railway in 1907, which linked it with Hungary proper via Šalovci to the north. The second event was ultimately even more significant for the city. With the formation of the Kingdom of Serbs, Croats and Slovenes in 1918 and the transfer of territory, Murska Sobota found itself more or less in the centre of Prekmurje and development really took off. The area was occupied by Hungary during WWII.

Orientation

Trg Zmage (Victory Square), the centre of Murska Sobota, lies southeast of large, shady

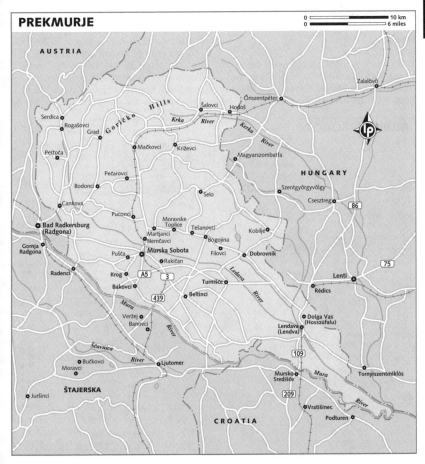

Mestni Park (City Park). The bus station is 400m to the south on Slomškova ulica next to the Hotel Diana. The train station is 700m southeast of Trg Zmage at the eastern end of Ulica Arhitekta Novaka.

Information

Dobra Knjiga (☎ 522 37 24; Slovenska ulica 9; ✆ 7am-6pm Mon-Fri, 8am-noon Sat) Central bookshop with regional maps for hiking in Prekmurje.

Nova Ljubljanska Banka (Trg Zmage 7; ✆ 8am-5pm Mon-Fri)

Post office (Trg Zmage 6)

SKB Banka (Kocljeva ulica 14; ✆ 8.30am-noon & 2-5pm Mon-Fri)

Tourist Information Centre Murska Sobota (☎ 534 11 30; tic.ms@siol.net; Slovenska ulica; ✆ 8am-6pm Mon-Fri, 8am-noon Sat) In a pavement kiosk southeast of Trg Zmage.

Sights

SOBOTA CASTLE

This sprawling manor house in the centre of Mestni Park dates from the mid-16th century. It houses the renovated **Murska Sobota Regional Museum** (Pokrajinski Muzej Murska Sobota; ☎ 527 17 06;

www.pok-muzej-ms.si; Trubarjev drevored 4; adult/student/child €2.50/2.10/1.70; ✆ 9am-5pm Tue-Fri, 9am-1pm Sat & Sun), which tells the story of life along the Mura River from prehistoric to present times in 15 rooms. The ethnographic section will look familiar to anyone who has visited such collections in southern Transdanubia just over the border; the farm implements, painted jugs, costumes and woodcarvings displayed in the vaulted rooms are almost identical to their Hungarian counterparts.

OTHER SIGHTS

At the eastern entrance to Mestni Park the **Victory Monument** is an impressive (if anachronistic) grouping of heavy artillery and Yugoslav and Soviet soldiers in stone that somehow remained while the rest of Slovenia was 'spring cleaning' after independence. Opposite the park is the neo-Gothic **Evangelical Church** (1910), the main Lutheran seat in Slovenia (the majority of Slovenian Protestants, who number about 16,000, live in Prekmurje). The interior, painted with geometric shapes and floral motifs in muted shades of blue and green, is a welcome change from the

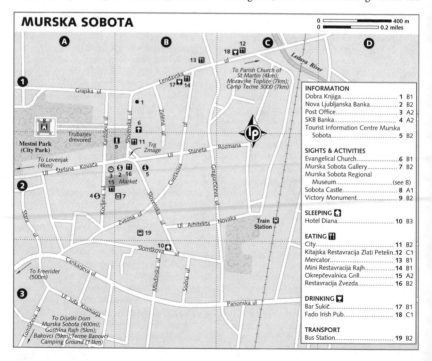

MURSKA SOBOTA

0   400 m
0   0.2 miles

Ledova River

To Parish Church of
St Martin (4km);
Moravske Toplice (7km);
Camp Terme 3000 (7km)

Mestni Park
(City Park)

To Lovenjak
(4km)

To Freerider
(500m)

Train Station

To Dijaški Dom
Murska Sobota (400m);
Gostilna Rajh (5km);
Bakovci (5km); Terme Banovci
Camping Ground (13km)

INFORMATION	
Dobra Knjiga	1 B1
Nova Ljubljanska Banka	2 B2
Post Office	3 A2
SKB Banka	4 A2
Tourist Information Centre Murska Sobota	5 B2

SIGHTS & ACTIVITIES	
Evangelical Church	6 B1
Murska Sobota Gallery	7 B2
Murska Sobota Regional Museum	(see 8)
Sobota Castle	8 A1
Victory Monument	9 B2

SLEEPING	
Hotel Diana	10 B3

EATING	
City	11 B2
Kitajska Restavracija Zlati Petelin	12 C1
Mercator	13 B1
Mini Restavracija Rajh	14 B1
Okrepčevalnica Grill	15 A2
Restavracija Zvezda	16 B2

DRINKING	
Bar Sukič	17 B1
Fado Irish Pub	18 C1

TRANSPORT	
Bus Station	19 B2

MILLS & THRILLS

Floating mills, which date back to Roman times, were very popular on rivers that changed their course abruptly or swelled rapidly after rainfall, as they allowed millers to move to the best possible spots for milling. In Slovenia, floating mills were largely built on the Mura River; there were dozens of them in operation up to WWII. Today, the only one left is the Babič Mill at Veržej, and even it cannot be classified as a fully 'floating mill' as only the mill wheel is in the water. The rest of it is firmly tethered to the riverbank.

overwrought baroque gold and marble decor found in most Catholic churches here.

The **Murska Sobota Gallery** (☎ 522 38 34; Kocljeva ulica 7; ✆ 10am-6pm Tue-Fri, 9am-noon Sat), the best gallery in Prekmurje, has rotating exhibits (admission varies).

The **Parish Church of St Martin** in **Martjanci** (population 490), 4km north of Murska Sobota on the road to Moravske Toplice, contains wonderful 14th-century frescoes by Johannes Aquila of Radgona, painted on the sanctuary's vaulted ceiling and walls. They depict angels bearing inscriptions, the Apostles, scenes from the life of St Martin and even a self-portrait of Master Johannes himself. Not to be outdone by the artist, the church's benefactor had his likeness appear in several scenes on the north arch and west wall.

Sleeping

The closest camping ground is at Camp Terme at Moravske Toplice (p269), 7km to the northeast.

Terme Banovci (☎ 513 14 00; www.terme-banovci.si; campsites €12-13; ✆ late Mar-Oct; P ✆) A quarter of the 210 sites at this small spa near Veržej, 13km south of Murska Sobota, are reserved for naturists. The price includes entry to the spa's thermal and swimming pools.

Dijaški Dom Murska Sobota (☎ 530 03 10; info@d-dom.ms.edus.si; Tomšičeva ulica 15; per person €16; ✆ late Jul-Aug; ✆ ✆) This 60-bed student dormitory southwest of the centre accepts travellers in summer only, although there is usually a handful of rooms available at other times as well. It has laundry facilities.

Hotel Diana (☎ 514 12 00; www.zvezda-diana.si in Slovene; Slovenska ulica 52; s/d/ste €43/71/79; P ✆ ✆ ✆ ✆)

The 95 rooms in Murska Sobota's only hotel are bright and airy but get no points for decor; they're in a garishly painted concrete block in the centre of town. It has a glassed-in swimming pool, sauna and fitness room as well as a decent pizzeria (pizzas €4.20 to €6.20) open seven days of the week.

Eating

City (Slovenska ulica 27; sandwiches from €1.50; ✆ 6am-9pm Mon-Fri, 6am-3pm Sat, 7am-1pm Sun) Essentially a stylish café with drinks, City also serves snacks and sandwiches and is a convenient distance to the museum.

Okrepčevalnica Grill (☎ 524 18 50; Kocljeva ulica 5; dishes from €2.50; ✆ 6am-6pm Mon-Fri, 6.30am-1pm Sat) This inexpensive *bife* (snack bar) in the market south of Trg Zmage serves fish dishes as well as Balkan-style grilled meats.

Mini Restavracija Rajh (☎ 523 12 38; Cvetkova ulica 21; starters €3.70-6.25, pizza & pasta €4.10-5.50; ✆ 10am-10pm Tue-Sun) A self-styled 'mini-restaurant' on the corner of Lendavska ulica, Rajh is an upmarket *špagetarija* and *picerija*.

Kitajska Restavracija Zlati Petelin (☎ 523 17 90; Lendavska ulica 39e; starters €3.55-4.10, mains €5-8.70) As its name indicates, the 'Golden Cock' is a Chinese restaurant serving up the usual range of rather toned-down Chinese dishes.

Gostilna Rajh (☎ 543 90 98; Soboška ulica 32; meals from €10.50; ✆ 10am-11pm Tue-Sat, 10am-4.30pm Sun) In Bakovci, a village 5km to the southwest, this *gostilna* (innlike restaurant) specialises in local dishes and boasts a large cellar of regional wines.

Restavracija Zvezda (☎ 514 18 61; Trg Zmage 8; meals €12.50; ✆ 6.30am-11pm Mon-Thu, 6.30am-1am Fri, 7am-1am Sat, 7am-10pm Sun) This renovated pub restaurant is very central, and in the warmer months

THE AUTHOR'S CHOICE

Lovenjak (☎ 525 21 53; Polana 40; starters €6.25-8.35, mains €7.50-10.80; ✆ 11am-10pm Mon-Thu, 11am-midnight Fri & Sat, 11am-6pm Sun) This excellent, very atmospheric *gostilna* in the tiny village of Polana, 4km northwest of Murska Sobota, serves such local favourites as *bograč golaž* (Hungarian-style goulash soup), roast suckling pig served with noodles, Gypsy-style pork with garlic, Prekmurje ham and, for dessert, the indecently rich *gibanica*. Be sure to book for Sunday lunch.

PREKMURJE

the outside terrace under the chestnut trees becomes the town's focal point. At weekends there always seems to be a function on.

Mercator (Lendavska ulica 21; ☺ 7am-9pm) This supermarket northeast of the centre is open daily.

Drinking

You'll find a couple of bars along Lendavska ulica, including the convivial **Fado Irish Pub** (☎ 523 14 11; Lendavska ulica 39a; ☺ 7am-11pm Mon-Thu, 7am-midnight Fri, 9am-midnight Sat, 8am-10pm Sun) and further west **Bar Sukič** (☎ 523 12 58; Lendavska ulica 14; ☺ 5.30am-10pm Mon-Thu, 5.30am-11pm Fri, 6am-3pm Sat) with a large open terrace.

Getting There & Around

Buses leave six to eight times a day for Dobrovnik (€2.60, 30 minutes, 18km), Gornja Radgona via Radenci (€2.15, 15 minutes, 13km), Maribor (€6.15, 1¼ hours, 60km), Lendava (€3.50, 30 minutes, 29km, half-houly) and Moravske Toplice (€1.70, 15 minutes, 10km). Other destinations include Hodoš (€3.50, 45 minutes, 27km, five a day on weekdays) and Ljubljana (€15.70, 4¼ hours, 187km, one or two a day) via Maribor. Departures for the capital are at 4.38am Monday to Saturday and 5.45am daily.

Murska Sobota is on a rail link that connects it with Ormož (€2.65 to €4, 45 minutes, 39km) on the main line to Ljubljana (€9.90 to €14.50, 4¼ hour, 216km) and Maribor (€5.50 to €7, 45 minutes, 98km) and Vienna. There are up to eight departures a day, and the train stops at Beltinci, Ljutomer and Veržej. From Murska Sobota the train carries on to Hodoš and Budapest.

Bikes can be rented from **Freerider** (☎ 524 15 66; Koroška ulica 41; regular/mountain bikes per hr €2.10/4.20, per day €8.35-16.70; ☺ 10am-6pm Mon-Sat, 10am-1pm Sat), which is 500km southwest of the centre.

RADENCI

☎ 02 / pop 2145 / elev 200m

Radenci is best known for its health resort, parts of which still feel like a full-of-itself 19th-century spa town. Indeed, as one Slovenian friend once said: 'Radenci remains the preserve of highbrow intellectuals and rumble-tumble chamber music'. But the town is equally celebrated for its Radenska Tri Srca – the Radenci Three Hearts mineral water that is bottled here and consumed throughout the land.

Strictly speaking, Radenci is not part of Prekmurje province as such because it is not 'beyond the Mura'. In fact, it lies about 1km from the river's right bank and is thus really 'on the Mura' (Pomurje). But let's not get technical…Radenci has always been closely tied historically and geographically with Prekmurje, and it is easily accessible from Murska Sobota, 13km to the east.

Information

Nova Ljubljanska Banka (Panonska cesta 7; ☺ 8.30am-noon & 2.30-5pm Mon-Fri) Opposite the main entrance to the spa.

Post office (Panonska cesta 5; ☺ 8am-6pm Mon-Fri, 8am-noon Sat) Next door to the bank.

Activities
TERME RADENCI

The **Radenci Thermal Spa** (☎ 520 10 00; www.terme-radenci.si; Zdraviliško naselje 12) has three claims to fame: water rich in carbon dioxide for drinking; mineral-laden thermal water (41°C) for bathing; and sulphurous mud from Lake Negova for therapeutic and beauty treatments.

Springs of mineral water were discovered in the early 19th century by an Austrian medical student, and the bottling of Radenska began in 1869. The spa itself opened in 1882.

Today, unattractive modern blocks overlook the few remaining older Victorian-style buildings and a large wooded park with paths, a chapel and pavilions. The complex has 10 **pools** (☺ 9am-9pm) of varying sizes, including large indoor and outdoor thermal pools with a temperature of about 34°C, and glassed-in swimming pools with normal water. Guests can use the pools at will; outsiders pay €9.20 per day, €7.10 for three hours, and €5.85 after 6pm. There are also a half-dozen different types of **sauna** (per day/3hr €16.70/12.50; ☺ 9am-9pm).

OTHER ACTIVITIES

The seven outdoor and indoor **tennis courts** just southeast of the hotel complex can be rented for €6.70/9.20 and €3.35/4.60 per hour during the day/night respectively. Rackets (€2) and balls are available from the **tennis school** (☺ 2.30-4pm Mon-Fri, 9am-1pm Sat).

Excellent **cycling excursions** can be made into the surrounding wine country; head southwest along the *vinska cesta* ('wine road') for about 4km to Janžev Vrh and an old vineyard cottage called Janžev Hram or even further south to Kapelski Vrh and Ivanjski Vrh. The region's most celebrated wine is a sparkling one: Zlata Radgonska Penina.

Sleeping

There are lots of private rooms available on Panonska cesta to the west and south of the spa's main entrance; **house No 23** (☎ 565 15 77) charges from about €18.

The cheapest of the four **spa hotels** (☎ 520 10 00; www.terme-radenci.si; P 🗙 🖵 🗈 🕭) is the two-star **Hotel Terapija** (s/d €74.50/100), a self-described 'old health resort-style hotel' that has seen better days. The other three have four stars and are much of a muchness. The **Hotel Radin Standard** (s/d €88/110), with 73 rooms, is the cheapest of the three whereas the smaller **Hotel Izvir** (s/d €110/138), with 60 rooms, and the 149-room **Hotel Radin Superior** (s/d €113/138) cost about 25% more.

Eating

Okrepčevalnica Zeton (☎ 524 18 50; Radgonska cesta 6; dishes from €3; 🕑 6am-8pm Mon-Thu, 6.30am-10pm Fri, noon-10pm Sat) This inexpensive *bife* is located in the small shopping centre, next to the bank and post office. It has simple dishes and grills.

Restavracija Park (☎ 520 10 00; meals from €16; 🕑 11am-10pm Tue-Sun) In the heart of the resort's large wooded park and serving local specialities, the aptly named Park is a pleasant place for a meal in summer.

You'll find a **Mercator** (Panonska cesta 145; 🕑 7am-7pm Mon-Fri, 7am-noon Sat) supermarket on the main road near the bank and post office.

Getting There & Away

There are daily buses to Gornja Radgona (€1.70, 10 minutes, 9km, hourly), Ljubljana (€15, four hours, 176km, one a day at 5.58am) via Celje (€9.30, 1¼ hours, 103km) and Maribor (€5.50, one hour, 48km, up to six a day). Murska Sobota (€2.15, 15 minutes, 13km) is served by between six and eight buses a day.

MORAVSKE TOPLICE

☎ 02 / pop 720 / elev 201m

The thermal spa of Moravske Toplice, 7km northeast of Murska Sobota, boasts the hottest water in Slovenia: 72°C at its source but cooled to a body temperature of 38°C for use in its many pools and basins. It's one of the newest spas in the country – the spring was only discovered in 1960 during exploratory oil drilling – and has enough upgraded recreational facilities to cater to all tastes.

Information

Nova Ljubljanska Banka (Kranjčeva ulica; 🕑 8.30am-noon & 2.30-5pm Mon-Fri) At the entrance to the spa.

Post office (Kranjčeva ulica 5; 🕑 8am-6pm Mon-Fri, 8am-noon Sat) Next to the tourist office.

Tourist Information Centre Moravske Toplice (☎ 538 15 20; www.moravske-toplice.com; Kranjčeva ulica 3; 🕑 8am-8pm Mon-Sat, 8am-2pm Sun Jun-Sep; 8am-6pm Mon-Sat, 8am-2pm Sun Oct-May) On the main road northwest of the entrance to the spa complex.

Activities

The renovated spa complex, **Terme 3000** (☎ 512 22 00; www.terme3000.si; Kranjčeva ulica 12; 🕑 8am-9pm Jun-Sep, 9am-9pm Oct-May), has 22 indoor and outdoor pools filled with thermal water, and two large outdoor ones with ordinary heated water, four slides, a water tower and – wait for it – sound and light special effects. The thermal water is recommended for relief of rheumatism and certain minor skin problems, and there are enough therapies and beauty treatments available to keep you occupied for a week. Guests at the resort have free use of the pools; otherwise you'll have to pay €11 to €12.50 (depending on the season) for the privilege. The spa resort also has an 18-hole golf course, three tennis courts, a fitness room and saunas.

Sleeping

The tourist office can organise private rooms for around €15 per person, while apartments for two work out to be between €34.50 and €41.50, depending on the length of stay (minimum three nights). If the office is closed you'll find rooms available nearby at Nos 3c, 13, 16 and 18 on Kranjčeva ulica.

All the accommodation at **Terme 3000** (☎ 512 22 00; www.terme3000.si; Kranjčeva ulica 12) shares the same contact numbers; prices vary according to the season. The spa's 5-hectare camping ground, **Camp Terme 3000** (per person €13-14), can accommodate 800 guests and is open year-round. Use of the swimming pool nearby is included in the price. The attractive **bungalows** (s €49-52, d €76-82; 🕑 Mar-Oct; P 🖵 🗈) at the resort's Prekmurje Village (Premurska Vas) are done up to look like traditional peasant cottages, with thatched roofs and cool whitewashed walls. They have a total of 78

PREKMURJE

WHITE STORKS

The white stork (bela štorklja) is Prekmurje's most beloved symbol. Country people consider it an honour for a pair to nest on the rooftop, and the distinctive birds with black and white feathers and long bills and legs are thought to bring good luck (not to mention babies). The storks arrive in spring – usually April – and spend the warm summer months here. When mid-August arrives, instinct tells the birds – some of them just a few months old – to fly south for a two- or three-year, 12,000km trek to sub-Saharan Africa, from where they return to Prekmurje when they are ready to breed.

Storks build their nests on church steeples, rooftops or telephone poles, and normally return to the same one every year. The nest is repaired or rebuilt every year, and some can weigh as much as 500kg. Storks live on a diet of worms, grasshoppers, frogs and small rodents, which are most easily found in the region's meadows. If food is scarce, however, it is not unknown for parents to turf their fledglings out of the nest.

The number of storks in Slovenia – currently around 200 pairs with 40% (80) breeding in Prekmurje – has grown over the past two decades as it has throughout Europe. Nevertheless, the white stork remains a vulnerable species primarily because its hunting and breeding grounds – the meadows – are being destroyed, dried out and regulated.

---

double rooms but are open only in the warmer months. At the **Hotel Termal** (s €63-68, d €100-110; P ✗ ✗ 🖳 🖳 ⬚) about half of the 139 rooms have balconies. The 157-room **Hotel Ajda** (s €73-78, d €116-128; P ✗ ✗ 🖳 🖳 ⬚) is in a large, three-winged modern building of little interest but, with four stars, was the best the resort had to offer until the opening of the five-star 221-bed Hotel Livada Prestige next door, in September 2006.

Eating

Gostišče Kamin (☎ 548 18 54; Dolga ulica 61; pizzas from €5; ☺ 10am-11pm Thu-Tue) This spot northeast of the tourist office and spa is popular for its pizza and pasta.

Gostilna Kuhar (☎ 548 12 15; Kranjčeva 13; meals from €10.50; ☺ 9am-11pm Tue-Sun) Next to the Evangelical church on the main road, Kuhar is a decent and – being opposite the spa's main entrance –

convenient place in which to sample Prekmurje's cuisine. It also has rooms.

Dobrovnik (population 935), about 12km southeast of Moravske Toplice, has a couple of decent roadside gostilna where a meal should cost less than €10. This includes **Pri Lujzi** (☎ 579 90 06; Dobrovnik 273a; starters €3-3.50, mains €3.75-5.45; ☺ 7am-1am Mon, Wed & Thu, 7am-2am Fri & Sat, 8am-1am Sun), with a small terrace overlooking the main road, and the larger (and more welcoming) **Lipot** (☎ 579 11 47; starters €3.55-5, mains €5-8.20; Dobrovnik 277a; ☺ 7am-11pm Tue-Sun).

Getting There & Around

Buses leave from Kranjčeva ulica up to six times a day for Murska Sobota (€1.70, 10 minutes, 7km) and Dobrovnik (€1.70, 10 minutes, 19km).

The resort rents bicycles for €2.25 an hour.

Directory

CONTENTS

ACCOMMODATION

Accommodation in Slovenia runs the gamut from riverside camping grounds, hostels, mountain huts (for pricing see boxed text, p44), cosy *gostišča* (inns) and farmhouses, to elegant castle hotels in Dolenjska and Štajerska, and five-star hotels in Ljubljana. Slovenia counts just under 80,000 beds in total – over a third of them in hotels – so you'll usually have little trouble finding accommodation to fit your budget, except at the height of the season (July and August) on the coast, at Bled or Bohinj, or in Ljubljana.

> **BOOK ACCOMMODATION ONLINE**
>
> For more accommodation reviews and recommendations by Lonely Planet authors, check out the online booking service at www.lonelyplanet.com. You'll find the true, insider lowdown on the best places to stay. Reviews are thorough and independent. Best of all, you can book online.

Accommodation listings throughout this guide are ordered by price – from the cheapest to the most expensive, even within budget, midrange and top-end categories. Very, very roughly, budget accommodation means a double room under €50, midrange is €51 to €100 and top end is €101 or more.

Bear in mind that virtually every municipality in the land levies a tourist tax of between €0.60 and €1.25 per person per night. For stays of less than three nights, many pensions and almost all private rooms charge 30% to 50% more, although the percentage usually drops on the second night.

Accommodation owners are required to register foreign visitors with the local town hall – an old socialist holdover – so many will insist on holding your passport or identity document during your stay. This can be inconvenient when trying to change money, although most places are happy to return the documents to you after registering your details.

Camping

In summer, camping is a great way to go if you're on a budget and would like to meet people. You'll find a conveniently located *kamp* (camping ground) in virtually every corner of the country, but there are about four-dozen official ones. And you don't always need a tent; a few grounds have inexpensive bungalows available for hire. Among the best camping grounds for those who want to experience the mountains are Camping Špik (p126) at Gozd Martuljek near Kranjska Gora, Kamp Triglav (p132) at Trenta and Kamp Polovnik (p137) at Bovec. On the coast, most of the camping grounds are *avtokampi*, catering more to camper vans and caravans than to motorists and pedestrians with tents. Places like Avtokamp Fiesa (p174) near Piran and Avtokamp Lucija (p179) near Portorož can be crammed to bursting in summer.

Prices vary according to the site and the season, but expect to pay anywhere from €5 to €15 per adult (children are usually charged 30% of the adult fee) on the coast or in the mountains at peak season. Many of the official camping grounds offer discounts of 5% to 10% to holders of the Camping Card International (CCI; see p276).

Almost all sites close between mid-October and mid-April. Camping 'rough' is illegal in Slovenia, and this is enforced, especially around Bled. Seek out the Slovenian Tourist Board's *Camping in Slovenia* pamphlet.

Farmhouses

Hundreds of working farms in Slovenia offer accommodation to paying guests, and for a truly relaxing break they can't be beaten. You stay either in private rooms in the farmhouse itself or in alpine-style guesthouses somewhere nearby. Many of the farms offer activities such as horse riding, kayaking, trekking or cycling and allow you to help out with the farm chores if you feel so inclined.

The farms themselves can range from places where Old MacDonald would feel at home to not much more than a modern guesthouse with a vegetable patch and orchard. The latter

is especially true around tourist destinations like Bled and near the coast. You'll find much more isolated farmsteads with livestock and vineyards in Štajerska, Dolenjska and Bela Krajina. For more information, contact the **Association of Tourist Farms of Slovenia** (Združenje Turističnih Kmetij Slovenije; ☎ 03-491 64 80; ztks@siol.net; Trnoveljska cesta 1, 3000 Celje) or check out the Slovenian Tourist Board's *Friendly Countryside* pamphlet, which lists upwards of 300 farms with accommodation (see p284. You can book through **ABC Farm & Countryside Holidays** (☎ 01-510 43 20; abc-tourism@europcar.si; Ulica Jožeta Jame 16) in Ljubljana.

Expect to pay about €13 per person in a room with shared bathroom and breakfast (from €17 for half-board) in the low season (September to mid-December and mid-January to June), rising in the high season (July and August) to a minimum €16 per person (from €23 for half-board). Apartments for groups of up to eight people are also available. There's no minimum stay, but you must pay 30% more if you stay fewer than three nights.

Hostels & Student Dormitories

Some 26 hostels in Ljubljana and the provinces are registered with or affiliated with the Maribor-based **Hostelling International Slovenia** (Popotniško Združenje Slovenije; ☎ 234 21 37; www.youth -hostel.si; Gosposvetska cesta 84). In Ljubljana contact Erazem (p68). You are not required to have a Hostelling International (HI) card to stay at hostels in Slovenia, but it sometimes earns you a discount or cancellation of the tourist tax. These hostels typically cost from €13 to €21, with prices at their highest in midsummer.

A large percentage of Slovenian pupils and students live away from home during the school year and sleep in a *dijaški dom* (college dormitory) or *študentski dom* (student residence). Dorms in Ljubljana, Maribor, Idrija and a number of other cities in Slovenia accept foreign travellers in summer for rates ranging from €10 for a bed in a dormitory to €30 for a single room with bathroom.

Hotels

Rates at Slovenia's hotels vary seasonally, with July and August the peak season and September/October and May/June the shoulder ones. Ski resorts such as Kranjska Gora and Maribor Pohorje also have a peak season from December to March. In Ljubljana prices are generally constant throughout the year. Many resort hotels, particularly on the coast, are closed in winter. As hotels seldom levy a surcharge for stays of one or two nights, they're worth considering if you're only passing through. Rates almost always include breakfast.

Despite a star system (one to five), as with many other countries in the region, hotel standards in Slovenia vary enormously and it's often difficult to tell what's what until you've stepped inside or spent the night. The Slovenian Tourist Board's annual *Hotel Rates* pamphlet, with pictures, rates and some description, might prove useful (see p284).

There's a new crop of destination hotels – places you'd travel a great distance just to stay in – coming up in Slovenia, places like Ljubljana's Antiq Hotel (p81) and the Dobra Vila (p137). Other fine and/or romantic places to stay include the country's castle hotels such as those at Otočec (p207) and Mokrice (p214).

Pensions & Guesthouses

Pensions and guesthouses go by several names in Slovenia. A *penzion* is, of course, a pension, but more commonly it's called a *gostišče* – a rustic (or made to look rustic) restaurant with *prenočišče* (accommodation) upstairs or somewhere in a separate building. They are more expensive than hostels but cheaper than hotels, and they might be your only option in small towns and villages. Generally speaking, a *gostilna* serves food and drink only, but some might have rooms as well. The distinction between a *gostilna* and a *gostišče* isn't very clear – even to most Slovenes.

Private Rooms & Apartments

You'll find private rooms and apartments available through tourist offices and travel agencies at most tourist towns. Make sure you understand exactly where you'll be staying; in cities some private rooms are located quite far from the centre. The Slovenian Tourist Board's brochure *Rates for Accommodation in Private Rooms and Apartments* is useful, as it provides a photo and the location of the house along with the rates of its rooms and/or apartments.

You don't have to go through agencies or tourist offices; any house with a sign reading 'Sobe' or 'Zimmer frei' means that rooms are available. The only advantage to this is that, depending on the season, you might save yourself a little money by going directly.

In Slovenia, *registered* private rooms and apartments are rated with from one to four stars. Those with one star have running water in the room and a shower or bathroom in the corridor, while those with two have their own shower or bath. Rooms with their own bath plus comfortable furnishings, TV, breakfast on offer and so on rate three stars while four stars (apartments only) adds large room sizes and great views to the three-star category. Prices vary greatly according to the town and season, but typical rates range from around €12 to €25 per person per night.

The price quoted is usually for a minimum stay of three nights. If you're staying a shorter time (and you are usually welcome to except in high season), you'll have to pay 30% and sometimes as much as 50% more the first night and 20% to 30% extra the second and third. The price of a private room never includes breakfast (from around €4.50 if available) or tourist tax. An extra bed in the room is usually 20% on top, as is single use of a room.

Some agencies and tourist offices also have holiday apartments available that can accommodate up to six people. One for two/four people could go for as low as €30/45.

ACTIVITIES

Known as 'Europe's activities playground', Slovenia offers an extensive range of outdoor activities, from skiing, climbing and cycling to bird-watching, diving and 'taking the waters' at one of the nation's many spas. For details, see the Great Outdoors chapter (p43).

BUSINESS HOURS

With rare exceptions, the *delovni čas* (opening times) of any concern are posted on the door. *Odprto* means 'open' while *zaprto* is 'closed'.

Grocery stores and supermarkets are usually open from 8am to 7pm on weekdays and 8am until 1pm on Saturday. In winter they may close an hour earlier. Some branches of the Mercator supermarket chain open from 8am to 11am on Sunday.

Restaurant hours vary tremendously across the country but essentially are from 10am or 11am to 10pm or 11pm daily. Bars are equally variable but are usually open 11am to midnight Sunday to Thursday and to 1am or 2am on Friday and Saturday.

Bank hours vary, but generally they're from 8am or 8.30am to 5pm weekdays (often with a lunchtime break from 12.30pm to 2pm) and (rarely these days) from 8am until noon or 1pm on Saturday. The main post office in any city or town (almost always the ones listed in this book in the Information sections of the individual towns and cities) is open from 8am to 7pm weekdays and 8am until noon or 1pm on Saturday.

Museums are usually open from 10am to 6pm Tuesday to Sunday. Winter opening hours may be shorter (or at weekends only) outside the big cities and towns.

CHILDREN

Successful travel with young children requires planning and effort. Don't try to overdo things; even for adults, packing too much into the time available can cause problems. And make sure the activities include the kids as well. Although the Slovenian Ethnographic Museum (p72) in Ljubljana has wonderful and very colourful hands-on exhibits for kids, balance a morning there with an afternoon at the zoo (p72) on Rožnik Hill or at the huge Atlantis water park (p77) in the BTC City mall. Include children in the trip planning; if they've helped to work out where you will be going, they'll be much more interested when they get there. Lonely Planet's *Travel with Children* is a good source of information.

Additionally, while most activities and sights have lower prices for children, readers have reported that many places don't charge entrance fees for children under the age of five.

All car-rental firms in Slovenia have children's safety seats for hire for about €20 per rental. Make sure you book them in advance; by law children must use such seats until age 12. The same goes for highchairs and cots (cribs); they're standard in some restaurants and hotels, but numbers are limited. The choice of baby food, infant formulas, soy and other types of milk, disposable nappies (diapers) and the like is as great in Slovenian supermarkets as it is back home, but the opening hours may be different. Don't be caught out at the weekend. Nappy-changing facilities, on the other hand, are few and far between.

CLIMATE CHARTS

In general, Slovenia is temperate with four distinct seasons, but the topography creates three individual climates. The northwest has an alpine climate with strong influences from the Atlantic and abundant precipitation. Temperatures in the alpine valleys are moderate in summer but cold in winter. The coast and a large part of Primorska as far as the Soča Valley has a Mediterranean climate with warm, sunny weather much of the year, and mostly mild winters (although the *burja*, a cold and dry northeasterly wind, can be fierce at times). Most of eastern Slovenia has a Continental climate with hot (and occasionally very hot) summers and cold winters.

Slovenia gets most of its rain in the late spring (May and June) and autumn (October and November); precipitation varies but averages about 900mm in the east, 1300mm to 1600mm in the centre (Ljubljana), 1100mm to 1300mm on the coast and up to 3500mm in the Alps. January is the coldest month, with an average annual temperature of -2°C, and July is the warmest (19°C to 23°C). The mean average temperature is around 10°C in Ljubljana, 7°C in the mountains and 13.5°C on the coast. The number of hours of sunshine per year ranges from 1500 to 2300, with Ljubljana at the low end of the scale and Portorož at the top. For more information on how the climate might affect your travel plans, see p12.

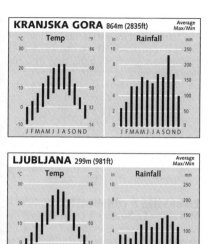

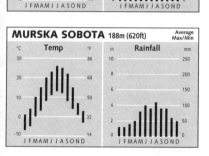

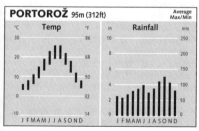

COURSES

The most famous and prestigious place to learn Slovene is the **Centre for Slovene as a Second/Foreign Language** (Center za Slovenščino kot Drugi/Tuji Jezik; Map p66; ☎ 01-241 86 77; www.centerslo.net; 2nd fl, Kongresni trg 12; 🕑 11am-1pm Mon, Tue, Thu & Fri, 11am-1pm & 3-5pm Wed) at the University of Ljubljana. There are a number of courses available, including a two-week winter course in January/February for €467, two- and four-week summer ones

in July for €467 and €789 respectively, and an intensive 14-week course running from October to January and February to May for €1168 per semester. Prices do not include room and board. The centre also sponsors free two-hour introductory lessons in Slovene for tourists once a week at the Slovenian Tourist Information Centre (p68) in Ljubljana.

Private schools offering courses in Slovene in Ljubljana include the academic **Miklošič Educational Centre** (Map pp62-3; ☎ 01-230 76 02; www.ism.si; Miklošičeva cesta 26), with courses of 30/85 hours starting at €160/395, and the upbeat **Mint International House Ljubljana** (Map pp62-3; ☎ 01-300 43 00; www.mint.si; 1st fl, Kersnikova ulica 1), with courses of 60/90 hours costing €399/598. Individual lessons cost from €29 an hour.

CUSTOMS

Duty-free shopping within the European Union was abolished in 1999, and Slovenia, as an EU member since 2004, now adheres to those rules. You cannot buy tax-free goods in, say, Austria, Italy or Hungary and take them to Slovenia. However, you can still enter Slovenia with duty-free items from countries outside the EU (eg Australia, the USA, Switzerland, Croatia etc). The usual allowances apply: 200 cigarettes, 50 cigars or 250g of loose tobacco; 2L of still wine and 1L of spirits; 50g of perfume and 250cc of eau de toilette.

DANGERS & ANNOYANCES

Slovenia is not a violent or dangerous society. Firearms are strictly controlled, the few drunks you'll encounter are sloppy but docile, and you'll see little of the vandalism that plagues cities like New York or London (although the incidence of graffiti in urban centres has risen astronomically in the years since independence). The organised crime that torments Russia and some Eastern European countries has arrived in Slovenia, notably in Ljubljana and Maribor, but not to the same degree.

EMERGENCY NUMBERS

Ambulance (Reševalci) ☎ 112
Fire brigade (Gasilci) ☎ 112
First aid (Prva pomoč) ☎ 112
Police (Policija) ☎ 113 (emergencies)
Road emergency or towing (AMZS)
☎ 1987

DIRECTORY

Police say that 90% of all crimes reported in Slovenia involve theft, so take the usual precautions. Be careful of your purse or wallet in busy areas like bus and train stations, and don't leave it unattended on the beach, or in a hut while hiking. Lock your car at all times, park in well-lit areas and do not leave valuables visible.

In cities like Ljubljana, Maribor or Celje you might be approached occasionally by beggars who ask for – and then demand money – but it's seldom anything dangerous. One problem can be drunks on the road – literally or behind the wheel – especially around St Martin's Day (Martinovanje; 11 November; see p278).

One particularly irksome law here is that alcohol may not be purchased from a shop, off-license or bar for consumption off the premises by anyone between the hours of 9pm and 7am. Of course you can drink to your heart's content in restaurants, bars, pubs and clubs until closing time, but not buy it outside. The ruling follows a number of horrific car accidents involving young people who had consumed alcohol bought at popular round-the-clock convenience stores.

DISCOUNT CARDS

For details about the excellent-value Ljubljana Card, see p65.

Camping Card International

The **Camping Card International** (CCI; www.camp ingcardinternational.com), which is basically a camping-ground ID, is available from local automobile clubs, local camping federations (eg the Caravan Club in the UK) and sometimes on the spot at selected camping grounds. They incorporate third-party insurance for damage you may cause, and some camping grounds in Slovenia offer discounts of 5% to 10% if you sign in with one. Contact the **Caravaning Club Slovenije** (CCS; info@ccs-si.com).

Hostel Card

No hostels in Slovenia actually require you to be a Hostelling International (HI) or associated member or cardholder, but they sometimes offer a discount if you are. Hostelling International Slovenia (see p272) in Maribor and Erazem (p68) in Ljubljana sell hostel cards for those aged up to 15 (€5.85), 16 to 29 (€7.50) and over 30 (€9.20).

Student, Youth & Teacher Cards

The **International Student Identity Card** (ISIC; www .isic.org; €7.10), a plastic ID-style card with your photograph, provides bona fide students many discounts on certain forms of transport and cheap admission to museums and other sights. If you're aged under 26 but not a student, you can apply for ISIC's International Youth Travel Card (IYTC; €7.10) or the Euro<26 card (€7.10) issued by the European Youth Card Association (EYCA), both of which offer the same discounts as the student card. Teachers can apply for the International Teacher Identity Card (ITIC; €8.35).

EMBASSIES & CONSULATES
Slovenian Embassies & Consulates

Slovenian representations abroad are listed on the website of the **Slovenian Foreign Ministry** (www .mzz.gov.si) and include the following embassies:
Australia Embassy (☎ 02-6243 4830; vca@gov.si; 6th fl, St George's Bldg, 60 Marcus Clarke St, Canberra ACT 2601); Sydney Consulate (☎ 02-9517 1591; slovcon@emona.com .au; 86 Parramatta Rd, Camperdown NSW 2050)
Austria Embassy (☎ 01-586 13 09; vdu@gov.si; Nibelungengasse 13, A-1010 Vienna)
Canada Embassy (☎ 613-565 5781; vot@gov.si; Suite 2101, 150 Metcalfe St, Ottawa K2P 1P1)
Croatia Embassy (☎ 01-63 11 000; vzg@gov.si; Savska cesta 41, 10000 Zagreb)
France Embassy (☎ 01-44 96 50 60; vpa@gov.si; 28 rue Bois-le-Vent 75116 Paris)
Germany Embassy (☎ 030-206 1450; vbn@gov.si; Hausvogteiplatz 3-4, D-10117 Berlin); Munich Consulate (☎ 089-543 9819; kmu@gov.si; PF 150829, Lindwurmstrasse 14, 80045 Munich)
Hungary Embassy (☎ 01-438 5600; vbp@gov.si; Cseppkő út 68, 1025 Budapest)
Ireland Embassy (☎ 01-670 5240; vdb@gov.si; 2nd fl, Morrison Chambers, 32 Nassau St, Dublin 2)
Italy Embassy (☎ 06-80 914 310; vri@gov.si; Via Leonardo Pisano 10, 00197 Rome)
Netherlands Embassy (☎ 070-310 86 90; vhg@gov.si; Anna Paulownastraat 11, 2518 BA Den Haag)
UK Embassy (☎ 020-7222 5400; vlo@gov.si; 10 Little College St, London SW1P 3SH)
USA Embassy (☎ 202-667 5363; vwa@gov.si; 1525 New Hampshire Ave NW, Washington, DC 20036); New York Consulate (☎ 212-370 3006; 600 Third Avenue, 21st fl, New York, NY 10016)

Embassies & Consulates in Slovenia

Selected countries with representation in Ljubljana – either full embassies or consulates – appear below. If telephoning from outside the

capital but still within Slovenia, remember to
dial 01 first. From outside Slovenia dial 386-01
then the number.

Australia Consulate (Map pp62-3; ☎ 425 42 52; 12th fl,
Trg Republike 3; ⏰ 9am-1pm Mon-Fri)

Austria Embassy (Map pp62-3; ☎ 479 07 00; Prešernova
cesta 23; ⏰ 8am-noon Mon-Thu, 8-11am Fri) Enter from
Veselova ul.

Canada Consulate (Map pp62-3; ☎ 430 35 70; Dunajska
cesta 22; ⏰ 9am-noon Mon-Fri)

Croatia Embassy (Map p75; ☎ 425 62 20; Gruberjevo
nabrežje 6; ⏰ 10am-1pm Mon-Fri); Consulate (☎ 02-234
66 80; Trg Svobode 3, Maribor; ⏰ 10am-1pm Mon-Fri)

France Embassy (Map p75; ☎ 479 04 00; Barjanska
cesta 1; ⏰ 8.30am-12.30pm Mon-Fri)

Germany Embassy (Map pp62-3; ☎ 479 03 00;
Prešernova cesta 27; ⏰ 9am-noon Mon-Thu, 9-11am Fri)

Hungary Embassy (Map pp62-3; ☎ 512 18 82; Ulica
Konrada Babnika 5; ⏰ 9am-noon Mon, Wed & Fri)

Ireland Embassy (Map pp62-3; ☎ 300 89 70; Poljanski
nasip 6; ⏰ 9am-12.30pm & 2.30-4.30pm Mon-Fri)

Italy Embassy (Map pp62-3; ☎ 426 21 94; Snežniška
ulica 8; ⏰ 9-11am Mon-Fri); Consulate (05-627 37 49;
Belveder 2, Koper; ⏰ 8.30am-noon Mon-Fri)

Netherlands Embassy (Map pp62-3; ☎ 420 14 61;
Poljanski nasip 6; ⏰ 9am-noon Mon-Fri)

New Zealand Consulate (Map pp62-3; ☎ 580 30 55;
Verovškova ulica 57; ⏰ 8am-3pm Mon-Fri)

South Africa Consulate (Map pp62-3; ☎ 200 63 00;
Pražakova ulica4; ⏰ 3-4pm Tue)

UK Embassy (Map pp62-3; ☎ 200 39 10; 4th fl, Trg
Republike 3; ⏰ 9am-noon Mon-Fri)

USA Embassy (Map pp62-3; ☎ 200 55 00; Prešernova
cesta 31; ⏰ 9-11.30am Mon-Fri)

FESTIVALS & EVENTS

Major cultural and sporting events are listed
in the Festivals & Events section of individual
towns and cities. The following abbreviated
list gives you a taste of what to expect. For a
fuller list look under 'Events' on the website
of the Slovenian Tourist Board (www.slovenia
-tourism.si) and in the STB's annual *Calendar
of Major Events in Slovenia*.

JANUARY
**Women's World Cup Slalom and Giant Slalom
Competition (Golden Fox), Pohorje** (www.pohorje
.org) One of the major international ski events for women.
Held on the slopes southwest of Maribor.

FEBRUARY
Kurentovanje, Ptuj (www.kurentovanje.net) A 'rite of
spring' celebrated for 10 days up to Shrove Tuesday (February
or early March) and the most popular Mardi Gras celebration

in Slovenia. Other important pre-Lenten festivals take place
in Cerknica in Notranjska and Cerkno in Primorska.

MARCH
Ski Jumping World Cup Championships, Planica
(www.planica.info) Three days of high flying on skis near
Kranjska Gora.

APRIL
**Spring Flower Show & Gardening Fair, Volčji
Potok** (www.arboretum-vp.si) Slovenia's largest flower
and gardening show at the arboretum near Kamnik.
Salt Works Festival, Piran & Sečovlje Country Park
(www.kpss.soline.si) Weekend festival held in both Piran
and at Sečovlje Saltworks Country Park to promote the
tradition of salt making and the uses of sea salt.

MAY
Druga Godba, Ljubljana (www.drugagodba.si) A
festival of alternative and world music in the Križanke in
late May/early June.

JUNE
International Rowing Regatta, Bled (www.bled.si)
One of the country's most exciting (and fastest) sporting
events. Held over three days in late June.
International Biennial of Graphic Arts, Ljubljana
(www.mglc-lj.si) Held at Ljubljana's International Centre
of Graphic Arts and other venues from late June to early
October in odd-numbered years (ie 2007, 2009 etc).
**Ana Desetnica International Festival of Street
Theatre, Ljubljana** (www.anadesetnica.org) One of
the largest outdoor theatre festivals in Europe held over a
week in late June/early July.
Festival Lent, Maribor (http://lent.slovenija.net) A
two-week extravaganza of folklore and culture in the Old
Town in late June/early July.
Brežice Festival of Early Music, Brežice (www.festival
brezice.com) Month-long series of concerts of ancient
music. Held from late June to late July.

JULY
Ljubljana Summer Festival (www.festival-lj.si) The
nation's premier cultural event (music, theatre and dance)
held from early July to late August.
Primorska Summer Festival (www.portoroz.si) Concerts,
theatre and dance events held in various venues in Piran,
Koper, Izola and Portorož from early July to mid-August.
Rock Otočec (www.rock-otocec.com) Three-day rock
concert in early July at Prečna airfield, 5km northwest of
Novo Mesto, and Slovenia's biggest open-air rock concert.

AUGUST
Okarina Etno Festival, Bled (www.bled.si) Two-day
international festival of folk and world music.

Erasmus Tournament, Predjama (www.postojna-cave .com) Jousting and other medieval shenanigans below Slovenia's most beguiling castle.

SEPTEMBER

Cows' Ball, Bohinj (www.bohinj.si) Zany weekend of folk dance, music, eating and drinking to mark the return of the cows from their high pastures to the valleys.

Dormouse Night, Cerknica (www.postojna-cave.com) A celebration and feast during the very short dormouse-hunting season in the forests around Snežnik Castle in late September.

OCTOBER

City of Women, Ljubljana (www.cityofwomen-a.si) International festival of contemporary arts, focusing on art and culture created by women.

Ljubljana Marathon (http://maraton.slo-timing.com) First run in 1996, this marathon draws an increasingly international field.

DECEMBER

Christmas concerts Held throughout Slovenia, especially Ljubljana, but the most famous are in Postojna Cave (www.postojna-cave.com), where you can also attend the Live Christmas Crib, a re-enactment of the Nativity with Christmas carols.

FOOD & DRINK

Slovenia has a highly developed and varied cuisine and a wine-making tradition that goes back to the time of the Romans. For details see the Food & Drink chapter (p49).

GAY & LESBIAN TRAVELLERS

Slovenia has no sodomy laws. There's a national gay rights law in place that bans discrimination in employment and other areas on the basis of sexual preference, and homosexuals are allowed in the military. Outside Ljubljana, however, there is little evidence of a gay presence, much less a lifestyle.

K4 Roza (Map pp62-3; ☎ 01-430 47 40; Kersnikova ul 4) in Ljubljana is made up of the gay and lesbian branches of Škuc (www.skuc.org), which stands for Študentski Kulturni Center (Student Cultural Centre) but is no longer student-orientated as such. It organises the **Gay & Lesbian Pride** event in June and the **Gay & Lesbian Film Festival** in December. The gay male branch, Magnus (skucmagnus@yahoo.com), deals with AIDS prevention, usually publishes a colour magazine of news, interviews and listings called *1XY* several times a year and runs the café-bar Tiffany (p87) in Ljubljana.

Lesbians can contact the Ljubljana-based and ŠKUC-affiliated LL through Monokel (p87).

Legebrita (www.ljudmila.org/siqrd/legebitra; PO Box 106, 1000 Ljubljana), affiliated with the Student Organisation of the University of Ljubljana (Študentska Organizacija Univerze Ljubljani; ŠOU) is a youth group for lesbians, gays, bisexuals and transsexuals under 26. ŠOU runs the gay and lesbian K4 Roza (p87) in Ljubljana. **GALfon** (☎ 01-432 40 89; ⏰ 7-10pm) is a hotline and general source of information for gays and lesbians. The website of the **Slovenian Queer Resources Directory** (www.ljudmila .org/siqrd) contains a lot of stuff, both organisational and serious, but is often out of date (or perhaps just 'archival'). **Out in Slovenia** (www .outinslovenija.com) is where to go for the latest on events, activities and venues.

HOLIDAYS

Slovenia celebrates 14 *prazniki* (holidays) a year. If any of the following fall on a Sunday, then the Monday becomes the holiday.

New Year's holidays 1 & 2 January
Prešeren Day (Slovenian Culture Day) 8 February
Easter & Easter Monday March/April
Insurrection Day 27 April
Labour Day holidays 1 & 2 May
National Day 25 June
Assumption Day 15 August
Reformation Day 31 October
All Saints' Day 1 November
Christmas Day 25 December
Independence Day 26 December

Although it's not a public holiday, St Martin's Day (11 November), the day that fermenting grape juice officially becomes new wine, is almost marked as such (p52), and just about everyone has to have a sip or three.

On the eve of St Gregory's Day (11 March), all the children in certain Gorenjska towns and villages – Železniki is the most famous one – set afloat hundreds of tiny boats bearing candles.

On Palm Sunday (the Sunday before Easter), people carry a complex arrangement of greenery, wood shavings and ribbons called a *butara* to church to be blessed. These *butare* end up as home decorations or are placed on the graves of relatives.

Many towns celebrate Midsummer's Night (Kresna Noč; 23 June) with a large bonfire, and St John's Eve (30 April) is the night for setting up the maypoles and more bonfires.

A *žegnanje* is a fair or celebration held on the feast day of a church's patron saint. Naturally a lot of them take place throughout Slovenia on 15 August, the feast of the Assumption of the Virgin Mary, especially at Ptujska Gora in Štajerska (p237) and at Sveta Gora (p142), north of Nova Gorica.

INSURANCE

A travel insurance policy to cover theft, loss and medical problems is a good idea. There is a wide variety of policies available, so check the small print. EU citizens on public health insurance schemes should note that they're generally covered by reciprocal arrangements in Slovenia; see p296.

Some insurance policies specifically exclude 'dangerous activities', which can include scuba diving, motorcycling, even trekking. A locally acquired motorcycle licence is not valid under some policies.

You may prefer a policy that pays doctors or hospitals directly rather than you having to pay on the spot and claim later. If you have to claim later, make sure you keep all documentation. Some policies ask you to call back (reverse charges) to a centre in your home country, where an immediate assessment of your problem is made. Check that the policy covers ambulances or an emergency flight home.

Paying for your airline ticket with a credit card often provides limited travel accident insurance, and you may be able to reclaim the payment if the operator doesn't deliver. Ask your credit-card company what it covers.

INTERNET ACCESS

The internet has arrived in a big way in Slovenia; 37% of the population uses it regularly. The useful **e-points in Slovenia from A to Ž** (http://e-tocke.gov.si in Slovene) and its website lists free access terminals, wi-fi hotspots and commercial cyber-cafés where you can log on across the nation. Many libraries in Slovenia have free terminals and most towns have at least one cyber-café. Check the Information section of cities and towns throughout the book.

Most hotels and hostels in Slovenia have some form of internet access available nowadays. We have included an internet icon (🖳) only if the hotel has wi-fi or allows guests to use a terminal free of charge in the lobby or reception room. Some establishments (usually hostels) charge their guests an access fee, which we have usually noted in the review text.

COMING OF AGE

The legal age for voting, driving an automobile and drinking alcohol is 18. According to Article 183 (1995) of the Penal Code of the Republic of Slovenia (Kazenski Zakonik Republike Slovenije), the age of consent for all sexual activity (ie heterosexual and homosexual) is 15 years.

If you're travelling with your own notebook or hand-held computer, remember that the power-supply voltage in Slovenia may vary from that at home, risking damage to your equipment. The best investment is a universal AC adaptor for your appliance, which will enable you to plug it in anywhere. You'll also need a plug adaptor for European outlets; it is often easiest to buy these before you leave home.

For the best sites to check out before arriving in Slovenia, see p14.

LAUNDRY

With a full 96% of all Slovenian households owning a washing machine, well, good luck trying to find a self-service laundrette… The best place to seek out do-it-yourself washers and dryers is at hostels, college dormitories and camping grounds, but even these are very limited. There are a few commercial laundries in Ljubljana (p65) that will do your laundry reasonably quickly, but they are expensive, charging from €3.80 per kilogram. Hotel laundry service is even more costly.

LEGAL MATTERS

Persons violating the laws of Slovenia, even unknowingly, may be expelled, arrested or imprisoned. Penalties for possession, use or trafficking in illegal drugs in Slovenia are strict, and convicted offenders can expect jail sentences and heavy fines. The permitted blood-alcohol level for motorists is 0.05%, and it is strictly enforced, especially on motorways.

MAPS

The **Geodesic Institute of Slovenia** (Geodetski Zavod Slovenije or GZS; www.gzs-dd.si in Slovene), the country's principal map-making company, which also runs the Kod & Kam (p61) shop in Ljubljana, produces national (1:300,000; €7.20) and regional maps. Some 17 excursion maps at a scale of 1:50,000 (€7.20) cover the whole country, and there are city plans

(€3.10 to €7.10) for all the major towns. GZS's *Ljubljana* map (1:20,000; €6.70) with street index is excellent. The **Alpine Association of Slovenia** (Planinska Zveza Slovenije or PZS; www.pzs.si) produces 30 hiking maps (€7.50) with scales as large as 1:25,000.

Anyone planning to do a lot of driving in the country should pick up a copy of the 1:300 000 *Turistični Atlas Slovenija* (Tourist Atlas of Slovenia; €19) from GZS, which includes 14 city plans, or the more detailed 1:100 000 *Avtoatlas Slovenija* (Road Atlas of Slovenia; €30), with 65 1:12,500 maps of Slovenian cities and towns.

MONEY

Slovenia traded the tolar (abbreviated SIT) for the euro (abbreviated € and pronounced *ew*-roh in Slovene) in January 2007, sharing the currency with 12 of the 25 other member-states of the EU (Austria, Belgium, Finland, France, Germany, Greece, Ireland, Italy, Luxembourg, Netherlands, Portugal and Spain). One euro is divided into 100 cents. There are seven euro notes in different colours and sizes; they come in denominations of €5, €10, €20, €50, €100, €200 and €500. The designs on the recto (generic windows or portals) and verso (imaginary bridges, a map of the EU) are exactly the same in all 13 countries and symbolise openness and cooperation.

The eight coins in circulation are in denominations of €2 and €1, then one, two, five, 10, 20 and 50 cents. The 'heads' side of the coin, on which the denomination is shown, is identical throughout the euro zone; the 'tails' side is peculiar to each member-state, though euro coins can be used anywhere where euros are legal tender, of course.

In Slovenia, the verso of the €2 coin (brassy centre ringed with silver) shows the poet France Prešeren (1800–49) and a line from his poem *Zdravljica,* which forms part of the national anthem. The €1 coin (silver centre with brassy ring) portrays the Protestant reformer and translator Primož Trubar (1508–86) and the Latin inscription *Stati Inu Obstati* (To Stand and Withstand).

On the three lowest-denomination coins – €0.01, €0.02 and €0.05 (all copper) – are a stork, the stone where the 8th-century Carantanian dukes were installed, and *The Sower* by painter Ivan Grohar (1867–1911). The other three coins are brass. On the €0.10 coin is a design for a parliament by architect Jože

Plečnik (1872–1957) that was never built and the words 'Katedrala Svobode' (Cathedral of Freedom). The €0.20 coin features a pair of Lipizzaner horses prancing together. The stunning and very symbolic €0.50 coin shows Mt Triglav, the Cancer constellation (under which independent Slovenia was born) and the words 'Oj Triglav moj dom' (O Triglav, my home).

Exchange rates are given on the inside front cover of this book. For a general idea on what you might spend while visiting Slovenia, see p13.

ATMs

Automated teller machines (ATMs) – called *bančni avtomat* – are ubiquitous throughout Slovenia. If you have a card linked to either the Visa/Electron/Plus or the MasterCard/Maestro/Cirrus network and a PIN (personal identification number), then you can withdraw euros from almost any ATM in the country. Both Abanka and SKB Banka ATMs are linked to both networks; all banks mentioned in this guide have an ATM unless otherwise indicated.

Although an English-language option is available on the ATM screen, the following are the Slovenian words you'll find on the buttons of the machines (in the order shown) and their English equivalents:

Popravek – Correction/Clear
Prekinitev – Cancel
Potrditev – Enter/Confirm

Cash

Nothing beats cash for convenience – or risk. It's always prudent to carry a little foreign cash, however, in case you can't find an ATM nearby or there's no bank or travel office open to cash your travellers cheques. You can always change cash at a hotel, though the commission will be high.

Credit Cards

Visa, MasterCard/Eurocard and American Express credit cards are widely accepted at hotels, restaurants, shops, car-rental firms, petrol stations and travel agencies. Diner's Club is also accepted but less frequently.

Visa cardholders can get cash advances from any Abanka branch, Eurocard/MasterCard holders from a Nova Ljubljanska Banka or SKB Banka. American Express clients can get an advance from the main office of **Atlas Express** (Map pp62-3; ☎ 01-430 77 20; Kolodvorska ulica

16; ☺ 8am-5pm Mon-Fri) in Ljubljana, but the amount is usually limited to US$600 in travellers cheques for Green Card holders and US$1200 for Gold Card holders. American Express customers who want to report a lost or stolen card or travellers cheques should also call here They can both replace cards (although you must know the account number) and make refunds for lost or stolen American Express travellers cheques.

If you have problems with your Visa card, call the **Visa Centre** (☎ 01-471 81 00) in Ljubljana. Eurocard and MasterCard holders should call **Nova Ljubljanska Banka** (☎ 01-477 20 00). **Diners Club** (☎ 01-589 61 11) is based in Bežigrad, a northern suburb of Ljubljana.

International Transfers

Nova Ljubljanska Banka (☎ 01-477 2001 for information) is an agent for Western Union, and you can have money wired to any of its branches throughout the country.

Moneychangers

It is easy to change cash and travellers cheques at banks, post offices, tourist offices, travel agencies and private exchange offices. Look for the words *menjalnica* or *devizna blagajna* to guide you to the correct place or window.

There's no black market in Slovenia, but exchange rates can vary substantially, so it pays to keep your eyes open. Banks take a *provizija* (commission) of 1% on travellers cheques and usually nothing at all on cash, but tourist offices, travel agencies and exchange bureaus usually charge around 3%. Hotels can take as much as 5%.

Taxes & Refunds

Value-added tax (known as *davek na dodano vrednost* or DDV in Slovenia) is applied to the purchase of most goods and services at a standard rate of 20% (eg on alcoholic drinks, petrol and so on) and a reduced rate of 8.5% (eg on hotel accommodation, food, books, museum entrance fees etc). It is usually included in the quoted price of goods, but not of some services, so beware.

Visitors who are not residents of the European Union can claim refunds on total purchases of €62.50 (not including tobacco products or spirits) issued on one or more receipts by the same retailer/shop on the same day as long as they take the goods out of the country (and the EU) within 90 days. In order to make the claim, you must have a DDV-VP form or Global Tax-Free Shopping refund cheque correctly filled out by the salesperson at the time of purchase and have it stamped by a Slovenian customs officer at the border. You can then collect your refund – minus handling fee from more than 30 post offices nationwide. You can also have it sent by bank cheque or deposited into your credit-card account. For information contact **Global Refund** (☎ 01-513 22 60; www.globalrefund.com; Goriška ulica 17) in Ljubljana.

Most towns and cities in Slovenia levy a 'tourist tax' on visitors staying overnight (typically €0.65 to €1.25 per person per night). This is not normally included in hotels' advertised rates and is never included in the rates quoted in this book.

Tipping

Tipping was not really very common at Slovenian restaurants, bars or hotels under the *ancien régime* but has become so since independence. When a gratuity is not included in your bill, which is usually the case, 10% is customary. If service is outstanding, you could go as high as 15%. With taxi drivers, you usually just round up the sum if you have been happy with the ride or for the sake of convenience.

Travellers cheques

Slovenian banks often give a better exchange rate for travellers cheques than for cash while some private exchange offices (not travel agencies) do the opposite. Post offices are not the best places to change money as many accept only cash, and when they do take travellers cheques it will be at a relatively poor rate.

PHOTOGRAPHY & VIDEO

Film and basic camera equipment are available throughout Slovenia, although the largest selection by far is in Ljubljana.

Film prices vary, but a 36-exposure roll of 200 ASA Kodak, Agfa or Fuji colour print film will cost about €3.25 to €3.75 and a disposable camera around €5.50 (€6.65 with flash). Slide film (36 exposures) is €6. **Foto Tivoli** (Map pp62-3; ☎ 01-438 40 00; www.foto-tivoli.si in Slovene; Slovenska cesta 58; ☺ 8am-7pm Mon-Fri, 8am-1pm Sat) in the lower level of a shopping arcade in Ljubljana stocks a wide range of cameras and photographic equipment.

DIRECTORY

There are processing labs in towns and cities nationwide where you can have your film developed and printed in a matter of hours. You'll have no problems having your digital photos transferred to CD, and the standard of printing is very high. Print processing costs from €2 per roll, and from €0.25 per print.

Labs with fast processing in Ljubljana include **Foto Grad** (Map pp62-3; ☎ 01-439 2910; Trg OF 13; ☻ 8am-7pm Mon-Thu, 8am-4pm Fri) opposite the train station and a **Foto Grad branch** (Map pp62-3; ☎ 01-439 29 00; Miklošičeva cesta 36; ☻ 8am-7pm Mon-Fri, 8am-1pm Sat) around the corner. Foto Grad can develop from all digital media as well.

Spare cassettes for video cameras are also widely available in photographic and electronic goods shops. A 60-minute 8mm cassette costs €5.20 while a 30-minute DVM is €7.50.

POST

The Slovenian postal system (Pošta Slovenije), recognised by its bright yellow logo, offers a wide variety of services – from selling stamps and telephone cards to making photocopies and changing money. The queues are never very long, but you can avoid a trip to the post office if you just want to mail a few postcards by buying *znamke* (stamps) at newsstands and dropping your mail into any of the yellow letterboxes on the street. Staff at post offices can sell you boxes and will even wrap the packages you want to send for you.

Something mailed within Slovenia takes only a day or two. Post to neighbouring countries and ones close by (eg Germany) should take about three days maximum. For the UK, you can count on about five days, and the USA between a week and 10 days. Mail to Asia and Australia takes between 10 days and two weeks.

Postal Rates
Domestic mail costs €0.20 for up to 20g, €0.40 for up to 50g and €0.50 for up to 100g. Postcards are a uniform €0.20. For international mail, the rate is €0.45 for 20g or less, €0.95 for up to 100g and €0.35 for a postcard. An aerogram costs €0.50.

Sending & Receiving Mail
Look for the sign 'Pisma – Paketi' if you've got a *pismo* (letter) or *paket* (parcel) to post.

Poštno ležeče (poste restante) is kept at the main post office of a city or town. In the capital, address it to Glavni Pošta, Slovenska cesta 32, 1101 Ljubljana, where it will be held for 30 days.

There are a lot of different words for 'street' in Slovene. You'll find all the various terms used to distinguish boulevards, roads and alleys in the Glossary (p306), while the accompanying boxed text might help with place names.

SHOPPING
Although Ljubljana has a nice array of craft and souvenir shops (p88), in general it's best to go to the source where you'll find the real

---

ADDRESSES & PLACE NAMES

Streets in Slovenian towns and cities are well signposted, although the numbering system can be a bit confusing with odd and even numbers sometimes running on the same sides of streets and squares.

In small towns and villages, streets are usually not named and houses are just given numbers. Thus Ribčev Laz 13 is house No 13 in the village of Ribčev Laz on Lake Bohinj. As Slovenian villages are frequently made up of one road with houses clustered on or just off it, this is seldom confusing.

Places with double-barrelled names such as Novo Mesto (New Town) and Črna Gora (Black Hill) start the second word in lower case (Novo mesto, Črna gora) in Slovene, almost as if the names were Newtown and Blackhill. This is the correct Slovene orthography, but we have opted to go with the English-language way of doing it to avoid confusion.

Slovene frequently uses the possessive (genitive) case in street names. Thus a road named after the poet Ivan Cankar is Cankarjeva ulica and a square honouring France Prešeren is Prešernov trg. Also, when nouns are turned into adjectives they often become unrecognisable. The town is 'Bled', for example, but 'Lake Bled' is Blejsko Jezero. A street leading to a castle (*grad*) is usually called Grajska ulica. A road going in the direction of Trieste (Trst) is Tržaška cesta. The words 'pri', 'pod' and 'na' in place names mean 'at the', 'below the' and 'on the' respectively.

thing and not mass-produced kitsch. In Gorenjska, go to Bohinj for carved wooden pipes with silver lids, and to Kropa for objects made of wrought iron. In Primorska go to Idrija or Železniki for lace. Ribnica in Dolenjska is famous for its *suha roba* (wooden household utensils), Rogaška Slatina in Štajerska for its crystal, and Prekmurje for its Hungarian-style black pottery. Some people think they're tacky, but traditional *panjske končnice* (beehive panels) painted with folk motifs make original and unusual souvenirs – especially the one showing a devil sharpening a gossip's tongue on a grindstone. I'm sure we all know a few people back home who should hang that one up as an icon.

The silver-filigree jewellery you'll see for sale in shops all over the country, but especially on the coast, is not distinctively Slovenian but a good buy nonetheless. Almost all of the shops are owned and run by ethnic Albanians who brought the craft here from Kosovo.

Ski equipment and ski-wear are of very high quality. Skis and snowboards are made by Elan (www.elan.si) in Begunje na Gorenjskem near Bled, and boots by Alpina (www.alpina.si) at Žiri, northeast of Idrija.

Natural remedies, herbal teas, sea salt and apian products, such as beeswax, honey, pollen, propolis and royal jelly, can be found in speciality shops around the country.

A bottle of quality Slovenian wine makes a great gift. Buy it from a *vinoteka* or a dealer with a large selection, such as Vinoteka Movia or Wine Cellars of Slovenia (Vinske Kleti Slovenije; p89). A couple of the monasteries found in Dolenjska – the Cistercian one at Stična near Ivančna Gorica and the Carthusian one at Pleterje – sell their own brand of firewater made from fruits and berries. It's fragrant and very potent stuff.

Two excellent books, well-illustrated works on the arts and crafts of Slovenia, both of them by ethnologist Janez Bogataj, are *Handicrafts of Slovenia* (Mojstrovine Slovenije; €66.50) and the broader-scoped *Creative Slovenia* (Ustvarjalna Slovenija; €54). Other sources of information include the **Craft Chamber of Slovenia** (Obrtna Zbornica Slovenije; www.ozs.si) and **Art & Craft Slovenija** (Rokodelstvo Slovenija; www.rokodelstvo.si in Slovene). No one sells classier and better-made Slovenian gift items, books and wine than Darila Rokus (p89), with outlets in Ljubljana.

Bargaining

As elsewhere in Eastern Europe, bargaining was not the done thing under communism; everyone paid the same amount by weight and volume. Nowadays people selling folk crafts on the street and especially vendors at flea markets will be very open to haggling. At hotels enjoying less-than-full occupancy during the off-season, you may be able to wangle a *popust* (discount) of up to 25%.

TELEPHONE

Public telephones in Slovenia don't accept coins; they require a *telefonska kartica* or *telekartica* (telephone card) available at all post offices and some newsstands. Phonecards cost €2.95/4.20/7.10/14.60 for 25/50/100/300 *impulzov* (impulses, or units). A three-minute local call will cost €0.08 during peak times (7am to 7pm weekdays) and €0.06 at off-peak times.

A three-minute call from Slovenia to Austria, Croatia, Italy or Hungary will cost €0.38; to much of Western Europe, including the UK, as well as Canada and the USA, it's €0.42; to Australia €1.14; and to New Zealand, South Africa and most of Asia €1.71. Rates are 20% cheaper on most calls between 7pm and 7am every day. Slovenian call boxes do not display their telephone numbers, so it's impossible for the other party to phone you back.

To call Slovenia from abroad, dial the international access code, ☎ 386 (the country code for Slovenia), the area code (minus the initial zero) and the number. There are six area codes in Slovenia (01 to 05 and 07), and these are listed at the beginning of each city and town section in this book. To call abroad from Slovenia, dial ☎ 00 followed by the country and area codes and then the number.

Mobile Phones

Many locals – just under 52% to be precise – have mobile phones, and network coverage amounts to more than 95% of the country. In fact, even certain businesses only quote

---

USEFUL TELEPHONE NUMBERS

General information ☎ 090-939 881
International directory assistance ☎ 1180
Domestic directory assistance ☎ 1188
International operator/collect calls ☎ 115
Time/speaking clock (in Slovene) ☎ 195

DIRECTORY

mobile numbers, identified by the prefix 031, 040, 041 and 051.

Slovenia uses GSM 900, which is compatible with the rest of Europe and Australia but not with the North American GSM 1900 or the totally different system in Japan. SIM cards with €4 credit are available for €12 from SiMobil (www.simobil.si) and for €15.40 from Mobitel (www.mobitel.si). Top-up cards, available at post offices, newsstands and petrol stations, cost €4.20, €10.40 and €21.

Both networks have outlets in virtually every city and town in Slovenia, including Ljubljana:

Mobitel Centre (Mobitelov Center; Map p66; ☎ 472 24 60; www.mobitel.si; Trg Ajdovščina 1; ☺ 8am-8pm Mon-Fri, 8am-1pm Sat)

SiMobil Slovenska cesta (Halo Centre; Map pp62-3; ☎ 430 01 75; www.simobil.si; Slovenska cesta 47; ☺ 8am-7pm Mon-Fri); Old Town (Map p66; ☎ 426 71 02; Mestni trg 19; ☺ 8am-8pm Mon-Fri, 8am-1pm Sat)

TIME

Slovenia lies in the Central European time zone. Winter time is GMT plus one hour while in summer it's GMT plus two hours. Clocks are advanced at 2am on the last Sunday in March and set back at the same time on the last Sunday in October.

Without taking daylight-saving times into account, when it's noon in Ljubljana, it's 11pm in Auckland, 1pm in Bucharest, 11am in London, 2pm in Moscow, 6am in New York, noon in Paris, 3am in San Francisco, 9pm in Sydney and 8pm in Tokyo.

Like a few other European languages, Slovene tells the time by making reference to the next hour – not the previous one as in English. Thus 1.15 is 'one-quarter of two', 1.30 is 'half of two' and 1.45 is 'three-quarters of two'.

TOILETS

Finding a public lavatory is not always easy in Slovenia, and when you do, you'll probably have to pay (€0.20) to use it. All train stations have toilets as do most shopping centres and department stores. The standard of hygiene is usually good.

TOURIST INFORMATION

The **Slovenian Tourist Board** (Slovenska Turistična Organizacija, STO; ☎ 01-589 18 40; www.slovenia.info; Dunajska cesta 156) based in Ljubljana is the umbrella organisation for tourist promotion in Slovenia, and it can handle requests for information

in writing or by email. The STO produces a number of excellent brochures, pamphlets and booklets in English, 17 of which can be ordered on its website. The site itself is not open to the public.

Walk-in visitors in Ljubljana can head to the **Slovenian Tourist Information Centre** (STIC; ☎ 306 45 75; stic@ljubljana-tourism.si; Krekov trg 10; ☺ 8am-9pm Jun-Sep, 8am-7pm Oct-May). In addition, the STO oversees another five dozen or so local tourist offices and bureaus called 'tourist information centres' (TICs) across the country; there are smaller, independent or community-run offices in other cities and towns. If the place you're visiting doesn't have either, seek assistance at a branch of one of the big travel agencies (eg Kompas or Globtour) or from hotel or museum staff.

The best office in Slovenia for face-to-face information is the **Ljubljana Tourist Information Centre** (TIC; ☎ 306 12 15; www.ljubljana-tourism.si; Kresija Bldg, Stritarjeva ulica; ☺ 8am-9pm Jun-Sep, 8am-7pm Oct-May) run by the Ljubljana Tourist Board (Zavod za Turizem Ljubljana). The staff know everything about the capital and almost as much about the rest of Slovenia. In summer the TIC employs students who are very enthusiastic about their country and your interest in it. There's a branch at the train station (p67).

TRAVELLERS WITH DISABILITIES

Disabled facilities found throughout Slovenia include public telephones with amplifiers, pedestrian crossings with beepers, Braille on maps at city bus stops, occasional lifts in pedestrian underpasses, sloped pavements and ramps in government buildings, and reserved spaces in many car parks. An increasing number of hotels (mostly top-end, although not always) have at least one room designed especially for disabled guests (bathrooms big enough for a wheelchair user to turn around in, access door on bath tubs, grip bars alongside toilets etc). These are noted in the text throughout the book with an icon (♿).

The **Paraplegics Association of Slovenia** (Zveza Paraplegikov Republike Slovenije; ☎ 01-432 71 38; www.zveza-paraplegikov.si; Štihova ulica 14) in Ljubljana looks after the interests and special needs of paraplegics, and produces a special guide for its members in Slovene only (although their website in English is fairly complete). Another active group is the Ljubljana-based **Slovenian Association of Disabled Students** (Društvo Študentov

Invalidov Slovenije; ☎ 01-565 33 51; www.dsis-drustvo.si; Kardeljeva ploščad 5). Some towns and cities produce useful brochures describing which local sights and attractions are accessible by wheelchair.

VISAS

Virtually everyone entering Slovenia must have a valid passport, although citizens of the EU as well as Switzerland need only produce their national identity card on arrival for stays of up to 30 days. It's a good idea to carry your passport or other identification at all times.

Citizens of virtually all European countries as well as Australia, Canada, Israel, Japan, New Zealand and the USA do not require visas to visit Slovenia for stays of up to 90 days. Those who do require visas (including South Africans) can get them at any Slovenian embassy or consulate (p276) for up to 90 days. They cost €35 regardless of the type or length of validity. You'll need confirmation of a hotel booking plus one photo and may have to show a return or onward ticket.

Your hotel, hostel, camping ground or private room arranged through an agency will register your name and address with the municipal *občina* (government) office as required by law. That's why they have to take your passport away – at least for the first night. If you are staying elsewhere (eg with relatives or friends), your host is supposed to take care of this for you within three days.

If you want to stay in Slovenia longer than three months, the easiest thing to do is simply cross the border into Croatia and return (it won't work with Austria, Italy or Hungary as they are all EU countries too). Otherwise you will have to apply for a temporary residence permit at the **Foreigners Office** (Urad za Tujce; ☎ 01-306 30 00; Proletarska ulica 1; ☼ 8am-3pm Mon, 8am-5pm Wed, 8am-1pm Fri) in Moste, northeast of Center in Ljubljana.

Contact any Slovenian embassy, consulate or tourist office abroad for any recent changes in the above regulations or check the website of the Foreign Ministry (www.mzz.gov.si).

VOLUNTEERING

Voluntariat (☎ 01-239 16 25, 031-813 939; www.zavod-voluntariat.si; Resljeva ulica 20; ☼ 9am-2pm Mon, 10am-2pm Tue, 1-5pm Wed, 9am-1pm Thu) in Ljubljana, which is part of the Service Civil International (SCI), organises summer work camps in Slovenia on projects ranging from ecology research in Novo Mesto to working with Roma (Gypsies) near Murska Sobota, as well as volunteer work camps abroad.

WOMEN TRAVELLERS

Travelling as a single woman in Slovenia is no different from travelling in most Western European countries. If you can handle yourself in the very occasional less-than-comfortable situation, you'll be fine.

In the event of an emergency call the **police** (☎ 113) any time or the **SOS Helpline** (☎ 080-11 55; www.drustvo-sos.si; ☼ noon-10pm Mon-Fri, 6-10pm Sat & Sun).

Transport

GETTING THERE & AWAY

ENTERING THE COUNTRY

Border formalities with Slovenia's three fellow European Union neighbours – Italy, Austria and Hungary – are now virtually nonexistent. However, as a member state that forms part of the EU's external frontier, Slovenia must implement the strict Schengen border rules, so expect a somewhat closer inspection of your documents – national ID (for EU citizens) or passport and, in some cases, visa (p285) when travelling to/from Croatia.

AIR
Airports & Airlines

Slovenia's only international airport receiving regular scheduled flights is **Brnik Airport** (airport code LJU; ☎ 04-206 10 00; www.lju-airport.si) at Brnik, 27km north of Ljubljana, though there are international airports handling special and charter flights at Maribor and Portorož as well. In the Brnik arrivals hall you'll find a branch of the **Slovenia Tourist Information Centre** (STIC; ☼ 11am-5.30pm Mon-Fri, to 4.30pm Sat), a hotel booking board with telephone, an ATM and a currency-exchange machine. In the departures area there is an information desk, a **post office** (☼ 7am-6pm Mon-Fri, to noon Sat), a branch of

Nova Ljubljanska Banka (☎ 8am-3pm Mon-Fri), an exchange bureau run by **Kompas** (☎ 04-201 42 88; ☼ 7am-7pm) and a row of car-rental agencies, including Europcar, Avis, Budget and Hertz.

From its base here, the Slovenian flag-carrier, **Adria Airways** (JP; ☎ 01-231 33 12, toll-free ☎ 080 13 00, airport ☎ 04-236 34 62; www.adria-airways.com; Gosposvetska cesta 6; ☼ 8am-7pm Mon-Fri, 8am-noon Sat) serves as many as two-dozen European destinations depending on the season. Adria flights can be remarkably good value, but with the arrival of easyJet and Wizz Air flights between the Slovenian capital and London, most British visitors are now weekend visitors on budget airlines. Adria connections include two to five per day from Frankfurt, three daily from Munich, one or two daily from Paris (Roissy Charles de Gaulle) and Zürich, daily from Istanbul and London Gatwick, four weekly from Amsterdam, twice weekly from Manchester, and useful connections to Pristina (Kosovo), Ohrid (Macedonia) and Tirana (Albania).

Other airlines serving Ljubljana include:
Air France (AF; ☎ 01-244 34 47, 04-202 36 50; www.airfrance.com) Daily flights to Paris (CDG)
Austrian Airlines (OS; ☎ 04-202 01 22; www.aua.com) Multiple daily flights to Vienna.
ČSA Czech Airlines (OK; ☎ 04-206 17 05; www.csa.cz) Flights to Prague.
EasyJet (EZY; ☎ 04-206 12 29; www.easyjet.com) Low-cost flights to London Stansted.
JAT Airways (JU; ☎ 01-231 43 40, 04-206 17 80; www.jat.com) Daily to Belgrade.
LOT Polish Airlines (LO; ☎ 04-202 0122; www.lot.com) Flights to Warsaw.

CLIMATE CHANGE & TRAVEL

Climate change is a serious threat to the ecosystems that humans rely upon, and air travel is the fastest-growing contributor to the problem. Lonely Planet regards travel, overall, as a global benefit, but believes we all have a responsibility to limit our personal impact on global warming.

Flying & Climate Change

Pretty much every form of motor transport generates CO_2 (the main cause of human-induced climate change) but planes are far and away the worst offenders, not just because of the sheer distances they allow us to travel, but because they release greenhouse gases high into the atmosphere. The statistics are frightening: two people taking a return flight between Europe and the US will contribute as much to climate change as an average household's gas and electricity consumption over a whole year.

Carbon Offset Schemes

Climatecare.org and other websites use 'carbon calculators' that allow travellers to offset the greenhouse gases they are responsible for with contributions to energy-saving projects and other climate-friendly initiatives in the developing world – including projects in India, Honduras, Kazakhstan and Uganda.

Lonely Planet, together with Rough Guides and other concerned partners in the travel industry, supports the carbon offset scheme run by climatecare.org. Lonely Planet offsets all of its staff and author travel.

For more information check out our website: www.lonelyplanet.com.

Malév Hungarian Airlines (MA; ☎ 04-206 16 76; www.malev.hu) Daily to Budapest.
Turkish Airlines (TK; ☎ 04-206 16 80, 031-285 753; www.turkishairlines.com) Flights to Istanbul.
Wizz Air (W6; ☎ 04-206 19 81; www.wizzair.com) Budget flights to London Luton and Brussels (Charleroi).

Australia

Flights to Ljubljana from Australia generally involve a combination of airlines, passing through one of the main European hubs. Return low-season fares from Sydney are from A$1865 to A$2300 and from Melbourne A$2100 to A$2400.

The following are well-known agents for competitive fares:
STA Travel (☎ 1300 733 035; www.statravel.com.au)
Flight Centre (☎ 133 133; www.flightcentre.com.au)

Continental Europe

Adria has at least one nonstop flight a day to Ljubljana from Brussels, Frankfurt, Istanbul, Moscow, Munich, Paris, Pristina, Sarajevo, Skopje, Vienna and Zürich, and one to five departures a week from Amsterdam, Barcelona, Belgrade, Copenhagen, Dublin, Manchester, Ohrid, Podgorica, Rome, Tirana and Warsaw.

Return flights from Frankfurt and Munich on an Adria-Lufthansa joint flight cost around €330 and €260 respectively. From Paris on Adria or Air France expect to pay about €240, and from Vienna (Adria or Austrian Airlines) from €185.

A few recommended travel agents include the following:
France Nouvelles Frontières (☎ 0 825 000 747; www.nouvelles-frontieres.com in French)
Germany Just Travel (☎ 089-747 3330; www.justtravel.de)
Netherlands NBBS Reizen (☎ 0900 1020 300; www.nbbs.nl in Dutch)

UK

Adria flies non-stop daily from London and once or twice a week from Manchester and Dublin during the summer. The cheapest return excursion ticket from London with Adria is UK£123, but the average two-week advance purchase excursion (APEX) fare is still around UK£165.

You'll do much better on **easyJet** (EZY; ☎ 0905 821 0905), which flies daily to Ljubljana from London's Stansted airport or **Wizz Air** (W6; ☎ Poland

---

DEPARTURE TAX

A departure tax of €16.75 is collected from everyone leaving Slovenia by air. This is usually included in the ticket price, but it's always best to check.

TRANSPORT

call centre +48 22 351 9499), with four flights a week from London Luton airport. Depending on the season and the day of the week, return fares can go as low as UK£40, including taxes.

An alternative budget option to Slovenia from London, especially if you want to concentrate on the coast is **Ryanair** (☎ 0871 246 0000 www.ryanair.com), which links London Stansted with Trieste's **Ronchi dei Legionari airport** (www.aeroporto.fvg.it). Trieste may (still) be in Italy, but it's much closer to Primorska than Ljubljana. From the Trieste airport terminal there is a daily **Terravision bus** (www.lowcostcoach.com; single/return €15/25) at 2.40pm to Koper (1½ hours, 56km), Izola (two hours, 61km), Portorož and Piran (2½ hours, 69km).

Competitive travel agencies include the following:

Flightbookers (☎ 0800 082 3000; www.ebookers.com)
STA Travel (☎ 0870 163 0026; www.statravel.co.uk)
Trailfinders (☎ 0845 058 5858; www.trailfinders.com)

USA & Canada

A return flight from New York to Ljubljana via Paris with Air France and Adria costs from US$1403. Return fares from Toronto start at about C$2010.

Competitive travel agents include:

Council on International Educational Exchange (☎ 1-800-407 8839; www.ciee.org) America's largest student travel organisation.
STA Travel (☎ 800 781 4040; www.statravel.com) Has offices around America.
Travel CUTS (☎ 1-866 246 9762; www.travelcuts.com) Canada's national student travel agency.

LAND

Slovenia is well connected by road and rail with its four neighbours. Note that bus and train timetables sometimes use Slovenian names for foreign cities (p307).

Bus

Most international buses arrive and depart from **Ljubljana bus station** (☎ 090 42 30, 090 42 40; www.ap-ljubljana.si).

Car & Motorcycle

Slovenia maintains about 150 border crossings with its neighbours, but not all are open to citizens of 'third countries' (not from either side). On country maps and atlases, those marked with a circle and a line are international ones; those with just a circle are local ones. Although a member of the EU since 2004, Slovenia only entered Schengen zone in October 2007. The 670km border it shares with Croatia is at present the 'last frontier' of the EU.

Train

Slovenian Railways (Slovenske Železnice, SŽ; ☎ 01-291 33 32; www.slo-zeleznice.si) links up with the European railway network via Austria (Villach, Salzburg, Graz, Vienna), Germany (Munich), Czech Republic (Prague), Croatia (Zagreb, Rijeka, Pula), Hungary (Budapest), Italy (Trieste, Venice), Switzerland (Zürich), Serbia (Belgrade, Niš), Macedonia (Skopje) and Greece (Thessaloniki). SŽ trains are clean and punctual; in recent years the acquisition of new rolling stock, including high-speed InterCity tilting

ROAD DISTANCES (KM)

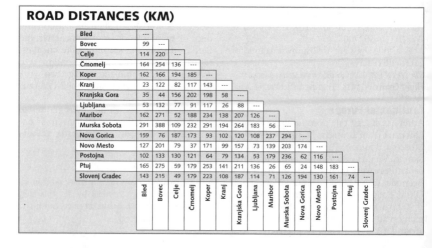

	Bled	Bovec	Celje	Črnomelj	Koper	Kranj	Kranjska Gora	Ljubljana	Maribor	Murska Sobota	Nova Gorica	Novo Mesto	Postojna	Ptuj	Slovenj Gradec
Bled	---														
Bovec	99	---													
Celje	114	220	---												
Črnomelj	164	254	136	---											
Koper	162	166	194	185	---										
Kranj	23	122	82	117	143	---									
Kranjska Gora	35	44	156	202	198	58	---								
Ljubljana	53	132	77	91	117	26	88	---							
Maribor	162	271	52	188	234	138	207	126	---						
Murska Sobota	291	388	109	232	291	194	264	183	56	---					
Nova Gorica	159	76	187	173	93	102	120	108	237	294	---				
Novo Mesto	127	201	79	37	171	99	157	73	139	203	174	---			
Postojna	102	133	130	121	64	79	134	53	179	236	62	116	---		
Ptuj	165	275	59	179	253	141	211	136	26	65	24	148	183	---	
Slovenj Gradec	143	215	49	179	223	108	187	114	71	126	194	130	161	74	---

trains, have brought the network firmly into the 21st century.

The international trains include EuroCity (EC) ones (*Mimara* linking Munich and Zagreb, *Agram* between Salzburg and Zagreb, *Zagreb and Croatia* between Vienna and Zagreb, *Emona* linking Vienna and Ljubljana, *Casanova* linking Venice and Ljubljana, *Goldoni* between Budapest and Venice via Ljubljana and Zagreb and the *Jože Plečnik* between Prague and Ljubljana), InterCity (IC) ones (*Citadella* between Budapest and Ljubljana, *Sava* linking Munich and Belgrade), EuroNight (EN) trains (*Venezia* between Budapest and Venice via Ljubljana and Zagreb) and expresses.

Seat reservations, compulsory on trains to and from Italy and on IC trains, cost €3 but it is usually included in the ticket price. On some trains, including the EN *Venezia,* sleepers and couchettes are available. When travelling on an international train within Slovenia a supplement of €1.45 and €1.70 is charged.

DISCOUNTS & PASSES

Undiscounted international tickets on SŽ trains are valid for two months. Certain fares bought at special offer are valid for one month, while others are valid only for the day and train indicated on the ticket; see the destinations below for details. Half-price tickets are available to children between the ages of six and 12 years on all trains.

SŽ sells **Inter-Rail** (www.interrailnet.com) passes to those under 26 – older travellers can get an Inter-Rail 26+ card, which is about 35% more expensive – though you must have resided in the country of purchase for six months and be able to prove it. Inter-Rail divides Europe into eight zones (A to H). Passes for one, two or all eight (global) are available. A 16-day pass valid in Zone G only, which includes Slovenia, Italy, Greece, the ferry company serving the last two, and Turkey, costs €195/286 for IR-26/IR+26; with another zone and valid 22 days it would cost €275/396. Global passes (€385/546) are valid for a month

The only ticket from USA-based **Eurail** (www.eurail.com), which make its passes available to European and non-European residents alike, that includes Slovenia is the Eurail Selectpass, which allows travel within three, four or five bordering countries for five, six, eight or 10 days within a two-month period. Thus a Eurail Selectpass valid for travel in Slovenia, Austria, Italy, Croatia and Hungary for five/10 days would cost adults US$473/670 in 1st class (only) and youths under 26 years of age US$306/433 in 2nd class.

For national rail passes valid within Slovenia only, see p295.

Croatia, Bosnia & Hercegovina, & Serbia
BUS

Koper, Piran and Portorož are the best ports of entry from Croatian Istria and points further south by bus.

A bus leaves Koper daily on weekdays for Rijeka (€7.60, two hours, 84km, 10.10am Monday to Friday) and there's a daily bus to Zagreb at 4.56am (€22, 4½ hours, 243km). There are also buses to Rovinj (€11.10, three hours, 129km, 3.55pm daily July & August) via Piran, Portorož and Poreč (€8, two hours, 88km), with another two or three buses to Poreč only, including one at 8.30am Monday to Friday.

Two daily buses link Zagreb (€11.25 to €13.25, 2½ hours, 154km, at 7.30am and 8pm) with Ljubljana. Count on at least two daily departures to Belgrade (€31.30 to €35, 8¼ hours, 549km, 10am and 7.45pm daily, 10.45pm Sunday to Friday). There is also a departure at 6.35am on Saturday for Varaždin (€19, five hours, 214km). Buses depart from Ljubljana at 3.30pm and 7.40pm daily for Rijeka (€9.50, 2½ hours, 136km); the second one carries on to Split (€34, 10 hours, 528km), where you can change for Dubrovnik (€15.60, four hours, 212km). A bus for Banja Luka (€30.25, 5½ hours, 336km, 12.57pm and 4pm daily) leaves twice a day and another one three times a week for Sarajevo (€35.65, 9½ hours, 554km, 7.15pm Monday, Wednesday and Friday)

Expect two buses a day from Maribor to Varaždin and Zagreb (€10.75, two hours, 119km, 5.35pm on Monday and 7pm Friday) and another bus once a day to Varaždin and Zagreb (€8.75, 1½ hours, 97km, 8am on Monday and Friday) from Ptuj.

TRAIN

There are eight trains a day to Ljubljana from Zagreb via Zidani Most (€11.90, two hours, 154km), two a day from Rijeka (€11.40, two hours, 136km) via Postojna, and five a day from Split (€44.10, eight to 12 hours, 456km), with a change at Zagreb. There are four trains a day from Belgrade (€41.80, nine to 10 hours,

549km) via Zagreb. There is also one train a day from Sarajevo (€35, 12 hours, 554km) with a change at Zagreb.

Germany, Austria & Czech Republic
BUS

Deutsche Touring (☎ 069-79 030 in Frankfurt; www .deutsche-touring.com) operates a daily overnight bus between Frankfurt and Ljubljana (adult one way/return €80/122, under 26/student €72/110; 12½ hours, 799km), leaving Frankfurt at 1pm and picking up passengers at Stuttgart (4.30pm), Ulm (6pm) and Munich (7.15pm). The northbound bus leaves Ljubljana at 7.30pm Sunday to Friday and at 9.30am on Saturday. A bus bound for Prague (€43.40, 12 hours, 659km, one a week on Sunday) departs Ljubljana between June and mid-October.

There are daily buses from Maribor to Munich, Stuttgart and Frankfurt (€78, 12½ hours, 778km, 6.50pm and 9.50pm daily) and another at 8.12am on Saturday.

TRAIN

There are three direct trains a day between Munich (€66, 6½ hours, 405km) and Ljubljana via Salzburg and Villach. The 8.17pm departure has sleeping carriages available. There is also a train from Salzburg only (€39, 4½ hours, 273km) to Ljubljana and another one just from Villach (€16.20, two hours, 96km).

To get to Vienna you have a choice between the morning ICS (InterCity Slovenia) and EC *Rogla Croatia* from Zagreb (change at Maribor) or the afternoon EC *Emona*. To get to Graz you have a choice between three connections per day (one with a change in Maribor).

Ljubljana–Vienna trains (€57, 6¼ hours, 385km) via Graz (€30, 200km, 3½ hours) are expensive though so-called SparSchiene fares as low as €29 (valid for travel in one direction in 2nd class) apply on certain trains at certain times. In summer passengers can travel with couchette for only €39 on specific trains. There is also a 'Praga Spezial' fare available on the *Jože Plečnik* train between Ljubljana and Prague for only €29.

Be aware that the number of these discounted tickets per train is limited.

Hungary
BUS

The Hungarian train station Rédics is only 7km to the north of Lendava, in northeastern

Slovenia, which can be reached from Murska Sobota (€3.50, 30 minutes, 29km, half-hourly). Two buses a day link Murska Sobota and Ljubljana (€16.50, four hours, 195km). From Rédics trains go to Zalaegerszeg (450Ft, 1¼ hours, 49km, six to eight daily), which is reached by three direct trains from Budapest (2226Ft, four hours, 252km) and a couple more requiring a change at Boba.

TRAIN
The EN *Venezia* and EC *Goldoni* link Ljubljana directly with Budapest (€58.60, 8¾ hours, 451km, three daily) via Zagreb and Koprivnica in Croatia. The IC Citadella goes via Ptuj and Hodoš in Slovenia's northeast. There are Budapest Spezial fares available as low as €39 on certain trains at certain times.

Italy
BUS
Buses from Koper to Trieste (€3, one hour, 23km, up to 13 daily) run along the coast via Ankaran and Muggia on weekdays only. There's a direct year-round service from Ljubljana to Trieste (€11.50, 2½ hours, 105km, 6.25am Monday to Saturday), with an additional departure at 8.15am Saturday between June and mid-October.

Hourly buses link the train stations in the Italian city of Gorizia with Nova Gorica (€1, 25 minutes), just across the border. Tarvisio (Trbiž) in northeast Italy is linked by bus with Ljubljana (€10.20, 2½ hours, 109km) via Kranj and Kranjska Gora Monday to Saturday.

TRAIN
There are several trains between Ljubljana and Venice (€25, four hours, 244km) to choose from, with special fares of only €15 available on some trains. Another possibility is to go first to Nova Gorica (€7.30, three hours, 153km, six daily), walk to Gorizia then take an Italian train to Venice (€7.90, 2¼ hours).

The EC *Casanova*, a high-speed Pendolino train, leaves Venice daily for Ljubljana via Sežana and Postojna at 3.44pm, arriving in Ljubljana at 7.42pm. It leaves Ljubljana at 10.28am, arriving in Venice at 2.21pm.

The EN *Venezia* runs between Venice and Budapest via Ljubljana. Departure from Ljubljana is at 1.47pm, arriving in Trieste (€15, 99km) at 4.52pm and Venice at 7.16pm. It departs from Venice at 9.04pm, arriving in Trieste at 11.13pm and in Ljubljana at 2.31am.

The EC *Goldoni* also runs between Venice and Budapest via Ljubljana. Departure from Ljubljana is at 4.16pm, with arrival in Venice at 8.31pm. It returns from Venice at 9am, reaching Ljubljana at 1.14pm.

SEA
The **Prince of Venice** (☎ 05-617 80 00; portoroz@kompas .si) is a 39m high-speed catamaran that runs day trips between Izola and Venice. It departs Izola at 8am and arrives in Venice at 10.30am; the return journey departs at 5pm and arrives back at Izola at 7.30pm. The schedule changes according to the season, but essentially there are sailings on Saturday from mid-April to October, with between two and three sailings a week from May to September. An adult return ticket costs €42 to €67 (children aged three to 14 pay half-price) depending on the season and day, including a guided tour of Venice, and there are various family packages available. An adult single costs €29.20 to €46.90. Tickets can be purchased at **Kompas** (www .kompas.si) travel outlets in Slovenia and various other agencies along the coast.

From mid-April to mid-October **Venezia Lines** (in Italy; ☎ 674 67 72; www.venezialines.com) runs a similar service from Piran, departing at 8.40am and returning at just after 7.30pm on Tuesday, with an occasional sailing on Thursday. Tickets, which cost €79 to €82 for an adult return (children aged three to 13 pay half-price), are available through several travel agencies in Piran and Portorož, including **Maona Tourist Agency** (www.maona.si).

GETTING AROUND

AIR
Slovenia has no scheduled domestic flights, but a division of Adria Airways called **Aviotaxi** (☎ 04-259 42 45, 041-636 420; www.adria-airways .com) flies chartered Piper Turbo Arrows on demand to airports and aerodromes around the country. Sample return fares for three passengers from Brnik airport are €83.70 to Bled, €1000.50 to Bled and Bohinj, €150.80 to Slovenj Gradec and €294 to Portorož or Maribor.

BICYCLE
Cycling is both a popular leisure pastime and a means of transport in Slovenia, and bikes can be carried free of charge in the baggage

TRANSPORT

compartments of InterCity and regional trains. On buses you can put your bike in the luggage compartment as long as there is space. Cycling is permitted on all roads except motorways. Many larger towns and cities, including Ljubljana, Maribor, Celje, Ptuj, Novo Mesto, Kranj and Murska Sobota, have dedicated bicycle lanes and special traffic lights.

Bicycle rental places are generally concentrated in the more popular tourist areas such as Ljubljana, Bled, Bovec and Piran though a fair few cycle shops and repair places hire them out as well. Expect to pay from €4.20 to €5.45 per day; some places may ask for a cash deposit or a piece of ID as security. Look in the Getting Around sections of the relevant towns for details.

BUS

You can buy your ticket at the *avtobusna postaja* (bus station) or simply pay the driver as you board. In Ljubljana you should book your seat (€1/3.60 domestic/international) one day in advance if you're travelling on Friday, or to destinations in the mountains or on the coast on a public holiday. Bus services are severely restricted on Sunday and holidays (less so on Saturday).

A range of bus companies serve the country, but prices are uniform: €3/5.50/9/16.50 for 25/50/100/200km. For sample domestic bus fares from the capital, see p90.

Some bus stations have a *garderoba* (left-luggage office) and charge €1.80 per hour. They often keep banker's hours; if it's an option, a better bet is to leave your things at the train station, which is usually nearby and keeps longer hours. If your bag has to go in the luggage compartment below the bus, it will cost €1.25 extra.

Bus Timetables

Timetables in the bus station, or posted on a wall or column outside, list all destinations and departure times. If you cannot find your bus listed or don't understand the schedule, get help from the *blagajna vozovnice* (information or ticket window), which are usually one and the same. *Odhodi* means 'departures' while *prihodi* is 'arrivals'.

Slovenian bus timetables use standard coloured text or abbreviation footnotes to denote which days of the week and during what seasons the buses run. The following lists cover most of the combinations you'll encounter.

Bus Timetable Colours

white or black	daily
green	Mon-Sat
blue	Mon-Fri
orange	Mon-Fri & working Sat
yellow	days when school is in session
red	Sun & public holidays

Bus Timetable Abbreviations

Č	Thu
D	workdays (Mon-Fri)
D+	Mon-Sat
N	Sun
NP	Sun &holidays
Pe	Fri
Po	Mon
PP	Mon-Fri
SN	Sat & Sun
So	Sat
ŠP	days when school is in session
Sr	Wed
To	Tue
V	daily

CAR & MOTORCYCLE
Automobile Association

Slovenia's national automobile club is the **AMZS** (Avto-Moto Zveza Slovenije; ☎ 530 53 00; www.amzs.si; Dunajska cesta 128; ☽ 7am-7.30pm Mon-Fri, to 12.30pm Sat) based in Ljubljana. For emergency roadside assistance, call the AMZS on ☎ 19 87 anywhere in Slovenia. All accidents should be reported to the police (☽ 113) immediately.

Driving Licence

If you don't hold a European driving licence and plan to drive in Slovenia, obtain an International Driving Permit (IDP) from your local automobile association before you leave – you'll need a passport photo and a valid licence. They are usually inexpensive and valid for one year only. Be aware, though, that an IDP is not valid unless accompanied by your original driver's licence.

Fuel

Petrol stations, which accept almost every credit card, are usually open from about 7am to 8pm Monday to Saturday, though larger towns have 24-hour services on the outskirts.

Bencin (petrol) has risen by almost 25% in the past three years, and the price is now on par with the rest of Continental Europe:

EuroSuper 95/SuperPlus98 costs €1.04/1.06 per litre, with diesel at €0.98.

Hire

Renting a car in Slovenia is recommended and can even save you money as you can access cheaper out-of-centre hotels and farm or village homestays. Car rentals from international firms such as Avis, Budget, Europcar and Hertz (all have offices in Ljubljana and in some provincial cities) vary in price. Expect to pay from €45/245 a day/week, including unlimited mileage, collision damage waiver (CDW), theft protection (TP), Personal Accident Insurance (PAI) and taxes. Some smaller agencies (p90) have somewhat more competitive rates.

Insurance

International vehicle insurance is compulsory in Slovenia. If you enter the country in your own car and it is registered in the EU, you are covered; Slovenia has concluded special agreements with certain other countries, including Croatia. Other motorists must buy a Green Card (www.cobx.org/public/NXhomeEng -Public.htm) valid for Slovenia at the border.

Parking

You must pay to park in the centre of most large Slovenian towns. In general you'll have to buy a special 'pay and display' parking coupon (from €0.45 per hour) from newsstands, kiosks or vending machines and display it on the dashboard. In Ljubljana there are underground car parks where fees are charged (€1.25 for the first hour and €0.85 per hour after that).

Road Conditions

Roads in Slovenia are generally good, well maintained and improving rapidly. Driving in the Alps can be hair-raising, with a gradient of up to 18% at the Korensko Sedlo Pass into Austria, and a series of 49 hairpin bends on the road over the Vršič Pass. Many mountain roads are closed in winter and some well into early spring. Motorways and highways are very well signposted, but secondary and tertiary roads are not always so; be sure to have a good map or atlas (see p279) at the ready.

Investments worth €5.4 billion have been earmarked over a 10-year period to 2013 for the expansion of Slovenia's motorway network – from 228km in 1990 to 483km by the end of 2004. There are two main motorway corridors – between Maribor and the coast (via the impressive new flyover at Črni Kal) and from the Karavanke Tunnel into Austria to Zagreb in Croatia – intersecting at the Ljubljana ring road, with a branch from Postojna to Nova Gorica. Motorways are numbered from A1 to A10 (for *avtocesta*), and a *cestnina* (toll) is payable (eg €4.40 from Ljubljana to Koper, €5.40 from Ljubljana to Maribor).

Major international roads are preceded by an 'E'. The most important of these are the E70 to Zagreb via Novo Mesto, the E61 to Villach via Jesenice and the Karavanke Tunnel, the E57 from Celje to Graz via Maribor, and the E59 from Graz to Zagreb via Maribor. National highways contain a single digit and link cities. Secondary and tertiary roads have two sets of numbers separated by a hyphen; the first number indicates the highway that the road runs into. Thus road No 10-5 from Nova Gorica and Ajdovščina joins the A10 motorway at Razdrto.

Private-car ownership in Slovenia exceeds that of the UK (457 vs 444 vehicles per 1000 inhabitants), so expect a lot of traffic congestion, especially in summer and on Friday afternoons when entire cities and towns head for the countryside. Work is being carried out on major roads throughout the country so factor in the possibility of delays and *obvozi* (diversions).

Road Rules

You must drive on the right. Speed limits for cars and motorcycles (less for buses) are 50km/h in towns and villages, 90km/h on secondary and tertiary roads, 100km/h on highways and 130km/h on motorways.

The use of seat belts is compulsory, and motorcyclists must wear helmets. Another law taken very seriously is the one requiring all motorists to illuminate their headlights throughout the day. The permitted blood-alcohol level for drivers is 0.05%.

HITCHING

Hitchhiking remains a popular way to get around for young Slovenes, and it's generally easy – except on Friday afternoon, before school holidays and on Sunday, when cars are often full of families.

Hitching from bus stops is fairly common. Otherwise use motorway access roads or other areas where the traffic will not be disturbed. For the best routes out of the Ljubljana, see p90.

TOURS

Many local travel agencies organise excursions and tours for both individuals and groups. **Kompas** (☎ 200 64 14; www.kompas-online .net) is just one example that has half-day and day trips to Bled (€46), Postojna Cave and Predjama Castle (€48), Lipica and Škocjan Caves (€60) and Maribor and Ptuj (€64). Tours last for between five and nine hours and include transport, guide and entrance fees.

A very welcome addition for travellers in Ljubljana anxious to see some of the rest of the country is **Roundabout** (☎ 051-427 624, www.roundabout.si), based in the capital. It's basically a hop-on, hop-off bus trip that does what it calls a Gorenjska trip (Škofja Loka, Bled and Bohinj; €35.50) on Tuesday, Thursday, Saturday and Sunday and a Primorska one (Predjama, Škocjan, Lipica and Piran; €39.60) on Monday, Wednesday, Friday and Sunday. You can either do the trip in one go or get off and wait for the next bus. A more ambitious trip is the two-day West Roundy one that takes in Bled, Bohinj, Bovec (where you stay overnight) Kobarid, Štanjel, Lipica, Piran and the Škocjan Caves before heading back to Ljubljana. The trip alone costs €66.80; with multibed apartment/hotel accommodation in Bovec added on it's €79.30/96.

TRAIN

Slovenian Railways (☎ 01-291 33 32; www.slo-zel eznice.si) runs trains on 1230km of track, about 40% of which is electrified. Very roughly, figure on covering about 60km/h to 65km/h except on the ICS express trains, which hurtle between Ljubljana and Maribor (€12.40, 1¾ hours) at an average speed of 90km/h. In the summer months an ICS train links Koper with Maribor (€21.70, four hours) via Ljubljana (€12.40, two hours).

Although many secondary lines serve provincial cities and towns only, the main ones converge on Ljubljana, and to get from A to B it's usually easier to go via the capital. Going from Maribor to Novo Mesto, for example, takes two or more changes if you refuse to backtrack.

The provinces are served by *regionalni vlaki* (regional trains) and *primestni vlaki* (city trains), but the fastest are InterCity trains (IC), which levy a surcharge of €1.45 to €1.80.

TIMETABLE SYMBOLS

╳	Mon-Sat (except public holidays)
✖	Mon-Fri (except public holidays)
⊗	Mon-Sat and public holidays
Ⓥ	Sat & Sun
❶	Sat, Sun & public holidays
7	Sun and public holidays
Ⓟ	No Sun service
†	Holiday service

An 'R' next to the train number on the timetable means seat reservations are available. If the 'R' is boxed, seat reservations are obligatory.

Purchase your ticket before you travel at the *železniška postaja* (train station) itself; buying it from the conductor on the train costs an additional €2.10. An invalid ticket or trying to avoid paying will earn you a fine of €33.50.

A *povratna vozovnica* (return ticket) costs double the price of a *enosmerna vozovnica* (a one-way or single ticket). A 1st-class ticket costs 50% more than a 2nd-class one.

Travelling by train in Slovenia works out to almost half the price of going by bus. In rough terms, a 100km journey costs €5.50 in 2nd class; see p90 for sample domestic fares out of the capital. There's a 30% discount on return weekend and ICS fares.

Seventeen stations around the country have left-luggage offices, and there are lockers at stations in Ljubljana, Maribor, Celje and Koper. The charge is €2 per piece of luggage or locker per day.

Train Timetables

Departures and arrivals are announced by loudspeaker or on an electronic board and are always on a printed timetable somewhere in the station. The yellow one with the heading *Odhod* or *Odhodi Vlakov* means 'Departures', and the white one with the words *Prihod* or *Prihodi Vlakov* is 'Arrivals'. Other important words that appear often are *čas* (time), *peron* (platform), *sedež* (seat), *smer* (direction) and *tir* (rail).

If you expect to use the train a lot in Slovenia, buy a copy of the official timetable, *Vozni Red Slovenske Železnice* (€4.20), which has explanatory notes in Slovene and German. An abridged version listing main routes only in Slovene is free.

Discounts & Passes

Slovenian Railways has its own Slovenian Rail Pass which allows three/four/five/six/seven/eight days of travel in 2nd class for €30/35/40/45/50/55 and in 1st class for €42/48/54/60/66/72. Travel is unlimited except on ICS trains, which levy a supplement of €1.90/4.40 on 2nd-/1st-class seats.

Euro Domino passes, allowing three to eight days of midnight-to-midnight travel over a one-month period, are also available to more than two-dozen European and North African countries A three-day adult/youth (ie under 26) pass for Slovenia costs €41/55, while one valid for eight days' travel within a month is €95/71. Euro Domino passes are available only to those who have resided in Europe for at least six consecutive months and must be purchased outside the country in which you intend to travel.

Steam Trains

SŽ has a stock of five steam locomotives and antique rolling stock – a trainspotter's dream come true – and several of them dating as far back as 1919 are put to good use in summer when the Old Timer Train (Muzejski Vlak) excursions depart. For details see p114.

TRANSPORT

Health

CONTENTS

Travel health depends on your predeparture preparations, your daily health care while travelling and the way you handle any medical problem that develops while you are on the road. Although the potential dangers might seem frightening, in reality few travellers experience anything more than an upset stomach. Tap water, for example, is 100% safe everywhere in Slovenia. Mosquitoes can be a real annoyance, however, especially around lakes and ponds in the warmer months.

BEFORE YOU GO

A little planning before departure, particularly for pre-existing illnesses or conditions, will save trouble later. See your dentist before a long trip, carry a spare pair of contact lenses or glasses, and take your optical prescription with you. Bring medications in their original, clearly labelled, containers. A signed and dated letter from your physician describing your medical conditions and medications, including their generic names, is also a good idea.

INSURANCE

EU citizens on public-health insurance schemes should note that they're generally covered by reciprocal arrangements in Slovenia. They should, however, carry

RECOMMENDED VACCINATIONS

While Slovenia does not require any vaccination of international travellers, the World Health Organisation (WHO) recommends that all travellers be covered for diphtheria, tetanus, measles, mumps, rubella and polio, regardless of their destination. Since most vaccines don't produce immunity until at least two weeks after they're given, visit a physician or clinic at least six weeks before departure.

their European Health Insurance Card. In the UK, application forms for such cards are available from any branch of the Department of Health (www.dh.gov.uk). In addition, citizens of certain other countries, including Bulgaria, Croatia, Macedonia and Romania, are guaranteed emergency medical assistance or subsequent treatment provided they submit the appropriate documentation. Citizens of other countries should check with their Ministry of Health or equivalent before setting out. Everyone else is entitled to emergency medical treatment in Slovenia, but they must pay for it. Check the website of the Health Insurance Institute of Slovenia (www.zzzs.si) for more information.

If you do need health insurance while travelling (p279), we strongly advise you to consider a policy that covers you for the worst possible scenario, such as an accident requiring an ambulance or an emergency flight home.

INTERNET RESOURCES

The World Health Organisation's (WHO) online publication *International Travel and Health* is revised annually and is available at www.who.int/ith.

Other useful websites:
www.ageconcern.org.uk Advice on travel for the elderly.
www.fitfortravel.scot.nhs.uk General travel advice for the layperson.
www.mariestopes.org.uk Information on women's health and contraception.
www.mdtravelhealth.com Travel-health recommendations for every country; updated daily.

It's usually a good idea to consult your government's travel health website before departure, if one is available:

Australia (www.dfat.gov.au/travel/)
Canada (www.travelhealth.gc.ca)
UK (www.dh.gov.uk/home/fs/en)
USA (www.cdc.gov/travel/)

IN TRANSIT

DEEP VEIN THROMBOSIS (DVT)

Blood clots may form in the legs (deep vein thrombosis or DVT) during plane flights, chiefly because of prolonged immobility. The longer the flight, the greater the risk. The chief symptom of DVT is swelling or pain in the foot, ankle or calf, usually – but not always – on just one side. When a blood clot travels to the lungs, it may cause chest pain and breathing difficulties. Travellers with any of these symptoms should seek medical attention immediately.

To prevent the development of DVT on long flights, you should walk about the cabin, contract the leg muscles while sitting, drink plenty of fluids and avoid alcohol.

JET LAG & MOTION SICKNESS

To avoid jet lag, which is common when crossing more than five time zones, try drinking plenty of nonalchoholic fluids and eating light meals. Upon arrival, get exposure to natural sunlight and readjust your schedule (for meals, sleep and so on) as soon as possible.

Antihistamines such as dimenhydrinate (Dramamine) and meclizine (Antivert, Bonine) are usually the first choice for treating motion sickness. A herbal alternative is ginger.

IN SLOVENIA

AVAILABILITY & COST OF HEALTH CARE

Medical care in Slovenia corresponds to European standards and is good. Every large town or city has a *zdravstveni dom* (health centre) or *klinični center* (clinic) that operates from 7am to at least 7pm. Treatment at a public outpatient clinic costs little or nothing; doctors working privately will charge much more. Very roughly, a consultation in a Slovenian doctor's surgery costs from €20.

Pharmacies are usually open from 7am to 8pm, and at least one in each community is open round the clock. A sign on the door of any *lekarna* (pharmacy) will help you find the nearest 24-hour one.

INFECTIOUS DISEASES

Lyme Disease

A tick-transmitted infection that is not unknown in Central and Eastern Europe, the illness usually begins with a spreading rash at the site of the tick bite. It is accompanied by fever, headache, extreme fatigue, aching joints and muscles, and mild neck stiffness. If untreated, these symptoms usually resolve over several weeks, but over subsequent weeks or months disorders of the nervous system, heart and joints might develop.

Poliomyelitis

This disease is spread through contaminated food and water. Children are vaccinated against it, but vaccination should be boosted every 10 years, either orally (a drop on the tongue) or as an injection.

Rabies

Contracted through bites or licks on broken skin from an infected animal, Rabies is always fatal unless treated. Three injections are needed over a month. If you have not been vaccinated and have been bitten, you will need a course of five injections starting within 24 hours or as soon as possible after the injury. If you have been vaccinated, you will need fewer injections and will have more time to seek medical help.

Tickborne Encephalitis

Another condition spread by tick bites, this is a serious infection of the brain. Vaccination is advised for those in risk areas – parts of Central and Eastern Europe, including Slovenia – who are unable to avoid tick bites (such as campers, forestry workers and ramblers). Two doses of vaccine will give a year's protection, three doses up to three years'. For up-to-date information, log on to www.masta.org/tickalert.

Typhoid & Hepatitis A

These are spread through contaminated food (particularly shellfish) and water. Typhoid can cause septicaemia; hepatitis A causes liver inflammation and jaundice. Neither is usually fatal, but recovery can be prolonged. Typhoid

HEALTH

vaccine (typhim Vi, typherix) will give protection for three years. In some countries, the oral vaccine Vivotif is also available. Hepatitis A vaccine (Avaxim, VAQTA, Havrix) is given as an injection; a single dose will give protection for up to a year, a booster after a year gives 10 years' protection. Hepatitis A and typhoid vaccines can also be given as a single-dose vaccine, hepatyrix or viatim.

ENVIRONMENTAL HAZARDS
Insect Bites & Stings
Mosquitoes are found in most parts of Europe; they might not carry malaria but can still cause irritation and infected bites. Just make sure you're armed with a DEET-based *prašek* (insect repellent) and wear long-sleeved shirts and long trousers around sundown.

Bees and wasps cause real problems only to those with a severe allergy (anaphylaxis) If you have a severe allergy to bee or wasp stings carry an 'epipen' or similar adrenaline injection.

Water
If you are hiking or camping in Slovenia's mountains and are unsure about the water, the simplest way of purifying it is to boil it for 10 minutes. Chlorine tablets will kill many pathogens. Iodine is more effective and is available in tablet form. Follow the directions carefully, and remember that too much iodine can be harmful.

TRAVELLING WITH CHILDREN
All travellers with children should know how to treat minor ailments and when to seek medical treatment. Make sure the children are up to date with routine vaccinations, and discuss possible travel vaccines well before departure as some vaccines are not suitable for children younger than a year.

Children should be encouraged to avoid and mistrust any dogs or other mammals because of the risk of rabies and other diseases. Any bite, scratch or lick from a warm-blooded, furry animal should immediately be thoroughly cleaned. If there is any possibility that the animal is infected with rabies, immediate medical assistance should be sought.

WOMEN'S HEALTH
If using oral contraceptives, remember that some antibiotics, diarrhoea and vomiting can stop the pill from working and lead to the risk of pregnancy. Time zones, gastrointestinal upsets and antibiotics do not affect injectable contraception.

Travelling during pregnancy is usually possible but always consult your doctor before planning your trip. The riskiest times for travel are during the first 12 weeks of pregnancy and after 30 weeks.

SEXUAL HEALTH
Emergency contraception is most effective if taken within 24 hours after unprotected sex. The International Planned Parent Federation (www.ippf.org) can advise about the availability of contraception in different countries.

When buying condoms, look for a European CE mark, which means they have been rigorously tested, and then keep them in a cool dry place; otherwise they might crack and split.

Language

CONTENTS

Slovene is the official language of the Republic of Slovenia. The forebears of today's Slovenians brought the language, with its roots in the Slavonic language, from their original homeland beyond the Carpathian Mountains.

The French novelist Charles Nodier (1780–1844), who lived and worked in Ljubljana for a couple of years in the early 19th century, once wrote that Slovenia was like 'an Academy of Arts and Sciences' because of the people's flair for speaking foreign languages. Monsieur Nodier would be happy to know that Slovenci still have that talent almost two centuries down the track.

Virtually everyone in Slovenia speaks at least one other language. Around 90% speak Croatian and Serbian, 45% speak German, 37% are conversant in English and 17% speak Italian.

German, once the language of education and the elite, is generally spoken only by older Slovenians these days, mostly in Koroška, Štajerska and northern Gorenjska. There may be fewer speakers of English than German overall, but it is definitely the preferred language of the young, with the vast majority of all students claiming some knowledge of it. Most speak English very well indeed, even if they pepper their speech with the odd bit of 'Slovenglish' slang, like 'full cool', meaning 'trendy' or 'fashionable'. Italian is really only useful in Primorska and small parts of Notranjska.

The fact that you'll rarely have difficulty making yourself understood and that you'll probably never 'need' Slovene shouldn't stop you from learning a few words and phrases of this rich and wonderful language. More than anything else, Slovene has kept the Slovenian *narod* (nation) alive and united as a culture over centuries of domination and brutality, so any effort on your part to speak it will be rewarded a hundred-fold.

PRONUNCIATION

No sounds in Slovene are difficult for a speaker of English to learn. The Slovenian alphabet consists of 25 letters. Each letter generally represents only one sound, with very few exceptions.

Vowels

a   as the 'u' in 'cut'
e   as the 'a' in 'hat'; as the 'e' in 'they'; when unstressed, as the 'a' in 'ago'
i   short, as in 'ink'; long as in 'marine' (written as **ee** in the pronunciation guides)
o   as in 'off'; also as in 'or' (written as **aw** in the pronunciation guides)
u   as in 'put' (written as **oo** in the pronunciation guides)

Consonants

c   as the 'ts' in 'cats' (written as **ts** in the pronunciation guides)
č   as the 'ch' in 'chip' (written as **ch** in the pronunciation guides)
g   as in 'gold'
j   as the 'y' in 'yellow' (written as **y** in the pronunciation guides)
r   a rolled 'r'
š   as the 'sh' in 'ship' (written as **sh** in the pronunciation guides)
ž   as the 's' in 'pleasure' (written as **zh** in the pronunciation guides)

Stress

Slovene has no fixed rule for word stress, so it simply has to be learned case by case.

LANGUAGE

We've made things easier for you in our pronunciation guides by marking the stressed syllable in italics.

ACCOMMODATION
I'm looking for a/the ...
Iščem ...   eesh·chem ...
   camping ground
   kamping   kam·ping
   guesthouse
   gostišče   gos·teesh·che
   hotel
   hotel   ho·tel
   manager/owner
   direktor/lastnik   de·rek·tor/last·neek
   youth hostel
   počitniški dom   po·cheet·neesh·kee dom

What's the address?
Kako je naslov?   ka·ko ye na·slaw?
Please write it down.
Prosim, napišite naslov.   pro·seem, na·pee·she·te na·slaw

I'd like a ...
Rad/Rada bi ... (m/f)   rad/ra·da bee ...
Do you have a ...?
Ali imate prosto ...?   a·lee ee·ma·te pro·sto ...?
   bed
   posteljo   po·stal·yo
   cheap room
   poceni sobo   po·tse·nee so·bo
   single room
   enoposteljno sobo   en·no·po·stel·no so·bo
   double room
   dvoposteljno sobo   dvo·po·stel·no so·bo
   room with a bathroom
   sobo z kopalnico   so·bo z ko·pal·nee·tso

I'd like to share a dorm.
Rad/Rada bi delil/a spalnico. (m/f)
rad/ra·da bee de·lee/lee·la spal·nee·ko

How much is it ...?
Koliko stane ...?   ko·lee·ko sta·ne ...?
   per night
   na noč   na noch
   per person
   po osebi   po o·se·bee

Is breakfast included?
Ali je zajtrk vključen?
a·lee ye zay·trk oo·klyoo·chen?
May I see the room?
Lahko vidim sobo?
lah·ko vee·deem so·bo?

Where is the bathroom?
Kje je kopalnica?
kye ye ko·pal·nee·ca?
Where's the toilet?
Kje je stranišče/WC?
kye ye stra·neesh·che/ve·tse?
I'm/We're leaving today.
Danes odhajam/odhajamo.
da·nes od·ha·yam/od·ha·ya·mo

CONVERSATION & ESSENTIALS
Good day/Hello.
Dober dan.   do·br dan
Hi.
Pozdravljeni (pol)/   poz·drav·lye·nee/
Pozdravljen. (inf)   poz·drav·lyen
Goodbye.
Nasvidenje.   nas·vee·da·nye
Please.
Prosim.   pro·seem
Thank you (very much).
Hvala (lepa).   hva·la (le·pa)
You're welcome. (Don't mention it.)
Dobrodošli. (Ni za kaj.)   do·bro·do·shlee! (nee za kay)
Yes.
Da/Ja. (pol/inf)   da/ya
No.
Ne.   ne
Excuse me.
Dovolite mi, prosim.   do·vo·lee·te mee, pro·seem
Sorry. (forgive me.)
Oprostite. (pol)   o·pro·stee·te
Oprosti. (inf)   o·pro·stee
What's your name?
Kako vam je ime? (pol)   ka·ko vam ye ee·me?
Kako ti je ime? (inf)   ka·ko tee ye ee·me?
My name's ...
Jaz sem ...   yas sam ...

Where are you from?
Od kod ste? od *kot* ste?
I'm from ...
Sem iz ... sam eez ...
May I?
Ali lahko? *a*·lee lah·*ko*?
No problem.
Brez problema. brez pro·*ble*·ma
I like (to do something).
Rad/Rada bi ... (m/f) rad/*ra*·da bee ...
I like (something).
Imam rad/rada ... (m/f) mam *rad/ra*·da ...
I don't like ...
Ne maram ... ne *ma*·ram ...

brother	*brat*	brat
daughter	*hči*	hchee
father	*oče*	*o*·che
husband	*mož*	mozh
mother	*mama*	*ma*·ma
sister	*sestra*	sas·tra
son	*sin*	seen
wife	*žena*	*zha*·na

DIRECTIONS
Where is ...?
Kje je ...? kye ye ...?
How do I get to ...?
Kako pridem do ...? ka·*ko* pree·dam do ...?
Is it near/far?
Ali je blizu/daleč? a·lee ye *blee*·zoo/*da*·lach?
(Go) straight ahead.
(Pojdite) naravnost (poy·*dee*·te) na·*raw*·nost
naprej. na·*pray*

(Turn) left/right at ...
(Obrnite) levo/desno pri ...
(o·*br*·nee·te) *le*·vo/*des*·no pree ...
  the corner
  vogalu vo·*ga*·loo
  the traffic lights
  semaforju se·ma·*for*·yoo

far (from)	*daleč (od)*	*da*·lech (od)
near (to)	*blizu (do)*	*blee*·zoo (do)
in front of	*spredaj*	*spre*·day
behind	*za (zadaj)*	za (*za*·day)
opposite	*nasproti*	nas·*pro*·tee
here/there	*tu/tam*	too/tam
north	*sever*	*se*·ver
south	*jug*	yoog
east	*vzhod*	ooz·*hod*
west	*zahod*	za·*hod*
beach	*plaža*	*pla*·zha
bridge	*most*	most

SIGNS

Informacije	Information
Izhod	Exit
Odprto/Zaprto	Open/Closed
Postaja	Station
Prepovedano	Prohibited
Vhod	Entrance
Železniška Blagajna	Ticket Office (Train)
Avtobusno Postajališče	Bus Stop
Carina	Customs
Proste Sobe	Rooms Available
Zasedeno	Full (No Vacancies)
Policija	Police
Stranišče	Toilets
Moški	Men
Ženske	Women

castle	*grad*	grad
cathedral	*stolnica*	*stol*·nee·tsa
church	*cerkev*	*tser*·koo
hospital	*bolnišnica*	bol·*neesh*·nee·tsa
lake	*jezero*	*ye*·ze·ro
main square	*glavni trg*	*glaw*·nee terg
market	*tržnica*	*terzh*·nee·tsa
palace	*palača*	pa·*la*·cha
ruins	*ruševine*	roo·she·*vee*·ne
tower	*stolp*	stolp

HEALTH
I'm sick.
Bolan/Bolna sem. (m/f) bo·*lan*/*baw*·na sam
Where's the nearest doctor?
Kje je najbližji kye ye nay·*bleezh*·yee
zdravnik? zdraw·*neek*?
Where's the nearest hospital?
Kje je najbližja bolnica? kye ye nay·*bleezh*·ya bol·nee·tsa?
I'm diabetic/epileptic/asthmatic.
Sem diabetik/epileptik/ sam dee·ya·*be*·teek/a·pee·*lep*·teek/
astmatik. ast·*ma*·teek
It hurts here.
Tukaj boli. *too*·kay bo·*lee*

I'm allergic to ...
Alergičen sem na ...
a·*ler*·gee·chen sem na ...
  penicillin
  penicilin pe·nee·tsee·*leen*
  antibiotics
  antibiotike an·tee·bee·*o*·tee·ke
  nuts
  orehe o·*re*·he
  peanuts
  kikiriki kee·kee·*ree*·kee

LANGUAGE

EMERGENCIES

Help!
Na pomoč!   na po·*moch*!
There's been an accident!
Nesreča se je zgodila!   ne·*sre*·cha se ye zgo·*dee*·la!
I'm lost.
Izgubil/a sem se. (m/f) eez·goo·*beel*/*bee*·la sam se
Could you please help me?
Mi lahko pomagate?   mee *lah*·ko po·*ma*·ga·te?
Go away!
Pojdite stran!   poy·*dee*·te stran!

Call ...!	*Pokličite ...!*	po·*klee*·chee·te ...!
a doctor	*zdravnika*	*zdraw*·*nee*·ka
the police	*policijo*	po·lee·*tsee*·yo

antiseptic	*antiseptik/ razkužilo*	an·tee·*sep*·teek/ raz·koo·*zhee*·lo
aspirin	*aspirin*	as·pee·*reen*
condoms	*kondomi*	kon·*do*·mee
contraceptive	*kontraceptivno sredstvo*	kon·tra·tsep·*teev*·no *sret*·stvo
diarrhoea	*driska*	*drees*·ka
medicine	*zdravilo*	zdra·*vee*·lo
nausea	*slabost*	sla·*bost*
sunblock cream	*krema za sončenje*	*kre*·ma za *son*·chan·ye
tampons	*tamponi*	tam·*po*·nee

LANGUAGE DIFFICULTIES

Do you speak English?
Govorite angleško?
go·vo·*ree*·te an·*glesh*·ko?
Does anyone here speak English?
Ali kdo tukaj govori angleško?
a·lee gdo *too*·kay go·vo·*ree* an·*glesh*·ko?
I understand.
Razumem.
ra·*zoo*·mem
I (don't) understand.
(Ne) razumem.
(ne) ra·*zoo*·mem
Could you repeat that, please?
Lahko ponovite?
lah·ko po·no·*vee*·te?
Could you write it down, please?
Lahko to napišete?
lah·ko to na·*pee*·she·te?
Can you show me (on the map)?
Mi lahko pokažete (na mapi)?
mee lah·*ko* po·*ka*·zhe·te (na *ma*·pee)?
How do you say ... (in Slovene)?
Kako se reče ... (na slovenskem)?
ka·*ko* se *ra*·che ... (na slo·ven·skem)

What does ... mean?
Kaj ... pomeni?
kay ... po·*me*·nee?

NUMBERS

0	*nula*	*noo*·la
1	*en/ena* (m/f)	en/*en*·na
2	*dva/dve* (m/f)	dva/dve
3	*trije/tri* (m/f)	*tree*·je/tree
4	*štirje/štiri* (m/f)	*shtee*·ree·ye/*shtee*·ree
5	*pet*	pet
6	*šest*	shest
7	*sedem*	se·*dem*
8	*osem*	*o*·sem
9	*devet*	de·*vet*
10	*deset*	de·*set*
11	*enajst*	en·*nayst*
12	*dvanajst*	dva·*nayst*
13	*trinajst*	tree·*nayst*
14	*štirinajst*	shtee·ree·*nayst*
15	*petnajst*	pet·na·yest
16	*šestnajst*	shest·*nayst*
17	*sedemnajst*	se·dem·*nayst*
18	*osemnajst*	o·sem·*nayst*
19	*devetnajst*	de·vet·*nayst*
20	*dvajset*	dvay·set
21	*enaindvajset*	e·na·een·dvay·set
22	*dvaindvajset*	dva·een·dvay·set
30	*trideset*	tree·de·set
40	*štirideset*	shtee·ree·de·set
50	*petdeset*	pet·de·set
60	*šestdeset*	shest·de·set
70	*sedemdeset*	se·dem·de·set
80	*osemdeset*	o·sem·de·set
90	*devetdeset*	de·vet·de·set
100	*sto*	sto
101	*sto ena*	sto en·na
110	*sto deset*	sto de·*set*
1000	*tisoč*	*tee*·soch

PAPERWORK

date/place of birth	*datum/kraj rojstva*	*da*·toom/kray *roy*·stva
given name	*ime*	ee·*me*
male/female	*moški/ženska*	*mosh*·kee/zhen·ska
nationality	*državljanstvo*	dr·zhav·*lyan*·stvo
passport	*potni list*	*pot*·nee leest
surname	*priimek*	pree·*ee*·mek

QUESTION WORDS

Who?	*Kdo?*	kdo?
What?	*Kaj?*	kay?
What is it?	*Kaj je to?*	kay ye to?
When?	*Kdaj?*	gday?
Where?	*Kje?*	kye?

Which?	*Kateri/ra?* (m/f)	ka·*te*·ree/ra?
Why?	*Zakaj?*	za·*kay*?
How?	*Kako?*	ka·*ko*?
How much/ many?	*Koliko?*	ko·*lee*·ko?

SHOPPING & SERVICES

I'm looking for a/the ...
Iščem ... — eesh·chem ...

Where is a/the ...?
Kje je ...? — kye ye ...?

bank
banka — ban·ka

bookshop
knjigarna — kn'ee·*gar*·na

chemist
lekarna — le·*kar*·na

church
cerkev — tser·koo

city centre
središče mesta — sre·*deesh*·che *mes*·ta

consulate
konzulat — kon·zoo·*lat*

embassy
ambasada — am·ba·*sa*·da

exchange office
menjalnica — men·*yal*·nee·tsa

grocery store
špecerija — shpe·tse·*ree*·ya

hospital
bolnica — bol·*nee*·tsa

laundry/laundrette
pralnica — pral·nee·tsa

market
tržnica — trzh·nee·tsa

museum
muzej — moo·*zey*

newsagency
časopisni kiosk — cha·so·*pees*·nee *kee*·yosk

police
policija — po·lee·*tsee*·ya

post office
pošta — posh·ta

public phone
javni telefon — yav·nee te·le·*fon*

public toilet
javno stranišče — yav·no stra·*neesh*·che

restaurant
restavracija — rest·taw·*ra*·tsee·ya

supermarket
samopostrežba — sa·mo·pos·*trezh*·ba

telephone centre
telefonska centrala — te·le·*fon*·ska tsen·*tra*·la

tourist office
turistični urad — too·*rees*·teech·nee oo·*rad*

What time does it open/close?
Kdaj se odpre/zapre? — gday se od·*pre*/za·*pre*?

I'd like to buy ...
Rad bi kupil/kupila ... — rad bee *koo*·poo/koo·*pee*·la ...

I'm just looking.
Samo gledam. — sa·*mo gle*·dam

How much is it?
Koliko stane? — ko·*lee*·ko *sta*·ne?

I don't like it.
Ni mi všeč. — nee mee oo·*shech*

It's too expensive for me.
Predrago je zame. — pra·*dra*·go ye za·me

It's cheap. (ie good value)
Poceni je. — po·*tse*·nee ye

May I look at it?
Ali lahko pogledam? — a·lee lah·*ko* po·*gle*·dam?

I'll take it.
Kupil/Kupila bom. (m/f) — koo·poo/koo·*pee*·la bom

more	*več*	vech
less	*manj*	man
bigger	*večje*	vech·ye
smaller	*manjše*	man·she

I'd like to change some ...
Rad bi zamenjal nekaj ...
rad bee za·men·yaw ne·kay ...

money
denarja — dan·*nar*·ya

travellers cheques
potovalnih čekov — po·to·*val*·neeh *che*·kaw

Do you accept credit cards?
Ali vzamete kreditne karte?
a·lee oo·*za*·me·te kre·*deet*·ne *kar*·te?

I want to make a telephone call.
Rad bi telefoniral. (m)
Rada bi telefonirala. (f)
rad bee te·le·fon·*nee*·ra·oo
ra·da bee te·le·fon·*nee*·ra·la

Where can I get Internet access?
Kje lahko pridem do interneta?
kye lah·*ko* pree·dem do *een*·ter·ne·ta?

TIME & DATES

What time is it?
Koliko je ura? — ko·*lee*·ko ye *oo*·ra?

It's ...
Ura je ... — *oo*·ra ye ...

(eight) o'clock
osem — *o*·sem

(one) o'clock
ena — en·na

seven thirty
pol osem — pol *o*·sem

a quarter to (hour)
četrt do (...) che·trt do (...)
a quarter past (hour)
(...) in četrt (...) een che·trt

in the morning	*zjutraj*	zyoot·ray
in the evening	*zvečer*	zve·cher
today	*danes*	da·nes
tonight	*nocoj*	no·tsoy
tomorrow	*jutri*	yoo·tree
yesterday	*včeraj*	oo·cher·ray

Monday	*ponedeljek*	po·ne·del·yek
Tuesday	*torek*	to·rek
Wednesday	*sreda*	sre·da
Thursday	*četrtek*	che·trt·tek
Friday	*petek*	pe·tek
Saturday	*sobota*	so·bo·ta
Sunday	*nedelja*	ne·del·ya

January	*januar*	ya·noo·ar
February	*februar*	fe·broo·ar
March	*marec*	ma·rets
April	*april*	a·preel
May	*maj*	may
June	*junij*	yoo·nee
July	*julij*	yoo·lee
August	*avgust*	aw·goost
September	*september*	sep·tem·ber
October	*oktober*	ok·to·ber
November	*november*	no·vem·ber
December	*december*	de·tsem·ber

TRANSPORT
Public Transport
What time does the ... leave?
Kdaj odpelje ...? gday od·pel·ye ...?
boat/ferry
ladja/trajekt la·dya/tra·yekt
bus
avtobus a·oo·to·boos
plane
avion a·vee·on
train
vlak vlak

I want to go to ...
Želim iti ...
zhe·leem ee·tee ...
Can you tell me when we get to ...?
Mi lahko poveste kdaj pridemo ...?
mee lah·ko po·ves·te gday pree·de·mo ...?
The train has been delayed.
Vlak ima zamudo.
vlak ee·ma za·moo·do

The train has been cancelled.
Ta vlak je odpovedan.
ta vlak ye od·po·ve·dan
Stop here, please.
Ustavite tukaj, prosim.
oos·ta·vee·te too·kay, pro·seem
How long does the trip take?
Koliko traja potovanje?
ko·lee·ko tra·ya po·to·van·ye?
Do I need to change?
Ali moram presesti?
a·lee mo·ram pre·ses·tee?

one way	*ena smer*	en·na smer
return	*povratna*	pov·rat·na
1st class	*prvi razred*	pr·vee raz·red
2nd class	*drugi razred*	droo·gee raz·red
the first	*prvi*	pree·vee
the last	*zadnji*	zad·nee

platform number
številka kolodvora shte·veel·ka ko·lo·dvo·ra
ticket office
prodaja vozovnic pro·da·ya vo·zov·neets
timetable
spored spo·red
train station
železniška postaja zhe·lez·neesh·ka pos·ta·ya
bus station
avtobusno postajališče aw·to·boos·no po·sta·ya·leesh·che

Private Transport
I'd like to hire a ...
Rad bi najel ... (m) rad bee na·ye·oo ...
Rada bi najela ... (f) rada bee na·ye·la ...
bicycle
kolo ko·lo
car
avto a·oo·to
4WD
terenski avto te·ren·skee a·oo·to
guide
vodiča vo·dee·cha
horse
konja ko·nya
motorcyle
motorno kolo mo·tor·no ko·lo

Is this the road to ...?
Ali je to cesta za ...? a·lee ye to tses·ta za ...?
Where's a service station?
Kje je pumpa? kye ye poom·pa?

ROAD SIGNS

Dajte Prednost	Give Way
Nevarnost	Danger
Prepovedano Parkiranje	No Parking
Obvoz	Detour
Vhod	Entry
Cestnina	Toll
Vozite Počasi	Slow Down
Prepovedan Vhod	No Entry
Ena Smer	One Way
Izhod	Exit
Prepovedano Vstavljanje	Keep Clear

Please fill it up.
Napolnite prosim.   na-*pol*-nee-te *pro*-seem
I'd like ... litres.
Prosim ... litrov.   *pro*-seem ... *leet*-raw
diesel
dizel   dee-zel
leaded petrol
benzin z svincem   ben-*zeen* z *sveen*-tsem
unleaded petrol
benzin brez svinca   ben-*zeen* brez sveen-tsa
(How long) Can I park here?
(Koliko časa) lahko   *(ko*-lee-ko *cha*-sa) lah-*ko*
tukaj parkiram?   *too*-kay par-*kee*-ram?
Where do I pay?
Kje plačam?   kye *pla*-cham?

Car Trouble

I need a mechanic.
Potrebujem mehanika.   po-tre-*boo*-yem me-*ha*-nee-ka
The car/motorbike has broken down (at ...)
Avto/motor se je pokvaril (pri ...)
a-oo-to/mo-*tor* se ye pok-*va*-reel (pree ...)
The car/motorbike won't start.
Avto/motor noče vžgati.
a-oo-to/mo-*tor* no-che oozh-*ga*-tee
I have a flat tyre.
Zračnica mi je počila.
zra-chnee-tsa mee ye po-chee-la

I've run out of petrol.
Nimam več benzina.
nee-mam vech ben-zee-na
I've had an accident.
Imel/Imela sem nesrečo. (m/f)
ee-*me*-oo/ee-*me*-la sem ne-*sre*-cho

TRAVEL WITH CHILDREN

Is there a/an ...?
Ali tukaj obstoja ...?
a-lee *too*-kay ob-*sto*-ya ...?
I need a ...
Potrebujem ...
po-tre-*boo*-yem ...
  baby change room
  prostor za previjanje   *pro*-stor za pre-*vee*-yan-ye
  dojenčka   do-*yench*-ka
  car baby seat
  sedež za dojenčka   se-dezh za do-*yench*-ka
  child-minding service
  nekoga da mi čuva   ne-ko-ga da mee *choo*-va
  otroka   ot-*ro*-ka
  children's menu
  otroški meni   ot-*rosh*-kee me-*nee*
  disposable nappies/diapers
  papirnate plenice   pa-*peer*-na-te ple-*nee*-tse
  infant milk formula
  formula za dojenčke   *for*-moo-la za do-*yench*-ke
  (English-speaking) babysitter
  otroško varovalko   ot-*rosh*-ko va-ro-*val*-ko
  (ki govori angleško)   (kee go-vo-*ree* an-*glesh*-sko)
  highchair
  visoki stol   vee-*so*-kee staw
  potty
  kahlico   *kahl*-tso
  stroller/pusher
  otroški voziček   ot-*rosh*-kee vo-*zee*-chek

Do you mind if I breastfeed here?
A lahko tukaj dojim?   a lah-*ko too*-kay do-*yeem*?
Are children allowed?
Ali je dovoljeno za   *a*-lee ye do-*vol*-ye-no za
otroke?   ot-*ro*-ke?

LANGUAGE

Also available from Lonely Planet:
Fast Talk Slovene and *Eastern Europe Phrasebook*

Glossary

Can't find the word you're looking for here? Try the Language chapter (p299) or the Slovene–English Glossary in the Food & Drink chapter (p49).

AMZS – Avto-Moto Zveza Slovenije (Automobile Association of Slovenia)
avtocesta – motorway, highway

bife – snack and/or drinks bar
bivak – bivouac (basic shelter in the mountains)
breg – river bank
burja – bora (cold northeast wind from the Adriatic)

čaj – tea
čakalnica – waiting room (eg in station)
cena – price
cerkev – church
cesta – road (abbreviated c)

DDV – davek na dodano vrednost (value added tax, or VAT)
delovni čas – opening/business hours
dijaški dom – student dormitory, hostel
dolina – valley
dom – house; mountain cottage or lodge
drevored – avenue
dvorana – hall
dvorišče – courtyard

fijaker – horse-drawn carriage

gaj – grove, park
garderoba – left-luggage office, coat check
gledališče – theatre
gora – mountain
gostilna – innlike restaurant
gostišče – innlike restaurant usually with accommodation
gozd – forest, grove
grad – castle
greben – ridge, crest
GRS – Gorska Reševalna Služba (Mountain Rescue Service)
GZS – Geodetski Zavod Slovenije (Geodesic Institute of Slovenia)

Hallstatt – early Iron Age Celtic culture (800–500 BC)
hiša – house
hrib – hill

izhod – exit
izvir – source (of a river, stream etc)

jama – cave
jedilni list – menu
jezero – lake
jug – south

Karst – limestone region of underground rivers and caves in Primorska
kavarna – coffee shop, café
klet – cellar
knjigarna – bookshop
knjižnica – library
koča – mountain cottage or hut
kosilo – lunch
kot – glacial valley, corner
kotlina – basin
kozolec – hayrack distinct to Slovenia
kras – karst
krčma – drinks bar (sometimes with food)

La Tène – late Iron Age culture (450–390 BC)
lekarna – pharmacy
LPP – Ljubljanski Potniški Promet (Ljubljana city bus network)

mali (m) **mala** (f) **malo** (n) – little
malica – midmorning snack
menjalnica – private currency exchange office
mesto – town
morje – sea
moški – men (toilet)
most – bridge
muzej – museum

na – on
nabrežje – embankment
narod – nation
naselje – colony, development, estate
nasip – dike, embankment
novi (m) **nova** (f) **novo** (n)– new

občina – administrative division; county or commune
obvoz – detour (road sign)
obvoznica – ring road, bypass
odhod – departure
odprto – open
okrepčevalnica – snack bar

Osvobodilne Fronte (OF) – Anti-Fascist Liberation Front during WWII
otok – island

panjska končnica – beehive panel painted with Slovenian folk motifs
peron – train-station platform
pivnica – pub, beer hall
pivo – beer
planina – Alpine pasture
planota – plateau
pod – under, below
podhod – pedestrian underpass (subway)
polje – collapsed limestone area under cultivation
pot – trail
potok – stream
potovanje – travel
prazniki – holidays
prehod – passage, crossing
prekop – canal
prenočišče – accommodation
prevoz – transport
pri – at, near, by
prihod – arrival
PZS – Planinska Zveza Slovenije (Alpine Association of Slovenia)

regija – province, region
reka – river
restavracija – restaurant
rini – push (door)
rob – escarpment, edge

samopostrežna restavracija – self-service restaurant
samostan – monastery
Secessionism – art and architectural style similar to Art Nouveau
sedežnica – chairlift
sedlo – pass, saddle
sever – north
SIT – international currency code for tolar, Slovenia's currency from 1992 to 2007
skanzen – open-air museum displaying village architecture
slaščičarna – shop selling ice cream, sweets
smučanje – skiing
SNTO – Slovenska Nacionalna Turistična Organizacija (Slovenian Tourist Board)
sobe – rooms (available)
soteska – ravine, gorge
sprehajališče – walkway, promenade
star(i/a/o) – old
stena – wall, cliff
steza – path

stolp – tower
štruklji – dumplings
Sv – Saint
SŽ – Slovenske Železnice (Slovenian Railways)

terme – Italian word for 'spa' used frequently in Slovenia
TIC – Tourist Information Centre
TNP – Triglavski Narodni Park (Triglav National Park)
toplar – double-linked hayrack unique to Slovenia
toplice – spa
trg – square

ulica – street (abbreviated ul)

vas – village
večerja – dinner, supper
veliki (m) **velika** (f) **veliko** (n) – great, big
vhod – entrance
vila – villa
vinoteka – wine bar
vinska cesta – wine road
vinska klet – wine cellar
vleci – pull (door)
vozni red – timetable
vozovnica – ticket
vrata – gate
vrh – summit, peak
vrt – garden, park
vrtača – sinkhole
vzhod – east
vzpenjača – cable car, gondola

zahod – west
zaprto – closed
zavetišče – mountain 'refuge' with refreshments and sometimes accommodation
zdravilišče – health resort, spa
zdravstveni dom – medical centre, clinic
žegnanje – a patron's festival at a church or chapel
ženske – women (toilet)
žičnica – cable car
zidanica – a cottage in one of the wine-growing regions
znamenje – wayside religious shrine

ALTERNATIVE PLACE NAMES
Abbreviations
(C) Croatian, (Cz) Czech, (E) English, (G) German, (H) Hungarian, (I) Italian, (P) Polish

Avstrija – Austria (E), Österreich (G)

Beljak – Villach (G)
Benetke – Venice (E), Venezia (I)

Bizeljsko – Wisell (G)
Bohinj – Wochain (G)
Brežice – Rhain (G)
Budimpešta – Budapest (H)

Čedad – Cividale (I)
Celovec – Klagenfurt (G)
Celje – Cilli (G)
Cerknica – Cirkniz (G)
Črna Gora – Montenegro (E)
Črnomelj – Tschernembl (G)

Dolenjska – Lower Carniola (E)
Dunaj – Vienna (E), Wien (G)

Gorenjska – Upper Carniola (E)
Gorica – Gorizia (I)
Gradec – Graz (G)
Gradež – Grado (I)

Hrvaška – Croatia (E), Hrvatska (C)

Idrija – Ydria (G)
Istra – Istria (E)
Italija – Italy (E), Italia (I)
Izola – Isola (I)

Jadran, Jadransko Morje – Adriatic Sea (E)

Kamnik – Stein (G)
Kobarid – Caporetto (I)
Koper – Capodistria (I)
Koroška – Carinthia (E), Kärnten (G)
Kostanjevica – Landstrass (G)
Kranj – Krainburg (G)
Kranjska – Carniola (E), Krain (G)
Kras – Karst (E)
Kropa – Cropp (G)
Krnski Grad – Karnburg (G)

Lendava – Lendva (H)
Lipnica – Leibnitz (G)
Ljubljana – Laibach (G), Liubliana (I)

Madžarska – Hungary (E), Magyarország (H)
Metlika – Möttling (G)

Milje – Muggia (I)
Murska Sobota – Muraszombat (H)

Notranjska – Inner Carniola (E)
Nova Gorica – Gorizia (I), Görz (G)

Otočec – Wördl (G)
Oglej – Aquileia (I)

Piran – Pirano (I)
Pleterje – Pletariach (G)
Pliberk – Bleiburg (G)
Portorož – Portorose (I)
Postojna – Adelsberg (G)
Praga – Prague (E), Praha (Cz)
Ptuj – Pettau (G)

Radgona – Bad Radkersburg (G)
Radovljica – Ratmansdorf (G)
Reka – Rijeka (C), Fiume (I)
Ribnica – Reiffniz (G)
Rim – Rome (E), Roma (I)
Rogaška Slatina – Rohitsch-Sauerbrunn (G)
Rosalnice – Rosendorf (G)

Seča – Sezza (I) Peninsula
Sečovlje – Sicciole (I)
Škocjan – San Canziano (I)
Štajerska – Styria (E), Steiermark (G)
Soča – Isonzo (I)
Srbija – Serbia (E)
Sredozemlje – Mediterranean (E)
Sredozemsko Morje – Mediterranean Sea (E)
Štajerska – Styria (E), Steiermark (G)
Stična – Sittich (G)
Strunjan – Strugnano (I)

Trbiž – Tarvisio (I)
Trst – Trieste (I)
Tržaški Zaliv – Gulf of Trieste (E), Golfo di Trieste (I)
Tržič – Monfalcone (I)

Varšava – Warsaw (E), Warszawa (P)
Videm – Udine (I)
Vinica – Weinitz (G)

Železna Kapla – Eisenkappel (G)

Behind the Scenes

THIS BOOK
This 5th edition of Lonely Planet's Slovenia was written by Steve Fallon. Steve also wrote the 4th, 2nd and the 1st edition, the first ever English-language guidebook to the country. Neil Wilson wrote the 3rd edition. The Health chapter was adapted from material written by Dr Caroline Evans. This guidebook was commissioned in Lonely Planet's London office and was produced by the following:

Commissioning Editors Fiona Buchan, Alan Murphy, William Gourlay
Coordinating Editor Stephanie Ong
Coordinating Cartographer Valentina Kremenchutskaya
Coordinating Layout Designer Yvonne Bischofberger
Assisting Layout Designer Evelyn Yee
Managing Editors Barbara Delissen, Geoff Howard
Managing Cartographer Mark Griffiths
Assisting Editors Simon Williamson, Sally O'Brien
Assisting Cartographers Andy Rojas, Katie Cason, Vicki-Ann Dimas
Cover Designer Rebecca Dandens
Project Manager Sarah Sloane
Language Content Coordinator Quentin Frayne

Thanks to Trent Paton, Gennifer Ciavarra, Kate Whitfield, Kate McLeod, Louise Clarke, Lyahna Spencer, Sally Darmody, Celia Wood

THANKS
STEVE FALLON
A number of people assisted in the research and writing of *Slovenia*, in particular my two very dear friends Verica Leskovar and Tatjana Radovič at the Ljubljana Tourist Board. Others to whom I'd like to say *najlepša hvala* include Valburga Baričević of Hoteli Piran; Tjaša Borštnik of the Ljubljana Tourist Board; Dušan Brejc of the Commercial Union for Viticulture and Wine of Slovenia, Ljubljana; Jelena Dašič of the Bovec Tourist Information Centre; Majda Rozina Dolenc of the Slovenian Tourist Board, Ljubljana; Marino Fakin of Slovenian Railways, Ljubljana; Darjono Husodo and Maja Tratar-Husodo of the Antiq Hotel, Ljubljana; Aleš Hvala of the Hvala hotel, Kobarid; Lado Leskovar of UNICEF and RTV, Ljubljana; Vojko Anzeljc and Tone Plankar at the Ljubljana bus station; Aleksander Riznič of Radio Odeon, Črnomelj; Petra Stušek of the Ljubljana Tourist Board; Eva Štravs of the Bled Tourist Information Centre; Brigita Zorec of Ljubljana Aerodrom; and Olga Žvanut of Slovenian Railways, Ljubljana. Mark Mocicka of Melbourne showed me a few places even I hadn't seen before and I am most grateful.

As always, my efforts here are dedicated to my partner, Michael Rothschild, an 'honest man' at last.

OUR READERS
Many thanks to the travellers who used the last edition and wrote to us with helpful hints, useful advice and interesting anecdotes:

Sandra Ager, Sylvio Amaral, Matt Ashworth, Chelsea Bagnard, Peter Baloh, Marcia Bennett, Erik Blatnik, Lee Bone, Ravter Bostjan, Graeme Brock, NR Brookehouse, Vesna Bukilica, Elaine Cass, Simon Cerne, Michael Chambers, Rex & Judy Chisholm, Samantha Collett, Pete Cull, Kerec Darko, Trevor Davis, Megan

THE LONELY PLANET STORY
The story begins with a classic travel adventure: Tony and Maureen Wheeler's 1972 journey across Europe and Asia to Australia. There was no useful information about the overland trail then, so Tony and Maureen published the first Lonely Planet guidebook to meet a growing need.

From a kitchen table, Lonely Planet has grown to become the largest independent travel publisher in the world, with offices in Melbourne (Australia), Oakland (USA) and London (UK). Today Lonely Planet guidebooks cover the globe. There is an ever-growing list of books and information in a variety of media. Some things haven't changed. The main aim is still to make it possible for adventurous travellers to get out there – to explore and better understand the world.

At Lonely Planet we believe travellers can make a positive contribution to the countries they visit – if they respect their host communities and spend their money wisely. Every year 5% of company profit is donated to charities around the world.

Dean, George Dehnel, Lee Delahay, Rachel Derrico, Matthew Dewar, Oran Erster, Paul Fatt, Janet Fearnley, Charles Featherstone, Niki Gal, Ben Gilbert, Cora Gilbey, Jim Gilchrist, Vid Gorjan, Anna Grundy, Gareth Hamilton, Kay Harrison, Jeni Holmes, Louise Hope, Rok Jarc, Matic Jesensek, Joan Joesting-Mahoney, Ian Juniper, Matthew Keane, Steven Keen, Becky Klugiewicz, Mark Koltun, Jan Kotuc, Jasmina Kristan, Debra Leonard, David Lewis, Manja Lilek, Chris Louie, Anna Macarthur, Mirek Marut, Damjana Mavric, Mark Mocicka, Chuck Muckle, Beth Mylius, John Neander, Barbara Olsen, David Pabst, Rolf Palmberg, Randy Patton, Samo Pecovnik, Brian Philpott, Sarah Pitt, Angie & Andy Polkey, Brian Pozun, Lance Ringel, Dave Sears, Philip & Kayti Selbie, Marian Smith, Vic Sofras, Martin Stanley, Mads Stjernø, Bepi Tissi, Theresa & David Truskinger, Ivan Valencic, Yves Vandijck, Colin Vickers, Simon Vrecar, Peter Weller, Joachim Whaley, Rolf Wrelf, David Wright

SEND US YOUR FEEDBACK

We love to hear from travellers – your comments keep us on our toes and help make our books better. Our well-travelled team reads every word on what you loved or loathed about this book. Although we cannot reply individually to postal submissions, we always guarantee that your feedback goes straight to the appropriate authors, in time for the next edition. Each person who sends us information is thanked in the next edition – and the most useful submissions are rewarded with a free book.

To send us your updates – and find out about Lonely Planet events, newsletters and travel news – visit our award-winning website: **www.lonelyplanet.com/contact**.

Note: we may edit, reproduce and incorporate your comments in Lonely Planet products such as guidebooks, websites and digital products, so let us know if you don't want your comments reproduced or your name acknowledged. For a copy of our privacy policy visit www.lonelyplanet.com/privacy.

312

Index

Bel   Bela Krajina
Dol   Dolenjska
Gor   Gorenjska
Kor   Koroska
Lju   Ljubljana
Not   Notranjska
Pre   Prekmurje
Pri   Primorska
Sta   Stajerska

A
accommodation 44, 271-3, *see also* camping
activities 14, 273-4, *see also individual activities*
Adlešiči (Bel) 221
air pollution 42
air travel 286-8
    airlines 286-7
    airports 286-7
    to/from Australia 287
    to/from continental europe 287
    to/from the UK 287-8
    to/from the USA & Canada 288
    within Slovenia 291
alcohol 276
animals 41, *see also individual animals*
Aquileia (ancient city) 23
architecture 36-9
art galleries 73, *see also* museums
    Božidar Jakac Gallery (Dol) 210
    Kamen Gallery (Gor) 108
    Koroška Gallery of Fine Arts 261
    Lamut Art Salon (Dol) 209
    Miha Maleš Gallery (Gor) 94
    National Gallery (Lju) 73-4
Art Nouveau, *see* Secessionist
arts 33-9
ATMs 280
Attila 21
attractions 14

000 Map pages
000 Photograph pages

B
ballooning 47
basketball 33
bears, brown 41
beehives 106, 107, 283
beer 52, 75
begging 276
Bela Krajina 192, 215-22, **215**
Belgrade 29-30
Beltinci (Pre) 18
billiards 76
bird-watching 48
Bizeljsko-Sremič wine district (Dol) 215
Blatnik, Andrej 35
Bled (Gor) 110-17, **111**
    accommodation 115-16
    attractions 112-13
    food 116-17
    travel to/from 117
Bled Island (Gor) 113, **155**
boating
    Bled (Gor) 114
    Bohinj (Gor) 121
    Ljubljana 76
    Otočec Ob Krki (Dol) 206
    Portorož (Pri) 177
Bogojina (Pre) 18
Bohinj (Gor) 118-24
books 13-14, *see also* literature
Bovec (Pri) 134-8, **135**, **157**
bowling 76
Brežice (Dol) 212-14, **213**
Brezje (Gor) 109
Bronze Age 21, 60
brown bears 41
Broz, Josip 27, *see* Tito
burek 53
bus travel 288
    to/from Croatia, Bosnia & Hercegovina, & Serbia 290
    to/from Germany, Austria & Czech Republic 290
    to/from Hungary 290-1
    to/from Italy 291
    within Slovenia 292
business hours 274

C
camping 271-2
Cankar, Ivan 26, 35

canoeing 46
    Bovec (Pri) 136-7
    Dolenjske Toplice (Dol) 201
    Kolpa Valley (Bel) 222
    Otočec Ob Krki (Dol) 206
    Žužemberk (Dol) 199
car travel 288, 292-3
    driving licence 292
    hire 293
    insurance 293
    road distance chart 288
    rules 293
Carinthia 22-3
castles
    Bled Castle (Gor) 112-13
    Bogenšperk Castle (Dol) 197-8
    Celje Old Castle (Sta) 251
    Črnomelj Castle (Bel) 219
    Dobrovo Castle (Pri) 144
    Khislstein Castle (Gor) 104
    Kostanjevica Castle (Dol) 209-10
    Little Castle (Gor) 94, 95
    Ljubljana Castle (Lju) 70-1, **5**, **153**
    Loka Castle (Gor) 99
    Maribor Castle (Sta) 239-41
    Metlika Castle (Bel) 215
    Mokrice Castle (Dol) 214
    Old Castle (Gor) 95
    Otočec Castle (Dol) 206
    Podčetrtek Castle (Sta) 224-6
    Podsreda Castle (Sta) 228, **160**
    Posavje Castle (Dol) 212, **159**
    Predjama Castle (Not) 187, **5**
    Ptuj Castle (Sta) 234-5, **160**
    Ribnica Castle (Dol) 193
    Snežnik Castle (Not) 190-1
    Sobota Castle (Pre) 266
    Stonič Castle (Bel) 219
    Vrbovec Castle (Sta) 255
    Žužemberk Castle (Dol) 199-200
cathedrals, *see* churches & cathedrals
Catholicism 33
caves
    Black Cave (Not) 186
    Divača Caves (Pri) 152
    Kostanjevica Cave (Dol) 210
    Križna Cave (Not) 191
    Krka Cave (Dol) 199
    Pivka Cave (Not) 186
    Planina Cave (Not) 186

INDEX

INDEX

MAP LEGEND

ROUTES

	Tollway		One-Way Street
	Freeway		Unsealed Road
	Primary Road		Street Mall/Steps
	Secondary Road		Tunnel
	Tertiary Road		Walking Tour
	Lane		Walking Tour Detour
	Under Construction		Walking Trail
	Track		Walking Path

TRANSPORT

	Ferry		Rail
	Ski Line		Rail (Underground)

HYDROGRAPHY

	River, Creek		Canal
	Lake (Salt)		Water

BOUNDARIES

	International		Regional, Suburb
	State, Provincial		Ancient Wall
	Disputed		Cliff

AREA FEATURES

	Airport		Land
	Beach, Desert		Mall
	Building		Park
	Campus		Rocks
	Cemetery, Christian		Sports
	Forest		Urban

POPULATION

●	CAPITAL (NATIONAL)	◉	CAPITAL (STATE)
●	Large City	●	Medium City
○	Small City	●	Town, Village

SYMBOLS

Sights/Activities
- Beach
- Castle, Fortress
- Christian
- Jewish
- Monument
- Museum, Gallery
- Point of Interest
- Pool
- Ruin
- Skiing
- Winery, Vineyard
- Zoo, Bird Sanctuary

Eating
- Eating

Drinking
- Drinking
- Café

Entertainment
- Entertainment

Shopping
- Shopping

Sleeping
- Sleeping
- Camping

Transport
- Airport, Airfield
- Border Crossing
- Bus Station
- Cycling, Bicycle Path
- General Transport
- Taxi Rank

Information
- Bank, ATM
- Embassy/Consulate
- Hospital, Medical
- Information
- Internet Facilities
- Parking Area
- Police Station
- Post Office, GPO
- Telephone
- Toilets

Geographic
- Lookout
- Mountain, Volcano
- National Park
- Pass, Canyon
- River Flow
- Waterfall

LONELY PLANET OFFICES

Australia
Head Office
Locked Bag 1, Footscray, Victoria 3011
☎ 03 8379 8000, fax 03 8379 8111
talk2us@lonelyplanet.com.au

USA
150 Linden St, Oakland, CA 94607
☎ 510 893 8555, toll free 800 275 8555
fax 510 893 8572
info@lonelyplanet.com

UK
72–82 Rosebery Ave,
Clerkenwell, London EC1R 4RW
☎ 020 7841 9000, fax 020 7841 9001
go@lonelyplanet.co.uk

Published by Lonely Planet Publications Pty Ltd
ABN 36 005 607 983

© Lonely Planet Publications Pty Ltd 2007

© photographers as indicated 2007

Cover photograph by Lonely Planet Images: Spire of the Church of the Assumption on Bled Island, with the Julian Alps in the background, Jon Davison. Many of the images in this guide are available for licensing from Lonely Planet Images: www.lonelyplanetimages.com.

Printed through The Bookmaker International Ltd.
Printed in China